Econometric Society Monographs No. 3(

Regression analysis of count data

Regression Analysis of Count Data

Students in both the natural and social sciences often seek regression models to explain the frequency of events, such as visits to a doctor, auto accidents, or new patents awarded. This analysis provides the most comprehensive and up-to-date account of models and methods to interpret such data. The authors have conducted research in the field for nearly 15 years and in this work combine theory and practice to make sophisticated methods of analysis accessible to practitioners working with widely different types of data and software. The treatment will be useful to researchers in areas such as applied statistics, econometrics, marketing, operations research, actuarial studies, demography, biostatistics, and quantitatively oriented sociology and political science. The book may be used as a reference work on count models or by students seeking an authoritative overview. The analysis is complemented by template programs available on the Internet through the authors' homepages.

A. Colin Cameron is Associate Professor of Economics at the University of California, Davis. He has also taught at the Ohio State University and held visiting positions at the Australian National University, Indiana University at Bloomington, and the University of New South Wales. His research on count data and microeconometrics has appeared in many leading econometrics journals.

Pravin K. Trivedi is Professor of Economics at Indiana University at Bloomington and previously taught at the Australian National University and University of Southampton. He has also held visiting positions at the European University Institute and the World Bank. His publications on count data and micro- and macro-econometrics have appeared in most leading econometrics journals.

Econometric Society Monographs

The Econometric Society is an international society for the advancement of economic theory in relation to statistics and mathematics. The Econometric Society Monograph Series is designed to promote the publication of original research contributions of high quality in mathematical economics and theoretical and applied econometrics.

Other titles in the series:

G.S. Maddala *Limited-dependent and qualitative variables in econometrics*, 0 521 33825 5
Gerard Debreu *Mathematical economics: Twenty papers of Gerard Debreu*, 0 521 33561 2
Jean-Michel Grandmont *Money and value: A reconsideration of classical and neoclassical monetary economics*, 0 521 31364 3
Franklin M. Fisher *Disequilibrium foundations of equilibrium economics*, 0 521 37856 7
Andreu Mas-Colell *The theory of general economic equilibrium: A differentiable approach*, 0 521 26514 2, 0 521 38870 8
Cheng Hsiao *Analysis of panel data*, 0 521 38933 X
Truman F. Bewley, Editor *Advances in econometrics – Fifth World Congress (Volume I)*, 0 521 46726 8
Truman F. Bewley, Editor *Advances in econometrics – Fifth World Congress (Volume II)*, 0 521 46725 X
Hervé Moulin *Axioms of cooperative decision making*, 0 52136055 2, 0 521 42458 5
L.G. Godfrey *Misspecification tests in econometrics: The Lagrange multiplier principle and other approaches*, 0 521 42459 3
Tony Lancaster *The econometric analysis of transition data*, 0 521 43789 X
Alvin E. Roth and Marilda A. Oliviera Sotomayor, Editors *Two-sided matching: A study in game-theoretic modeling and analysis*, 0 521 43788 1
Wolfgang Härdle *Applied nonparametric regression*, 0 521 42950 1
Jean-Jacques Laffont, Editor *Advances in economic theory – Sixth World Congress (Volume I)*, 0 521 48459 6
Jean-Jacques Laffont, Editor *Advances in economic theory – Sixth World Congress (Volume II)*, 0 521 48460 X
Halbert White *Estimation, inference and specification analysis*, 0 521 25280 6, 0 521 57446 3
Christopher Sims, Editor *Advances in econometrics – Sixth World Congress (Volume I)*, 0 521 56610 X

(Series list continues on page after index.)

Regression Analysis of Count Data

A. Colin Cameron

Pravin K. Trivedi

CAMBRIDGE
UNIVERSITY PRESS

PUBLISHED BY THE PRESS SYNDICATE OF THE UNIVERSITY OF CAMBRIDGE
The Pitt Building, Trumpington Street, Cambridge, United Kingdom

CAMBRIDGE UNIVERSITY PRESS
The Edinburgh Building, Cambridge CB2 2RU, UK http: //www.cup.cam.ac.uk
40 West 20th Street, New York, NY 10011-4211, USA http: //www.cup.org
10 Stamford Road, Oakleigh, Melbourne 3166, Australia

First published 1998

Printed in the United States of America

Typeset in Times Roman 10/12 pt. in LaTeX 2_{ε} [TB]

A catalog record for this book is available from the British Library

Library of Congress Cataloging-in-Publication Data

Cameron, Adrian Colin.

Regression analysis of count data / A. Colin Cameron, Pravin K. Trivedi.

p. cm.

Includes bibliographical references.

ISBN 0-521-63201-3 (hb). – ISBN 0-521-63567-5 (pb)

1. Regression analysis. 2. Econometrics. I. Trivedi, P. K. II. Title.

CA278.2.C36 1998
519.5′36 – dc21 98–15184
CIP

ISBN 0 521 63201 3 hardback
ISBN 0 521 63567 5 paperback

To Michelle and Bhavna

Contents

List of Figures

List of Tables

1996. The second author thanks Indiana University and the European University Institute, Florence, for support during his tenure as Jean Monnet Fellow in 1996, which permitted a period away from regular duties. For shorter periods of stay that allowed us to work jointly, we thank the Department of Economics at Indiana University, SELAPO at University of Munich, and the European University Institute.

Finally we would both like to thank our families for their patience and forbearance, especially during the periods of intensive work on the book. This work would not have been possible at all without their constant support.

A. Colin Cameron
Davis, California

Pravin K. Trivedi
Bloomington, Indiana

CHAPTER 1

Introduction

God made the integers, all the rest is the work of man.
Kronecker

This book is concerned with models of event counts. An event count refers to the number of times an event occurs, for example the number of airline accidents or earthquakes. An event count is the realization of a nonnegative integer-valued random variable. A *univariate* statistical model of event counts usually specifies a probability distribution of the number of occurrences of the event known up to some parameters. Estimation and inference in such models are concerned with the unknown parameters, given the probability distribution and the count data. Such a specification involves no other variables and the number of events is assumed to be independently identically distributed (iid). Much early theoretical and applied work on event counts was carried out in the univariate framework. The main focus of this book, however, is *regression analysis* of event counts.

The statistical analysis of counts within the framework of discrete parametric distributions for univariate iid random variables has a long and rich history (Johnson, Kotz, and Kemp, 1992). The Poisson distribution was derived as a limiting case of the binomial by Poisson (1837). Early applications include the classic study of Bortkiewicz (1898) of the annual number of deaths from being kicked by mules in the Prussian army. A standard generalization of the Poisson is the negative binomial distribution. It was derived by Greenwood and Yule (1920), as a consequence of apparent contagion due to unobserved heterogeneity, and by Eggenberger and Polya (1923) as a result of true contagion. The biostatistics literature of the 1930s and 1940s, although predominantly univariate, refined and brought to the forefront seminal issues that have since permeated regression analysis of both counts and durations. The development of the counting process approach unified the treatment of counts and durations. Much of the vast literature on iid counts, which addresses issues such as heterogeneity and overdispersion, true versus apparent contagion, and identifiability of Poisson mixtures, retains its relevance in the context of count data regressions. This leads to models such as the negative binomial regression model.

Significant early developments in count models took place in actuarial science, biostatistics, and demography. In recent years these models have also been used extensively in economics, political science, and sociology. The special features of data in their respective fields of application have fueled developments that have enlarged the scope of these models. An important milestone in the development of count data regression models was the emergence of the "generalized linear models," of which the Poisson regression is a special case, first described by Nelder and Wedderburn (1972) and detailed in McCullagh and Nelder (1989). Building on these contributions, the papers by Gourieroux, Monfort, and Trognon (1984a, b), and the work on longitudinal or panel count data models of Hausman, Hall, and Griliches (1984), have also been very influential in stimulating applied work in the econometric literature.

Regression analysis of counts is motivated by the observation that in many, if not most, real-life contexts, the iid assumption is too strong. For example, the mean rate of occurrence of an event may vary from case to case and may depend on some observable variables. The investigator's main interest therefore may lie in the role of covariates (regressors) that are thought to affect the parameters of the conditional distribution of events, given the covariates. This is usually accomplished by a regression model for event count. At the simplest level we may think of this in the conventional regression framework in which the dependent variable, y, is restricted to be a nonnegative random variable whose conditional mean depends on some vector of regressors, $\mathbf{x}$.

At a different level of abstraction, an event may be thought of as the realization of a point process governed by some specified *rate of occurrence* of the event. The number of events may be characterized as the total number of such realizations over some unit of time. The dual of the event count is the *interarrival time*, defined as the length of the period between events. Count data regression is useful in studying the occurrence rate per unit of time conditional on some covariates. One could instead study the distribution of interarrival times conditional on covariates. This leads to regression models of *waiting times* or *durations*. The type of data available, cross-sectional, time series, or longitudinal, will affect the choice of the statistical framework.

An obvious first question is whether "special" methods are required to handle count data or whether the standard Gaussian linear regression may suffice. More common regression estimators and models, such as the ordinary least squares in the linear regression model, ignore the restricted support for the dependent variable. This leads to significant deficiencies unless the mean of the counts is high, in which case normal approximation and related regression methods may be satisfactory.

The Poisson (log-linear) regression is motivated by the usual considerations for regression analysis but also seeks to preserve and exploit as much as possible the nonnegative and integer-valued aspect of the outcome. At one level one might simply regard this as a special type of *nonlinear* regression that respects the discreteness of the count variable. In some analyses this specific distributional assumption may be given up, while preserving nonnegativity.

In econometrics the interest in count data models is a reflection of the general interest in modeling discrete aspects of individual economic behavior. For example, Pudney (1989) characterizes a large body of microeconometrics as "econometrics of corners, kinks and holes." Count data models are specific types of discrete data regressions. Discrete and limited dependent variable models have attracted a great deal of attention in econometrics and have found a rich set of applications in microeconometrics (Maddala, 1983), especially as econometricians have attempted to develop models for the many alternative types of sample data and sampling frames. Although the Poisson regression provides a starting point for many analyses, attempts to accommodate numerous real-life conditions governing observation and data collection lead to additional elaborations and complications.

The scope of count data models is very wide. This monograph addresses issues that arise in the regression models for counts, with a particular focus on features of economic data. In many cases, however, the material covered can be easily adapted for use in social and natural sciences, which do not always share the peculiarities of economic data.

1.1 Poisson Distribution

The benchmark model for count data is the Poisson distribution. It is useful at the outset to review some fundamental properties and characterization results of the Poisson distribution (for derivations see Taylor and Karlin, 1994).

If the discrete random variable Y is Poisson-distributed with intensity or rate parameter μ, $\mu > 0$, and t is the *exposure*, defined as the length of time during which the events are recorded, then Y has density

$$\Pr[Y = y] = \frac{e^{-\mu t}(\mu t)^y}{y!}, \qquad y = 0, 1, 2, \ldots \tag{1.1}$$

where $\mathsf{E}[Y] = \mathsf{V}[Y] = \mu t$. If we set the length of the exposure period t equal to unity, then

$$\Pr[Y = y] = \frac{e^{-\mu}\mu^y}{y!}, \qquad y = 0, 1, 2, \ldots \tag{1.2}$$

This distribution has a single parameter μ, and we refer to it as $\mathsf{P}[\mu]$. Its kth raw moment, $\mathsf{E}[Y^k]$, may be derived by differentiating the moment generating function (mgf) k times

$$\mathsf{M(t)} \equiv \mathsf{E}[e^{tY}] = \exp\{\mu(e^t - 1)\},$$

with respect to t and evaluating at $t = 0$. This yields the following four raw moments:

$$\begin{aligned}
\mu_1' &= \mu \\
\mu_2' &= \mu + \mu^2 \\
\mu_3' &= \mu + 3\mu^2 + \mu^3 \\
\mu_4' &= \mu + 7\mu^2 + 6\mu^3 + \mu^4.
\end{aligned}$$

Following convention, raw moments are denoted by primes, and central moments without primes. The central moments around μ can be derived from the raw moments in the standard way. Note that the first two central moments, denoted μ_1 and μ_2, respectively, are equal to μ. The central moments satisfy the recurrence relation

$$\mu_{r+1} = r\mu\mu_{r-1} + \mu\frac{\partial\mu_r}{\partial\mu}, \quad r = 1, 2, \ldots. \tag{1.3}$$

where $\mu_0 = 0$.

Equality of the mean and variance will be referred to as the *equidispersion* property of the Poisson. This property is frequently violated in real-life data. *Overdispersion* (*underdispersion*) means the variance exceeds (is less than) the mean.

A key property of the Poisson distribution is additivity. This is stated by the following *countable additivity theorem* (for a mathematically precise statement see Kingman, 1993).

Theorem. If $Y_i \sim \mathsf{P}[\mu_i]$, $i = 1, 2, \ldots$ are independent random variables, and if $\sum \mu_i < \infty$, then $S_Y = \sum Y_i \sim \mathsf{P}[\sum \mu_i]$.

The binomial and the multinomial can be derived from the Poisson by appropriate conditioning. Under the conditions stated,

$$\begin{aligned}
&\Pr[Y_1 = y_1, Y_2 = y_2, \ldots, Y_n = y_n \mid S_Y = s] \\
&\quad = \left[\prod_{j=1}^{n} \frac{e^{-\mu_j}\mu_j^{y_j}}{y_j!}\right] \Bigg/ \left[\frac{\left(\sum \mu_i\right)^s e^{-\sum \mu_i}}{s!}\right] \\
&\quad = \frac{s!}{y_1!y_2!\ldots y_n!}\left(\frac{\mu_1}{\sum \mu_i}\right)^{y_1}\left(\frac{\mu_2}{\sum \mu_i}\right)^{y_2}\cdots\left(\frac{\mu_n}{\sum \mu_i}\right)^{y_n}. \\
&\quad = \frac{s!}{y_1!y_2!\ldots y_n!}\pi_1^{y_1}\pi_2^{y_2}\ldots\pi_n^{y_n},
\end{aligned} \tag{1.4}$$

where $\pi_j = \mu_j / \sum \mu_i$. This is the multinomial distribution $\mathsf{m}[s; \pi_1, \ldots, \pi_n]$. The binomial is the case $n = 2$.

There are many characterizations of the Poisson distribution. Here we consider four. The first, the law of rare events, is a common motivation for the

Poisson. The second, the Poisson counting process, is very commonly encountered in introduction to stochastic processes. The third is simply the dual of the second, with waiting times between events replacing the count. The fourth characterization, Poisson-stopped binomial, treats the number of events as repetitions of a binomial outcome, with the number of repetitions taken as Poisson distributed.

1.1.1 *Poisson as the "Law of Rare Events"*

The *law of rare events* states that the total number of events will follow, approximately, the Poisson distribution if an event may occur in any of a large number of trials but the probability of occurrence in any given trial is small.

More formally, let $Y_{n,\pi}$ denote the total number of successes in a large number n of independent Bernoulli trials with success probability π of each trial being small. Then

$$\Pr[Y_{n,\pi} = k] = \binom{n}{k}\pi^k(1-\pi)^{n-k}, \qquad k = 0, 1, \ldots, n.$$

In the limiting case where $n \to \infty$, $\pi \to 0$, and $n\pi = \mu > 0$, that is, the average μ is held constant while $n \to \infty$, we have

$$\lim_{n\to\infty}\left[\binom{n}{k}\left(\frac{\mu}{n}\right)^k\left(1-\frac{\mu}{n}\right)^{n-k}\right] = \frac{\mu^k e^{-\mu}}{k!},$$

the Poisson probability distribution with parameter μ, denoted as $\mathsf{P}[\mu]$.

1.1.2 *Poisson Process*

The Poisson distribution has been described as characterizing "complete randomness" (Kingman, 1993). To elaborate this feature the connection between the Poisson distribution and the *Poisson process* needs to be made explicit. Such an exposition begins with the definition of a *counting process*.

A stochastic process $\{N(t), t \geq 0\}$ is defined to be a counting process if $N(t)$ denotes an event count up to time t. $N(t)$ is nonnegative and integer-valued and must satisfy the property that $N(s) \leq N(t)$ if $s < t$, and $N(t) - N(s)$ is the number of events in the interval $(s, t]$. If the event counts in disjoint time intervals are independent, the counting process is said to have independent increments. It is said to be stationary if the distribution of the number of events depends only on the length of the interval.

The Poisson process can be represented in one dimension as a set of points on the time axis representing a random series of events occurring at points of time. The Poisson process is based on notions of independence and the Poisson distribution in the following sense.

Define μ to be the constant rate of occurrence of the event of interest, and $N(s, s+h)$, to be the number of occurrence of the event in the time interval

$(s, s+h]$. A (pure) Poisson process of rate μ occurs if events occur independently with constant probability equal to μ times the length of the interval. The numbers of events in disjoint time intervals are independent, and the distribution of events in each interval of unit length is $\mathsf{P}[\mu]$. Formally, as the length of the interval $h \to 0$,

$$\begin{aligned} \Pr[N(s, s+h) = 0] &= 1 - \mu h + o(h) \\ \Pr[N(s, s+h) = 1] &= \mu h + o(h), \end{aligned} \tag{1.5}$$

where $o(h)$ denotes a remainder term with the property $o(h)/h \to 0$ as $h \to 0$. $N(s, s+h)$ is statistically independent of the number and position of events in $(s, s+h]$. Note that in the limit the probability of two or more events occurring is zero; 0 and 1 events occur with probabilities of, respectively, $(1-\mu h)$ and μh. For this process it can be shown (Taylor and Karlin, 1994) that the number of events occurring in the interval $(s, s+h]$, for nonlimit h, is Poisson distributed with mean μh and probability

$$\Pr[N(s, s+h) = r] = \frac{e^{-\mu h}(\mu h)^r}{r!} \qquad r = 0, 1, 2, \ldots \tag{1.6}$$

Normalizing the length of the exposure time interval to be unity, $h = 1$, leads to the Poisson density given previously. In summary, the counting process $N(t)$ with stationary and independent increments and $N(0) = 0$, which satisfies (1.5), generates events that follow the Poisson distribution.

1.1.3 *Waiting Time Distributions*

We now consider a characterization of the Poisson that is the flip side of that given in the immediately preceding paragraph. Let W_1 denote the time of the first event, and W_r, $r \geq 1$, the time between the $(r-1)^{th}$ and r^{th} event. The nonnegative random sequence $\{W_r, r \geq 1\}$ is called the sequence of *interarrival times*, *waiting times*, *durations*, or *sojourn times*. In addition to, or instead of, analyzing the number of events occurring in the interval of length h, one can analyze the duration of time between successive occurrences of the event, or the time of occurrence of the rth event, W_r. This requires the distribution of W_r, which can be determined by exploiting the duality between event counts and waiting times. This is easily done for the Poisson process.

The outcome $\{W_1 > t\}$ occurs only if no events occur in the interval $(0, t]$. That is,

$$\Pr[W_1 > t] = \Pr[N(t) = 0] = e^{-\mu t}, \tag{1.7}$$

which implies that W_1 has exponential distribution with mean $1/\mu$. The waiting time to the first event, W_1, is exponentially distributed with density $f_{W_1}(t) = \mu e^{-\mu t}$, $t \geq 0$. Also,

$$\begin{aligned} \Pr[W_2 > t | W_1 = s] &= \Pr[N(s, s+t) = 0 \mid W_1 = s] \\ &= \Pr[N(s, s+t) = 0] \\ &= e^{-\mu t}, \end{aligned}$$

using the properties of independent stationary increments. This argument can be repeated for W_r to yield the result that $W_r, r = 1, 2, \ldots,$ are iid exponential random variables with mean $1/\mu$. This result reflects the property that the Poisson process has no memory.

In principle, the duality between number of occurrences and time between occurrences suggests that count and duration data should be covered in the same framework. Consider the arrival time of the rth event, denoted S_r,

$$S_r = \sum_{i=1}^{r} W_i, \qquad r \geq 1. \tag{1.8}$$

It can be shown using results on sums of random variables that S_r has gamma distribution

$$f_{S_r}(t) = \frac{\mu^r t^{r-1}}{(r-1)!} e^{-\mu t}, \qquad t \geq 0. \tag{1.9}$$

The above result can also be derived by observing that

$$N(t) \geq r \Leftrightarrow S_r \leq t. \tag{1.10}$$

Hence

$$\begin{aligned} \Pr[N(t) \geq r] &= \Pr[S_r \leq t] \\ &= \sum_{j=r}^{\infty} e^{-\mu t} \frac{(\mu t)^j}{j!}. \end{aligned} \tag{1.11}$$

To obtain the density of S_r, the cumulative density function (cdf) given above is differentiated with respect to t. Thus, the Poisson process may be characterized in terms of the implied properties of the waiting times.

Suppose one's main interest is in the role of the covariates that determine the Poisson process rate parameter μ. For example, let $\mu = \exp(\mathbf{x}'\boldsymbol{\beta})$. Hence, the mean waiting time is given by $1/\mu = \exp(-\mathbf{x}'\boldsymbol{\beta})$, confirming the intuition that the covariates affect the mean number of events and the waiting times in opposite directions. This illustrates that from the viewpoint of studying the role of covariates, analyzing the frequency of events is the dual complement of analyzing the waiting times between events.

The Poisson process is often too restrictive in practice. Mathematically tractable and computationally feasible common links between more general count and duration models are hard to find (see Chapter 4).

In the waiting time literature, emphasis is on estimating the hazard rate, the conditional instantaneous probability of the event occurring given that it has not yet occurred, controlling for censoring due to not always observing occurrence of the event. Fleming and Harrington (1991) and Andersen, Borgan, Gill, and Keiding (1993) present, in great detail, models for censored duration data based on application of martingale theory to counting processes.

We focus on counts. Even if duration is the more natural entity for analysis, it may not be observed. If only event counts are available, count regressions still provide an opportunity for studying the role of covariates in explaining the mean rate of event occurrence. However, count analysis leads in general to a loss of efficiency (Dean and Balshaw, 1997).

1.1.4 *Binomial Stopped by the Poisson*

Yet another characterization of the Poisson involves mixtures of the Poisson and the binomial. Let n be the actual (or true) count process taking nonnegative integer values with $\mathsf{E}[n] = \mu$, and $\mathsf{V}[n] = \sigma^2$. Let $B_1, B_2, \ldots, B_n$ be a sequence of n independent and identically distributed Bernoulli trials, in which each B_j takes one of only two values, 1 or 0, with probabilities π and $1-\pi$, respectively. Define the count variable $Y = \sum_{i=1}^{n} B_i$. For n given, Y follows a binomial distribution with parameters n and π. Hence,

$$\begin{aligned}\mathsf{E}[Y] &= \mathsf{E}[\mathsf{E}[Y \mid n]] = \mathsf{E}[n\pi] = \pi\mathsf{E}[n] = \mu\pi \\ \mathsf{V}[Y] &= \mathsf{V}[\mathsf{E}[Y \mid n]] + \mathsf{E}[\mathsf{V}[Y \mid n]] = (\sigma^2 - \mu)\pi^2 + \mu\pi.\end{aligned} \tag{1.12}$$

The actual distribution of Y depends on the distribution of n. For Poisson-distributed n it can be found using the following lemma.

Lemma. If π is the probability that $B_i = 1, i = 1, \ldots, n$, and $1-\pi$ the probability that $B_i = 0$, and $n \sim \mathsf{P}[\mu]$, then $Y \sim \mathsf{P}[\mu\pi]$.

To derive this result begin with the probability generating function (pgf), defined as $g(s) = \mathsf{E}[s^B]$, of the Bernoulli random variable

$$g(s) = (1-\pi) + \pi s, \tag{1.13}$$

for any real s. Let $f(s)$ denote the pgf of the Poisson variable n, $\mathsf{E}[s^n]$, that is,

$$f(s) = \exp(-\mu + \mu s). \tag{1.14}$$

Then the pgf of Y is obtained as

$$\begin{aligned}f(g(s)) &= \exp[-\mu + \mu g(s)] \\ &= \exp[-\mu\pi + \mu\pi s],\end{aligned} \tag{1.15}$$

which is the pgf of Poisson-distributed Y with parameter $\mu\pi$. This characterization of the Poisson has been called the Poisson-*stopped* binomial. This characterization is useful if the count is generated by a random number of repetitions of a binary outcome.

1.2 Poisson Regression

The approach taken to the analysis of count data, especially the choice of the regression framework, sometimes depends on how the counts are assumed to arise. There are two common formulations. In the first, they arise from a direct observation of a point process. In the second, counts arise from discretization ("ordinalization") of continuous latent data. Other less-used formulations appeal, for example, to the law of rare events or the binomial stopped by Poisson.

1.2.1 *Counts Derived from a Point Process*

Directly observed counts arise in many situations. Examples are the number of telephone calls arriving at a central telephone exchange, the number of monthly absences at the place of work, the number of airline accidents, the number of hospital admissions, and so forth. The data may also consist of interarrival times for events. In the simplest case, the underlying process is assumed to be stationary and homogeneous, with iid arrival times for events and other properties stated in the previous section.

1.2.2 *Counts Derived from Continuous Data*

Count-type variables sometimes arise from categorization of a latent continuous variable as the following example indicates. Credit rating of agencies may be stated as "AAA," "AAB," "AA," "A," "BBB," "B," and so forth, where "AAA" indicates the greatest credit worthiness. Suppose we code these as $y = 0, 1, \ldots, m$. These are pseudocounts that can be analyzed using a count regression. But one may also regard this as an ordinal ranking that can be modeled using a suitable latent variable model such as ordered probit. Chapter 3 provides a more detailed exposition.

1.2.3 *Regression Specification*

The standard model for count data is the *Poisson regression model*, which is a nonlinear regression model. This regression model is derived from the Poisson distribution by allowing the intensity parameter μ to depend on covariates (regressors). If the dependence is parametrically exact and involves exogenous covariates but no other source of stochastic variation, we obtain the standard Poisson regression. If the function relating μ and the covariates is stochastic, possibly because it involves unobserved random variables, then one obtains a *mixed Poisson* regression, the precise form of which depends on the assumptions about the random term. Chapter 4 deals with several examples of this type.

A standard application of Poisson regression is to cross-section data. Typical cross-section data for applied work consist of n independent observations, the ith of which is $(y_i, \mathbf{x}_i)$. The scalar dependent variable, y_i, is the number of occurrences of the event of interest, and $\mathbf{x}_i$ is the vector of linearly independent regressors that are thought to determine y_i. A regression model based on this distribution follows by conditioning the distribution of y_i on a k-dimensional vector of covariates, $\mathbf{x}_i' = [x_{1i}, \ldots, x_{ki}]$, and parameters $\boldsymbol{\beta}$, through a continuous function $\mu(\mathbf{x}_i, \boldsymbol{\beta})$, such that $\mathsf{E}[y_i \mid \mathbf{x}_i] = \mu(\mathbf{x}_i, \boldsymbol{\beta})$.

That is, y_i given $\mathbf{x}_i$ is Poisson-distributed with density

$$f(y_i \mid \mathbf{x}_i) = \frac{e^{-\mu_i}\mu_i^{y_i}}{y_i!}, \qquad y_i = 0, 1, 2, \ldots \tag{1.16}$$

In the log-linear version of the model the mean parameter is parameterized as

$$\mu_i = \exp(\mathbf{x}_i'\boldsymbol{\beta}), \tag{1.17}$$

to ensure $\mu > 0$. Equations (1.16) and (1.17) jointly define the Poisson (log-linear) regression model. If one does not wish to impose any distributional assumptions, the Eq. (1.17) by itself may be used for (nonlinear) regression analysis.

For notational economy we write $f(y_i \mid \mathbf{x}_i)$ in place of the more formal $f(Y_i = y_i \mid \mathbf{x}_i)$, which distinguishes between the random variable Y and its realization y. By the property of the Poisson, $\mathsf{V}[y_i \mid \mathbf{x}_i] = \mathsf{E}[y_i \mid \mathbf{x}_i]$, implying that the conditional variance is not a constant, and hence the regression is intrinsically heteroskedastic. In the log-linear version of the model the mean parameter is parameterized as (1.17), which implies that the conditional mean has a multiplicative form given by

$$\begin{aligned}\mathsf{E}[y_i \mid \mathbf{x}_i] &= \exp\left(\mathbf{x}_i'\boldsymbol{\beta}\right)\\ &= \exp(x_{1i}\beta_1)\exp(x_{2i}\beta_2)\cdots\exp(x_{ki}\beta_k),\end{aligned}$$

with interest often lying in changes in this conditional mean due to changes in the regressors. The additive specification, $\mathsf{E}[y_i \mid \mathbf{x}_i] = \mathbf{x}_i'\boldsymbol{\beta} = \sum_{j=1}^{k} x_{ji}\beta_i$, is likely to be unsatisfactory because certain combinations of β_i and $\mathbf{x}_i$ will violate the nonnegativity restriction on μ_i.

The Poisson model is closely related to the models for analyzing counted data in the form of proportions or ratios of counts sometimes obtained by grouping data. In some situations, for example when the population "at risk" is changing over time in a known way, it is helpful to reparameterize the model as follows. Let y be the observed number of events (e.g., accidents), N the known total exposure to risk (i.e., number "at risk"), and $\mathbf{x}$ the known set of k explanatory variables. The mean number of events μ may be expressed as the product of N and π, the probability of the occurrence of event, sometimes also called the *hazard rate*. That is, $\mu(\mathbf{x}) = N(\mathbf{x})\pi(\mathbf{x}, \boldsymbol{\beta})$. In this case the probability π is parameterized in terms of covariates. For example, $\pi = \exp(\mathbf{x}'\boldsymbol{\beta})$. This leads to a *rate* form of the Poisson model with the density

$$\Pr[Y = y \mid N(\mathbf{x}), \mathbf{x}] = \frac{e^{-\mu(\mathbf{x})}\mu(\mathbf{x})^y}{y!}, \qquad y = 0, 1, 2, \ldots \tag{1.18}$$

Variants of the Poisson regression arise in a number of ways. As was mentioned previously, the presence of an unobserved random error term in the conditional mean function, denoted ν_i, implies that we specify it as $\mathsf{E}[y_i \mid \mathbf{x}_i, \nu_i]$. The marginal distribution of y_i will involve the moments of the distribution of ν_i. This is one way in which mixed Poisson distributions may arise.

1.3 Examples

Patil (1970) gives numerous applications of count data analysis in the sciences. This earlier work is usually not in the regression context. There are now many examples of count data regression models in statistics and econometrics which use cross-sectional, time series or longitudinal data. For example, models of counts of doctor visits and other types of health care utilization; occupational injuries and illnesses; absenteeism in the workplace; recreational or shopping trips; automobile insurance rate making; labor mobility; entry and exits from industry; takeover activity in business; mortgage prepayments and loan defaults; bank failures; patent registration in connection with industrial research and development; and frequency of airline accidents. There are many applications also in demographic economics, in crime victimology, in marketing, political science and government, sociology and so forth. Many of the earlier applications are univariate treatments, not regression analyses.

The data used in many of these applications have certain commonalities. Events considered are often rare. The "law of rare events" is famously exemplified by Bortkiewicz's 1898 study of the number of soldiers kicked to death in Prussian stables. Zero event counts are often dominant, leading to a skewed distribution. Also, there may be a great deal of unobserved heterogeneity in the individual experiences of the event in question. Unobserved heterogeneity leads to overdispersion; that is, the actual variance of the process exceeds the nominal Poisson variance even after regressors are introduced.

Several examples are described in the remainder of this section. Some of these examples are used for illustrative purposes throughout this book. Figure 1.1 illustrates some features of the data for four of these examples.

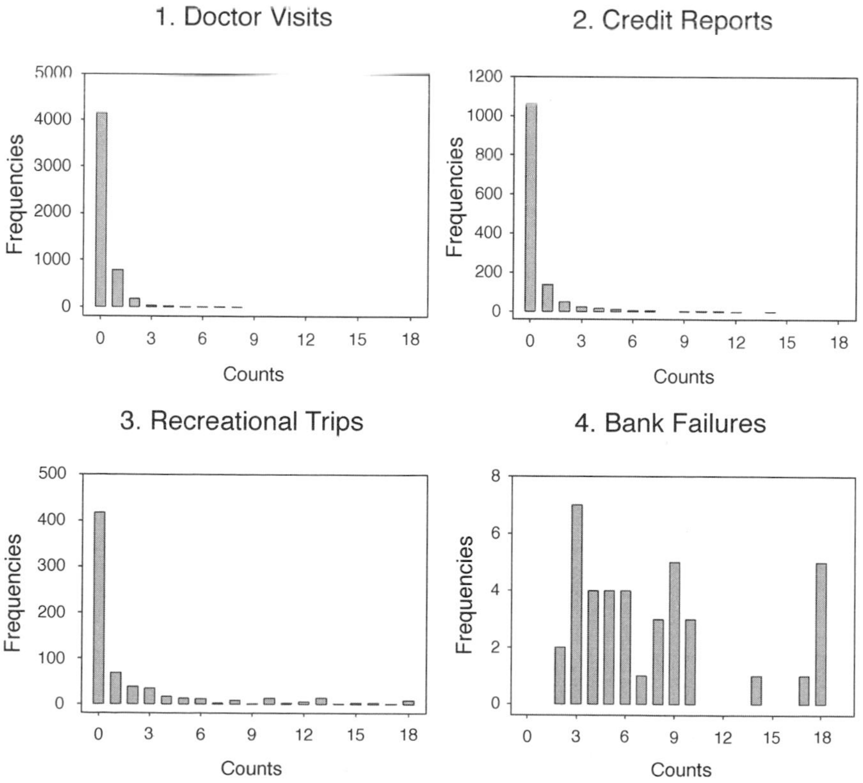

Figure 1.1. Frequency distribution of counts for four types of events.

1.3.1 *Health Services*

Health economics research is often concerned with the link between health-service utilization and economic variables such as income and price, especially the latter, which can be lowered considerably by holding a health insurance policy. Ideally one would measure utilization by expenditures, but if data come from surveys of individuals it is more common to have data on the number of times that health services are consumed, such as the number of visits to a doctor in the past month and the number of days in hospital in the past year, because individuals can better answer such questions than those on expenditure.

Data sets with healthcare utilization measured in counts include the National Health Interview Surveys and the Surveys on Income and Program Participation in the United States, the German Socioeconomic Panel (Wagner, Burkhauser, and Behringer, 1993), and the Australian Health Surveys (Australian Bureau of Statistics, 1978). Data on the number of doctor consultations in the past 2 weeks from the 1977–78 Australian Health Survey (see Figure 1.1) are analyzed using cross-section Poisson and negative binomial models by Cameron and Trivedi (1986) and Cameron, Trivedi, Milne, and Piggott (1988). Figure 1.1 highlights overdispersion in the form of excess zeros.

1.3.2 *Patents*

The link between research and development and product innovation is an important issue in empirical industrial organization. Product innovation is difficult to measure, but the number of patents is one indicator of it. This measure is commonly analyzed. Panel data on the number of patents received annually by firms in the United States are analyzed by Hausman, Hall, and Griliches (1984) and in many subsequent studies.

1.3.3 *Recreational Demand*

In environmental economics one is often interested in alternative uses of a natural resource such as forest or parkland. To analyze the valuation placed on such a resource by recreational users, economists often model the frequency of the visits to particular sites as a function of the cost of usage and the economic and demographic characteristics of the users. For example, Ozuna and Gomaz (1995) analyze 1980 survey data on the number of recreational boating trips to Lake Somerville in East Texas. Again, Figure 1.1 displays overdispersion and excess zeros.

1.3.4 *Takeover Bids*

In empirical finance the bidding process in a takeover is sometimes studied either using the probability of any additional takeover bids, after the first, using a binary outcome model, or using the number of bids as a dependent variable in a count regression. Jaggia and Thosar (1993) use cross-section data on the number of bids received by 126 U.S. firms that were targets of tender offers during the period between 1978 and 1985 and were actually taken over within 52 weeks of the initial offer. The dependent count variable y_i is the number of bids after the initial bid received by the target firm. Interest centers on the role of management actions to discourage takeover, the role of government regulators, the size of the firm, and the extent to which the firm was undervalued at the time of the initial bid.

1.3.5 *Bank Failures*

In insurance and finance, the frequency of the failure of a financial institution or the time to failure of the institution are variables of interest. Davutyan (1989) estimates a Poisson model for data summarized in Figure 1.1 on the annual number of bank failures in the United States over the period from 1947 to 1981. The focus is on the relation between bank failures and overall bank profitability, corporate profitability, and bank borrowings from the Federal Reserve Bank. The sample mean and variance of bank failures are, respectively, 6.343 and 11.820, suggesting some overdispersion. More problematic is the time series nature of the data, which is likely to violate the Poisson process framework.

1.3.6 *Accident Insurance*

In the insurance literature the frequency of accidents and the cost of insurance claims are often the variables of interest because they have an important impact on insurance premiums. Dionne and Vanasse (1992) use data on the number of accidents with damage in excess of $250 reported to police between August 1982 and July 1983 by 19,013 drivers in Quebec. The frequencies are very low, with a sample mean of 0.070. The sample variance of 0.078 is close to the mean. The paper uses cross-section estimates of the regression to derive predicted claims frequencies, and hence insurance premiums, from data on different individuals with different characteristics and records.

1.3.7 *Credit Rating*

How frequently mortgagees or credit-card holders fail to meet their financial obligations is a subject of interest in credit ratings. Often the number of defaulted payments are studied as a count variable. Greene (1994) analyzes the number of major derogatory reports, made after a delinquency of 60 days or more on a credit account, on 1319 individual applicants for a major credit card. Major derogatory reports are found to decrease with increases in the expenditure–income ratio (average monthly expenditure divided by yearly income); age, income, average monthly credit-card expenditure, and whether the individual holds another credit card are statistically insignificant. As seen in Figure 1.1, the data are overdispersed, calling for alternatives to the Poisson regression.

1.3.8 *Presidential Appointments*

Univariate probability models and time-series Poisson regressions have been used to model the frequency with which U.S. presidents were able to appoint U.S. Supreme Court Justices (King, 1987a). King's regression model uses the exponential conditional mean function, with the number of presidential appointments per year as the dependent variable. Explanatory variables are the number of previous appointments, the percentage of population that was in the military on active duty, the percentage of freshman in the House of Representatives, and the log of the number of seats in the court. It is argued that the presence of lagged appointments in the mean function permits a test for serial independence. King's results suggest negative dependence. However, it is an interesting issue whether the lagged variable should enter multiplicatively or additively. Chapter 7 considers this issue.

1.3.9 *Criminal Careers*

Nagin and Land (1993) use longitudinal data on 411 men for 20 years to study the number of recorded criminal offenses as a function of observable traits of criminals. The latter include psychological variables (e.g., IQ, risk preference, neuroticism), socialization variables (e.g., parental supervision or attachments), and family background variables. The authors model an individual's mean rate of offending in a period as a function of time-varying and time-invariant characteristics, allowing for unobserved heterogeneity among the subjects. Further, they also model the probability that the individual may be criminally "inactive" in the given period. Finally, the authors adopt a nonparametric treatment of unobserved interindividual differences (see Chapter 4 for details). This sophisticated modeling exercise allows the authors to classify criminals into different groups according to their propensity to commit crime.

1.3.10 *Doctoral Publications*

Using a sample of about 900 doctoral candidates, Long (1997) analyzes the relation between the number of doctoral publications in the final three years of Ph.D. studies and gender, marital status, number of young children, prestige of Ph.D. department, and number of articles by mentor in the preceding three years. He finds evidence that the scientists fall into two well-defined groups, "publishers" and "nonpublishers." The observed nonpublishers are drawn from both groups because some potential publishers may not have published just by chance, swelling the numbers who will "never" publish. The author argues that the results are plausible, as "there are scientists who, for structural reasons, will not publish" (Long, 1997, p. 249).

1.3.11 *Manufacturing Defects*

The number of defects per area in a manufacturing process are studied by Lambert (1992) using data from a soldering experiment at AT&T Bell Laboratories.

In this application components are mounted on printed wiring boards by soldering their leads onto pads on the board. The covariates in the study are qualitative, being five types of board surface, two types of solder, nine types of pads, and three types of panel. A high proportion of soldered areas had no defects, leading the author to generalize the Poisson regression model to account for excess zeros, meaning more zeros than are consistent with the Poisson formulation. The probability of zero defects is modeled using a logit regression, jointly with the Poisson regression for the mean number of defects.

1.4 Overview of Major Issues

We have introduced a number of important terms, phrases, and ideas. We now indicate where in this book these are further developed.

Chapter 2 covers issues of estimation and inference that are relevant to the rest of the monograph but also arise more generally. One issue concerns the two leading frameworks for parametric estimation and inference, namely, maximum likelihood and the moment-based methods. The former requires specification of the joint density of the observations, and hence implicitly of all population moments, whereas the latter requires a limited specification of a certain number of moments, usually the first one or two only, and no further information about higher moments. The discussion in Chapter 1 has focused on distributional models. The latter approach makes weaker assumptions but generally provides less information about the data distribution. Important theoretical issues concern the relative properties of these two broad approaches to estimation and inference. There are also issues of the ease of computation involved. Chapter 2 addresses these general issues and reviews some of the major results that are used in later chapters. This makes the monograph relatively self-contained.

Chapter 3 is concerned with the Poisson and the negative binomial models for the count regression. These models have been the most widely used starting points for empirical work. The Poisson density is only a one-parameter density and is generally found to be too restrictive. A first step is to consider less restrictive models for count data, such as the negative binomial and generalized linear models, which permit additional flexibility by introducing an additional parameter or parameters and breaking the equality restriction between the conditional mean and the variance. Chapter 3 provides a reasonably self-contained treatment of estimation and inference for these two basic models, which can be easily implemented using widely available packaged software. This chapter also includes issues of practical importance such as interpretation of coefficients and comparison and evaluation of goodness of fit of estimated models. For many readers this material will provide an adequate introduction to single-equation count regressions.

Chapter 4 deals with mixed Poisson and related parametric models that are particularly helpful when dealing with overdispersed data. One interpretation of such processes is as *doubly stochastic Poisson processes* with the Poisson parameter treated as stochastic (see Kingman, 1993, chapter 6). Chapter 4 deals with a leading case of the mixed Poisson, the negative binomial. Overdispersion is closely related to the presence of unobserved interindividual heterogeneity, but it can also arise from occurrence dependence between events. Using cross-section data it may be practically impossible to identify the underlying source of overdispersion. These issues are tackled in Chapter 4, which deals with models, especially overdispersed models, that are motivated by "non-Poisson" features of data that can occur separately or jointly with overdispersion, for example, an excess of zero observations relative to either the Poisson or the negative binomial, or the presence of censoring or truncation.

Chapter 5 deals with statistical inference and model evaluation for single-equation count regressions estimated using the methods of earlier chapters. The objective is to provide the user with specification tests and model evaluation procedures that are useful in empirical work based on cross-section data. As in Chapter 2, the issues considered in this chapter have relevance beyond count-data models.

Chapter 6 provides detailed analyses of two empirical examples to illustrate the single-equation modeling approaches of earlier chapters and especially the interplay of estimation and model evaluation that dominates empirical modeling.

Chapter 7 deals with time series analysis of event counts. A time series count regression is relevant if data are T observations, the tth of which is $(y_t, \mathbf{x}_t)$, $t = 1, \ldots, T$. If $\mathbf{x}_t$ includes past values of y_t, we refer to it as a *dynamic* count regression. This involves modeling the serial correlation in the count process. The static time series count regression as well as dynamic regression models are studied. This topic is still relatively underdeveloped.

Multivariate count models are considered in Chapter 8. An m-dimensional *multivariate* count model is based on data on $(\mathbf{y}_i, \mathbf{x}_i)$ where $\mathbf{y}_i$ is an $(m \times 1)$ vector of variables that may all be counts or may include counts as well as other discrete or continuous variables. Unlike the familiar case of the multivariate Gaussian distribution, the term *multivariate* in the case of count models covers a number of different definitions. Hence, Chapter 8 deals more with a number of special cases and provides relatively few results of general applicability.

Another class of multivariate models uses *longitudinal* or *panel data*, which are analyzed in Chapter 9. Longitudinal count models have attracted much attention in recent work, following the earlier work of Hausman, Hall, and Griliches (1984). Such models are relevant if the regression analysis is based on $(y_{it}, \mathbf{x}_{it})$, $i = 1, \ldots, n$; $t = 1, \ldots, T$, where i and t are individual and time subscripts, respectively. Dynamic panel data models also include lagged y variables. Unobserved random terms may also appear in multivariate and panel data models. The usefulness of longitudinal data is that without such data it is extremely difficult to distinguish between true contagion and apparent contagion.

Chapters 10 through 12 contain material based on more recent developments and areas of current research activity. Some of these issues are actively under investigation; their inclusion is motivated by our desire to inform the reader about the state of the literature and to stimulate further effort. Chapter 10 deals with the effects of measurement errors in either exposure or covariates, and with the problem of underrecorded counts. Chapter 11 deals with models with simultaneity and nonrandom sampling, including sample selection. Such models are usually estimated with nonlinear instrumental variable estimators.

In the final chapter, Chapter 12, we review several flexible modeling approaches to count data, some of which are based on series expansion methods. These methods permit considerable flexibility in the variance–mean relationships and in the estimation of probability of events. Some of them might also be described as "semiparametric."

We have attempted to structure this monograph keeping in mind the interests of researchers, practitioners, and new entrants to the field. The last group may wish to gain a relatively quick understanding of the standard models and methods; practitioners may be interested in the robustness and practicality of methods; and researchers wishing to contribute to the field presumably want an up-to-date and detailed account of the different models and methods. Wherever possible we have included illustrations based on real data. Inevitably, in places we have compromised, keeping in mind the constraints on the length of the monograph. We hope that the bibliographic notes and exercises at the ends of chapters will provide useful complementary material for all users.

In cross-referencing sections we use the convention that, for example, *section 3.4* refers to section 4 in Chapter 3.

Appendix A lists the acronyms that are used in the book. Some basic mathematical functions and distributions and their properties are summarized in Appendix B. Appendix C provides some software information.

Vectors are defined as column vectors, with transposition giving a row vector, and are printed in bold lowercase. Matrices are printed in bold uppercase.

1.5 Bibliographic Notes

Johnson, Kotz, and Kemp (1992) is an excellent reference for statistical properties of the univariate Poisson and related models. A lucid introduction to Poisson processes is in earlier sections of Kingman (1993). A good introductory textbook treatment of Poisson processes and renewal theory is Taylor and Karlin (1994). A more advanced treatment is in Feller (1971). Another comprehensive reference on Poisson and related distributions with full bibliographic details until 1967 is Haight (1967). Early applications of the Poisson regression include Cochran (1940) and Jorgenson (1961). Count data analysis in the sciences is surveyed in a comprehensive three-volume collective work edited by Patil (1970). Although volume 1 is theoretical, the remaining two volumes cover many applications in the natural sciences.

There are a number of surveys for count data models; for example, Cameron and Trivedi (1986), Gurmu and Trivedi (1994), and Winkelmann and Zimmermann (1995). In both biostatistics and econometrics, and especially in health, labor, and environmental economics, there are many applications of count models, which are mentioned throughout this book and especially in Chapter 6. Examples of applications in criminology, sociology, political science, and international relations arc Grogger (1990), Nagin and Land (1993), Hannan and Freeman (1987), and King (1987a, b). Examples of application in finance are Dionne, Artis and Guillen (1996) and Schwartz and Torous (1993).

CHAPTER 2

Model Specification and Estimation

2.1 Introduction

The general modeling approaches most often used in count data analysis – likelihood-based, generalized linear models, and moment-based – are presented in this chapter. Statistical inference for these nonlinear regression models is based on asymptotic theory, which is also summarized.

The models and results vary according to the strength of the distributional assumptions made. Likelihood based models and the associated maximum likelihood estimator require complete specification of the distribution. Statistical inference is usually performed under the assumption that the distribution is correctly specified.

A less parametric analysis assumes that some aspects of the distribution of the dependent variable are correctly specified while others are not specified, or if specified are potentially misspecified. For count data models considerable emphasis has been placed on analysis based on the assumption of correct specification of the conditional mean, or on the assumption of correct specification of both the conditional mean and the conditional variance. This is a nonlinear generalization of the linear regression model, where consistency requires correct specification of the mean and efficient estimation requires correct specification of the mean and variance. It is a special case of the class of generalized linear models, widely used in the statistics literature. Estimators for generalized linear models coincide with maximum likelihood estimators if the specified density is in the linear exponential family. But even then the analytical distribution of the same estimator can differ across the two approaches if different second moment assumptions are made. The term *pseudo-* (or *quasi-*) *maximum likelihood estimation* is used to describe the situation in which the assumption of correct specification of the density is relaxed. Here the first moment of the specified linear exponential family density is assumed to be correctly specified, while the second and other moments are permitted to be incorrectly specified.

An even more general framework, which permits estimation based on any specified moment conditions, is that of moment-based models. In the statistics literature this approach is known as estimating equations. In the econometrics literature this approach leads to generalized method of moments estimation, which is particularly useful if regressors are not exogenous.

Results for hypothesis testing also depend on the strength of the distributional assumptions. The classical statistical tests – Wald, likelihood ratio, and Lagrange multiplier (or score) – are based on the likelihood approach. Analogues of these hypothesis tests exist for the generalized method of moments approach. Finally, the moments approach introduces a new class of tests of model specification, not just of parameter restrictions, called *conditional moment tests*.

Section 2.2 presents the simplest count model and estimator, the maximum likelihood estimator of the Poisson regression model. Notation used throughout the book is also explained. The three main approaches – maximum likelihood, generalized linear models, and moment-based models – and associated estimation theory are presented in, respectively, sections 2.3 through 2.5. Testing using these approaches is summarized in section 2.6. Throughout, statistical inference based on first-order asymptotic theory is given, with results derived in section 2.7. Small sample refinements such as the bootstrap are deferred to later chapters.

Basic count data analysis uses maximum likelihood extensively, and also generalized linear models. For more complicated data situations presented in the latter half of the book, generalized linear models and moment-based models are increasingly used.

This chapter is a self-contained source, to be referred to as needed in reading later chapters. It is also intended to provide a bridge between the statistics and econometrics literatures. The presentation is of necessity relatively condensed and may be challenging to read in isolation, although motivation for results is given. A background at the level of Greene (1997a) or Johnston and DiNardo (1997) is assumed.

2.2 Example and Definitions

2.2.1 *Example*

The starting point for cross-section count data analysis is the Poisson regression model. This assumes that y_i, given the vector of regressors $\mathbf{x}_i$, is independently Poisson distributed with density

$$f(y_i \,|\, \mathbf{x}_i) = \frac{e^{-\mu_i}\mu_i^{y_i}}{y_i!}, \qquad y_i = 0, 1, 2, \ldots, \tag{2.1}$$

and mean parameter

$$\mu_i = \exp(\mathbf{x}_i'\boldsymbol{\beta}), \tag{2.2}$$

where $\boldsymbol{\beta}$ is a $k \times 1$ parameter vector. Counting process theory provides a motivation for choosing the Poisson distribution; taking the exponential of $\mathbf{x}_i'\boldsymbol{\beta}$ in

(2.2) ensures that the parameter μ_i is nonnegative. This model implies that the conditional mean is given by

$$\mathsf{E}[y_i \mid \mathbf{x}_i] = \exp(\mathbf{x}_i'\boldsymbol{\beta}), \tag{2.3}$$

with interest often lying in changes in this conditional mean due to changes in the regressors. It also implies a particular form of heteroskedasticity, due to equidispersion or equality of conditional variance and conditional mean,

$$\mathsf{V}[y_i \mid \mathbf{x}_i] = \exp(\mathbf{x}_i'\boldsymbol{\beta}). \tag{2.4}$$

The standard estimator for this model is the maximum likelihood estimator (MLE). Given independent observations, the log-likelihood function is

$$\mathcal{L}(\boldsymbol{\beta}) = \sum_{i=1}^{n} \left\{ y_i\mathbf{x}_i'\boldsymbol{\beta} - \exp(\mathbf{x}_i'\boldsymbol{\beta}) - \ln y_i! \right\}. \tag{2.5}$$

Differentiating (2.5) with respect to $\boldsymbol{\beta}$ yields the Poisson MLE $\hat{\boldsymbol{\beta}}$ as the solution to the first-order conditions

$$\sum_{i=1}^{n} (y_i - \exp(\mathbf{x}_i'\boldsymbol{\beta}))\mathbf{x}_i = \mathbf{0}. \tag{2.6}$$

These k equations are nonlinear in the k unknowns $\boldsymbol{\beta}$, and there is no analytical solution for $\hat{\boldsymbol{\beta}}$. Iterative methods, usually gradient methods such as Newton-Raphson, are needed to compute $\hat{\boldsymbol{\beta}}$. Such methods are given in standard texts.

Another consequence of there being no analytical solution for $\hat{\boldsymbol{\beta}}$ is that exact distributional results for $\hat{\boldsymbol{\beta}}$ are difficult to obtain. Inference is accordingly based on asymptotic results, presented in the remainder of this chapter. There are several ways to proceed. First, we can view $\hat{\boldsymbol{\beta}}$ as the estimator maximizing (2.5) and apply maximum likelihood theory. Second, we can view $\hat{\boldsymbol{\beta}}$ as being defined by (2.6). These equations have similar interpretation to those for the ordinary least squares (OLS) estimator. That is, the unweighted residual $(y_i - \mu_i)$ is orthogonal to the regressors. It is therefore possible that, as for OLS, inference can be performed under assumptions about just the mean and possibly variance. This is the generalized linear models approach. Third, because (2.3) implies $\mathsf{E}[(y_i - \exp(\mathbf{x}_i'\boldsymbol{\beta}))\mathbf{x}_i] = \mathbf{0}$, we can define an estimator that is the solution to the corresponding moment condition in the sample, that is, the solution to (2.6). This is the moment-based models approach.

2.2.2 *Definitions*

We use the generic notation $\boldsymbol{\theta} \in R^q$ to denote the $q \times 1$ parameter vector to be estimated. In the Poisson regression example the only parameters are the regression parameters, so $\boldsymbol{\theta} = \boldsymbol{\beta}$ and $q = k$. In the simplest extensions an additional scalar dispersion parameter α is introduced, so $\boldsymbol{\theta}' = (\boldsymbol{\beta}'\alpha)'$ and $q = k + 1$.

We consider random variables $\hat{\boldsymbol{\theta}}$ that converge in probability to a value $\boldsymbol{\theta}_*$,

$$\hat{\boldsymbol{\theta}} \xrightarrow{p} \boldsymbol{\theta}_*,$$

or equivalently the probability limit (plim) of $\hat{\boldsymbol{\theta}}$ equals $\boldsymbol{\theta}_*$,

$$\operatorname{plim} \hat{\boldsymbol{\theta}} = \boldsymbol{\theta}_*.$$

The probability limit $\boldsymbol{\theta}_*$ is called the pseudotrue value. If the data generating process (dgp) is a model with $\boldsymbol{\theta} = \boldsymbol{\theta}_0$, and the pseudotrue value actually equals $\boldsymbol{\theta}_0$, so $\boldsymbol{\theta}_0 = \boldsymbol{\theta}_*$, then $\hat{\boldsymbol{\theta}}$ is said to be consistent for $\boldsymbol{\theta}_0$.

Estimators $\hat{\boldsymbol{\theta}}$ used are usually root-n consistent for $\boldsymbol{\theta}_*$ and asymptotically normally distributed. Then the random variable $\sqrt{n}(\hat{\boldsymbol{\theta}} - \boldsymbol{\theta}_*)$ converges in distribution to the multivariate normal distribution with mean $\mathbf{0}$ and variance $\mathbf{C}$,

$$\sqrt{n}(\hat{\boldsymbol{\theta}} - \boldsymbol{\theta}_*) \xrightarrow{d} \mathsf{N}[\mathbf{0}, \mathbf{C}], \tag{2.7}$$

where $\mathbf{C}$ is a finite positive definite matrix. It is sometimes notationally convenient to express (2.7) in the simpler form

$$\hat{\boldsymbol{\theta}} \overset{a}{\sim} \mathsf{N}[\boldsymbol{\theta}_*, \mathbf{D}], \tag{2.8}$$

where $\mathbf{D} = \frac{1}{n}\mathbf{C}$. That is, $\hat{\boldsymbol{\theta}}$ is asymptotically normal distributed with mean $\boldsymbol{\theta}_*$ and variance $\mathbf{D} = \frac{1}{n}\mathbf{C}$. The division of the finite matrix $\mathbf{C}$ by the sample size makes it clear that as the sample size goes to infinity the variance matrix $\frac{1}{n}\mathbf{C}$ goes to zero, which is to be expected because $\hat{\boldsymbol{\theta}} \xrightarrow{p} \boldsymbol{\theta}_*$.

The variance matrix $\mathbf{C}$ may depend on unknown parameters, and the result (2.8) is operationalized by replacing $\mathbf{C}$ by a consistent estimator $\hat{\mathbf{C}}$. In many cases $\mathbf{C} = \mathbf{A}^{-1}\mathbf{B}\mathbf{A}'^{-1}$, where $\mathbf{A}$ and $\mathbf{B}$ are finite positive definite matrices. Then $\hat{\mathbf{C}} = \hat{\mathbf{A}}^{-1}\hat{\mathbf{B}}\hat{\mathbf{A}}'^{-1}$, where $\hat{\mathbf{A}}$ and $\hat{\mathbf{B}}$ are consistent estimators of $\mathbf{A}$ and $\mathbf{B}$. This is called the *sandwich* form, because $\mathbf{B}$ is sandwiched between $\mathbf{A}^{-1}$ and $\mathbf{A}^{-1}$ transposed. A more detailed discussion is given in section 2.5.1.

Results are expressed using matrix calculus. In general the derivative $\partial g(\boldsymbol{\theta})/\partial\boldsymbol{\theta}$ of a scalar function $g(\boldsymbol{\theta})$ with respect to the $q \times 1$ vector $\boldsymbol{\theta}$ is a $q \times 1$ vector with j^{th} entry $\partial g(\boldsymbol{\theta})/\partial\theta_j$. The derivative $\partial\mathbf{h}(\boldsymbol{\theta})/\partial\boldsymbol{\theta}'$ of a $r \times 1$ vector function $\mathbf{h}(\boldsymbol{\theta})$ with respect to the $1 \times q$ vector $\boldsymbol{\theta}'$ is an $r \times q$ matrix with jk^{th} entry $\partial h_j(\boldsymbol{\theta})/\partial\theta_k$.

2.3 Likelihood-Based Models

Likelihood-based models are models in which the joint density of the dependent variables is specified. For completeness a review is presented here, along with results for the less standard case of maximum likelihood with the density function misspecified.

We assume that the scalar random variable y_i, given the vector of regressors $\mathbf{x}_i$ and parameter vector $\boldsymbol{\theta}$, is distributed with density $f(y_i \mid \mathbf{x}_i, \boldsymbol{\theta})$. The likelihood principle chooses as estimator of $\boldsymbol{\theta}$ the value that maximizes the joint probability of observing the sample values $y_1, \ldots, y_n$. This probability, viewed as a function of parameters conditional on the data, is called the *likelihood function* and is denoted

$$\mathsf{L}(\boldsymbol{\theta}) = \prod_{i=1}^{n} f(y_i \mid \mathbf{x}_i, \boldsymbol{\theta}), \tag{2.9}$$

where we suppress the dependence of $\mathsf{L}(\boldsymbol{\theta})$ on the data and have assumed independence over i. This definition implicitly assumes cross-section data but can easily accommodate time series data by extending $\mathbf{x}_i$ to include lagged dependent and independent variables.

Maximizing the likelihood function is equivalent to maximizing the log-likelihood function

$$\mathcal{L}(\boldsymbol{\theta}) = \ln \mathsf{L}(\boldsymbol{\theta}) = \sum_{i=1}^{n} \ln f(y_i \mid \mathbf{x}_i, \boldsymbol{\theta}). \tag{2.10}$$

In the following analysis we consider the local maximum, which we assume to also be the global maximum.

2.3.1 *Regularity Conditions*

The standard results on consistency and asymptotic normality of the MLE hold if the so-called regularity conditions are satisfied. Furthermore, the MLE then has the desirable property that it attains the Cramer-Rao lower bound and is fully efficient. The following regularity conditions, given in Crowder (1976), are used in many studies.

1. The pdf $f(y, \mathbf{x}, \boldsymbol{\theta})$ is globally identified and $f(y, \mathbf{x}, \boldsymbol{\theta}^{(1)}) \neq f(y, \mathbf{x}, \boldsymbol{\theta}^{(2)})$, for all $\boldsymbol{\theta}^{(1)} \neq \boldsymbol{\theta}^{(2)}$.
2. $\boldsymbol{\theta} \in \boldsymbol{\Theta}$, where $\boldsymbol{\Theta}$ is finite dimensional, closed, and compact.
3. Continuous and bounded derivatives of $\mathcal{L}(\boldsymbol{\theta})$ exist up to order three.
4. The order of differentiation and integration of the likelihood may be reversed.
5. The regressor vector $\mathbf{x}_i$ satisfies
   (a) $\mathbf{x}_i'\mathbf{x}_i < \infty$
   (b) $\frac{\mathsf{E}[w_i^2]}{\sum_i \mathsf{E}[w_i^2]} = 0$ for all i, where $w_i \equiv \mathbf{x}_i' \frac{\partial \ln f(y_i \mid \mathbf{x}_i, \boldsymbol{\theta})}{\partial \boldsymbol{\theta}}$
   (c) $\lim_{n\to\infty} \frac{\sum_{i=1}^{n} \mathsf{E}[w_i^2 \mid \Omega_{i-1}]}{\sum_{i=1}^{n} \mathsf{E}[w_i^2]} = 1$ where $\Omega_{i-1} = (\mathbf{x}_1, \mathbf{x}_2, \ldots, \mathbf{x}_{i-1})$.

The first condition is an obvious identification condition, which ensures that the limit of $\frac{1}{n}\mathcal{L}$ has a unique maximum. The second condition rules out possible problems at the boundary of $\boldsymbol{\Theta}$ and can be relaxed if, for example, $\mathcal{L}$ is globally concave. The third condition can often be relaxed to existence up to second order. The fourth condition is a key condition that rules out densities for which the range of y_i depends on $\boldsymbol{\theta}$. The final condition rules out any observation making too large a contribution to the likelihood. For further details on regularity conditions for commonly used estimators, not just the MLE, see Newey and McFadden (1994).

2.3.2 *Maximum Likelihood*

We consider only the case in which the limit of $\frac{1}{n}\mathcal{L}$ is maximized at an interior point of Θ. The MLE $\hat{\boldsymbol{\theta}}_{\mathsf{ML}}$ is then the solution to the first-order conditions

$$\frac{\partial \mathcal{L}}{\partial \boldsymbol{\theta}} = \sum_{i=1}^{n} \frac{\partial \ln f_i}{\partial \boldsymbol{\theta}} = \mathbf{0}, \tag{2.11}$$

where $f_i = f(y_i \,|\, \mathbf{x}_i, \boldsymbol{\theta})$ and $\partial \mathcal{L}/\partial \boldsymbol{\theta}$ is a $q \times 1$ vector.

The asymptotic distribution of the MLE is usually obtained under the assumption that the density is correctly specified. That is, the dgp for y_i has density $f(y_i \,|\, \mathbf{x}_i, \boldsymbol{\theta}_0)$, where $\boldsymbol{\theta}_0$ is the true parameter value. Then, under the regularity conditions, $\hat{\boldsymbol{\theta}} \xrightarrow{p} \boldsymbol{\theta}_0$, so the MLE is consistent for $\boldsymbol{\theta}_0$. Also,

$$\sqrt{n}(\hat{\boldsymbol{\theta}}_{\mathsf{ML}} - \boldsymbol{\theta}_0) \xrightarrow{d} \mathsf{N}[\mathbf{0}, \mathbf{A}^{-1}], \tag{2.12}$$

where the $q \times q$ matrix $\mathbf{A}$ is defined as

$$\mathbf{A} = -\lim_{n\to\infty} \frac{1}{n} \mathsf{E}\left[\sum_{i=1}^{n} \left. \frac{\partial^2 \ln f_i}{\partial \boldsymbol{\theta} \partial \boldsymbol{\theta}'} \right|_{\boldsymbol{\theta}_0} \right]. \tag{2.13}$$

A consequence of regularity conditions three and four is the *information matrix equality*

$$\mathsf{E}\left[\frac{\partial^2 \mathcal{L}}{\partial \boldsymbol{\theta} \partial \boldsymbol{\theta}'} \right] = -\mathsf{E}\left[\frac{\partial \mathcal{L}}{\partial \boldsymbol{\theta}} \frac{\partial \mathcal{L}}{\partial \boldsymbol{\theta}'} \right], \tag{2.14}$$

for all values of $\boldsymbol{\theta} \in \Theta$. This is derived in section 2.7. Assuming independence over i and defining

$$\mathbf{B} = \lim_{n\to\infty} \frac{1}{n} \mathsf{E}\left[\sum_{i=1}^{n} \left. \frac{\partial \ln f_i}{\partial \boldsymbol{\theta}} \frac{\partial \ln f_i}{\partial \boldsymbol{\theta}'} \right|_{\boldsymbol{\theta}_0} \right], \tag{2.15}$$

the information equality implies $\mathbf{A} = \mathbf{B}$.

To operationalize these results one needs a consistent estimator of the variance matrix in Eq. (2.12). There are many possibilities. The (expected) *Fisher information estimator* takes the expectation in (2.13) under the assumed density and evaluates at $\hat{\boldsymbol{\theta}}$. The *Hessian estimator* simply evaluates (2.13) at $\hat{\boldsymbol{\theta}}$ without taking the expectation. The *outer-product estimator* evaluates (2.15) at $\hat{\boldsymbol{\theta}}$ without taking the expectation. It was proposed by Berndt, Hall, Hall, and Hausman (1974) and is also called the BHHH *estimator*. A more general form of the variance matrix of $\hat{\boldsymbol{\theta}}_{\mathsf{ML}}$, the sandwich form, is used if the assumption of correct specification of the density is relaxed (see section 2.3.4).

As an example, consider the MLE for the Poisson regression model presented in section 2.1. In this case $\partial\mathcal{L}/\partial\boldsymbol{\beta} = \sum_i (y_i - \exp(\mathbf{x}_i'\boldsymbol{\beta}))\mathbf{x}_i$ and

$$\partial^2\mathcal{L}/\partial\boldsymbol{\beta}\partial\boldsymbol{\beta}' = -\sum_i \exp\left(\mathbf{x}_i'\boldsymbol{\beta}\right)\mathbf{x}_i\mathbf{x}_i'.$$

It follows that we do not even need to take the expectation in (2.13) to obtain

$$\mathbf{A} = \lim_{n\to\infty} \frac{1}{n}\left[\sum_i \exp\left(\mathbf{x}_i'\boldsymbol{\beta}_0\right)\mathbf{x}_i\mathbf{x}_i'\right].$$

Assuming $\mathsf{E}[(y_i - \exp(\mathbf{x}_i'\boldsymbol{\beta}_0))^2|\mathbf{x}_i] = \exp(\mathbf{x}_i'\boldsymbol{\beta}_0)$, that is, correct specification of the variance, leads to the same expression for $\mathbf{B}$. The result is most conveniently expressed as

$$\hat{\boldsymbol{\beta}}_{\mathsf{ML}} \overset{a}{\sim} \mathsf{N}\left(\boldsymbol{\beta}_0, \left(\sum_{i=1}^{n} \exp\left(\mathbf{x}_i'\boldsymbol{\beta}_0\right)\mathbf{x}_i\mathbf{x}_i'\right)^{-1}\right). \tag{2.16}$$

In this case the Fisher information and Hessian estimators of $\mathsf{V}[\hat{\boldsymbol{\theta}}_{\mathsf{ML}}]$ coincide, and differ from the outer-product estimator.

2.3.3 *Profile Likelihood*

Suppose the likelihood depends on a parameter vector $\boldsymbol{\lambda}$ in addition to $\boldsymbol{\theta}$, so the likelihood function is $\mathcal{L}(\boldsymbol{\theta}, \boldsymbol{\lambda})$. The *profile likelihood* or *concentrated likelihood* eliminates $\boldsymbol{\lambda}$ by obtaining the restricted MLE $\hat{\boldsymbol{\lambda}}(\boldsymbol{\theta})$ for fixed $\boldsymbol{\theta}$. Then

$$\mathcal{L}_{\text{pro}}(\boldsymbol{\theta}) = \mathcal{L}(\boldsymbol{\theta}, \hat{\boldsymbol{\lambda}}(\boldsymbol{\theta})). \tag{2.17}$$

This approach can be used in all situations, but it is important to note that $\mathcal{L}_{\text{pro}}(\boldsymbol{\theta})$ is not strictly a log-likelihood function and that the usual results need to be adjusted in this case (see, for example, Davidson and MacKinnon, 1993, chapter 8).

The profile likelihood is useful if $\boldsymbol{\lambda}$ is a nuisance parameter. For example, interest may lie in modeling the conditional mean parameterized by $\boldsymbol{\theta}$, with variance parameters $\boldsymbol{\lambda}$ not intrinsically of interest. In such circumstances there is advantage to attempting to estimate $\boldsymbol{\theta}$ alone, especially if $\boldsymbol{\lambda}$ is of high dimension.

For scalar θ the profile likelihood can be used to form a likelihood ratio $100(1-\alpha)\%$ confidence region for θ, $\{\theta : \mathcal{L}_{\text{pro}}(\theta) > \mathcal{L}(\hat{\theta}, \hat{\boldsymbol{\lambda}}) - \chi_1^2(\alpha)\}$, where $\mathcal{L}(\hat{\theta}, \hat{\boldsymbol{\lambda}})$ is the unconstrained maximum likelihood. This need not be symmetric around $\hat{\theta}$, unlike the usual confidence interval $\hat{\theta} \pm z_{\alpha/2}\mathsf{se}[\hat{\theta}]$, where $\mathsf{se}[\hat{\theta}]$ is the standard error of $\hat{\theta}$.

Other variants of the likelihood approach can be used to eliminate nuisance parameters in some special circumstances. The *conditional likelihood* is the joint density of $\boldsymbol{\theta}$ conditional on a sufficient statistic for the nuisance parameters and is used, for example, to estimate the fixed effects Poisson model for panel data. The *marginal likelihood* is the likelihood for a subset of the data that may depend on $\boldsymbol{\theta}$ alone. For further discussion see McCullagh and Nelder (1989, chapter 7).

2.3.4 *Misspecified Density*

A weakness of the ML approach is that it assumes correct specification of the complete density. To see the role of this assumption, it is helpful to begin with an informal proof of consistency of the MLE in the usual case of correctly specified density.

The MLE solves the sample moment condition $\partial \mathcal{L}/\partial \boldsymbol{\theta} = \mathbf{0}$, so an intuitive necessary condition for consistency is that the same moment condition holds in the population or $\mathsf{E}[\partial \mathcal{L}/\partial \boldsymbol{\theta}] = \mathbf{0}$, which holds if $\mathsf{E}[\partial \ln f_i/\partial \boldsymbol{\theta}] = \mathbf{0}$. Any density $f(y \mid \mathbf{x}, \boldsymbol{\theta})$ satisfying the regularity conditions has the property that

$$\int \frac{\partial \ln f(y \mid \boldsymbol{\theta})}{\partial \boldsymbol{\theta}} f(y \mid \boldsymbol{\theta})\, dy = \mathbf{0}; \tag{2.18}$$

see section 2.7 for a derivation. The consistency condition $\mathsf{E}[\partial \ln f(y \mid \mathbf{x}, \boldsymbol{\theta})/\partial \boldsymbol{\theta}] = \mathbf{0}$ is implied by (2.18), if the expectations operator is taken using the assumed density $f(y \mid \mathbf{x}, \boldsymbol{\theta})$.

Suppose instead that the dgp is the density $f^*(y_i \mid \mathbf{z}_i, \boldsymbol{\gamma})$ rather than the assumed density $f(y_i \mid \mathbf{x}_i, \boldsymbol{\theta})$. Then, Eq. (2.18) no longer implies the consistency condition $\mathsf{E}[\partial \ln f(y \mid \mathbf{x}, \boldsymbol{\theta})/\partial \boldsymbol{\theta}] = \mathbf{0}$, which now becomes

$$\int \frac{\partial \ln f(y \mid \mathbf{x}, \boldsymbol{\theta})}{\partial \boldsymbol{\theta}} f^*(y \mid \mathbf{z}, \boldsymbol{\gamma})\, dy = \mathbf{0},$$

as the expectation should be with respect to the dgp density, not the assumed density. Thus, misspecification of the density may lead to inconsistency.

White (1982), following Huber (1967), obtained the distribution of the MLE if the density function is incorrectly specified. In general $\hat{\boldsymbol{\theta}}_{\mathsf{ML}} \xrightarrow{p} \boldsymbol{\theta}_*$, where the pseudotrue value $\boldsymbol{\theta}_*$ is the value of $\boldsymbol{\theta}$ that maximizes $\text{plim}\, \frac{1}{n}\sum_{i=1}^{n} \ln f(y_i \mid \mathbf{x}_i, \boldsymbol{\theta})$ and the probability limit is obtained under the dgp $f^*(y_i \mid \mathbf{z}_i, \boldsymbol{\gamma})$. Under suitable assumptions,

$$\sqrt{n}(\hat{\boldsymbol{\theta}}_{\mathsf{ML}} - \boldsymbol{\theta}_*) \xrightarrow{d} \mathsf{N}\left[\mathbf{0}, \mathbf{A}_*^{-1}\mathbf{B}_*\mathbf{A}_*^{-1}\right], \tag{2.19}$$

where

$$\mathbf{A}_* = -\lim_{n\to\infty} \frac{1}{n} \mathsf{E}_* \left[\sum_{i=1}^{n} \left. \frac{\partial^2 \ln f_i}{\partial \boldsymbol{\theta} \partial \boldsymbol{\theta}'} \right|_{\boldsymbol{\theta}_*} \right] \tag{2.20}$$

and

$$\mathbf{B}_* = \lim_{n\to\infty} \frac{1}{n} \mathsf{E}_* \left[\sum_{i=1}^{n} \frac{\partial \ln f_i}{\partial \boldsymbol{\theta}} \frac{\partial \ln f_i}{\partial \boldsymbol{\theta}'} \bigg|_{\boldsymbol{\theta}_*} \right], \tag{2.21}$$

where $f_i = f(y_i \mid \mathbf{x}_i, \boldsymbol{\theta})$ and the expectations E_* are with respect to the dgp $f^*(y_i \mid \mathbf{z}_i, \gamma)$.

The essential point is that if the density is misspecified the ML estimator is in general inconsistent. Generalized linear models, presented next, are the notable exception. A second point is that the MLE has the more complicated variance function with the sandwich form (2.19), because the information matrix equality (2.14) no longer holds. The *sandwich estimator* of the variance matrix of $\hat{\boldsymbol{\theta}}_{\mathsf{ML}}$ is $\hat{\mathbf{A}}^{-1}\hat{\mathbf{B}}\hat{\mathbf{A}}^{-1}$. Different estimates of $\hat{\mathbf{A}}$ and $\hat{\mathbf{B}}$ can be used (see section 2.3.2) depending on whether or not the expectations in $\mathbf{A}_*$ and $\mathbf{B}_*$ are taken before evaluation at $\hat{\boldsymbol{\theta}}_{\mathsf{ML}}$. The *robust sandwich estimator* does not take expectations.

2.4 Generalized Linear Models

Although the MLE is in general inconsistent if the density is incorrectly specified, for some specified densities consistency may be maintained even given partial misspecification of the model. A leading example is maximum likelihood estimation in the linear regression model under the assumption that y_i is independently $\mathsf{N}[\mathbf{x}_i'\beta_0, \sigma^2]$ distributed. Then $\hat{\beta}_{\mathsf{ML}}$ equals the OLS estimator, which may be consistent even given nonnormality and heteroskedasticity, as the essential requirement for consistency is correct specification of the conditional mean: $\mathsf{E}[y_i \mid \mathbf{x}_i] = \mathbf{x}_i'\beta_0$. A similar situation arises for the Poisson regression model. Consistency essentially requires that the population analogue of Eq. (2.6) holds:

$$\mathsf{E}[(y_i - \exp(\mathbf{x}_i'\beta_0))\mathbf{x}_i] = \mathbf{0}.$$

This is satisfied, however, if $\mathsf{E}[y_i \mid \mathbf{x}_i] = \exp(\mathbf{x}_i'\beta_0)$. More generally such results hold for maximum likelihood estimation of models with specified density a member of the linear exponential family, and estimation of the closely related class of generalized linear models.

Although consistency in these models requires only correct specification of the mean, misspecification of the variance leads to invalid statistical inference due to incorrect reported t-statistics and standard errors. For example, in the linear regression model the usual reported standard errors for OLS are incorrect if the error is heteroskedastic rather than homoskedastic. Adjustment to the usual computer output needs to be made to ensure correct standard errors. Furthermore, more efficient generalized least squares (GLS) estimation is possible.

We begin with a presentation of results for weighted least squares for linear models, results that carry over to generalized linear models. We then introduce generalized linear models by considering linear exponential family models.

These models are based on a one-parameter distribution, which in practice is too restrictive. Extensions to two-parameter models have been made in two ways – the linear exponential family with nuisance parameter and generalized linear models. Further results for generalized linear models are then presented before concluding with extended generalized linear models.

2.4.1 *Weighted Linear Least Squares*

Consider the linear regression model for y_i with nonstochastic regressors $\mathbf{x}_i$. In the linear model the regression function is $\mathbf{x}_i'\beta_0$. Suppose it is believed that heteroskedasticity exists and as a starting point can be approximated by $\mathsf{V}[y_i] = v_i$ where v_i is known. Then one uses the *weighted least squares* (WLS) estimator with weights $1/v_i$, which solves the first-order conditions

$$\sum_{i=1}^{n} \frac{1}{v_i}(y_i - \mathbf{x}_i'\beta)\mathbf{x}_i = \mathbf{0}. \tag{2.22}$$

We consider the distribution of this estimator if the mean is correctly specified but the variance is not necessarily v_i. It is helpful to express the first-order conditions in matrix notation as

$$\mathbf{X}'\mathbf{V}^{-1}(\mathbf{y} - \mathbf{X}\beta) = \mathbf{0}, \tag{2.23}$$

where $\mathbf{y}$ is the $n \times 1$ vector with i^{th} entry y_i, $\mathbf{X}$ is the $n \times k$ matrix with i^{th} row $\mathbf{x}_i'$, and $\mathbf{V}$ is the $n \times n$ weighting matrix with i^{th} diagonal entry v_i. These equations have the analytical solution

$$\hat{\beta}_{\mathsf{WLS}} = (\mathbf{X}'\mathbf{V}^{-1}\mathbf{X})^{-1}\mathbf{X}'\mathbf{V}^{-1}\mathbf{y}.$$

To obtain the mean and variance of $\hat{\beta}_{\mathsf{WLS}}$ we assume $\mathbf{y}$ has mean $\mathbf{X}\beta_0$ and variance matrix $\mathbf{\Omega}$. Then it is a standard result that $\mathsf{E}[\hat{\beta}_{\mathsf{WLS}}] = \beta_0$ and

$$\mathsf{V}[\hat{\beta}_{\mathsf{WLS}}] = (\mathbf{X}'\mathbf{V}^{-1}\mathbf{X})^{-1}\mathbf{X}'\mathbf{V}^{-1}\mathbf{\Omega}\mathbf{V}^{-1}\mathbf{X}(\mathbf{X}'\mathbf{V}^{-1}\mathbf{X})^{-1}. \tag{2.24}$$

One familiar example of this is OLS. Then $\mathbf{V} = \sigma^2\mathbf{I}$ and $\mathsf{V}[\hat{\beta}_{\mathsf{WLS}}] = (\mathbf{X}'\mathbf{X})^{-1}$ $\mathbf{X}'\mathbf{\Omega}\mathbf{X}(\mathbf{X}'\mathbf{X})^{-1}$, which simplifies to $\sigma^2(\mathbf{X}'\mathbf{X})^{-1}$ if $\mathbf{\Omega} = \sigma^2\mathbf{I}$. A second familiar example is GLS, with $\mathbf{V} = \mathbf{\Omega}$, in which case $\mathsf{V}[\hat{\beta}_{\mathsf{WLS}}] = (\mathbf{X}'\mathbf{\Omega}^{-1}\mathbf{X})^{-1}$.

It is important to note that the general result (2.24) represents a different situation to that in standard textbook treatments. One begins with a working hypothesis about the form of the heteroskedasticity, say v_i, leading to a *working variance matrix* $\mathbf{V}$. If $\mathbf{V}$ is misspecified then $\hat{\beta}_{\mathsf{WLS}}$ is still unbiased, but it is inefficient and most importantly has a variance matrix of the general form (2.24), which does not impose $\mathbf{V} = \mathbf{\Omega}$. One way to estimate $\mathsf{V}[\hat{\beta}_{\mathsf{WLS}}]$ is to specify $\mathbf{\Omega}$ to be a particular function of regressors and parameters and obtain consistent estimates of these parameters and hence a consistent estimator $\hat{\mathbf{\Omega}}$ of $\mathbf{\Omega}$. Alternatively, White (1980) (see also Eicker, 1967) gave conditions under which one need not specify the functional form for the variance matrix $\mathbf{\Omega}$ but can instead use the matrix $\tilde{\boldsymbol{\Omega}} = \mathsf{Diag}[(y_i - \mathbf{x}_i'\hat{\beta}_{\mathsf{WLS}})^2]$, where $\mathsf{Diag}[a_i]$ denotes the diagonal matrix with i^{th} diagonal entry a_i. The justification is that even though $\tilde{\boldsymbol{\Omega}}$ is not consistent for $\boldsymbol{\Omega}$, the difference between the $k \times k$ matrices $\frac{1}{n}\mathbf{X}'\mathbf{V}^{-1}\tilde{\boldsymbol{\Omega}}\mathbf{V}^{-1}\mathbf{X}$ and $\frac{1}{n}\mathbf{X}'\mathbf{V}^{-1}\boldsymbol{\Omega}\mathbf{V}^{-1}\mathbf{X}$ has probability limit zero.

These same points carry over to generalized linear models. One specifies a working variance assumption such as variance–mean equality for the Poisson. The dependence of v_i on μ_i does not change the result (2.24). Hence failure of this assumption does not lead to inconsistency if the mean is correctly specified but will lead to incorrect inference if one does not use the general form (2.24). Generalized linear models have an additional complication, because the mean function is nonlinear. This can be accommodated by generalizing the first-order conditions (2.22). Because in the linear case $\mu_i = \mathbf{x}_i'\beta$, (2.22) can be reexpressed as

$$\sum_{i=1}^{n} \frac{1}{v_i}(y_i - \mu_i)\frac{\partial \mu_i}{\partial \beta} = \mathbf{0}. \tag{2.25}$$

The first-order conditions for generalized linear models such as the Poisson are of the form (2.25). It can be shown that the discussion above still holds, with the important change that the matrix $\mathbf{X}$ in (2.23) and (2.24) is now defined to have i^{th} row $\partial \mu_i / \partial \beta'$.

There is considerable overlap in the next three subsections, which cover different representations and variations of essentially the same model. In sections 2.4.2 and 2.4.3 the density is parameterized in terms of the mean parameter; in section 2.4.4 the density is parameterized in terms of the so-called canonical parameter. The latter formulation is used in the generalized linear models literature. To those unfamiliar with this literature the mean parameter formulation may be more natural. For completeness both presentations are given here. Other variations, such as different ways nuisance scale parameters are introduced, are discussed at the end of section 2.4.4.

2.4.2 *Linear Exponential Family Models*

The presentation follows Cameron and Trivedi (1986), whose work was based on Gourieroux, Monfort, and Trognon (1984a). A density $f_{\mathsf{LEF}}(y \mid \mu)$ is a member of a *linear exponential family* (LEF) with mean parameterization if

$$f_{\mathsf{LEF}}(y \mid \mu) = \exp\{a(\mu) + b(y) + c(\mu)y\}, \tag{2.26}$$

where $\mu = \mathsf{E}[y]$, and the functions $a(\cdot)$ and $c(\cdot)$ are such that

$$\mathsf{E}[y] = -[c'(\mu)]^{-1}a'(\mu), \tag{2.27}$$

where $a'(\mu) = \partial a(\mu)/\partial \mu$ and $c'(\mu) = \partial c(\mu)/\partial \mu$, and

$$\mathsf{V}[y] = [c'(\mu)]^{-1}. \tag{2.28}$$

The function $b(\cdot)$ is a normalizing constant. Different functional forms for $a(\cdot)$ and $c(\cdot)$ lead to different LEF models. Special cases of the LEF include the normal (with σ^2 known), Poisson, geometric, binomial (with number of trials fixed), exponential, and one-parameter gamma.

For example, the Poisson density can be written as $\exp\{-\mu + y \ln \mu - \ln y!\}$, which is an LEF model with $a(\mu) = -\mu$, $c(\mu) = \ln \mu$ and $b(y) = -\ln y!$ Then $a'(\mu) = -1$ and $c'(\mu) = 1/\mu$, so $\mathsf{E}[y] = \mu$ from Eq. (2.27) and $\mathsf{V}[y] = \mu$ from (2.28).

Members of the exponential family have density $f(y \mid \lambda) = \exp\{a(\lambda) + b(y) + c(\lambda)t(y)\}$. The LEF is the special case $t(y) = y$, hence the qualifier linear. The natural exponential family has density $f(y \mid \lambda) = \exp\{a(\lambda) + \lambda y\}$. Other exponential families come from the natural exponential family by one-to-one transformations $x = t(y)$ of y.

A regression model is formed by specifying the density to be $f_{\mathsf{LEF}}(y_i \mid \mu_i)$ where

$$\mu_i = \mu(\mathbf{x}_i, \boldsymbol{\beta}), \tag{2.29}$$

for some specified mean function $\mu(\cdot)$. The MLE based on an LEF, $\hat{\boldsymbol{\beta}}_{\mathsf{LEF}}$, maximizes

$$\mathcal{L}_{\mathsf{LEF}} = \sum_{i=1}^{n} \{a(\mu_i) + b(y_i) + c(\mu_i) y_i\}. \tag{2.30}$$

The first-order conditions using Eqs. (2.27) and (2.28) can be rewritten as

$$\sum_{i=1}^{n} \frac{1}{v_i}(y_i - \mu_i)\frac{\partial \mu_i}{\partial \boldsymbol{\beta}} = \mathbf{0}, \tag{2.31}$$

where

$$v_i = [c'(\mu_i)]^{-1} \tag{2.32}$$

is the specified variance function which is a function of μ_i and hence $\boldsymbol{\beta}$. These first-order conditions are of the form (2.25), and as seen subsequently we obtain results similar to (2.24).

It is helpful at times to rewrite (2.31) as

$$\sum_{i=1}^{n} \frac{(y_i - \mu_i)}{\sqrt{v_i}} \frac{1}{\sqrt{v_i}} \frac{\partial \mu_i}{\partial \boldsymbol{\beta}} = \mathbf{0}, \tag{2.33}$$

which shows that the standardized residual is orthogonal to the standardized regressor.

Under the standard assumption that the density is correctly specified, so the dgp is $f_{\mathsf{LEF}}(y_i \mid \mu(\mathbf{x}_i, \boldsymbol{\beta}_0))$, application of (2.12) and (2.13) yields

$$\sqrt{n}(\hat{\boldsymbol{\beta}}_{\mathsf{LEF}} - \boldsymbol{\beta}_0) \xrightarrow{d} \mathsf{N}[\mathbf{0}, \mathbf{A}^{-1}], \tag{2.34}$$

where

$$\mathbf{A} = \lim_{n\to\infty} \frac{1}{n} \sum_{i=1}^{n} \frac{1}{v_i} \frac{\partial \mu_i}{\partial \boldsymbol{\beta}} \frac{\partial \mu_i}{\partial \boldsymbol{\beta}'}\bigg|_{\boldsymbol{\beta}_0}. \tag{2.35}$$

Now consider estimation if the density is misspecified. Gourieroux et al. (1984a) call the estimator in this case the *pseudomaximum likelihood* (PML) *estimator*. Other authors call such an estimator a *quasimaximum likelihood estimator*. Throughout this book we use the term PML to avoid confusion with the conceptually different quasilikelihood introduced in section 2.4.5.

Assume $(y_i, \mathbf{x}_i)$ is independent over i, the conditional mean of y_i is correctly specified as $\mathsf{E}[y_i \mid \mathbf{x}_i] = \mu(\mathbf{x}_i, \boldsymbol{\beta}_0)$, and

$$\mathsf{V}[y_i \mid \mathbf{x}_i] = \omega_i \tag{2.36}$$

is finite, but $\omega_i \neq v_i$ necessarily. Thus the mean is correctly specified but other features of the distribution such as the variance and density are potentially misspecified. Then Gourieroux et al. (1984a) show that $\hat{\boldsymbol{\beta}}_{\mathsf{LEF}} \xrightarrow{p} \boldsymbol{\beta}_0$, so the MLE is still consistent for $\boldsymbol{\beta}_0$. The intuition is that consistency of $\hat{\boldsymbol{\beta}}_{\mathsf{LEF}}$ essentially requires that

$$\mathsf{E}\left[\frac{1}{v_i}(y_i - \mu_i)\frac{\partial \mu_i}{\partial \boldsymbol{\beta}}\bigg|_{\boldsymbol{\beta}_0}\right] = \mathbf{0},$$

so that the conditions (2.31) hold in the population. This is the case if the conditional mean is correctly specified because then $\mathsf{E}[y_i - \mu(\mathbf{x}_i, \boldsymbol{\beta}_0) \mid \mathbf{x}_i] = 0$. Also

$$\sqrt{n}(\hat{\boldsymbol{\beta}}_{\mathsf{LEF}} - \boldsymbol{\beta}_0) \xrightarrow{d} \mathsf{N}[\mathbf{0}, \mathbf{A}^{-1}\mathbf{B}\mathbf{A}^{-1}], \tag{2.37}$$

where $\mathbf{A}$ is defined in Eq. (2.35) and

$$\mathbf{B} = \lim_{n\to\infty} \frac{1}{n} \sum_{i=1}^{n} \frac{\omega_i}{v_i^2} \frac{\partial \mu_i}{\partial \boldsymbol{\beta}} \frac{\partial \mu_i}{\partial \boldsymbol{\beta}'}\bigg|_{\boldsymbol{\beta}_0}. \tag{2.38}$$

Note that v_i is the working variance, the variance in the specified LEF density for y_i, while ω_i is the variance for the true dgp. Note also that (2.37) equals (2.24) where $\mathbf{X}$ is the $n \times k$ matrix with i^{th} row $\partial\mu_i/\partial\boldsymbol{\beta}'$, $\mathbf{V} = \text{diag}[v_i]$ and $\boldsymbol{\Omega} = \text{diag}[\omega_i]$, confirming the link with results for weighted linear least squares.

There are three important results. First, regardless of other properties of the true dgp for y, the PML estimator based on an assumed LEF is consistent provided the conditional mean is correctly specified. This result is sometimes misinterpreted. It should be clear that it is the assumed density that must be LEF, while the true dgp need not be LEF.

Second, correct specification of the mean and variance is sufficient for the usual maximum likelihood output to give the correct variance matrix for the PML estimator based on an assumed LEF density. Other moments of the distribution may be misspecified.

Third, if the only part of the model that is correctly specified is the conditional mean, the MLE is consistent, but the usual maximum likelihood output gives an inconsistent estimate of the variance matrix, because it uses $\mathbf{A}^{-1}$ rather than the sandwich form $\mathbf{A}^{-1}\mathbf{B}\mathbf{A}^{-1}$. This is correct only if $\mathbf{B}=\mathbf{A}$, which requires $\omega_i = v_i$, that is, correct specification of the conditional variance of the dependent variable.

Correct standard errors are obtained by using as variance matrix $\frac{1}{n}\hat{\mathbf{A}}^{-1}\hat{\mathbf{B}}\hat{\mathbf{A}}^{-1}$ where $\hat{\mathbf{A}}$ and $\hat{\mathbf{B}}$ equal $\mathbf{A}$ and $\mathbf{B}$ defined in, respectively, (2.35) and (2.37), evaluated at $\hat{\mu}_i = \mu(\mathbf{x}_i, \hat{\boldsymbol{\beta}}_{\mathsf{LEF}})$, $\hat{v}_i^2 = [c'(\hat{\mu}_i)]^{-1}$ and ω_i. The estimate of the true variance $\hat{\omega}_i$ can be obtained in two ways. First, if no assumptions are made about the variance one can use $\hat{\omega}_i = (y_i - \hat{\mu}_i)^2$ by extension of results for the OLS estimator given by White (1980). Even though $\hat{\omega}_i$ does not converge to ω_i, under suitable assumptions $\hat{\mathbf{B}} \xrightarrow{p} \mathbf{B}$. Secondly, a structural model for the variance can be specified, say as $\omega_i = \omega(\mathbf{x}_i, \boldsymbol{\beta}, \boldsymbol{\alpha})$, where $\boldsymbol{\alpha}$ is a finite dimensional nuisance parameter. Then we can use $\hat{\omega}_i = \omega(\mathbf{x}_i, \hat{\boldsymbol{\beta}}_{\mathsf{LEF}}, \hat{\boldsymbol{\alpha}})$ where $\hat{\boldsymbol{\alpha}}$ is a consistent estimate of $\boldsymbol{\alpha}$. Particularly convenient is $\omega_i = \alpha v_i$, as then $\mathbf{B} = \alpha\mathbf{A}$ so that $\mathbf{A}^{-1}\mathbf{B}\mathbf{A}^{-1} = \alpha\mathbf{A}^{-1}$.

As an example, consider the Poisson regression model with exponential mean function $\mu_i = \exp(\mathbf{x}_i'\boldsymbol{\beta})$. Then $\partial\mu_i/\partial\boldsymbol{\beta} = \mu_i\mathbf{x}_i$. The Poisson specifies the variance to equal the mean, so $v_i = \omega_i$. Substituting in (2.35) yields

$$\mathbf{A} = \lim \frac{1}{n}\sum_i \mu_i \mathbf{x}_i \mathbf{x}_i',$$

and similarly (2.38) yields

$$\mathbf{B} = \lim \frac{1}{n}\sum_i \omega_i \mathbf{x}_i \mathbf{x}_i'.$$

In general for correctly specified conditional mean the Poisson PML estimator is asymptotically normal with mean $\boldsymbol{\beta}_0$ and variance $\frac{1}{n}\mathbf{A}^{-1}\mathbf{B}\mathbf{A}^{-1}$. If additionally $\omega_i = v_i = \mu_i$ so that the conditional variance of y_i is correctly specified, then $\mathbf{A} = \mathbf{B}$ and the variance of the estimator simplifies to $\frac{1}{n}\mathbf{A}^{-1}$.

2.4.3 *LEF with Nuisance Parameter*

Given specification of a true variance function, so $\omega_i = \omega(\cdot)$, one can potentially obtain a more efficient estimator, in the same way that specification of the functional form of heteroskedasticity in the linear regression model leads to the more efficient GLS estimator.

Gourieroux et al. (1984a) introduced the more general variance function

$$\omega_i = \omega(\mu(\mathbf{x}_i, \boldsymbol{\beta}), \alpha) \tag{2.39}$$

by defining the LEF *with nuisance parameter* (LEFN)

$$f_{\mathsf{LEFN}}(y \mid \mu, \alpha) = \exp\{a(\mu, \alpha) + b(y, \alpha) + c(\mu, \alpha)y\}, \tag{2.40}$$

where $\mu = \mathsf{E}[y]$, $\omega(\mu, \alpha) = \mathsf{V}[y]$, and $\alpha = \psi(\mu, \omega)$ where $\psi(\cdot)$ is a differentiable function of α and ω and $\psi(\cdot)$ defines for any given μ a one-to-one relationship between α and ω. For given α this is an LEF density, so the functions $a(\cdot)$ and $c(\cdot)$ satisfy (2.27) and (2.28), with $c(\mu, \alpha)$ and $a(\mu, \alpha)$ replacing $c(\mu)$ and $a(\mu)$.

Gourieroux et al. (1984a) proposed the *quasigeneralized pseudomaximum likelihood* (QGPML) estimator $\hat{\boldsymbol{\beta}}_{\mathsf{LEFN}}$ based on LEFN, which maximizes with respect to $\boldsymbol{\beta}$

$$\mathcal{L}_{\mathsf{LEFN}} = \sum_{i=1}^{n} \{a(\mu_i, \omega(\tilde{\mu}_i, \tilde{\alpha})) + b(y_i, \omega(\tilde{\mu}_i, \tilde{\alpha})) + c(\mu_i, \omega(\tilde{\mu}_i, \tilde{\alpha}))y_i\} \tag{2.41}$$

where $\tilde{\mu}_i = \mu(\mathbf{x}_i, \tilde{\boldsymbol{\beta}})$ and $\tilde{\boldsymbol{\beta}}$ and $\tilde{\alpha}$ are root-n consistent estimates of $\boldsymbol{\beta}$ and α. The first-order conditions can be reexpressed as

$$\sum_{i=1}^{n} \frac{1}{\tilde{\omega}_i}(y_i - \mu_i)\frac{\partial \mu_i}{\partial \boldsymbol{\beta}} = \mathbf{0}. \tag{2.42}$$

Assume $(y_i, \mathbf{x}_i)$ is independent over i, and the conditional mean and variance of y_i are correctly specified, so $\mathsf{E}[y_i \mid \mathbf{x}_i] = \mu(\mathbf{x}_i, \boldsymbol{\beta}_0)$ and $\mathsf{V}[y_i \mid \mathbf{x}_i] = \omega(\mu(\mathbf{x}_i, \boldsymbol{\beta}_0), \alpha_0)$. Then $\hat{\boldsymbol{\beta}}_{\mathsf{LEFN}} \xrightarrow{p} \boldsymbol{\beta}_0$, so the QGPML estimator is consistent for $\boldsymbol{\beta}_0$. Also

$$\sqrt{n}(\hat{\boldsymbol{\beta}}_{\mathsf{LEFN}} - \boldsymbol{\beta}_0) \xrightarrow{d} \mathsf{N}[\mathbf{0}, \mathbf{A}^{-1}], \tag{2.43}$$

where

$$\mathbf{A} = \lim_{n\to\infty} \frac{1}{n} \sum_{i=1}^{n} \frac{1}{\omega_i} \frac{\partial \mu_i}{\partial \boldsymbol{\beta}} \frac{\partial \mu_i}{\partial \boldsymbol{\beta}'}\bigg|_{\boldsymbol{\beta}_0}. \tag{2.44}$$

A consistent estimate for the variance matrix is obtained by evaluating $\mathbf{A}$ at $\hat{\mu}_i = \mu(\mathbf{x}_i, \hat{\boldsymbol{\beta}}_{\mathsf{LEFN}})$ and $\hat{\omega}_i = \omega(\hat{\mu}_i, \tilde{\alpha})$. One can, of course, guard against possible misspecification of ω_i in the same way that possible misspecification of v_i was handled in the previous subsection.

The negative binomial model with mean μ and variance $\mu + \alpha\mu^2$ is an example of an LEFN model. The QGPMLE of this model is considered in section 3.3.

2.4.4 *Generalized Linear Models*

Generalized linear models (GLMs), introduced by Nelder and Wedderburn (1972), are closely related to the LEFN model. Differences include a notational one due to use of an alternative parameterization of the exponential family, and several simplifications including the use of more restrictive parameterizations of the conditional mean and variance than (2.29) and (2.39). A very useful simple summary of GLMs is presented in McCullagh and Nelder (1989, chapter 2).

A density $f_{\mathsf{GLM}}(y \mid \theta, \phi)$ is a member of a linear exponential family with *canonical* (or *natural*) *parameter* θ and *nuisance parameter* ϕ if

$$f_{\mathsf{GLM}}(y \mid \theta, \phi) = \exp\left\{\frac{\theta y - b(\theta)}{a(\phi)} + c(y, \phi)\right\}. \tag{2.45}$$

The function $b(\cdot)$ is such that

$$\mathsf{E}[y] = b'(\theta), \tag{2.46}$$

where $b'(\theta) = \partial b(\theta)/\partial\theta$. The function $a(\phi)$ is such that

$$\mathsf{V}[y] = a(\phi)b''(\theta), \tag{2.47}$$

where $b''(\theta) = \partial^2 b(\theta)/\partial\theta^2$. Usually $a(\phi) = \phi$. The function $c(\cdot)$ is a normalizing constant. Different functional forms for $a(\cdot)$ and $b(\cdot)$ lead to different GLMs. Note that the functions $a(\cdot)$, $b(\cdot)$, and $c(\cdot)$ for the GLM are different from the functions $a(\cdot)$, $b(\cdot)$, and $c(\cdot)$ for the LEF and LEFN.

As an example, the Poisson is the case $b(\theta) = \exp(\theta)$, $a(\phi) = 1$, and $c(y, \phi) = \ln y!$. Then (2.46) and (2.47) yield $\mathsf{E}[y] = \mathsf{V}[y] = \exp(\theta)$.

Regressors are introduced in the following way. Define the *linear predictor*

$$\eta = \mathbf{x}'\boldsymbol{\beta}. \tag{2.48}$$

The *link function* $\eta = \eta(\mu)$ relates the linear predictor to the mean μ. For example, the Poisson model with mean $\mu = \exp(\mathbf{x}'\boldsymbol{\beta})$ corresponds to the log link function $\eta = \ln\mu$. A special case of the link function of particular interest is the *canonical link function*, when

$$\eta = \theta. \tag{2.49}$$

For the Poisson the log link function is the canonical link function, because $b(\theta) = \exp(\theta)$ implies $\mu = b'(\theta) = \exp(\theta)$, so $\eta = \ln\mu = \ln(\exp(\theta)) = \theta$.

The concept of link function can cause confusion. It is more natural to consider the inverse of the link function, which is the conditional mean function. Thus, for example, the log link function is best thought of as being an exponential conditional mean function. The canonical link function is most easily thought of as leading to the density (2.45) being evaluated at $\theta = \mathbf{x}'\boldsymbol{\beta}$.

The MLE based on a GLM, $\hat{\boldsymbol{\beta}}_{\mathsf{GLM}}$, maximizes

$$\mathcal{L}_{\mathsf{GLM}} = \sum_{i=1}^{n}\left\{\frac{\theta(\mathbf{x}_i'\boldsymbol{\beta})y_i - b(\theta(\mathbf{x}_i'\boldsymbol{\beta}))}{a(\phi)} + c(y_i, \phi)\right\}. \tag{2.50}$$

The first-order conditions can be reexpressed as

$$\sum_{i=1}^{n}\frac{1}{\omega_i}(y_i - \mu_i)\frac{\partial\mu_i}{\partial\boldsymbol{\beta}} = \mathbf{0}, \tag{2.51}$$

where the variance function

$$\omega_i = a(\phi)\upsilon\big(\mu(\mathbf{x}_i'\boldsymbol{\beta})\big), \tag{2.52}$$

and

$$\upsilon(\mu_i) = b''(\theta_i). \tag{2.53}$$

The first-order conditions (2.51) for the GLM are of similar form to the first-order conditions (2.42) for the LEFN. This is because these two models are essentially the same. To link the two models, invert $\mu = b'(\theta)$ to obtain $\theta = d(\mu)$. Then (2.45) can be rewritten as

$$f_{\mathsf{GLM}}(y \mid \mu, \phi) = \exp\left\{\frac{-b(d(\mu))}{a(\phi)} + c(y, \phi) + \frac{d(\mu)}{a(\phi)}y\right\}, \tag{2.54}$$

which is clearly of the form (2.40), with the restriction that in (2.45) $a(\mu, \phi) = a_1(\mu)/a_2(\phi)$ and $c(\mu, \phi) = c_1(\mu)/c_2(\phi)$. This simplification implies that the GLM variance function $\omega(\mu(\mathbf{x}_i'\boldsymbol{\beta}), \phi)$ is multiplicative in ϕ, so that the first-order conditions can be solved for $\boldsymbol{\beta}$ without knowledge of ϕ. This is not necessarily a trivial simplification. For example, for Poisson with a nuisance parameter the GLM model specifies the variance function to be of multiplicative form $a(\psi)\mu$. The LEFN model allows, however, variance functions such as the quadratic form $\mu + \phi\mu^2$.

The same asymptotic theory as in section 2.4.3 therefore holds. Assume $(y_i, \mathbf{x}_i)$ is independent over i, and the conditional mean and variance of y_i are correctly specified, so $\mathsf{E}[y_i \mid \mathbf{x}_i] = \mu(\mathbf{x}_i, \boldsymbol{\beta}_0)$ and $\mathsf{V}(y_i \mid \mathbf{x}_i) = a(\phi_0)\upsilon(\mu(\mathbf{x}_i, \boldsymbol{\beta}_0))$. Then $\hat{\boldsymbol{\beta}}_{\mathsf{GLM}} \xrightarrow{p} \boldsymbol{\beta}_0$, so the MLE is consistent for $\boldsymbol{\beta}_0$. Also

$$\sqrt{n}(\hat{\boldsymbol{\beta}}_{\mathsf{GLM}} - \boldsymbol{\beta}_0) \xrightarrow{d} \mathsf{N}[\mathbf{0}, \mathbf{A}^{-1}] \tag{2.55}$$

where

$$\mathbf{A} = \lim_{n\to\infty} \frac{1}{n} \sum_{i=1}^{n} \frac{1}{\omega_i} \frac{\partial \mu_i}{\partial \boldsymbol{\beta}} \frac{\partial \mu_i}{\partial \boldsymbol{\beta}'}\bigg|_{\boldsymbol{\beta}_0}. \tag{2.56}$$

A consistent estimate of the variance matrix is obtained by evaluating $\mathbf{A}$ at $\hat{\mu}_i = \mu(\mathbf{x}_i, \hat{\boldsymbol{\beta}}_{\mathsf{GLM}})$ and $\hat{\omega}_i = a(\hat{\phi})\upsilon(\hat{\mu}_i)$. The standard estimate of ϕ is obtained from

$$\widehat{a(\phi)} = \frac{1}{n-k} \sum_{i=1}^{n} \frac{(y_i - \hat{\mu}_i)^2}{\upsilon(\hat{\mu}_i)}. \tag{2.57}$$

Usually $a(\phi) = \phi$.

In summary, the basic GLM model is based on the same density as the LEF and LEFN models presented in sections 2.4.2 through 2.4.3. It uses a different parameterization of the LEF, canonical and not mean, that is less natural if interest lies in modeling the conditional mean. The only real difference in the models is that the basic GLM model of Nelder and Wedderburn (1972) imposes some simplifying restrictions on the LEFN model that Gourieroux et al. (1984a) consider.

First, the conditional mean function $\mu(\mathbf{x}_i, \boldsymbol{\beta})$ is restricted to be a function of a linear combination of the regressors and so is of the simpler form $\mu(\mathbf{x}_i'\boldsymbol{\beta})$. This specialization to a single-index model simplifies interpretation of coefficients (see section 3.5) and permits computation of $\hat{\boldsymbol{\beta}}_{\mathrm{GLM}}$ using an iterative weighted least squares procedure that is detailed in McCullagh and Nelder (1989, chapter 2) and is presented for the Poisson model in section 3.8. Thus GLMs can be implemented even if one has access to just an OLS procedure. Given the computational facilities available at the time the GLM model was introduced, this was a considerable advantage.

Second, a particular parameterization of the conditional mean function, one that corresponds to the canonical link, is preferred. It can be shown that then $\partial\mu_i/\partial\boldsymbol{\beta} = \upsilon(\mu_i)\mathbf{x}_i$, so the first-order conditions (2.51) simplify to

$$\sum_{i=1}^{n}(y_i - \mu_i)\mathbf{x}_i = \mathbf{0}, \tag{2.58}$$

which makes computation especially easy. The QGPML estimator for the LEFN defined in (2.42) does not take advantage of this simplification and instead solves

$$\sum_{i=1}^{n}\frac{1}{\upsilon(\tilde{\mu}_i)}(y_i - \mu_i)\upsilon(\mu_i)\mathbf{x}_i = \mathbf{0}.$$

It is, however, asymptotically equivalent.

Third, the GLM variance function is of the simpler form $\omega_i = a(\phi)\upsilon(\mu_i)$, which is multiplicative in the nuisance parameter. Then one can estimate $\hat{\boldsymbol{\beta}}_{\mathrm{GLM}}$ without first estimating ϕ. A consequence is that with this simplification the QGPML estimator of $\boldsymbol{\beta}$ equals the PML estimator. Both can be obtained by using a maximum likelihood routine, with correct standard errors (or t-statistics) obtained by multiplying (or dividing) the standard maximum likelihood output by the square root of the scalar $\widehat{a(\phi)}$, which is easily estimated using (2.57).

2.4.5 *Extensions*

The LEFN and GLM densities permit more flexible models of the variance than the basic LEF density. Extensions to the LEF density that permit even greater flexibility in modeling the variance, particularly regression models for the variance, are extended quasilikelihood (Nelder and Pregibon, 1987), double exponential families (Efron, 1986), exponential dispersion models (Jorgensen, 1987), and varying dispersion models (Smyth, 1989). A survey is provided by Jorgensen (1997).

The presentation of GLMs has been likelihood-based, in that the estimator of $\boldsymbol{\beta}$ maximizes a log-likelihood function, albeit one possibly misspecified. An alternative way to present the results is to take as starting point the first-order conditions (2.51)

$$\sum_{i=1}^{n} \frac{1}{\omega_i}(y_i - \mu_i)\frac{\partial \mu_i}{\partial \boldsymbol{\beta}} = \mathbf{0}. \tag{2.59}$$

One can define an estimator of $\boldsymbol{\beta}$ to be the solution to these equations, without defining an underlying objective function whose derivative with respect to $\boldsymbol{\beta}$ is (2.59). These estimating equations have many properties similar to those of a log-likelihood derivative, and accordingly the left-hand side of (2.59) is called a *quasiscore function*. For completeness one can attempt to integrate this to obtain a *quasilikelihood function*. Accordingly, the solution to (2.59) is called the *quasilikelihood* (QL) *estimator*. For further details, see McCullagh and Nelder (1989, chapter 9).

It follows that the estimator of $\boldsymbol{\beta}$ in the GLM model can be interpreted either as a pseudo-MLE or quasi-MLE, meaning that it is an MLE based on a possibly misspecified density, or as a QL estimator, meaning that it is the solution to estimating equations that look like those from maximization of an unspecified log-likelihood function. It should be clear that in general the terms PML and QL have different meanings.

Recognition that it is sufficient to simply define the QL estimating equations (2.59) has led to generalizations of (2.59) and additional estimating equations to permit, for example, more flexible models of the variance functions that do not require specification of the density. These and other contributions of GLM are deferred to subsequent chapters.

2.5 Moment-Based Models

The first-order conditions (2.6) for the Poisson MLE can be motivated by noting that the specification of the conditional mean, $\mathsf{E}[y_i \mid \mathbf{x}_i] = \exp(\mathbf{x}_i'\boldsymbol{\beta})$, implies the unconditional population moment condition

$$\mathsf{E}\left[\left(y_i - \exp(\mathbf{x}_i'\boldsymbol{\beta})\right)\mathbf{x}_i\right] = \mathbf{0}.$$

A method of moments estimator for $\boldsymbol{\beta}$ is the solution to the corresponding sample moment condition

$$\sum_{i=1}^{n} \left(y_i - \exp(\mathbf{x}_i'\boldsymbol{\beta})\right)\mathbf{x}_i = \mathbf{0}.$$

In this example, the number of moment conditions equals the number of parameters, so a numerical solution for $\hat{\boldsymbol{\beta}}$ is possible. This is a special case of the estimating-equations approach, presented in section 2.5.1. More generally, there may be more moment conditions than parameters. Then we use the generalized method of moments estimator, which minimizes a quadratic function of the moment conditions and is presented in section 2.5.2.

2.5.1 *Estimating Equations*

We consider the q population moment conditions

$$\mathsf{E}[\mathbf{g}_i(y_i, \mathbf{x}_i, \boldsymbol{\theta})] = \mathbf{0}, \qquad i = 1, \ldots, n, \tag{2.60}$$

where $\mathbf{g}_i$ is a $q \times 1$ vector with the same dimension as $\boldsymbol{\theta}$. The estimator $\hat{\boldsymbol{\theta}}_{\mathsf{EE}}$ solves the corresponding estimating equations

$$\sum_{i=1}^{n} \mathbf{g}_i(y_i, \mathbf{x}_i, \boldsymbol{\theta}) = \mathbf{0}, \tag{2.61}$$

a system of q equations in q unknowns.

If (2.60) holds at $\boldsymbol{\theta}_0$ and regularity conditions are satisfied,

$$\sqrt{n}(\hat{\boldsymbol{\theta}}_{\mathsf{EE}} - \boldsymbol{\theta}_0) \stackrel{d}{\to} \mathsf{N}[\mathbf{0}, \mathbf{A}^{-1}\mathbf{B}\mathbf{A}^{-1}], \tag{2.62}$$

where

$$\mathbf{A} = \lim_{n\to\infty} \frac{1}{n} \mathsf{E}\left[\sum_{i=1}^{n} \left. \frac{\partial \mathbf{g}_i(y_i, \mathbf{x}_i, \boldsymbol{\theta})}{\partial \boldsymbol{\theta}'} \right|_{\boldsymbol{\theta}_0} \right] \tag{2.63}$$

$$\mathbf{B} = \lim_{n\to\infty} \frac{1}{n} \mathsf{E}\left[\sum_{i=1}^{n} \left. \mathbf{g}_i(y_i, \mathbf{x}_i, \boldsymbol{\theta}) \mathbf{g}_i(y_i, \mathbf{x}_i, \boldsymbol{\theta})' \right|_{\boldsymbol{\theta}_0} \right]. \tag{2.64}$$

The variance matrix in (2.62) is consistently estimated by $\hat{\mathbf{A}}^{-1}\hat{\mathbf{B}}\hat{\mathbf{A}}'^{-1}$, where $\hat{\mathbf{A}}$ and $\hat{\mathbf{B}}$ are any consistent estimates of $\mathbf{A}$ and $\mathbf{B}$. Such estimators are called sandwich estimators, because $\hat{\mathbf{B}}$ is sandwiched between $\hat{\mathbf{A}}^{-1}$ and $\hat{\mathbf{A}}'^{-1}$. Throughout the book we use the term *robust sandwich* (RS) estimator for the special case when the consistent estimators of $\mathbf{A}$ and $\mathbf{B}$ are

$$\hat{\mathbf{A}} = \frac{1}{n} \sum_{i=1}^{n} \left. \frac{\partial \mathbf{g}_i(y_i, \mathbf{x}_i, \boldsymbol{\theta})}{\partial \boldsymbol{\theta}'} \right|_{\hat{\boldsymbol{\theta}}_{\mathsf{EE}}}, \tag{2.65}$$

and, assuming independence of the data over i,

$$\hat{\mathbf{B}} = \frac{1}{n} \sum_{i=1}^{n} \mathbf{g}_i(y_i, \mathbf{x}_i, \hat{\boldsymbol{\theta}}_{\mathsf{EE}}) \mathbf{g}_i(y_i, \mathbf{x}_i, \hat{\boldsymbol{\theta}}_{\mathsf{EE}})'. \tag{2.66}$$

This has the special property that it is *robust* to misspecification of the dgp, in the sense that the expectations in (2.63) and (2.64) have been dropped.

For example, the OLS estimator sets $\mathbf{g}_i(y_i, \mathbf{x}_i, \boldsymbol{\beta}) = (y_i - \mathbf{x}_i'\boldsymbol{\beta})\mathbf{x}_i$; see (2.22) with $v_i = 1$. Then

$$\mathbf{B} = \frac{1}{n} \sum_i \mathsf{E}\left[(y_i - \mathbf{x}_i'\boldsymbol{\beta})^2 \right] \mathbf{x}_i \mathbf{x}_i'.$$

A consistent estimator of $\mathbf{B}$ that makes no assumptions on $\mathsf{E}[(y_i - \mathbf{x}_i'\beta)^2]$ is

$$\hat{\mathbf{B}} = \frac{1}{n}\sum_i \left(y_i - \mathbf{x}_i'\hat{\beta}\right)^2 \mathbf{x}_i\mathbf{x}_i'.$$

White (1980), building on work by Eicker (1967), proposed this estimator to guard against heteroskedasticity in models assuming homoskedasticity. Huber (1967) and White (1982) proposed the sandwich estimator (see [2.19]) to guard against misspecification of the density in the maximum likelihood framework. The robust sandwich estimator is often called the Huber estimator or Eicker-White estimator.

The estimating equation approach is general enough to include maximum likelihood and GLM as special cases. Extension to longitudinal data, due to Liang and Zeger (1986), is presented in Chapter 9. Optimal estimating equations based on the first few moments of the dependent variable are given in Chapter 12. Such extensions have tended to be piecemeal and assume the number of moment conditions equals the number of parameters. A very general framework, widely used in econometrics but rarely used in other areas of statistics, is generalized methods of moments. This is now presented.

2.5.2 *Generalized Methods of Moments*

We consider the r population moment (or orthogonality) conditions

$$\mathsf{E}[\mathbf{h}_i(y_i, \mathbf{x}_i, \boldsymbol{\theta})] = \mathbf{0}, \qquad i = 1, \ldots, n, \tag{2.67}$$

where $\mathbf{h}_i$ is an $r \times 1$ vector and $r \geq q$, so that the number of moment conditions potentially exceeds the number of parameters. Meaningful examples where $r \geq q$ are presented in later chapters.

Hansen (1982) proposed the *generalized methods of moments* (GMM) estimator $\hat{\boldsymbol{\theta}}_{\mathsf{GMM}}$, which makes the sample moment corresponding to (2.67) as small as possible in the quadratic norm

$$\left[\sum_{i=1}^{n} \mathbf{h}_i(y_i, \mathbf{x}_i, \boldsymbol{\theta})\right]' \mathbf{W}_n \left[\sum_{i=1}^{n} \mathbf{h}_i(y_i, \mathbf{x}_i, \boldsymbol{\theta})\right], \tag{2.68}$$

where $\mathbf{W}_n$ is a possibly stochastic symmetric positive definite $r \times r$ weighting matrix, which converges in probability to a nonstochastic matrix $\mathbf{W}$. The GMM estimator is calculated as the solution to the resulting first-order conditions

$$\left[\sum_{i=1}^{n} \frac{\partial \mathbf{h}_i'}{\partial \boldsymbol{\theta}}\right] \mathbf{W}_n \left[\sum_{i=1}^{n} \mathbf{h}_i\right] = \mathbf{0}, \tag{2.69}$$

where $\mathbf{h}_i = \mathbf{h}_i(y_i, \mathbf{x}_i, \boldsymbol{\theta})$. The solution will generally require an iterative technique. The parameter $\boldsymbol{\theta}$ is identified if (2.67) has a unique solution.

Under suitable assumptions $\hat{\boldsymbol{\theta}} \xrightarrow{p} \boldsymbol{\theta}_0$, where $\boldsymbol{\theta}_0$ is the value of $\boldsymbol{\theta}$ that minimizes the probability limit of n^{-2} times the objective function (2.68). Also,

$$\sqrt{n}(\hat{\boldsymbol{\theta}}_{\mathsf{GMM}} - \boldsymbol{\theta}_0) \xrightarrow{d} \mathsf{N}[\mathbf{0}, \mathbf{A}^{-1}\mathbf{B}\mathbf{A}^{-1}], \tag{2.70}$$

where the formulas for $\mathbf{A}$ and $\mathbf{B}$ are

$$\mathbf{A} = \mathbf{H}'\mathbf{W}\mathbf{H} \tag{2.71}$$

$$\mathbf{B} = \mathbf{H}'\mathbf{W}\mathbf{S}\mathbf{W}\mathbf{H} \tag{2.72}$$

where

$$\mathbf{H} = \lim_{n\to\infty} \frac{1}{n} \mathsf{E}\left[\sum_{i=1}^{n} \left. \frac{\partial \mathbf{h}_i}{\partial \boldsymbol{\theta}'} \right|_{\boldsymbol{\theta}_0} \right] \tag{2.73}$$

$$\mathbf{S} = \lim_{n\to\infty} \frac{1}{n} \mathsf{E}\left[\sum_{i=1}^{n} \sum_{j=1}^{n} \left. \mathbf{h}_i \mathbf{h}_j' \right|_{\boldsymbol{\theta}_0} \right]. \tag{2.74}$$

The expression for $\mathbf{S}$ permits possible correlation across i and j, and hence covers the case of time series. Note that substitution of (2.71) and (2.72) into (2.70) yields an expression for the variance matrix of the GMM estimator of the same form as (2.24) for the linear WLS estimator.

For given choice of population moment condition $\mathbf{h}_i(y_i, \mathbf{x}_i, \boldsymbol{\theta})$ in (2.67), the optimal choice of weighting matrix $\mathbf{W}_n$ in (2.68) is the inverse of a consistent estimator $\hat{\mathbf{S}}$ of $\mathbf{S}$. The optimal GMM estimator $\hat{\boldsymbol{\theta}}^{\text{opt}}_{\mathsf{GMM}}$ minimizes

$$\left[\sum_{i=1}^{n} \mathbf{h}_i(y_i, \mathbf{x}_i, \boldsymbol{\theta}) \right]' \hat{\mathbf{S}}^{-1} \left[\sum_{i=1}^{n} \mathbf{h}_i(y_i, \mathbf{x}_i, \boldsymbol{\theta}) \right]. \tag{2.75}$$

Then

$$\sqrt{n}\left(\hat{\boldsymbol{\theta}}^{\text{opt}}_{\mathsf{GMM}} - \boldsymbol{\theta}_0\right) \xrightarrow{d} \mathsf{N}[\mathbf{0}, \mathbf{A}^{-1}], \tag{2.76}$$

where

$$\mathbf{A} = \mathbf{H}'\mathbf{S}^{-1}\mathbf{H}. \tag{2.77}$$

A standard procedure is to first estimate the model by GMM with weighting matrix $\mathbf{W}_n = \mathbf{I}_r$ to obtain initial consistent estimates of $\boldsymbol{\theta}$. These are used to form $\hat{\mathbf{S}}$ needed for optimal GMM.

It is important to note that this optimality is limited, as it is for given moment condition $\mathbf{h}_i(y_i, \mathbf{x}_i, \boldsymbol{\theta})$. Some choices of $\mathbf{h}_i(y_i, \mathbf{x}_i, \boldsymbol{\theta})$ are better than others. If the distribution is completely specified, the MLE is optimal and

$$\mathbf{h}_i(y_i, \mathbf{x}_i, \boldsymbol{\theta}) = \frac{\partial \ln f(y_i \mid \mathbf{x}_i, \boldsymbol{\theta})}{\partial \boldsymbol{\theta}}.$$

The relevant theory was presented by Hansen (1982), based on earlier work on instrumental variables by Amemiya (1974) in the nonlinear case and Sargan (1958) in the linear case.

In particular, Amemiya (1974) proposed the *nonlinear two-stage least squares* or *nonlinear instrumental variables* (NLIV) estimator, which minimizes

$$\left[\sum_{i=1}^{n}(y_i - \mu(\mathbf{x}_i'\boldsymbol{\beta}))\mathbf{z}_i'\right]\left[\sum_{i=1}^{n}\mathbf{z}_i\mathbf{z}_i'\right]^{-1}\left[\sum_{i=1}^{n}(y_i - \mu(\mathbf{x}_i'\boldsymbol{\beta}))\mathbf{z}_i\right], \tag{2.78}$$

where $\mathbf{z}_i$ is an $r \times 1$ set of instruments such that $\mathsf{E}[y_i - \mu(\mathbf{x}_i'\boldsymbol{\beta}) \mid \mathbf{z}_i] = 0$. This is a GMM estimator where $\mathbf{h}_i(y_i, \mathbf{x}_i, \boldsymbol{\theta}) = (y_i - \mu(\mathbf{x}_i'\boldsymbol{\beta}))\mathbf{z}_i$ in (2.68). The weighting matrix in (2.78) is optimal if $\mathsf{V}[y_i \mid \mathbf{z}_i] = \sigma^2$, because then $\mathbf{S} = \sigma^2 \lim \frac{1}{n}\sum_{i=1}^{n} \mathbf{z}_i\mathbf{z}_i'$, and the variance of the estimator from (2.77) is $\mathbf{H}'\mathbf{S}^{-1}\mathbf{H}$ where $\mathbf{H} = \lim \frac{1}{n}\sum_{i=1}^{n} \mathbf{z}_i\,\partial\mu_i/\partial\boldsymbol{\beta}'$. This estimator is used, for example, in section 11.3, which also considers extension to heteroskedastic errors. The linear instrumental variables or two-stage least squares estimator is the specialization $\mu(\mathbf{x}_i'\boldsymbol{\beta}) = \mathbf{x}_i'\boldsymbol{\beta}$.

Smith (1997) summarizes recent research that places GMM in the likelihood framework. For example, Qin and Lawless (1994) propose an estimator, asymptotically equivalent to GMM, that maximizes the empirical likelihood subject to moment conditions of the form (2.68).

To operationalize these results requires consistent estimates of $\mathbf{H}$ and $\mathbf{S}$. For $\mathbf{H}$ use

$$\hat{\mathbf{H}} = \frac{1}{n}\sum_{i=1}^{n}\left.\frac{\partial\mathbf{h}_i}{\partial\boldsymbol{\theta}'}\right|_{\hat{\boldsymbol{\theta}}_{\mathsf{GMM}}}. \tag{2.79}$$

When observations are independent over i one uses

$$\hat{\mathbf{S}} = \frac{1}{n}\sum_{i=1}^{n}\left.\mathbf{h}_i\mathbf{h}_i'\right|_{\hat{\boldsymbol{\theta}}_{\mathsf{GMM}}}. \tag{2.80}$$

In the time series case observations are dependent over i. It is simplest to assume that only observations up to m periods apart are correlated, as is the case for a vector moving average process of order m. Then (2.74) simplifies to $\mathbf{S} = \boldsymbol{\Omega}_0 + \sum_{j=1}^{m}(\boldsymbol{\Omega}_j + \boldsymbol{\Omega}_j')$, where $\boldsymbol{\Omega}_j = \lim_{n\to\infty}\frac{1}{n}\mathsf{E}[\sum_{i=j+1}^{n}\mathbf{h}_i\mathbf{h}_{i-j}']$. Newey and West (1987a) proposed the estimator

$$\hat{\mathbf{S}} = \hat{\boldsymbol{\Omega}}_0 + \sum_{j=1}^{m}\left(1 - \frac{j}{m+1}\right)(\hat{\boldsymbol{\Omega}}_j + \hat{\boldsymbol{\Omega}}_j'), \tag{2.81}$$

where

$$\hat{\boldsymbol{\Omega}}_j = \frac{1}{n}\sum_{i=j+1}^{n}\left.\mathbf{h}_i\mathbf{h}_{i-j}'\right|_{\hat{\boldsymbol{\theta}}_{\mathsf{GMM}}}. \tag{2.82}$$

This estimator of $\mathbf{S}$ is the obvious estimator of this quantity, aside from multiplication by $(1 - j/(m+1))$, which ensures that $\hat{\mathbf{S}}$ is positive definite. Care needs to be used to ensure consistency before applying this last result. In particular, in the time series case if the regressors include lagged dependent variables and the $\mathbf{h}_i$ are serially correlated then the GMM estimator will be inconsistent.

The GMM results simplify if $r = q$, in which case we have the estimating equations presented in the previous subsection. Then $\mathbf{h}_i(y_i, \mathbf{x}_i, \boldsymbol{\theta}) = \mathbf{g}_i(y_i, \mathbf{x}_i, \boldsymbol{\theta})$, $\mathbf{H} = \mathbf{A}$, $\mathbf{B} = \mathbf{S}$, where $\mathbf{B}$ assumes independence over i, and the results are invariant to choice of weighting matrix $\mathbf{W}_n$. The estimating equations estimator defined by (2.61) is the GMM estimator which minimizes

$$\left[\sum_{i=1}^{n} \mathbf{g}_i(y_i, \mathbf{x}_i, \boldsymbol{\theta})\right]' \left[\sum_{i=1}^{n} \mathbf{g}_i(y_i, \mathbf{x}_i, \boldsymbol{\theta})\right].$$

Unlike the general case $r > q$, this quadratic objective function takes value 0 at the optimal value of $\boldsymbol{\theta}$ when $r = q$.

2.5.3 *Optimal GMM*

We have already considered a limited form of optimal GMM. Given a choice of $\mathbf{h}(y_i, \mathbf{x}_i, \boldsymbol{\theta})$ in (2.67), the optimal GMM estimator is $\hat{\boldsymbol{\theta}}_{\mathsf{GMM}}^{\text{opt}}$, defined in (2.75), which uses as weighting matrix a consistent estimate of $\mathbf{S}$ defined in (2.74).

Now we consider the more difficult question of optimal specification of $\mathbf{h}(y_i, \mathbf{x}_i, \boldsymbol{\theta})$, in the cross-section case or panel case where $y_i, \mathbf{x}_i$ are iid. This is analyzed by Chamberlain (1987) and Newey (1990a), with an excellent summary given in Newey (1993). Suppose interest lies in estimation based on the conditional moment restriction

$$\mathsf{E}[\boldsymbol{\rho}(y_i, \mathbf{x}_i, \boldsymbol{\theta}) \mid \mathbf{x}_i] = \mathbf{0}, \qquad i = 1, \ldots, n, \tag{2.83}$$

where $\boldsymbol{\rho}(\cdot)$ is a residual-type $s \times 1$ vector function.

For example, let $s = 2$ with the components of $\boldsymbol{\rho}(\cdot)$ being $\rho_1(y_i, \mathbf{x}_i, \boldsymbol{\theta}) = y_i - \mu_i$ and $\rho_2(y_i, \mathbf{x}_i, \boldsymbol{\theta}) = (y_i - \mu_i)^2 - \sigma_i^2$, where $\mu_i = \mu(\mathbf{x}_i, \boldsymbol{\theta})$ and $\sigma_i^2 = \omega(\mathbf{x}_i, \boldsymbol{\theta})$ are specified conditional mean and variance functions.

Typically s is less than the number of parameters, so GMM estimation based on (2.83) is not possible. Instead we introduce an $r \times s$ matrix of functions $\mathbf{D}(\mathbf{x}_i)$, where $r \geq q$, and note that by the law of iterated expectations,

$$\mathsf{E}[\mathbf{D}(\mathbf{x}_i)\boldsymbol{\rho}(y_i, \mathbf{x}_i, \boldsymbol{\theta})] = \mathbf{0}, \qquad i = 1, \ldots, n. \tag{2.84}$$

$\boldsymbol{\theta}$ can be estimated by GMM based on (2.84), because there are now $r \geq q$ moment conditions.

The variance of the GMM estimator can be shown to be minimized, given (2.83), by choosing $\mathbf{D}(\mathbf{x}_i)$ equal to the $q \times s$ matrix

$$\mathbf{D}^*(\mathbf{x}_i) = \mathsf{E}\left[\left.\frac{\partial \boldsymbol{\rho}(y_i, \mathbf{x}_i, \boldsymbol{\theta})'}{\partial \boldsymbol{\theta}}\right| \mathbf{x}_i\right] \{\mathsf{E}[\boldsymbol{\rho}(y_i, \mathbf{x}_i, \boldsymbol{\theta})\boldsymbol{\rho}(y_i, \mathbf{x}_i, \boldsymbol{\theta})' \mid \mathbf{x}_i]\}^{-1}.$$

Premultiplication of $\mathbf{D}^*(\mathbf{x}_i)$ by an $s \times s$ matrix of constants (not depending on $\mathbf{x}_i$) yields an equivalent optimal estimator. It follows that the optimal choice of $\mathbf{h}(y_i, \mathbf{x}_i, \boldsymbol{\theta})$ for GMM estimation, given (2.83), is

$$\mathbf{h}_i^*(y_i, \mathbf{x}_i, \boldsymbol{\theta}) = \mathsf{E}\left[\frac{\partial \rho(y_i, \mathbf{x}_i, \boldsymbol{\theta})'}{\partial \boldsymbol{\theta}}\bigg| \mathbf{x}_i\right] \times \{\mathsf{E}[\rho(y_i, \mathbf{x}_i, \boldsymbol{\theta})\rho(y_i, \mathbf{x}_i, \boldsymbol{\theta})' \,|\, \mathbf{x}_i]\}^{-1} \rho(y_i, \mathbf{x}_i, \boldsymbol{\theta}). \tag{2.85}$$

Note that here $r = q$, so $\mathbf{h}_i^*(y_i, \mathbf{x}_i, \boldsymbol{\theta})$ is $q \times q$ and the estimating equation results of section 2.5.1 are applicable. The optimal GMM estimator is the solution to

$$\sum_{i=1}^{n} \mathbf{h}_i^*(y_i, \mathbf{x}_i, \boldsymbol{\theta}) = \mathbf{0}.$$

The limit distribution is given in (2.62) through (2.64), with $\mathbf{g}_i(\cdot) = \mathbf{h}_i^*(\cdot)$.

This optimal GMM estimator is applied, for example, to models with specified conditional mean and variance functions in section 12.2.2.

2.5.4 *Sequential Two-Step Estimators*

The GMM framework is quite general. One example of its application is to sequential two-step estimators. Consider the case in which a model depends on vector parameters $\boldsymbol{\theta}_1$ and $\boldsymbol{\theta}_2$, and the model is estimated sequentially: (1) Obtain a root-n consistent estimate $\tilde{\boldsymbol{\theta}}_1$ of $\boldsymbol{\theta}_1$ that solves $\sum_{i=1}^{n} \mathbf{h}_{1i}(y_i, \mathbf{x}_i, \tilde{\boldsymbol{\theta}}_1) = \mathbf{0}$; and (2) Obtain a root-$n$ consistent estimate $\hat{\boldsymbol{\theta}}_2$ of $\boldsymbol{\theta}_2$ given $\tilde{\boldsymbol{\theta}}_1$ that solves $\sum_{i=1}^{n} \mathbf{h}_{2i}(y_i, \mathbf{x}_i, \tilde{\boldsymbol{\theta}}_1, \hat{\boldsymbol{\theta}}_2) = \mathbf{0}$.

In general the distribution of $\hat{\boldsymbol{\theta}}_2$ given estimation of $\tilde{\boldsymbol{\theta}}_1$ differs from, and is more complicated than, the distribution of $\hat{\boldsymbol{\theta}}_2$ if $\boldsymbol{\theta}_1$ is known. Statistical inference is invalid if it fails to take into account this complication. Newey (1984) proposed obtaining the distribution of $\hat{\boldsymbol{\theta}}_2$ by noting that $(\boldsymbol{\theta}_1, \boldsymbol{\theta}_2)$ jointly solve the equations

$$\sum_{i=1}^{n} \mathbf{h}_{1i}(y_i, \mathbf{x}_i, \boldsymbol{\theta}_1) = \mathbf{0}$$

and

$$\sum_{i=1}^{n} \mathbf{h}_{2i}(y_i, \mathbf{x}_i, \boldsymbol{\theta}_1, \boldsymbol{\theta}_2) = \mathbf{0}.$$

This is simply a special case of

$$\sum_{i=1}^{n} \mathbf{h}_i(y_i, \mathbf{x}_i, \boldsymbol{\theta}) = \mathbf{0},$$

defining $\boldsymbol{\theta} = (\boldsymbol{\theta}_1' \quad \boldsymbol{\theta}_2')'$ and $\mathbf{h}_i = (\mathbf{h}_{1i}' \quad \mathbf{h}_{2i}')'$. This is a GMM estimator with $\mathbf{W}_n = \mathbf{W} = \mathbf{I}$. Applying (2.70) with $\mathbf{A}$ and $\mathbf{B}$ partitioned similar to $\boldsymbol{\theta}$ and $\mathbf{h}_i$ yields a variance matrix for $\hat{\boldsymbol{\theta}}_2$, which is quite complicated even though simplification occurs because $\partial \mathbf{h}_{1i}(\boldsymbol{\theta})/\partial \boldsymbol{\theta}_2' = \mathbf{0}$. The expression is given in Newey (1984), Murphy and Topel (1985), Pagan (1986), and Greene (1997a). See also Pierce (1982).

A well-known exception to the need to take account of the randomness due to estimation of $\tilde{\boldsymbol{\theta}}_1$ is feasible GLS, where $\tilde{\boldsymbol{\theta}}_1$ corresponds to the first-round estimates used to consistently estimate the variance matrix, and $\hat{\boldsymbol{\theta}}_2$ corresponds to the second-round feasible GLS estimates of the regression parameters for the conditional mean.

Such simplification occurs whenever $\mathsf{E}[\partial \mathbf{h}_{2i}(\boldsymbol{\theta})/\partial \boldsymbol{\theta}_1'] = \mathbf{0}$. This simplification holds for the GLM and LEFN models. To see this for LEFN, from (2.42) with $\hat{\boldsymbol{\theta}}_2 = \hat{\beta}_{\mathsf{LEFN}}$ and $\tilde{\boldsymbol{\theta}}_1 = \tilde{\alpha}$ and

$$\mathbf{h}_{2i}(\boldsymbol{\theta}) = \frac{1}{\tilde{\omega}_i(\tilde{\boldsymbol{\theta}}_1)}(y_i - \mu_i(\boldsymbol{\theta}_2))\frac{\partial \mu_i(\boldsymbol{\theta}_2)}{\partial \boldsymbol{\theta}_2},$$

it follows that $\mathsf{E}[\partial \mathbf{h}_{2i}(\boldsymbol{\theta})/\partial \boldsymbol{\theta}_1'] = \mathbf{0}$.

This simplification also arises in the ML framework for jointly estimated $\boldsymbol{\theta}_1$ and $\boldsymbol{\theta}_2$ if the information matrix is block-diagonal. Then the variance of $\hat{\boldsymbol{\theta}}_{1,\mathsf{ML}}$ is the inverse of $-\mathsf{E}[\partial^2 \mathcal{L}(\boldsymbol{\theta})/\partial \boldsymbol{\theta}_1 \partial \boldsymbol{\theta}_1'] = \mathsf{E}[\partial(\partial \mathcal{L}(\boldsymbol{\theta})/\partial \boldsymbol{\theta}_1)/\partial \boldsymbol{\theta}_1']$. An example is the negative binomial distribution model with quadratic variance function (see Section 3.3.1).

2.6 Testing

2.6.1 *Likelihood-Based Models*

There is a well-developed theory for testing hypotheses in models in which the likelihood function is specified. Then there are three "classical" statistical techniques for testing hypotheses – the likelihood ratio, Wald, and Lagrange multiplier (or score) tests.

Let the null hypothesis be

$$H_0 : \mathbf{r}(\boldsymbol{\theta}_0) = \mathbf{0},$$

where $\mathbf{r}$ is an $h \times 1$ vector of possibly nonlinear restrictions on $\boldsymbol{\theta}$, $h \leq q$. Let the alternative hypothesis be

$$H_a : \mathbf{r}(\boldsymbol{\theta}_0) \neq \mathbf{0}.$$

For example, $r_l(\boldsymbol{\theta}) = \theta_3\theta_4 - 1$ if the lth restriction is $\theta_3\theta_4 = 1$. We assume the restrictions are such that the $h \times q$ matrix $\partial \mathbf{r}(\boldsymbol{\theta})/\partial \boldsymbol{\theta}'$, with the lj^{th} element $\partial r_l(\boldsymbol{\theta})/\partial \theta_j$, has full rank h. This is the analogue of the assumption of linearly independent restrictions in the case of linear restrictions.

Let $\mathsf{L}(\boldsymbol{\theta})$ denote the likelihood function, $\hat{\boldsymbol{\theta}}_u$ denote the unrestricted MLE that maximizes $\mathcal{L}(\boldsymbol{\theta}) = \ln \mathsf{L}(\boldsymbol{\theta})$, and $\tilde{\boldsymbol{\theta}}_r$ denote the restricted MLE under H_0 that maximizes $\mathcal{L}(\boldsymbol{\theta}) - \boldsymbol{\lambda}'\mathbf{r}(\boldsymbol{\theta})$ where $\boldsymbol{\lambda}$ is an $h \times 1$ vector of Lagrangian multipliers.

We now present the three standard test statistics. Under the regularity conditions they are all asymptotically $\chi^2(h)$ under H_0, and H_0 is rejected at significance level α if the computed test statistic exceeds $\chi^2(h;\alpha)$.

The likelihood ratio (LR) test statistic

$$\mathsf{T_{LR}} = -2[\mathcal{L}(\tilde{\boldsymbol{\theta}}_r) - \mathcal{L}(\hat{\boldsymbol{\theta}}_u)]. \tag{2.86}$$

The motivation for $\mathsf{T_{LR}}$ is that if H_0 is true, the unconstrained and constrained maxima of the likelihood function should be the same and $\mathsf{T_{LR}} \simeq 0$. The test is called the likelihood ratio test because $\mathsf{T_{LR}}$ equals minus two times the logarithm of the likelihood ratio $\mathsf{L}(\tilde{\boldsymbol{\theta}}_r)/\mathsf{L}(\hat{\boldsymbol{\theta}}_u)$.

The Wald test statistic is

$$\mathsf{T_W} = \mathbf{r}(\hat{\boldsymbol{\theta}}_u)'\left\{\left.\frac{\partial \mathbf{r}(\boldsymbol{\theta})'}{\partial \boldsymbol{\theta}}\right|_{\hat{\boldsymbol{\theta}}_u}\left[\frac{1}{n}\,\hat{\mathbf{A}}(\hat{\boldsymbol{\theta}}_u)^{-1}\right]\left.\frac{\partial \mathbf{r}(\boldsymbol{\theta})}{\partial \boldsymbol{\theta}'}\right|_{\hat{\boldsymbol{\theta}}_u}\right\}^{-1}\mathbf{r}(\hat{\boldsymbol{\theta}}_u), \tag{2.87}$$

where $\hat{\mathbf{A}}(\hat{\boldsymbol{\theta}}_u)$ is a consistent estimator of the variance matrix defined in (2.13) evaluated at the unrestricted MLE. This tests how close $\mathbf{r}(\hat{\boldsymbol{\theta}}_u)$ is to the hypothesized value of $\mathbf{0}$ under H_0. By a first-order Taylor series expansion of $\mathbf{r}(\hat{\boldsymbol{\theta}}_u)$ about $\boldsymbol{\theta}_0$ it can be shown that under H_0, $\mathbf{r}(\hat{\boldsymbol{\theta}}_u) \overset{a}{\sim} \mathsf{N}[\mathbf{0}, \mathsf{V}_r]$ where V_r is the matrix in braces in (2.87). This leads to the chi-square statistic (2.87).

The Lagrange multiplier (LM) test statistic is

$$\mathsf{T_{LM}} = \sum_{i=1}^{n}\left.\frac{\partial \ln f_i}{\partial \boldsymbol{\theta}'}\right|_{\tilde{\boldsymbol{\theta}}_r}\left[\frac{1}{n}\tilde{\mathbf{A}}(\tilde{\boldsymbol{\theta}}_r)\right]^{-1}\sum_{i=1}^{n}\left.\frac{\partial \ln f_i}{\partial \boldsymbol{\theta}}\right|_{\tilde{\boldsymbol{\theta}}_r} \tag{2.88}$$

where $\tilde{\mathbf{A}}(\tilde{\boldsymbol{\theta}}_r)$ is a consistent estimator of the variance matrix defined in (2.13) evaluated at the restricted MLE. Motivation of $\mathsf{T_{LM}}$ is given below.

To motivate $\mathsf{T_{LM}}$ first define the score vector

$$\mathbf{s}(\boldsymbol{\theta}) = \frac{\partial \mathcal{L}}{\partial \boldsymbol{\theta}} = \sum_{i=1}^{n}\frac{\partial \ln f_i}{\partial \boldsymbol{\theta}}. \tag{2.89}$$

For the unrestricted MLE the score vector $\mathbf{s}(\hat{\boldsymbol{\theta}}_u) = \mathbf{0}$. These are just the first-order conditions (2.11) that define the estimator. If H_0 is true, then this maximum should also occur at the restricted MLE, as imposing the constraint will then have little impact on the estimated value of $\boldsymbol{\theta}$. That is, $\mathbf{s}(\tilde{\boldsymbol{\theta}}_r) = \mathbf{0}$. $\mathsf{T_{LM}}$ measures the closeness of this derivative to zero. The distribution of $\mathsf{T_{LM}}$ follows from $\mathbf{s}(\tilde{\boldsymbol{\theta}}_r) \overset{a}{\sim} N(\mathbf{0}, \frac{1}{n}\mathbf{A})$ under H_0. Using this motivation, $\mathsf{T_{LM}}$ is called the *score test* because $\mathbf{s}(\boldsymbol{\theta})$ is the score vector.

An alternative motivation for $\mathsf{T_{LM}}$ is to measure the closeness to zero of the expected value of the Lagrange multipliers of the constrained optimization problem for the restricted MLE. Maximizing $\mathcal{L}(\mathbf{y}, \boldsymbol{\theta}) - \boldsymbol{\lambda}'\mathbf{r}(\boldsymbol{\theta})$, the first-order conditions with respect to $\boldsymbol{\theta}$ imply $\mathbf{s}(\tilde{\boldsymbol{\theta}}_r) = \mathbf{R}(\tilde{\boldsymbol{\theta}}_r)\tilde{\boldsymbol{\lambda}}$, where $\mathbf{R}(\boldsymbol{\theta}) = [\partial \mathbf{r}(\boldsymbol{\theta})'/\partial \boldsymbol{\theta}]$.

Tests based on $\mathbf{s}(\tilde{\boldsymbol{\theta}}_r)$ are equivalent to tests based on the estimated Lagrange multipliers $\tilde{\boldsymbol{\lambda}}$ because $\mathbf{R}(\tilde{\boldsymbol{\theta}}_r)$ is of full rank. So T_{LM} is also called the *Lagrange multiplier test*. Throughout this book we refer to T_{LM} as the LM test. It is exactly the same as the score test, an alternative label widely used in the statistics literature.

In addition to being asymptotically $\chi^2(h)$ under H_0, all three test statistics are noncentral $\chi^2(h)$ with the same noncentrality parameter under local alternatives $H_a : \mathbf{r}(\boldsymbol{\theta}) = n^{-1/2}\boldsymbol{\delta}$, where $\boldsymbol{\delta}$ is a vector of constants. So they all have the same local power. The choice of which test statistic to use is therefore mainly one of convenience in computation or of small sample performance.

T_{LR} requires estimation of $\boldsymbol{\theta}$ under both H_0 and H_a. If this is easily done, then the test is very simple to implement, as one need only read off the log-likelihood statistics routinely printed out, subtract, and multiply by 2. T_{W} requires estimation only under H_a and is best to use if the unrestricted model is easy to estimate. T_{LM} requires estimation only under H_0 and is attractive if the restricted model is easy to estimate.

An additional attraction of the LM test is easy computation. Let $\mathbf{s}_i(\tilde{\boldsymbol{\theta}}_r)$ be the ith component of the summation forming the score vector (2.89) for the unrestricted density evaluated at the restricted MLE. An asymptotically equivalent version of T_{LM} can be computed as the uncentered explained sum of squares, or n times the uncentered R^2, from the auxiliary OLS regression

$$1 = \mathbf{s}_i(\tilde{\boldsymbol{\theta}}_r)'\gamma + u_i. \tag{2.90}$$

The uncentered explained sum of squares from regression of $\mathbf{y}$ on $\mathbf{X}$ is $\mathbf{y}'\mathbf{X}$ $(\mathbf{X}'\mathbf{X})^{-1}$ $\mathbf{X}'\mathbf{y}$ and the uncentered R^2 is $\mathbf{y}'\mathbf{X}(\mathbf{X}'\mathbf{X})^{-1}\mathbf{X}'\mathbf{y}/\mathbf{y}'\mathbf{y}$.

2.6.2 *General Models*

The preceding results are restricted to hypothesis tests based on MLEs. The Wald test can be extended to any consistent estimator $\hat{\boldsymbol{\theta}}$ that does not impose the restrictions being tested. The only change in (2.87) is that $\hat{\boldsymbol{\theta}}$ replaces $\hat{\boldsymbol{\theta}}_u$ and $\mathsf{V}[\hat{\boldsymbol{\theta}}]$ replaces $\frac{1}{n}\hat{\mathbf{A}}(\hat{\boldsymbol{\theta}}_u)^{-1}$. We test $H_0 : \mathbf{r}(\boldsymbol{\theta}_0) = \mathbf{0}$ using

$$\mathsf{T}_{\mathsf{W}} = \mathbf{r}(\hat{\boldsymbol{\theta}})' \left\{ \left.\frac{\partial \mathbf{r}(\boldsymbol{\theta})'}{\partial \boldsymbol{\theta}}\right|_{\hat{\theta}} \mathsf{V}[\hat{\boldsymbol{\theta}}] \left.\frac{\partial \mathbf{r}(\boldsymbol{\theta})}{\partial \boldsymbol{\theta}'}\right|_{\hat{\theta}} \right\}^{-1} \mathbf{r}(\hat{\boldsymbol{\theta}}), \tag{2.91}$$

which is $\chi^2(h)$ under H_0. Reject $H_0 : \mathbf{r}(\boldsymbol{\theta}_0) = \mathbf{0}$ against $H_0 : \mathbf{r}(\boldsymbol{\theta}_0) \neq \mathbf{0}$ if $\mathsf{T}_{\mathsf{W}} > \chi^2_\alpha(h)$. Although such generality is appealing, a weakness of the Wald test is that in small samples it is not invariant to the parameterization of the model, whereas LR and LM tests are invariant.

For multiple exclusion restrictions, such as testing whether a set of indicator variables for occupation or educational level are jointly statistically significant, $H_0 : \mathbf{R}\boldsymbol{\theta} = \mathbf{0}$, where $\mathbf{R}$ is an $h \times q$ matrix whose rows each have entries of zero except for one entry of unity corresponding to one of the components of $\boldsymbol{\beta}$ that is being set to zero. Then $\mathbf{r}(\boldsymbol{\theta}) = \mathbf{R}\boldsymbol{\theta}$ and one uses (2.91) with $\mathbf{r}(\hat{\boldsymbol{\theta}}) = \mathbf{R}\hat{\boldsymbol{\theta}}$

and $\partial \mathbf{r}(\boldsymbol{\theta})'/\partial\boldsymbol{\theta} = \mathbf{R}$. This is the analog of the F test in the linear model under normality.

The usual t test for significance of the jth regressor is the square root of the Wald chi-square test. To see this note that for $H_0 : \theta_j = 0$, $\mathbf{r}(\boldsymbol{\theta}) = \theta_j$, $\partial\mathbf{r}(\boldsymbol{\theta})/\partial\boldsymbol{\theta}$ is a $q \times 1$ vector with unity in the jth row and zeros elsewhere, and (2.91) yields $\mathsf{T_W} = \hat{\theta}_j\, [\hat{\mathsf{V}}_{jj}]^{-1}\, \hat{\theta}_j$ where $\hat{\mathsf{V}}_{jj}$ is the jth diagonal entry in $\mathsf{V}[\hat{\boldsymbol{\theta}}]$ or the estimated variance of $\hat{\theta}_j$. The square root of $\mathsf{T_W}$,

$$\mathsf{T_Z} = \frac{\hat{\theta}_j}{\sqrt{\hat{\mathsf{V}}_{jj}}}, \tag{2.92}$$

is standard normal (the square root of $\chi^2[1]$). We reject H_0 against $H_a : \theta_j \neq 0$ at significance level α if $|\mathsf{T_Z}| > z_{\alpha/2}$. This test is called a t test, following the terminology for the corresponding test in the linear model under normality. It is more appropriately called a z test, as the justification for this test statistic in nonlinear models such as count models is asymptotic and it is in general not t-distributed in small samples.

The test statistic $\mathsf{T_Z}$ can be used in one-sided tests. Reject $H_0 : \theta_j = 0$ against $H_a : \theta_j > 0$ at significance level α if $\mathsf{T_Z} > z_\alpha$, and reject $H_0 : \theta_j = 0$ against $H_a : \theta_j < 0$ at significance level α if $\mathsf{T_Z} < -z_\alpha$.

The Wald approach can be adapted to obtain the distribution of nonlinear functions of parameter estimates, such as individual predictions of the conditional mean. Suppose interest lies in the function $\boldsymbol{\lambda} = \mathbf{r}(\boldsymbol{\theta})$, and we have available the estimator $\hat{\boldsymbol{\theta}} \overset{a}{\sim} \mathsf{N}[\boldsymbol{\theta}, \mathsf{V}[\hat{\boldsymbol{\theta}}]]$. By the *delta method*

$$\hat{\boldsymbol{\lambda}} = \mathbf{r}(\hat{\boldsymbol{\theta}}) \overset{a}{\sim} \mathsf{N}[\boldsymbol{\lambda}, \mathsf{V}[\hat{\boldsymbol{\lambda}}]], \tag{2.93}$$

where

$$\mathsf{V}[\hat{\boldsymbol{\lambda}}] = \left.\frac{\partial r(\boldsymbol{\theta})'}{\partial\boldsymbol{\theta}}\right|_{\hat{\theta}} \mathsf{V}[\hat{\boldsymbol{\theta}}] \left.\frac{\partial r(\boldsymbol{\theta})}{\partial\boldsymbol{\theta}'}\right|_{\hat{\theta}}. \tag{2.94}$$

This can be used in the obvious way to get standard errors and construct confidence intervals for $\boldsymbol{\lambda}$. For example, if λ is scalar, then a 95% confidence interval for λ is $\hat{\lambda} \pm 1.96$ se $(\hat{\lambda})$ where se$(\hat{\lambda})$ equals the square root of the scalar in the right-hand side of (2.94).

The LM and LR hypothesis tests have been extended to GMM estimators by Newey and West (1987b). See this reference or Davidson and MacKinnon (1993) for further details.

2.6.3 *Conditional Moment Tests*

The results so far have been restricted to tests of hypotheses on the parameters. The moment-based framework can be used to instead perform tests of model specification. A model may impose a number of moment conditions, not all of which are used in estimation. For example, the Poisson regression model imposes the constraint that the conditional variance equals the conditional mean, which implies

$$\mathsf{E}\left[\left(y_i - \exp(\mathbf{x}_i'\boldsymbol{\theta})\right)^2 - y_i\right] = 0.$$

Because this constraint is not imposed by the MLE, the Poisson model could be tested by testing the closeness to zero of the sample moment

$$\sum_{i=1}^{n} \left\{\left(y_i - \exp\left(\mathbf{x}_i'\hat{\boldsymbol{\theta}}\right)\right)^2 - y_i\right\}.$$

Such tests, called *conditional moment tests*, provide a general framework for model specification tests. These tests were introduced by Newey (1985) and Tauchen (1985) and are given a good presentation in Pagan and Vella (1989). They nest hypothesis tests such as Wald, LM, and LR, and specification tests such as information matrix tests. This unifying element is emphasized in White (1994).

Suppose a model implies the population moment conditions

$$\mathsf{E}[\mathbf{m}_i(y_i, \mathbf{x}_i, \boldsymbol{\theta}_0)] = \mathbf{0}, \qquad i = 1, \ldots, n, \tag{2.95}$$

where $\mathbf{m}_i(\cdot)$ is an $r \times 1$ vector function. Let $\hat{\boldsymbol{\theta}}$ be a root-n consistent estimator that converges to $\boldsymbol{\theta}_0$, obtained by a method that does not impose the moment condition (2.95). The notation $\mathbf{m}_i(\cdot)$ denotes moments used for the tests; $\mathbf{g}_i(\cdot)$ or $\mathbf{h}_i(\cdot)$ denote moments used in estimation.

The correct specification of the model can be tested by testing the closeness to zero of the corresponding sample moment

$$\mathbf{m}(\hat{\boldsymbol{\theta}}) = \sum_{i=1}^{n} \mathbf{m}_i(y_i, \mathbf{x}_i, \hat{\boldsymbol{\theta}}). \tag{2.96}$$

Suppose $\hat{\boldsymbol{\theta}}$ is the solution to the first-order conditions

$$\sum_{i=1}^{n} \mathbf{g}_i(y_i, \mathbf{x}_i, \hat{\boldsymbol{\theta}}) = \mathbf{0}.$$

If $\mathsf{E}[\mathbf{g}_i(y_i, \mathbf{x}_i, \boldsymbol{\theta}_0)] = \mathbf{0}$ and (2.95) holds, then

$$n^{-1/2}\mathbf{m}(\hat{\boldsymbol{\theta}}) \xrightarrow{d} \mathsf{N}[\mathbf{0},\ \mathbf{V}_m] \tag{2.97}$$

where

$$\mathbf{V}_m = \mathbf{H}\mathbf{J}\mathbf{H}', \tag{2.98}$$

$$\mathbf{J} = \lim_{n\to\infty} \frac{1}{n}\mathsf{E}\left[\begin{array}{cc|} \sum_{i=1}^{n} \mathbf{m}_i\mathbf{m}_i' & \sum_{i=1}^{n} \mathbf{m}_i\mathbf{g}_i' \\ \sum_{i=1}^{n} \mathbf{g}_i\mathbf{m}_i' & \sum_{i=1}^{n} \mathbf{g}_i\mathbf{g}_i' \end{array}_{\boldsymbol{\theta}_0}\right], \tag{2.99}$$

the vectors $\mathbf{m}_i = \mathbf{m}_i(y_i, \mathbf{x}_i, \boldsymbol{\theta})$ and $\mathbf{g}_i = \mathbf{g}_i(y_i, \mathbf{x}_i, \boldsymbol{\theta})$,

$$\mathbf{H} = [\mathbf{I}_r \quad -\mathbf{C}\mathbf{A}^{-1}], \tag{2.100}$$

$$\mathbf{C} = \lim_{n\to\infty} \frac{1}{n} \mathsf{E}\left[\sum_{i=1}^{n} \left. \frac{\partial \mathbf{m}_i}{\partial \boldsymbol{\theta}'} \right|_{\boldsymbol{\theta}_0} \right], \tag{2.101}$$

$$\mathbf{A} = \lim_{n\to\infty} \frac{1}{n} \mathsf{E}\left[\sum_{i=1}^{n} \left. \frac{\partial \mathbf{g}_i}{\partial \boldsymbol{\theta}'} \right|_{\boldsymbol{\theta}_0} \right]. \tag{2.102}$$

The formula for $\mathbf{V}_m$ is quite cumbersome because there are two sources of stochastic variation in $\mathbf{m}(\hat{\boldsymbol{\theta}})$ – the dependent variable y_i and the estimator $\hat{\boldsymbol{\theta}}$. See Section 2.7.5 for details.

The *conditional moment* (CM) *test* statistic

$$\mathsf{T}_{\mathsf{CM}} = n\, \mathbf{m}(\hat{\boldsymbol{\theta}})'\hat{\mathbf{V}}_m{}^{-1}\mathbf{m}(\hat{\boldsymbol{\theta}}), \tag{2.103}$$

where $\hat{\mathbf{V}}_m$ is consistent for $\mathbf{V}_m$, is asymptotically $\chi^2(r)$. Moment condition (2.95) is rejected at significance level α if the computed test statistic exceeds $\chi^2(r;\alpha)$. Rejection is interpreted as indicating model misspecification, although it is not always immediately apparent in what direction the model is misspecified.

Although the CM test is in general difficult to implement due to the need to obtain the variance $\mathbf{V}_m$, it is simple to compute in two leading cases.

First, if the moment $\mathbf{m}_i(\cdot)$ satisfies

$$\mathsf{E}\left[\frac{\partial \mathbf{m}_i}{\partial \boldsymbol{\theta}'} \right] = \mathbf{0}, \tag{2.104}$$

then from section 2.7.5 $\mathbf{V}_m = \lim \frac{1}{n}\mathsf{E}[\sum_i \mathbf{m}_i\mathbf{m}_i']$, which can be consistently estimated by $\hat{\mathbf{V}}_m = \frac{1}{n}\sum_i \hat{\mathbf{m}}_i\hat{\mathbf{m}}_i'$. For cross-section data, this means

$$\mathsf{T}_{\mathsf{CM}} = \sum_{i=1}^{n} \hat{\mathbf{m}}_i' \left[\sum_{i=1}^{n} \hat{\mathbf{m}}_i\hat{\mathbf{m}}_i' \right]^{-1} \sum_{i=1}^{n} \hat{\mathbf{m}}_i. \tag{2.105}$$

This can be computed as the uncentered explained sum of squares, or as n times the uncentered R^2, from the auxiliary regression

$$1 = \mathbf{m}_i(y_i, \mathbf{x}_i, \hat{\boldsymbol{\theta}})'\boldsymbol{\gamma} + u_i. \tag{2.106}$$

If $\mathsf{E}[\mathbf{m}_i\mathbf{m}_i']$ is known, the statistic

$$\sum_{i=1}^{n} \hat{\mathbf{m}}_i' \left[\sum_{i=1}^{n} \left. \mathsf{E}[\mathbf{m}_i\mathbf{m}_i'] \right|_{\hat{\boldsymbol{\theta}}} \right]^{-1} \sum_{i=1}^{n} \hat{\mathbf{m}}_i$$

is an alternative to (2.105).

A second case in which the CM test is easily implemented is if $\hat{\boldsymbol{\theta}}$ is the MLE. Then it can be shown that an asymptotically equivalent version of the CM test can be calculated as the uncentered explained sum of squares, or equivalently as n times the uncentered R^2, from the auxiliary regression

$$1 = \mathbf{m}_i(y_i, \mathbf{x}_i, \hat{\boldsymbol{\theta}})'\gamma_1 + \mathbf{s}_i(y_i, \mathbf{x}_i, \hat{\boldsymbol{\theta}})'\gamma_2 + u_i, \tag{2.107}$$

where $\mathbf{s}_i$ is the ith component of the score vector (2.89) and uncentered R^2 is defined after (2.90). This auxiliary regression is a computational device with no physical interpretation. It generalizes the regression (2.90) for the LM test. Derivation uses the *generalized information matrix equality* that

$$\mathsf{E}\left[\frac{\partial \mathbf{m}_i(\boldsymbol{\theta})}{\partial \boldsymbol{\theta}'}\right] = -\mathsf{E}\left[\mathbf{m}_i(\boldsymbol{\theta})\frac{\partial \ln f_i(\boldsymbol{\theta})}{\partial \boldsymbol{\theta}'}\right], \tag{2.108}$$

provided $\mathsf{E}[\mathbf{m}_i(\boldsymbol{\theta})] = \mathbf{0}$. The resulting test is called the *outer product of the gradient* (OPG) form of the test because it sums $\mathbf{m}_i(\boldsymbol{\theta}) \times \partial \ln f_i(\boldsymbol{\theta})/\partial \boldsymbol{\theta}'$ evaluated at $\hat{\boldsymbol{\theta}}$.

A leading example of the CM test is the *information matrix* IM test of White (1982). This tests whether the information matrix equality holds, or equivalently whether the moment condition

$$\mathsf{E}\left[\text{vech}\left(\frac{\partial^2 \ln f_i}{\partial \boldsymbol{\theta} \partial \boldsymbol{\theta}'} + \frac{\partial \ln f_i}{\partial \boldsymbol{\theta}}\frac{\partial \ln f_i}{\partial \boldsymbol{\theta}'}\right)\right] = \mathbf{0}$$

is satisfied, where $f_i(y, \boldsymbol{\theta})$ is the specified density. The vector-half operator vech($\cdot$) stacks the components of the symmetric $q \times q$ matrix into a $q(q+1)/2 \times 1$ column vector. The OPG form of the IM test is especially advantageous in this example, as otherwise one needs to obtain $\partial \mathbf{m}_i(\boldsymbol{\theta})/\partial \boldsymbol{\theta}'$, which entails third derivatives of the log density (Lancaster, 1984).

Despite their generality, CM tests other than the three classical tests (Wald, LM, and LR) are rarely exploited in applied work, for three reasons. First, the tests are unconventional in that there is no explicit alternative hypothesis. Rejection of the moment condition may not indicate how one should proceed to improve the model. Second, implementation of the CM test is in general difficult, aside from the MLE case in which a simple auxiliary regression can be run. But this OPG form of the test has been shown to have poor small sample properties in some leading cases (see Davidson and MacKinnon, 1993, chapter 13). Third, with real data and a large sample, testing at a fixed significance level that does not vary with sample size will always lead to rejection of sample moment conditions implied by a model, and to a conclusion that the model is inadequate. A similar situation also exists in more classical testing situations. With a large enough sample, regression coefficients will always be significantly different from zero. But this may be precisely the news that researchers want to hear.

2.7 Derivations

Formal proofs of convergence in probability of an estimator $\hat{\boldsymbol{\theta}}$ to a fixed value $\boldsymbol{\theta}_*$ are generally difficult and not reproduced here. A clear treatment is given in

Amemiya (1985, chapter 4), references to more advanced treatment are given in Davidson and MacKinnon (1993, p. 591), and a comprehensive treatment is given in Newey and McFadden (1994). If $\hat{\boldsymbol{\theta}}$ maximizes or minimizes an objective function, then $\boldsymbol{\theta}_*$ is the value of $\boldsymbol{\theta}$ that maximizes the probability limit of the objective function, where the objective function is appropriately scaled to ensure that the probability limit exists. For example, for maximum likelihood the objective function is the sum of n terms and is therefore divided by n. Then $\hat{\boldsymbol{\theta}}$ converges to $\boldsymbol{\theta}_*$, which maximizes plim $\frac{1}{n}\sum_{i=1}^{n} \ln f_i$, where the probability limit is taken with respect to the dgp which is not necessarily f_i.

It is less difficult and more insightful to obtain the asymptotic distribution of $\hat{\boldsymbol{\theta}}$. This is first done in a general framework, with specialization to likelihood-based models, generalized linear models, and moment-based models in remaining subsections.

2.7.1 *General Framework*

A framework that covers the preceding estimators, except GMM, is that the estimator $\hat{\boldsymbol{\theta}}$ of the $q \times 1$ parameter vector $\boldsymbol{\theta}$ is the solution to the equation

$$\sum_{i=1}^{n} \mathbf{g}_i(\boldsymbol{\theta}) = \mathbf{0}, \tag{2.109}$$

where $\mathbf{g}_i(\boldsymbol{\theta}) = \mathbf{g}_i(y_i, \mathbf{x}_i, \boldsymbol{\theta})$ is a $q \times 1$ vector, and we suppress dependence on the dependent variable and regressors. In typical applications (2.109) are the first-order conditions from maximization or minimization of a scalar objective function, and $\mathbf{g}_i$ is the vector of first derivatives of the ith component of the objective function with respect to $\boldsymbol{\theta}$. The first-order conditions (2.6) for the Poisson MLE are an example of (2.109).

By an exact first-order Taylor series expansion of the left-hand side of (2.109) about $\boldsymbol{\theta}_*$, the probability limit of $\hat{\boldsymbol{\theta}}$, we have

$$\sum_{i=1}^{n} \mathbf{g}_i(\boldsymbol{\theta}_*) + \sum_{i=1}^{n} \left.\frac{\partial \mathbf{g}_i(\boldsymbol{\theta})}{\partial \boldsymbol{\theta}'}\right|_{\boldsymbol{\theta}_{**}} (\hat{\boldsymbol{\theta}} - \boldsymbol{\theta}_*) = \mathbf{0}, \tag{2.110}$$

for some $\boldsymbol{\theta}_{**}$ between $\hat{\boldsymbol{\theta}}$ and $\boldsymbol{\theta}_*$. Solving for $\hat{\boldsymbol{\theta}}$ and rescaling by $\sqrt{n}$ yields

$$\sqrt{n}(\hat{\boldsymbol{\theta}} - \boldsymbol{\theta}_*) = -\left(\frac{1}{n}\sum_{i=1}^{n} \left.\frac{\partial \mathbf{g}_i(\boldsymbol{\theta})}{\partial \boldsymbol{\theta}'}\right|_{\boldsymbol{\theta}_{**}}\right)^{-1} \frac{1}{\sqrt{n}} \sum_{i=1}^{n} \mathbf{g}_i(\boldsymbol{\theta}_*) \tag{2.111}$$

where it is assumed that the inverse exists.

It is helpful at this stage to recall the proof of the asymptotic normality of the OLS estimator in the linear regression model. In that case

$$\sqrt{n}(\hat{\boldsymbol{\theta}} - \boldsymbol{\theta}_*) = \left(\frac{1}{n}\sum_{i=1}^{N} \mathbf{x}_i \mathbf{x}_i'\right)^{-1} \frac{1}{\sqrt{n}} \sum_{i=1}^{N} \mathbf{x}_i (y_i - \mathbf{x}_i' \boldsymbol{\theta}),$$

which is of the same form as (2.111). We therefore proceed in the same way as in the OLS case, where the first term in the right-hand side converges in probability to a fixed matrix and the second term in the right-hand side converges in distribution to the normal distribution.

Specifically, assume the existence of the $q \times q$ matrix

$$\mathbf{A} = -\text{plim}\frac{1}{n}\sum_{i=1}^{n}\left.\frac{\partial \mathbf{g}_i(\boldsymbol{\theta})}{\partial \boldsymbol{\theta}'}\right|_{\boldsymbol{\theta}_*}, \tag{2.112}$$

where $\mathbf{A}$ is positive definite for a minimization problem and negative definite for a maximization problem. Also assume

$$\frac{1}{\sqrt{n}}\sum_{i=1}^{n}\mathbf{g}_i(\boldsymbol{\theta}_*) \xrightarrow{d} \mathsf{N}[\mathbf{0}, \mathbf{B}], \tag{2.113}$$

where

$$\mathbf{B} = \text{plim}\frac{1}{n}\sum_{i=1}^{n}\sum_{j=1}^{n}\left.\mathbf{g}_i(\boldsymbol{\theta})\mathbf{g}_j(\boldsymbol{\theta})'\right|_{\boldsymbol{\theta}_*} \tag{2.114}$$

is a positive definite $q \times q$ matrix.

From (2.112) through (2.114), $\sqrt{n}(\hat{\boldsymbol{\theta}} - \boldsymbol{\theta}_*)$ in (2.111) is an $\mathsf{N}[\mathbf{0}, \mathbf{B}]$ distributed random variable premultiplied by minus the inverse of a random matrix that converges in probability to a matrix $\mathbf{A}$. Under appropriate conditions

$$\sqrt{n}(\hat{\boldsymbol{\theta}} - \boldsymbol{\theta}_*) \xrightarrow{d} \mathsf{N}[\mathbf{0}, \mathbf{A}^{-1}\mathbf{B}\mathbf{A}'^{-1}], \tag{2.115}$$

or

$$\hat{\boldsymbol{\theta}} \overset{a}{\sim} \mathsf{N}\left[\boldsymbol{\theta}_*, \frac{1}{n}\mathbf{A}^{-1}\mathbf{B}\mathbf{A}'^{-1}\right]. \tag{2.116}$$

The assumption (2.112) is verified by a law of large numbers because the right-hand side of (2.112) is an average. The assumption (2.113) is verified by a multivariate central limit theorem because the left-hand side of (2.113) is a rescaling of an average. This average is centered around zero (see below), and hence

$$\mathsf{V}\left[\frac{1}{\sqrt{n}}\sum_{i=1}^{n}\mathbf{g}_i\right] = \mathsf{E}\left[\frac{1}{n}\sum_i\sum_j \mathbf{g}_i\mathbf{g}_j'\right],$$

which is finite if there is not too much correlation between $\mathbf{g}_i$ and $\mathbf{g}_j$, $i \neq j$. Note that the definition of $\mathbf{B}$ in (2.114) permits correlation across observations, and the result (2.116) can potentially be applied to time series data.

Finally, note that by (2.111) convergence of $\hat{\boldsymbol{\theta}}$ to $\boldsymbol{\theta}_*$ requires centering around zero of $\frac{1}{\sqrt{n}}\sum_i \mathbf{g}_i(\boldsymbol{\theta}_*)$. An informal proof of convergence for estimators defined by (2.109) is therefore to verify that $\mathsf{E}_*[\sum_i \mathbf{g}_i(\boldsymbol{\theta}_*)] = \mathbf{0}$, where the expectation is taken with respect to the dgp.

2.7.2 *Likelihood-Based Models*

For the MLE given in section 2.3, (2.111) becomes

$$\sqrt{n}(\hat{\boldsymbol{\theta}}_{\mathsf{ML}} - \boldsymbol{\theta}_*) = -\left(\frac{1}{n}\sum_{i=1}^{n} \frac{\partial^2 \ln f_i}{\partial \boldsymbol{\theta} \partial \boldsymbol{\theta}'}\bigg|_{\boldsymbol{\theta}_{**}}\right)^{-1} \frac{1}{\sqrt{n}}\sum_{i=1}^{n} \frac{\partial \ln f_i}{\partial \boldsymbol{\theta}}\bigg|_{\boldsymbol{\theta}_*}, \tag{2.117}$$

where $f_i = f(y_i \mid \mathbf{x}_i, \boldsymbol{\theta})$. An informal proof of consistency of $\hat{\boldsymbol{\theta}}$ to $\boldsymbol{\theta}_0$, that is $\boldsymbol{\theta}_* = \boldsymbol{\theta}_0$, requires $\mathsf{E}[\partial \ln f_i / \partial \boldsymbol{\theta}|_{\boldsymbol{\theta}_0}] = \mathbf{0}$. This is satisfied if the density is correctly specified, so the expectation is taken with respect to $f(y_i \mid \mathbf{x}_i, \boldsymbol{\theta}_0)$, and the density satisfies the fourth regularity condition.

To see this, note that any density $f(y \mid \boldsymbol{\theta})$ satisfies $\int f(y \mid \boldsymbol{\theta})\, dy = 1$. Differentiating with respect to $\boldsymbol{\theta}$, $\frac{\partial}{\partial \boldsymbol{\theta}} \int f(y \mid \boldsymbol{\theta})\, dy = \mathbf{0}$. If the range of y does not depend on $\boldsymbol{\theta}$, the derivative can be taken inside the integral and $\int (\partial f(y \mid \boldsymbol{\theta})/\partial \boldsymbol{\theta})\, dy = \mathbf{0}$, which can be reexpressed as $\int (\partial \ln f(y \mid \boldsymbol{\theta})/\partial \boldsymbol{\theta})\, f(y \mid \boldsymbol{\theta})\, dy = \mathbf{0}$, because $\partial \ln f(y \mid \boldsymbol{\theta})/\partial \boldsymbol{\theta} = (\partial f(y \mid \boldsymbol{\theta})/\partial \boldsymbol{\theta})(1/f(y \mid \boldsymbol{\theta}))$. Then $\mathsf{E}[\partial \ln f(y \mid \boldsymbol{\theta})/\partial \boldsymbol{\theta}] = \mathbf{0}$, where E is taken with respect to $f(y \mid \boldsymbol{\theta})$.

The variance matrix of $\hat{\boldsymbol{\theta}}_{\mathsf{ML}}$ is $\frac{1}{n}\mathbf{A}^{-1}\mathbf{B}\mathbf{A}^{-1}$ where $\mathbf{A}$ and $\mathbf{B}$ are defined in (2.112) and (2.114) with $g(y_i \mid \mathbf{x}_i, \boldsymbol{\theta}) = \partial \ln f(y_i \mid \mathbf{x}_i, \boldsymbol{\theta})/\partial \boldsymbol{\theta}$. Simplification occurs if the density is correctly specified and the range of y does not depend on $\boldsymbol{\theta}$. Then the information matrix equality $\mathbf{A} = \mathbf{B}$ holds.

To see this, differentiating $\int (\partial \ln f(y \mid \boldsymbol{\theta})/\partial \boldsymbol{\theta})\, f(y \mid \boldsymbol{\theta})\, dy = \mathbf{0}$ with respect to $\boldsymbol{\theta}$ yields

$$\mathsf{E}[\partial^2 \ln f(y \mid \boldsymbol{\theta})/\partial \boldsymbol{\theta} \partial \boldsymbol{\theta}'] = -\mathsf{E}[\partial \ln f(y \mid \boldsymbol{\theta})/\partial \boldsymbol{\theta}\, \partial \ln f(y \mid \boldsymbol{\theta})/\partial \boldsymbol{\theta}']$$

after some algebra, where E is taken with respect to $f(y \mid \boldsymbol{\theta})$.

If the density is misspecified it is no longer the case that such simplifications occur, and the results of section 2.7.1 for $g(\boldsymbol{\theta}) = \ln f(y_i \mid \mathbf{x}_i, \boldsymbol{\theta})$ yield the result given in section 2.3.4.

2.7.3 *Generalized Linear Models*

For the PML estimator for the LEF given in section 2.4.2, (2.111) becomes

$$\begin{aligned}\sqrt{n}(\hat{\boldsymbol{\beta}}_{\mathsf{LEF}} - \boldsymbol{\beta}_0) = &-\left[\frac{1}{n}\sum_{i=1}^{n} \frac{1}{v_i}\left\{-\frac{\partial \mu_i}{\partial \boldsymbol{\beta}}\frac{\partial \mu_i}{\partial \boldsymbol{\beta}'} + (y_i - \mu_i)\frac{\partial^2 \mu_i}{\partial \boldsymbol{\beta} \partial \boldsymbol{\beta}'}\right.\right.\\ &\left.\left. - \frac{y_i - \mu_i}{v_i}\frac{\partial \mu_i}{\partial \boldsymbol{\beta}}\frac{\partial v_i}{\partial \boldsymbol{\beta}'}\right\}\bigg|_{\boldsymbol{\beta}_0}\right]^{-1}\\ &\times \frac{1}{\sqrt{n}}\sum_{i=1}^{n} \frac{1}{v_i}\{y_i - \mu_i\}\frac{\partial \mu_i}{\partial \boldsymbol{\beta}}\bigg|_{\boldsymbol{\beta}_0}.\end{aligned} \tag{2.118}$$

An informal proof of convergence of $\hat{\beta}_{\mathsf{LEF}}$ to β_0 is that the second term in the right-hand side is centered around $\mathbf{0}$ if $\mathsf{E}[y_i - \mu(\mathbf{x}_i, \beta_0)] = 0$, or that the conditional mean is correctly specified. The first term on the right-hand side converges to

$$\mathbf{A} = \lim \frac{1}{n} \sum_{i=1}^{n} \frac{1}{v_i} \frac{\partial \mu_i}{\partial \boldsymbol{\beta}} \frac{\partial \mu_i}{\partial \boldsymbol{\beta}'} \bigg|_{\beta_0}$$

because $\mathsf{E}[y_i - \mu(\mathbf{x}_i, \beta_0)] = 0$, and the second term converges to the normal distribution with variance matrix

$$\mathbf{B} = \lim \frac{1}{n} \sum_{i=1}^{n} \frac{\omega_i}{v_i^2} \frac{\partial \mu_i}{\partial \boldsymbol{\beta}} \frac{\partial \mu_i}{\partial \boldsymbol{\beta}'} \bigg|_{\beta_0},$$

where $\omega_i = \mathsf{E}[(y_i - \mu(\mathbf{x}_i, \beta_0))^2]$. Then $\mathsf{V}[\hat{\beta}_{\mathsf{LEF}}] = \frac{1}{n}\mathbf{A}^{-1}\mathbf{B}\mathbf{A}^{-1}$.

For the QGPML estimator for the LEFN density in section 2.4.3 we have

$$\begin{aligned} &\sqrt{n}(\hat{\beta}_{\mathsf{LEFN}} - \beta_0) \\ &= -\left[\frac{1}{n} \sum_{i=1}^{n} \frac{1}{\tilde{\omega}_i} \left\{ - \frac{\partial \mu_i}{\partial \boldsymbol{\beta}} \frac{\partial \mu_i}{\partial \boldsymbol{\beta}'} + (y_i - \mu_i) \frac{\partial^2 \mu_i}{\partial \boldsymbol{\beta} \partial \boldsymbol{\beta}'} \right\} \bigg|_{\beta_0} \right]^{-1} \\ &\quad \times \frac{1}{\sqrt{n}} \sum_{i=1}^{n} \frac{1}{\tilde{\omega}_i} (y_i - \mu_i) \frac{\partial \mu_i}{\partial \boldsymbol{\beta}} \bigg|_{\beta_0} \end{aligned} \tag{2.119}$$

where $\tilde{\omega}_i = \omega(\mu(\mathbf{x}_i, \tilde{\beta}), \tilde{\alpha})$. Then v_i in $\mathbf{A}$ and $\mathbf{B}$ above is replaced by ω_i, which implies $\mathbf{A} = \mathbf{B}$.

Derivation for the estimator in the GLM of section 2.4.4 is similar.

2.7.4 *Moment-Based Models*

Results for estimating equations given in section 2.5.1 follow directly from section 2.7.1.

The GMM estimator given in section 2.5.2 solves the equations

$$\left[\frac{1}{n} \sum_{i=1}^{n} \frac{\partial \mathbf{h}_i(y_i, \mathbf{x}_i, \boldsymbol{\theta})'}{\partial \boldsymbol{\theta}} \right] \mathbf{W}_n \left[\frac{1}{\sqrt{n}} \sum_{i=1}^{n} \mathbf{h}_i(y_i, \mathbf{x}_i, \boldsymbol{\theta}) \right] = \mathbf{0}, \tag{2.120}$$

on multiplying by an extra scaling parameter $n^{-3/2}$. Taking a Taylor series expansion of the third term similar to (2.110) yields

$$\begin{aligned} &\left[\frac{1}{n} \sum_{i=1}^{n} \frac{\partial \mathbf{h}_i'}{\partial \boldsymbol{\theta}} \right] \mathbf{W}_n \left[\frac{1}{\sqrt{n}} \sum_{i=1}^{n} \mathbf{h}_i \bigg|_{\boldsymbol{\theta}_*} \right. \\ &\qquad \left. + \frac{1}{n} \sum_{i=1}^{n} \frac{\partial \mathbf{h}_i}{\partial \boldsymbol{\theta}'} \bigg|_{\boldsymbol{\theta}_{**}} \sqrt{n}(\hat{\boldsymbol{\theta}}_{\mathsf{GMM}} - \boldsymbol{\theta}_*) \right] = \mathbf{0}, \end{aligned}$$

where $\mathbf{h}_i = \mathbf{h}_i(y_i, \mathbf{x}_i, \boldsymbol{\theta})$. Solving yields

$$\sqrt{n}(\hat{\boldsymbol{\theta}}_{\mathsf{GMM}} - \boldsymbol{\theta}_*) = \left(\left[\frac{1}{n} \sum_{i=1}^{n} \frac{\partial \mathbf{h}_i'}{\partial \boldsymbol{\theta}} \right] \mathbf{W}_n \left[\frac{1}{n} \sum_{i=1}^{n} \left. \frac{\partial \mathbf{h}_i}{\partial \boldsymbol{\theta}'} \right|_{\boldsymbol{\theta}_*} \right] \right)^{-1}$$

$$\times \left[\frac{1}{n} \sum_{i=1}^{n} \frac{\partial \mathbf{h}_i'}{\partial \boldsymbol{\theta}} \right] \mathbf{W}_n \frac{1}{\sqrt{n}} \sum_{i=1}^{n} \left. \mathbf{h}_i \right|_{\boldsymbol{\theta}_{**}}. \tag{2.121}$$

Equation (2.121) is the key result for obtaining the variance of the GMM estimator. It is sufficient to obtain the probability limit of the first five terms and the limit distribution of the last term in the right-hand side of (2.121). Both $\frac{1}{n}\sum_i \partial \mathbf{h}_i/\partial \boldsymbol{\theta}'$ and $\frac{1}{n}\sum_i \partial \mathbf{h}_i/\partial \boldsymbol{\theta}'|_{\boldsymbol{\theta}_*}$ converge in probability to the matrix $\mathbf{H}$ defined in (2.73), and by assumption plim$\mathbf{W}_n = \mathbf{W}$. By a central limit theorem $\frac{1}{\sqrt{n}}\sum_i \mathbf{h}_i|_{\boldsymbol{\theta}_{**}}$ converges in distribution to $\mathsf{N}[\mathbf{0}, \mathbf{S}]$ where

$$\mathbf{S} = \lim_{n\to\infty} \frac{1}{n} \mathsf{E}\left[\sum_i \sum_j \left. \mathbf{h}_i \mathbf{h}_j' \right|_{\boldsymbol{\theta}_*} \right].$$

Thus from (2.121) $\sqrt{n}(\hat{\boldsymbol{\theta}}_{\mathsf{GMM}} - \boldsymbol{\theta}_*)$ has the same limit distribution as $(\mathbf{H}'\mathbf{W}\mathbf{H})^{-1}\mathbf{H}'\mathbf{W}$ times a random variable that is $\mathsf{N}[\mathbf{0}, \mathbf{S}]$. Equivalently, $\sqrt{n}(\hat{\boldsymbol{\theta}} - \boldsymbol{\theta}_*) \stackrel{d}{\to} \mathsf{N}[\mathbf{0}, \mathbf{A}^{-1}\mathbf{B}\mathbf{A}^{-1}]$ where $\mathbf{A} = \mathbf{H}'\mathbf{W}\mathbf{H}$ and $\mathbf{B} = \mathbf{H}'\mathbf{W}\mathbf{S}\mathbf{W}\mathbf{H}$.

The optimal GMM estimator can be motivated by noting that the variance is exactly the same matrix form as that of the linear WLS estimator given in (2.24), with $\mathbf{X} = \mathbf{H}$, $\mathbf{V}^{-1} = \mathbf{W}$ and $\boldsymbol{\Omega} = \mathbf{S}$. For given $\mathbf{X}$ and $\boldsymbol{\Omega}$ the linear WLS variance is minimized by choosing $\mathbf{V} = \boldsymbol{\Omega}$. By the same matrix algebra, for given $\mathbf{H}$ and $\mathbf{S}$ the GMM variance is minimized by choosing $\mathbf{W} = \mathbf{S}^{-1}$. Analogously to feasible GLS one can equivalently use $\mathbf{W}_n = \hat{\mathbf{S}}^{-1}$ where $\hat{\mathbf{S}}$ is consistent for $\mathbf{S}$.

2.7.5 *Conditional Moment Tests*

For the distribution of the conditional moment test statistic (2.96), we take a first-order Taylor series expansion about $\boldsymbol{\theta}_0$

$$\frac{1}{\sqrt{n}} \mathbf{m}(\hat{\boldsymbol{\theta}}) = \frac{1}{\sqrt{n}} \sum_{i=1}^{n} \mathbf{m}_i(\boldsymbol{\theta}_0) + \frac{1}{n} \sum_{i=1}^{n} \frac{\partial \mathbf{m}_i(\boldsymbol{\theta}_0)}{\partial \boldsymbol{\theta}'} \sqrt{n}(\hat{\boldsymbol{\theta}} - \boldsymbol{\theta}_0), \tag{2.122}$$

where $\mathbf{m}_i(\boldsymbol{\theta}_0) = \mathbf{m}_i(y_i, \mathbf{x}_i, \boldsymbol{\theta}_0)$ and $\partial \mathbf{m}_i(\boldsymbol{\theta}_0)/\partial \boldsymbol{\theta}' = \partial \mathbf{m}_i(y_i, \mathbf{x}_i, \boldsymbol{\theta}_0)/\partial \boldsymbol{\theta}'|_{\boldsymbol{\theta}_0}$. We suppose $\hat{\boldsymbol{\theta}}$ is the solution to the first-order conditions

$$\sum_{i=1}^{n} \mathbf{g}_i(\hat{\boldsymbol{\theta}}) = \mathbf{0},$$

where $\mathbf{g}_i(\boldsymbol{\theta}) = \mathbf{g}_i(y_i, \mathbf{x}_i, \boldsymbol{\theta})$. Replacing $\sqrt{n}(\hat{\boldsymbol{\theta}} - \boldsymbol{\theta}_0)$ by the right-hand side of (2.111) yields

$$\frac{1}{\sqrt{n}}\mathbf{m}(\hat{\theta}) = \frac{1}{\sqrt{n}}\sum_{i=1}^{n}\mathbf{m}_i(\boldsymbol{\theta}_0) - \frac{1}{n}\sum_{i=1}^{n}\frac{\partial \mathbf{m}_i(\boldsymbol{\theta}_0)}{\partial \boldsymbol{\theta}'}$$

$$\times\left(\frac{1}{n}\sum_{i=1}^{n}\frac{\partial \mathbf{g}_i(\boldsymbol{\theta}_0)}{\partial \boldsymbol{\theta}'}\right)^{-1}\frac{1}{\sqrt{n}}\sum_{i=1}^{n}\mathbf{g}_i(\boldsymbol{\theta}_0). \tag{2.123}$$

It follows on some algebra that

$$\frac{1}{\sqrt{n}}\mathbf{m}(\hat{\theta}) \overset{LD}{=} [\mathbf{I}_r \quad -\mathbf{C}\mathbf{A}^{-1}]\begin{bmatrix}\frac{1}{\sqrt{n}}\sum_{i=1}^{n}\mathbf{m}_i(\boldsymbol{\theta}_0)\\ \frac{1}{\sqrt{n}}\sum_{i=1}^{n}\mathbf{g}_i(\boldsymbol{\theta}_0)\end{bmatrix} \tag{2.124}$$

where $\overset{LD}{=}$ means *has the same limit distribution as*, and

$$\mathbf{C} = \lim_{n\to\infty}\frac{1}{n}\mathsf{E}\left[\sum_{i=1}^{n}\left.\frac{\partial \mathbf{m}_i}{\partial \boldsymbol{\theta}'}\right|_{\boldsymbol{\theta}_0}\right],$$

and

$$\mathbf{A} = \lim_{n\to\infty}\frac{1}{n}\mathsf{E}\left[\sum_{i=1}^{n}\left.\frac{\partial \mathbf{g}_i}{\partial \boldsymbol{\theta}'}\right|_{\boldsymbol{\theta}_0}\right].$$

Equation (2.124) is the key to obtaining the distribution of the CM test statistic. By a central limit theorem the second term in the right-hand side of (2.124) converges to $\mathsf{N}[\mathbf{0}, \mathbf{J}]$ where

$$\mathbf{J} = \lim_{n\to\infty}\frac{1}{n}\mathsf{E}\left.\begin{bmatrix}\sum_{i=1}^{n}\mathbf{m}_i\mathbf{m}_i' & \sum_{i=1}^{n}\mathbf{m}_i\mathbf{g}_i'\\ \sum_{i=1}^{n}\mathbf{g}_i\mathbf{m}_i' & \sum_{i=1}^{n}\mathbf{g}_i\mathbf{g}_i'\end{bmatrix}\right|_{\boldsymbol{\theta}_0}.$$

It follows that $n^{-1/2}\mathbf{m}(\hat{\boldsymbol{\theta}}) \overset{d}{\to} \mathsf{N}[\mathbf{0}, \mathbf{V}_m]$ where

$$\mathbf{V}_m = \mathbf{HJH}',$$

$\mathbf{J}$ is defined already, and

$$\mathbf{H} = \left[\mathbf{I}_r \quad -\mathbf{C}\mathbf{A}^{-1}\right].$$

The CM test can be operationalized by dropping the expectation and evaluating the expressions above at $\hat{\boldsymbol{\theta}}$.

In the special case in which (2.104) holds, that is, $\mathsf{E}[\partial\mathbf{m}_i/\partial\boldsymbol{\theta}'] = \mathbf{0}$, $\mathbf{C} = \mathbf{0}$ so $\mathbf{V}_m = \mathbf{HJH}' = \lim \frac{1}{n}\mathsf{E}[\sum_{i=1}^{n}\mathbf{m}_i\mathbf{m}_i']$ leading to the simplification (2.105). For the OPG auxiliary regression (2.107) if $\hat{\boldsymbol{\theta}}$ is the MLE, see, for example, Pagan and Vella (1989).

2.8 Bibliographic Notes

Standard references for estimation theory are Amemiya (1985) and Davidson and MacKinnon (1993), and a comprehensive treatment is given in Newey and McFadden (1994). For maximum likelihood estimation see also Hendry (1995). The two-volume work by Gourieroux and Montfort (1995) presents estimation and testing theory in considerable detail, with considerable emphasis on the PML framework. Reference to GLM is generally restricted to the statistics literature, even though it nests many common nonlinear regression models, including the linear, logit, probit, and Poisson regression models. Key papers are Nelder and Wedderburn (1972), Wedderburn (1974), and McCullagh (1983); the standard reference is McCullagh and Nelder (1989). The book by Fahrmeir and Tutz (1994) presents the GLM framework and recent advances in a form amenable to econometricians. This may encourage more social science analyses to take advantage of results for GLM models, especially for more complicated forms of data. The estimating equation approach is summarized by Carroll, Ruppert, and Stefanski (1995). For GMM the paper by Hansen (1982) and other references are generally written at an advanced level. These include Newey and West (1987a), for a relatively brief statement of the estimator and its distribution, and detailed textbook treatments by Ogaki (1993), Hamilton (1994, chapter 14), and Davidson and MacKinnon (1993, chapter 17).

2.9 Exercises

2.1 Let the dgp for $\mathbf{y}$ be $\mathbf{y} = \mathbf{X}\beta_0 + \mathbf{u}$, where $\mathbf{X}$ is nonstochastic and $\mathbf{u} \sim (\mathbf{0}, \boldsymbol{\Omega})$. Show by substituting out $\mathbf{y}$ that the WLS estimator defined in (2.23) can be expressed as $\hat{\beta}_{\mathsf{WLS}} = \beta_0 + (\mathbf{X}'\mathbf{V}^{-1}\mathbf{X})^{-1}\mathbf{X}'\mathbf{V}^{-1}\mathbf{u}$. Hence, obtain $\mathsf{V}[\hat{\beta}_{\mathsf{WLS}}]$ given in (2.24).

2.2 Let y have the LEF density $f(y \mid \mu)$ given in (2.26), where the range of the y does not depend on $\mu \equiv \mathsf{E}[y]$. Show by differentiating with respect to μ the identity $\int f(y \mid \mu)\, dy = 1$ that $\mathsf{E}[a'(\mu) + c'(\mu)y] = 0$. Hence obtain $\mathsf{E}[y]$ given in (2.27). Show by differentiating with respect to μ the identity $\int y f(y \mid \mu)\, dy = \mu$ that $\mathrm{E}[a'(\mu)y + c'(\mu)y^2] = 1$. Hence, obtain $\mathsf{V}[y]$ given in (2.28).

2.3 For the LEF log-likelihood defined in (2.29) and (2.30) obtain the first-order conditions for the MLE $\hat{\beta}_{\mathsf{ML}}$. Show that these can be reexpressed as (2.31) using (2.27) and (2.28). From (2.31) obtain the first-order conditions for the MLE of the Poisson regression model with exponential mean function.

2.4 Consider the geometric density $f(y \mid \mu) = \mu^y(1+\mu)^{-y-1}$, where $y = 0, 1, 2, \ldots$ and $\mu = \mathsf{E}[y]$. Write this density in the LEF form (2.26). Hence, obtain the formula for $\mathsf{V}[y]$ using (2.28). In the regression case in which $\mu_i = \exp(\mathbf{x}_i'\beta)$ obtain the first-order conditions for the MLE for β. Give the distribution for this estimator, assuming correct specification of the variance.

2.5 Consider the geometric density $f(y \mid \mu) = \mu^y(1+\mu)^{-y-1}$, where $y = 0, 1, 2, \ldots$ and $\mu = \mathsf{E}[y]$. Write this density in the canonical form of the LEF (2.45). Hence, obtain the formula for $\mathsf{V}[y]$ using (2.47). Obtain the canonical link function for thc geometric, verifying that it is not the log link function. In the regression case with the canonical link function obtain the first-order conditions for the MLE for $\boldsymbol{\beta}$. Give the distribution for this estimator, assuming correct specification of the variance.

2.6 Models with exponential mean function $\exp(\mathbf{x}_i'\boldsymbol{\beta})$, where $\boldsymbol{\beta}$ and $\mathbf{x}_i$ are $k \times 1$ vectors, satisfy $\mathsf{E}[(y_i - \exp(\mathbf{x}_i'\boldsymbol{\beta}))\mathbf{x}_i] = \mathbf{0}$. Obtain the first-order conditions for the GMM estimator that minimizes (2.68), where $h(y_i, \mathbf{x}_i, \boldsymbol{\beta}) = (y_i - \exp(\mathbf{x}_i'\boldsymbol{\beta}))\mathbf{x}_i$ and $\mathbf{W}$ is $k \times k$ of rank k. Show that these first-order conditions are a full-rank $k \times k$ matrix transformation of the first-order conditions (2.6) for the Poisson MLE. What do you conclude?

2.7 For the Poisson regression model with exponential mean function $\exp(\mathbf{x}_i'\boldsymbol{\beta})$, consider tests for exclusion of the subcomponent $\mathbf{x}_{2i}$ of $\mathbf{x}_i = [\mathbf{x}_{1i}', \mathbf{x}_{2i}']'$, which are tests of $\boldsymbol{\beta}_2 = \mathbf{0}$. Obtain the test statistic T_{LM} given (2.88). State how to compute an asymptotically equivalent version of the LM test using an auxiliary regression. State how to alternatively implement Wald and LR tests of $\boldsymbol{\beta}_2 = \mathbf{0}$.

2.8 Show that variance–mean equality in the Poisson regression model with exponential mean implies that $\mathsf{E}[\{y_i - \exp(\mathbf{x}_i'\boldsymbol{\beta})^2 - y_i\}^2] = 0$. Using this moment condition obtain the conditional moment test statistic T_{CM} given in (2.105), first showing that the simplifying condition (2.104) holds if $y_i \sim \mathsf{P}[\exp(\mathbf{x}_i'\boldsymbol{\beta})]$. State how to compute T_{CM} by an auxiliary regression. Does $\hat{\boldsymbol{\beta}}$ need to be the MLE here, or will any $\sqrt{n}$-consistent estimator do?

CHAPTER 3

Basic Count Regression

3.1 Introduction

This chapter is intended to provide a self-contained treatment of basic cross-section count data regression analysis. It is analogous to a chapter in a standard statistics text that covers both homoskedastic and heteroskedastic linear regression models.

The most commonly used count models are Poisson and negative binomial. For readers interested only in these models it is sufficient to read sections 3.1 through 3.5, along with preparatory material in sections 1.2 and 2.2 in previous chapters.

Additional regression models for cross-section count data are given in the remainder of Chapter 3, most notably the ordered probit and logit models. These additional models generally ignore the count nature of the data. Still further models, such as the hurdle model, which do explicitly treat the data as count data, are given in Chapter 4. Some model diagnostic methods are presented in Chapter 3, but most are deferred to Chapter 5.

As indicated in Chapter 2, the properties of an estimator vary with the assumptions made on the dgp. By correct specification of the conditional mean or variance or density, we mean that the functional form and explanatory variables in the specified conditional mean or variance or density are those of the dgp.

The simplest regression model for count data is the Poisson regression model. For the Poisson MLE it can be shown that:

1. Consistency requires correct specification of the conditional mean. It does not require that the dependent variable y be Poisson distributed.
2. Valid statistical inference using computed maximum likelihood standard errors and t statistics requires correct specification of both the conditional mean and variance. This requires equidispersion, that is, equality of conditional variance and mean, but not Poisson distribution for y.
3. Valid statistical inference using appropriately modified maximum likelihood output is still possible if data are not equidispersed, provided the conditional mean is correctly specified.

4. More efficient estimators than Poisson MLE can be obtained if data are not equidispersed.

Properties 1 through 4 are similar to those of the OLS estimator in the classical linear regression model, which is the MLE if errors are iid normal. The Poisson restriction of equidispersion is directly analogous to homoskedasticity in the linear model. If errors are heteroskedastic in the linear model, one would use alternative t statistics to those from the usual OLS output (property 3) and preferably estimate by WLS (property 4).

In many applications count data are overdispersed, with conditional variance exceeding conditional mean. One response is to nonetheless use Poisson regression, because as already noted it still yields consistent estimates provided the conditional mean is correctly specified. It is necessary, however, to adjust standard error estimates. This leads to estimators closely related to the Poisson MLE, which differ according to assumptions made about the dgp. Specializing the GLM results from Section 2.4 to the Poisson case, we have

1. Poisson MLE with statistical inference based on the assumption that the data are Poisson.
2. Poisson pseudo-MLE (PMLE), which is the Poisson MLE with statistical inference based on the correct specification of the mean but not assuming equidispersion.
3. Poisson GLM estimator, quasigeneralized PMLE (QGPMLE), and GMM estimator, which are all based on correct specification of the mean and variance.

Results vary with the specified variance function. By far the simplest assumption is that the variance is a multiple of the mean. In this case the Poisson maximum likelihood and GLM coefficient estimates are identical, and the usual Poisson maximum likelihood standard errors and t statistics can be used after appropriate rescaling.

An alternative to Poisson regression is to specify a more general distribution than the Poisson that does not impose equidispersion and to perform standard maximum likelihood inference. The standard distribution used is the negative binomial, with variance assumed to be a quadratic function of the mean.

It is important that such modifications to Poisson MLE be made. Count data are often very overdispersed, which causes computed Poisson maximum likelihood t statistics to be considerably overinflated. This can lead to very erroneous and overly optimistic conclusions of statistical significance of regressors.

The various Poisson regression estimators are presented in section 3.2; negative binomial regression is given in section 3.3. Tests for overdispersion are presented in section 3.4. Practical issues of interpretation of coefficients with an exponential, rather than linear, specification of the conditional mean, and use of estimates for prediction, are presented in section 3.5. An alternative approach to count data is to assume an underlying continuous latent process, with higher counts arising as the continuous variable passes successively higher thresholds. Ordered probit and related discrete choice models are presented in section 3.6. Least-squares methods are the focus of section 3.7. These include nonlinear least squares with exponential conditional mean function, and OLS with the dependent variable a transformation of the count data y to reduce heteroskedasticity and asymmetry. Throughout this chapter the methods presented are applied to a regression model for the number of doctor visits, introduced in section 3.2.6.

For completeness many different models, regression parameter estimators, and standard error estimators are presented in this chapter. The models considered are the Poisson and two variants of the negative binomial – NB1 and NB2. The estimators considered include MLE, PMLE, and QGPMLE. An acronym such as NB1 MLE is shorthand for the NB1 model estimated by maximum likelihood.

For many analyses the Poisson PMLE with corrected standard errors, the negative binomial MLE, and the ordered probit MLE are sufficient. The most common departure from these is the hurdle model, presented in the next chapter.

3.2 Poisson MLE, PMLE, and GLM

Many of the algebraic results presented in this chapter need to be modified if the conditional mean function is not exponential.

3.2.1 *Poisson MLE*

From section 1.2.3, the Poisson regression model specifies that y_i given $\mathbf{x}_i$ is Poisson distributed with density

$$f(y_i \mid \mathbf{x}_i) = \frac{e^{-\mu_i}\mu_i^{y_i}}{y_i!}, \qquad y_i = 0, 1, 2, \ldots \tag{3.1}$$

and mean parameter

$$\mathsf{E}[y_i \mid \mathbf{x}_i] = \mu_i = \exp(\mathbf{x}_i'\boldsymbol{\beta}). \tag{3.2}$$

The specification (3.2) is called the *exponential mean function*. The model comprising (3.1) and (3.2) is usually referred to as the Poisson regression model, a terminology we also use, although more precisely it is the Poisson regression model with exponential mean function. In the statistics literature the model is also called a *log-linear model*, because the logarithm of the conditional mean is linear in the parameters: $\ln \mathsf{E}[y_i \mid \mathbf{x}_i] = \mathbf{x}_i'\boldsymbol{\beta}$.

Given independent observations, the log-likelihood is

$$\ln \mathsf{L}(\boldsymbol{\beta}) = \sum_{i=1}^{n} \{y_i\mathbf{x}_i'\boldsymbol{\beta} - \exp(\mathbf{x}_i'\boldsymbol{\beta}) - \ln y_i!\}. \tag{3.3}$$

The Poisson MLE $\hat{\boldsymbol{\beta}}_{\mathsf{P}}$ is the solution to the first-order conditions

$$\sum_{i=1}^{n} \left(y_i - \exp\left(\mathbf{x}_i'\boldsymbol{\beta}\right)\right)\mathbf{x}_i = \mathbf{0}. \tag{3.4}$$

Note that if the regressors include a constant term then the residuals $y_i - \exp(\mathbf{x}_i'\boldsymbol{\beta})$ sum to zero by (3.4).

The standard method for computation of $\hat{\boldsymbol{\beta}}_{\mathsf{P}}$ is the Newton-Raphson iterative method. Convergence is guaranteed, because the log-likelihood function is globally concave. In practice often fewer than ten iterations are needed. The Newton-Raphson method can be implemented by iterative use of OLS as presented in section 3.8.

If the dgp for y_i is indeed Poisson with mean (3.2) we can apply the usual maximum likelihood theory as in section 2.3.2. This yields

$$\hat{\boldsymbol{\beta}}_{\mathsf{P}} \overset{a}{\sim} \mathsf{N}[\boldsymbol{\beta}, \mathsf{V}_{\mathsf{ML}}[\hat{\boldsymbol{\beta}}_{\mathsf{P}}]] \tag{3.5}$$

where

$$\mathsf{V}_{\mathsf{ML}}[\hat{\boldsymbol{\beta}}_{\mathsf{P}}] = \left(\sum_{i=1}^{n} \mu_i \mathbf{x}_i \mathbf{x}_i'\right)^{-1}, \tag{3.6}$$

using $\mathsf{E}[\partial^2 \ln \mathsf{L}/\partial\boldsymbol{\beta}\partial\boldsymbol{\beta}'] = -\sum_{i=1}^{n} \mu_i \mathbf{x}_i \mathbf{x}_i'$. Strictly speaking we should assume that the dgp evaluates $\boldsymbol{\beta}$ at the specific value $\boldsymbol{\beta}_0$ and replace $\boldsymbol{\beta}$ by $\boldsymbol{\beta}_0$ in (3.5). This more formal presentation is used in Chapter 2. In the rest of the book we use a less formal presentation, provided the estimator is indeed consistent.

Most statistical programs use Hessian maximum likelihood (MLH) standard errors using (3.6) evaluated at $\hat{\mu}_i = \exp(\mathbf{x}_i'\hat{\boldsymbol{\beta}}_{\mathsf{P}})$. By the information matrix equality one can instead use the summed outer product of the first derivatives (see section 2.3.2), leading to the maximum likelihood outer product (MLOP) estimator

$$\hat{\mathsf{V}}_{\mathsf{MLOP}}[\hat{\boldsymbol{\beta}}_{\mathsf{P}}] = \left(\sum_{i=1}^{n} (y_i - \mu_i)^2 \mathbf{x}_i \mathbf{x}_i'\right)^{-1}, \tag{3.7}$$

evaluated at $\hat{\mu}_i$. A general optimization routine may provide standard errors based on (3.7), which asymptotically equals (3.6) if data are equidispersed.

3.2.2 *NB1 and NB2 Variance Functions*

In the Poisson regression model y_i has mean $\mu_i = \exp(\mathbf{x}_i'\boldsymbol{\beta})$ and variance μ_i. We now relax the variance assumption, because data almost always reject the restriction that the variance equals the mean, and we maintain the assumption that the mean is $\exp(\mathbf{x}_i'\boldsymbol{\beta})$.

We use the general notation

$$\omega_i = \mathsf{V}[y_i \mid \mathbf{x}_i] \tag{3.8}$$

to denote the conditional variance of y_i. It is natural to continue to model the variance as a function of the mean, with

$$\omega_i = \omega(\mu_i, \alpha) \tag{3.9}$$

for some specified function $\omega(\cdot)$ and where α is a scalar parameter. Most models specialize this to the general variance function

$$\omega_i = \mu_i + \alpha\mu_i^p, \tag{3.10}$$

where the constant p is specified. Analysis is usually restricted to two special cases, in addition to the Poisson case of $\alpha = 0$.

First, the NB1 variance function sets $p = 1$. Then the variance

$$\omega_i = (1 + \alpha)\mu_i \tag{3.11}$$

is a multiple of the mean. In the GLM framework this is usually rewritten as

$$\omega_i = \phi\mu_i, \tag{3.12}$$

where $\phi = 1 + \alpha$.

Second, the NB2 variance function sets $p = 2$. Then the variance is quadratic in the mean:

$$\omega_i = \mu_i + \alpha\mu_i^2. \tag{3.13}$$

In both cases the *dispersion parameter* α is to be estimated.

Cameron and Trivedi (1986), in the context of negative binomial models, used the terminology *NB1 model* to describe the case $p = 1$ and *NB2 model* to describe the case $p = 2$. Here we have extended this terminology to the variance function itself.

3.2.3 *Poisson PMLE*

The assumption of a Poisson distribution is stronger than necessary for statistical inference based on $\hat{\beta}_P$ defined by (3.4). As discussed in section 2.4.2, whose results are used extensively in this subsection, consistency holds for the MLE of any specified LEF density such as the Poisson, provided the conditional mean function (3.2) is correctly specified. An intuitive explanation is that consistency requires the left-hand side of the first-order conditions (3.4) to have expected value zero. This is the case if $\mathsf{E}[y_i \mid \mathbf{x}_i] = \exp(\mathbf{x}_i'\beta)$, because then $\mathsf{E}[(y_i - \exp(\mathbf{x}_i'\beta))\mathbf{x}_i] = \mathbf{0}$.

Given this robustness to distributional assumptions, we can continue to use $\hat{\beta}_P$ even if the dgp for y_i is not the Poisson. If an alternative dgp is entertained, the estimator defined by the Poisson maximum likelihood first-order conditions (3.4) is called the *Poisson pseudo-MLE* (PMLE) or the *Poisson quasi*-MLE. This terminology means that the estimator is like the Poisson MLE in that the Poisson model is used to motivate the first-order condition defining the estimator, but it is unlike the Poisson MLE in that the dgp used to obtain the distribution of the estimator need not be the Poisson. Here we assume the Poisson mean but relax the Poisson restriction of equidispersion.

The Poisson PMLE $\hat{\beta}_{\mathsf{P}}$ is defined to be the solution to (3.4). If (3.2) holds then

$$\hat{\beta}_{\mathsf{P}} \overset{a}{\sim} \mathsf{N}[\beta, \mathsf{V}_{\mathsf{PML}}[\hat{\beta}_{\mathsf{P}}]], \tag{3.14}$$

where

$$\mathsf{V}_{\mathsf{PML}}[\hat{\beta}_{\mathsf{P}}] = \left(\sum_{i=1}^{n} \mu_i \mathbf{x}_i \mathbf{x}_i'\right)^{-1} \left(\sum_{i=1}^{n} \omega_i \mathbf{x}_i \mathbf{x}_i'\right) \left(\sum_{i=1}^{n} \mu_i \mathbf{x}_i \mathbf{x}_i'\right)^{-1} \tag{3.15}$$

and ω_i is the conditional variance of y_i defined in (3.8). Implementation of (3.15) depends on what functional form, if any, is assumed for ω_i.

Poisson PMLE with Poisson Variance Function

If the conditional variance of y_i is that for the Poisson, so $\omega_i = \mu_i$, then the variance matrix (3.15) simplifies to (3.6). Thus the usual Poisson maximum likelihood inference is valid provided the first two moments are correctly specified.

Poisson PMLE with NB1 Variance Function

The simplest generalization of $\omega_i = \mu_i$ is the NB1 variance function (3.12). Because $\omega_i = \phi\mu_i$ the variance matrix in (3.15) simplifies to

$$\mathsf{V}_{\mathsf{NB1}}[\hat{\beta}_{\mathsf{P}}] = \phi \left(\sum_{i=1}^{n} \mu_i \mathbf{x}_i \mathbf{x}_i'\right)^{-1} = \phi \mathsf{V}_{\mathsf{ML}}[\hat{\beta}_{\mathsf{P}}], \tag{3.16}$$

where $\mathsf{V}_{\mathsf{ML}}[\hat{\beta}_{\mathsf{P}}]$ is the maximum likelihood variance matrix given in (3.6). Thus, the simplest way to handle overdispersed or underdispersed data is to begin with the computed Poisson maximum likelihood output. Then, multiply maximum likelihood output by ϕ to obtain correct variance matrix, multiply by $\sqrt{\phi}$ to obtain correct standard errors, and divide by $\sqrt{\phi}$ to get correct t statistics.

The standard estimator of ϕ is

$$\hat{\phi}_{\mathsf{NB1}} = \frac{1}{n-k} \sum_{i=1}^{n} \frac{(y_i - \hat{\mu}_i)^2}{\hat{\mu}_i}. \tag{3.17}$$

The motivation for this estimator is that variance function (3.12) implies $\mathsf{E}[(y_i - \mu_i)^2] = \phi\mu_i$ and hence $\phi = \mathsf{E}[(y_i - \mu_i)^2/\mu_i]$. The corresponding sample moment is (3.17) where division by $(n-k)$ rather than n is a degrees-of-freedom correction. This approach to estimation is the GLM approach presented in section 2.4.3; see also section 3.2.4. Poisson regression packages using the

GLM framework automatically use (3.16) for standard errors; most others instead use (3.6).

Poisson PMLE with NB2 Variance Function

A common alternative specification for the variance of y_i is the NB2 variance function (3.13). Then, because $\omega_i = \mu_i + \alpha\mu_i^2$, the variance matrix (3.15) becomes

$$\mathsf{V}_{\mathsf{NB2}}[\hat{\beta}_{\mathsf{P}}] = \left(\sum_{i=1}^{n} \mu_i \mathbf{x}_i \mathbf{x}_i'\right)^{-1} \left(\sum_{i=1}^{n} (\mu_i + \alpha\mu_i^2)\mathbf{x}_i \mathbf{x}_i'\right)\left(\sum_{i=1}^{n} \mu_i \mathbf{x}_i \mathbf{x}_i'\right)^{-1}. \tag{3.18}$$

This does not simplify and computation requires matrix routines. One of several possible estimators of α is

$$\hat{\alpha}_{\mathsf{NB2}} = \frac{1}{n-k} \sum_{i=1}^{n} \frac{\{(y_i - \hat{\mu}_i)^2 - \hat{\mu}_i\}}{\hat{\mu}_i^2}. \tag{3.19}$$

The motivation for this estimator of α is that (3.13) implies $\mathsf{E}[(y_i - \mu_i)^2 - \mu_i] = \alpha\mu_i^2$ and hence $\alpha = \mathsf{E}[\{(y_i - \mu_i)^2 - \mu_i\}/\mu_i^2]$. The corresponding sample moment with degrees-of-freedom correction is (3.19). This estimator was proposed by Gourieroux et al. (1984a, 1984b).

Alternative estimators of ϕ and α for NB1 and NB2 variance functions are given in Cameron and Trivedi (1986). In practice studies do not present estimated standard errors for $\hat{\phi}_{\mathsf{NB1}}$ and $\hat{\alpha}_{\mathsf{NB2}}$, although these can be obtained using the delta method given in section 2.6.2. A series of papers by Dean (1993, 1994) and Dean, Eaves and Martinez (1995) consider different estimators for the dispersion parameter and consequences for variance matrix estimation.

Poisson PMLE with Unspecified Variance Function

The variance matrix (3.15) can be consistently estimated without specification of a functional form for ω_i. We need to estimate for unknown ω_i the middle term in $\mathsf{V}_{\mathsf{PML}}[\hat{\beta}_{\mathsf{P}}]$ defined in (3.15). Formally, a consistent estimate of $\lim \frac{1}{n} \sum_{i=1}^{n} \mathsf{E}[(y_i - \mu_i)^2 \mid \mathbf{x}_i]\mathbf{x}_i\mathbf{x}_i'$ is needed. It can be shown that if $(y_i, \mathbf{x}_i)$ are iid this $k \times k$ matrix is consistently estimated by $\frac{1}{n}\sum_{i=1}^{n}(y_i - \hat{\mu}_i)^2\mathbf{x}_i\mathbf{x}_i'$, even though it is impossible to consistently estimate each of the n scalars ω_i^2 by $(y_i - \hat{\mu}_i)^2$. This yields the variance matrix estimate

$$\mathsf{V}_{\mathsf{RS}}[\hat{\beta}_{\mathsf{P}}] = \left(\sum_{i=1}^{n} \mu_i \mathbf{x}_i \mathbf{x}_i'\right)^{-1} \left(\sum_{i=1}^{n} (y_i - \mu_i)^2 \mathbf{x}_i \mathbf{x}_i'\right)\left(\sum_{i=1}^{n} \mu_i \mathbf{x}_i \mathbf{x}_i'\right)^{-1}, \tag{3.20}$$

which is evaluated at $\hat{\mu}_i$.

The estimator (3.20) is the RS estimator discussed in section 2.5.1. It builds on work by Eicker (1967), who obtained a similar result in the nonregression case, and White (1980), who obtained this result in the OLS regression case and popularized its use in econometrics. See Robinson (1987) for a history of this approach and for further references. This method is used extensively throughout this book, in settings much more general than the Poisson PMLE with cross-section data. As shorthand we refer to standard errors as *robust standard errors* whenever a similar approach is used to obtain standard errors without specifying functional forms for the second moments of the dependent variable.

An alternative way to proceed when the variance function ω_i is not specified is to *bootstrap*. This estimates properties of the distribution of $\hat{\boldsymbol{\beta}}_{\mathsf{P}}$ and performs statistical inference on $\boldsymbol{\beta}$ by resampling from the original data set. The standard procedure for linear regression is to bootstrap residuals $(y_i - \hat{\mu}_i)$. This procedure cannot be applied to residuals from Poisson regression, however, as $(y_i - \mu_i)$ is then heteroskedastic, and noninteger values of y_i would arise. Instead for Poisson regression we bootstrap the pairs $(y_i, \mathbf{x}_i)$. A detailed discussion of the bootstrap is given in section 5.5.1.

3.2.4 *Poisson GLM*

Generalized linear models are defined in section 2.4.4. For the Poisson with mean function (3.2), which is the canonical link function for this model, the Poisson GLM density is

$$f(y_i \mid \mathbf{x}_i) = \exp\left\{\frac{\mathbf{x}_i'\boldsymbol{\beta} y_i - \exp\left(\mathbf{x}_i'\boldsymbol{\beta}\right)}{\phi} + c(y_i, \phi)\right\}, \tag{3.21}$$

where $c(y_i, \phi)$ is a normalizing constant. Then $\mathsf{V}[y_i] = \phi\mu_i$, which is the NB1 variance function.

The Poisson GLM estimator $\hat{\boldsymbol{\beta}}_{\mathsf{PGLM}}$ maximizes with respect to $\boldsymbol{\beta}$ the corresponding log-likelihood, with first-order conditions

$$\sum_{i=1}^{n} \frac{1}{\phi}\left(y_i - \exp\left(\mathbf{x}_i'\boldsymbol{\beta}\right)\right)\mathbf{x}_i = \mathbf{0}. \tag{3.22}$$

These coincide with (3.4) for the Poisson PML, except for scaling by the constant ϕ. Consequently $\hat{\boldsymbol{\beta}}_{\mathsf{PGLM}} = \hat{\boldsymbol{\beta}}_{\mathsf{P}}$, and the variance matrix is the same as (3.16) for the Poisson PML with NB1 variance function

$$\mathsf{V}[\hat{\boldsymbol{\beta}}_{\mathsf{PGLM}}] = \phi\left(\sum_{i=1}^{n} \mu_i \mathbf{x}_i \mathbf{x}_i'\right)^{-1}. \tag{3.23}$$

To implement this last result for statistical inference on $\boldsymbol{\beta}$, GLM practitioners use the consistent estimate $\hat{\phi}_{\mathsf{NB1}}$ defined in (3.17).

A more obvious approach to estimating the nuisance parameter ϕ is to maximize the log-likelihood based on (3.21) with respect to both β and ϕ. Differentiation with respect to ϕ requires an expression for the normalizing constant $c(y_i, \phi)$, however, and the restriction that probabilities sum to unity,

$$\sum_{y_i=0}^{\infty} \exp\left\{\frac{1}{\phi}\left(\mathbf{x}_i'\boldsymbol{\beta} y_i - \exp\left(\mathbf{x}_i'\boldsymbol{\beta}\right)\right) + c(y_i, \phi)\right\} = 1,$$

has no simple solution for $c(y_i, \phi)$. One therefore uses the estimator (3.17), which is based on assumptions about the first two moments rather than the density. More generally the density (3.21) is best thought of as merely giving a justification for the first-order conditions (3.22), rather than as a density that would be used, for example, to predict the probabilities of particular values of y.

3.2.5 *Poisson EE*

A quite general estimation procedure is to use the estimating equation presented in section 2.4.5,

$$\sum_i \frac{1}{\omega_i}(y_i - \mu_i)\frac{\partial \mu_i}{\partial \boldsymbol{\beta}} = \mathbf{0},$$

which generalizes linear WLS. Consider a specific variance function of the form $\omega_i = \omega(\mu_i, \alpha)$, and let $\tilde{\alpha}$ be a consistent estimator of α. For the exponential mean function $\partial \mu_i / \partial \boldsymbol{\beta} = \mu_i \mathbf{x}_i$, so $\hat{\boldsymbol{\beta}}_{\mathsf{EE}}$ solves the first-order conditions

$$\sum_{i=1}^{n} \frac{1}{\omega(\mu_i, \tilde{\alpha})}(y_i - \mu_i)\mu_i \mathbf{x}_i = \mathbf{0}. \tag{3.24}$$

If the variance function is correctly specified then it follows that

$$\mathsf{V}_{\mathsf{EE}}[\hat{\boldsymbol{\beta}}_{\mathsf{EE}}] = \left(\sum_{i=1}^{n} \frac{1}{\omega(\mu_i, \alpha)}\mu_i^2 \mathbf{x}_i \mathbf{x}_i'\right)^{-1}. \tag{3.25}$$

Because this estimator is motivated by specification of the first two moments, it can also be viewed as a method-of-moments estimator, a special case of GMM whose more general framework is unnecessary here as the number of equations (3.24) equals the number of unknowns. The first-order conditions nest as special cases those for the Poisson MLE and GLM, which replace $\omega(\mu_i, \tilde{\alpha})$ by μ_i.

3.2.6 *Example: Doctor Visits*

Consider the following example of the number of doctor visits in the past 2 weeks for a single-adult sample of size 5190 from the Australian Health Survey 1977–78. This and several other measures of health service utilization such as

Table 3.1. *Doctor visits: actual frequency distribution*

Count	0	1	2	3	4	5	6	7	8	9
Frequency	4141	782	174	30	24	9	12	12	5	1
Relative frequency	.798	.151	.033	.006	.005	.002	.002	.002	.001	.000

Table 3.2. *Doctor visits: variable definitions and summary statistics*

Variable	Definition	Mean	Standard deviation
DVISITS	Number of doctor visits in past 2 weeks	.302	.798
SEX	Equals 1 if female	.521	.500
AGE	Age in years divided by 100	.406	.205
AGESQ	*AGE* squared	.207	.186
INCOME	Annual income in tens of thousands of dollars	.583	.369
LEVYPLUS	Equals 1 if private health insurance	.443	.497
FREEPOOR	Equals 1 if free government health insurance due to low income	.043	.202
FREEREPA	Equals 1 if free government health insurance due to old age, disability or veteran status	.210	.408
ILLNESS	Number of illnesses in past 2 weeks	1.432	1.384
ACTDAYS	Number of days of reduced activity in past 2 weeks due to illness or injury	.862	2.888
HSCORE	General health questionnaire score using Goldberg's method	1.218	2.124
CHCOND1	Equals 1 if chronic condition not limiting activity	.403	.491
CHCOND2	Equals 1 if chronic condition limiting activity	.117	.321

days in hospital and number of medicines taken were analyzed in Cameron, Trivedi, Milne, and Piggott (1988) in the light of an economic model of joint determination of health service utilization and health insurance choice. The particular data presented here were also studied by Cameron and Trivedi (1986). The analysis of this example in this chapter (see also sections 3.3, 3.4, 3.5.1, and 3.7.4) is more detailed and covers additional methods.

The dependent variable *DVISITS* is summarized in Table 3.1. There are few large counts, with 98% of the sample taking values of 0, 1, or 2. The mean number of doctor visits is .302 with variance .637. The raw data are therefore overdispersed, although inclusion of regressors may eliminate the overdispersion.

The variables are defined and summary statistics given in Table 3.2. Regressors can be grouped into four categories: socioeconomic: *SEX*, *AGE*, *AGESQ*, *INCOME*; health insurance status indicators: *LEVYPLUS*, *FREEPOOR*, and *FREEREPA*, with *LEVY* (government Medibank health insurance) the omitted category; recent health status measures: *ILLNESS*, *ACTDAYS*; and long-term health status measures: *HSCORE*, *CHCOND1*, *CHCOND2*.

Table 3.3. *Doctor visits: Poisson PMLE with different standard error estimates*

Variable	Coefficient, Poisson PMLE	Standard errors MLH	MLOP	NB1	NB2	RS	Boot	t Statistic, NB1
ONE	−2.224	.190	.144	.219	.207	.254	.265	−10.16
SEX	.157	.056	.041	.065	.062	.079	.076	2.42
AGE	1.056	1.001	.750	1.153	1.112	1.364	1.411	.92
AGESQ	−.849	1.078	.809	1.242	1.210	1.460	1.547	−.68
INCOME	−.205	.088	.062	.102	.096	.129	.130	−2.02
LEVYPLUS	.123	.072	.056	.083	.077	.095	.101	1.49
FREEPOOR	−.440	.180	.116	.207	.188	.290	.294	−2.12
FREEREPA	.080	.092	.070	.106	.102	.126	.133	.75
ILLNESS	.187	.018	.014	.021	.021	.024	.025	8.88
ACTDAYS	.127	.005	.004	.006	.006	.008	.008	21.87
HSCORE	.030	.010	.007	.012	.012	.014	.015	2.59
CHCOND1	.114	.066	.051	.077	.071	091	.087	1.48
CHCOND2	141	.083	.059	.096	.092	.122	.121	1.47
−ln L	3355.5							

Note: Different standard error estimates due to different specifications of ω, the conditional variance of y. MLH, $\omega = \mu$ hessian estimate; MLOP, $\omega = \mu$ summed outer product of first derivatives estimate; NB1, $\omega = \phi\mu = (1+\alpha)\mu$ where here $\alpha = .328$; NB2, $\omega = \mu + \alpha\mu^2$ where here $\alpha = .286$; RS, unspecified ω robust sandwich estimate; Boot, unspecified ω bootstrap estimate.

The Poisson maximum likelihood estimates defined by (3.4) are given in the first column of Table 3.3. These estimates are by definition identical to the Poisson PML estimates. Various estimates of the standard errors are given in the remainder of the table, under different assumptions about the variance of y, where throughout it is assumed that the conditional mean is correctly specified as in (3.2). Standard errors are presented rather than t statistics to allow comparison with the precision of alternative estimators given in later tables.

The MLH standard errors are the usual maximum likelihood standard errors using the inverse of the Hessian (3.6). If instead one uses the summed outer product of the first derivatives, the resulting MLOP standard errors using (3.7) are in this example on average 25% lower than MLH standard errors. Comparison of (3.6) and (3.7) shows that this is consistent with $\mathsf{E}[(y_i - \mu_i)^2 \mid \mathbf{x}_i] = \phi\mu_i$ where $1/\sqrt{\phi} \simeq .75$ or $\alpha = (\phi - 1) \simeq .78$. More generally for overdispersed data the MLOP standard errors will be biased downward even more than are the usual MLH standard errors (3.6).

The columns labeled *MLH*, *NB1*, and *NB2* specify that the variance of y equals, respectively, the mean, a multiple of the mean, and a quadratic function of the mean. The standard errors NB1 are 1.152 times MLH standard errors, because $\hat{\phi}_{\mathsf{NB1}} = 1.328$ using (3.17), which has square root 1.152. The standard errors NB2 are obtained using (3.15), where (3.19) yields $\hat{\alpha}_{\text{NB2}} = 0.286$. These estimated values of α are not reported in the table, as they are not used in forming an estimate of $\boldsymbol{\beta}$. They are used only to obtain standard errors of the PMLE of $\boldsymbol{\beta}$.

Other count applications yield similar results. In the usual case in which data are overdispersed, the MLH and MLOP standard errors are smaller than NB1 and NB2 standard errors and should not be used. The differences can be much greater than in this example if data are greatly overdispersed. One should never use MLH or MLOP here.

The column labeled *RS* uses the robust sandwich estimates given in (3.20). These are roughly 20 percent larger than NB1 and NB2 standard errors. One possibility is that the robust sandwich estimates are biased, due to being influenced by outliers that can lead to large values of $(y_i - \hat{\mu}_i)^2$ in (3.20), even in a sample as large as 5190. One way to assess this is through a bootstrap. The bootstrap standard errors in this situation can be shown to be small-sample–corrected estimates of the robust sandwich standard errors. The column Boot uses bootstrap estimates with 200 replications. The bootstrap procedure to estimate standard errors, and to conduct hypothesis tests, is detailed in section 5.5.1. The bootstrap standard errors are generally within 5 percent of RS, indicating little bias in standard error estimation for this example with $n = 5190$.

Which standard errors should be used? If one is willing to specify that $\omega_i = \phi\mu_i$ (or $\omega_i = \mu_i + \alpha\mu_i^2$), then one can use NB1 (or NB2) standard errors. If one is unwilling to impose such variance functions, then one can use RS standard errors in large samples and bootstrap in small samples. In practice NB1 standard errors are very appealing, due to the computational advantage of being a simple rescaling of MLH standard errors often reported by maximum likelihood routines. This is also the GLM approach. It seems to work well in practice and clearly is far superior to using maximum likelihood standard errors, although there appears to be scope for further analysis.

The final column of Table 3.3 gives t statistics based on the NB1 standard errors. By far the most statistically significant determinants of doctor visits in the past 2 weeks are recent health status measures – number of illnesses and days of reduced activity in the past 2 weeks – with positive coefficients, confirming that sicker people are more likely to visit a doctor. The long-term health status measure *HSCORE* and the socioeconomic variable *SEX* are also statistically significant. Discussion of the impact of these variables on the number of doctor visits is deferred to section 3.5.

3.3 Negative Binomial MLE and QGPMLE

The Poisson PML estimator handles overdispersion or underdispersion by moving away from complete distributional specification to specification of the first two moments. Alternatively one can specify a distribution that permits more flexible modeling of the variance than the Poisson.

The standard parametric model to account for overdispersion is the negative binomial. There are a number of ways that this distribution can arise, with two quite different derivations given in Chapter 4. The most common is that the data are Poisson, but there is gamma-distributed unobserved individual heterogeneity reflecting the fact that the true mean is not perfectly observed. An alternative derivation of the negative binomial assumes a particular form of dependence for the underlying stochastic process, with occurrence of an event increasing the probability of further occurrences. Cross-section data on counts are insufficient on their own to discriminate between the two.

3.3.1 *NB2 Model and MLE*

The most common implementation of the *negative binomial* is the NB2 model, with NB2 variance function $\mu + \alpha\mu^2$ defined in (3.13). It has density

$$f(y \mid \mu, \alpha) = \frac{\Gamma(y+\alpha^{-1})}{\Gamma(y+1)\Gamma(\alpha^{-1})}\left(\frac{\alpha^{-1}}{\alpha^{-1}+\mu}\right)^{\alpha^{-1}}\left(\frac{\mu}{\alpha^{-1}+\mu}\right)^{y},$$
$$\alpha \geq 0, \qquad y = 0, 1, 2, \ldots \tag{3.26}$$

This reduces to the Poisson if $\alpha = 0$ (see section 3.3.3).

The function $\Gamma(\cdot)$ is the gamma function, defined in Appendix B, where it is shown that $\Gamma(y+a)/\Gamma(a) = \prod_{j=0}^{y-1}(j+a)$, if y is an integer. Thus,

$$\ln\left(\frac{\Gamma(y+\alpha^{-1})}{\Gamma(\alpha^{-1})}\right) = \sum_{j=0}^{y-1}\ln(j+\alpha^{-1}). \tag{3.27}$$

Substituting (3.27) into (3.26), the log-likelihood function for exponential mean $\mu_i = \exp(\mathbf{x}_i'\boldsymbol{\beta})$ is therefore

$$\ln \mathsf{L}(\alpha, \beta) = \sum_{i=1}^{n}\left\{\left(\sum\nolimits_{j=0}^{y_i-1}\ln(j+\alpha^{-1})\right) - \ln y_i! \right.$$
$$\left. -(y_i+\alpha^{-1})\ln\left(1+\alpha\exp\left(\mathbf{x}_i'\boldsymbol{\beta}\right)\right) + y_i\ln\alpha + y_i\mathbf{x}_i'\boldsymbol{\beta}\}\right\}. \tag{3.28}$$

The NB2 MLE $(\hat{\boldsymbol{\beta}}_{\mathsf{NB2}}, \hat{\alpha}_{\mathsf{NB2}})$ is the solution to the first-order conditions

$$\sum_{i=1}^{n}\frac{y_i-\mu_i}{1+\alpha\mu_i}\mathbf{x}_i = \mathbf{0}$$
$$\sum_{i=1}^{n}\left\{\frac{1}{\alpha^2}\left(\ln(1+\alpha\mu_i) - \sum_{j=0}^{y_i-1}\frac{1}{(j+\alpha^{-1})}\right) + \frac{y_i-\mu_i}{\alpha(1+\alpha\mu_i)}\right\} = 0. \tag{3.29}$$

Given correct specification of the distribution

$$\begin{bmatrix} \hat{\beta}_{\mathsf{NB2}} \\ \hat{\alpha}_{\mathsf{NB2}} \end{bmatrix} \overset{a}{\sim} \mathsf{N}\left(\begin{bmatrix} \beta \\ \alpha \end{bmatrix}, \begin{bmatrix} \mathsf{V}_{\mathsf{ML}}[\hat{\beta}_{\mathsf{NB2}}] & \mathsf{Cov}_{\mathsf{ML}}[\hat{\beta}_{\mathsf{NB2}}, \hat{\alpha}_{\mathsf{NB2}}] \\ \mathsf{Cov}_{\mathsf{ML}}[\hat{\beta}_{\mathsf{NB2}}, \hat{\alpha}_{\mathsf{NB2}}] & \mathsf{V}_{\mathsf{ML}}[\hat{\alpha}_{\mathsf{NB2}}] \end{bmatrix} \right) \tag{3.30}$$

where

$$\mathsf{V}_{\mathsf{ML}}[\hat{\beta}_{\mathsf{NB2}}] = \left(\sum_{i=1}^{n} \frac{\mu_i}{1+\alpha\mu_i} \mathbf{x}_i \mathbf{x}_i' \right)^{-1}, \tag{3.31}$$

$$\mathsf{V}_{\mathsf{ML}}[\hat{\alpha}_{\mathsf{NB2}}] = \left(\sum_{i=1}^{n} \frac{1}{\alpha^4} \left(\ln(1+\alpha\mu_i) - \sum_{j=0}^{y_i-1} \frac{1}{(j+\alpha^{-1})} \right)^2 + \frac{\mu_i}{\alpha^2(1+\alpha\mu_i)} \right)^{-1} \tag{3.32}$$

and

$$\mathsf{Cov}_{\mathsf{ML}}[\hat{\beta}_{\mathsf{NB2}}, \hat{\alpha}_{\mathsf{NB2}}] = \mathbf{0}. \tag{3.33}$$

This result is obtained by noting that the information matrix is block-diagonal, because differentiating the first term in (3.29) with respect to α yields

$$\mathsf{E}\left[\frac{\partial^2 \ln \mathsf{L}}{\partial \beta \partial \alpha} \right] = \mathsf{E}\left[-\sum_{i=1}^{n} \frac{y_i - \mu_i}{(1+\alpha\mu_i)^2} \mu_i \mathbf{x}_i \mathbf{x}_i' \right] = \mathbf{0} \tag{3.34}$$

as $\mathsf{E}[y_i \mid \mathbf{x}_i] = \mu_i$. This simplifies analysis as then the general result in section 2.3.2 for the maximum likelihood variance matrix specializes to

$$\begin{bmatrix} \mathsf{E}\left[\frac{\partial^2 \ln \mathsf{L}}{\partial \beta \partial \beta'}\right] & \mathbf{0} \\ \mathbf{0} & \mathsf{E}\left[\frac{\partial^2 \ln \mathsf{L}}{\partial \alpha^2}\right] \end{bmatrix}^{-1} = \begin{bmatrix} \left[\mathsf{E}\left[\frac{\partial^2 \ln \mathsf{L}}{\partial \beta \partial \beta'}\right]\right]^{-1} & \mathbf{0} \\ \mathbf{0} & \left[\mathsf{E}\left[\frac{\partial^2 \ln \mathsf{L}}{\partial \alpha^2}\right]\right]^{-1} \end{bmatrix}.$$

Several packages offer this negative binomial model as a standard option. Alternatively, one can use a maximum likelihood routine with user-provided log-likelihood function and possibly derivatives. In this case potential computational problems can be avoided by using the form of the log-likelihood function given in (3.28), or by using the log-gamma function rather than first calculating the gamma function and then taking the natural logarithm. If instead one tries to directly compute the gamma functions, numerical calculation of $\Gamma(z)$ with large values of z may cause an overflow, for example, if $z > 169$ in the matrix program GAUSS. The restriction to α positive can be ensured by instead estimating $\alpha^* = \ln \alpha$ and then obtaining $\alpha = \exp(\alpha^*)$.

3.3.2 NB2 Model and QGPMLE

The NB2 density can be reexpressed as

$$f(y \mid \mu, \alpha) = \exp\left\{-\alpha^{-1}\ln(1+\alpha\mu) + \ln\left(\frac{\Gamma(y+\alpha^{-1})}{\Gamma(y+1)\Gamma(\alpha^{-1})}\right)\right.$$
$$\left. + y\ln\left(\frac{\alpha\mu}{1+\alpha\mu}\right)\right\}. \tag{3.35}$$

If α is known this is an LEF density defined in section 2.4.2 with $a(\mu) = -\alpha^{-1}\ln(1+\alpha\mu)$ and $c(\mu) = \ln(\alpha\mu/(1+\alpha\mu))$. Because $a'(\mu) = -1/(1+\alpha\mu)$ and $c'(\mu) = 1/\mu(1+\alpha\mu)$ it follows that $\mathsf{E}[y] = \mu$ and $\mathsf{V}[y] = \mu + \alpha\mu^2$, which is the NB2 variance function.

If α is unknown this is an LEFN density defined in section 2.4.3. Given a consistent estimator $\tilde{\alpha}$ of α, such as (3.19), the QGPMLE $\hat{\beta}_{\mathsf{QGPML}}$ maximizes

$$\ln \mathsf{L}_{\mathsf{LEFN}} = \sum_{i=1}^{n}\left\{-\tilde{\alpha}^{-1}\ln(1+\tilde{\alpha}\mu_i) + y_i\ln\left(\frac{\tilde{\alpha}\mu_i}{1+\tilde{\alpha}\mu_i}\right) + b(y_i, \tilde{\alpha})\right\}. \tag{3.36}$$

For exponential mean (3.4) the first-order conditions are

$$\sum_{i=1}^{n}\frac{y_i - \mu_i}{1+\tilde{\alpha}\mu_i}\mathbf{x}_i = \mathbf{0}. \tag{3.37}$$

Using results from section 2.4.3, or noting that (3.37) is a special case of the estimating equation (3.24), $\hat{\beta}_{\mathsf{QGPML}}$ is asymptotically normal with mean $\mathbf{0}$ and variance

$$\mathsf{V}[\hat{\beta}_{\mathsf{QGPML}}] = \left(\sum_{i=1}^{n}\frac{\mu_i}{1+\alpha\mu_i}\mathbf{x}_i\mathbf{x}_i'\right)^{-1}. \tag{3.38}$$

This equals $\mathsf{V}_{\mathsf{ML}}[\hat{\beta}_{\mathsf{NB2}}]$ defined in (3.31), so that $\hat{\beta}_{\mathsf{QGPML}}$ is fully efficient for β if the density is NB2, although $\tilde{\alpha}$ is not necessarily fully efficient for α.

3.3.3 NB1 Model and MLE

Cameron and Trivedi (1986) considered a more general class of negative binomial models with mean μ_i and variance function $\mu_i + \alpha\mu_i^p$. The NB2 model, with $p = 2$, is the standard formulation of the negative binomial model. Models with other values of p have the same density as (3.26), except that α^{-1} is replaced everywhere by $\alpha^{-1}\mu^{2-p}$.

The NB1 model, which sets $p = 1$, is also of interest because it has the same variance function, $(1+\alpha)\mu_i = \phi\mu_i$, as that used in the GLM approach. The

NB1 log-likelihood function is

$$\ln \mathsf{L}(\alpha, \beta) = \sum_{i=1}^{n} \left\{ \left(\sum_{j=0}^{y_i-1} \ln \left(j + \alpha^{-1} \exp \left(\mathbf{x}_i'\beta\right)\right) \right) - \ln y_i! \right.$$
$$\left. - \left(y_i + \alpha^{-1} \exp(\mathbf{x}_i'\beta)\right) \ln (1 + \alpha) + y_i \ln \alpha \right\}.$$

The NB1 MLE solves the associated first-order conditions

$$\sum_{i=1}^{n} \left\{ \left(\sum_{j=0}^{y_i-1} \frac{\alpha^{-1}\mu_i}{(j + \alpha^{-1}\mu_i)} \right) \mathbf{x}_i + \alpha^{-1}\mu_i \mathbf{x}_i \right\} = \mathbf{0}$$
$$\sum_{i=1}^{n} \frac{1}{\alpha^2} \left\{ - \left(\sum_{j=0}^{y_i-1} \frac{\mu_i}{(j + \alpha^{-1})} \right) - \alpha^{-2}\mu_i \ln (1 + \alpha) \right.$$
$$\left. - \frac{\alpha}{1+\alpha} + y_i \alpha \right\} = 0.$$

Estimation based on the first two moments of the NB1 density yields the Poisson GLM estimator, which we also call the NB1 GLM estimator.

3.3.4 *Discussion*

One can clearly consider negative binomial models other than NB1 and NB2. The generalized event count model, presented in section 4.4.1, includes the negative binomial with mean μ_i and variance function $\mu_i + \alpha\mu_i^p$, where p is estimated rather than set to the value 1 or 2.

The NB2 model has a number of special features not shared by other models in this class, including block diagonality of the information matrix, being a member of the LEF if α is known, robustness to distributional misspecification, and nesting as a special case the Geometric distribution if $\alpha = 1$.

The NB2 MLE is robust to distributional misspecification, due to membership in the LEF for specified α. Thus, provided the conditional mean is correctly specified the NB2 MLE is consistent for β. This can be seen by directly inspecting the first-order conditions for β given in (3.29), whose left-hand side has expected value zero if the mean is correctly specified. This follows because $\mathsf{E}[y_i - \mu_i \mid \mathbf{x}_i] = 0$.

The associated maximum likelihood standard errors of the NB2 MLE will, however, generally be inconsistent if there is any distributional misspecification. First, they are inconsistent if (3.13) does not hold, so the variance function is incorrectly specified. Second, even if the variance function is correctly specified, in which case it can be shown that $\mathsf{V}[\hat{\beta}_{\mathsf{NB2}}]$ is again that given in (3.31), failure of the negative binomial assumption leads to evaluation of (3.31) at an inconsistent estimate of α. From (3.29) consistency of $\hat{\alpha}_{\mathsf{NB2}}$ requires both $\mathsf{E}[y_i - \mu_i \mid \mathbf{x}_i] = 0$

for the NB2 variance function the maximum-likelihood and moment-based estimates $\hat{\alpha}$, respectively, 1.077 and .286, are quite different. The moment-based estimates for NB1 and NB2 use, respectively, (3.17) and (3.19). Another moment-based method, that given in Cameron and Trivedi (1986, p. 46), yields for NB1 and NB2 variance functions estimates of, respectively, .218 and .490. Such differences in estimates of α have received little attention in the literature, in part because interest lies in estimation of $\boldsymbol{\beta}$, with α a nuisance parameter. But even then they are important, as the standard error estimates of $\hat{\boldsymbol{\beta}}$ depend on $\hat{\alpha}$.

Within the maximum likelihood framework the NB2 model is preferred here to NB1 as it has higher log-likelihood, $-3198.7 > -3226.6$, with the same number of parameters. In practice, most studies use either NB2 MLE or NB1 GLM.

3.4 Overdispersion Tests

Failure of the Poisson assumption of equidispersion has similar qualitative consequences to failure of the assumption of homoskedasticity in the linear regression model. But the magnitude of the effect on reported standard errors and t statistics can be much larger. To see this suppose $\omega_i = 4\mu_i$. Then by equation (3.16) the variance matrix of the Poisson PML estimator is four times reported maximum likelihood standard errors using (3.6). As a result the reported Poisson maximum likelihood t statistics need to be deflated by a factor of two. Overdispersion as large as $\omega_i = 4\mu_i$ arises, for example, in the recreational trips data (see section 1.3) and in health services data on length of hospitalization.

Data are overdispersed if the conditional variance exceeds the conditional mean. An indication of the magnitude of overdispersion or underdispersion can be obtained simply by comparing the sample mean and variance of the dependent count variable. Subsequent Poisson regression decreases the conditional variance of the dependent variable somewhat. The average of the conditional mean will be unchanged, however, as the average of the fitted means equals the sample mean. This follows because Poisson residuals sum to zero if a constant term is included. If the sample variance is less than the sample mean, the data necessarily are even more underdispersed once regressors are included. If the sample variance is more than twice the sample mean, then data are likely to remain overdispersed after inclusion of regressors. This is particularly so for cross-section data, for which regressors usually explain less than half the variation in the data.

The standard models for overdispersion have already been presented. These are the NB1 variance function $\omega_i = \mu_i + \alpha\mu_i$ as in (3.11) or NB2 variance function $\omega_i = \mu_i + \alpha\mu_i^2$ as in (3.13). If one takes the partially parametric mean–variance approach (GLM) it is much easier to use the NB1 variance function. If one takes the fully parametric negative binomial approach it is customary to use NB2. Note that if $\alpha = 0$ the negative binomial reduces to the Poisson.

A sound practice is to estimate both Poisson and negative binomial models if software is readily available. The Poisson is the special case of the negative binomial with $\alpha = 0$. The null hypothesis $H_0 : \alpha = 0$ can be tested against the alternative $\alpha > 0$ using the hypothesis test methods presented in section 2.6.1. An LR test uses -2 times the difference in the fitted log-likelihoods of the two models. Alternatively a Wald test can by performed, using the reported t statistic for the estimated α in the negative binomial model.

The distribution of these statistics is nonstandard, due to the restriction that α cannot be less than zero. This complication is usually not commented on, a notable exception being Lawless (1987b). One way to see problems that arise is to consider constructing a Monte Carlo experiment to obtain the distribution of the test statistic. We would draw samples from the Poisson, because this is the model under the null hypothesis of no overdispersion. Roughly half the time the data will be underdispersed. Then the negative binomial MLE for α is zero, the negative binomial parameter estimates equal the Poisson estimates, and the LR test statistic takes a value of 0. Clearly this test statistic is not χ^2 distributed, because half its mass is at zero. Similar problems arise for the Wald test statistic. A general treatment of hypothesis testing at boundary values is given by Moran (1971). The asymptotic distribution of the LR test statistic has probability mass of one half at zero and a half-$\chi^2(1)$ distribution above 0. This means that if testing at level δ, where $\delta > 0.5$, one rejects H_0 if the test statistic exceeds $\chi^2_{1-2\delta}(1)$ rather than $\chi^2_{1-\delta}(1)$. The Wald test is usually implemented as a t test statistic, which here has mass of one half at zero and a normal distribution for values above zero. In this case one continues to use the usual one-sided test critical value of $z_{1-\delta}$. Essentially the only adjustment that needs to be made is an obvious one to the χ^2 critical values, which arises due to performing a one-sided rather than two-sided test.

If a package program for negative binomial regression is unavailable, one can still test for overdispersion by estimating the Poisson model, constructing fitted values $\hat{\mu}_i = \exp(\mathbf{x}_i'\hat{\beta})$, and performing the auxiliary OLS regression (without constant)

$$\frac{(y_i - \hat{\mu}_i)^2 - y_i}{\hat{\mu}_i} = \alpha \hat{\mu}_i + u_i, \tag{3.39}$$

where u_i is an error term. The reported t statistic for α is asymptotically normal under the null hypothesis of no overdispersion against the alternative of overdispersion of the NB2 form. To test overdispersion of the NB1 form, replace (3.39) with

$$\frac{(y_i - \hat{\mu}_i)^2 - y_i}{\hat{\mu}_i} = \alpha + u_i. \tag{3.40}$$

These auxiliary regression tests coincide with the score or LM test for Poisson against negative binomial but additionally test for underdispersion and can be given a more general motivation based on using only the specified mean and variance (see Chapter 5).

Beyond rejection or nonrejection of the null hypothesis of equidispersion, interest may lie in interpreting the magnitude of departures from equidispersion.

Estimates of α for the NB1 variance function $(1+\alpha)\mu_i$ are easily interpreted, with underdispersion if $\alpha < 0$, modest overdispersion when, say, $0 < \alpha < 1$, and considerable overdispersion if, say, $\alpha > 1$. For the NB2 variance function $\mu_i + \alpha\mu_i^2$ underdispersion also occurs if $\alpha < 0$. The NB2 variance function can be inappropriate for underdispersed data, as the estimated variance is negative for observations with $\alpha < -1/\mu_i$. For interpretation of the magnitude of overdispersion it is helpful to rewrite the NB2 variance as $(1+\alpha\mu_i)\ \mu_i$. Then values of considerable overdispersion arise if, say, $\alpha\mu_i > 1$, because then the multiplier $1+\alpha\mu_i > 2$. Thus a value of α equal to 0.5 would indicate modest overdispersion if the dependent variable took mostly values of 0, 1 and 2, but great overdispersion if counts of 10 or more were often observed.

Most often count data are overdispersed rather than underdispersed, and tests for departures from equidispersion are usually called overdispersion tests. Note that the negative binomial model can only accommodate overdispersion.

Example: Doctor Visits (Continued)

From Table 3.1 the data before inclusion of regressors are overdispersed, with variance–mean ratio of $.637/.302 = 2.11$. The only question is whether this overdispersion disappears on inclusion of regressors.

We first consider tests of Poisson against NB2 at significance level 1%. Given the results in Tables 3.3 and 3.4 the LR test statistic is $2(3355.5 - 3198.7) = 313.6$, which exceeds the 1% critical value of $\chi^2_{.98}(1) = 5.41$. The Wald test statistic from Table 3.4 is $1.077/.098 = 10.99$, which exceeds the 1% critical value of $z_{.99} = 2.33$. Finally, the LM test statistic computed using the auxiliary regression (3.39) is 7.51, and exceeds the 1% critical value of $z_{.99} = 2.33$. Therefore all three tests strongly reject the null hypothesis of Poisson, indicating the presence of overdispersion. Note that these tests are asymptotically equivalent, yet there is quite a difference in their realized values of $\sqrt{313.6} = 17.69$, 10.9, and 7.51.

Similar test statistics for Poisson against NB1 are $T_{LR} = 2 \times (3355.5 - 3226.6) = 257.8$, $T_W = .455/.041 = 11.10$ and $T_{LM} = 6.543$ on running auxiliary regression (3.40). These again strongly reject equidispersion.

Clearly some control is necessary for overdispersion. Possibilities include the Poisson PML, see Table 3.3, which corrects the standard errors for overdispersion, and the various NB1 and NB2 estimators presented in Table 3.4.

3.5 Use of Regression Results

The techniques presented to date allow estimation of count data models and performance of tests of statistical significance of regression coefficients. We have focused on tests on individual coefficients. Tests of joint hypotheses such as overall significance can be performed using the Wald, LM, and LR tests presented in section 2.6.1. Confidence intervals for functions of parameters can be formed using the delta method in section 2.6.2.

We now turn to interpretation of regression coefficients and prediction of the dependent variable.

3.5.1 *Interpretation of Coefficients*

An important issue is interpretation of regression coefficients. For example, what does $\hat{\beta}_j = 0.2$ mean? This is straightforward in the linear regression model $\mathsf{E}[y \mid \mathbf{x}] = \mathbf{x}'\boldsymbol{\beta}$. Then $\partial\mathsf{E}[y \mid \mathbf{x}]/\partial\mathbf{x}_j = \beta_j$, so $\hat{\beta}_j = 0.2$ means that a one-unit change in the jth regressor increases the conditional mean by 0.2 units.

We consider the exponential conditional mean

$$\mathsf{E}[y \mid \mathbf{x}] = \exp(\mathbf{x}'\boldsymbol{\beta}), \tag{3.41}$$

where for exposition the subscript i is dropped. Let the scalar x_j denote the jth regressor. Differentiating

$$\frac{\partial\mathsf{E}[y \mid \mathbf{x}]}{\partial x_j} = \beta_j \exp\left(\mathbf{x}_i'\boldsymbol{\beta}\right). \tag{3.42}$$

For example, if $\hat{\beta}_j = 0.2$ and $\exp(\mathbf{x}_i'\hat{\boldsymbol{\beta}}) = 2.5$, then a one-unit change in the jth regressor increases the expectation of y by 0.5 units.

Calculated values differ across individuals, however, due to different values of $\mathbf{x}$. This makes interpretation more difficult.

One procedure is to aggregate over all individuals and calculate the average response

$$\frac{1}{n}\sum_{i=1}^{n}\frac{\partial\mathsf{E}[y_i \mid \mathbf{x}_i]}{\partial x_{ij}} = \frac{1}{n}\sum_{i=1}^{n}\beta_j \exp\left(\mathbf{x}_i'\boldsymbol{\beta}\right). \tag{3.43}$$

In the special case that one uses the Poisson MLE or PMLE, and the regression includes an intercept term, this expression simplifies to

$$\frac{1}{n}\sum_{i=1}^{n}\frac{\partial\mathsf{E}[y_i \mid \mathbf{x}_i]}{\partial x_{ij}} = \beta_j \bar{y} \tag{3.44}$$

because the first-order conditions imply $\sum_i \exp(\mathbf{x}_i'\boldsymbol{\beta}) = \sum_i y_i$.

A second procedure is to calculate the response for the individual with average characteristics

$$\left.\frac{\partial\mathsf{E}[y \mid \mathbf{x}]}{\partial x_j}\right|_{\bar{\mathbf{x}}} = \beta_j \exp(\bar{\mathbf{x}}'\boldsymbol{\beta}). \tag{3.45}$$

Because $\exp(\cdot)$ is a convex function, by Jensen's inequality the average of $\exp(\cdot)$ evaluated at several points exceeds $\exp(\cdot)$ evaluated at the average of the same points. So (3.45) gives responses smaller than (3.43). Due to the need for less calculation, it is common in nonlinear regression to report responses at the sample mean of regressors. It is conceptually better, however, to report the average response (3.43) over all individuals. And it is actually easier in the special case of Poisson with intercept included, as (3.44) can be used.

A third procedure is to calculate (3.42) for select values of $\mathbf{x}_j$ of particular interest. This is perhaps the best method. The actual values of $\mathbf{x}_j$ of particular interest vary from application to application.

It is useful to note that direct interpretation of the coefficients is possible without such additional computations.

- The coefficient β_j equals the proportionate change in the conditional mean if the jth regressor changes by one unit. This follows from rewriting (3.42) as $\partial \mathsf{E}[y \mid \mathbf{x}]/\partial x_j = \beta_j \mathsf{E}[y \mid \mathbf{x}]$, using (3.41), and hence

$$\beta_j = \frac{\partial \mathsf{E}[y \mid \mathbf{x}]}{\partial x_j} \frac{1}{\mathsf{E}[y \mid \mathbf{x}]}. \tag{3.46}$$

  This is a semielasticity, which can alternatively be obtained by rewriting (3.41) as $\ln \mathsf{E}[y \mid \mathbf{x}] = \mathbf{x}'\boldsymbol{\beta}$ and differentiating with respect to x_j.
- The sign of the response $\partial \mathsf{E}[y \mid \mathbf{x}]/\partial x_j$ is given by the sign of β_j, because the response is β_j times the scalar $\exp(\mathbf{x}_i'\boldsymbol{\beta})$, which is always positive.
- If one regression coefficient is twice as large as another, then the effect of a one-unit change of the associated regressor is double that of the other. This result follows from

$$\frac{\partial \mathsf{E}[y \mid \mathbf{x}]/\partial x_j}{\partial \mathsf{E}[y \mid \mathbf{x}]/\partial x_k} = \frac{\beta_j \exp(\mathbf{x}'\boldsymbol{\beta})}{\beta_k \exp(\mathbf{x}'\boldsymbol{\beta})} = \frac{\beta_j}{\beta_k}. \tag{3.47}$$

A *single-index model* is one for which $\mathsf{E}[y \mid \mathbf{x}] = g(\mathbf{x}'\boldsymbol{\beta})$, for monotonic function $g(\cdot)$. The last two properties hold more generally for any single-index model.

Sometimes regressors enter logarithmically in (3.41). For example, we may have

$$\begin{aligned} \mathsf{E}[y \mid \mathbf{x}] &= \exp\left(\beta_1 \ln(x_1) + \mathbf{x}_2'\boldsymbol{\beta}_2\right) \\ &= x_1^{\beta_1} \exp\left(\mathbf{x}_2'\boldsymbol{\beta}_2\right). \end{aligned}$$

Then β_1 is an elasticity, giving the percentage change in $\mathsf{E}[y \mid \mathbf{x}]$ for a 1% change in x_1. This formulation is particularly appropriate if x_1 is a measure of exposure, such as number of miles driven if modeling the number of automobile accidents or population if modeling the incidence of a disease. Then we expect β_1 to be close to unity.

The conditional mean function may include *interaction terms*. For example, suppose

$$\mathsf{E}[y \mid \mathbf{x}] = \exp(\beta_1 + \beta_2 x_2 + \beta_2 x_3 + \beta_4 x_2 x_3).$$

Then the proportionate change in the conditional mean due to a one-unit change in x_3 equals $(\beta_2 + \beta_4 x_2)$, because

$$\frac{\partial \mathsf{E}[y \mid \mathbf{x}]}{\partial x_3} \frac{1}{\mathsf{E}[y \mid \mathbf{x}]} = (\beta_2 + \beta_4 x_2).$$

Thus even the semielasticity measuring the effect of changes in x_3 varies according to the value of regressors – here x_2.

The calculus methods above are appropriate for continuous regressors. Now consider an *indicator variable* regressor d that takes only values 0 and 1, and suppose

$$\mathsf{E}[y \mid d, \mathbf{x}_2] = \exp\left(\beta_1 d + \mathbf{x}_2' \boldsymbol{\beta}_2\right).$$

Then

$$\frac{\mathsf{E}[y \mid d = 1, \mathbf{x}_2]}{\mathsf{E}[y \mid d = 0, \mathbf{x}_2]} = \frac{\exp\left(\beta_1 + \mathbf{x}_2' \boldsymbol{\beta}_2\right)}{\exp\left(\mathbf{x}_2' \boldsymbol{\beta}_2\right)} = \exp(\beta_1).$$

So the conditional mean is $\exp(\beta_1)$ times larger if the indicator variable is unity rather than zero. If we instead use calculus methods then (3.46) predicts a proportionate change of β_1, or equivalently that the conditional mean is $(1+\beta_1)$ times larger. This is a good approximation for small β_1, say $\beta_1 < 0.1$, as then $\exp(\beta_1) \simeq 1 + \beta_1$.

The preceding discussion has considered the effect of a one-unit change in $\mathbf{x}$, which is not free of the units used to measure $\mathbf{x}$. One method is to scale by the sample mean of x_j, so use $\hat{\beta}_j \bar{x}_j$, which given (3.42) is a measure of the elasticity of $\mathsf{E}[y \mid \mathbf{x}]$ with respect to x_j. An alternative method is to consider semistandardized coefficients that give the effect of a one-standard-deviation change in x_j, so use $\hat{\beta}_j s_j$, where s_j is the standard deviation of x_j. Such adjustments, of course, need to be made even for the linear regression model.

Example: Doctor Visits (Continued)

Various measures of the magnitude of the response of the number of doctor visits to changes in regressors are given in Table 3.5. These measures are based on the Poisson PMLE estimates given earlier in Table 3.3.

The coefficient estimates given in the column labeled PMLE using (3.46) can be interpreted as giving the proportionate change in number of doctor visits due to a one-unit change in the regressors. If we consider *ACTDAYS*, the most highly statistically significant regressor, an increase of 1 day of reduced activity in the preceding 2 weeks leads to a .127 proportionate change or 12.7% change in the expected number of doctor visits. More complicated is the effect of age, which appears through both *AGE* and *AGESQ*. For a 40-year-old person, *AGE* = .4 and *AGESQ* = .16, and an increase of 1 year or 0.01 units leads to a $0.01 \times (1.056 - 2 \times .849 \times .40) = .0038$ proportionate change or .38% change in the expected number of doctor visits.

Table 3.5. *Doctor visits: Poisson PMLE mean effects and scaled coefficients*

Variable	Coefficient, PMLE	Mean effect: Ave	Mean effect: At Ave	Mean effect: OLS	Scaled coefficients: Elast	Scaled coefficients: SSC	Summary stats: Mean	Summary stats: Standard deviation
ONE	−2.224							
SEX	.157	.047	.035	.034	.082	.078	.521	.500
AGE	1.056	.319	.241	.203	.430	.216	.406	.205
AGESQ	−.849	−.256	−.193	−.062	−.176	−.157	.207	.186
INCOME	−.205	−.062	−.047	−.057	−.120	−.076	.583	.369
LEVYPLUS	.123	.037	.028	.035	.055	.061	.443	.497
FREEPOOR	−.440	−.133	−.100	−.103	−.019	−.089	.043	.202
FREEREPA	.080	.024	−.018	.033	.017	.033	.210	.408
ILLNESS	.187	.056	.043	.060	.268	.259	1.432	1.384
ACTDAYS	.127	.038	.029	.103	.109	.366	.862	2.888
HSCORE	.030	.009	.007	.017	.037	.064	1.218	2.124
CHCOND1	.114	.034	.026	.004	.046	.056	.403	.491
CHCOND2	.141	.043	.032	.042	.016	.045	.117	.321

Note: Ave, average over sample of effect of y of a one-unit change in x; At Ave, effect on y of a one-unit change in x evaluated at average regressors; OLS, OLS coefficients; Elast, coefficients scaled by sample mean of x; SSC, coefficients scaled by standard deviation of x.

The columns *Ave* and *At Ave* give two different measures of the change in the number of doctor visits due to a one-unit change in regressors. First, the column *Ave* gives the average of the individual responses, using (3.44). Second, the column *At Ave* gives the response for the individual with regressors equal to the sample mean values, computed using (3.45). The preferred *Ave* estimates are about 30% larger than those of the "representative" individual, a consequence of the convexity of the exponential mean function. An increase of 1 day of reduced activity in the preceding 2 weeks, for example, leads on average to an increase of .038 doctor visits.

The column *OLS* gives coefficient estimates from OLS of y on $\mathbf{x}$. Like the preceding two columns these give estimates of the effects of a one-unit change of x_j on $\mathrm{E}[y]$, the only difference being in whether an exponential or linear mean function is specified. The three columns are generally similar, although OLS gives a much larger effect of an increase of .103 in the number of doctor visits due to 1 more day of reduced activity.

All these measures consider the effect of a one-unit change in x_j, but it is not always clear whether such a change is a large or small change. The *Elast* column gives $\hat{\beta}_j \bar{x}_j$, where $\bar{x}_j$ is given in the second-to-last column of the table. Given the exponential mean function, this measures the elasticity of $\mathrm{E}[y]$ with respect to changes in regressors. The SSC column gives $\hat{\beta}_j s_j$, which instead scales by the standard deviation of the regressors, given in the last column of the table. Both measures highlight the importance of the health status measures *ILLNESS*, *ACTDAYS*, and *HSCORE* much more clearly than the raw coefficient estimates and the estimates of $\partial \mathsf{E}[y]/\partial x_j$. For example, the estimates imply that a 1% increase in illness days leads to a .268% increase in expected doctor visits, while a one-standard-deviation increase in activity days leads to a .259% increase in expected doctor visits.

3.5.2 *Prediction*

We begin by considering, for an individual observation with $\mathbf{x} = \mathbf{x}_p$, prediction of the conditional mean $\mu_p = \mathsf{E}[y \mid \mathbf{x} = \mathbf{x}_p]$.

For the exponential conditional mean function, the mean prediction is

$$\hat{\mu}_p = \exp(\mathbf{x}_p' \hat{\boldsymbol{\beta}}). \tag{3.48}$$

A 95% confidence interval, which allows for the imprecision in the estimate $\hat{\boldsymbol{\beta}}$, can be obtained using the delta method given in section 2.6.2. Consider estimation procedures that additionally estimate a scalar nuisance parameter α, to accommodate overdispersion. Because $\partial \mu_p / \partial \boldsymbol{\beta} = \mu_p \mathbf{x}_p$ and $\partial \mu_p / \partial \alpha = 0$, we obtain

$$\mu_p \in \hat{\mu}_p \pm z_{.025} \sqrt{\hat{\mu}_p^2 \mathbf{x}_p' \mathsf{V}[\hat{\boldsymbol{\beta}}] \mathbf{x}_p}, \tag{3.49}$$

for estimator $\hat{\boldsymbol{\beta}} \overset{a}{\sim} \mathsf{N}[\boldsymbol{\beta}, \mathsf{V}[\hat{\boldsymbol{\beta}}]]$. As expected, greater precision in the estimation of $\boldsymbol{\beta}$ leads to a narrower confidence interval.

One may also wish to predict the actual value of y, rather than its predicted mean. This is considerably more difficult, as the randomness of y needs to be accounted for, in addition to the randomness in the estimator $\hat{\boldsymbol{\beta}}$. For low counts in particular, individual values are poorly predicted due to the intrinsic randomness of y.

For an individual observation with $\mathbf{x} = \mathbf{x}_p$, and using the exponential conditional mean function, the individual prediction is

$$\hat{y}_p = \exp(\mathbf{x}_p' \hat{\boldsymbol{\beta}}). \tag{3.50}$$

Note that while $\hat{y}_p$ equals $\hat{\mu}_p$, it is being used as an estimate of y_p rather than μ_p. If we consider variance functions of the form (3.9), the estimated variance of y_p is $\omega(\hat{\mu}_p, \hat{\alpha})$. Adding this to the earlier variance due to imprecision in the estimate $\hat{\boldsymbol{\beta}}$, the variance of $\hat{y}_p$ is consistently estimated by $\omega(\hat{\mu}_p, \hat{\alpha}) + \hat{\mu}_p^2 \mathbf{x}_p' \mathsf{V}[\hat{\boldsymbol{\beta}}] \mathbf{x}_p$. A two-standard error interval is

$$y_p \in \hat{y}_p \pm 2 \sqrt{\omega(\hat{\mu}_p, \hat{\alpha}) + \hat{\mu}_p^2 \mathbf{x}_p' \mathsf{V}[\hat{\boldsymbol{\beta}}] \mathbf{x}_p}. \tag{3.51}$$

This can be used as a guide but is not formally a 95% confidence interval because y_p is not normally distributed even in large samples.

The width of this interval is increasing in $\hat{\mu}_p$, because $\omega(\hat{\mu}_p, \hat{\alpha})$ is increasing in $\hat{\mu}_p$. The interval is quite wide, even for low counts. For example, consider the Poisson distribution, so $\omega(\mu, \alpha) = \mu$, and assume a large sample size, so that $\boldsymbol{\beta}$ is very precisely estimated and $\mathsf{V}[\hat{\boldsymbol{\beta}}] \simeq \mathbf{0}$. Then (3.51) becomes $y_p \in \hat{y}_p \pm 2\sqrt{\hat{y}_p}$.

Even for $\hat{y}_p = 4$ this yields (0, 8). If y is Poisson and β is known it is better to directly use this knowledge, rather than the approximation (3.51). Then because $\Pr[1 \leq y_p \leq 8] = .0397$ when y_p is Poisson-distributed with $\mu_p = 4$, a 96.03% confidence interval for y_p is (1,8).

Interest can also lie in predicting the probabilities of particular values of y occurring, for an individual observation with $\mathbf{x} = \mathbf{x}_p$. Let p_k denote the probability that $y_p = k$ if $\mathbf{x} = \mathbf{x}_p$. For the Poisson, for example, this is estimated by $\hat{p}_k = \exp(-\hat{\mu}_p)\hat{\mu}_p^k/k!$, where $\hat{\mu}_p$ is given in (3.48). The delta method can be used to obtain a confidence interval for p_k. Most parametric models include an overdispersion parameter α. Because $\partial p_k/\partial \alpha \neq 0$ the delta method does not yield an interval as simple as (3.49).

A fourth quantity that might be predicted is the change in the conditional mean if the jth regressor changes by one unit. From (3.42) the predicted change is $\hat{\beta}_j \hat{\mu}_p$. Again the delta method can be used to form a confidence interval.

As the sample size gets very large the variance of $\hat{\beta}$ goes to zero and the confidence intervals for predictions of the conditional mean, individual probabilities, and changes in predicted probabilities collapse to a point. The confidence intervals for predictions of individual values of y, however, can remain wide as demonstrated above. Thus, within-sample individual predictions of y differ considerably from the actual values of y, especially for small counts. If interest is in assessing the usefulness of model predictions, it can be better to consider predictions at a more aggregated level. This is considered in Chapter 5.

The preceding methods require use of a computer program that saves the variance matrix of the regression parameters and permits matrix multiplication. It is generally no more difficult to instead use the bootstrap, which has the additional advantages of providing asymmetric confidence intervals and potentially better small-sample performance.

More problematic in practice is deciding what values of $\mathbf{x}_p$ to use in prediction. If, for example, there are just two regressors, both binary, one would simply predict for each of the four distinct values of $\mathbf{x}$. But in practice there are many different distinct values of $\mathbf{x}$, and it may not be obvious which few values to focus on. Such considerations also arise in the linear regression model.

3.6 Ordered and Other Discrete-Choice Models

Count data can alternatively be modeled using discrete choice methods surveyed in Maddala (1983). This is particularly natural if most observed counts take values 0 and 1, with few counts in excess of 1. Then one might simply model whether the count is zero or nonzero, using a binary choice model such as logit or probit. This leads, however, to a loss of precision in estimation.

Now suppose most observed counts take values 0, 1, or 2, with few counts in excess of 2. For data with three choices, in this case 0, 1, and 2 or more, the standard discrete choice model is the multinomial logit model, but this has deficiencies given subsequently here. It is better to use an ordered model, such as ordered probit or ordered logit.

Ordered discrete-choice models treat the data as generated by a continuous unobserved latent variable, which on crossing a threshold leads to an increase of one in the observed number of events. This is a representation of the dgp quite different from the Poisson process, which leads to the Poisson density for counts. In theory, one should use an ordered model for data for which the dgp is felt to be a continuous latent variable. In practice, ordered models have been rarely applied to count data outside the cross-section setting.

3.6.1 *Binary-Choice Models*

Let y_i be the count variable of interest. Define the indicator variable

$$\begin{aligned} d_i &= 1 \quad \text{if } y_i > 0 \\ &= 0 \quad \text{if } y_i = 0. \end{aligned} \tag{3.52}$$

This equals the count variable except that y_i values of 2 or more are recoded to 1. Other partitions are possible, such as $y_i > k$ and $y_i \leq k$.

The general form of such a binary choice model is

$$\begin{aligned} \Pr[d_i = 1] &= F(\mathbf{x}_i'\boldsymbol{\beta}) \\ \Pr[d_i = 0] &= 1 - F(\mathbf{x}_i'\boldsymbol{\beta}), \end{aligned} \tag{3.53}$$

where $0 < F(\cdot) < 1$. It is customary to let the probability be a transformation of a linear combination of the regressors rather than use the more general functional form $F(\mathbf{x}_i, \boldsymbol{\beta})$. By construction the probabilities sum to one. A parsimonious way to write the density given by (3.53) is $F(\mathbf{x}_i'\boldsymbol{\beta})^{d_i}\,(1 - F(\mathbf{x}_i'\boldsymbol{\beta}))^{1-d_i}$, which leads to the log-likelihood function

$$\ln \mathsf{L} = \sum_{i=1}^{n} d_i \ln F(\mathbf{x}_i'\boldsymbol{\beta}) + (1 - d_i) \ln \left(1 - F(\mathbf{x}_i'\boldsymbol{\beta})\right). \tag{3.54}$$

Different binary choice models correspond to different choice of the function $F(\cdot)$. Standard choices include the *logit model*, which corresponds to $F(z) = \exp(z)/(1 + \exp(z))$; and the *probit model*, which corresponds to $F(z) = \Phi(z)$ where $\Phi(\cdot)$ is the standard normal cdf.

There is a loss of efficiency due to combining all counts in excess of zero into a single category. Suppose y_i are Poisson distributed with mean μ_i. Then $\Pr[d_i = 1] = \Pr[y_i > 0] = 1 - \exp(-\mu_i)$, so for $\mu_i = \exp(\mathbf{x}_i'\boldsymbol{\beta})$.

$$F(\mathbf{x}_i'\boldsymbol{\beta}) = 1 - \exp(-\exp(\mathbf{x}_i'\boldsymbol{\beta})).$$

The binary Poisson MLE $\hat{\boldsymbol{\beta}}_{\mathsf{BP}}$ maximizes (3.54) with this choice of $F(\cdot)$. It can be shown that

$$\mathsf{V}[\hat{\boldsymbol{\beta}}_{\mathsf{BP}}] = \left(\sum_{i=1}^{n} c_i \mu_i \mathbf{x}_i \mathbf{x}_i'\right)^{-1},$$

where $c_i = \mu_i \exp(-\mu_i)/(1 - \exp(-\mu_i))$. $\mathsf{V}[\hat{\beta}_{\mathsf{BP}}]$ exceeds $(\sum_{i=1}^{n} \mu_i \mathbf{x}_i \mathbf{x}_i')^{-1}$, the variance matrix of the Poisson MLE from (3.6), because $c_i < 1$ for $\mu_i > 0$. As expected, the relevant efficiency loss is increasing in the Poisson mean. For example, for $\mu_i = .5$ and 1, respectively, $c_i = .77$ and .58. In the Poisson iid case with $\mu = .5$, the standard error of $\hat{\beta}_{\mathsf{BP}}$ is $\sqrt{1/.77} = 1.14$ times that of the Poisson MLE, even though less than 10% of the counts will exceed unity.

3.6.2 *Ordered Probit*

The Poisson and negative binomial models treat discrete data as being the result of an underlying point process. One could instead model the number of doctor visits, for example, as being due to a continuous process that on crossing a threshold leads to a visit to a doctor. Crossing further thresholds leads to additional doctor visits. Before specializing to threshold models such as ordered probit, we first present general results for multinomial models.

Suppose the count variable y_i takes values $0, 1, 2, \ldots, m$. Define the $m + 1$ indicator variables

$$\begin{aligned} d_{ij} &= 1 \quad y_i =, j \\ &= 0 \quad y_i \neq j. \end{aligned} \tag{3.55}$$

Also define the corresponding probabilities

$$\Pr[d_{ij} = 1] = p_{ij}, \qquad j = 0, \ldots, m, \tag{3.56}$$

where p_{ij} may depend on regressors and parameters. Then the density function for the ith observation can be written as

$$f(y_i) = f(d_{i0}, d_{i1}, \ldots, d_{im}) = \prod_{j=0}^{m} p_{ij}^{d_{ij}}, \tag{3.57}$$

and the log-likelihood function is

$$\ln \mathsf{L} = \sum_{i=1}^{n} \sum_{j=0}^{m} d_{ij} \ln p_{ij}. \tag{3.58}$$

Different multinomial models arise from different specification of the probabilities p_{ij}. The most common is the multinomial logit model, which specifies $p_{ij} = \exp(\mathbf{x}_i'\boldsymbol{\beta}_j)/\,(\sum_{k=0}^{m} \mathbf{x}_i'\boldsymbol{\beta}_k)$ in (3.58). This model is inappropriate for count data for which the outcome, the number of occurrences of an event, is naturally ordered. One way to see this is to note that a property of multinomial logit is that the relative probabilities of any two outcomes are independent of the probabilities of other outcomes. For example, the probability of one doctor visit, conditional on the probability of zero or one visit, would not depend on the probability of two visits. But one expects that this conditional probability will be higher the higher the probability of two visits. It is better to use a multinomial model that explicitly incorporates the ordering of the data.

The *ordered probit* model, presented for example in Maddala (1983), introduces a latent (unobserved) random variable

$$y_i^* = \mathbf{x}_i'\boldsymbol{\beta} + \varepsilon_i, \tag{3.59}$$

where ε_i is N[0, 1]. The observed discrete data variable y_i is generated from the unobserved y_i^* in the following way:

$$y_i = j \quad \text{if} \quad \alpha_j < y_i^* \leq \alpha_{j+1}, \qquad j = 0, \ldots, m, \tag{3.60}$$

where $\alpha_0 = -\infty$ and $\alpha_{m+1} = \infty$. It follows that

$$\begin{aligned} p_{ij} &= \Pr\left[\alpha_j < y_i^* \leq \alpha_{j+1}\right] \\ &= \Pr\left[\alpha_j - \mathbf{x}_i'\boldsymbol{\beta} < \varepsilon_i \leq \alpha_{j+1} - \mathbf{x}_i'\boldsymbol{\beta}\right] \\ &= \Phi\left(\alpha_{j+1} - \mathbf{x}_i'\boldsymbol{\beta}\right) - \Phi\left(\alpha_j - \mathbf{x}_i'\boldsymbol{\beta}\right), \end{aligned} \tag{3.61}$$

where $\Phi(\cdot)$ is the standard normal cdf, $j = 0, 1, 2, \ldots, m$, and $\alpha_{m+1} = \infty$. The log-likelihood function (3.58) with probabilities (3.61) is

$$\ln \mathsf{L} = \sum_{i=1}^{n} \sum_{j=0}^{m} d_{ij} \ln\left[\Phi\left(\alpha_{j+1} - \mathbf{x}_i'\boldsymbol{\beta}\right) - \Phi\left(\alpha_j - \mathbf{x}_i'\boldsymbol{\beta}\right)\right]. \tag{3.62}$$

Estimation of $\boldsymbol{\beta}$ and $\alpha_1, \ldots, \alpha_m$ by maximum likelihood is straightforward. Identification requires a normalization, such as 0, for one of $\alpha_1, \ldots, \alpha_m$ or the intercept term in $\boldsymbol{\beta}$.

If there are many counts or few observations for a given count then some aggregation of count data may be necessary. For example, if there are few observations larger than three one might have categories of *0, 1, 2,* and *3 or more*. As an alternative to the ordered probit one can use the *ordered logit* model, in which case $\Phi(\cdot)$ is replaced by the logistic cdf $L(z) = e^z/(1 + e^z)$. More generally if ε_i in (3.59) has a nonnormal distribution the log-likelihood function is (3.62) with $\Phi(\cdot)$ replaced by the cdf of ε_i.

The ordered discrete choice model has the additional attraction of being applicable to count data that are negative. Such data may arise if instead of directly modeling a count variable, one differences and models the change in the count. For example, some U.S. stock prices are a count, as they are measured in units of a *tick*, or one eighth of a dollar. Hausman, Lo, and MacKinlay (1992) modeled price changes in consecutive time-stamped trades of a given stock using the ordered probit model, generalized to allow ε_i to be N[0, σ_i^2] where the variance σ_i^2 is itself modeled by a regression equation.

3.7 Other Models

In this section we consider whether least-squares methods might be usefully applied to count data y. Three variations of least squares are considered. The first is linear regression of y on $\mathbf{x}$, making no allowance for the count nature of the data aside from using heteroskedasticity robust standard errors. The second is linear regression of a nonlinear transformation of y on $\mathbf{x}$, for which the transformation leads to a dependent variable that is close to homoskedastic and symmetric. Third, we consider nonlinear least squares regression with conditional mean of y specified to be $\exp(\mathbf{x}'\boldsymbol{\beta})$.

The section finishes with a discussion of estimation using duration data, rather than count data, if the data are generated by a Poisson process.

3.7.1 *OLS without Transformation*

The OLS estimator is clearly inappropriate as it specifies a conditional mean function $\mathbf{x}'\boldsymbol{\gamma}$ that may take negative values and a variance function that is homoskedastic. If the conditional mean function is in fact $\exp(\mathbf{x}'\boldsymbol{\beta})$, the OLS estimator is inconsistent for $\boldsymbol{\beta}$ and the computed OLS output gives the wrong asymptotic variance matrix.

Nonetheless, OLS estimates in practice give results qualitatively similar to those for Poisson and other estimators using the exponential mean. The ratio of OLS slope coefficients is often similar to the ratio of Poisson slope coefficients, with the OLS slope coefficients approximately $\bar{y}$ times the Poisson slope coefficients, and the most highly statistically significant regressors from OLS regression, using usual OLS output t statistics, are in practice the most highly significant using Poisson regression. This is similar to comparing different models for binary data such as logit, probit, and OLS. In all cases the conditional mean is restricted to be of form $g(\mathbf{x}'\boldsymbol{\beta})$, which is a monotonic transformation of a linear combination of the regressors. The only difference across models is the choice of function g, which leads to a different scaling of the parameters $\boldsymbol{\beta}$.

A first-order Taylor series expansion of the exponential mean $\exp(\mathbf{x}'\boldsymbol{\beta})$ around the sample mean $\bar{y}$, that is, around $\mathbf{x}'\boldsymbol{\beta} = \ln \bar{y}$, yields $\exp(\mathbf{x}'\boldsymbol{\beta}) = \bar{y} + \bar{y}(\mathbf{x}'\boldsymbol{\beta} - \ln \bar{y})$. For models with intercept, this can be rewritten as $\exp(\beta_1 + \mathbf{x}_2'\boldsymbol{\beta}_2) = \gamma_1 + \mathbf{x}_2'\boldsymbol{\gamma}_2$, where $\gamma_1 = \bar{y} + \beta_1\bar{y} - \ln \bar{y}$ and $\boldsymbol{\gamma}_2 = \boldsymbol{\beta}_2\bar{y}$. So linear mean slope coefficients are approximately $\bar{y}$ times exponential slope coefficients. This approximation will be more reasonable the less dispersed the predicted values $\exp(\mathbf{x}_i'\hat{\boldsymbol{\beta}})$ are about $\bar{y}$.

The OLS estimator can be quite useful for preliminary data analysis, such as determining key variables, in simple count models. Dealing with more complicated count models for which no off-the-shelf software is readily available is easier if one first ignores the count aspect of the data and does the corresponding adjustment to OLS. For example, if the complication is endogeneity, then do linear two-stage least squares as a potential guide to the impact of endogeneity. But experience is sufficiently limited that one cannot advocate this approach.

3.7.2 *OLS with Transformation*

For skewed continuous data such as that on individual income or on housing prices a standard transformation is the *log transformation*. For example, if y is log-normal-distributed then $\ln y$ is by definition exactly normally distributed, so the log transformation induces constant variance and eliminates skewness.

The log transformation may also be used for count data that are often skewed. Because $\ln 0$ is not defined, a standard solution is to add a constant term, such as 0.5, and to model $\ln(y+.5)$ by OLS. This model has been criticized by King (1989b) as performing poorly.

An alternative transformation is the *square-root transformation*. Following McCullagh and Nelder (1989, p. 236), let $y=\mu(1+\varepsilon)$. Then a fourth-order Taylor series expansion around $\varepsilon=0$ yields

$$y^{1/2} \simeq \mu^{1/2}\left(1+\frac{1}{2}\varepsilon-\frac{1}{8}\varepsilon^2+\frac{1}{16}\varepsilon^3-\frac{5}{128}\varepsilon^4\right).$$

For the Poisson, $\varepsilon=(y-\mu)/\mu$ has first four moments $0, 1/\mu, 1/\mu^2$, and $(3/\mu^2+1/\mu^3)$. It follows that $\mathsf{E}[\sqrt{y}] \simeq \sqrt{\mu}(1-1/8\mu+O(1/\mu^2))$, $\mathsf{V}[\sqrt{y}] \simeq (1/4)(1+3/8\mu+O(1/\mu^2))$, and $\mathsf{E}[(\sqrt{y}-\mathsf{E}[\sqrt{y}])^3] \simeq -(1/16\sqrt{\mu})(1+O(1/\mu))$. Thus if y is Poisson then $\sqrt{y}$ is close to homoskedastic and is close to symmetric. The skewness index is the third central moment divided by variance raised to the power 1.5. Here it is less than $-(1/16\sqrt{\mu})/(1/4)^{1.5}=-1/2\sqrt{\mu}$. By comparison for the Poisson y is heteroskedastic with variance μ and asymmetric with skewness index $1/\sqrt{\mu}$. The square-root transformation works quite well for large μ.

One therefore models $\sqrt{y}$ by OLS, regressing $\sqrt{y_i}$ on $\mathbf{x}_i$. The usual OLS t statistics can be used for statistical inference. More problematic is the interpretation of coefficients. These give the impact of a one-unit change in x_j on $\mathsf{E}[\sqrt{y}]$ rather than $\mathsf{E}[y]$, and by Jensen's inequality $\mathsf{E}[y] \neq (\mathsf{E}[\sqrt{y}])^2$. A similar problem arises in prediction, although the method of Duan (1983) can be used to predict $\mathsf{E}[y_i]$, given the estimated model for $\sqrt{y_i}$.

3.7.3 *Nonlinear Least Squares*

The nonlinear least squares (NLS) estimator with exponential mean minimizes the sum of squared residuals $\sum_i(y_i-\exp(\mathbf{x}_i'\boldsymbol{\beta}))^2$. The estimator $\hat{\boldsymbol{\beta}}_{\mathsf{NLS}}$ is the solution to the first-order conditions

$$\sum_{i=1}^{n} \mathbf{x}_i\left(y_i-\exp\left(\mathbf{x}_i'\boldsymbol{\beta}\right)\right)\exp\left(\mathbf{x}_i'\boldsymbol{\beta}\right)=\mathbf{0}. \tag{3.63}$$

This estimator is consistent if the conditional mean of y_i is $\exp(\mathbf{x}_i'\boldsymbol{\beta})$. It is inefficient, however, as the errors are certainly not homoskedastic, and the usual reported NLS standard errors are inconsistent. $\hat{\boldsymbol{\beta}}_{\mathsf{NLS}}$ is asymptotically normal with variance

$$\mathsf{V}[\hat{\boldsymbol{\beta}}_{\mathsf{NLS}}]=\left(\sum_{i=1}^{n}\mu_i^2\mathbf{x}_i\mathbf{x}_i'\right)^{-1}\left(\sum_{i=1}^{n}\omega_i\mu_i^2\mathbf{x}_i\mathbf{x}_i'\right)\left(\sum_{i=1}^{n}\mu_i^2\mathbf{x}_i\mathbf{x}_i'\right)^{-1}, \tag{3.64}$$

where $\omega_i = \mathsf{V}[y_i \mid \mathbf{x}_i]$. The robust sandwich estimate of $\mathsf{V}[\hat{\beta}_{\mathsf{NLS}}]$ is (3.64), with μ_i and ω_i replaced by $\hat{\mu}_i$ and $(y_i - \hat{\mu}_i)^2$.

The NLS estimator can therefore be used, but more efficient estimates can be obtained using the estimators given in sections 3.2 and 3.3.

Example: Doctor Visits (Continued)

Coefficient estimates of binary Poisson, ordered probit, OLS, OLS of transformations of y (both $\ln[y + 0.1]$ and $\sqrt{y}$), Poisson PMLE, and NLS with exponential mean are presented in Table 3.6. The associated t statistics reported are based on RS standard errors, except for binary Poisson and ordered probit. The skewness and kurtosis measures given are for model residuals $z_i - \hat{z}_i$ where z_i is the dependent variable, for example, $z_i = \sqrt{y_i}$, and are estimates of, respectively, the third central moment divided by s^3 and the fourth central moment divided by s^4, where s^2 is the estimated variance. For the standard normal distribution the kurtosis measure is 3.

We begin with estimation of a binary choice model for the recoded variable $d = 0$ if $y = 0$ and $d = 1$ if $y \geq 1$. To allow direct comparison with Poisson estimates, we estimate the nonstandard binary Poisson model introduced in section 3.6.1. Compared with Poisson estimates in the *Poiss* column, the *BP* results for health status measures are similar, although for the statistically insignificant socioeconomic variables *AGE*, *AGESQ*, and *INCOME* there are sign changes. Similar sign changes for *AGE* and *AGESQ* occur in Table 3.4 and are discussed there. The log-likelihood for *BP* exceeds that for Poisson, but this comparison is meaningless due to the different dependent variable. Logit and probit, not reported, lead to similar log-likelihood and qualitatively similar estimates to those from binary Poisson, so differences between binary Poisson and Poisson can be attributed to aggregating all positive counts into one value.

The ordered probit model normalizes the error variance to 1. To enable comparison with OLS estimates we multiply these by $s = .714$, the estimated standard deviation of the residual from OLS regression. Also, as only one observation took the value 9, this was combined into a category of *8 or more*. The rescaled threshold parameter estimates are .67, 1.08, 1.22, 1.39, 1.49, 1.67, and 1.99, with t statistics all in excess of 18 and all at least two standard errors apart. Despite the rescaling there is still considerable difference from the OLS estimates. It is meaningful to compare the ordered-probit log-likelihood with that of other count data models; the change of one observation from *9* to *8 or more* in the ordered probit should have little effect. The log-likelihood is higher for this model than for NB2, because $-3138.1 > -3198.7$, although six more parameters are estimated.

The log transformation $\ln(y + 0.1)$ was chosen on grounds of smaller skewness and kurtosis than $\ln(y + 0.2)$ or $\ln(y + 0.4)$. The skewness and kurtosis are somewhat smaller for $\ln y$ than $\sqrt{y}$. Both transformations appear quite successful in moving towards normality, especially compared with residuals from OLS or Poisson regression with y as dependent variables. Much of this gain appears

Table 3.6. *Doctor visits: alternative estimates and t ratios*

	Discrete choice		Estimators and t statistics OLS of transformations			Exponential mean	
Variable	BP	OrdProb	y	$\ln y$	$\sqrt{y}$	Poiss	NLS
ONE	−.905	−.980	.028	−2.115	.070	−2.224	−2.234
	(6.66)	(9.29)	(.38)	(21.43)	(1.55)	(8.74)	(6.14)
SEX	.136	.094	.034	.081	.034	.157	−.057
	(3.39)	(3.03)	(1.47)	(2.73)	(2.48)	(1.98)	(.42)
AGE	−1.356	−.381	.203	−.566	−.161	1.056	3.626
	(1.76)	(.46)	(.46)	(.97)	(.60)	(.77)	(1.82)
AGESQ	1.842	.611	−.062	.877	.292	−.849	−3.676
	(2.15)	(.65)	(.12)	(1.31)	(.94)	(.58)	(1.70)
INCOME	.007	−.044	−.057	−.019	−.168	−.205	−.394
	(.12)	(.95)	(1.65)	(.43)	(.80)	(1.59)	(2.02)
LEVYPLUS	.136	.098	.035	.080	.337	.123	.214
	(2.80)	(2.45)	(1.62)	(2.58)	(2.41)	(1.29)	(1.48)
FREEPOOR	−.265	−.245	−.103	−.182	−.081	−.440	−.232
	(2.55)	(2.75)	(2.17)	(3.17)	(3.00)	(1.52)	(.54)
FREEREPA	.223	.127	.033	.139	.054	.080	−.003
	(3.16)	(2.37)	(.77)	(2.45)	(2.06)	(.63)	(.02)
ILLNESS	.148	.107	.060	.110	.048	.187	.140
	(9.12)	(9.23)	(6.04)	(8.53)	(8.12)	(7.81)	(3.63)
ACTDAYS	.117	.072	.103	.106	.054	.127	.121
	(14.47)	(18.35)	(10.61)	(13.57)	(13.06)	(16.33)	(14.21)
HSCORE	.034	.023	.017	.029	.013	.030	.023
	(3.64)	(3.54)	(2.37)	(3.31)	(3.17)	(2.11)	(1.03)
CHCOND1	.042	.044	.004	.022	.009	.114	.079
	(.94)	(1.23)	(.20)	(.70)	(.61)	(1.25)	(.55)
CHCOND2	.141	.096	.042	.102	.043	.141	−.055
	(2.11)	(2.06)	(.90)	(1.81)	(1.62)	(1.15)	(.31)
−ln L	2246.9	3138.1					
Skewness			3.6	1.2	1.4	3.1	
Kurtosis			26.4	4.0	5.5	26.0	

Note: BP, MLE for binary poisson; OrdProb, MLE for rescaled ordered probit; y, OLS for y; $\ln y$, OLS for $\ln(y+0.1)$; $\sqrt{y}$, OLS for $\sqrt{y}$; Poiss, Poisson PMLE; NLS, NLS with exponential mean. The t statistics are robust sandwich for all but BP and OrdProb. Skewness and kurtosis are for model residuals.

even before inclusion of regressors, as inclusion of regressors reduces skewness and kurtosis by about 20% in this example. All models give similar results regarding the statistical significance of regressors, although interpretation of the magnitude of the effect of regressors is more difficult if the dependent variable is $\ln(y+0.1)$ or $\sqrt{y}$.

The NLS estimates for exponential mean lead to similar conclusions as Poisson for the health-status variables, but quite different conclusions for socioeconomic variables with considerably larger coefficients and t statistics for *AGE*, *AGESQ*, and *INCOME* and a sign change for *SEX*.

3.7.4 *Exponential Duration Model*

For a Poisson point process the number of events in a given interval of time is Poisson distributed. The duration of a spell, the time from one occurrence to the next, is exponentially distributed. Here we consider modeling durations rather than counts.

Suppose that for each individual in a sample of n individuals we observe the duration of one complete spell, generated by a Poisson point process with rate parameter γ_i. Then t_i has exponential density $f(t_i) = \gamma_i \exp(-\gamma_i t_i)$ with mean $\mathsf{E}[t_i] = 1/\gamma_i$. For regression analysis it is customary to specify $\gamma_i = \exp(\mathbf{x}_i'\boldsymbol{\beta})$. The exponential MLE, $\hat{\boldsymbol{\beta}}_{\mathsf{E}}$, maximizes the log-likelihood function

$$\ln \mathsf{L} = \sum_{i=1}^{n} \mathbf{x}_i'\boldsymbol{\beta} - \exp(\mathbf{x}_i'\boldsymbol{\beta}) t_i. \tag{3.65}$$

The first-order conditions can be expressed as

$$\sum_{i=1}^{n} (1 - \exp(\mathbf{x}_i'\boldsymbol{\beta}) t_i) \mathbf{x}_i = \mathbf{0}, \tag{3.66}$$

and application of the usual maximum likelihood theory yields

$$\mathsf{V}_{\mathsf{ML}}[\hat{\boldsymbol{\beta}}_{\mathsf{E}}] = \left(\sum_{i=1}^{n} \mathbf{x}_i \mathbf{x}_i' \right)^{-1}. \tag{3.67}$$

If instead we modeled the number of events from a Poisson point process with rate parameter $\gamma_i = \exp(\mathbf{x}_i'\boldsymbol{\beta})$ we obtain

$$\mathsf{V}_{\mathsf{ML}}[\hat{\boldsymbol{\beta}}_{\mathsf{P}}] = \left(\sum_{i=1}^{n} \gamma_i \mathbf{x}_i \mathbf{x}_i' \right)^{-1}.$$

The two variance matrices coincide if $\gamma_i = 1$. Thus if we choose intervals for each individual so that individuals on average experience one event such as a doctor visit, the count data have the same information content, in terms of precision of estimation of $\boldsymbol{\beta}$, as observing for each individual one completed spell such as time between successive visits to the doctor. More simply, one count conveys the same information as the length of one complete spell.

3.8 Iteratively Reweighted Least Squares

Most of the models and estimators in this book require special statistical packages for nonlinear models. An exception is the Poisson PMLE, which can be computed in the following way.

In general at the sth iteration, the Newton-Raphson method updates the current estimate $\hat{\boldsymbol{\beta}}_s$ by the formula $\hat{\boldsymbol{\beta}}_{s+1} = \hat{\boldsymbol{\beta}}_s - \hat{\mathbf{H}}_s^{-1}\hat{\mathbf{g}}_s$, where $\mathbf{g} = \partial \ln \mathsf{L}/\partial \boldsymbol{\beta}$ and

$\mathbf{H} = \partial^2 \ln \mathsf{L}/\partial\boldsymbol{\beta}\partial\boldsymbol{\beta}'$ are evaluated at $\hat{\boldsymbol{\beta}}_s$. Here this becomes

$$\hat{\boldsymbol{\beta}}_{s+1} = \hat{\boldsymbol{\beta}}_s + \left[\sum_{i=1}^{n} \hat{\mu}_{is}\mathbf{x}_i\mathbf{x}_i'\right]^{-1} \sum_{i=1}^{n} \mathbf{x}_i(y_i - \hat{\mu}_{is}),$$

where we consider the exponential mean function so $\hat{\mu}_{is} = \exp(\mathbf{x}_i'\hat{\boldsymbol{\beta}}_s)$. This can be rewritten as

$$\hat{\boldsymbol{\beta}}_{s+1} = \left[\sum_{i=1}^{n} \left(\sqrt{\hat{\mu}_{is}}\mathbf{x}_i\right)\left(\sqrt{\hat{\mu}_{is}}\mathbf{x}_i\right)'\right]^{-1} \sum_{i=1}^{n} \left(\sqrt{\hat{\mu}_{is}}\mathbf{x}_i\right) \left\{\sqrt{\hat{\mu}_{is}}\frac{(y_i - \hat{\mu}_{is})}{\hat{\mu}_{is}} + \sqrt{\hat{\mu}_{is}}\mathbf{x}_i'\hat{\boldsymbol{\beta}}_s\right\},$$

which is the formula for the OLS estimator from the regression

$$\sqrt{\hat{\mu}_{is}}\left\{\frac{(y_i - \hat{\mu}_{is})}{\hat{\mu}_{is}} + \mathbf{x}_i'\hat{\boldsymbol{\beta}}_s\right\} = \left(\sqrt{\hat{\mu}_{is}}\mathbf{x}_i\right)'\boldsymbol{\beta}_{s+1} + u_i, \tag{3.68}$$

where u_i is an error term. Thus the Poisson PMLE can be calculated by this iterative OLS regression. Equivalently, it can be estimated by WLS regression of $\{((y_i - \hat{\mu}_{is})/\hat{\mu}_{is}) + \mathbf{x}_i'\hat{\boldsymbol{\beta}}_s\}$ on $\mathbf{x}_i$, where the weights $\sqrt{\hat{\mu}_{is}}$ change at each iteration.

For the general conditional mean function $\hat{\mu}_i = \mu(\mathbf{x}_i, \boldsymbol{\beta})$, the method of scoring, which replaces $\mathbf{H}$ by $\mathsf{E}[\mathbf{H}]$, yields a similar regression, with the dependent variable $\hat{\mu}_{is}^{-1/2}\{(y_i - \hat{\mu}_{is}) + \partial\mu_i/\partial\boldsymbol{\beta}'|_{\hat{\boldsymbol{\beta}}_s}\hat{\boldsymbol{\beta}}_s\}$ and regressor $\hat{\mu}_{is}^{-1/2}\partial\mu_i/\partial\boldsymbol{\beta}'|_{\hat{\boldsymbol{\beta}}_s}$.

3.9 Bibliographic Notes

An early application of the Poisson regression model is by Jorgenson (1961). In the statistical literature much of the work on the Poisson uses the GLM approach. The key reference is McCullagh and Nelder (1989), with Poisson regression detailed in Chapter 6. In biostatistics a brief survey with reference to clinical trials and epidemiological studies is provided by Kianifard and Gallo (1995). An early review of count models in marketing is Morrison and Schmittlein (1988). In econometrics early influential papers were by Gourieroux et al. (1984a, 1984b). The first paper presented the general theory for LEFN models; the second paper specialized analysis to count data. Cameron and Trivedi (1986) presented both LEFN and negative binomial maximum likelihood approaches, with a detailed application to the doctor visits data used in this chapter. The paper by Hausman, Hall, and Griliches (1984) is also often cited. It considers the more difficult topic of panel count data and is discussed in Chapter 9. The books by Maddala (1983), Gourieroux and Montfort (1995), and Greene (1997a) give a brief treatment of Poisson regression. More recent surveys by Winkelmann and Zimmermann (1995), Cameron and Trivedi (1996), and Winkelmann (1997), cover the material in Chapter 3 and also some of the material in Chapter 4. The survey by Gurmu and Trivedi (1994) provides a condensed treatment of many aspects of count data regression.

3.10 Exercises

3.1 The first-order conditions for the Poisson PMLE are $\sum_{i=1}^{n} \mathbf{g}_i(\boldsymbol{\beta}) = \mathbf{0}$, where $\mathbf{g}_i(\boldsymbol{\beta}) = (y_i - \exp(\mathbf{x}_i'\boldsymbol{\beta}))\mathbf{x}_i$. Find $\mathsf{E}[\sum_{i=1}^{n} \partial \mathbf{g}_i(\boldsymbol{\beta})/\partial \boldsymbol{\beta}']$ and $\mathsf{E}[\sum_{i=1}^{n} \mathbf{g}_i(\boldsymbol{\beta}) g_i(\boldsymbol{\beta})']$ if y_i has mean μ_i and variance ω_i. Hence verify that the asymptotic variance is (3.15), using the general results in section 2.7.1.

3.2 Obtain the expression for the asymptotic variance of $\hat{\phi}_{\mathsf{NB1}}$ defined in (3.17), using the delta method given in section 2.6.2.

3.3 The geometric model is the special case of NB2 if $\alpha = 1$. Give the density of the geometric model if $\mu_i = \exp(\mathbf{x}_i'\boldsymbol{\beta})/[1 - \exp(\mathbf{x}_i'\boldsymbol{\beta})]$, and obtain the first-order conditions for the MLE of $\boldsymbol{\beta}$. This functional form for the conditional mean corresponds to the canonical link function.

3.4 Using a similar approach to that of Exercise 3.1, obtain the asymptotic variance for the QGPMLE of the NB2 model defined as the solution to (3.37) if in fact y_i has variance ω_i rather than $(\mu_i + \alpha\mu_i^2)$. Hence, give the RS estimator for the variance matrix.

3.5 For regression models with exponential conditional mean function, use the delta method in section 2.6.2 to obtain the formula for a 95% confidence interval for the change in the conditional mean if the jth regressor changes by one unit.

3.6 For the ordered probit model give the log-likelihood function if $\varepsilon_i \sim \mathsf{N}[0, \sigma_i^2]$ rather than $\varepsilon_i \sim \mathsf{N}[0, 1]$.

3.7 Consider the NLS estimator that minimizes $\sum_i (y_i - \exp(\mathbf{x}_i'\boldsymbol{\beta}))^2$. Show that the first-order conditions for $\boldsymbol{\beta}$ are shown in (3.63). Using a similar approach to that of Exercise 3.1, show that the asymptotic variance of the NLS estimator is (3.64).

CHAPTER 4

Generalized Count Regression

4.1 Introduction

This chapter deals with departures from the Poisson regression. One reason for the failure of the Poisson regression is unobserved heterogeneity, which contributes additional randomness. Mixture models obtained by averaging with respect to unobserved heterogeneity generally are not Poisson. A second reason is the failure of the Poisson process assumption and its replacement by a more general stochastic process.

Section 4.2 deals with the negative binomial model. One characterization of this is as a Poisson–gamma mixture. In Section 4.3 we examine the relation between waiting times and counts introduced in Chapter 1. Section 4.4 considers flexible functional forms which are alternatives to the Poisson. Sections 4.5 and 4.6 consider the case in which the range of observed counts is further restricted by either truncation or censoring. Section 4.7 considers an empirically important class of *hurdle* models that give a special treatment to zero counts. This class combines elements both of truncation and mixtures. Section 4.8 provides a detailed treatment of the finite mixture latent class model that is empirically implemented in Chapter 6. Section 4.9 gives an introduction to estimation by simulation. In the remainder of this section we summarize the motivation underlying the models analyzed in this chapter.

The leading motivation for considering parametric distributions other than the Poisson is that they have the potential to accommodate features of data that are inconsistent with the Poisson assumption. Some common departures from the standard Poisson regression are as follows.

1. The failure of the mean equals variance restriction: Frequently the conditional variance of data exceeds the conditional mean, which is usually referred to as *extra-Poisson variation* or *overdispersion* relative to the Poisson model. If the conditional variance is less than the mean, we have *underdispersion*. Overdispersion may result from neglected or unobserved heterogeneity that is inadequately captured by the covariates in the conditional mean function. Hence, it is common to allow for random variation in the Poisson conditional mean by

introducing a multiplicative error term. This leads to families of mixed Poisson models.

2. Truncation and censoring: The observed counts may be left truncated (zero truncation is quite common) leading to small counts being excluded, or right-censored, by having counts exceeding some value being aggregated.
3. The "excess zeros" or "zero inflation" problem: The observed data may show a higher relative frequency of zeros, or some other integer, than is consistent with the Poisson model (Mullahy, 1986; Lambert, 1992). The higher relative frequency of zeros is a feature of all Poisson mixtures obtained by convolution.
4. Multimodality: Observed univariate count distributions are sometimes bimodal or multimodal. If this is also a feature of the conditional distribution of counts, perhaps because observations may be drawn from different populations, then extensions of the Poisson are desirable.
5. Trends: The mean rate of event occurrence, the intensity function, may have a trend or some other deterministic form of time dependence that violates the simple Poisson process assumption.
6. Simultaneity and sample selection: Some covariates may be jointly determined with the dependent variable, or the included observations may be subject to a sample selection rule.
7. The failure of the conditional independence assumption: Event counts, especially if they are a time series, may be dependent.

The last three considerations have to do with the failure of the Poisson process assumption, whereas the first four are concessions to the characteristics of observed data. Extensions and generalizations of the basic Poisson model are numerous, and an encyclopedic coverage is not feasible. Our choice has been influenced by models that have gained a wide usage, models that have interesting properties and are potentially useful, or those that elucidate important issues. In the remainder of this chapter we consider the parametric approach to accommodate the first four issues. The remaining three are dealt with in later chapters.

4.2 Mixture Models for Unobserved Heterogeneity

In a Poisson regression without heterogeneity the distribution of $(y_i \mid \mathbf{x}_i)$ is specified conditional on observable covariates $\mathbf{x}_i$. This is equivalent to specifying the conditional mean function as a nonstochastic function of $\mathbf{x}_i$. In mixture models we instead specify the distribution of $(y_i \mid \mathbf{x}_i, \nu_i)$ where ν_i denotes an unobserved heterogeneity term for observation i. Simply, individuals are assumed to differ randomly in a manner not fully accounted for by the observed covariates. The marginal distribution of y_i is obtained by averaging with respect to ν_i. It may be helpful to regard this as a type of random-effects model. If the event distribution is conditionally $\mathsf{P}[\mu]$, but μ is treated as stochastic, the process has been called *doubly stochastic Poisson* by Cox (1955) and the *Cox process* by Kingman (1993).

The precise functional form linking y_i and $(\mathbf{x}_i, \nu_i)$ must be specified. A commonly used functional form is the exponential mean with a multiplicative error. That is, $\mathsf{E}[y_i \mid \mathbf{x}_i, \nu_i] = \exp(\mathbf{x}_i'\boldsymbol{\beta})\nu_i$, where the stochastic term ν_i is independent of the regressors. The multiplicative heterogeneity assumption is very special, but it is mathematically convenient and more attractive than an additive error that could lead to violation of the nonnegativity of y_i. A standard approach involves postulating a distribution for ν_i and then deriving the marginal distribution of y_i.

4.2.1 *Unobserved Heterogeneity and Overdispersion*

Mixing based on multiplicative heterogeneity has two important and related consequences. First, the variance of the mixture, conditional on the observable variables, exceeds the variance of the parent Poisson distribution conditional on both the observables and heterogeneity. This is the basis of the common interpretation of overdispersion as a result of neglected unobserved heterogeneity in the phenomenon being modeled. Replace $\mu_i = \exp(\mathbf{x}_i'\boldsymbol{\beta})$ by

$$\mu_i^* = \mathsf{E}[y_i \mid \mu_i, \nu_i] = \mu_i \nu_i, \tag{4.1}$$

where the unobserved heterogeneity term $\nu_i = \exp(\varepsilon_i)$ could reflect a specification error such as unobserved omitted exogenous variables. However, randomness in the heterogeneity term ν_i is distinguished from the intrinsic randomness in the endogenous count variate y_i. It is usually assumed that ν_is are iid, possibly with a known parametric distribution, and that they are independent of the $\mathbf{x}_i$.

For example, assume that ν_i is iid with $\mathsf{E}[\nu_i] = 1$ and $\mathrm{var}(\nu_i) = \sigma_\nu^2$. The assumption that $\mathsf{E}[\nu_i] = 1$ is made for identification purposes and only affects the intercept term, assuming the exponential mean specification. Also assume that $\mathsf{E}[y_i \mid \mathbf{x}_i, \nu_i] = \mathrm{var}[y_i \mid \mathbf{x}_i, \nu_i] = \mu_i$, as in the Poisson. The moments of y_i can be derived as

$$\mathsf{E}[y_i \mid \mathbf{x}_i] = \mu_i, \tag{4.2}$$

$$\mathsf{V}[y_i \mid \mathbf{x}_i] = \mu_i\left[1 + \sigma_\nu^2 \mu_i\right] > \mathsf{E}[y_i \mid \mathbf{x}_i], \tag{4.3}$$

where the second line is obtained using the result

$$\mathsf{V}[y \mid \mathbf{x}] = \mathsf{E}_\nu[\mathsf{V}_{y|\nu,\mathbf{x}}(y \mid \nu, \mathbf{x})] + \mathsf{V}_\nu[\mathsf{E}_{y|\nu,\mathbf{x}}(y \mid \nu, \mathbf{x})]. \tag{4.4}$$

See, for example Gourieroux et al. (1984b).* In this setup, ν_i leads to overdispersed y_i without affecting $\mathsf{E}[y_i \mid \mathbf{x}_i]$. Note also that this variance function is the same as for the NB2 model in Chapter 3.

* These moments also provide the basis of sequential quasilikelihood estimation (McCullagh, 1983; Gourieroux et al., 1984b; Cameron and Trivedi, 1986) and moment estimation (Moore, 1986) in count models. See section 2.5.

From (4.3) and (4.4), a fully parametric mixture is based on full specification of the density functions of $(y_i \mid \mathbf{x}_i, \nu_i)$ and ν_i. Specifically, let $f(y_i \mid \mathbf{x}_i, \nu_i)$ be the probability function obtained by replacing μ_i in (1.17) by μ_i^*, and let $g(\nu_i)$ denote the probability density function of ν_i. The mixed marginal density of $(y \mid \mathbf{x})$ is then derived by integrating with respect to ν_i, thus:

$$h(y \mid \mu) = \int f(y \mid \mu, \nu) g(\nu)\, d\nu. \tag{4.5}$$

Although precise form of this mixed Poisson distribution depends on the specific choice of $g(\nu_i)$, the general property of overdispersion does not depend on $g(\nu_i)$. If $g(\cdot)$ and $f(\cdot)$ are conjugate families, the resulting compound model is expressible in a closed form.

The second related consequence is that mixing causes the proportion of zero counts to increase. It exceeds the corresponding proportion of zeros in the parent distribution. Thus overdispersion and excess of zeros, relative to the Poisson, are related consequences of unobserved heterogeneity. That is, irrespective of the form of $g(\nu_i)$ for the mixture, and provided it is nondegenerate, for the parent and mixture distributions with the same mean μ_i, it is true that,

$$f(y_i = 0 \mid \mu_i) \equiv f(0 \mid \mu_i) > f(y_i = 0 \mid \mu_i, \nu_i) = f(0 \mid \mu_i, \nu_i). \tag{4.6}$$

Feller (1943) and Mullahy (1997b) have provided proofs of this result. Mullahy shows that the feature of $f(y_i \mid \mu_i, \nu_i)$ that yields this property is its strict convexity in μ. It is also the case that in most instances the frequency of $y = 1$ is less in the mixture distribution than in the parent distribution,

$$f(y_i = 1 \mid \mu_i) = f(1 \mid \mu_i) < f(y_i = 1 \mid \mu_i, \nu_i) \equiv f(1 \mid \mu_i, \nu_i). \tag{4.7}$$

Finally, the mixture exhibits thicker right tail than the parent distribution. These properties of the Poisson mixtures may be used for constructing specification tests of departures from the Poisson (Mullahy, 1997b). The result is a special case of a general result on exponential family mixtures referred to as the Two Crossings Theorem by Shaked (1980).

Two Crossings Theorem. For the random variable y, continuous or discrete, let $f(y \mid \mathbf{x}, \nu)$ denote an exponential family conditional (on ν) model density and let $\mathsf{E}[\nu] = 1$, $\mathsf{V}[\nu] = \sigma^2 > 0$. Then the mixed (marginal with respect to ν) distribution $h(y \mid \mathbf{x}) = \mathsf{E}_\nu f(y \mid \mathbf{x}, \nu)$ will have heavier tails than $f(y \mid \mathbf{x}, \nu)$ in the sense that the sign pattern of marginal minus the conditional, $h(y \mid \mathbf{x}) - f(y \mid \mathbf{x}, \nu)$, is $\{+, -, +\}$ as y increases on its support.

That is, for the same mean, any marginal distribution must "cross" the conditional distribution twice, first from above and then from below, the first crossing accounting for a relative excess of zeros, and the second for the thickness of the right tail. A sketch of the proof of this theorem is given in section 4.10.

As an example, compare Figure 4.1, which shows the Poisson–gamma mixture, or negative binomial, with mean 10 and $\sigma_\nu^2 = 0.2$ with the Poisson distribution with mean 10.

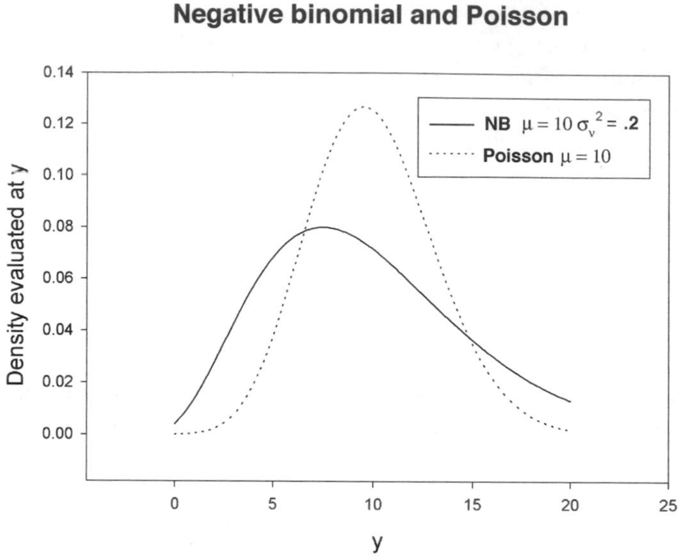

Figure 4.1. Negative binomial compared with Poisson.

4.2.2 *Negative Binomial Model*

The interpretation and derivation of the negative binomial as a Poisson–gamma mixture is an old result that can be algebraically derived in several different ways (Greenwood and Yule, 1920). Here we approach the problem directly in terms of a mixture distribution.

Suppose the distribution of a random count y is conditionally Poisson:

$$f(y_i \mid \theta_i) = \frac{\exp(-\theta_i) \cdot \theta_i^{y_i}}{y_i!}, \qquad y_i = 0, 1, \ldots. \tag{4.8}$$

Suppose the parameter θ_i has a random intercept term, and the random term enters the conditional mean function multiplicatively, that is,

$$\begin{aligned} \theta_i &= \exp\left(\beta_0 + \mathbf{x}_i'\boldsymbol{\beta}_1 + \varepsilon_i\right) \\ &= e^{\mathbf{x}_i'\beta_1} e^{(\beta_0+\varepsilon_i)} \\ &= e^{(\beta_0+\mathbf{x}_i'\beta_1)} e^{\varepsilon_i} \\ &= \mu_i \nu_i, \end{aligned} \tag{4.9}$$

where $\exp(\beta_0 + \varepsilon_i)$ is interpreted as random intercept, $\mu_i = e^{(\beta_0+\mathbf{x}_i'\beta_1)}$, and $\nu_i = e^{\varepsilon_i}$.

The marginal distribution of y is obtained by integrating out ν_i,

$$\begin{aligned} h(y_i \mid \mu_i) &= \int f(y_i \mid \mu_i, \nu_i) g(\nu_i)\, d\nu_i \\ &\equiv \mathsf{E}_\nu[f(y_i \mid \mu_i, \nu_i)], \end{aligned} \tag{4.10}$$

where $g(\nu_i)$ is a mixing distribution. For specific choices of $f(\cdot)$ and $g(\cdot)$, for example Poisson and gamma densities respectively, the integral has an explicit solution. This is shown shortly.

From here on the i subscript is omitted if there is no ambiguity. Suppose that the variable ν has a two-parameter gamma distribution $g(\nu; \delta, \phi)$

$$g(\nu, \delta, \phi) = \frac{\delta^{\phi}}{\Gamma(\delta)} \nu^{\delta-1} e^{-\nu\phi}, \quad \delta > 0, \phi > 0, \tag{4.11}$$

where $\mathsf{E}[\nu] = \delta/\phi$, and $\mathsf{V}[\nu] = \delta/\phi^2$. The intercept identification condition is $\mathsf{E}[\nu] = 1$ which is obtained by setting $\delta = \phi$, which implies a one-parameter gamma family with $\mathsf{V}[\nu] = 1/\delta \equiv \alpha$. We transform from ν to θ using $\theta = \mu\nu$, and noting that the Jacobian transformation term is $(1/\mu)$. This yields the pdf for θ,

$$\begin{aligned} g(\theta \mid \mu, \delta) &= \frac{1}{\mu} \frac{\delta^{\delta}}{\Gamma(\delta)} \left(\frac{\theta}{\mu} \right)^{\delta-1} e^{-\frac{\theta}{\mu}\delta} \\ &= \frac{(\delta/\mu)^{\delta}}{\Gamma(\delta)} \theta^{\delta-1} e^{-\frac{\theta\delta}{\mu}}. \end{aligned} \tag{4.12}$$

The marginal distribution of y is given by

$$h(y \mid \mu, \delta) = \int \frac{\exp(-\theta) \cdot \theta^{y}}{y!} \frac{(\delta/\mu)^{\delta}}{\Gamma(\delta)} \theta^{\delta-1} e^{-\frac{\theta\delta}{\mu}} \, d\theta. \tag{4.13}$$

Using the following definitions this integral can be expressed in a closed form:

$$\Gamma(a) = \int_0^{\infty} t^{a-1} e^{-t} dt, \quad \text{for any } a > 0$$

$$\Gamma(y-1) = y!$$

$$\Gamma(a)/b^a = \int_0^{\infty} t^{a-1} e^{-bt} dt, \quad \text{for any } b > 0.$$

Substituting these into (4.13) we obtain

$$\begin{aligned} h(y \mid \mu, \delta) &= \frac{(\delta/\mu)^{\delta}}{\Gamma(\delta)\Gamma(y+1)} \int \exp\left(-\theta\left(1 + \frac{\delta}{\mu}\right)\right) \theta^{y+\delta-1} d\theta \\ &= \frac{\left(\frac{\delta}{\mu}\right)^{\delta} \left(1 + \frac{\delta}{\mu}\right)^{-(\delta+y)} \Gamma(\delta + y)}{\Gamma(\delta)\Gamma(y+1)} \\ &= \frac{\Gamma(\alpha^{-1} + y)}{\Gamma(\alpha^{-1})\Gamma(y+1)} \left(\frac{\alpha^{-1}}{\alpha^{-1} + \mu} \right)^{\alpha^{-1}} \left(\frac{\mu}{\mu + \alpha^{-1}} \right)^{y}, \end{aligned} \tag{4.14}$$

where the second line follows after noting that the integral in the preceding expression is $(1 + \delta/\mu)^{-(\delta+y)}\Gamma(\delta + y)$ and we use $1/\delta = \alpha$. The marginal distribution is the negative binomial with the first two moments

$$\mathsf{E}[y \mid \mu, \alpha] = \mu,$$

$$\mathsf{V}[y \mid \mu, \alpha] = \mu(1 + \alpha\mu) > \mu, \quad \text{if } \alpha > 0.$$

Maximum likelihood estimation of this currently popular model and several variants of it was discussed in section 3.3.

4.2.3 *Other Characterizations of NB*

The characterization of the NB distribution as a Poisson–gamma mixture is only one of a number of chance mechanisms that can generate that distribution. Boswell and Patil (1970) list 13 distinct stochastic mechanisms for generating the NB. These include the NB as a waiting time distribution, as a Poisson sum of a logarithmic series random variables, as a linear birth and death process, as the equilibrium of a Markov chain, and as a group-size distribution.

A special mention should be made of Eggenberger and Polya's (1923) derivation of the NB as a limit of an urn scheme. The idea here is that an urn scheme can be used to model true contagion in which the occurrence of an event affects the probability of later events.

Consider an urn containing N balls of which a fraction p are red and fraction $q = 1 - p$ are black. A random sample of size n is drawn. After each draw the ball drawn is replaced and $k = \theta N$ balls of the same color are added to the urn. Let Y be the number of red balls in n trials. Then the distribution of Y is the Polya distribution defined as

$$\Pr[Y = y] = \binom{n}{y} \times \frac{p(p+\theta)\cdots[p+(y-1)\theta]q(q+\theta)\cdots[q+(n-y)\theta]}{1(1+\theta)\cdots[1+(n-1)\theta]}, \quad y = 0, 1, \ldots, n.$$

Let $n \to \infty$, $p \to 0$, $\theta \to 0$, with $np \to \eta$ and $\theta n \to b\eta$, for some constant b. Then the limit of the Polya distribution can be shown to be the NB with parameters $k \equiv 1/b$ and $1/(1 + b\eta)$; that is,

$$\Pr[Y = y] = \binom{k + y - 1}{k - 1} \left(\frac{k}{\eta}\right)^y \left(\frac{\eta}{\eta - k}\right)^{-k},$$

where for convenience we take k to be an integer (see Boswell and Patil, 1970; Feller, 1968, pp. 118–145).

The Polya urn scheme can be interpreted in terms of occurrence of social or economic events. Suppose an event of interest, such as an accident, corresponds to drawing a red ball from an urn. Suppose that subsequent to each such occurrence, social or economic behavior increases the probability of the next occurrence. This is analogous to a scheme for replacing the red ball drawn from the urn in such a way that the proportion of red balls to black balls increases. If, however, after a ball is drawn, more balls of opposite color are added to the urn, then the drawing of a ball reduces the probability of a repeat occurrence at the next draw.

Of course, there can be many possible replacement schemes in the urn problem. Which scheme one uses determines the nature of the dependence between one event and the subsequent ones. This shows that the NB distribution can reflect true contagion or occurrence dependence. By contrast, an example of spurious contagion results if we consider that different individuals, for example, workers, experience an event, such as an accident at the workplace, with constant but different probabilities. This is analogous to individuals having their separate urns with red and black balls in different proportions. For each person the probability of drawing a red ball is constant, but there is a distribution across individuals. In the aggregate one observes apparent dependence, or spurious contagion, due to heterogeneity.

4.2.4 *General Mixture Results*

The statistics literature contains many examples of generalized count models generated by mixtures. An historical account can be found in Johnson, Kotz, and Kemp (1992). Although the negative binomial is one of the oldest and most popular in applied work, other mixtures that have been used include Poisson-inverse Gaussian mixture (Dean, Lawless, and Willmot, 1989), discrete log-normal (Shaban, 1988), generalized Poisson (Consul, 1989; Consul and Jain, 1973), and Gauss-Poisson (Johnson, Kotz, and Kemp, 1992). Additional flexibility due to the presence of parameters of the mixing distribution generally improves the fit of the resulting distribution to observed data.

Many general probability distributions can collapse to special forms under restrictions on a subset of parameters. These then provide natural generalizations of the restrictive cases. One of the oldest approaches to the generalization of the Poisson is based on mixtures and convolutions. Of course, the same distribution could be postulated directly as a more flexible functional form. Furthermore, a particular mixture could arise from component distributions in more than one way; that is, it may not be a unique convolution.

It is useful to distinguish between continuous mixtures (convolutions) and finite mixtures.

Definition. Suppose $F(y \mid \theta)$ is a parametric distribution depending on θ, and let $\pi(\theta \mid \alpha)$ define a continuous mixing distribution. Then a convolution or a continuous mixture is defined by $F(y \mid \alpha) = \int_{-\infty}^{\infty} \pi(\theta \mid \alpha) F(y \mid \theta)\, d\theta$.

Definition. If $F_j(y \mid \theta_j)$, $j = 1, 2, \ldots, m$, is a distribution function then $F(y \mid \pi_j) = \sum_{j=1}^{m} \pi_j F_j(y \mid \theta_j)$, $0 < \pi_j < 1$, $\sum_{j=1}^{m} \pi_j = 1$, defines m-component finite mixture.

Note that although these definitions are stated in terms of the cdf rather than the pdf, definitions in terms of the latter are feasible. The second definition is a special case of the first, if $\pi(\theta \mid \alpha)$ is discrete and assigns positive probability to a finite number of parameter values $\theta_1, \ldots, \theta_m$. In this case π_j, the mixing proportion, is the probability that an observation comes from the jth population. By contrast, in a continuous mixture the parameter θ of the conditional density is subject to chance variation described by a density with an infinite number of support points. Estimation and inference for convolutions involves (θ, α) and for finite mixtures $(\pi_j, \theta_j;\ j = 1, \ldots, m)$.

4.2.5 *Identification*

The identifiability, or unique characterization, of mixtures should be established prior to estimation and inference. A mixture is identifiable if there is a unique correspondence between the mixture and the mixing distribution, usually in the presence of some a priori constraints (Teicher, 1961).

The pgf of a mixed Poisson model, denoted $\mathsf{P}(z)$, can be expressed as the convolution integral

$$\mathsf{P}(z) = \int_0^\infty \exp(\mu(z-1)) f(\mu)\, d\mu, \tag{4.15}$$

where $\exp(\mu(z-1))$ is the pgf of the Poisson distribution and $f(\mu)$ is the assumed distribution for μ. The mixture models, being akin to "reduced form" models, are subject to an identification problem. The same distribution can be obtained from a different mixture. For example, the negative binomial mixture can be generated as a Poisson–gamma mixture by allowing the Poisson parameter μ to have a gamma distribution (see section 4.2). It can also be generated by taking a random sum of independent random variables in which the number of terms in the sum has a Poisson distribution; if each term is discrete and has a logarithmic distribution and if the number of terms has a Poisson distribution, the mixture is negative binomial (Daley and Vere-Jones, 1988).

Identification may be secured by restricting the conditional event distribution to be Poisson. This follows from the uniqueness property of exponential mixtures (Jewel, 1982).

A practical consideration is that in applied work, especially that based on small samples, it may be difficult to distinguish between alternative mixing distributions, and the choice may be largely based on the ease of computation. Most of the issues are analogous to those that have been discussed extensively in the duration literature.* In the examples in the duration literature finiteness of the mean of the mixing distribution is required for identifiability of the mixture. This issue is illustrated by comparing the Poisson–gamma and Poisson–inverse Gaussian (PIG) mixtures. The latter is generated from the convolution integral $\int f(y_i \mid \mu_i, \nu_i) g(\nu_i)\, d\nu_i$ with $f(\cdot)$ as Poisson and $g(\cdot)$ as inverse Gaussian with

* Lancaster (1990, chapter 7) provides an excellent discussion of the identification conditions for the proportional hazard models and gives an example of a nonidentifiable model.

density

$$g(\nu) = (2\pi\delta^{-1}\nu^3)\exp\left[\frac{-\delta(\nu-1)^2}{2\nu}\right], \tag{4.16}$$

where $\mathsf{E}[\nu] = 1$, $\mathsf{V}[\nu] = \delta^{-1} \equiv \alpha$. Although the convolution integral does not have a closed form, note that the first two moments of the mixing inverse Gaussian distribution are the same as those of the gamma distribution in (4.11). Consequently, the first two moments of the Poisson–gamma and PIG mixtures are equal. Hence, the two mixing distributions can only be distinguished using information about higher moments. In small samples such information is imprecise, and attempts to distinguish empirically between competing alternatives may yield inconclusive results.

Although more flexible count distributions are usually derived by mixing, it may sometimes be appropriate to directly specify flexible functional forms for counts, without the intermediate step of introducing a distribution of unobserved heterogeneity (e.g., in aggregate time series applications). In microeconometric applications, however, mixing seems a natural way of handling heterogeneity.

As an example, Dean, Lawless, and Wilmot (1989) use the PIG mixture to study the frequency of insurance claims. They analyze data on the number of accident claims on third-party motor insurance policies in Sweden during 1977 in each of 315 risk groups. The counts take a wide range of values – the median is 10, the maximum is 2127 – so there is clearly a need to control for the size of risk group. This is done by defining the mean to equal $T_i \exp(\mathbf{x}_i\beta)$, where T_i is the number of insured automobile-years for the group, which is equivalent to including $\ln T_i$ as a regressor and constraining its coefficient to equal unity. Even after including this and other regressors, the data are overdispersed. The authors estimate a mixed PIG model, with overdispersion modeled by a quadratic variance function. These maximum likelihood estimates are within 1% of estimates from solving equations that use only the first two moments.

4.2.6 *Consequences of Misspecified Heterogeneity*

In the duration literature, in which the shape of the hazard function is of central interest, there has been an extensive discussion of how misspecified unobserved heterogeneity can lead to inconsistent estimates of the hazard function (see Heckman and Singer, 1984, and Lancaster, 1990, pp. 294–305 for a summary). Under our assumptions, misspecification of the heterogeneity distribution implies that the variance function, and the marginal distribution of counts, are misspecified. The consequences of this misspecification are dealt with in Chapter 2. A particular parametric assumption of heterogeneity is not easy to justify except as an approximation. Obviously, the more flexible is the assumption, the less likely is a serious misspecification error. Certain variance functions have been found to be good approximations to arbitrary variance functions in the sense that the improvement in fit of the model achieved by freeing up the form of the variance function further may be slight. An example is NB2 quadratic variance function. Also see Bourlange and Doz (1988).

4.3 Models Based on Waiting-Time Distributions

Chapter 1 sketches the duality between waiting-time distributions and event count distributions in a simple case. We pursue this issue in greater detail here. Some useful insights into the dispersion properties of counts are obtained by examining the duality between waiting times and event counts in a model in which the waiting times are dependent.

4.3.1 *True and Apparent Contagion*

The discussion of heterogeneity and overdispersion is related to a long-standing discussion in the biostatistics literature on *true* and *apparent contagion*. True contagion refers to dependence between the occurrence of successive events. The occurrence of an event, such as an accident or illness, may change the probability of subsequent occurrence of similar events. True positive contagion implies that the occurrence of an event shortens the expected waiting time to the next occurrence of the event, whereas true negative contagion implies that the expected waiting time to the next occurrence of the event is longer. The alleged phenomenon of accident proneness can be interpreted in terms of true contagion as suggesting that an individual who has experienced an accident is more likely to experience another accident. Apparent contagion arises from the recognition that sampled individuals come from a heterogeneous population in which individuals have constant but different propensity to experience accidents. For a given individual, occurrence of an accident does not make it more or less likely that another accident will occur. But aggregation across heterogeneous individuals generates the statistical finding that occurrence of an accident increases the probability of another accident.

Yet another mode of dynamic dependence is present in the notion that events occur in "spells" that themselves occur independently according to some probability law. Events within a given spell follow a different probability law and may be dependent. Serial dependence can be shown to lead to overdispersion in the counts. However, as was shown previously, overdispersion can also be a consequence of population heterogeneity or differences among individuals in their propensity to experience an event. Thus, the mere presence of overdispersion in the data does not preclude the possibility that for a given individual there may be no serial dependence in event occurrence. This second situation is therefore referred to as apparent contagion.

The discussion of accident proneness of individuals in the early statistical literature emphasized the difficulty of distinguishing between true accident proneness and effects of interindividual heterogeneity. In reference to Neyman (1939), Feller (1943) pointed out that the same negative binomial model had been derived by Greenwood and Yule (1920) using the assumption of population heterogeneity and by Eggenberger and Polya (1923), who assumed true contagion. He observed, "Therefore, the possibility of its interpretation in two ways, diametrically opposite in their nature as well as their implications is of greatest statistical significance" (Feller, 1943, p. 389). Neyman (1965, p. 6) emphasized that the distinction between true and apparent contagion would become possible "if one has at one's disposal data on accidents incurred by each individual separately for two periods of six months each"; clearly this refers to longitudinal data. These issues are further pursued in Chapter 9.

4.3.2 *Renewal Process*

Renewal theory deals with functions of iid nonnegative random variables that represent time intervals between successive events (renewals). The topic is introduced in Chapter 1.

Consider the counting process, $\{N(t), t \geq 0\}$, which measures the successive occurences of an event in the time interval $(0, t]$. Denote by W_r the length of time between the occurrences of events $(r - 1)$ and r, by $F_n(t)$ the cdf of $(W_1, \ldots, W_n)$, and by S_n the sum of waiting times, $\sum_{k=1}^{n} W_k$, for n events, $n \geq 1$. Renewal theory derives properties of random variables associated with the number of events, $N(t)$, or waiting times, S_n, given the specification of $F_n(t)$. An example of a statistic of major interest is the mean number of occurrences in the interval $(0, t]$, denoted as $m(t)$ and called the *renewal function,* which is related to $F_n(t)$. This is evaluated at $t = T$,

$$\begin{aligned} m(t) &= \mathsf{E}[N(T)] \\ &= \sum_{n=1}^{\infty} n \Pr[N(T) = n] \\ &= \sum_{n=1}^{\infty} n[F_n(T) - F_{n+1}(T)] \\ &= \sum_{n=1}^{\infty} F_n(T). \end{aligned} \tag{4.17}$$

Thus, the mean of the count variable is $\sum_{n=1}^{\infty} F_n(T)$ and its variance is given by

$$\mathsf{V}[N] = \sum_{n=1}^{\infty} n^2[F_n(T) - F_{n+1}(T)] - \left(\sum_{n=1}^{\infty} F_n(T)\right)^2. \tag{4.18}$$

4.3.3 *Waiting-Time Distribution*

Here we consider the mathematical relation between counts and waiting times that was introduced in Chapter 1. Although a general formulation is possible, it does not produce easily interpretable results. Instead we present a specific example, due to Winkelmann (1995), that illustrates both the issues and the method.

For events that occur randomly over time, the count point process is $\{\mathsf{N}(t), t > 0\}$. Let $N(t)$ represent the number of events between 0 and T. For fixed t, $N(t)$ is a count variable. This can be transformed into the sequence of interevent waiting times, denoted W_r for the time interval between the $(r-1)^{th}$ and r^{th} events. The arrival time of the rth event is given by $S_r = \sum_{j=1}^{r} W_j$. For a renewal process, the distribution of S_r can be derived by using Laplace transforms.

Given the definitions, $N_T < r$ iff $S_r > T$. Let $F_r(T)$ denote the cumulative distribution of S_r. Then

$$\begin{aligned}\Pr[N(T) < r] &= \Pr[S_r \geq T] \\ &= 1 - F_r(T)\end{aligned} \tag{4.19}$$

and

$$\begin{aligned}\Pr[N(T) = r] &= \Pr[N(T) < r + 1] - \Pr[N(T) < r] \\ &= F_r(T) - F_{r+1}(T) \\ &= \int_0^T [1 - F_r(T - z)]\, dF_r(z),\end{aligned} \tag{4.20}$$

which is the fundamental relation between the distribution of waiting times and that of event counts. This relation may form the basis of a count model corresponding to an arbitrary waiting-time model. Conditioning on exogenous variable $\mathbf{x}_i$, the likelihood for the m independent observations is defined by

$$\mathsf{L} = \prod_{i=1}^{m} \left[F_{n_i}(T \mid \mathbf{x}_i) - F_{n_i+1}(T \mid \mathbf{x}_i)\right]. \tag{4.21}$$

The practical utility of this formulation in part depends on whether the cdf of S_n can be easily evaluated. Even if no closed form expression for the cdf is available, computer-intensive methods can be used as suggested by Lee (1997). Further, the approach can be extended to generalized renewal processes; for example, we may allow the waiting-time distribution of the first event to differ from that of subsequent events (Ross, 1996) – a case analogous to the hurdle count model. Another potential advantage is that the approach can exploit the availability of structurally and behaviorally richer specifications of waiting-time models.

One approach is to begin by specifying parametric regression models for waiting times. For example, a broad class of parametric waiting-time models is defined by the regression

$$\ln t_i = \mathbf{x}_i'\boldsymbol{\beta} + \sigma\varepsilon_i \tag{4.22}$$

where the distribution of ε_i is specified. We consider some special cases.

- The exponential duration model (and the Poisson model for counts) follows from the assumption that $\sigma = 1$, and ε_i follow the extreme value distribution.
- A less restrictive model is

$$\ln t_i = \mathbf{x}_i'\beta + \varepsilon_i - u_i$$

  where the ε_i are iid extreme value distributed and u_i is a log-gamma random variable.* This choice corresponds to the negative binomial distribution for counts (Lee, 1997).
- Equation (4.22) corresponds to the popular Weibull waiting-time distribution with an additional free parameter that allows duration dependence. In this case there is no closed form expression for the distribution of counts.

In the following subsection we consider an interesting special case analyzed by Winkelmann (1995), which illustrates some of the problems and possibilities of this approach.

4.3.4 *Gamma Waiting Times*

Winkelmann (1995) considered the gamma waiting-time distribution, which admits monotonic increasing or decreasing hazards. Then the density of W is given by

$$f(W \mid \phi, \alpha) = \frac{\alpha^\phi}{\Gamma(\phi)} W^{\alpha-1} e^{-\alpha W}, \qquad W > 0. \tag{4.23}$$

The corresponding *hazard function*, which describes the underlying dependence of the process, is defined as

$$\begin{aligned} h(W) &= \frac{f(W)}{1 - F(W)} \\ &= -\frac{d}{dW} \ln(1 - F(W)) \\ &= \left[\int_0^\infty e^{-\alpha u}(1 + u/W)^{\phi-1}\, du \right]^{-1}. \end{aligned}$$

The hazard function does not have a closed-form expression but can be shown to be monotonically increasing for $\alpha > 1$. This implies positive duration dependence or increasing hazards. The function is monotonic decreasing for $\alpha < 1$, which implies negative duration dependence or decreasing hazards. The slope of the hazard function, $\partial h(W)/\partial W$, reflects the dependence of the

* The density of u is defined by $f(v) = \exp[v/\eta - \exp(v)]/\Gamma(1/\eta)$ where $u = \ln \eta + v$ (Kalbfleish and Prentice, 1980; Lee, 1997).

process; negative slope implies that waiting time is less likely to end, the longer it lasts, whereas positive slope implies that the transition out of the current state is more probable the longer the duration in that state. Hazard function may be nonmonotonic; for example, it may have an inverse bathtub shape.

We first obtain the distribution of S_r given the distribution (4.23). To do so we use the Laplace transform, which for nonnegative random variables is the analog of the moment-generating function. The Laplace transform of the gamma-distributed random variables is defined as

$$\begin{aligned} \mathsf{L}_W(z) &= \int_0^\infty e^{-zW} f(W) \\ &= (1 + z/\alpha)^{-\alpha}. \end{aligned} \tag{4.24}$$

The Laplace transform of $S_r = \sum_{j=1}^r W_j$, $r = 1, 2, \ldots,$ is given by

$$\begin{aligned} \mathsf{L}_{S_r}(z) &= \prod_{i=1}^r \mathsf{L}_{S_i}(z) \\ &= (1 + z/\alpha)^{-r\alpha}, \end{aligned} \tag{4.25}$$

so that the density of S_r is obtained by replacing ϕ in the density for W_i by $r\phi$. Hence,

$$f_r(S \mid \phi, \alpha) = \frac{\alpha^{r\phi}}{\Gamma(r\phi)} S^{r\phi-1} e^{-\alpha S}. \tag{4.26}$$

To deploy the fundamental relation (4.20), using the corresponding cumulative distribution function we obtain

$$\begin{aligned} F_r(T \mid \alpha, \phi) &= \int_0^T \frac{\alpha^{r\phi}}{\Gamma(r\phi)} S^{r\phi-1} e^{-\alpha S} dS \\ &= \frac{1}{\Gamma(r\phi)} \int_0^{\alpha T} u^{r\phi-1} e^{-u} du \\ &\equiv G(r\phi, \alpha T), \end{aligned} \tag{4.27}$$

where the second equality uses the change of variable to $u = \alpha S$. The right-hand side is an incomplete gamma integral that can be numerically evaluated. Finally using the fundamental relation between durations and counts, we obtain the corresponding count distribution

$$\Pr[N = r] = \begin{cases} 1 - G(\phi, \alpha) & \text{for } r = 0 \\ G(r\phi, \alpha) - G(r\phi + \phi, \alpha) & \text{for } r = 1, 2, \ldots. \end{cases} \tag{4.28}$$

where $G(0, \alpha T) = 1$ and we normalize $T = 1$. This simplifies to the Poisson with parameter α if $\phi = 1$ but allows for positive duration dependence if $\alpha > 1$

and negative duration dependence if $\alpha < 1$ (Winkelmann, 1995). For any $\phi > 0$, it can be shown that $\alpha > 1$ leads to underdispersion and $\alpha < 1$ to overdispersion. Using (4.21) the likelihood function can be formed. Each term in the likelihood involves an integral that can be evaluated numerically.

4.3.5 *Dependence and Dispersion*

It can be shown that this result is not specific to gamma waiting times; it applies whenever the hazard function is monotonic. Let the mean and variance of waiting-time distributions be denoted, respectively, μ_w and σ_w^2. Cox (1962b, p. 40) shows that the asymptotic distribution of the number of events N_T in the interval $(0, T)$ is approximately normal with mean T/μ_w and variance $T\sigma_w^2/\mu_w^3$, and the approximation is good if $\mathsf{E}[w]$ is small relative to T. If CV denotes the coefficient of variation, then

$$\mathsf{CV}^2 = \frac{\sigma_w^2}{\mu_w^2}. \tag{4.29}$$

For waiting-time distributions with monotonic hazards, it can be shown (Barlow and Proschan, 1965, p. 33) that

$$\mathsf{CV} < 1 \Rightarrow \text{increasing duration dependence}$$

$$\mathsf{CV} > 1 \Rightarrow \text{decreasing duration dependence.}$$

This result indicates that overdispersion (underdispersion, equidispersion) in count models is consistent with negative- (positive-, zero-) duration dependence of waiting times. Although this result provides a valuable connection between models of counts and durations, the usefulness of the result for interpreting estimated count models depends on whether the underlying assumption of monotone hazards and absence of other types of model misspecification is realistic.

Another form of overdispersion is sometimes observed in the form of clustering. For instance, a particular cause (e.g., illness) may generate a cluster of correlated events (e.g., doctor visits). Over some period of time such as a year, one may observe several clusters for an individual, with correlation within but not between clusters. One way to model dependence between events in a cluster is to begin with the binomial-stopped-by-Poisson characterization of Chapter 1. One then allows the binary outcome variable to be correlated, as in the *correlated binomial* model, denoted $\mathsf{CB}[n, \pi, \rho]$. In this case the count is $Y = \sum_{i=1}^{n} B_i$, B_i is a binary 0/1 random variable that, if the event occurs, takes the value 1 with probability π. The pair (B_i, B_j), $i \neq j$, has covariance $\rho\pi(1-\pi)$, $0 \leq \rho < 1$ (Dean, 1992; Luceño, 1995). That is, all (i, j) pairs have constant correlation ρ. Assuming a random number of events in a given period, the $\mathsf{CB}[n, \pi, \rho]$ model generates the *correlated Poisson* model, denoted $\mathsf{CP}[\mu(1-\rho), (1-\rho)(\mu + \rho\mu^2)]$. The arguments in the latter are the mean and the variance, respectively, and $\mu = \lim(n\pi)$. Note that the variance–mean ratio in this case has the same form as the NB2 model, with ρ replacing the parameter

α. Clearly, clumping or correlation of events can generate overdispersion. This phenomenon is of potential interest in time series count models.

4.4 Katz, Double Poisson, and Generalized Poisson

Multiplicative mixtures lead to overdispersion. However, sometimes it is not evident that overdispersion is present in the data. It is then of interest to consider models that have variance functions flexible enough to cover both over- and underdispersion. In this section we consider several count models that are not generated by mixtures or non-Poisson processes and that have this property. Additional cross-sectional models with a similar underlying motivation are also discussed in Chapter 12.

4.4.1 *The Katz System*

Some extensions of the Poisson model that permit both over- and underdispersion can be obtained by introducing a variance function with additional parameters. Cameron and Trivedi (1986) suggested the variance function

$$\mathsf{V}[y_i \mid \mathbf{x}_i] = \mathsf{E}[y_i \mid \mathbf{x}_i] + \alpha \mathsf{E}[y_i \mid \mathbf{x}_i]^{2-k_1}, \qquad \alpha > 0. \tag{4.30}$$

This specializes to that for the Poisson, NB1, and NB2 as $k_1 = 2$, 1, and 0, respectively. Motivated by the desire to specify a variance function that would cover overdispersion as well as underdispersion, Winkelmann and Zimmermann (1991), following King (1989b), reparameterized (note that $-k_1 = k_2 - 1$ and $\alpha = \sigma_2^2 - 1$) this as

$$\mathsf{V}[y_i \mid \mathbf{x}_i] = \mathsf{E}[y_i \mid \mathbf{x}_i] + \left(\sigma_2^2 - 1\right) \mathsf{E}[y_i \mid \mathbf{x}_i]^{k_2+1}, \qquad \sigma_2^2 > 1, \tag{4.31}$$

and proposed to treat k_2 as an unknown parameter. The restriction $\sigma_2^2 - 1 = 0$ yields the Poisson case, $\alpha > 0$ implies overdispersion, and $0 < \sigma_2^2 < 1$ and $\mathsf{E}[y_i \mid \mathbf{x}_i]^{k_2} \leq -1/(\sigma_2^2 - 1)$ implies underdispersion. However, it is useful to know where (4.31) comes from if we are to ensure that the above variance function is consistent with a particular pdf of y_i. This can be done using the Katz family of distributions.

Katz (1963) studied the system of discrete distributions defined by the probability recursion

$$\Pr[y+1] = \Pr[y] \frac{\omega + \gamma y}{1 + y}, \qquad \omega + \gamma y \geq 0, \mu > 0, \gamma < 1, \tag{4.32}$$

which has mean $\mu = \omega/(1 - \gamma)$ and variance $\omega/(1 - \gamma)^2$. This includes as special cases the Poisson ($\gamma = 0$) and the negative binomial ($0 < \gamma < 1$). Setting $\omega/(1 - \gamma)^2$ equal to the right-hand side of (4.31) and solving for (ω, γ) yields

$$\gamma = \frac{\alpha \mu^{k_2}}{\alpha \mu^{k_2} + 1}; \qquad \omega = \frac{\mu}{\alpha \mu^{k_2} + 1}.$$

Substituting these back into (4.31) and solving for the pdf of y yields the so-called generalized event count (GEC[k]) density (Winkelmann and Zimmermann, 1995),

$$f(y \mid \mu, \alpha, k_2) = C_i \times \begin{cases} \prod_{j=1}^{y} \left[\frac{\mu + \alpha(j-1)\mu^{k_2}}{[\alpha\mu^{k_2}+1]j} \right] & \text{for } y = 1, 2, \ldots \\ 1 & \text{for } y = 0, \end{cases} \tag{4.33}$$

where

$$C_i = \begin{cases} \left(\alpha\mu_i^{k_2} + 1\right)^{\zeta_i} & \text{for } \alpha \geq 0 \\ \left(\alpha\mu_i^{k_2} + 1\right)^{\zeta_i} D_i^{-1} & \text{for } 0 < \alpha - 1 < 1;\ \mu_i^{k_2} \leq 1/\alpha; \\ & \quad y_i \leq int^*(\zeta_i) \\ 0 & \text{otherwise} \end{cases}$$

$$\zeta_i = -\mu_i^{k_2-1}/\alpha$$

$$D_i = \sum_{m=0}^{int^*(\zeta_i)} f_{binomial}(m \mid \mu, \alpha, k_2),$$

$$int^*(y) = \begin{cases} int(y) + 1 & \text{for } int(y) < y \\ int(y) & \text{for } int(y) = y. \end{cases}$$

From a computational viewpoint this is an awkward density to work with. Analytical discussion of the properties of the MLE based on this density is complicated by the fact that the range of y depends on the unknown parameters, which violates the fourth regularity condition mentioned in section 2.3. There are a number of examples in the econometric literature of models estimated by maximum likelihood based on this density (Winkelmann and Zimmermann, 1991). This appears to fit better than the Poisson, but there are very few examples where the GEC(k) fits better than NB2. This may be interpreted to mean either that the quadratic variance function of the NB2 model is a good approximation in practice, or that the departures from the quadratic variance function are difficult to detect unless the sample is sufficiently large.

4.4.2 *Example: Doctor Visits*

How much difference can different variance functions generate in estimates? In Table 4.1 we present estimates of three alternative specifications, Poisson, GEC(k), and gamma, using the Australian doctor-consultation data. All models are estimated by maximum likelihood. The gamma model is estimated using (4.28) with $\phi_i = \alpha \exp(\mathbf{x}_i'\boldsymbol{\beta})$.

The GEC(k) model allows us to evaluate the adequacy of the Poisson and the NB specifications. The estimated value of the k_1 parameter is close to 1. This indicates that a variance function linear in the mean fits the data. The α

Table 4.1. *Doctor visits: generalized event count (GEC[k]) and gamma MLE and t ratios*

	Poisson		GEC(k)		Gamma	
Variable	Coefficient	$\|t\|$	Coefficient	$\|t\|$	Coefficient	$\|t\|$
ONE	−2.264	8.740	−2.172	9.29	−8.281	3.634
SEX	0.157	1.980	0.224	3.229	.470	2.141
AGE	1.056	.774	−.379	.293	3.606	1.028
AGESQ	−.849	.581	.805	.564	−3.190	.870
INCOME	−.205	1.589	−.138	1.273	−.591	1.737
LEVYPLUS	.123	1.295	.106	1.240	0.353	1.301
FREEPOOR	−.440	1.517	−.495	2.430	−1.396	1.816
FREEREPA	.080	.630	.141	1.200	.215	.680
ILLNESS	.187	7.810	.216	8.804	.510	4.106
ACTDAYS	.127	16.327	.150	15.054	.323	4.414
HSCORE	.030	2.113	.039	2.751	.068	2.048
CHCOND1	.114	1.256	.094	1.200	.523	1.803
CHCOND2	.141	1.150	.199	1.894	.552	1.680
α			2.130	18.775	.235	3.821
k_1			1.138	10.194		
$-\ln L$	3355.		3198.		3261.	

parameter is close to 2, indicating the presence of significant overdispersion. These two results together can be interpreted to mean that the NB2 model should fit the data well. This is confirmed by a comparison of the results with those from NB2 in Table 3.4. The log-likelihood values for the two models are very close, as are also most of the parameters. Clearly, empirically the two are almost equivalent, and the NB2 is easier to estimate. In terms of log-likelihood the gamma model does not fit as well as the GEC(k) formulation, but it provides a different interpretation of overdispersion in the data. It indicates negative duration dependence, meaning that the probability of an additional doctor consultation declines following the occurrence of a consultation.

4.4.3 *Double Poisson Model*

The double Poisson distribution was proposed by Efron (1986) within the context of the double exponential family. This distribution is obtained as an exponential combination of two Poisson distributions, $\mathsf{P}[\mu]$ and $\mathsf{P}[y]$, as in

$$f(y, \mu, \phi) = K(\mu, \phi)[\mathsf{P}[\mu]]^{\phi}[\mathsf{P}[y]]^{1-\phi},$$

where ϕ is a dispersion parameter, and $K(\mu, \phi)$ is a normalizing constant whose exact value depends on μ and ϕ. Expanded, the double Poisson density becomes

$$f(y, \mu, \phi) = K(\mu, \phi)\phi^{1/2} \exp(-\phi\mu) \exp(-y)y^y \left(\frac{e\mu}{y}\right)^{\phi y}, \qquad (4.34)$$

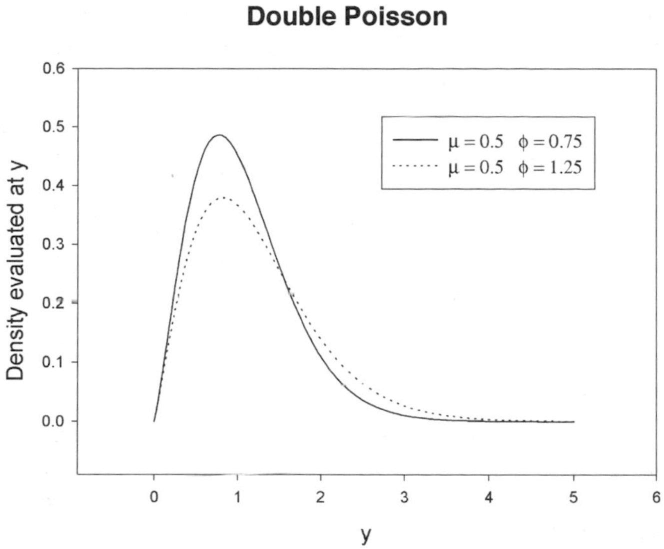

Figure 4.2. Two examples of double Poisson.

where

$$\frac{1}{K(\mu, \phi)} \simeq 1 + \frac{1-\phi}{12\phi\mu}\left(1 + \frac{1}{\phi\mu}\right)$$

ensures $f(\cdot)$ sums to unity. This distribution has mean value approximately μ and variance approximately μ/ϕ (Efron, 1986, p. 715). The parameter μ is similar to the Poisson mean parameter. Efron (1986) shows that the constant $K(\mu, \phi)$ in (4.34) nearly equals 1. Because it is a source of significant nonlinearity, the approximate density obtained by suppressing it may be used in approximate maximum likelihood estimation. The Poisson model is nested in the double Poisson model for $\phi = 1$. The double Poisson model allows for overdispersion ($\phi < 1$) as well as underdispersion ($\phi > 1$). Another advantage of the double Poisson regression model is that both the mean and the dispersion parameters may depend on observed explanatory variables. Thus, it is possible to model the mean and dispersion structure separately as is sometimes done for a heteroskedastic normal linear regression model.* Figure 4.2 shows the densities for two combinations of (μ, ϕ), (0.5, 1.25) and (0.5, 0.75), both leading to underdispersed outcomes with a relatively low frequency of zeros.

Let $\mu_i = \exp(\mathbf{x}_i'\boldsymbol{\beta})$. The first-order conditions for maximum likelihood estimation of $\boldsymbol{\beta}$ are

$$\sum \frac{(y_i - \mu_i)}{(\mu_i/\phi_i)} \frac{\partial \mu_i}{\partial \boldsymbol{\beta}} = \mathbf{0},$$

* This extension takes us into the realm of exponential dispersion models considered by Jorgensen (1987).

which are the same as for the PML if ϕ_i is a constant and does not involve covariates. If ϕ is a constant, the maximum likelihood estimate ϕ is simply the average value of the deviance measure,

$$\hat{\phi} = n^{-1} \sum y_i \ln y_i / \hat{\mu}_i - (y_i - \hat{\mu}_i). \tag{4.35}$$

Because the estimating equations for β are the same as in the Poisson case, PML is consistent even if the dgp is double Poisson. A simple way of adjusting its variance is to scale the estimated variance matrix by multiplying by $1/\hat{\phi}$. However, to calculate the event probabilites, the expression in (4.34) should be used.

4.4.4 *Neyman's Contagious Distributions*

Neyman (1939) developed type A, type B, and type C distributions to handle a form of clustering that is common in the biological sciences. The univariate version of type A has been used with success, but we are unaware of any regression applications. Johnson, Kotz, and Kemp (1992) give an excellent account of its properties and further references.

These distributions can be thought of as compound Poisson distributions that involve two processes. For example, suppose that the number of events (e.g., doctor visits) within a spell (of illness), denoted y, follows the Poisson distribution, and the random number of spells within a specified period, denoted z, follows some other discrete distribution. Then the marginal distribution of events is compound Poisson. One variant of Neyman type A with two parameters is obtained if both y and z have independent Poisson distributions parameters (say) μ and λ, respectively. The expression for the compound distribution can be obtained by specializing the general result in (4.15).

In univariate cases Neyman type A and negative binomial have been compared. They are close competitors. Because the latter is better established in regression contexts, we shall not devote further space to Neyman type A.

4.4.5 *Consul's Generalized Poisson*

Consul (1989) has proposed a distribution that can accommodate both over- and underdispersion. The distribution is

$$f(y_i \mid x_i) = \begin{cases} \frac{\exp(-\mu_i - \gamma y_i)(\mu_i + \gamma y_i)^{y_i - 1}}{y_i!}, & y_i = 0, 1, \ldots, \\ 0 \quad \text{for } y > N, & \text{when } \gamma < 0, \end{cases} \tag{4.36}$$

where $\max(-1, -\mu/N) < \gamma \leq 1$ and N is the largest positive integer that satisfies the inequality $\mu + N\gamma > 0$ if μ is large. Because $\mathsf{E}[y_i] = \mu(1-\gamma)^{-1}$ and $\mathsf{V}[y_i] = \mu(1-\gamma)^{-3}$, the distribution can display under- and equidispersion as $\max(-1, -\mu/N) < \gamma \leq 0$, and $\gamma = 0$, and overdispersion for $0 < \gamma < 1$.

This model does not appear to have been much used in regression contexts (see Consul and Famoye, 1992). Because for this distribution the range of the random variable depends on the unknown parameter γ, one of the standard conditions for consistency and asymptotic normality of the maximum likelihood estimation is violated. The importance of this violation is a matter for future investigation.

4.5 Truncated Counts

The models allowing for truncation are required if observations $(y_i, \mathbf{x}_i)$ in some range are totally lost and the distribution of observed counts is restricted. In some studies involving count data, inclusion in the sample requires that sampled individuals have been engaged in the activity of interest or, as Johnson and Kotz (1969, p. 104) put it, "the observational apparatus become active only when a specified number of events (usually one) occurs." Examples of truncated counts include the number of bus trips made per week in surveys taken on buses, the number of shopping trips made by individuals sampled at a mall, and the number of unemployment spells among a pool of unemployed. These are examples of left truncation or truncation from below. Right truncation, or truncation from above, may result if high counts are not observed. In the special case of a "positive Poisson" model zeros are not observed.

Truncated count models are discrete counterparts of truncated and censored models for continuous variables, particularly the Tobit models for normally distributed data, that have been used extensively in the economics literature (Amemiya, 1984; Maddala, 1983). The sample selection counterparts of the model are discussed in Chapter 11. Truncated models are also related to the hurdle model discussed in section 4.7.

4.5.1 *Standard Truncated Models*

For simplicity, only truncation from below is considered. Analogous results for right truncation can be derived by adapting those for left truncation. The following general framework for truncated count models is used. Let

$$H(y_i, \boldsymbol{\Lambda}) = \Pr[Y_i \leq y_i]$$

denote the cdf of the discrete random variable with pdf $h(y_i, \boldsymbol{\Lambda})$, where $\boldsymbol{\Lambda}$ is a parameter vector. If realizations of y less than a positive integer r are omitted, the ensuing distribution is called *left-truncated* (or *truncated from below*). The left-truncated count distribution is given by

$$f(y_i, \boldsymbol{\Lambda} \mid y_i \geq r) = \frac{h(y_i, \boldsymbol{\Lambda})}{1 - H(r-1, \boldsymbol{\Lambda})}, \qquad y_i = r, \; r+1, \ldots. \tag{4.37}$$

A special case is the left-truncated negative binomial for which

$$h(y_i, \mathbf{\Lambda}) = \frac{\Gamma(y_i + \alpha^{-1})}{\Gamma(\alpha^{-1})\Gamma(y_i + 1)}(\alpha\mu_i)^{y_i}(1 + \alpha\mu_i)^{-(y_i+\alpha^{-1})},$$

where $\mathbf{\Lambda} \equiv (\mu_i, \alpha)$. The truncated mean and variance are defined by

$$\begin{aligned}
\theta_i &= \mu_i + \delta_i \\
\sigma_i^2 &= \mu_i + \alpha\mu_i^2 - \delta_i(\mu_i - r) \\
\delta_i &= \mu_i[1 + \alpha(r - 1)]\lambda(r - 1, \mu_i, \alpha) \\
\lambda(r - 1, \mu_i, \alpha) &= h(r - 1, \mu_i)/1 - H(r - 1, \mu_i).
\end{aligned} \tag{4.38}$$

The left-truncated NB incorporates overdispersion in the sense that truncated variance of the NB exceeds the truncated variance of the Poisson. The latter is a limiting case obtained as $\alpha \to 0$.

For the Poisson pdf $h(y_i, \mu_i) = \exp(-\mu_i)\mu_i^{y_i}/y_i!$ the left truncated Poisson density, obtained as a limiting case, is

$$f(y_i, \mu_i \mid y_i \geq r) = \frac{\mu_i^{y_i}}{\left[e^{\mu_i} - \sum_{j=0}^{r-1} \frac{\mu_i^j}{j!}\right] y_i!}, \qquad y_i = r, r+1, \ldots. \tag{4.39}$$

whose (truncated) mean (θ_i) and (truncated) variance (σ_i^2) are given by

$$\begin{aligned}
\theta_i &= \mu_i + \delta_i \\
\sigma_i^2 &= \mu_i - \delta_i(\mu_i - r) \\
\delta_i &= \mu_i\lambda(r - 1, \mu_i) \\
\lambda(r - 1, \mu_i) &= h(r - 1, \mu_i)/1 - H(r - 1, \mu_i),
\end{aligned} \tag{4.40}$$

which shows that the mean of the left-truncated random variable exceeds the corresponding mean of the untruncated distribution model, whereas the truncated variance is smaller. The relation between the truncated mean and the mean of the parent distribution can be expressed as

$$\mathsf{E}[y_i \mid y_i \geq r] = \mathsf{E}[y_i] + \delta_i, \qquad \delta_i > 0,$$

where δ_i, the difference between the truncated and untruncated means, depends on the parameters of the models and on $\lambda(r - 1, \mu_i)$. The adjustment factor plays a useful role, analogous to the Mill's ratio in continuous models, in the estimation and testing of count models.

The most common form of truncation in count models is left truncation at zero, $r = 1$ (Gurmu, 1991). That is, observation apparatus is activated only by the occurrence of an event. In the special case of Poisson-without-zeros, the moments are

$$\mathsf{E}[y_i \mid y_i > 0] = \frac{\mu_i}{1 - e^{-\mu_i}}$$

and

$$\begin{aligned}\mathsf{V}[y_i \mid y_i > 0] &= \mathsf{E}[y_i \mid y_i > 0][1 - \Pr[y = 0]\mathsf{E}[y_i \mid y_i > 0]] \\ &= \frac{\mu_i}{1 - e^{-\mu_i}}\left[1 - \frac{\mu_i e^{-\mu_i}}{1 - e^{-\mu_i}}\right]. \end{aligned} \tag{4.41}$$

It is clear that the truncated Poisson, unlike the Poisson, does not have equal first and second moments. Furthermore, misspecification of the distribution implies that the first conditional truncated moment, which depends on the correct probability of zero value, will also be misspecified. This results in inconsistent estimates of μ_i if the parent distribution is incorrectly specified.

Truncated Poisson may be interpreted as a specialization of the truncated negative binomial. The without-zeros variant of the NB2 has the following first two moments:

$$\mathsf{E}[y_i \mid y_i > 0] = \frac{\mu_i}{1 - (1 + \alpha\mu_i)^{-\frac{1}{\alpha}}} \tag{4.42}$$

$$\begin{aligned}\mathsf{V}[y_i \mid y_i > 0] &= \frac{\mu_i}{1 - (1 + \alpha\mu_i)^{-\frac{1}{\alpha}}} \\ &\quad \times \left[1 - (1 + \alpha\mu_i)^{-\frac{1}{\alpha}} \frac{\mu_i}{1 - (1 + \alpha\mu_i)^{-\frac{1}{\alpha}}}\right]. \end{aligned} \tag{4.43}$$

Briefly consider right truncation. Suppose the omitted values of y_i consist of values greater than c. Let $f(y_i, \boldsymbol{\Lambda}) = \Pr[Y_i \leq y_i \mid Y_i < c]$; then the right-truncated (or truncated from above) probability distribution and the truncated mean are

$$f(y_i, \boldsymbol{\Lambda} \mid y_i \leq c) = \frac{h(y_i, \boldsymbol{\Lambda})}{H(c, \boldsymbol{\Lambda})}, \qquad y_i = 0, 1, \ldots, c, \tag{4.44}$$

and

$$\begin{aligned}\mathsf{E}[y_i \mid y_i \leq c] &= \mathsf{E}[y_i] + \delta_{1i} \qquad \delta_{1i} < 0 \\ \theta_{1i} &= \mu_i + \delta_{1i}, \end{aligned} \tag{4.45}$$

where $\delta_{1i} = -\mu_i \lambda_1(c, \mu_i)$, which depends on the parameters of the model and $\lambda_1(c, \boldsymbol{\Lambda}) = h(c, \boldsymbol{\Lambda})/H(c, \boldsymbol{\Lambda})$.

Right *censoring*, often resulting from aggregation of counts above a specified value, is usually more common than right truncation. Moments of the right-truncated distribution can be obtained from the corresponding moments of the left-truncated distribution by simply replacing $r-1$, θ, and δ by c, θ_1, and δ_1, respectively. Right truncation results in a smaller mean and variance relative to the parent distribution. Detailed analysis of the moments of left- and right-truncated negative binomial models is given in Gurmu and Trivedi (1992).

4.5.2 *Maximum Likelihood Estimation*

We consider the maximum likelihood estimation of left-truncated Poisson models. Using (4.39), the log-likelihood $\mathcal{L}(\boldsymbol{\beta})$ based on n independent observations is

$$\mathcal{L}(\boldsymbol{\beta})=\sum_{i=1}^{n}\Bigg[y_i \ln(\mu_i)-\mu_i - \ln\left(1-\exp(-\mu_i)\sum_{j=0}^{r-1}\mu_i^j \Big/ j!\right)-\ln(y_i!)\Bigg]. \tag{4.46}$$

The MLE of $\boldsymbol{\beta}$ is the solution of the following equation:

$$\sum_{i=1}^{n}[y_i-\mu_i-\delta_i]\mu_i^{-1}\frac{\partial\mu_i}{\partial\boldsymbol{\beta}}=0, \tag{4.47}$$

where

$$\delta_i=\frac{\mu_i h(r,\mu_i)}{[1-H(r-1,\mu_i)]}.$$

Rewriting this as

$$\sum_{i=1}^{n}\left[\frac{y_i-\mu_i-\delta_i}{\sqrt{\mu_i}}\right]\left(\frac{1}{\sqrt{\mu_i}}\frac{\partial\mu_i}{\partial\boldsymbol{\beta}}\right)=0 \tag{4.48}$$

yields the interpretation that the score equation is an orthogonality condition between the standardized truncated residual and standardized gradient vector of the conditional mean. This interpretation parallels that for the normal truncated regression. For the exponential specification $\mu_i=\exp(\mathbf{x}_i'\boldsymbol{\beta})$, $\partial\mu_i/\partial\boldsymbol{\beta}=\mu_i\mathbf{x}_i$. So (4.47) reduces to an orthogonality condition between the $\mathbf{x}_i$ and the generalized residuals. The information matrix is

$$\mathcal{I}(\boldsymbol{\beta})=-\mathsf{E}\left[\frac{\partial^2\mathcal{L}(\boldsymbol{\beta})}{\partial\boldsymbol{\beta}\partial\boldsymbol{\beta}'}\right]=\sum_{i=1}^{n}[\mu_i-\delta_i(\mu_i+\delta_i-r)]\mu_i^{-2}\frac{\partial\mu_i}{\partial\boldsymbol{\beta}}\frac{\partial\mu_i}{\partial\boldsymbol{\beta}'}. \tag{4.49}$$

The MLE $\hat{\boldsymbol{\beta}}$ is asymptotically normal with mean $\boldsymbol{\beta}$ and variance matrix $\mathcal{I}(\boldsymbol{\beta})^{-1}$.

In maximum likelihood estimation of truncated models a misspecification of the underlying distribution leads to inconsistency due to the presence of the adjustment factor. A comparison of (4.40) with (4.38) shows that the conditional means in the two cases are different. Suppose that the counts in the parent distribution are conditionally NB distributed and $\alpha > 0$. If the distribution is misspecified as the truncated Poisson, rather than truncated NB, then the conditional mean is misspecified and the MLE will be inconsistent. To reiterate, ignoring overdispersion in the truncated count model leads to inconsistency, not just inefficiency. Thus, the result that neglected overdispersion does not affect the consistency property of the correctly specified untruncated Poisson conditional mean function does not carry over to the truncated Poisson. Hence, the left-truncated NB is a better starting point for analyzing the data that might be overdispersed.

Given estimates of the truncated Poisson, the mean of the parent distribution may be written as a product of two terms:

$$\mathsf{E}[y_i] = \mathsf{E}[y_i \mid y_i > 0] \Pr[y > 0].$$

Assuming again that $\mu_i = \exp(\mathbf{x}_i'\boldsymbol{\beta})$, the partial response of $\mathsf{E}[y_i]$ to a unit change in the continuous covariate x_j may be decomposed into the part that affects the mean of the currently untruncated part of the distribution and the part that affects the probability of truncation.

4.6 Censored Counts

Models allowing for censoring are required if observations $(y_i, \mathbf{x}_i)$ are available for a restricted range of y_i, but those for $\mathbf{x}_i$ are always observed. This is in contrast to truncation, where all observations are lost for some range of values of y. Hence, censoring involves loss of information less serious than truncation.

Censoring of count observations may arise from aggregation or may be imposed by survey design; see, for example, Terza (1985). Alternatively, censored samples may result if high counts are not observed.* Consider count models that are censored from above at point c. An implicit regression model for a latent count variable y_i^* is

$$y_i^* = \mu(\mathbf{x}_i, \boldsymbol{\beta}) + u_i, \tag{4.50}$$

where u_i is a disturbance term with $\mathsf{E}[u_i] = 0$. For a right-censored count model, the latent endogenous variable y_i^* is related to the observed dependent variable y_i as follows:

$$y_i^* = \begin{cases} y_i & \text{if } y_i^* < c, \\ c & \text{if } y_i^* \geq c, \end{cases}$$

* Applications of censored count models include provision of hospital beds for emergency admissions (Newell, 1965) and number of shopping trips (Terza, 1985; Okoruwa, Terza, and Nourse, 1988).

where c is a known positive integer. Define a latent categorical variable as follows: $d_i = 1$ if $y_i^* < c$, and 0 if $y_i^* \geq c$. The probablity of censoring the ith observation is

$$\Pr\left[y_i^* \geq c\right] = \Pr[d_i = 0] = 1 - \Pr[d_i = 1] = 1 - \mathsf{E}[d_i].$$

It is assumed that $\{\mathbf{x}_i\}$ are observed for all i and that the censoring mechanism and the data-generation process for the count variable are independent. The log-likelihood function for n independent observations from model (4.50) is

$$\begin{aligned}\mathcal{L}(\mathbf{\Lambda}) &= \sum_{i=1}^{n}\left[\ln[h(y_i, \mathbf{\Lambda})]^{d_i} + \ln[1 - H(c-1, \mathbf{\Lambda})]^{1-d_i}\right] \\ &= \sum_{i=1}^{n}[d_i \ln(h(y_i, \mathbf{\Lambda})) + (1 - d_i)\ln(1 - H(c-1, \mathbf{\Lambda})], \qquad (4.51)\end{aligned}$$

where $h(y_i;\ \mathbf{\Lambda})$ is the pdf of y_i and

$$H(y_i; c-1, \mathbf{\Lambda}) = \Pr[Y_i \leq c-1],$$

respectively.

Maximization of the likelihood given above is straightforward using gradient-based methods. Another approach is to use the expectation-maximization (EM) algorithm based on *expected likelihood*. Expected likelihood, $\mathcal{EL}(\mathbf{\Lambda})$, is obtained by replacing d_i by $\mathsf{E}[d_i]$, which denotes (1 − Pr[censoring]).

$$\mathcal{EL}(\mathbf{\Lambda}) = \sum_{i=1}^{n}[\mathsf{E}[d_i]\ln(h(y_i, \mathbf{\Lambda})) + (1 - \mathsf{E}[d_i])\ln(1 - H(c-1, \mathbf{\Lambda})].$$

The expected likelihood is a weighted sum of pdf and cdf with censoring probability as the weight. In the EM algorithm the estimates are obtained iteratively by replacing d_i by their expectations and then maximizing the expected likelihood with respect to $\mathbf{\Lambda}$. Given $\mathbf{\Lambda}$, the expected value of d_i, or the probability of censoring, can be recomputed. The expected likelihood is then defined using this new value and another estimate of $\mathbf{\Lambda}$ obtained. This iterative algorithm is the well-known EM method, which has been used in other contexts, for example in estimation of the Tobit model. Gradient methods may be computationally more efficient. Maximum likelihood estimation of censored count models raises issues similar to those in Tobit models (Terza, 1985; Gurmu, 1993).

For the right censored Poisson model the maximum likelihood estimating equation is:

$$\sum_{i=1}^{n}[d_i(y_i - \mu_i) + (1 - d_i)\delta_i]\mu_i^{-1}\frac{\partial \mu_i}{\partial \boldsymbol{\beta}} = \mathbf{0},$$

where

$$\delta_i = \mu_i \cdot h(c-1, \mu_i)/[1 - H(c-1, \mu_i)]$$

is the adjustment factor associated with the left-truncated Poisson model. Because $(y_i - \mu_i)$ is the error for the uncensored Poisson model and

$$\mathsf{E}[y_i - \mu_i \mid y_i \geq c] = \delta_i,$$

the expression, $d_i(y_i - \mu_i) + (1 - d_i)\delta_i$, given above is interpreted as the generalized error (Gourieroux et al., 1987a) for the right-censored Poisson model. The score equations imply that the vector of generalized residuals is orthogonal to the vector of exogenous variables.

4.7 Hurdle and Zero-Inflated Models

In this section we discuss modified count models that are closely related to truncated models. They also involve discrete mixtures, as against continuous mixtures that are exemplified by the Poisson–gamma. The first of these is the hurdle model and the second is the zero-inflated count (or with-zeros) model. The principle motivation for these models is that real-life data frequently display overdispersion through excess zeros. This refers to observing more zero observations than is consistent with the Poisson or another baseline model such as the mixed Poisson. The latter would in any case have a higher proportion of zeros than the parent Poisson distribution.

The hurdle model has an interpretation as a two-part model. The first part is a binary outcome model, and the second part is a truncated count model. Such a partition permits the interpretation that positive observations arise from crossing the zero hurdle or the zero threshold. The first part models the probability that the threshold is crossed. In principle, the threshold need not be at zero; it could be any value. Further, it need not be treated as known. The zero value has special appeal because in many situations it partitions the population into subpopulations in a meaningful way.

4.7.1 *With Zeros and Hurdle Models*

In some cases the dgp adds additional mass at the zero (or some other positive) value resulting in higher probability of this value than is consistent with the Poisson or some other specified distribution. This happens because zeros may arise from two sources. For instance, in response to the question, "How many times did you go fishing in the past 2 months?" zero responses would be recorded from those who never fish and from those who do but who did not do so in the past 2 months. Thus the sample is a *mixture*. It would be a misspecification to assume in this instance that the zeros and the nonzeros (positives) come from the same dgp. A hurdle specification deals with mixtures whose moments are allowed to differ from those of the parent distribution. That is,

$$\Pr[y=0] = f_1(0)$$
$$\Pr[y=j] = \frac{1-f_1(0)}{1-f_2(0)} f_2(y), \qquad j>0, \tag{4.52}$$

which collapses to the standard model only if $f_1(\cdot) = f_2(\cdot)$.

This is a modified count model in which the two processes generating the zeros and the positives are not constrained to be the same. In the context of a censored normal density (the Tobit model) the idea for a hurdle model was developed by Cragg (1971). The basic idea is that a binomial probability governs the binary outcome of whether a count variate has a zero or a positive realization. If the realization is positive, the "hurdle is crossed," and the conditional distribution of the positives is governed by a truncated-at-zero count data model. Mullahy (1986) provided the general form of hurdle count regression models, together with applications to daily consumption of various beverages. The hurdle model is the dual of the split-population survival time model (Schmidt and Witte, 1989), in which the probability of an eventual death and the timing of death depend separately on individual characteristics.

The hurdle model is a finite mixture generated by combining the zeros generated by one density with the zeros and positives generated by a second zero-truncated density. Hence, the moments of the hurdle model are determined by the probability of crossing the threshold, and by the moments of the zero-truncated density. That is,

$$\mathsf{E}[y \mid \mathbf{x}] = \Pr[y>0 \mid \mathbf{x}]\mathsf{E}_{y>0}[y \mid y>0, \mathbf{x}], \tag{4.53}$$

where the second expectation is taken relative to the zero-truncated density. The variance can be shown to be

$$\mathsf{V}[y \mid \mathbf{x}] = \Pr[y>0 \mid \mathbf{x}]\mathsf{V}_{y>0}[y \mid y>0, \mathbf{x}]$$
$$+ \Pr[y=0 \mid \mathbf{x}]\mathsf{E}_{y>0}[y \mid y>0 \mid \mathbf{x}]. \tag{4.54}$$

The full model with the zeros and the positives is then used to identify the parameters of both densities. Finite mixtures considered elsewhere, by contrast, combine both zeros and positives from two or more densities.

Consider the hurdle version of the NB2 model. Let $\mu_{1i} = \exp(\mathbf{x}_i'\boldsymbol{\beta}_1)$ be the NB2 mean parameter for the case of zero counts. Similarly, let $\mu_{2i} = \mu_2(\mathbf{x}_i'\boldsymbol{\beta}_2)$ for the positive set $\mathsf{J} = \{1, 2, \ldots\}$. Further define the indicator function $1[\, y_i \in \mathsf{J}] = 1$ if $y_i \in \mathsf{J}$ and $1[\, y_i \in \mathsf{J}] = 0$ if $y_i = 0$. From the NB distribution with a quadratic variance function, the following probabilities can be obtained:

$$\Pr[y_i = 0 \mid \mathbf{x}_i] = (1+\alpha_1\mu_{1i})^{-1/\alpha_1}; \tag{4.55}$$

$$1 - \Pr[y_i = 0 \mid \mathbf{x}_i] = \sum_{y_i \in \mathsf{J}} h(y_i \mid \mathbf{x}_i) = 1 - (1+\alpha_1\mu_{1i})^{-1/\alpha_1}; \tag{4.56}$$

$$\Pr[y_i \mid \mathbf{x}_i, y_i > 0] = \frac{\Gamma(y_i + \alpha_2^{-1})}{\Gamma(\alpha_2^{-1})\Gamma(y_i + 1)} \left(\frac{1}{(1 + \alpha_2 \mu_{2i})^{1/\alpha_2} - 1} \right)^{-\alpha_2^{-1}} \times \left(\frac{\mu_{2i}}{\mu_{2i} + \alpha_2^{-1}} \right)^{y_i}. \tag{4.57}$$

The equation in (4.55) gives the probability of zero counts, while (4.56) is the probability that the threshold is crossed. Equation (4.57) is the truncated-at-zero NB2 distribution. The log-likelihood function for the observations splits into two components, thus:

$$\mathcal{L}_1(\beta_1, \alpha_1) = \sum_{i=1}^{n} [(1 - 1[y_i \in \mathrm{J}]) \ln \Pr[y_i = 0 \mid \mathbf{x}_i]] + \sum_{i=1}^{n} 1[y_i \in \mathrm{J}] \ln(1 - \Pr[y_i = 0 \mid \mathbf{x}_i]),$$

and

$$\begin{aligned} \mathcal{L}_2(\beta_2, \alpha_2) &= \sum_{i=1}^{n} 1[y_i \in \mathrm{J}] \ \ln[\Pr y_i \mid \mathbf{x}_i, y_i > 0] \\ \mathcal{L}(\beta_1, \beta_2, \alpha_1, \alpha_2) &= \mathcal{L}_1(\beta_1, \alpha_1) + \mathcal{L}_2(\beta_2, \alpha_2). \end{aligned} \tag{4.58}$$

Here $\mathcal{L}_1(\beta_1, \alpha_1)$ is the log-likelihood for the binary process that splits the observations into zeros and positives, and $\mathcal{L}_2(\beta_2, \alpha_2)$ is the likelihood function for the truncated negative binomial part for the positives. Because the two mechanisms are assumed (functionally) independent, the joint likelihood is maximized by separately maximizing each component. Practically this means that the hurdle model can be estimated using software that may not explicitly include the hurdles option. The Poisson hurdle and the geometric hurdle models examined in Mullahy (1986) can be obtained from (4.55) through (4.57) by setting $\alpha_1 = \alpha_2 = 0$ and $\alpha_1 = \alpha_2 = 1$, respectively. Note that when $\alpha_1 = 1$, $\Pr[y_i = 0 \mid \mathbf{x}_i] = (1 + \mu_{1i})^{-1}$, so that if $\mu_{1i} = \exp(\mathbf{x}_{1i}'\beta_1)$, the binary process model is a logit model.

4.7.2 *Zero-Inflated Counts*

Zero-inflated count models provide another way to model excess zeros. Consider the following:

$$\begin{aligned} \Pr[y_i = 0] &= \varphi_i + (1 - \varphi_i) e^{-\mu_i}, \\ \Pr[y_i = r] &= (1 - \varphi_i) \frac{e^{-\mu_i} \mu_i^r}{r!}, \qquad r = 1, 2, \ldots. \end{aligned} \tag{4.59}$$

This distribution can also be interpreted as a finite mixture with a degenerate distribution whose mass is concentrated at zero (see the next section). In (4.59) the proportion of zeros, φ_i, is added to the $\mathsf{P}[\mu_i]$ distribution, and other frequencies are reduced by a corresponding amount. One possible justification for this is the case of misrecorded observations, where the misrecording is concentrated exclusively in the zero class. The proportion φ_i may be further parameterized by a (logistic) transformation of $\mathbf{z}_i\gamma$. The objective is to estimate (β, γ). Assume identifiability. Because

$$\begin{aligned} \mathsf{V}[y_i] &= (1-\varphi_i)\left(\mu_i + \varphi_i\mu_i^2\right) \\ &> \mu_i(1-\varphi_i) = \mathsf{E}[y_i], \end{aligned}$$

excess zeros imply overdispersion.

Lambert (1992) introduced the zero-inflated Poisson (ZIP) model in which $\mu_i = \mu(\mathbf{x}_i, \beta)$ and the probability φ_i is parameterized as a logistic function of the observable vector of covariates $\mathbf{z}_i$, thereby ensuring nonnegativity of φ_i; that is,

$$\begin{aligned} y_i &= 0 \qquad \text{with probability } \varphi_i \\ y_i &\sim \mathsf{P}[\mu_i] \qquad \text{with probability } (1-\varphi_i) \\ \varphi_i &= \frac{\exp\left(\mathbf{z}_i'\gamma\right)}{1+\exp\left(\mathbf{z}_i'\gamma\right)}. \end{aligned} \tag{4.60}$$

Although the logistic functional form is convenient, generalizations of the logistic such as Prentice's F distribution (Stukel, 1988) may also be used. Identifiability of any additional parameters thereby introduced should be verified.

Let $1(y_i = 0)$ denote an indicator variable that takes value 1 if $y_i = 0$, and zero otherwise. The joint likelihood function after omitting constants is given by

$$\begin{aligned} \mathcal{L}(\beta,\gamma) &= \sum_{i=1}^{n} 1(y_i = 0)\ln\left(\exp(\mathbf{z}_i'\gamma) + \exp\left(-\exp(\mathbf{x}_i'\beta)\right)\right) \\ &\quad + \sum_{i=1}^{n}(1 - 1(y_i = 0))\left(y_i\mathbf{x}_i'\beta - \exp(\mathbf{x}_i'\beta)\right) \\ &\quad - \sum_{i=1}^{n}\ln\left(1 + \exp(\mathbf{z}_i'\gamma)\right). \end{aligned}$$

Lambert suggested using the EM algorithm to maximize the likelihood. As in the censored regression case, this uses expected likelihood formulation. If the indicator variables are replaced by their expected values, the expected likelihood function is obtained. The expected value may be treated as a parameter and replaced by an estimate if an initial estimate of γ is available. The expected likelihood function, $\mathcal{EL}(\beta, \gamma)$, may then be maximized for the unknown parameters β. Given the functional independence of the μ_i and φ_i components, the joint likelihood can be maximized by the EM algorithm (Lambert, 1992); in practice, convergence is also fairly rapid even if the Newton-Raphson algorithm is used. The model can be extended to the negative binomial case. Further, the logistic specification may be replaced by $\varphi_i = F(\mathbf{z}_i'\gamma)$ where $F(\cdot)$ is any valid cdf. This latter approach works most satisfactorily if the correlation between the $\mathbf{x}$ and $\mathbf{z}$ variables is small. In practice, variables that enter φ function may also determine μ, making it harder to identify their individual roles.

Both the hurdles and ZIP models allow for two sources of overdispersion. One of these allows for extra (or too few) zeros; the second allows for overdispersion induced by individual heterogeneity in the positive set. The hurdle model can also explain too few zeros. For example, the hurdle Poisson explains too few if $\mu_1 > \mu_2$ (then $e^{-\mu_1} < e^{-\mu_2}$). The with-zeros model cannot, although it can if we change from $0 \leq \varphi \leq 1$ to $-f(0)/(1 - f(0)) \leq \varphi \leq 1$. The increased generality comes at the cost of a more heavily parameterized model, some of whose parameters can be subject to difficulties of identification. Consequently in maximum likelihood estimation convergence may be slow.

4.7.3 *Example: Hurdles and Two-Part Decisionmaking*

In a recent application, Pohlmeier and Ulrich (1995) develop a count model of the two-part decisionmaking process in the demand for health care in West Germany. Cross-section data from the West German Socioeconomic Panel are used to estimate the model. The model postulates that "while at the first stage it is the patient who determines whether to visit the physician (contact analysis), it is essentially up to the physician to determine the intensity of the treatment (frequency analysis)" (Pohlmeier and Ulrich, 1995, p. 340). Thus the analysis is in the principal–agent framework in which the physician (the agent) determines utilization on behalf of the patient (the principal). This contrasts with the approach in which the demand for health care is determined primarily by the patient.

Pohlmeier and Ulrich estimate an NB1 hurdle model, a generalization of Mullahy (1986), in which the first step is the binary outcome model of the contact decision, which separates the full sample (5096) into those who had zero demand for physician and specialist consultations during the period under study, and the second stage, which estimates the left- (zero-) truncated negative binomial model for those who had at least one physician (or specialist) consultation (2125 or 1640). The authors point out that, under the then-prevalent system in West Germany, the insured individual was required to initiate the demand for covered services by first obtaining a sickness voucher from the sickness fund each quarter. The demand for specialist services was based on a referral from a general practitioner to the specialist. The authors argue that such an institutional set-up supports a hurdles-type model, which allows contacts and frequency to be determined independently.

The authors test the Poisson hurdle and NB1 against the Poisson and reject the latter. Then the first two models are tested against a less restrictive NB1 hurdle model, which is preferred to all restrictive alternatives using Wald and

Hausman specification tests. The authors report "important differences between the two-part decisionmaking stages"; for example, the physician-density variable, which reflects accessibility to service, has no significant impact on the contact decision but has a significant positive impact on the frequency decision in the general practitioner and the specialist equations. However, with more than 20 coefficients in each of the two parts of the model, the NB1 hurdle model could lead to overparameterization.

4.8 Finite Mixtures and Latent Class Analysis

A zero-inflated count model is a special case of a finite mixture model considered in this section. The formal definition of a finite mixture is given in section 4.2.3. The latter formulation is more general because it allows mixing with respect to both zeros and positives, whereas the zero-inflated model only permits mixing with respect to zeros. The assumption that mixing takes place with respect to zeros only is relatively more attractive if the population can be realistically divided into two components. Members of one subpopulation are "never at risk" and hence never experience a positive number of events. Those of the second are "at risk" and may experience a positive number of events.

4.8.1 *Finite Mixtures*

In a finite mixture model a random variable is postulated as a draw from a superpopulation that is an additive mixture of C distinct populations in proportions $\pi_1, \ldots, \pi_C$, where $\sum_{j=1}^{C} \pi_j = 1,\ \pi_j \geq 0\,(j = 1, \ldots, C)$. The mixture density is given by

$$f(y_i \mid \Theta) = \sum_{j=1}^{C-1} \pi_j f_j(y_i \mid \boldsymbol{\theta}_j) + \pi_C f_C(y_i \mid \boldsymbol{\theta}_C), \tag{4.61}$$

where each term in the sum on the right-hand side is the product of mixing probability π_j and the component (subpopulation) density $f_j(y_i \mid \boldsymbol{\theta}_j)$. In general the π_j are unknown and hence to be estimated along with all other parameters, denoted $\boldsymbol{\Theta}$. Also $\pi_C = (1 - \sum_{j=1}^{C-1} \pi_j)$. For identifiability, we use the labeling restriction that $\pi_1 \geq \pi_2 \geq \ldots \geq \pi_C$, which can always be satisfied by rearrangement postestimation. This model has a long history in statistics; see McLachlan and Basford (1988), Titterington, Smith, and Makov (1985), Everitt and Hand (1981). To date, univariate formulations have been more popular. The identification and estimation of the model is complex (Lindsay, 1995).

The parameter π_j may be further parameterized using, for example, the logit function. Thus $\pi_j = \exp(\lambda_j)/(1+\exp(\lambda_j))$ and λ_j in turn may be parameterized in terms of further observable covariates.

Although in principle the component distributions may be different parametric families, in practice it is usual to restrict them to be the same. Despite this, the finite mixture class offers a flexible way of specifying mixtures. There are a number of advantages of using a discrete rather than a continuous mixing distribution. The finite mixture representation provides a natural and intuitively attractive representation of heterogeneity in a finite, usually small, number of latent classes, each of which may be regarded as a "type," or a "group." The choice of the number of components in the mixture determines the number of "types," but the choice of the functional form for the density can accommodate heterogeneity within each component. A finite mixture characterization is attractive if the mixture components have a natural interpretation. However, this is not essential. A finite mixture may be simply a way of flexibly and parsimoniously modeling the data, with each mixture component providing a local approximation in some part of the true distribution. As such the approach is an alternative to nonparametric estimation.

Second, the finite mixture approach is semiparametric: It does not require any distributional assumptions for the mixing variable. Third, the results of Laird (1978) and Heckman and Singer (1984) suggest that estimates of such finite mixture models may provide good numerical approximations even if the underlying mixing distribution is continuous. Finally, the choice of a continuous mixing density for some parametric count models is sometimes restrictive and computationally intractable except if the conditional (kernel) and mixing densities are from conjugate families, because otherwise the marginal density does not have a closed form. By contrast, there are several promising approaches available for estimating finite mixture models (Böhning, 1995).

Some special cases are of interest; for example, the random intercept model in which the jth component of the density has intercept parameter θ_j and the slope parameters are restricted to be equal. That is, subpopulations are assumed to differ randomly only with respect to their location parameter. This is sometimes referred to as a "semiparametric" representation of unobserved heterogeneity because a parametric assumption about the distribution of the error term is avoided, by assuming that individuals fall randomly into C categories with probabilities $\pi_1, \pi_2, \ldots, (1-\sum_{i=1}^{C-1} \pi_i)$. The more general model allows for full heterogeneity by permitting all parameters in the C components to differ. This case is sometimes referred to as a mixture with random effects in the intercept and the slope parameters (Wedel, Desarbo, Bult, and Ramaswamy, 1993).

Finite mixtures of some standard univariate count models are discussed in Titterington et al. (1985). The finite mixture model is somewhat different from the heterogeneous Poisson model because it changes the conditional mean specification of the model, not just the variance function for a given mean. Its relevance in the present context arises from practical difficulties of distinguishing between alternative mixtures. If, however, the observed distribution is strongly multimodal, there may be a good case for a finite mixture model. Denote by $\mathsf{P}[\mu]$ the Poisson distribution with parameter μ. Figure 4.3 shows two bimodal univariate mixtures $.75\mathsf{P}[5] + .25\mathsf{P}[1]$ and $.5\mathsf{P}[10] + .5\mathsf{P}[1]$. Both are bimodal to an extent that depends on the closeness of the component means.

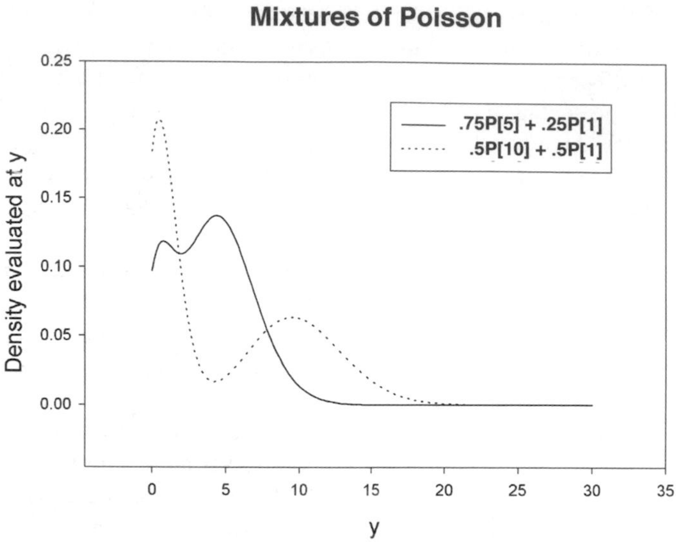

Figure 4.3. Two univariate two-component mixtures of Poisson.

The uncentered ("raw") moments of a finite mixture distribution may be derived using the general formula

$$\mu'_r(y) = \mathsf{E}[y^r] = \sum_{j=1}^{C} \pi_j \mu'_r[y \mid f_j(y)], \tag{4.62}$$

where μ'_r denotes the rth uncentered moment and $f_j(y)$ denotes the jth component (Johnson, Kotz, and Kemp, 1992). The central moments of the mixture can then be derived using standard relations between the raw and central moments.

4.8.2 *Nonparametric Maximum Likelihood*

Let $\mathsf{L}(\pi, \Theta, C \mid \mathbf{y})$ denote the likelihood based on (4.61) with C distinct parametrically specified components. The probability distribution $f(y_i \mid \hat{\Theta}; \hat{C})$ that maximizes $\mathcal{L}(\pi, \Theta, C \mid \mathbf{y})$ is called the *semiparametric maximum likelihood estimator*. Lindsay (1995) has discussed its properties. In some cases C may be given. Then the problem is to maximize $\mathcal{L}(\pi, \Theta \mid C, \mathbf{y})$. It is easier to handle estimation by maximizing log-likelihood for a selection of values of C and then using model selection criteria to choose among estimated models.

4.8.3 *Latent Class Analysis*

The finite mixture model is related to latent class analysis (Aitkin and Rubin, 1985, Wedel et al., 1993). In practice the number of latent components has to be estimated, but initially we assume that the number of components in the mixture, C, is given. Let $\mathbf{d}_i = (d_{i1}, \ldots, d_{iC})$ define an indicator (dummy) variable such that $d_{ij} = 1; \sum_j d_{ij} = 1$, indicating that y_i was drawn from the jth (latent) group or class for $i = 1, \ldots, n$. That is, each observation may be regarded as a draw from one of the C latent classes or "types," each with its own distribution. The finite mixture model specifies that $(y_i \mid \mathbf{d}_i, \boldsymbol{\theta}, \boldsymbol{\pi})$ are independently distributed with densities

$$\sum_{j=1}^{C} d_{ij} f(y_i \mid \boldsymbol{\theta}_j) = \prod_{i=1}^{C} f(y_i \mid \boldsymbol{\theta}_j)^{d_{ij}},$$

and $(d_{ij} \mid \boldsymbol{\theta}, \boldsymbol{\pi})$ are iid with multinomial distribution

$$\prod_{j=1j}^{C} \pi_j^{d_{ij}}, \qquad 0 < \pi_j < 1, \qquad \sum_{j=1}^{C} \pi_j = 1.$$

The last two relations imply that

$$(y_i \mid \boldsymbol{\theta}, \boldsymbol{\pi}) \overset{\text{iid}}{\sim} \sum_{j=1}^{C} \pi_j^{d_{ij}} f_j(y; \boldsymbol{\theta}_j), \qquad 0 < \pi_j < 1, \qquad \sum_{j=1}^{C} \pi_j = 1,$$

where $\boldsymbol{\pi}' = [\pi_1, \ldots, \pi_C]$ and $\boldsymbol{\theta} = [\boldsymbol{\theta}_1, \ldots, \boldsymbol{\theta}_C]$. Hence the likelihood function is

$$\mathsf{L}(\boldsymbol{\theta}, \boldsymbol{\pi} \mid \mathbf{y}) = \prod_{i=1}^{n} \sum_{j=1}^{C} \pi_j^{d_{ij}} [f_j(\mathbf{y}; \boldsymbol{\theta}_j)]^{d_{ij}}, \quad 0 < \pi_j < 1, \quad \sum_{j=1}^{C} \pi_j = 1. \tag{4.63}$$

If π_j, $j = 1, \ldots, C$, is given, the posterior probability that observation y_i belongs to the population j, $j = 1, 2, \ldots, C$, denoted z_{ij}, is given by

$$z_{ij} \equiv \Pr[y_i \in \text{ population } j] = \frac{\pi_j f_j(y_i \mid \mathbf{x}_i', \boldsymbol{\theta}_j)}{\sum_{j=1}^{C} \pi_j f_j(y_i \mid \mathbf{x}_i', \boldsymbol{\theta}_j)}. \tag{4.64}$$

The average value of z_{ij} over i is the probability that a randomly chosen individual belongs to subpopulation j. This equals π_j:

$$\mathsf{E}[z_{ij}] = \pi_j.$$

4.8.4 *Estimation*

A widely recommended procedure for estimating the finite mixture model is the EM procedure, which is structured as follows. Given an initial estimate $[\boldsymbol{\pi}^{(0)}, \boldsymbol{\theta}^{(0)}]$, the likelihood function (4.63) may be maximized directly or using the EM algorithm in which the variables d_{ij} are treated as missing data. If the d_{ij} were observable the log-likelihood of the model would be

$$\mathcal{L}(\pi, \Theta \mid \mathbf{y}) = \sum_{i=1}^{n}\sum_{j=1}^{C} d_{ij}[\ln f_j(y_i; \boldsymbol{\theta}_j) + \ln \pi_j]. \tag{4.65}$$

Replacing d_{ij} by its expected value, $\mathsf{E}[d_{ij}]$, yields the expected log-likelihood,

$$\mathcal{EL}(\Theta \mid \mathbf{y}, \pi) = \sum_{i=1}^{n}\sum_{j=1}^{C} \hat{z}_{ij}[\ln f_j(y_i; \boldsymbol{\theta}_j) + \ln \pi_j], \tag{4.66}$$

where

$$\mathsf{E}[d_{ij}] = \hat{z}_{ij}.$$

The M step of the EM procedure maximizes (4.66) by solving the first-order conditions

$$\hat{\pi}_j - \frac{\sum_{i=1}^{n} \hat{z}_{ij}}{n} = 0, \qquad j = 1, .., C \tag{4.67}$$

$$\sum_{i=1}^{n}\sum_{j=1}^{C} \hat{z}_{ij} \frac{\partial \ln f_j(y_i; \boldsymbol{\theta}_j)}{\partial \boldsymbol{\theta}_j} = \mathbf{0}. \tag{4.68}$$

The marginal probability that an observation comes from the subpopulation j is the average of all individual observation probabilities of coming from the jth population. The E step of the EM procedure obtains new values of $\mathsf{E}[d_{ij}]$ using (4.64).

The EM algorithm may be slow to converge, especially if the starting values are not good. Other approaches such as the Newton-Raphson or Broyden-Fletcher-Goldfarb-Shanno may also be worth considering. A discussion of reliable algorithms is in Böhning (1995). The applications reported in Chapter 6 use Newton-Raphson with numerically estimated gradients.

For C given, the covariance matrix of estimated parameters is obtained by specializing the results in section 2.3.2. Alternative estimators for the variance, including the sandwich and robust sandwich estimators, are also available. However, these should be used with caution, especially if C is likely to be misspecified. Treating C as known, if in fact it is not, means that the estimated variances are conditional quantities.

4.8.5 *Inference on C*

The preceding account has not dealt with the choice of the parameter C. Two approaches have been widely considered in the literature. The first is to use likelihood ratio to test $C = C^*$ versus $C = C^* + 1$. This is equivalent to the test of $H_0 : \pi_{C^*+1} = 0$ versus $H_1 : \pi_{C^*+1} \neq 0$. Unfortunately, the likelihood ratio test statistic in this case does not have the standard chi-squared distribution because the regularity conditions for likelihood-based inference are violated.

For example, let $C = 2$. We wish to test

$$H_0 : f(y_i \mid \Theta) = \mathsf{P}[\theta_1]$$

against

$$H_1 : f(y_i \mid \Theta) = (1 - \pi)\,\mathsf{P}[\theta_1] + \pi\,\mathsf{P}[\theta_2].$$

where $\Theta = (\pi, \theta_1, \theta_2) \in [0, 1] \times (0, \infty) \times (0, \infty)$, where $\theta_1 \not< \theta_2$. The null holds if either $\pi = 0$ or $\theta_1 = \theta_2$. That is, the parameter space where H_0 holds is

$$\Theta_0 = (\pi, \theta) = [0] \times (0, \infty) \times (0, \infty) \cup [0, 1] \times (0, \infty),$$

where $\theta_1 = \theta_2 = \theta$. This is the entire θ space if $\pi = 0$, and the line segment $[0, 1]$ if $\theta_1 = \theta_2$. Under the null hypothesis the parameter π is not identifiable because it is on the boundary of the parameter space. The standard assumption for likelihood-based testing assumes regularity conditions stated in section 2.3. This includes the condition that Θ is in the interior of parameter space. Hence, the standard asymptotic distribution theory does not apply. Specifically, the likelihood ratio test statistic does not have the chi-squared distribution under the null. Hence, the standard critical values are inappropriate. One solution to this problem is to use a parametric bootstrap to obtain the critical values (Feng and McCulloch, 1996; see also section 6.4). This computer-intensive technique has not been widely used in the Poisson regression context.

A second, simpler approach is to first fix the largest value of C one is prepared to accept. Often this is a small number like 2, 3, or 4. The model is estimated for all values of $C \leq C^*$. Information criteria are used to select C (see Chapter 5). Chapter 6 contains examples and further discussion.

In an unconstrained model, adding additional components can easily lead to overparameterization in two senses. The total number of parameters may be large. Then the number of components may also be too large relative to the information in the data. Because the problem is akin to classification into "types," doing so reliably requires that interindividual differences are large in the relevant sense. In the case of a constrained mixture, such as the random intercept model, the resulting increase in the number of parameters is small, but in the unconstrained model in which all parameters are allowed to vary, the total number of parameters can be quite large (see Chapter 6 for an example).

If the model is overparameterized, one can expect difficulties in estimation due to flat log-likelihood. This problem is further compounded by the possible multimodality of the mixture likelihood. Thus it is possible for an estimation algorithm to converge to a local rather than a global maximum. In practical applications of finite mixtures, therefore, it is important to test for the presence of mixture components. If the evidence for mixture is weak, identification is a problem. It is also important to test whether a global maximum of the likelihood is attained. These important issues are reconsidered in Chapter 6.

4.9 Estimation by Simulation

The specific parametric models of heterogeneity considered in this chapter have the convenient feature that they generate a closed-form marginal distribution, which then forms the basis of the likelihood. Such an outcome is somewhat artificially generated. In many otherwise appealing models a closed-form marginal density may not be generated. It is still possible to estimate the parameters of the mixture distribution using computer-intensive methods such as *simulated maximum likelihood* or *simulated method of moments* (Gourieroux and Monfort, 1997). The approach is illustrated using a Poisson–normal mixture.

Consider the Poisson model with normally distributed multiplicative heterogeneity term

$$y_i \mid \mu_i, \nu_i \sim \mathsf{P}\left[y_i \mid \exp\left(\mathbf{x}_i'\boldsymbol{\beta} + \sigma\nu_i\right)\right],$$
$$\nu_i \sim \mathsf{N}[0, 1].$$

The marginal distribution is

$$\begin{aligned} h(y_i \mid \mu_i) &= \mathsf{E}_\nu\left[f\left[y_i \mid \exp\left(\mathbf{x}_i'\boldsymbol{\beta} + \sigma\nu_i\right)\right]\right] \\ &= \int_{-\infty}^{\infty} f\left[y_i \mid \exp\left(\mathbf{x}_i'\boldsymbol{\beta} + \sigma\nu_i\right)\right]\phi(\nu_i)\, d\nu_i \\ &= \int_{-\infty}^{\infty} \frac{1}{y_i!} \exp\left(-\exp\left[\mathbf{x}_i'\boldsymbol{\beta} + \sigma\nu_i\right]\right) \\ &\quad \times \exp\left[\left(\mathbf{x}_i'\boldsymbol{\beta} + \sigma\nu_i\right)^{y_i}\right] \frac{1}{\sqrt{2\pi}} e^{-\nu^2/2}\, d\nu_i, \end{aligned} \tag{4.69}$$

where the third line follows because $\phi(\nu)$ is the standard normal density. There is no closed-form solution for $h(y_i \mid \mu_i)$, unlike for the gamma heterogeneity term considered in section 4.2.

An alternative approach is to use simulation. Because the marginal distribution is a mathematical expectation, the expression can be approximated by replacing the n-element vector $\boldsymbol{\nu}$ by draws from the $\mathsf{N}[0, 1]$ distribution. Then

$$h(y_i \mid \mu_i) \approx \frac{1}{S} \sum_{s=1}^{S} f\left[y_i \mid \exp\left(\mathbf{x}_i'\boldsymbol{\beta} + \sigma\nu_i^{(s)}\right)\right]. \tag{4.70}$$

This method is also called *Monte Carlo integration*. The simulated likelihood function can be built up using n terms like that above. To intuitively understand the procedure note that if the heterogenenity term were observable then the likelihood could be constructed directly. In the absence of such information, we use S draws from a pseudorandom number generator to approximate the term. Simulated maximum likelihood estimates are obtained by maximizing the log-likelihood function

$$\mathcal{L}(\beta, \sigma) = \sum_{i=1}^{n} \ln \frac{1}{S} \sum_{s=1}^{S} f\left[y_i \mid \exp\left(\mathbf{x}_i'\beta + \sigma v_i^{(s)}\right)\right]. \tag{4.71}$$

It is known that if S is held fixed while $n \to \infty$, the resulting estimator of (β, σ) is biased (McFadden and Ruud, 1994; Gourieroux and Monfort, 1997) However, if S and n tend to infinity in such a way that $\sqrt{S}/n \to 0$, the estimator is both consistent and asymptotically efficient. An active area of research, for problems in which it is computationally burdensome to let S go to infinity, is to incorporate a bias correction in the expression for the density and then build the likelihood from it. For relatively simple problems such as this example, however, there is no need to do this, as there is no practical problem in using a very high value of S.

An alternative estimation procedure may be based on numerical integration. Here the integration is replaced by an H-point Gaussian quadrature with quadrature points (nodes) v_h and weights w_h,

$$h(y_i \mid \mu_i) \approx \frac{1}{\sqrt{\pi}} \sum_{h=1}^{H} w_h[f[y_i \mid \mu_i, v_h]].$$

This approach was used by Hinde (1982) for Poisson-normal model. The table of weights for Gaussian quadrature can be found in Stroud and Secrest (1966).

The simulation approach is flexible and potentially very useful in the context of truncated or censored models with unobserved heterogeneity and also structural models. An example is given in Chapter 11. The simulation approach is now also widely used in Bayesian analyses of posterior distributions that may not possess a closed form.

4.10 Derivations

We sketch a proof of the Two Crossings Theorem, following Shaked (1980). For simplicity, we consider only a one-parameter exponential family, which covers distributions other than the Poisson, which is of main interest here.

For the random variable y, $y \in \mathcal{R}_y$, let

$$f(y; \theta) = \exp\{a(\theta) + c(\theta)y\}$$

denote the density. We consider mixing with respect to θ, $\theta \in \mathcal{R}_\theta$, given $\pi(\theta)$, a nondegenerate distribution with mean

$$\mu = \int_{R_\theta} \theta\pi(\theta)\, d\theta.$$

The mixture density,

$$h(y) = \int_{R_\theta} \exp\{a(\theta) + c(\theta)y\}\pi(\theta)\, d\theta,$$

is approximated by

$$f(y) \equiv f(y \mid \mu) = \exp\{a(\mu) + c(\mu)y\},$$

obtained by replacing θ by its mean μ in $f(y;\theta)$. The Two Crossings Theorem studies the sign pattern of $h(y) - f(y)$, assuming that the parent and the mixture distributions have the same mean; that is,

$$\int y f(y \mid \mu)\, dy = \int y h(y)\, dy. \tag{4.72}$$

Let $S^-(h - f)$ denote the number of sign changes in $h - y$ over the set $\mathcal{R}(y)$. The number of sign changes of $h - f$ is the same as the number of sign changes of the function

$$\begin{aligned} r(y) &= \frac{h(y)}{f(y)} - 1 \\ &= \int_{R(\theta)} \exp\{(a(\theta) - a(\mu)) + (c(\theta) - c(\mu))y\}\pi(\theta)\, d\theta - 1. \end{aligned}$$

Because $r(y)$ is convex on the set $\mathcal{R}_y$ it is implied that $S^-(h - f) \leq 2$. Obviously $S^-(h - f) \neq 0$. To show that $S^-(h - f) \neq 1$, assume, on the contrary that $S^-(h - f) = 1$. If the sign sequence is $\{+, -\}$ then the cdf $H(y) = \int h(y)\, dy$ and $F(y) = \int f(y)\, dy$ satisfy

$$F(y) \geq H(y)$$

for all y. This result, together with $h \neq f$, implies

$$\int y h(y)\, dy < \int y f(y)\, dy,$$

which contradicts the assumption of equal means, (4.72). Similarly if the sequence is $\{-, +\}$, (4.72) is also contradicted. Thus $S^-(h - f) \neq 1$ and hence $S^-(h - f) = 2$. The sign sequence $\{+, -, +\}$ follows from the convexity of $r(y)$.

4.11 Bibliographic Notes

Feller (1971) is a classic reference for several topics discussed in this chapter. Cox processes are concisely discussed in Kingman (1993, pp. 65–72). A recent accessible discussion of the Two Crossings Theorem of Shaked (1980) is by Mullahy (1997b). Shaked's analysis applies to a one-parameter exponential family. The two-crossings result is extended by Gelfand and Dalal (1990, p. 57) to a two-parameter exponential family by exploiting convexity as in section 8.9.

Chapters 4 and 5 in Lancaster (1990) contain material complementary to that in sections 4.2 and 4.3. Our material in section 2.3.5 borrows heavily from Winkelmann (1995), who provides a useful discussion of dependence and dispersion. Lee (1997) provides a further development and important extensions of this approach using simulated maximum likelihood to estimate the model. Gourieroux and Visser (1997) also use the duration model to define a count model; they also consider the heterogeneity distribution arising from the presence of both individual and spell-specific components.

Lucerño (1995) examines several models in which clustering leads to overdispersion. An application of truncated Poisson is Grogger and Carson (1991). See also Creel and Loomis (1990) and Brännäs (1992). The monograph by McLachlan and Basford (1988) provides a good treatment of finite mixtures, and Wedel et al. (1993) and Deb and Trivedi (1997) are econometric applications. Brännäs and Rosenqvist (1994) and Böhning (1995) have outlined the computational properties of alternative algorithms. Finite mixtures can be handled in a Bayesian framework using Markov chain Monte Carlo methods as in Robert (1996). Detailed analysis of the moment properties of truncated count regression models include Gurmu (1991), who considers the zero-truncated Poisson, and Gurmu and Trivedi (1992), who deal with left or right truncation in general and who also deal with tests of overdispersion in the truncated Poisson regression. Censored Poisson regression was analyzed in some detail by Gurmu (1993), who uses the EM algorithm. Amemiya (1985) provides a good exposition of the EM algorithm. Crepon and Duguet (1997b) apply the simulation-based estimator to a panel model. Treatment of heterogeneity based on simulation is quite general in Gourieroux and Monfort (1991). A flexible approach to count models based on series expansions is given later in Chapter 12, which also gives further references. Some background material for this is in Chapter 8.

4.12 Exercises

4.1 The Katz family of distributions is defined by the probability recursion

$$\frac{\Pr[y+1]}{\Pr[y]} = \frac{\mu + \gamma y}{1+y} \quad \text{for } y = 0, 1, \ldots, \quad \text{and} \quad \mu + \gamma y \geq 0.$$

Show that this yields overdispersed distributions for $0 < \gamma < 1$, and underdispersed distributions for $\gamma < 0$.

4.2 Using the NB2 density show that the density collapses to that of the Poisson as the variance of the mixing distribution approaches zero.

4.3 The Poisson-lognormal mixture is obtained by considering the following model in which μ is normally distributed with mean $\mathbf{x}'\boldsymbol{\beta}$ and variance 1. That is, given $y \mid \mu_\nu \sim \mathsf{P}[\mu_\nu]$, $\ln \mu_\nu = \mathbf{x}'\boldsymbol{\beta} + \sigma\nu$, $\nu \sim \mathsf{N}[0, 1]$, show that although the Poisson-lognormal mixture cannot be written in a closed form, the mean of the mixture distribution is shifted by a constant. Show that the first two moments of the marginal distribution are:

$$\mathsf{E}[y \mid \mathbf{x}] = \exp\left(\mathbf{x}'\boldsymbol{\beta} + \frac{1}{2}\sigma^2\right)$$

$$\mathsf{V}[y \mid \mathbf{x}] = \exp(2\mathbf{x}'\boldsymbol{\beta})[\exp(2\sigma^2) - \exp(\sigma^2)] + \exp\left(\mathbf{x}'\boldsymbol{\beta} + \frac{1}{2}\sigma^2\right).$$

4.4 Compare the variance function obtained in 4.3 with the quadratic variance function in the NB2 case.

4.5 (**a**) Suppose y takes values 0, 1, 2, ... with density $f(y)$ and mean μ. Find $\mathsf{E}[y \mid y > 0]$.

(**b**) Suppose y takes values 0, 1, 2, ... with hurdle density given by

$$\Pr[y=0]=f_1(0) \quad \text{and}$$
$$\Pr[y=k]=(1-f_1(0))/(1-f_2(0))f_2(0), \quad k=1,2,\ldots$$

where the density $f_2(y)$ has untruncated mean μ_2, i.e., $\sum_{k=0}^{\infty} kf(k) = \mu_2$. Find $\mathsf{E}[y]$.

(**c**) Introducing regressors, suppose the zeros are given by a logit model and positives by a Poisson model, i.e.,

$$f_1(0)=1/[1+\exp(\mathbf{x}'\boldsymbol{\beta}_1)]$$

$$f(k)=\exp[-\exp(\mathbf{x}'\boldsymbol{\beta}_2)][\exp(\mathbf{x}'\boldsymbol{\beta}_2)^k/y!], \quad k=1,2,\ldots;$$

give an expression for $\mathsf{E}[y \mid \mathbf{x}]$.

(**d**) Hence obtain an expression for $\partial\mathsf{E}[y \mid \mathbf{x}]/\partial\mathbf{x}$ for the hurdle model.

4.6 Derive the information matrix for μ and ϕ in the double-Poisson case. Show how its block-diagonal structure may be exploited in devising a computer algorithm for estimating these parameters.

4.7 Let y denote the zero-truncated Poisson-distributed random variable with density

$$f(y \mid \mu)=\mu^y e^{-\mu}/[y!(1-e^{-\mu})], \quad \mu > 0.$$

Let μ be a random variable with distribution

$$g(\mu)=c(1-e^{-\mu})e^{-\theta\mu}\mu^{\eta-1}/y!$$

where the normalizing constant $c=\Gamma(\eta)\theta^{-\eta}[1+[\theta/(1+\theta)]^{\eta}]$. Show that the marginal distribution of y is zero-truncated NB distribution. (This example is due to Boswell and Patil (1970), who emphasized that in this case the mixing distribution is not a gamma distribution.)

CHAPTER 5

Model Evaluation and Testing

5.1 Introduction

It is desirable to analyze count data using a cycle of model specification, estimation, testing, and evaluation. This cycle can go from specific to general models – for example, it can begin with Poisson and then test for negative binomial – or one can use a general to specific approach – for example, begin with negative binomial and then test the restrictions imposed by Poisson. For inclusion of regressors in a given count model either approach might be taken; for choice of the count data model itself other than simple choices such as Poisson or negative binomial the former approach is most often useful. For example, if the negative binomial model is inadequate, there is a very wide range of models that might be considered, rendering a general-to-specific approach difficult to implement.

The preceding two chapters have presented the specification and estimation components of this cycle for cross-section count data. In this chapter we focus on the testing and evaluation aspects of this cycle. This includes residual analysis, goodness-of-fit measures, and moment-based specification tests, in addition to classical statistical inference.

Residual analysis, based on a range of definitions of the residual for heteroskedastic data such as counts, is presented in section 5.2. A range of measures of goodness of fit, including pseudo R-squareds and a chi-square goodness-of-fit statistic, are presented in section 5.3. Likelihood-based hypothesis tests for overdispersion, introduced in section 3.4, are discussed more extensively in section 5.4. Small-sample corrections, including the bootstrap pairs procedure for quite general cross-section data models, are presented in section 5.5. Moment-based tests, using the conditional moment test framework, are presented in section 5.6. Discrimination among nonnested models is the subject of section 5.7. Many of the methods are illustrated using a regression model for the number of takeover bids, which is introduced in section 5.2.5.

The presentation here is in places very detailed. For the practitioner, the use of simple residuals such as Pearson residuals is well-established and can be quite informative. For overall model fit in fully parametric models, chi-square goodness-of-fit measures are straightforward to implement. In testing for overdispersion in the Poisson model, the overdispersion tests presented already in section 3.4 often are adequate. The current chapter gives a more theoretical treatment. Bootstrap methods, such as those outlined here, should be performed if more refined small-sample inference is desired. Conditional moment tests are easily implemented, but their interpretation if they are applied to count data is quite subtle due to the inherent heteroskedasticity. Finally, the standard methods for discriminating between nonnested models have been adapted to count data.

The treatment of many of these topics, as with estimation, varies according to whether we use a fully parametric maximum likelihood framework or a conditional moment approach based on specification of the first one or two moments of the dependent variable. Even within this classification results may be specialized, notably maximum likelihood methods to LEF and moment methods to GLMs. Also, most detailed analysis is restricted to cross-section data. Many of the techniques presented here have been developed only for such special cases and their generality is not always clear. There is considerable scope for generalization and application to a broader range of count data models.

5.2 Residual Analysis

Residuals measure the departure of fitted values from actual values of the dependent variable. They can be used to detect model misspecification; to detect outliers, or observations with poor fit; and to detect influential observations, or observations with a big impact on the fitted model.

Residual analysis, particularly visual analysis, can potentially indicate the nature of misspecification and ways that it may be corrected, as well as provide a feel for the magnitude of the effect of the misspecification. By contrast, formal statistical tests of model misspecification can be black boxes, producing only a single number that is then compared to a critical value. Moreover, if one tests at the same significance level (usually 5%) without regard to sample size, any model using real data will be rejected with a sufficiently large sample even if it does fit the data well.

For linear models a residual is easily defined as the difference between actual and fitted value. For nonlinear models the very definition of a residual is not unique. Several residuals have been proposed for the Poisson and other GLMs. These residuals do not always generalize in the presence of common complications, such as censored or hurdle models, for which it may be more fruitful to appeal to residuals proposed in the duration literature. We present many candidate definitions of residuals and stress that at this stage there appears to be no one single residual that can be used in all contexts.

We also give a brief treatment of detection of outliers and influential observations. This topic is less important in applications in which data sets are large and the relative importance of individual observations is small. And if data sets are small and an influential or outlying observation is detected, it is not always clear how one should proceed. Dropping the observation or adapting the model simply to better fit one observation creates concerns of data-mining and overfitting.

5.2.1 *Pearson, Deviance, and Anscombe Residuals*

The natural residual is the *raw residual*

$$r_i = (y_i - \hat{\mu}_i), \tag{5.1}$$

where the fitted mean $\hat{\mu}_i$ is the conditional mean $\mu_i = \mu(\mathbf{x}_i'\beta)$ evaluated at $\beta = \hat{\beta}$. Asymptotically this residual behaves as $(y_i - \mu_i)$, because $\hat{\beta} \xrightarrow{p} \beta$ implies $\hat{\mu}_i \xrightarrow{p} \mu_i$. For the classical linear regression model with normally distributed homoskedastic error $(y - \mu) \sim \mathsf{N}[0, \sigma^2]$, so that in large samples the raw residual has the desirable properties of being symmetrically distributed around zero with constant variance. For count data, however, $(y - \mu)$ is heteroskedastic and asymmetric. For example, if $y \sim \mathsf{P}[\mu]$ then $(y - \mu)$ has variance μ and third moment μ. So the raw residual even in large samples is heteroskedastic and asymmetric.

For count data there is no one residual that has zero mean, constant variance, and symmetric distribution. This leads to several different residuals according to which of these properties is felt to be most desirable.

The obvious correction for heteroskedasticity is the *Pearson residual*

$$p_i = \frac{(y_i - \hat{\mu}_i)}{\sqrt{\hat{\omega}_i}}, \tag{5.2}$$

where $\hat{\omega}_i$ is an estimate of the variance ω_i of y_i. The sum of the squares of these residuals is the Pearson statistic, defined in (5.16). For the Poisson, GLM, and NB2 models, respectively, one uses $\omega = \mu$, $\omega = \alpha\mu$ and $\omega = \mu + \alpha\mu^2$. In large samples this residual has zero mean and is homoskedastic (with variance unity), but it is asymmetrically distributed. For example, if y is Poisson then $\mathsf{E}[(y - \mu)^3/\sqrt{\mu}] = 1/\sqrt{\mu}$.

If y is generated by an LEF density one can use the *deviance residual*, which is

$$d_i = \text{sign}\,(y_i - \hat{\mu}_i)\sqrt{2\{l(y_i) - l(\hat{\mu}_i)\}}, \tag{5.3}$$

where $l(\hat{\mu})$ is the log-density of y evaluated at $\mu = \hat{\mu}$ and $l(y)$ is the log-density evaluated at $\mu = y$. A motivation for the deviance residual is that the sum of squares of these residuals is the deviance statistic, defined in (5.18), which is the generalization for LEF models of the sum of raw residuals in the linear model. Thus, for the normal distribution with σ^2 known, $d_i = (y_i - \mu_i)/\sigma$, the usual standardized residual. For the Poisson this residual equals

$$d_i = \text{sign}\,(y_i - \hat{\mu}_i)\sqrt{2\{y_i \ln(y_i/\hat{\mu}_i) - (y_i - \hat{\mu}_i)\}}, \tag{5.4}$$

where $y \ln y = 0$ if $y = 0$. Most other count data models are not GLMs, so this residual cannot be used. A notable exception is the NB2 model with α known. Then

$$d_i = \text{sign}(y_i - \hat{\mu}_i) \times \sqrt{2\{y_i \ln(y_i/\hat{\mu}_i) - (y_i + \alpha^{-1}) \ln((y_i + \alpha^{-1})/(\hat{\mu}_i + \alpha^{-1}))\}}. \tag{5.5}$$

The *Anscombe residual* is defined to be the transformation of y that is closest to normality, then standardized to mean zero and variance 1. This transformation has been obtained for LEF densities. If y is Poisson-distributed, the function $y^{2/3}$ is closest to normality and the Anscombe residual is

$$a_i = \frac{1.5\left(y_i^{2/3} - \mu_i^{2/3}\right)}{\mu_i^{1/6}}. \tag{5.6}$$

The Pearson, deviance, and Anscombe residuals for the Poisson can all be reexpressed as a function of y/μ alone. McCullagh and Nelder (1989, p. 39) tabulate these residuals for selected values of $c = y/\mu$. Here we present this graphically in Figure 5.1. All three residuals are zero when $y = \mu$, i.e., $c = 1$, and are increasing in y/μ. It is clear that there is very little difference between the deviance and Anscombe residuals. The Pearson residuals are scaled differently, though also increase with c, and are roughly twice as big for $c > 1$. Pierce and Schafer (1986) consider these residuals in some detail.

5.2.2 *Generalized Residuals*

Cox and Snell (1968) define a *generalized residual* to be any function

$$R_i = R_i(\mathbf{x}_i, \hat{\boldsymbol{\theta}}, y_i), \tag{5.7}$$

subject to some weak restrictions. This quite broad definition includes Pearson, deviance, and Anscombe residuals as special cases.

Many other possible residuals satisfy (5.7). For example, consider a count data model with conditional mean function $\mu(\mathbf{x}_i, \boldsymbol{\theta})$ and multiplicative error, that is, $y_i = \mu(\mathbf{x}_i, \boldsymbol{\theta})\varepsilon_i$ where $\mathsf{E}[\varepsilon_i \mid \mathbf{x}_i] = 1$. Solving for $\varepsilon_i = y_i/\mu(\mathbf{x}_i, \boldsymbol{\theta})$ suggests the residual $R_i = y_i/\mu(\mathbf{x}_i, \hat{\boldsymbol{\theta}})$. An additive error leads one instead to the raw residual $y_i - \mu(\mathbf{x}_i, \hat{\boldsymbol{\theta}})$ presented in the previous section.

Another way to motivate a generalized residual is to make comparison to least-squares first-order conditions. For single-index models with log-density $l_i = l(y_i, \eta(\mathbf{x}_i, \boldsymbol{\theta}))$ the first-order conditions are

$$\sum_{i=1}^{n} \frac{\partial \eta_i}{\partial \boldsymbol{\theta}} \frac{\partial l_i}{\partial \eta_i} = \mathbf{0}. \tag{5.8}$$

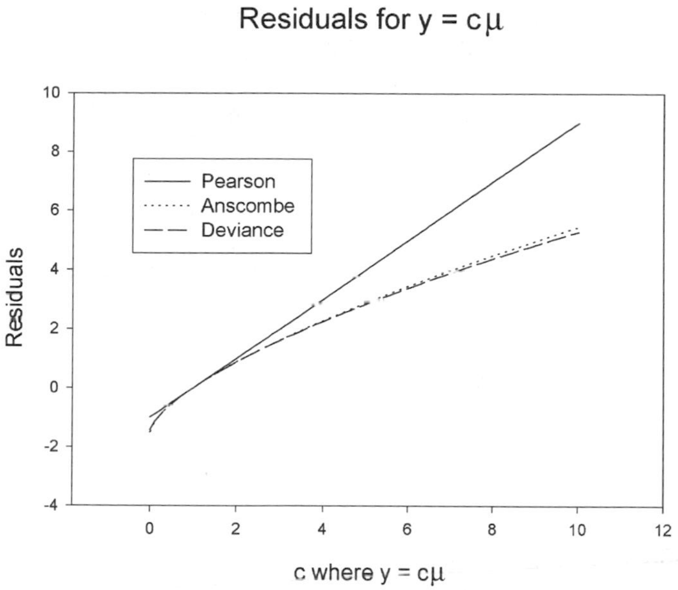

Figure 5.1. Comparison of Pearson, deviance, and Anscombe residuals.

Comparison with $\sum_{i=1}^{n} \mathbf{x}_i(y_i - \mathbf{x}_i'\boldsymbol{\beta}) = \mathbf{0}$ for the linear model suggests interpreting $\partial\eta_i/\partial\boldsymbol{\theta}$ as the regressors and using

$$R_i = \partial l_i/\partial\eta_i \tag{5.9}$$

as a generalized residual. For the Poisson model with $\eta_i = \mu_i = \mu(\mathbf{x}_i, \boldsymbol{\theta})$ this leads to the residual $(y_i - \mu_i)/\mu_i$. The Pearson residual $(y_i - \mu_i)/\sqrt{\mu_i}$ arises if R_i is standardized to have unit variance. This last result, that the Pearson residual equals $\partial l_i/\partial\eta_i/\sqrt{\mathsf{V}[\partial l_i/\partial\eta_i]}$, holds for all LEF models. More problematic is how to proceed in models more general than single-index models. For the NB2 and ordered-probit models the log-density is of the form $l_i = l(y_i, \eta(\mathbf{x}_i, \boldsymbol{\beta}), \boldsymbol{\alpha})$ and one might again use $R_i = \partial l_i/\partial\eta_i$ by considering the first-order conditions with respect to $\boldsymbol{\beta}$ only.

For regression models based on a normal latent variable several authors have proposed residuals. Chesher and Irish (1987) propose using as residual $R_i = \mathsf{E}[\varepsilon_i^* \mid y_i]$ as the residual where $\varepsilon_i^* = y_i^* - \mu_i$, y_i^* is an unobserved variable that is distributed as $\mathsf{N}[\mu_i, \sigma^2]$, and the observed variable $y_i = g(y_i^*)$. Different functions $g(\cdot)$ lead to probit, censored tobit, and grouped normal models. This approach can be applied to ordered probit (or logit) models for count data. Gourieroux, Monfort, Renault, and Trognon (1987a) generalize this approach to LEF densities. Thus, let the log of the LEF density of the latent variable be $l_i^* = l^*(y_i^*, \eta(\mathbf{x}_i, \boldsymbol{\theta}))$. If y_i^* was observed one could use $R_i^* = \partial l_i^*/\partial\eta_i$ as a generalized residual. Instead one uses $R_i = \mathsf{E}[R_i^* \mid y_i]$. An interesting result for LEF densities is that $R_i = \partial l_i/\partial\eta_i$, where l_i is the log-density of the observed variable. Thus the same residual is obtained by applying (5.9) to the latent variable model and then conditioning on observed data as is obtained by directly applying (5.9) to the observed variable.

A count application is the left-truncated Poisson model, studied by Gurmu and Trivedi (1992), whose results were summarized in section 4.5. Then $y_i^* \sim \mathsf{P}[\mu_i]$ and we observe $y_i = y_i^*$ if $y_i^* \geq r$. For the latent variable model $R_i^* = (y_i^* - \mu_i)/\mu_i$. Because $\mathsf{E}[y_i^* \mid y_i^* \geq r] = \mu_i + \delta_i$, where the correction factor δ_i is given in section 4.5.1, the residual for the observed variable is $R_i = \mathsf{E}[R_i^* \mid y_i^* \geq r] = (y_i - \mu_i - \delta_i)/\mu_i$. Alternatively, inspection of the maximum-likelihood first-order conditions given in section 4.5.2 also leads to this residual.

5.2.3 *Using Residuals*

Perhaps the most fruitful way to use residuals is by plotting residuals against other variables of interest. Such plots include residuals plotted against predicted values of the dependent variable, for example to see whether the fit is poor for small or large values of the dependent variable; against omitted regressors, to see whether there is any relationship in which case the residuals should be included; and against included regressors, to see whether regressors should enter through a different functional form than that specified.

For the first plot it is tempting to plot residuals against the actual value of the dependent variable, but such a plot is not informative for count data. To see this, consider this plot using the raw residual. Because $\mathsf{Cov}[y - \mu, y] = \mathsf{V}[y]$, which equals μ for Poisson data, there is a positive relationship between $y - \mu$ and y. Such plots are more useful for the linear regression model under classical assumptions, in which case $\mathsf{V}[y]$ is a constant and any pattern in the relationship between $y - \mu$ and y is interpreted as indicating heteroscedasticity. For counts we instead plot residuals against predicted means and note that $\mathsf{Cov}[y - \mu, \mu] = 0$. A variation is to plot the actual value of y against the predicted value. This plot is difficult to interpret, however, if the dependent variable takes only a few values.

If there is little variation in predicted means the residuals may also be lumpy due to lumpiness in y, making plots of the residuals against the fitted mean difficult to interpret. A similar problem arises in the logit and other discrete choice models. Landwehr, Pregibon, and Shoemaker (1984) propose graphical smoothing methods (see also Chesher and Irish, 1987). For the probit model based on a normal latent variable, Gourieroux, Monfort, Renault, and Trognon (1987b) propose use of simulated residuals as a way to overcome lumpiness, but this adds considerable noise. The approach could be applied to ordered probit and logit models for count data for which the underlying latent variable is discrete.

Even if the variables being plotted are not lumpy it can still be difficult to detect a relationship, and it is preferable to perform a nonparametric regression of R on x, where R denotes the residual being analyzed and x is the variable it is being plotted against. One can then plot the predictions $\hat{R}$ against x, where $\hat{R}$ is the estimate of the potentially nonlinear mean $\mathsf{E}[R \mid x]$.

There are a number of methods for such nonparametric regression. Let y_i be a dependent variable, in the preceding discussion a model residual, and x_i be a regressor, in the preceding discussion the dependent variable, fitted mean, or model regressor. We wish to estimate $\mathsf{E}[y_l \mid x_l]$, where the evaluation points x_l may or may not be actual sample values of x. The nonparametric estimator of the regression function is

$$\hat{y}_l = \hat{\mathsf{E}}[y_l \mid x_l] = \left(\sum_{i=1}^{n} w_{il} y_i\right) \Bigg/ \left(\sum_{i=1}^{n} w_{il}\right) \tag{5.10}$$

where the weights w_{il} are decreasing functions of $|x_i - x_l|$. Different methods lead to different weighting functions, with kernel and nearest-neighbors methods particularly popular. A more recent method that is easy to implement and appears to perform well is weighted local linear regression, proposed by Fan (1992).

An overall test of adequacy of a model may be to see how close the residuals are to normality. This can be done by a normal scores plot, which orders the residuals r_i from smallest to largest and plots them against the values predicted if the residuals were exactly normally distributed, that is, plot the ordered r_i against

$$rnorm_i = \bar{r} + s_r \Phi^{-1}((i - .5)/n), \tag{5.11}$$

$i = 1, \ldots, n$, where s_r is the sample standard deviation of r and Φ^{-1} is the inverse of the standard normal cdf. If the residuals are exactly normal this produces a straight line. Davison and Gigli (1989) advocate using such normal scores plots with deviance residuals to check distributional assumptions.

5.2.4 *Small Sample Corrections and Influential Observations*

The preceding motivations for the various residuals have implicitly treated $\hat{\mu}_i$ as μ_i, ignoring estimation error in $\hat{\mu}_i$. Estimation error can lead to quite different small-sample behavior between, for example, the raw residual $(y_i - \hat{\mu}_i)$ and $(y_i - \mu_i)$ just as it does in the linear regression model.

In the linear model, $\mathbf{y} = \mathbf{x}_i'\boldsymbol{\beta} + \mathbf{u}$, it is a standard result that the OLS residual vector $(\mathbf{y} - \hat{\boldsymbol{\mu}}) = (\mathbf{I} - \mathbf{H})\mathbf{u}$, where $\mathbf{H} = \mathbf{X}(\mathbf{X}'\mathbf{X})^{-1}\mathbf{X}'$. Under classic assumptions that $\mathsf{E}[\mathbf{uu}'] = \sigma^2\mathbf{I}$ it follows that $\mathsf{E}[(\mathbf{y} - \hat{\boldsymbol{\mu}})(\mathbf{y} - \hat{\boldsymbol{\mu}})'] = \sigma^2(\mathbf{I} - \mathbf{H})$. Therefore, $(y_i - \hat{\mu}_i)$ has variance $(1 - h_{ii})\sigma^2$, where h_{ii} is the ith diagonal entry of $\mathbf{H}$. For very large n, $h_{ii} \rightarrow 0$ so the OLS residual has variance σ^2 as expected. But for small n the variance may be quite different and it is best to use the standardized residual $(y_i - \hat{\mu}_i)/\sqrt{(1 - h_{ii})s^2}$.

The matrix $\mathbf{H}$ also appears in detecting influential observations. Because in the linear model $\hat{\boldsymbol{\mu}} = \hat{\mathbf{y}} = \mathbf{Hy}$, $\mathbf{H}$ is called the *hat matrix*. If h_{ii}, the ith diagonal entry in $\mathbf{H}$, is large, then the design matrix $\mathbf{X}$, which determines $\mathbf{H}$, is such that y_i has a big influence on its own prediction.

Pregibon (1981) generalized this analysis to the logit model. The logit results in turn have been extended to GLMs (see for example Williams, 1987, and McCullagh and Nelder, 1989 for a summary). For GLMs the hat matrix is

$$\mathbf{H} = \mathbf{W}^{1/2}\mathbf{X}(\mathbf{X}'\mathbf{W}\mathbf{X})^{-1}\mathbf{X}'\mathbf{W}^{1/2}, \tag{5.12}$$

where $\mathbf{W} = \mathsf{Diag}[w_i]$, a diagonal matrix with i^{th} entry w_i, and $w_i = (\partial\mu_i / \partial\mathbf{x}_i'\boldsymbol{\beta})^2/\mathsf{V}[y_i]$. For the Poisson with exponential mean function $w_i = \mu_i$, so $\mathbf{H}$ is easily calculated. As in the linear model the $n \times n$ matrix $\mathbf{H}$ is idempotent with trace equal to its rank k, the number of regressors. So the average value of h_{ii} is k/n, and values of h_{ii} in excess of $2k/n$ are viewed as having high leverage. The *studentized Pearson residual* is

$$p_i^* = p_i/\sqrt{1 - h_{ii}} \tag{5.13}$$

and the *studentized deviance residual* is

$$d_i^* = d_i/\sqrt{1 - h_{ii}}. \tag{5.14}$$

Other small-sample corrections for generalized residuals are given by Cox and Snell (1968). See also Davison and Snell (1991), who consider GLM and more general residuals.

A practical problem in implementing these methods is that $\mathbf{H}$ is of dimension $n \times n$, so that if one uses the obvious matrix commands to compute $\mathbf{H}$ the data set cannot be too large, due to the need to compute a matrix with n^2 elements. Even $n = 100$ may lead to problems in some programs that support matrix commands, and some ingenuity may be needed to calculate the diagonal entries in $\mathbf{H}$.

These asymptotic approximations are for small n. Some authors also consider so-called small-m asymptotics, which correct for not having multiple observations on y for each value of the regressors. Such corrections lead to an adjusted deviance residual that is closer to the normal distribution than the deviance residual. For the Poisson the adjusted deviance residual is

$$dadj_i = d_i + 1/(6\sqrt{\mu_i}). \tag{5.15}$$

Pierce and Schafer (1986) find that the adjusted deviance residual is closest to normality, after taking account of the discreteness by making a continuity correction that adds or subtracts 0.5 to or from y, toward the center of the distribution.

5.2.5 *Example: Takeover Bids*

Jaggia and Thosar (1993) model the number of bids received by 126 U.S. firms that were targets of tender offers during the period from 1978 through 1985 and were actually taken over within 52 weeks of the initial offer. The dependent

Table 5.1. *Takeover bids: actual frequency distribution*

Count	0	1	2	3	4	5	6	7	8	9	10
Frequency	9	63	31	12	6	1	2	1	0	0	1
Relative frequency	.071	.500	.246	.095	.048	.008	.016	.008	.001	.000	.008

Table 5.2. *Takeover bids: variable definitions and summary statistics*

Variable	Definition	Mean	Standard deviation
NUMBIDS	Number of takeover bids	1.738	1.432
LEGLREST	Equals 1 if legal defense by lawsuit	.429	.497
REALREST	Equals 1 if proposed changes in asset structure	.183	.388
FINREST	Equals 1 if proposed changes in ownership structure	.103	.305
WHITEKNT	Equals 1 if management invitation for friendly third-party bid	.595	.493
BIDPREM	Bid price divided by price 14 working days before bid	1.347	.189
INSTHOLD	Percentage of stock held by institutions	.252	.186
SIZE	Total book value of assets in billion of dollars	1.219	3.097
SIZESQ	*SIZE* squared	10.999	59.915
REGULATN	Equals 1 if chronic condition limiting activity	.270	.446

count variable is the number of bids after the initial bid (*NUMBIDS*) received by the target firm. These data are also analyzed at the end of section 5.3.4.

Data on the number of bids are given in Table 5.1. Less than 10% of the firms received zero bids, one half of the firms received exactly one bid (after the initial bid), a further one quarter received exactly two bids, and the remainder of the sample received between three and ten bids. The mean number of bids is 1.738 and the sample variance is 2.050. This is only a small amount of overdispersion $(2.050/1.738 = 1.18)$, which can be expected to disappear as regressors are added.

The variables are defined and summary statistics given in Table 5.2. Regressors can be grouped into three categories: (1) defensive actions taken by management of the target firm: *LEGLREST*, *REALREST*, *FINREST*, *WHITEKNT*; (2) firm-specific characteristics: *BIDPREM*, *INSTHOLD*, *SIZE*, *SIZESQ*; and (3) intervention by federal regulators: *REGULATN*. The defensive action variables are expected to decrease the number of bids, aside from *WHITEKNT*, which may increase bids as it is itself a bid. With greater institutional holdings it is expected that outside offers are more likely to be favorably received, which encourages more bids. As size of the firm increases there are expected to be more bids, up to a point where the firm gets so large that few others are capable of making a credible bid. This is captured by the quadratic in firm size. Regulator intervention is likely to discourage bids.

The Poisson PML estimates are given in Table 5.3, along with standard errors

Table 5.3. *Takeover bids: Poisson* PMLE *with* NB1 *standard errors and t ratios*

	Poisson PMLE		
Variable	Coefficient	Standard errors	t statistic
ONE	.986	.461	2.14
LEGLREST	.260	.130	2.00
REALREST	−.196	.166	−1.18
FINREST	.074	.187	.40
WHITEKNT	.481	.137	3.51
BIDPREM	−.678	.326	−2.08
INSTHOLD	−.362	.367	−.99
SIZE	.179	.052	3.44
SIZESQ	−.008	.003	−2.81
REGULATN	−.029	.139	−.21
$-\ln$ L	185.0		

and t statistics assuming an NB1 variance function. The estimated value of the overdispersion parameter α is 0.746, which is considerably less than unity. At the same time, a formal test of underdispersion using the LM test does not reject the null hypothesis of no overdispersion, leading Jaggia and Thosar (1993) to prefer the Poisson estimator.

The defensive action variables are generally statistically insignificant at 5% except for *LEGLREST*, which actually has an unexpected positive effect. While the coefficient of *WHITEKNT* is statistically different from zero at 5%, its coefficient implies that the number of bids increases by $0.481 \times 1.738 \simeq .84$ of a bid. This effect is not statistically significantly different from unity. (If a white-knight bid has no effect on bids by other potential bidders we expect it to increase the number of bids by one.) The firm-specific characteristics with the exception of *INSTHOLD* are statistically significant with the expected signs. *BIDPREM* has a relatively modest effect, with an increase in the bid premium of 0.2, which is approximately one standard deviation of *BIDPREM*, or 20%, leading to a decrease of $0.2 \times 0.677 \times 1.738 \simeq .24$ in the number of bids. Bids first increase and then decrease as firm size increases. Government-regulator intervention has very little effect on the number of bids.

Summary statistics for different definitions of residuals from the same Poisson PML estimates are given in Table 5.4. These residuals are the raw, Pearson, deviance, and Anscombe residuals defined in, respectively, (5.1), (5.2), (5.4), and (5.6), small-sample corrected or studentized Pearson and deviance residuals (5.13) and (5.14) obtained by division by $\sqrt{1-h_{ii}}$, and the adjusted deviance residual (5.15).

The various residuals are intended to be closer to normality, that is, with no skewness and kurtosis equal to 3, than the raw residual if the data are $\mathsf{P}[\mu_i]$. For these real data, which are not exactly $\mathsf{P}[\mu_i]$, this is the case for all except

Table 5.4. *Takeover bids: descriptive statistics for various residuals*

Residual	Mean	Standard deviation	Skewness	Kurtosis	Minimum	10%	90%	Maximum
r	.00	1.23	1.4	7.4	−3.22	−1.30	1.27	5.57
p	.00	.83	1.1	4.9	−1.61	−.96	.99	3.03
p*	−.00	.89	1.1	5.1	−1.87	−1.02	1.02	3.11
d	−.05	.96	.7	9.4	−3.65	−.95	.56	4.07
d*	−.05	1.03	.7	9.7	−3.80	−1.06	.58	4.28
dadj	.09	.96	.6	9.3	−3.55	−.86	.69	4.19
a	−.10	.85	.2	3.9	−2.41	−1.16	.89	2.41

Note: r, raw; p, Pearson; p*, studentized Pearson; d, deviance; d*, studentized deviance; dadj, adjusted deviance; a, Anscombe residual.

Table 5.5. *Takeover bids: correlations of various residuals*

Residual	r	p	p*	d	d*	dadj	a
r	1.000						
p	.976	1.000					
p*	.983	.998	1.000				
d	.919	.917	.918	1.000			
d*	.925	.913	.918	.998	1.000		
dadj	.920	.917	.919	1.000	.988	1.000	
a	.951	.980	.977	.934	.928	.934	1.000

Note: r, raw; p, Pearson; p*, studentized Pearson; d, deviance; d*, studentized deviance; dadj, adjusted deviance; a, Anscombe residual.

the deviance residual, which has quite high kurtosis. The Anscombe residual is clearly preferred on these criteria. Studentizing makes little difference. It is expected that it will make little difference for most observations, because the average $h_{ii} = 10/126 = .079$ leading to a small correction. For this sample even the second largest value of $h_{ii} = .321$ only leads to division of Pearson and deviance residuals by .82, not greatly different from unity.

The similarity between the residuals is also apparent from Table 5.5, which gives correlation amongst the various residuals. The correlations between the residuals are all in excess of 0.9, and small-sample corrected residuals have correlation of 0.998 or more with the corresponding uncorrected residual.

We conclude that for this sample the various residuals should all tell a similar story. We focus on the Anscombe residual a_i, since this is the closest to normality. Various residual plots are presented in Figure 5.2.

Panel 1 of Figure 5.2 plots the Anscombe residual against the dependent variable. This shows the expected positive relationship, explained earlier. It is better to plot against the predicted mean, which is done in panel 2. It is difficult to visually detect a relationship.

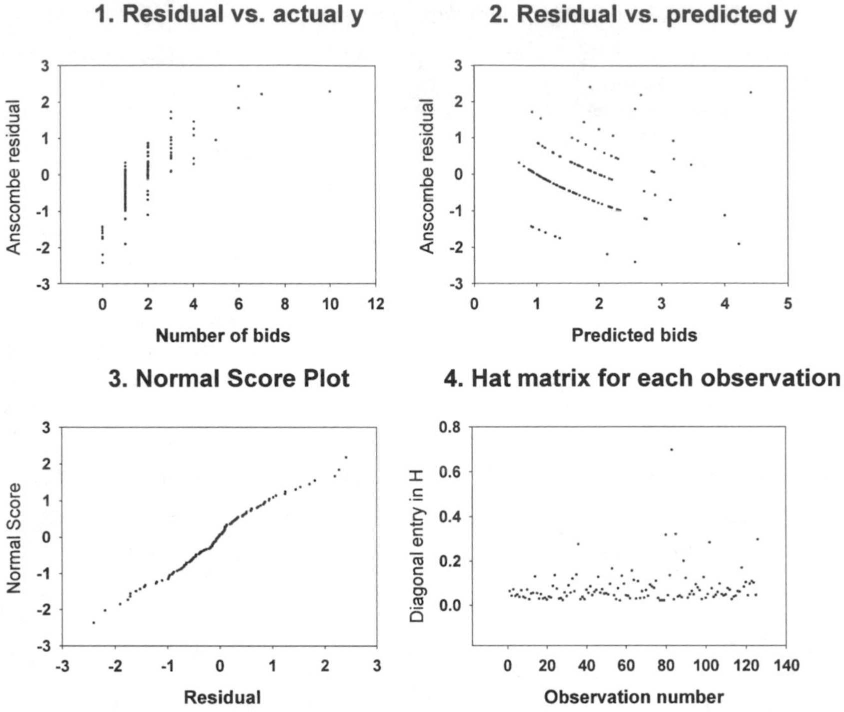

Figure 5.2. Takeover bids: residual plots.

A normal score plot of the Anscombe residual, that is, a plot of the residual against the prediction (5.11) if the residual is normally distributed, is given in panel 3 of Figure 5.2. The relationship is close to linear, although the high values of the Anscombe residuals are above the line, suggesting higher-than-expected residuals for large values of the dependent variable.

The hat matrix defined in (5.12) can be used for detecting influential observations. A plot of the ith diagonal entry h_{ii} against observation number is given in panel 4 of Figure 5.2. For this sample there are six observations with $h_{ii} > 3k/n = .24$. These are observations 36, 80, 83, 85, 102, and 126 with h_{ii} of, respectively, .28, .32, .70, .32, .28, and .30. If instead we use the OLS leverage measures, $\mathbf{H} = \mathbf{X}(\mathbf{X}'\mathbf{X})^{-1}\mathbf{X}'$, the corresponding diagonal entries are .18, .27, .45, .58, .18, and .16, so that one would come to similar conclusions.

On dropping these six observations the coefficients of the most highly statistically significant variables change by around 30%. The major differences are a change in the sign of *SIZESQ*, and that both *SIZE* and *SIZESQ* become very statistically insignificant. Further investigation of the data reveals that these six observations are for the six largest firms, and that the size distribution has a very fat tail with the kurtosis of *SIZE* equal to 31, explaining the high leverage of these observations. The leverage measures very strongly alert one to the problem, but the solution is not so clear. Dropping the observations with large *SIZE* is not desirable if one wants to test the hypothesis that, other things being equal, very large firms attract fewer bids than medium-size firms. Different functional forms for *SIZE* might be considered, such as log(*SIZE*) and its square, or an indicator variable for large firms might be used.

For this example there is little difference in the usefulness of the various standardized residuals. The sample size with 126 observations regressors is relatively small for statistical inference based on asymptotic theory, especially with 10 regressors, yet is sufficiently large that small-sample corrections made virtually no difference to the residuals. Using the hat matrix to detect influential observations was useful in suggesting possible changes to the functional form of the model.

5.3 Goodness of Fit

In the preceding section the focus was on evaluating the performance of the model in fitting individual observations. Now we consider the overall performance of the model. Common goodness-of-fit measures for GLMs are the Pearson and deviance statistics, which are weighted sums of residuals. These can be used to form pseudo R-squared measures, with those based on deviance statistics preferred. A final measure is comparison of average predicted probabilities of counts with empirical relative frequencies, using a chi-square goodness-of-fit test that controls for estimation error in the regression coefficients.

5.3.1 *Pearson Statistic*

A standard measure of goodness of fit for any model of y_i with mean μ_i and variance ω_i is the *Pearson statistic*

$$P = \sum_{i=1}^{n} \frac{(y_i - \hat{\mu}_i)^2}{\hat{\omega}_i}, \tag{5.16}$$

where $\hat{\mu}_i$ and $\hat{\omega}_i$ are estimates of μ_i and ω_i. If the mean and variance are correctly specified then $\mathsf{E}[\sum_{i=1}^{n}(y_i - \mu_i)^2/\omega_i] = n$, because $\mathsf{E}[(y_i - \mu_i)^2/\omega_i] = 1$. In practice P is compared with $(n-k)$, reflecting a degrees of freedom correction due to estimation of μ_i.

The simplest count application is to the Poisson regression model. This sets $\omega_i = \mu_i$, so that

$$P_{\mathsf{P}} = \sum_{i=1}^{n} \frac{(y_i - \hat{\mu}_i)^2}{\hat{\mu}_i}. \tag{5.17}$$

In the GLM literature it is standard to interpret $P_{\mathsf{P}} > n - k$ as evidence of overdispersion – that is, the true variance exceeds the mean, which implies $\mathsf{E}[(y_i - \mu_i)^2/\mu_i] > 1$; $P_{\mathsf{P}} < n - k$ indicates underdispersion. Note that this interpretation presumes correct specification of μ_i. In fact $P_{\mathsf{P}} \neq n - k$ may instead indicate misspecification of the conditional mean.

In practice even the simplest count data models make some correction for overdispersion. In the GLM literature the variance is a multiple of the mean as in section 3.2.4. Then $\hat{\omega}_i = \hat{\phi}\hat{\mu}_i$ where $\hat{\phi} = \hat{\phi}_{\mathsf{NB1}} = (n-k)^{-1}\sum_{i=1}^{n}\{(y_i - \hat{\mu}_i)^2/\hat{\mu}_i\}$. But this implies that P always equals $(n-k)$, so P is no longer a useful diagnostic. If instead one uses the NB2 model, $\hat{\omega}_i = \hat{\mu}_i + \hat{\alpha}\hat{\mu}_i^2$, with $\hat{\alpha}$ the maximum likelihood estimate of α from section 3.3.1, then P is still a useful diagnostic. So the Pearson statistic cannot be used to test whether overdispersion is adequately modeled in the GLM framework but can be used if the NB2 MLE is used. Even here, departures of P from $(n-k)$ may actually reflect misspecification of the conditional the mean.

Some references to the Pearson statistic suggest that it is asymptotically chi-square distributed, but this is only true in the special case of grouped data with multiple observations for each μ_i. McCullagh (1986) gives the distribution in the more common case of ungrouped data, in which case one needs to account for the dependence of $\hat{\mu}_i$ on $\hat{\beta}$. This distribution can be obtained by appeal to the results on CM tests given in section 2.6.3. Thus $\mathsf{T_P} = P'\hat{\mathsf{V}}_P^{-1}P \overset{a}{\sim} \chi^2(1)$, where the formula for the variance V_P is quite cumbersome. For the NB2 model estimated by maximum likelihood one can use the simpler OPG form of the CM test. Then an asymptotically equivalent version of $\mathsf{T_P}$ is n times the uncentered R^2 from auxiliary regression of 1 on the $k+2$ regressors $(y_i - \hat{\mu}_i)^2/(\hat{\mu}_i + \hat{\alpha}\hat{\mu}_i^2)$, $(y_i - \hat{\mu}_i)/(1+\hat{\alpha}\hat{\mu}_i)\mathbf{x}_i$ and $\{\hat{\alpha}^{-2}[\ln(1+\hat{\alpha}\hat{\mu}_i) - \sum_{j=0}^{y_i-1}(j+\hat{\alpha}^{-1})] + (y_i - \hat{\mu}_i)/\alpha(1+\hat{\alpha}\hat{\mu}_i)\}$. Studies very seldom implement such a formal test statistic.

5.3.2 *Deviance Statistic*

A second measure of goodness of fit, restricted to GLMs, is the deviance. Let $\mathcal{L}(\boldsymbol{\mu}) \equiv \ln \mathsf{L}(\boldsymbol{\mu})$ denote the log-likelihood function for a LEF density, defined in section 2.4, where $\boldsymbol{\mu}$ is the $n \times 1$ vector with i^{th} entry μ_i. Then the fitted log-likelihood is $\mathcal{L}(\hat{\boldsymbol{\mu}})$, and the maximum log-likelihood achievable, that in a full model with n parameters, can be shown to be $\mathcal{L}(\mathbf{y})$, where $\hat{\boldsymbol{\mu}}$ and $\mathbf{y}$ are the $n \times 1$ vectors with i^{th} entries $\hat{\mu}_i$ and y_i. The *deviance* is defined to be

$$D(\mathbf{y}, \hat{\boldsymbol{\mu}}) = 2\{\mathcal{L}(\mathbf{y}) - \mathcal{L}(\hat{\boldsymbol{\mu}})\}, \tag{5.18}$$

which is twice the difference between the maximum log-likelihood achievable and the log-likelihood of the fitted model.

GLMs additionally introduce a dispersion parameter ϕ, with variance scaled by $a(\phi)$. Then the log-likelihood is $\mathcal{L}(\boldsymbol{\mu}, \phi)$, and the scaled deviance is defined to be

$$SD(\mathbf{y}, \hat{\boldsymbol{\mu}}, \phi) = 2\{\mathcal{L}(\mathbf{y}, \phi) - \mathcal{L}(\hat{\boldsymbol{\mu}}, \phi)\}. \tag{5.19}$$

For GLM densities $SD(\mathbf{y}, \hat{\boldsymbol{\mu}}, \phi)$ equals a function of $\mathbf{y}$ and $\hat{\boldsymbol{\mu}}$ divided by $a(\phi)$. It is convenient to multiply $SD(\mathbf{y}, \hat{\boldsymbol{\mu}}, \phi)$ by the dispersion factor $a(\phi)$, and the deviance is defined as

$$D(\mathbf{y}, \hat{\boldsymbol{\mu}}) = 2a(\phi)\{\mathcal{L}(\mathbf{y}, \phi) - \mathcal{L}(\hat{\boldsymbol{\mu}}, \phi)\}. \tag{5.20}$$

The left-hand side of (5.20) is not a function of ϕ because the terms in ϕ in the right-hand side cancel. McCullagh (1986) gives the distribution of the deviance.

For the linear regression model under normality, the deviance equals the residual sum of squares $\sum_{i=1}^{n}(y_i - \hat{\mu}_i)^2$. This has led to the deviance being used in the GLM framework as a generalization of the sum of squares. This provides the motivation for the deviance residual defined in section 5.2.1. To compare sequences of nested GLMs, the analysis of deviance generalizes the analysis of variance.

For the Poisson model

$$D_{\mathrm{P}} = \sum_{i=1}^{n} \left\{ y_i \ln\left(\frac{y_i}{\hat{\mu}_i}\right) - (y_i - \hat{\mu}_i) \right\}, \tag{5.21}$$

where $y \ln y = 0$ if $y = 0$. This statistic is also called the *G-squared statistic*; see Bishop, Feinberg, and Holland (1975). Because Poisson residuals sum to zero if an intercept is included and the exponential mean function is used, D_{P} can more easily be calculated as $\sum_i y_i \ln(y_i/\hat{\mu}_i)$. For the NB2 model with α known,

$$D_{\mathrm{NB2}} = \sum_{i=1}^{n} \left\{ y_i \ln\left(\frac{y_i}{\hat{\mu}_i}\right) - (y_i + \alpha^{-1}) \ln\left[\frac{y_i + \alpha^{-1}}{\hat{\mu}_i + \alpha^{-1}}\right] \right\}. \tag{5.22}$$

5.3.3 *Pseudo R-Squared Measures*

There is no universal definition of R squared in nonlinear models. A number of measures can be proposed. This indeterminedness is reflected in use of "pseudo" as a qualifier. Pseudo R-squareds usually have the property that, on specialization to the linear model, they coincide with an interpretation of the linear model R squared.

The attractive features of the linear model R-squared measure disappear in nonlinear regression models. In the linear regression model, the starting point for obtaining R^2 is decomposition of the total sum of squares. In general,

$$\begin{aligned}\sum_{i=1}^{n}(y_i - \bar{y})^2 &= \sum_{i=1}^{n}(y_i - \hat{\mu}_i)^2 + \sum_{i=1}^{n}(\hat{\mu}_i - \bar{y})^2 \\ &\quad + 2\sum_{i=1}^{n}(y_i - \hat{\mu}_i)(\hat{\mu}_i - \bar{y}).\end{aligned} \tag{5.23}$$

The first three summations are, respectively, the total sum of squares (TSS), residual sum of squares (RSS), and explained sum of squares (ESS). The final summation is zero for OLS estimates of the linear regression model if an intercept is included. It is nonzero, however, for virtually all other estimators and models, including the Poisson and NLS with exponential conditional mean. This leads to different measures according to whether one uses $R^2 = 1-$ RSS/TSS or $R^2 =$ ESS/TSS. Furthermore, because estimators such as the Poisson MLE do not minimize RSS, these R squareds need not necessarily increase as regressors are added, and even if an intercept is included the first of these may be negative and the second may exceed unity.

The deviance is the GLM generalization of the sum of squares, as noted in the previous subsection. Cameron and Windmeijer (1996, 1997) propose a pseudo-R^2 based on decomposition of the deviance. Then

$$D(\mathbf{y}, \bar{\mathbf{y}}) = D(\mathbf{y}, \hat{\boldsymbol{\mu}}) + D(\hat{\boldsymbol{\mu}}, \bar{\mathbf{y}}), \tag{5.24}$$

where $D(\mathbf{y}, \bar{\mathbf{y}})$ is the deviance in the intercept-only model, $D(\mathbf{y}, \hat{\boldsymbol{\mu}})$ is the deviance in the fitted model, and $D(\hat{\boldsymbol{\mu}}, \bar{\mathbf{y}})$ is the explained deviance. One uses

$$R^2_{\mathsf{DEV}} = 1 - \frac{D(\mathbf{y}, \hat{\boldsymbol{\mu}})}{D(\mathbf{y}, \bar{\mathbf{y}})}, \tag{5.25}$$

which measures the reduction in the deviance due to inclusion of regressors. This equals $D(\hat{\boldsymbol{\mu}}, \bar{\mathbf{y}})/D(\mathbf{y}, \bar{\mathbf{y}})$, the R^2 based instead on the explained deviance. It lies between 0 and 1, increases as regressors are added, and can be given an information-theoretic interpretation as the proportionate reduction in Kullback-Liebler divergence due to inclusion of regressors. Only the last of these properties actually requires correct specification of the distribution of y.

This method can be applied to models for which the deviance is defined. For the Poisson linear regression model the deviance is given in (5.21) leading to

$$R^2_{\mathsf{DEV,P}} = \frac{\sum_{i=1}^n y_i \ln\left(\frac{\hat{\mu}_i}{\bar{y}}\right) - (y_i - \hat{\mu}_i)}{\sum_{i=1}^n y_i \ln\left(\frac{y_i}{\bar{y}}\right)}, \tag{5.26}$$

where $y \ln y = 0$ if $y = 0$. The same measure is obtained for the Poisson GLM with NB1 variance function. For maximum likelihood estimation of the negative binomial with NB2 variance function the *deviance pseudo-*R^2 is

$$R^2_{\mathsf{DEV,NB2}} = 1 - \frac{\sum_{i=1}^n y_i \ln\left(\frac{\hat{\mu}_i}{\bar{y}}\right) - (y_i + \hat{a}) \ln\left(\frac{y_i + \hat{a}}{\hat{\mu}_i + \hat{a}}\right)}{\sum_{i=1}^n y_i \ln\left(\frac{\hat{y}_i}{\bar{y}}\right) - (y_i + \hat{a}) \ln\left(\frac{y_i + \hat{a}}{\bar{y} + \hat{a}}\right)} \tag{5.27}$$

where $\hat{a} = 1/\hat{\alpha}$ and $\hat{\alpha}$ is the estimate of α in the fitted model. Note that $R^2_{\mathsf{DEV,P}}$ and $R^2_{\mathsf{DEV,NB2}}$ have different denominators and are not directly comparable. In particular it is possible, and indeed likely for data that are considerably overdispersed, that $R^2_{\mathsf{DEV,P}} > R^2_{\mathsf{DEV,NB2}}$. One can instead modify the deviance pseudo-R^2 measures to have common denominator $\sum_{i=1}^n y_i \ln(y_i/\bar{y})$, in which case the intercept-only Poisson is being used as the benchmark model. The NB1 model is not a GLM model, although Cameron and Windmeijer (1996) nonetheless propose a deviance-type R^2 measure in this case.

Cameron and Windmeijer (1996) motivate the deviance R^2 measures as measures based on residuals; one uses deviance residuals rather than raw residuals. One can alternatively view these measures in terms of the fraction of the potential log-likelihood gain that is achieved with inclusion of regressors. Formally,

$$R^2 = \frac{\mathcal{L}_{\text{fit}} - \mathcal{L}_0}{\mathcal{L}_{\max} - \mathcal{L}_0} = 1 - \frac{\mathcal{L}_{\max} - \mathcal{L}_{\text{fit}}}{\mathcal{L}_{\max} - \mathcal{L}_0}, \tag{5.28}$$

where $\mathcal{L}_{\text{fit}}$ and $\mathcal{L}_0$ denote the log-likelihood in the fitted and intercept-only models and $\mathcal{L}_{\max}$ denotes the maximum log-likelihood achievable. In (5.28), $(\mathcal{L}_{\max} - \mathcal{L}_0)$ is the potential log-likelihood gain and $(\mathcal{L}_{\max} - \mathcal{L}_{\text{fit}})$ is the log-likelihood gain achieved. This approach was taken by Merkle and Zimmermann (1992) for the Poisson model. The difficult part in implementation to more general models is defining $\mathcal{L}_{\max}$. For some models $\mathcal{L}_{\max}$ is unbounded, in which case any model has an R^2 of zero. For GLM models $\mathcal{L}_{\max} = \mathcal{L}(\mathbf{y})$ is finite and the approach is useful.

For nonlinear models some studies have proposed instead using the pseudo-R^2 measure $R^2 = 1 - (\mathcal{L}_{\text{fit}}/\mathcal{L}_0)$, sometimes called the *likelihood ratio index*. This is the same as (5.28) in the special case $\mathcal{L}_{\max} = 0$, which is the case for binary logit. More generally, however, the likelihood ratio index can be considerably less than unity for discrete densities, regardless of how good the fit is, because $\mathcal{L}_{\max} \leq 0$. Also, for continuous densities, problems may arise as $\mathcal{L}_{\text{fit}} > 0$ and negative R^2 values are possible.

Poisson packages usually report $\mathcal{L}_{\text{fit}}$ and $\mathcal{L}_0$. Using (5.28), $R^2_{\text{DEV,P}}$ can be computed if one additionally computes $\mathcal{L}_{\max} = \sum_i \{y_i \log y_i - y_i - \log y_i!\}$. The measure can also be clearly applied to truncated and censored variants of these models.

Cameron and Windmeijer (1996) also consider a similar R^2 measure based on Pearson residual. For models with variance function $\omega(\mu, \alpha)$

$$R^2_{\text{PEARSON}} = 1 - \sum_{i=1}^{n} \frac{(y_i - \hat{\mu}_i)^2}{\omega(\hat{\mu}_i, \hat{\alpha})} \Bigg/ \sum_{i=1}^{n} \frac{(y_i - \hat{\mu}_0)^2}{\omega(\hat{\mu}_0, \hat{\alpha})}, \tag{5.29}$$

where $\hat{\alpha}$ is the estimate of α in the fitted model and $\hat{\mu}_0 = \hat{\mu}_0(\hat{\alpha})$ denotes the predicted mean in the intercept-only model estimated under the constraint that $\alpha = \hat{\alpha}$. For Poisson and NB2 models $\hat{\mu}_0 = \bar{y}$. This measure has the attraction of requiring only mean–variance assumptions and being applicable to a wide range of models. This measure can be negative, however, and can decrease as regressors are added. These weaknesses are not just theoretical, as they are found to arise often in simulations and in applications. Despite its relative simplicity and generality, use of R^2_{PEARSON} is not recommended.

5.3.4 *Chi-Square Goodness of Fit Test*

For fully parametric models such as Poisson and negative binomial maximum likelihood, a crude diagnostic is to compare fitted probabilities with actual frequencies, where the fitted frequency distribution is computed as the average over observations of the predicted probabilities fitted for each count.

Suppose the count y_i takes values $0, 1, \ldots, m$ where $m = \max_i(y_i)$. Let the observed frequencies (i.e., the fraction of the sample with $y = j$) be denoted by $\bar{p}_j$ and the corresponding fitted frequencies be denoted $\hat{p}_j$, $j = 0, \ldots, m$. For the Poisson, for example, $\hat{p}_j = n^{-1} \sum_{i=1}^{n} \exp(-\hat{\mu}_i)\hat{\mu}_i^j / j!$. Comparison of $\hat{p}_j$ with $\bar{p}_j$ can be useful in displaying poor performance of a model, in highlighting ranges of the counts for which the model has a tendency to underpredict or overpredict, and for allowing a simple comparison of the predictive performance of competing models. Without doing a formal test, however, it is not clear when $\hat{p}_j$ is "close" enough to $\bar{p}_j$ for one to conclude that the model is a good one.

Formal comparison of $\hat{p}_j$ and $\bar{p}_j$ can be done using a CM test. We consider a slightly more general framework than the above, where the range of y is broken into J mutually exclusive cells, where each cell may include more than one value of y and the J cells span all possible values of y. For example, in data where only low values are observed, the cells may be $\{0\}$, $\{1\}$, $\{2, 3\}$ and $\{4, 5, \ldots\}$. Let $d_{ij}(y_i)$ be an indicator variable with $d_{ij} = 1$ if y_i falls in the jth set and $d_{ij} = 0$ otherwise. Let $p_{ij}(\mathbf{x}_i, \boldsymbol{\theta})$ denote the predicted probability that observation i falls in the jth set, where to begin with we assume the parameter vector $\boldsymbol{\theta}$ is known. Consider testing whether $d_{ij}(y_i)$ is centered around $p_{ij}(\mathbf{x}_i, \boldsymbol{\theta})$,

$$\mathsf{E}[d_{ij}(y_i) - p_{ij}(\mathbf{x}_i, \boldsymbol{\theta})] = 0, \qquad j = 1, \ldots, J, \tag{5.30}$$

or stacking all J moments in obvious vector notation

$$\mathsf{E}[\mathbf{d}_i(y_i) - \mathbf{p}_i(\mathbf{x}_i, \boldsymbol{\theta})] = \mathbf{0}. \tag{5.31}$$

This hypothesis can be tested by testing the closeness to zero of the corresponding sample moment

$$\mathbf{m}(\hat{\boldsymbol{\theta}}) = \sum_{i=1}^{n} (\mathbf{d}_i(y_i) - \mathbf{p}_i(\mathbf{x}_i, \hat{\boldsymbol{\theta}})). \tag{5.32}$$

This is clearly a CM test, presented in section 2.6.3. The CM test statistic is

$$\mathsf{T}_{\chi^2} = \mathbf{m}(\hat{\boldsymbol{\theta}})' \hat{\mathbf{V}}_m^{-} \mathbf{m}(\hat{\boldsymbol{\theta}}), \tag{5.33}$$

where $\hat{\mathbf{V}}_m$ is a consistent estimate of $\mathbf{V}_m$, the asymptotic variance matrix of $\mathbf{m}(\hat{\boldsymbol{\theta}})$, and $\hat{\mathbf{V}}_m^{-}$ is the Moore-Penrose generalized inverse of $\hat{\mathbf{V}}_m$. The generalized inverse is used because the $J \times J$ matrix $\mathbf{V}_m$ may not be of full rank. Under the null hypothesis that the density is correctly specified, that is, that $p_{ij}(\mathbf{x}_i, \boldsymbol{\theta})$ gives the correct probabilities, the test statistic is chi-square distributed with $\mathsf{rank}[\hat{\mathbf{V}}_m]$ degrees of freedom.

The results in section 2.6.3 can be used to obtain $\mathbf{V}_m$, which here usually has $\mathsf{rank}[\mathbf{V}_m] = J - 1$ rather than J as a consequence of the probabilities over all J cells summing to one. This entails considerable algebra, and it is easiest to instead use the asymptotically equivalent OPG form of the test, which is appropriate because fully parametric models are being considered here so that $\hat{\boldsymbol{\theta}}$ will be the MLE. The test is implemented calculating n times the uncentered R^2 from the artificial regression of 1 on the scores $\mathbf{s}_i(y_i, \mathbf{x}_i, \hat{\boldsymbol{\theta}})$ and $d_{ij}(y_i) - p_{ij}(\mathbf{x}_i, \hat{\boldsymbol{\theta}})$, $j = 1, \ldots, J-1$, where one cell has been dropped due to rank$[\mathbf{V}_m] = J-1$. In some cases rank$[\mathbf{V}_m] < J-1$. This occurs if the estimator $\hat{\boldsymbol{\theta}}$ is the solution to first-order conditions that set a linear transformation of $\mathbf{m}(\hat{\boldsymbol{\theta}})$ equal to zero or is asymptotically equivalent to such an estimator. An example is the multinomial model, with an extreme case being the binary logit model whose first-order conditions imply $\sum_{i=1}^{n}(d_{ij}(y_i) - p_{ij}(\mathbf{x}_i, \hat{\boldsymbol{\theta}})) = 0$, $j = 0, 1$.

The test statistic (5.33) is called the *chi-square goodness-of-fit test*, as it is a generalization of Pearson's chi-square test,

$$\sum_{j=1}^{J} \frac{(n\bar{p}_j - n\hat{p}_j)^2}{n\hat{p}_j}. \tag{5.34}$$

In an exercise it is shown that (5.34) can be rewritten as (5.33) in the special case in which $\mathbf{V}_m$ is a diagonal matrix with i^{th} entry $\sum_{i=1}^{n} p_{ij}(\mathbf{x}_i, \boldsymbol{\theta})$. Although this is the case in the application originally considered by Pearson – y_i is iid and takes only J discrete values and a multinomial MLE is used – in most regression applications the more general form (5.33) must be used. The generalization of Pearson's original chi-square test by Heckman (1984), Tauchen (1985), Andrews (1988a, 1988b), and others is reviewed in Andrews (1988b, pp. 140–141). For simplicity we have considered partition of the range of y into J cells. More generally the partition may be over the range of $(y, \mathbf{x})$.

Example: Takeover Bids (Continued)

We consider goodness-of-fit measures for the Poisson estimates given in Table 5.3. The Pearson statistic (5.17) is 72.52, much less than its theoretical value of $n - k = 116$, indicating underdispersion. The deviance statistic (5.21) is 75.87. The Poisson deviance R^2 given in (5.26) equals .25 while the Pearson R^2 given in (5.29) equals .35. Note that these two R^2 measures are still valid if the conditional variance equals $\alpha\mu_i$ rather than μ_i and can be easily computed using knowledge of the deviance and Pearson statistics plus the frequency distribution given in Table 5.1. Although experience with these R^2 measures is limited, it seems reasonable to conclude that the fit is quite good for cross-section data. If one instead runs an OLS regression, the R^2 equals .24.

Before performing a formal chi-square goodness-of-fit test, it is insightful to compare predicted relative frequencies $\hat{p}_j$ with actual relative frequencies $\bar{p}_j$. These are given in Table 5.6, where counts of five or more are grouped into the one cell to prevent cell sizes from getting too small. Clearly the Poisson overpredicts greatly the number of zeros and underpredicts the number of ones.

Table 5.6. *Takeover bids: Poisson MLE predicted and actual probabilities*

Counts	Actual	Predicted	|Diff|	Pearson
0	.0714	.2132	.1418	11.81
1	.5000	.2977	.2020	17.32
2	.2460	.2327	.0133	.10
3	.0952	.1367	.0415	1.58
4	.0476	.0680	.0204	.77
≥5	.0397	.0517	.0120	.00

Note: Actual, actual relative frequency; Predicted, predicted relative frequency; |Diff|, absolute difference between predicted and actual probabilities; Pearson, contribution to Pearson's chi-square test.

The last column of Table 5.6 gives $n(\bar{p}_j - \hat{p}_j)^2/\hat{p}_j$, which is the contribution of count j to Pearson's chi-square test statistic (5.34). Although this test statistic, whose value is 31.58, is inappropriate due to failure to control for estimation error in $\hat{p}_j$, it does suggest that the major contributors to the formal test will be the predictions for zeros and ones. The formal chi-square test statistic (5.33) yields a value 48.66 compared to a $\chi^2(5)$ critical value of 9.24 at 5%. The Poisson model is strongly rejected.

We conclude that the Poisson is an inadequate fully parametric model, due to its inability to model the relatively few zeros in the sample. Analysis of the data by Cameron and Johansson (1997) using alternative parametric models – Katz, hurdle, double-Poisson, and a flexible parametric model – is briefly discussed in section 12.3.3. Interestingly, none of the earlier diagnostics, such as residual analysis, detected this weakness in the Poisson estimates.

5.4 Hypothesis Tests

Hypothesis tests on regression coefficients and dispersion parameters in count data models involve straightforward application of the theory in section 2.6. A general approach is the Wald test. If the maximum likelihood framework is used, for example a negative binomial model, one can additionally use LR and LM tests. This theory has already been applied in Chapter 3 to basic count data models and is not presented here.

In this section we present only test statistics which are not straightforward to obtain. These are hypothesis tests of the Poisson restriction of variance–mean equality in the likelihood framework, notably the LM test against the Katz system (which includes negative binomial), and the closely related LM test due to Cox (1983) which does not require specification of the complete distribution under the alternative hypothesis. These tests are revisited in section 5.6, in the context of moment-based rather than likelihood-based tests.

5.4.1 *LM Test for Overdispersion against Katz System*

Tests for overdispersion are tests of the variance–mean equality imposed by the Poisson against the alternative that the variance exceeds the mean. These are implemented by tests of the Poisson with mean μ_i and variance μ_i, against the negative binomial with mean

$$\mathsf{E}[y_i \mid \mathbf{x}_i] = \mu_i = \mu(\mathbf{x}_i, \boldsymbol{\beta}) \tag{5.35}$$

and variance

$$\mathsf{V}[y_i \mid \mathbf{x}_i] = \mu_i + \alpha g(\mu_i), \tag{5.36}$$

for specified function $g(\mu_i)$. Usually $g(\mu_i) = \mu_i$ or $g(\mu_i) = \mu_i^2$. The null hypothesis is

$$H_0 : \alpha = 0. \tag{5.37}$$

Such tests are easily implemented as LR, Wald, or LM tests of H_0 against $H_a : \alpha > 0$. These tests are presented in Chapter 3. As noted there, the usual critical values of the LR and Wald cannot be used, and adjustment needs to be made because the null hypothesis $\alpha = 0$ lies on the boundary of the parameter space for the negative binomial, which does not permit underdispersion.

Tests for underdispersion, or variance less than the mean, can be constructed in a similar manner. One needs a distribution that permits underdispersion and nests the Poisson. The Katz system, defined in Chapter 4, has this property. For overdispersed data it equals the commonly used negative binomial. For underdispersed data, however, the Katz system model is not offered as a standard model in count-data packages. The LM test, which requires estimation only under the null hypothesis of Poisson, is particularly attractive for the underdispersed case.

Derivation of the LM test of Poisson against the Katz system, due to Lee (1986), who considered $g(\mu_i) = \mu_i$ and $g(\mu_i) = \mu_i^2$, is not straightforward. In section 5.8 it is shown that for the Katz system density with mean μ_i and variance $\mu_i + \alpha g(\mu_i)$

$$\begin{aligned}
\left.\frac{\partial \mathcal{L}}{\partial \boldsymbol{\beta}}\right|_{\alpha=0} &= \sum_{i=1}^{n} \mu_i^{-1}(y - \mu_i)\frac{\partial \mu_i}{\partial \boldsymbol{\beta}} \\
\left.\frac{\partial \mathcal{L}}{\partial \alpha}\right|_{\alpha=0} &= \sum_{i=1}^{n} \frac{1}{2}\mu_i^{-2} g(\mu_i)\{(y_i - \mu_i)^2 - y_i\}.
\end{aligned} \tag{5.38}$$

The LM test is based on these derivatives evaluated at the restricted MLE, which is $\hat{\boldsymbol{\theta}} = (\hat{\boldsymbol{\beta}}'\ \hat{\alpha})' = (\hat{\boldsymbol{\beta}}'\ 0)'$ where $\hat{\boldsymbol{\beta}}$ is the Poisson MLE. But the first summation in (5.38) equals the derivative with respect to $\boldsymbol{\beta}$ of the Poisson log-likelihood with general conditional mean $\mu_i(\boldsymbol{\beta})$, so $\partial \mathcal{L}/\partial \boldsymbol{\beta}|_{\boldsymbol{\beta}=\hat{\boldsymbol{\beta}},\alpha=0} = \mathbf{0}$ and hence

$$\left.\frac{\partial \mathcal{L}}{\partial \boldsymbol{\theta}}\right|_{\boldsymbol{\beta}=\hat{\boldsymbol{\beta}},\alpha=0} = \begin{bmatrix} \mathbf{0} \\ \sum_{i=1}^{n} \hat{\mu}_i^{-2} g(\hat{\mu}_i)\frac{1}{2}\{(y_i - \hat{\mu}_i)^2 - y_i\} \end{bmatrix}. \tag{5.39}$$

To construct the LM test stated earlier in section 2.6.1, we additionally need a consistent estimate of the variance matrix, which by the information matrix equality is the limit of $T^{-1}\mathsf{E}[(\partial\mathcal{L}/\partial\boldsymbol{\theta}|_{\alpha=0})(\partial\mathcal{L}/\partial\boldsymbol{\theta}'|_{\alpha=0})]$. Now under the null hypothesis that $y \sim \mathsf{P}[\mu]$,

$$\begin{aligned} &\mathsf{E}[(y-\mu)^2] = \mu \\ &\mathsf{E}[\{(y-\mu)^2 - y\}(y-\mu)] = 0 \\ &\mathsf{E}[\{(y-\mu)^2 - y\}^2] = 2\mu^2. \end{aligned} \tag{5.40}$$

This implies

$$\mathsf{E}\left[\left.\frac{\partial^2\mathcal{L}}{\partial\boldsymbol{\theta}\partial\boldsymbol{\theta}'}\right|_{\alpha=0}\right] = \begin{bmatrix} \sum_{i=1}^n \mu_i^{-1}\frac{\partial\mu_i}{\partial\beta}\frac{\partial\mu_i}{\partial\beta'} & \mathbf{0} \\ \mathbf{0} & \sum_{i=1}^n \frac{1}{2}\mu_i^{-2}g^2(\mu_i) \end{bmatrix}. \tag{5.41}$$

Given (5.39) and (5.41) the LM test statistic in section 2.6.1 is constructed. This will be a $(k+1) \times (k+1)$ matrix with zeros everywhere except for the last diagonal entry. Taking the square root of this scalar yields

$$\mathsf{T}_{\mathsf{LM}} = \left[\sum_{i=1}^n \frac{1}{2}\hat{\mu}_i^{-2}g^2(\hat{\mu}_i)\right]^{-1/2} \sum_{i=1}^n \frac{1}{2}\hat{\mu}_i^{-2}g(\hat{\mu}_i)\{(y_i-\hat{\mu}_i)^2 - y_i\}. \tag{5.42}$$

Because the negative binomial is the special case $\alpha > 0$ of the Katz system, this statistic is the LM test for Poisson against both negative binomial overdispersion and Katz system underdispersion. At significance level .05, for example, the null hypothesis of equidispersion is rejected against the alternative hypothesis of overdispersion if $\mathsf{T}_{\mathsf{LM}} > z_{.05}$, underdispersion if $\mathsf{T}_{\mathsf{LM}} < -z_{.05}$ and over- or underdispersion if $|\mathsf{T}_{\mathsf{LM}}| > z_{.025}$.

Clearly one can obtain different LM test statistics by nesting the Poisson in other distributions. In particular Gurmu and Trivedi (1993) nest the Poisson in the double-Poisson, a special case of nesting the LEF in the extended LEF, which they more generally consider, and obtain a test statistic for overdispersion that is a function of the deviance statistic.

The LM test for Poisson against negative binomial has been extended to positive Poisson models by Gurmu (1991) and to left- and right-truncated Poisson models by Gurmu and Trivedi (1992). These extensions involve a number of complications, including non–block-diagonality of the information matrix so that the off-diagonal elements in the generalization of (5.41) are nonzero.

5.4.2 *Auxiliary Regressions for LM Test*

As is usual for test statistics, there are many asymptotically equivalent versions under H_0 of the overdispersion test statistic T_{LM} given in (5.42). Several of these can be easily calculated from many different auxiliary OLS regressions. Like T_{LM} they are distributed as N[0, 1], or $\chi^2(1)$ on squaring, under H_0.

The auxiliary OPG regression for the LM test given in section 2.6.1 uses the uncentered explained sums of squares from OLS regression of 1 on $\frac{1}{2}\hat{\mu}_i^{-2}g(\hat{\mu}_i)\{(y_i - \hat{\mu}_i)^2 - y_i\}$ and $\hat{\mu}_i^{-1}(y_i - \hat{\mu}_i)\partial\mu_i/\partial\beta|_{\hat{\beta}}$. The square root of this is asymptotically equivalent to T_{LM}.

An asymptotically equivalent variant of this auxiliary regression is to use the uncentered explained sums of squares from OLS regression of 1 on $\frac{1}{2}\hat{\mu}_i^{-2}g(\hat{\mu}_i)\{(y_i - \hat{\mu}_i)^2 - y_i\}$ alone. This simplification is possible, as $\frac{1}{2}\hat{\mu}_i^{-2}g(\hat{\mu}_i)\{(y_i - \hat{\mu}_i)^2 - y_i\}$ and $\hat{\mu}_i^{-1}(y_i - \hat{\mu}_i)\partial\mu_i/\partial\beta|_{\hat{\beta}}$ are asymptotically uncorrelated because for the Poisson $\mathsf{E}[\{(y_i - \mu_i)^2 - y_i\}(y_i - \mu_i)] = 0$ by (5.40), and because $\sum_{i=1}^n \hat{\mu}_i^{-1}(y_i - \hat{\mu}_i)\partial\mu_i/\partial\beta|_{\hat{\beta}} = 0$ by the first-order conditions for the H_0 Poisson MLE. The square root of the explained sum of squares is

$$T^*_{LM} = \left[\sum_{i=1}^n \left(\frac{1}{2}\right)^2 \hat{\mu}_i^{-4} g^2(\hat{\mu}_i)\{(y_i - \hat{\mu}_i)^2 - y_i\}^2\right]^{-1/2} \times \sum_{i=1}^n \frac{1}{2}\hat{\mu}_i^{-2} g(\hat{\mu}_i)\{(y_i - \hat{\mu}_i)^2 - y_i\}, \tag{5.43}$$

using the result that the square root of the uncentered explained sum of squares from regression of y_i^* on the scalar x_i is $(\sum_i x_i^2)^{-1/2}\sum_i x_i y_i^*$. This test is asymptotically equivalent to T_{LM}, as for the Poisson

$$\mathsf{E}\left[\frac{1}{2}\mu_i^{-2}\{(y_i - \mu_i)^2 - y_i\}^2\right] = 1, \tag{5.44}$$

by the last equation in (5.40).

In the special case $g(\mu_i) = \mu_i^l$, Cameron and Trivedi (1986) proposed using an alternative variant of T_{LM}. For general $g(\mu_i)$ this variant becomes

$$T^{**}_{LM} = \left[\frac{1}{n}\sum_{i=1}^n \frac{1}{2}\hat{\mu}_i^{-2}\{(y - \hat{\mu}_i)^2 - y_i\}^2\right]^{-1/2} \left[\sum_{i=1}^n \frac{1}{2}\hat{\mu}_i^{-2} g^2(\hat{\mu}_i)\right]^{-1/2} \times \sum_{i=1}^n \frac{1}{2}\hat{\mu}_i^{-2} g(\hat{\mu}_i)\{(y_i - \hat{\mu}_i)^2 - y_i\}. \tag{5.45}$$

This is asymptotically equivalent to T_{LM} because the first term in parentheses has plim unity by (5.44). This can be computed as the square root of n times the uncentered explained sum of squares from the OLS regression of $\frac{1}{2}\hat{\mu}_i^{-1}\{(y_i - \hat{\mu}_i)^2 - y_i\}$ against $\frac{1}{2}\hat{\mu}_i^{-1}g(\hat{\mu}_i)$.

In general the t test from the regression $y_i^* = \alpha x_i + u_i$, where x_i is a scalar, can be shown to equal $(1/s)(\sum_i x_i^2)^{-1/2}\sum_i x_i y_i^*$, where s is the standard error of this regression. For the regression

$$(\sqrt{2}\hat{\mu}_i)^{-1}\{(y_i - \hat{\mu}_i)^2 - y_i\} = (\sqrt{2}\hat{\mu}_i)^{-1} g(\hat{\mu}_i)\alpha + v_i, \tag{5.46}$$

it follows that the t statistic for $\alpha = 0$ is

$$\mathsf{T}^{***}_{\mathsf{LM}} = \left[s^2 \sum_{i=1}^{n} \frac{1}{2} \hat{\mu}_i^{-2} g^2(\hat{\mu}_i) \right]^{-1/2} \sum_{i=1}^{n} \frac{1}{2} \hat{\mu}_i^{-2} g(\hat{\mu}_i) \{(y_i - \hat{\mu}_i)^2 - y_i\}, \tag{5.47}$$

where

$$s^2 = \frac{1}{n-1} \sum_{i=1}^{n} (\sqrt{2}\hat{\mu}_i)^{-2} \{(y_i - \hat{\mu}_i)^2 - y_i - g(\hat{\mu}_i)\hat{\alpha}\}^2. \tag{5.48}$$

This test is asymptotically equivalent to T_{LM}, because plim $s^2 = 1$ under H_0 on setting $\alpha = 0$ and using the moment condition (5.44). This is the regression given in section 3.4, on elimination of $\frac{1}{2}$ from both sides of the regression and letting $g(\mu_i) = \mu_i^2$ for tests against NB2 and $g(\mu_i) = \mu_i$ for tests against NB1.

In principle the LM test statistic can be computed using any of these many auxiliary regressions, as they are all asymptotically equivalent under H_0. In practice the computed values can differ significantly. This is made clear by noting that asymptotic equivalence is established using assumptions, such as $\mathsf{E}[\{(y_i - \mu_i)^2 - y_i\}^2] = 2\mu_i$, which hold only under H_0.

The regression (5.46) has a physical interpretation, in addition to being a computational device. It can be viewed as a WLS regression based on testing whether $\alpha = 0$ in the population moment condition

$$\mathsf{E}[(y_i - \mu_i)^2 - y_i] = \alpha g(\mu_i). \tag{5.49}$$

This moment condition is implied by the alternative hypothesis given by (5.35) and (5.36). Tests based on (5.49) of overdispersion or underdispersion, under much weaker stochastic assumptions than Poisson against the Katz system, were proposed by Cameron and Trivedi (1985, 1990a). Their testing approach is presented in section 5.6.

5.4.3 *LM Test against Local Alternatives*

Cox (1983) proposed a quite general method to construct the LM test statistic without completely specifying the density under the alternative hypothesis. The general result is presented before specialization to overdispersion tests.

Let y have density $f(y \mid \lambda)$, where the scalar parameter λ is itself a random variable, distributed with density $p(\lambda \mid \mu, \tau)$ where μ and τ denote the mean and variance of λ. This mixture distribution approach has already been presented in Chapter 4. For example, if y is Poisson-distributed with parameter λ where λ is gamma-distributed, then y is negative binomial distributed, conditional on the gamma distribution parameters.

Interest lies in the distribution of y given μ and τ

$$h(y \mid \mu, \tau) = \int f(y \mid \lambda) p(\lambda \mid \mu, \tau)\, d\lambda. \tag{5.50}$$

A second-order Taylor series expansion of $f(y \mid \lambda)$ about $\lambda = \mu$ yields

$$h(y \mid \mu, \tau) = \int \{f(y \mid \mu) + f'(y \mid \mu)(\lambda - \mu) + \frac{1}{2} f''(y \mid \mu)(\lambda - \mu)^2 + R\} p(\lambda \mid \mu, \tau)\, d\lambda \qquad (5.51)$$

where $f'(\cdot)$ and $f''(\cdot)$ denote the first and second derivatives, respectively, and R is a remainder term. Cox (1983) considered only small departures of λ from its mean of μ, specifically $\mathsf{V}[\lambda] = \tau = \delta/\sqrt{n}$, where δ is finite nonzero. After considerable algebra, given in section 5.8, this can be reexpressed as

$$h(y \mid \mu, \tau) = f(y \mid \mu) \exp\left[\frac{1}{2}\tau\left\{\frac{\partial^2 \ln f(y \mid \mu)}{\partial \mu^2} + \left(\frac{\partial \ln f(y \mid \mu)}{\partial \mu}\right)^2\right\}\right] + O(n^{-1}). \qquad (5.52)$$

Cox (1983) considered LM (or score) tests against this approximation to the alternative hypothesis density, which from 5.52 reduces to the null hypothesis density $f(y \mid \mu)$ if $\tau = 0$.

For application to the Poisson we suppose $\mathsf{V}[\lambda] = \tau = \delta g(\mu)/\sqrt{n}$, which implies $\mathsf{V}[y] = \mu + \delta g(\mu)/\sqrt{n}$. Then in (5.36) we are considering local alternatives $\alpha = \delta/\sqrt{n}$. The log-likelihood under local alternatives is $\mathcal{L} = \sum_{i=1}^{n} \ln h(y_i \mid \mu_i, \tau)$ and

$$\left.\frac{\partial \mathcal{L}}{\partial \alpha}\right|_{\alpha=0} = \sum_{i=1}^{n} \frac{1}{2} g(\mu_i) \left\{\frac{\partial^2 \ln f(y_i \mid \mu_i)}{\partial \mu_i^2} + \left(\frac{\partial \ln f(y_i \mid \mu_i)}{\partial \mu_i}\right)^2\right\}. \qquad (5.53)$$

If $f(y_i \mid \mu_i)$ is the Poisson density this yields

$$\left.\frac{\partial \mathcal{L}}{\partial \alpha}\right|_{\alpha=0} = \sum_{i=1}^{n} \frac{1}{2} g(\mu_i) \mu_i^{-2} \{(y_i - \mu_i)^2 - y_i\}, \qquad (5.54)$$

which is exactly the same as the second term in (5.38). The first term, $\partial \mathcal{L}/\partial \beta|_{\alpha=0}$ is also the same as in (5.38), and the LM test statistic is T_{LM}, given in (5.42).

The approach of Cox (1983) demonstrates that T_{LM} in (5.42) is valid for testing Poisson against all local alternatives satisfying (5.35) and (5.36), not just the Katz system. The general form (5.52) for the density under local alternatives is clearly related to the information matrix equality. In section 5.6.5 we make the connection between the Cox test and the information matrix test.

5.5 Inference with Finite Sample Corrections

A brief discussion of small-sample performance of hypothesis tests in the Poisson and negative binomial models is given by Lawless (1987b). He concluded that the LR test was preferable for tests on regression coefficients, although none of the methods worked badly in small samples. There was, however, considerable small-sample bias in testing dispersion parameters.

The standard general procedure to handle small-sample bias in statistical inference is the bootstrap, proposed by Efron (1979) and presented in the next subsection. This method has to date not been widely applied to count models. One potential complication is that the bootstrap requires resampling from an iid distribution, but the errors in cross-section count data models are typically not identically distributed.

The main application of small-sample corrections for count data analysis has been a method quite different from the bootstrap, one proposed by Dean and Lawless (1989a) for LM tests of overdispersion. This method has been applied in several studies, which find in simulations that the improved size performance is small except if sample sizes are small, say less than 30 observations.

5.5.1 *Bootstrap*

The bootstrap, introduced by Efron (1979), is a method to obtain the distribution of a statistic by resampling from the original data set. An introductory treatment is given by Efron and Tibsharani (1993). An excellent treatment with emphasis on common regression applications is given by Horowitz (1997). Here we focus on application to cross-section count data regression models, particularly the Poisson PMLE, using the bootstrap pairs procedure under the assumption that $(y_i, \mathbf{x}_i)$ is iid.

Reasons for performing a bootstrap in estimation and statistical inference include weaker stochastic assumptions, simpler computation, and potentially better small-sample performance. The first two reasons are often compelling reasons for using the bootstrap in applied work even if small-sample performance gains are not achieved. An example of using the bootstrap under weaker stochastic assumptions has been given in section 3.2.6, where the standard error of the Poisson PMLE was obtained under the assumption that $(y_i, \mathbf{x}_i)$ is iid and $\mathsf{E}[y_i \mid \mathbf{x}_i] = \exp(\mathbf{x}_i'\boldsymbol{\beta})$. Here $\mathsf{V}[y_i \mid \mathbf{x}_i]$ is not specified, and the distributional assumptions are similar to those made in obtaining the robust sandwich standard errors. Examples of simpler computation include obtaining the distribution of $\mathbf{r}(\hat{\boldsymbol{\theta}})$, in applications in which $\mathbf{r}(\cdot)$ is a complicated function of $\boldsymbol{\theta}$, by bootstrap rather than the delta method given in section 2.6.2; and obtaining the distribution of a sequential two-step estimator by bootstrap, rather than the method discussed in section 2.5.3 and detailed in Newey (1984). Despite these other advantages, the statistical literature has focused on small-sample performance of the bootstrap.

The bootstrap can be applied to estimation of moments of the distribution of a statistic, testing hypotheses, and construction of confidence intervals.

We begin with use of the bootstrap to estimate standard errors. Let $\hat{\theta}_j$ denote the estimator of the jth component of the parameter vector $\boldsymbol{\theta}$. The bootstrap procedure is as follows:

1. Form a new pseudosample of size n, $(y_l^*, \mathbf{x}_l^*)$, $l = 1, \ldots, n$, by sampling with replacement from the original sample $(y_i, \mathbf{x}_i)$, $i = 1, \ldots, n$.
2. Obtain the estimator, say $\hat{\boldsymbol{\theta}}_1$ with j^{th} component $\hat{\theta}_{j,1}$, using the pseudosample data.
3. Repeat steps 1 and 2 B times giving B estimates $\hat{\theta}_{j,1}, \ldots, \hat{\theta}_{j,B}$.
4. Estimate the standard deviation of $\hat{\theta}_j$ using the usual formula for the sample standard deviation of $\hat{\theta}_{j,1}, \ldots, \hat{\theta}_{j,B}$, or

$$\mathsf{se}_{\mathsf{Boot}}[\hat{\theta}_j] = \sqrt{\frac{1}{B-1}\sum_{b=1}^{B}(\hat{\theta}_{j,b} - \bar{\theta}_j)^2} \tag{5.55}$$

where $\bar{\theta}_j$ is the usual sample mean $\bar{\theta}_j = (1/B)\sum_{b=1}^{B}\hat{\theta}_{j,b}$. The estimated standard error is the square root of $\mathsf{V}_{\mathsf{Boot}}[\hat{\theta}_{\mathsf{P},j}]$.

The bootstrap is very easy to implement in this example, given a resampling algorithm and a way to save parameter estimates from the B simulations. The only drawback is that if estimating the model once takes a long time, estimating it B times may be too computationally burdensome. Efron and Tibshirani (1993, p. 52) state that $B = 200$ is generally sufficient for standard error estimation. The method is easily adapted to statistics other than an estimator – replace $\hat{\boldsymbol{\theta}}$ by the statistic of interest, and to estimates of moments other than the sample standard deviation.

The bootstrap can additionally provide improved estimation of the distribution of a statistic in small samples, in the sense that as $n \to \infty$ the bootstrap estimator converges faster than the usual first-order asymptotic theory. These gains occur because in some cases it is possible to construct the bootstrap as a numerical method to implement an Edgeworth expansion, which is a more refined asymptotic theory than the usual first-order theory. A key requirement for improved small-sample performance of the bootstrap is that the statistic being considered is *asymptotically pivotal*, which means that the asymptotic distribution of the statistic does not depend on unknown parameters.

We present a version of the bootstrap for hypothesis tests that yields improved small-sample performance. Consider testing the hypothesis $H_0 : \theta_j = \theta_{j0}$ against $H_0 : \theta_j \neq \theta_{j0}$, where estimation is by the Poisson PMLE. The t statistic used is $t_j = (\hat{\theta}_j - \theta_{j0})/s_j$, where s_j is the robust sandwich standard error estimate for $\hat{\theta}_j$ which assumes that $(y_i, \mathbf{x}_i)$ is iid. On the basis of first-order asymptotic theory, we would reject H_0 at level α if $|t_j| > z_{\alpha/2}$.

The bootstrap procedure to test H_0 is as follows:

1. Form a new pseudosample of size n, $(y_l^*, \mathbf{x}_l^*)$, $l = 1, \ldots, n$, by sampling with replacement from the original sample $(y_i, \mathbf{x}_i)$, $i = 1, \ldots, n$.
2. Obtain the estimator $\hat{\theta}_{j,1}$, the standard error $s_{j,1}$, and the t statistic $t_{j,1} = (\hat{\theta}_{j,1} - \theta_{j0})/s_{j,1}$ for the pseudosample data.
3. Repeat steps 1 and 2 B times, yielding $t_{j,1}, \ldots, t_{j,B}$.
4. Order these B t statistics and calculate $t_{j,[\alpha/2]}$ and $t_{j,[1-\alpha/2]}$, the lower and upper $\alpha/2$ percentiles of $t_{j,1}, \ldots, t_{j,B}$.

5. Reject H_0 at level α if t_j, the t statistic from the original sample, falls outside the interval $(t_{j,[\alpha/2]}, t_{j,[1-\alpha/2]})$.

For confidence intervals the same bootstrap procedure is used, except that at step 2 one forms $t^*_{j,1} = (\hat{\theta}_{j,1} - \hat{\theta}_j)/s_{j,1}$, centering around the estimate of θ_j from the original example, and at the last stage one constructs the $100(1-\alpha)\%$ confidence interval $(\hat{\theta}_j - t^*_{j,[\alpha/2]}s_j, \hat{\theta}_j + t^*_{j,[1-\alpha/2]}s_j)$.

This bootstrap procedure leads to an improved small-sample performance in the following sense. Let α be the nominal size for a test procedure. Usual asymptotic theory produces t tests with actual size $\alpha + O(n^{-1/2})$, whereas this bootstrap produces t tests with actual size $\alpha + O(n^{-1})$. This refinement is possible because it is the t statistic, whose asymptotic distribution does not depend on unknown parameters, that is bootstrapped. For both hypothesis tests and confidence intervals the number of iterations should be larger than for standard error estimation, say $B = 1000$.

An alternative bootstrap method is the percentile method. This calculates $\theta_{j,[\alpha/2]}$ and $\theta_{j,[1-\alpha/2]}$, the lower and upper $\alpha/2$ percentiles of $\hat{\theta}_{j,1}, \ldots, \hat{\theta}_{j,B}$. Then one rejects $H_0 : \theta_j = \theta_{j0}$ against $H_a : \theta_j \neq \theta_{j0}$ if θ_{j0} does not lie in $(\theta_{j,[\alpha/2]}, \theta_{j,[1-\alpha/2]})$, and one uses $(\theta_{j,[\alpha/2]}, \theta_{j,[1-\alpha/2]})$ as the $100(1-\alpha)\%$ confidence interval. This alternative procedure is asymptotically valid but is no better than using the usual asymptotic theory because it is based on the distribution of $\hat{\theta}_j$, which unlike t_j depends on unknown parameters. Similarly, using the usual hypothesis tests and confidence intervals, with the one change that s_j is replaced by a bootstrap estimate, is asymptotically valid but no better than the usual first-order asymptotic methods.

These alternative approaches illustrate the need to bootstrap the right statistic to achieve small-sample performance gains. Theoretically inferior methods may still be very useful in actual applications, however, as they do not require computation of s_j using potentially complicated asymptotic results. Also, for very large samples there may be little need for asymptotic refinements.

The bootstrap can also be used for bias correction. Consider estimation of θ_j, the jth component of $\boldsymbol{\theta}$. Let $\hat{\theta}_j$ denote the usual estimator of θ_j using the original sample, and let $\bar{\theta}_j$ denote the average over B bootstrap replications of the bootstrap estimates. The estimator $\bar{\theta}_j$ is a bootstrap measure of $E[\hat{\theta}_j]$, so the bootstrap estimate of bias is $(\bar{\theta}_j - \hat{\theta}_j)$. Before giving a general formula, consider a specific example of bias correction in which $\hat{\theta}_j = 4$ and $\bar{\theta}_j = 5$. Then $\hat{\theta}_j$ is upward-biased with bias of 1 because the bootstrap estimate of $E[\hat{\theta}_j]$ is 5. To correct for this upwards bias in the estimator $\hat{\theta}_j$ we subtract the bias from the sample estimate $\hat{\theta}_j$, giving a bias-corrected estimate of 3. More generally, the bias-corrected estimate of θ_j is $\hat{\theta}_j - (\bar{\theta}_j - \hat{\theta}_j) = 2\hat{\theta}_j - \bar{\theta}_j$. Note that the bias-corrected estimate of θ_j is not $\bar{\theta}_j$. Efron and Tibsharani (1993, p. 138) provide several other caveats on using the bootstrap for bias correction.

A key requirement for validity of the bootstrap is that resampling be done on a quantity that is iid. The bootstrap pairs procedure ensures this, resampling jointly the pairs $(y_i, \mathbf{x}_i)$, which are assumed to be iid. In the linear model with homoskedastic errors an alternative and more commonly used procedure is to bootstrap or resample the residuals. Efron and Tibshirani (1993, p. 113) discuss bootstrapping pairs, rather than residuals, for the linear model with iid errors where both approaches are possible. For count data, bootstrapping the residuals is not valid as the errors are heteroskedastic, for example, and therefore not iid.

Horowitz (1997) gives a detailed example of bootstrap hypothesis tests for the linear model with heteroskedasticity. In addition to bootstrap pairs, he uses the wild bootstrap of Liu (1988); see also Mammen, 1993), which imposes on the bootstrap the restriction that the conditional mean of the error is zero. The wild bootstrap performs considerably better than bootstrapping pairs. These methods can be adapted to the Poisson PMLE. Presumably further gains can be obtained by imposing any additional moment assumptions that might be made, such as the GLM assumption that the variance is a multiple of the mean. For fully parametric models such as the hurdle model one can perform hypothesis tests using a parametric bootstrap.

For time series data, dependence is a potential problem. In the linear model it is accounted for by assuming an autoregressive moving average error structure and resampling the underlying white noise error, or by using the moving-blocks bootstrap in which blocks are independent but the correlation structure within blocks is preserved. These time series methods are in their infancy.

5.5.2 *Other Corrections*

Small-sample corrections to testing in count data models have rarely been done, although this should change rapidly as the bootstrap becomes increasingly used. To date the leading example of small-sample correction in count models has been to LM tests for overdispersion, using an approach due to Dean and Lawless (1989a), which differs from the Edgeworth expansion and bootstrap. This method can be applied to any GLM, not just the Poisson.

Dean and Lawless (1989a) considered the LM test statistic for Poisson against NB2 given in (5.42). The starting point is the result in McCullagh and Nelder (1983, appendix C) that for GLM density with mean μ_i and variance $\mathsf{V}[y_i]$, the residual $(y_i - \hat{\mu}_i)$ has approximate variance $(1 - h_{ii})\mathsf{V}[y_i]$, where h_{ii} is the ith diagonal entry of the hat matrix $\mathbf{H}$ defined in (5.12). Applying this result to the Poisson, it follows that

$$\mathsf{E}[(y_i - \hat{\mu}_i)^2 - y_i] \simeq (1 - \hat{h}_{ii})\hat{\mu}_i - \hat{\mu}_i \simeq -h_{ii}\hat{\mu}_i. \tag{5.56}$$

This leads to small-sample bias under $H_0 : \mathsf{E}[(y_i - \mu_i)^2 - y_i]$, which can be corrected by adding $\hat{h}_{ii}\hat{\mu}_i$ to components of the sum in the numerator of (5.42), yielding the adjusted LM test statistic

$$\mathsf{T}^{\mathsf{a}}_{\mathsf{LM}} = \left[\sum_{i=1}^{n} \frac{1}{2}\hat{\mu}_i^{-2} g^2(\hat{\mu}_i)\right]^{-1/2} \times \sum_{i=1}^{n} \frac{1}{2}\hat{\mu}_i^{-2} g(\hat{\mu}_i)\{(y_i - \hat{\mu}_i)^2 - y_i + \hat{h}_{ii}\hat{\mu}_i\}. \tag{5.57}$$

For the Poisson with exponential mean function, $\hat{h}_{ii}$ is the ith diagonal entry in $\mathbf{W}^{1/2}\mathbf{X}(\mathbf{X}'\mathbf{W}\mathbf{X})^{-1}\mathbf{X}'\mathbf{W}^{1/2}$ where $\mathbf{W} = \mathsf{Diag}[\hat{\mu}_i]$ and $\mathbf{X}$ is the matrix of regressors.

Dean and Lawless (1989a) considered tests of Poisson against NB2 overdispersion, $g(\mu_i) = \mu_i^2$. The method has also been applied to other GLM models. Application to overdispersion in the binomial model is relatively straightforward and is presented in Dean (1992). Application to a truncated Poisson model, also a GLM, is considerably more complex and is given by Gurmu and Trivedi (1992). For data left-truncated at r, meaning only $y_i \geq r$ is observed, the adjusted LM test for Poisson against negative binomial is

$$\mathsf{T}^{\mathsf{a}}_{\mathsf{LM}} = [\hat{\mathcal{I}}^{\alpha\alpha}]^{-1/2} \sum_{i=1}^{n} \frac{1}{2} \hat{\mu}_i^{-2} g(\hat{\mu}_i)$$
$$\times \{(y_i - \hat{\mu}_i)^2 - y_i + (2y_i - \hat{\mu}_i - r + 1)\lambda(r - 1, \hat{\mu}_i)\hat{\mu}_i\},$$

where $\hat{\mathcal{I}}^{\alpha\alpha}$ is the scalar subcomponent for α of the inverse of the information matrix $-\mathsf{E}[\partial^2 \mathcal{L}/\partial\boldsymbol{\theta}\partial\boldsymbol{\theta}']$ evaluated at $\hat{\boldsymbol{\theta}} = (\hat{\boldsymbol{\beta}}', 0)'$, see Gurmu and Trivedi (1992, p. 350), and $\lambda(r - 1, \mu) = f(y, \mu)/1 - F(y, \mu)$ where $f(\cdot)$ and $F(\cdot)$ are the untruncated Poisson density and cdf.

The procedure has a certain asymmetry in that a small-sample correction is made only to the term in the numerator of the score test statistic. Conniffe (1990) additionally considered correction to the denominator term.

This method for small-sample correction of heteroskedasticity tests is much simpler than using the Edgeworth expansion, which from Honda (1988) is surprisingly complex even for the linear regression model under normality. The method cannot be adapted to tests of the regression coefficients themselves, however, as the score test in this case involves a weighted sum of $(y_i - \hat{\mu}_i)$ and the above method yields a zero asymptotic bias for $(y_i - \hat{\mu}_i)$. Small-sample adjustments are most easily done using the bootstrap, which as already noted is actually an empirical implementation of an Edgeworth expansion.

5.6 Conditional Moment Specification Tests

Likelihood-based hypothesis tests, for overdispersion, were presented in section 5.4. In this section we instead take a moment-based approach to hypothesis testing, using the CM test framework. The general approach is outlined in section 5.6.1. See also section 2.6.3 for motivation and general theory. The focus is on CM tests of correct specification of the mean and variance. Key results, and links to the LM tests presented earlier, are given in section 5.6.2. Generalization of these results to general cross-section models is given in section 5.6.3. In section 5.6.4 we present CM tests based on orthogonal polynomials in $(y - \mu)$, an alternative way to use the low-order moments of y. Two commonly used CM tests, the Hausman test and the information test, are presented in, respectively, sections 5.6.5 and 5.6.6.

One conclusion from this section is that many insights gained from the linear regression model with homoskedastic errors require substantial modification before being applied to even the simple Poisson model models. This is because the Poisson has complications of both nonlinear conditional mean function and heteroskedasticity that is a function of that mean. A better guide is provided by a binary choice model, such as logit or probit. But even this is too limited as the variance function cannot be misspecified in binary choice models, because it is always the mean times one minus the mean, whereas with count data the variance function is not restricted to being that imposed by the Poisson regression model.

5.6.1 *Introduction*

Suppose a model implies the population moment condition

$$\mathsf{E}[\mathbf{m}_i(y_i, \mathbf{x}_i, \boldsymbol{\theta})] = \mathbf{0}, \qquad i = 1, \ldots, n, \tag{5.58}$$

where $\mathbf{m}_i(\cdot)$ is an $r \times 1$ vector function. A CM test of this moment condition is based on the closeness to zero of the corresponding sample moment condition, that is

$$\mathbf{m}(\hat{\boldsymbol{\theta}}) = \sum_{i=1}^{n} \hat{\mathbf{m}}_i,$$

where $\hat{\mathbf{m}}_i = \mathbf{m}_i(y_i, \mathbf{x}_i, \hat{\boldsymbol{\theta}})$. The CM test statistic in general is

$$\sum_{i=1}^{n} \hat{\mathbf{m}}_i' \left\{ \mathsf{V}\left[\sum_{i=1}^{n} \hat{\mathbf{m}}_i \right] \right\}^{-1} \sum_{i=1}^{n} \hat{\mathbf{m}}_i,$$

and is asymptotically chi-square distributed.

Two issues arise in applying CM tests. First is choice of the function $\mathbf{m}_i(\cdot)$. Here we focus on tests based on the first two moments of count data regression models. Second is choosing how to implement the test. Several asymptotically equivalent versions are available, some of which can be computed using an auxiliary regression. Here we focus on applications in which the moment condition is chosen so that $\mathbf{m}_i(\cdot)$ satisfies

$$\mathsf{E}\left[\frac{\partial \mathbf{m}_i(y_i, \mathbf{x}_i, \boldsymbol{\theta})}{\partial \boldsymbol{\theta}'} \right] = \mathbf{0}. \tag{5.59}$$

Then from section 2.6.3 the CM test statistic simplifies to

$$\sum_{i=1}^{n} \hat{\mathbf{m}}_i' \left[\sum_{i=1}^{n} \mathsf{E}[\mathbf{m}_i \mathbf{m}_i']|_{\hat{\boldsymbol{\theta}}} \right]^{-1} \sum_{i=1}^{n} \hat{\mathbf{m}}_i. \tag{5.60}$$

If $m_i(\cdot)$ is a scalar, taking the square root of (5.60) yields the test statistic

$$\mathsf{T}_{\mathsf{CM}} = \left[\sum_{i=1}^{n} \mathsf{E}[m_i^2]|_{\hat{\theta}}\right]^{-1/2} \sum_{i=1}^{n} \hat{m}_i, \tag{5.61}$$

which is asymptotically $\mathsf{N}[0, 1]$ if (5.58) and (5.59) hold. An asymptotically equivalent version is

$$\mathsf{T}^*_{\mathsf{CM}} = \left[\sum_{i=1}^{n} \hat{m}_i^2\right]^{-1/2} \sum_{i=1}^{n} \hat{m}_i. \tag{5.62}$$

Even if (5.59) does not hold, implementation is still simple, provided $\hat{\boldsymbol{\theta}}$ is the MLE. Then a chi-square test statistic is the uncentered explained sum of squares from regression of 1 on $\hat{\mathbf{m}}_i$ and $\hat{\mathbf{s}}_i$, where $\hat{\mathbf{s}}_i = \partial \ln f(y_i \mid \mathbf{x}_i, \boldsymbol{\theta})/\partial\boldsymbol{\theta}|_{\hat{\boldsymbol{\theta}}}$.

If possible CM tests are compared to the LM test, which is a special case of a CM test and is, of course, the most powerful test if a fully parametric approach is taken. Particular interest lies in tests of correct specification of the conditional mean and variance.

For the Poisson regression, the LM test for exclusion of the subcomponent $\mathbf{x}_{2i}$ of $\mathbf{x}_i = [\mathbf{x}'_{1i}, \mathbf{x}'_{2i}]'$ model is a CM test of

$$\mathsf{E}[\mathbf{m}_i(y_i, \mathbf{x}_i, \boldsymbol{\beta}_1)] = \mathsf{E}[(y_i - \mu_{1i})\mathbf{x}_{2i}] = \mathbf{0}, \tag{5.63}$$

where $\mu_{1i} = \exp(\mathbf{x}'_{1i}\boldsymbol{\beta}_1)$.

For overdispersion, the test of Poisson with variance $\mu_i = \mu(\mathbf{x}'_i\boldsymbol{\beta})$ against the Katz system with variance function $\mu_i + \alpha g(\mu_i)$ is from (5.39) a CM test of

$$\mathsf{E}[m_i(y_i, \mathbf{x}_i, \boldsymbol{\beta})] = \mathsf{E}[\{(y_i - \mu_i)^2 - y_i\}\mu_i^{-2} g(\mu_i)] = 0. \tag{5.64}$$

Note that the simplifying condition (5.59) holds for $m_i(y_i, \mathbf{x}_i, \boldsymbol{\beta})$ in (5.64), provided (5.64) holds and $\mathsf{E}[y_i - \mu_i] = 0$. It can be shown that for the moment condition (5.64) the test statistic (5.61) yields T_{LM} given in (5.42), and the test statistic (5.62) yields $\mathsf{T}^*_{\mathsf{LM}}$ given in (5.43).

CM tests can be obtained under relatively weak stochastic assumptions. Several examples are given here, beginning with one in which a regression provides the motivation or basis for the test rather than just providing a way to calculate a test statistic.

5.6.2 *Regression-Based Tests for Overdispersion*

Consider cross-section data $(y_i, \mathbf{x}_i)$ where under the null hypothesis the first two moments are those of the Poisson regression model

$$H_0 : \mathsf{E}[y_i \mid \mathbf{x}_i] = \mu_i = \mu(\mathbf{x}_i, \boldsymbol{\beta}), \quad \mathsf{V}[y_i \mid \mathbf{x}_i] = \mu_i, \tag{5.65}$$

while under the alternative hypothesis

$$H_a : \mathsf{E}[y_i \mid \mathbf{x}_i] = \mu_i = \mu(\mathbf{x}_i, \boldsymbol{\beta}), \quad \mathsf{V}[y_i \mid \mathbf{x}_i] = \mu_i + \alpha g(\mu_i), \tag{5.66}$$

where $g(\mu_i)$ is a specified function such as μ_i or μ_i^2. The moments (5.66) are those of, for example, the negative binomial models presented in section 3.3.

The moment condition (5.66) implies

$$H_a : \mathsf{E}[\{(y_i - \mu_i)^2 - y_i\}|\mathbf{x}_i] = \alpha g(\mu_i), \tag{5.67}$$

while H_0 imposes the constraint that $\alpha = 0$. If μ_i is known one could perform a t test of $\alpha = 0$ based on regression of $(y_i - \mu_i)^2 - y_i$ on $g(\mu_i)$. Two complications are that μ_i is unknown and that the error term in this regression is in general heteroskedastic as the conditional variance of $(y_i - \mu_i)^2 - y_i$ is a function of μ_i, say

$$\omega_i = \omega(\mu_i) = \mathsf{V}[(y_i - \mu_i)^2 - y_i|\mathbf{x}_i]. \tag{5.68}$$

The null hypothesis

$$H_0 : \alpha = 0 \tag{5.69}$$

can be tested by the t test of $\alpha = 0$ in the LS regression

$$\sqrt{\hat{\omega}_i}\{(y_i - \hat{\mu}_i)^2 - y_i\} = \alpha \sqrt{\hat{\omega}_i}\, g(\hat{\mu}_i) + u_i, \tag{5.70}$$

where $\hat{\mu}_i = \mu(\mathbf{x}_i'\hat{\boldsymbol{\beta}})$, $\hat{\omega}_i = \omega(\hat{\mu}_i)$ and $\hat{\boldsymbol{\beta}}$ is a consistent estimator of $\boldsymbol{\beta}$ under H_0. The WLS regression is used as it yields the most efficient least-squares regression estimator of α and hence the most powerful or optimal test. In principle replacing μ_i by $\hat{\mu}_i$ leads to a more complicated distribution for $\hat{\alpha}$. This is not a problem in this particular application, however, essentially because $\partial\{(y_i - \mu_i)^2 - y_i\}/\partial\boldsymbol{\beta} = -2(y_i - \mu_i)\partial\mu_i/\partial\boldsymbol{\beta}$ has expected value $\mathbf{0}$ so (5.59) holds.

Standard results for OLS yields the t test statistic $\hat{\alpha}/\sqrt{\hat{\mathsf{V}}[\hat{\alpha}]}$ or

$$\mathsf{T}_{\mathsf{CM}}^{\mathsf{OLS}} = \left[s^2 \sum_{i=1}^{n} \hat{\omega}_i^{-1} g^2(\hat{\mu}_i)\right]^{-1/2} \sum_{i=1}^{n} \hat{\omega}_i^{-1} g(\hat{\mu}_i)\{(y_i - \hat{\mu}_i)^2 - y_i\}, \tag{5.71}$$

where

$$s^2 = \frac{1}{n-1} \sum_{i=1}^{n} \hat{\omega}_i^{-1}\{(y_i - \hat{\mu}_i)^2 - y_i - g(\hat{\mu}_i)\,\hat{\alpha}\}^2.$$

Under H_0, plim $s^2 = 1$ as $\alpha = 0$, and one can equivalently use

$$\mathsf{T}_{\mathsf{CM}} = \left[\sum_{i=1}^{n} \hat{\omega}_i^{-1} g^2(\hat{\mu}_i)\right]^{-1/2} \sum_{i=1}^{n} \hat{\omega}_i^{-1} g(\hat{\mu}_i)\{(y - \hat{\mu}_i)^2 - y_i\}. \tag{5.72}$$

Advantages of this approach to testing, beyond simplicity of use, include

1. If the first four moments of y_i under the null hypothesis are those of the Poisson, T_{CM} equals the optimal LM test statistic for testing Poisson against the Katz system.
2. The test is easily adapted to situations in which assumptions on only the first two moments are made.
3. The test can be given a simple interpretation as a CM test based on the first two moments of y_i.
4. The test is computed from an OLS regression that has interpretation as a model, rather than merely a computational device to compute the statistic.
5. The approach can be generalized to other testing situations.

These points are made clear in the following discussion.

First, in the fully parametric situation in which $y_i \sim \mathsf{P}[\mu_i]$, using formulae for the first four moments of the Poisson one obtains $\omega_i = 2\mu_i^2$. But then $\mathsf{T}_{\mathsf{CM}}^{\mathsf{OLS}}$ in (5.71) equals $\mathsf{T}_{\mathsf{LM}}^{***}$, the LM test for Poisson against negative binomial presented in (5.47), while T_{CM} in (5.72) equals T_{LM} given in (5.42).

Second, consider adaptation of the test statistic (5.71) in the case in which only the first two moments of y_i are assumed. Then ω_i in (5.68) is unknown. The least-squares regression (5.70) is again run, but with weighting function $\hat{\omega}_i$ replaced by $\hat{v}_i$. One might choose $\hat{v}_i = 2\hat{\mu}_i^2$, although one should note that it is no longer assumed that $\omega_i = 2\mu_i^2$. Now the error u_i has heteroskedasticity of unknown functional form, so the t test of $\alpha = 0$ uses robust sandwich standard errors. The test statistic is

$$\mathsf{T}_{\mathsf{CM}}^{\mathsf{Robust}} = \left[\sum_{i=1}^{n} \hat{u}_i^2 \hat{v}_i^{-1} g^2(\hat{\mu}_i) \right]^{-1/2} \sum_{i=1}^{n} \hat{v}_i^{-1} g(\hat{\mu}_i) \{(y_i - \hat{\mu}_i)^2 - y_i\}, \tag{5.73}$$

where $\hat{u}_i^2 = \{(y_i - \hat{\mu}_i)^2 - y_i - \hat{\alpha} g(\hat{\mu}_i)\}^2$ and $\hat{\alpha}$ is the least-squares estimator in (5.70) with $\hat{\omega}_i$ replaced by $\hat{v}_i$. Under H_0, $\mathsf{T}_{\mathsf{CM}}^{\mathsf{Robust}}$ is asymptotically $\mathsf{N}[0, 1]$.

In the special case in which $\hat{v}_i = 2\hat{\mu}_i^2$ the test statistic (5.73) provides a variant of the LM test statistic for overdispersion given in section 5.4 that is robust to misspecification of the third and fourth moments of y_i. This is directly analogous to the modification of the Breusch-Pagan LM test for heteroskedasticity in the regression model under normality proposed by Koenker (1982) to allow for nonconstant fourth moments of the dependent variable.

Third, consider a CM test for variance–mean equality. The null hypothesis (5.65) implies that

$$\mathsf{E}[\{(y_i - \mu_i)^2 - y_i\} | \mathbf{x}_i] = 0, \tag{5.74}$$

which in turn implies

$$\mathsf{E}[h(\mu_i)\{(y_i - \mu_i)^2 - y_i\}] = 0, \tag{5.75}$$

where we let $h(\mu_i)$ be a specified scalar function. The test based on closeness to zero of $\sum_{i=1}^{n} h(\hat{\mu}_i)\{(y_i - \hat{\mu}_i)^2 - y_i\}$ is a special case of the CM chi-square test statistic given in section 2.6.3. Because $\partial\{(y_i - \mu_i)^2 - y_i\}/\partial\boldsymbol{\beta} = -2(y_i - \mu_i)\partial\mu_i/\partial\boldsymbol{\beta}$ has expected value $\mathbf{0}$ and so (5.59) holds, one can use T_{CM} given in (5.61)

$$\mathsf{T}_{\mathsf{CM}} = \left[\sum_{i=1}^{n} h^2(\hat{\mu}_i)\hat{\omega}_i\right]^{-1/2} \sum_{i=1}^{n} h(\hat{\mu}_i)\{(y_i - \hat{\mu}_i)^2 - y_i\}, \qquad (5.76)$$

where $\omega_i = \mathsf{E}[\{(y_i - \mu_i)^2 - y_i\}^2|\mathbf{x}_i]$. T_{CM} is asymptotically $\mathsf{N}[0, 1]$ under (5.74). This test specifies only a moment condition under H_0. Different choices of function $h(\mu_i)$ will test in different directions away from H_0, with the optimal choice of $h(\mu_i)$ depending on the particular alternative to (5.74). The regression-based approach makes it clear that if the alternative is (5.67) then the optimal choice is $h(\mu_i) = \omega_i^{-1}g(\mu_i)$.

Fourth, consider calculation of overdispersion test statistics by an auxiliary regression. The usual approach is to obtain a CM or LM test statistic and then give ways to calculate the statistic or an asymptotically equivalent variant of the statistic by an auxiliary regression. This regression has no physical interpretation, being merely a computational device. Such tests are best called *regression-implemented* tests, although they are often called *regression-based* because their computation is based on a regression. By comparison the overdispersion test statistic given in this subsection is regression-based in the stronger sense that there is a regression motivation for the test statistic.

The final point, that this *regression-based* or *regression-motivated* test approach generalizes to other testing situations, is outlined in the next subsection.

Regression-based tests for overdispersion were proposed by Cameron and Trivedi (1985, 1990a). In addition to the regression (5.70) they also considered the t test of $\alpha = 0$ in the least-squares regression

$$\sqrt{\hat{\omega}_i}\{(y_i - \hat{\mu}_i)^2 - \hat{\mu}_i\} = \alpha\sqrt{\hat{\omega}_i}g(\hat{\mu}_i) + u_i. \qquad (5.77)$$

This replaces y_i by $\hat{\mu}_i$ in the left-hand side, the rationale being that the moment condition (5.66) implies not only (5.67) but also

$$H_a : \mathsf{E}[\{(y_i - \mu_i)^2 - \mu_i\} \,|\, \mathbf{x}_i] = \alpha g(\mu_i). \qquad (5.78)$$

The test based on the regression (5.77) is more difficult to implement because replacing μ_i by $\hat{\mu}_i$ makes a difference in this regression, because $\partial\{(y_i - \mu_i)^2 - \mu_i\}/\partial\boldsymbol{\beta} = -\{2(y_i - \mu_i) + 1\}\partial\mu_i/\partial\boldsymbol{\beta}$ has nonzero expected value. Cameron and Trivedi (1985) show that the analog of (5.72) is

$$\mathsf{T}_{\mathsf{CM},2} = \left[\sum_{i=1}^{n}\sum_{j=1}^{n} \hat{w}_{ij}g(\hat{\mu}_i)g(\hat{\mu}_j)\right]^{-1/2} \times \sum_{i=1}^{n}\sum_{j=1}^{n} \hat{w}_{ij}g(\hat{\mu}_i)\{(y_j - \hat{\mu}_j)^2 - \hat{\mu}_j\}, \qquad (5.79)$$

where w_{ij} is the ij^{th} entry in $\mathbf{W} = [\mathbf{D} - \mathbf{\Delta}(\mathbf{\Delta}'\mathbf{D}_\mu^{-1}\mathbf{\Delta})^{-1}\mathbf{\Delta}']^{-1}$, $\mathbf{D}$ and $\mathbf{D}_\mu$ are $n \times n$ diagonal matrices with i^{th} entries $(2\mu_i^2 + \mu_i)$ and μ_i, respectively, and $\mathbf{\Delta}$ is an $n \times k$ matrix with i^{th} row $\partial\mu_i/\partial\boldsymbol{\beta}'$.

The test $\mathsf{T}_{\mathsf{CM},2}$ is a different test from T_{CM} in (5.72), with different power properties. In particular $\mathsf{T}_{\mathsf{CM},2}$ is the LM test, and hence the most powerful test, for testing $\mathsf{N}[\mu_i, \mu_i]$ against $\mathsf{N}[\mu_i, \mu_i + \alpha g(\mu_i)]$. It has already been shown that T_{CM} is the LM test for $\mathsf{P}[\mu_i]$ against NB2. In addition to greater power in the standard setup for overdispersion tests, T_{CM} has the advantage of being easier to implement.

5.6.3 *Regression-Based CM Tests*

Suppose that a specified model imposes the conditional moment restriction

$$\mathsf{E}[r(y_i, \mathbf{x}_i, \boldsymbol{\theta}) \mid \mathbf{x}_i] = 0, \tag{5.80}$$

where for simplicity $r(\cdot)$ is a scalar function. Suppose we wish to test this restriction against the specific alternative conditional expected value for $r(y_i, \mathbf{x}_i, \boldsymbol{\theta})$

$$\mathsf{E}[r(y_i, \mathbf{x}_i, \boldsymbol{\theta}) \mid \mathbf{x}_i] = \mathbf{g}(\mathbf{x}_i, \boldsymbol{\theta})'\boldsymbol{\alpha}, \tag{5.81}$$

where $\mathbf{g}(\cdot)$ and $\boldsymbol{\alpha}$ are $p \times 1$ vectors.

The moment condition (5.80) can be tested against (5.81) by test of $\boldsymbol{\alpha} = \mathbf{0}$ in the regression

$$r(y_i, \mathbf{x}_i, \boldsymbol{\theta}) = \mathbf{g}(\mathbf{x}_i, \boldsymbol{\theta})'\boldsymbol{\alpha} + \varepsilon_i. \tag{5.82}$$

The most powerful test of $\boldsymbol{\alpha} = \mathbf{0}$ is based on the efficient GLS estimator, which for data independent over i is the WLS estimator

$$\hat{\boldsymbol{\alpha}} = \left[\sum_{i=1}^{n} \frac{1}{\sigma^2(\mathbf{x}_i, \boldsymbol{\theta})} \mathbf{g}(\mathbf{x}_i, \boldsymbol{\theta})\mathbf{g}(\mathbf{x}_i, \boldsymbol{\theta})'\right]^{-1} \times \sum_{i=1}^{n} \frac{1}{\sigma^2(\mathbf{x}_i, \boldsymbol{\theta})} \mathbf{g}(\mathbf{x}_i, \boldsymbol{\theta}) r(y_i, \mathbf{x}_i, \boldsymbol{\theta}), \tag{5.83}$$

where

$$\sigma^2(\mathbf{x}_i, \boldsymbol{\theta}) = \mathsf{E}_0[r(y_i, \mathbf{x}_i, \boldsymbol{\theta})^2 \mid \mathbf{x}_i] \tag{5.84}$$

is the conditional variance of $r(y_i, \mathbf{x}_i, \boldsymbol{\theta})$ under the null hypothesis model.

Tests based on $\hat{\boldsymbol{\alpha}}$ are equivalent to tests based on any full rank transformation of $\hat{\boldsymbol{\alpha}}$. Most simply multiply by $\sum_{i=1}^{n} \sigma^{-2}(\mathbf{x}_i, \boldsymbol{\theta})\mathbf{g}(\mathbf{x}_i, \boldsymbol{\theta}) r(y_i, \mathbf{x}_i, \boldsymbol{\theta})$. This is equivalent to a CM test of the unconditional moment condition

$$\mathsf{E}[\mathbf{m}(y_i, \mathbf{x}_i, \boldsymbol{\theta})] = \mathsf{E}\left[\frac{1}{\sigma^2(\mathbf{x}_i, \boldsymbol{\theta})} \mathbf{g}(\mathbf{x}_i, \boldsymbol{\theta}) r(y_i, \mathbf{x}_i, \boldsymbol{\theta})\right] = \mathbf{0}. \tag{5.85}$$

Note that the unconditional moment (5.85) for the CM test is obtained as a test of the conditional moment condition (5.80) against the alternative (5.81).

An example already considered is testing variance–mean equality, in which case $r(y_i, \mathbf{x}_i, \boldsymbol{\beta}) = (y_i - \mu_i)^2 - y_i$ and $g(\mathbf{x}_i, \boldsymbol{\beta})'\alpha = \alpha\mu_i^2$ in the case of overdispersion of NB2 form. If the Poisson assumption is maintained under the null, then $\sigma^2(\mathbf{x}_i, \boldsymbol{\beta}) = 2\mu_i^2$ and the CM test based on the unconditional moment (5.85) simplifies to a test of

$$\mathsf{E}[(y_i - \mu_i)^2 - y_i] = 0. \tag{5.86}$$

Now consider a CM test based on an unconditional moment condition that can be partitioned into a product of the form

$$\mathsf{E}[\mathbf{m}^*(y_i, \mathbf{x}_i, \boldsymbol{\theta})] = \mathsf{E}[\mathbf{g}^*(\mathbf{x}_i, \boldsymbol{\theta})r^*(y_i, \mathbf{x}_i, \boldsymbol{\theta})], \tag{5.87}$$

where y_i only appears through the scalar function $r^*(\cdot)$. A simple interpretation of this test is that it is testing failure of the conditional moment condition

$$\mathsf{E}[r^*(y_i, \mathbf{x}_i, \boldsymbol{\theta}) \mid \mathbf{x}_i] = 0, \tag{5.88}$$

in the direction $\mathbf{g}^*(\mathbf{x}_i, \boldsymbol{\theta})$. A much more specific interpretation of the direction of the test, using (5.85), is that it is testing (5.88) against the conditional moment condition

$$\mathsf{E}[r^*(y_i, \mathbf{x}_i, \boldsymbol{\theta}) \mid \mathbf{x}_i] = \sigma^{*2}(\mathbf{x}_i, \boldsymbol{\theta})\mathbf{g}^*(\mathbf{x}_i, \boldsymbol{\theta})'\boldsymbol{\alpha}, \tag{5.89}$$

where

$$\sigma^{*2}(\mathbf{x}_i, \boldsymbol{\theta}) = \mathsf{V}[r^*(y_i, \mathbf{x}_i, \boldsymbol{\theta}) \mid \mathbf{x}_i].$$

Considering again the test of overdispersion of NB2 form, it is not immediately apparent what form of overdispersion is being tested by the CM test of (5.86). Using (5.89), however, the test can be viewed as a test against the alternative $\mathsf{E}[(y_i - \mu_i)^2 - y_i] = \alpha{\mu_i}^2$, where this interpretation uses the result that the null hypothesis Poisson model implies $\mathsf{V}[(y_i - \mu_i)^2 - y_i] = 2\mu_i^2$.

To summarize, in the usual case in which interest lies in the expected value of a scalar function $r(y_i, \mathbf{x}_i, \boldsymbol{\theta})$ of the dependent variable, CM tests of an explicit null against an explicit alternative conditional expected value of $r(y_i, \mathbf{x}_i, \boldsymbol{\theta})$ are easily developed. Going the other way, a CM test for zero unconditional expected value of the product of $r(y_i, \mathbf{x}_i, \boldsymbol{\theta})$ and a specified function of $\mathbf{x}_i$ and $\boldsymbol{\theta}$ can be interpreted as a test of an explicit null against an explicit alternative conditional expected value of $r(y_i, \mathbf{x}_i, \boldsymbol{\theta})$.

This approach, called *regression-based CM tests* by Cameron and Trivedi (1990c), therefore provides a link between the standard formulation of CM tests as model misspecification tests in no particular direction and formal hypothesis tests which test against an explicit alternative hypothesis. Several applications, and extension to the case in which $\mathbf{r}(y_i, \mathbf{x}_i, \boldsymbol{\theta})$ is a vector, are given in Cameron and Trivedi (1990c).

The preceding discussion looks only at the formation of the moment for the CM test. For actual implementation one can either run regression (5.82), that is, replace $\boldsymbol{\theta}$ by $\hat{\boldsymbol{\theta}}$ and use weights $\sigma^{-1}(\mathbf{x}_i, \hat{\boldsymbol{\theta}})$, or form a test based on the sample analog of (5.85), $\sum_{i=1}^{n} \sigma^{-2}(\mathbf{x}_i, \hat{\boldsymbol{\theta}})\mathbf{g}(\mathbf{x}_i, \hat{\boldsymbol{\theta}})r(y_i, \mathbf{x}_i, \hat{\boldsymbol{\theta}})$. In either case the distribution is most easily obtained if condition (5.59) holds, which is the case if in addition to (5.80)

$$\mathsf{E}\left[\frac{\partial r(y_i, \mathbf{x}_i, \boldsymbol{\theta})}{\partial \boldsymbol{\theta}'}\right] = \mathbf{0}. \tag{5.90}$$

For example, in testing variance–mean equality, the choice $r_i(y_i, \mathbf{x}_i, \boldsymbol{\theta}) = \{(y_i - \mu_i)^2 - \mu_i\}$ satisfies (5.90).

In other testing situations it is also possible to construct tests in which (5.90) holds. In particular, for testing that the correct model for heteroskedasticity is a specified function $v(\mu_i)$ against the alternative that $\mathsf{V}[y_i \mid \mathbf{x}_i] = v(\mu_i) + \alpha g(\mu_i)$, where $\mathsf{E}[y_i \mid \mathbf{x}_i] = \mu_i = \mu(\mathbf{x}_i, \boldsymbol{\beta})$, the choice

$$r(y_i, \mathbf{x}_i, \boldsymbol{\beta}) = (y_i - \mu_i)^2 - \frac{\partial v(\mu_i)}{\partial \mu_i}(y_i - \mu_i) - v(\mu_i), \tag{5.91}$$

satisfies (5.90). The regression-based CM test using (5.91) not only is easy to implement but also coincides with the LM test of Poisson against negative binomial, the LM test of binomial against the beta binomial, and the Breusch-Pagan (Breusch and Pagan, 1979) test of normal homoskedastic error against normal heteroskedastic error (in which case $v(\mu_i) = v(\mu_i, \sigma^2) = \sigma^2$). For details see Cameron (1991).

Further examples of regression-based CM tests are given here.

5.6.4 *Orthogonal Polynomial Tests*

In the CM test framework it is natural to focus on tests of correct specification of the first few conditional moments of the dependent variable. One possibility is to construct a sequence of tests based on whether the expected values of y_i^k equal those imposed by the model, for $k = 1, 2, 3, \ldots$. Another is to use central moments, in which case the sequence is of the expected values of $(y_i - \mu_i)^k$ for $k = 1, 2, 3, \ldots$.

An alternative approach, proposed by Cameron and Trivedi (1990b), is to consider a sequence of *orthogonal polynomial* functions in y_i, in which case terms in the sequence are uncorrelated. One can additionally consider *orthonormal polynomials*, for which terms are orthogonal and normalized to have unit variance.

For the Poisson density, the orthonormal polynomials are called the *Gram-Charlier polynomial series*, with first three terms

$$\begin{aligned} Q_1(y) &= (y - \mu)/\sqrt{\mu} \\ Q_2(y) &= \{(y - \mu)^2 - y\}/\sqrt{2}\mu \\ Q_3(y) &= \{(y - \mu)^3 - 3(y - \mu)^2 \\ &\quad - (3\mu - 2)(y - \mu) + 2\mu\}/\sqrt{6\mu^3}. \end{aligned} \tag{5.92}$$

Further terms are obtained using $Q_j(y) = \partial\{(1+z)^y \exp(-\mu z)\}/\partial z|_{z=0}$. Note that $\mathsf{E}[Q_j(y)] = 0$. These polynomials have the property of orthogonality, that is, $\mathsf{E}[Q_j(y)Q_k(y)] = 0$ for $j \neq k$, and are normalized so that $\mathsf{E}[Q_j^2(y)] = 1$. These properties hold if y is $\mathsf{P}[\mu]$, and also hold for the first j terms under the weaker assumption that y has the same first $j+k$ moments as $\mathsf{P}[\mu]$ for orthogonality, and the same first $2j$ moments as $\mathsf{P}[\mu]$ for orthonormality.

The orthonormal polynomials can be used directly for CM tests. Thus, to test correct specification of the jth moment of y_i, assuming correct specification of the first $(j-1)$ moments, use

$$\mathsf{E}[\mathbf{m}_j(y_i, \mathbf{x}_i, \boldsymbol{\beta})] = \mathsf{E}[Q_j(y_i, \mathbf{x}_i, \boldsymbol{\beta})\, \mathbf{g}_j(\mathbf{x}_i, \boldsymbol{\beta})] = \mathbf{0}, \tag{5.93}$$

where for regression applications $Q_j(y_i, \mathbf{x}_i, \boldsymbol{\beta})$ is $Q_j(y)$ in (5.92) evaluated at $\mu_i = \mu(\mathbf{x}_i, \boldsymbol{\beta})$. Using the regression-based interpretation of the CM test in (5.88) and (5.89), this is a test of $\mathsf{E}[Q_j(y_i, \mathbf{x}_i, \boldsymbol{\beta}) \mid \mathbf{x}_i] = 0$ against $\mathsf{E}[Q_j(y_i, \mathbf{x}_i, \boldsymbol{\beta}) \mid \mathbf{x}_i] = \mathbf{g}(\mathbf{x}_i, \boldsymbol{\beta})'\boldsymbol{\alpha}_j$, where simplification occurs because $\mathsf{V}[Q_j(y_i)] = 1$ due to orthonormality. Define the jth central moment of the Poisson to be $\mu'_j = \mathsf{E}[(y-\mu)^j]$. Then, equivalently, given the assumption of correct assumption of the first $(j-1)$ moments, the CM test (5.93) is a test of $\mathsf{E}[(y_i-\mu_i)^j] = \mu'_j$ against $\mathsf{E}[(y_i-\mu_i)^j] = \mu'_j + \mathbf{g}(\mathbf{x}_i, \boldsymbol{\beta})'\boldsymbol{\alpha}_j$. These CM tests are easy to compute, because for the Poisson the orthonormal polynomials satisfy $\mathsf{E}[\partial Q_j(y)/\partial\mu] = 0$, so (5.59) holds.

The orthonormal polynomials can also be used to construct LM tests for the Poisson against series expansions around a baseline Poisson density. A property of orthogonal polynomials is that a general density $g(y)$ can be represented as the following series expansion around the baseline density $f(y)$

$$g(y) = f(y)\left[1 + \sum_{j=1}^{\infty} a_j Q_j(y)\right],$$

where $a_j = \int Q_j(y)g(y)\,dy$ and $g(y)$ is assumed to satisfy the boundedness condition $\int \{g(y)/f(y)\}^2 f(y)\,dy < \infty$. Then, because $\ln g(y) = \ln f(y) + \ln[1 + \sum_{j=1}^{\infty} a_j Q_j(y)]$,

$$\left.\frac{\partial \ln g(y)}{\partial a_j}\right|_{a_1=0, a_2=0, \ldots} = Q_j(y), \qquad j = 1, 2, \ldots.$$

This suggests a sequence of score tests for the null hypothesis that the Poisson density is correctly specified

$$\mathsf{E}[Q_j(y_i, \mathbf{x}_i, \boldsymbol{\beta})] = 0, \qquad j = 1, 2, \ldots. \tag{5.94}$$

For the Poisson, the tests based on orthonormal polynomials equal the standard LM tests for correct specification of the first two moments. Thus tests based on $Q_1(y_i) = (y_i - \mu_i)$ coincide with the LM test (5.63) for excluded variables, while tests based on $Q_2(y_i) = (y_i - \mu_i)^2 - y_i$ correspond to the LM test (5.64) for Poisson against the Katz system. Non-Poisson skewness can be tested using $Q_3(y_i)$ given in (5.92). This is essentially the same test as that of Lee (1986) for the Poisson against truncated Gram-Charlier series expansion.

The CM tests proposed here differ in general from those obtained by considering only the jth central moment. For example, consider a CM test of the second moment of the Poisson, conditional on correct specification of the first. Then, because $\mathsf{E}[(y-\mu)^2] = \mu$ for $y \sim \mathsf{P}[\mu]$, the CM test based on the second central moment is

$$\mathsf{E}[\{(y_i - \mu(\mathbf{x}_i, \boldsymbol{\beta}))^2 - \mu(\mathbf{x}_i, \boldsymbol{\beta})\}\, \mathbf{g}_2(\mathbf{x}_i, \boldsymbol{\beta})] = \mathbf{0}.$$

The test based on the second orthogonal polynomial from (5.92) is

$$\mathsf{E}[\{(y_i - \mu(\mathbf{x}_i, \boldsymbol{\beta}))^2 - y_i\}\, \mathbf{g}_2(\mathbf{x}_i, \boldsymbol{\beta})] = \mathbf{0}.$$

As pointed out at the end of section 5.6.2 for overdispersion tests with $\mathbf{g}_2(\mathbf{x}_i, \boldsymbol{\beta}) = \mu_i^{-2} g(\mu_i)$, these different moment conditions lead to quite different tests.

Key properties of orthogonal and orthonormal polynomials are summarized in Cameron and Trivedi (1993) and also discussed in Chapter 8. The discussion here has focused on the Poisson. The properties that the resulting CM tests coincide with standard LM tests for mean and variance, and that the tests are easy to implement as (5.59) holds, carry over to the LEF with quadratic variance function (QVF). For the LEF-QVF the variance is a quadratic function of the mean, $\mathsf{V}[y] = v_0 + v_1\mu + v_2\mu^2$, where various possible choices of the coefficients v_0, v_1, and v_2 lead to six exponential families, five of which, the normal, Poisson, gamma, binomial, and negative binomial, constitute the Meixner class. This is discussed in detail in Cameron and Trivedi (1990b).

Finally, although results are especially straightforward for LEF-QVF densities, one can construct orthogonal polynomial sequences for any assumed model. In particular, letting $\mu = \mathsf{E}[y]$ and $\mu_j = \mathsf{E}[(y-\mu)^j]$ for $j = 2, 3$, the first two orthogonal polynomials are

$$\begin{aligned} P_1(y) &= y - \mu \\ P_2(y) &= (y-\mu)^2 - \frac{\mu_3}{\mu_2}(y-\mu) - \mu_2. \end{aligned} \tag{5.95}$$

These can be used for tests of the specified conditional mean and variance in general settings.

5.6.5 *Information Matrix Tests*

The IM test, introduced in section 2.6.3, is a CM test for fully parametric models of whether the information matrix equality holds, that is, whether

$$\mathsf{E}\left[\operatorname{vech}\left(\frac{\partial^2 \ln f_i}{\partial\boldsymbol{\theta}\partial\boldsymbol{\theta}'} + \frac{\partial \ln f_i}{\partial\boldsymbol{\theta}}\frac{\partial \ln f_i}{\partial\boldsymbol{\theta}'}\right)\right] = \mathbf{0}, \tag{5.96}$$

where $f_i = f_i(y_i, \mathbf{x}_i, \boldsymbol{\theta})$ is the density. This can be applied in a straightforward manner to any specified density for count data, such as negative binomial and hurdle, and is easily computed using the OPG regression given in section 2.6.3.

An interesting question is what fundamental features of the model are being tested by an IM test. Chesher (1984) showed that quite generally the IM test is a test for random parameter heterogeneity; Hall (1987) showed that for the linear model under normality, subcomponents of the IM test were tests of heteroskedasticity, symmetry, and kurtosis. Here we focus on Poisson regression.

For the Poisson regression model with exponential mean function, substitution into (5.96) of the first and second derivatives of the log-density with respect to $\boldsymbol{\theta}$ yields

$$\mathsf{E}\left[\{(y_i - \mu_i)^2 - \mu_i\}\mathrm{vech}\left(\mathbf{x}_i\mathbf{x}_i'\right)\right] = \mathbf{0}. \tag{5.97}$$

The IM test is a CM test of (5.97). If only the component of the IM test based on the intercept term is considered, the IM test coincides with the LM test of overdispersion of form $\mathsf{V}[y_i] = \mu_i + \alpha\mu_i^2$, because the test is based on $\sum_{i=1}^n (y_i - \hat{\mu}_i)^2 - \hat{\mu}_i$, which equals $\sum_{i=1}^n (y_i - \hat{\mu}_i)^2 - y_i$ as the Poisson first order conditions imply $\sum_{i=1}^n (y_i - \hat{\mu}_i) = 0$.

Considering all components of the IM test, (5.97) is of the form (5.87). Using $\mathsf{E}[\{(y_i - \mu_i)^2 - \mu_i\}^2] = 2\mu_i^2$, this leads to the interpretation of the IM test as a test of $\mathsf{E}[\{(y_i - \mu_i)^2 - \mu_i\} \mid \mathbf{x}_i] = 0$ against $\mathsf{E}[\{(y_i - \mu_i)^2 - \mu_i\} \mid \mathbf{x}_i] = \mu_i^2\, \mathrm{vech}(\mathbf{x}_i\mathbf{x}_i')'\boldsymbol{\alpha}$. So the IM test is a test against overdispersion of form $\mathsf{V}[y_i] = \mu_i + \mu_i^2\, \mathrm{vech}(\mathbf{x}_i\mathbf{x}_i')'\boldsymbol{\alpha}$. This result is analogous to the result of Hall (1987) for the regression parameters subcomponent for the linear regression model under normality. Note, however, that $\mathrm{vech}(\mathbf{x}_i\mathbf{x}_i')'\boldsymbol{\alpha}$ is weighted by μ_i^2, whereas in the linear model the test is simply against $\mathsf{V}[y_i] = \sigma^2 + \mathrm{vech}(\mathbf{x}_i\mathbf{x}_i')'\boldsymbol{\alpha}$.

The result (5.97) holds only for an exponential conditional mean. If the conditional mean is of general form $\mu_i = \mu(\mathbf{x}_i'\boldsymbol{\beta})$ then the IM test can be shown to be a CM test of

$$\mathsf{E}\left[\frac{y_i - \mu_i}{\mu_i}\mathrm{vech}\left(\frac{\partial^2\mu_i}{\partial\boldsymbol{\beta}\partial\boldsymbol{\beta}'}\right)\right] + \mathsf{E}\left[\left\{\frac{(y_i - \mu_i)^2 - y_i}{\mu_i^2}\right\}\mathrm{vech}\left(\mathbf{x}_i\mathbf{x}_i'\right)\right] = \mathbf{0}. \tag{5.98}$$

This tests both the specification of the variance, through the second term, and the more fundamental condition that the conditional mean is misspecified. Similar results for LEF models in general are given in Cameron and Trivedi (1990d).

The Poisson regression model is a special case of a model in which the underlying distribution of y_i depends only on the scalar μ_i, which is then parameterized to depend on a function of k regression parameters, meaning that the density is of the special form $f(y_i \mid \mu(\mathbf{x}_i, \boldsymbol{\beta}))$. It follows that $\partial \ln f_i/\partial\boldsymbol{\beta} =$

$(\partial \ln f_i/\partial\mu_i)(\partial\mu_i/\partial\boldsymbol{\beta})$ and the IM test (5.96) can be expressed as a test of

$$\mathsf{E}\left[\frac{\partial \ln f_i}{\partial \mu_i}\text{vech}\left(\frac{\partial^2\mu_i}{\partial\boldsymbol{\beta}\partial\boldsymbol{\beta}'}\right)\right] + \mathsf{E}\left[\left\{\frac{\partial^2 \ln f_i}{\partial\mu_i^2}+\left(\frac{\partial \ln f_i}{\partial\mu_i}\right)^2\right\}\text{vech}\left(\frac{\partial\mu_i}{\partial\boldsymbol{\beta}}\frac{\partial\mu_i}{\partial\boldsymbol{\beta}'}\right)\right]=\mathbf{0}. \tag{5.99}$$

There are clearly two components to the IM test. The first component is a test of whether $\mathsf{E}[\partial \ln f_i/\partial\mu_i]=0$, required for consistency of the MLE which solves $\sum_{i=1}^n \partial \ln f_i/\partial\mu_i(\partial\mu_i/\partial\boldsymbol{\beta}) = \mathbf{0}$. The second component is a test of the IM equality in terms of the underlying parameter μ_i rather than the regression parameter $\boldsymbol{\beta}$.

Setting $\tau = \text{vech}((\partial\mu_i/\partial\boldsymbol{\beta})(\partial\mu_i/\partial\boldsymbol{\beta}'))'\boldsymbol{\alpha}/\sqrt{n}$ in (5.52) yields a LM test of $\boldsymbol{\alpha} = \mathbf{0}$, which equals the second component of the IM test. It follows that the second component of the IM test is an LM test that the density is $f(y_i|\mu_i)$ where $\mu_i = \mu(\mathbf{x}_i, \beta)$, against the alternative that it is $f(y_i \mid \lambda_i)$ where λ_i is a random variable with mean μ_i and variance $\text{vech}((\partial\mu_i/\partial\boldsymbol{\beta})(\partial\mu_i/\partial\boldsymbol{\beta}'))'\boldsymbol{\alpha}/\sqrt{n}$. Cameron and Trivedi (1990d) show that the complete IM test, with both components, is a test against the alternative that y_i has density $f(y_i \mid \lambda_i)$ where λ_i is a random variable with mean $\mu_i + \text{vech}(\partial^2\mu_i/\partial\boldsymbol{\beta}\partial\boldsymbol{\beta}')/\sqrt{n}$ and variance $\text{vech}((\partial\mu_i/\partial\boldsymbol{\beta})(\partial\mu_i/\partial\boldsymbol{\beta}'))'\boldsymbol{\alpha}/\sqrt{n}$. So the IM test additionally tests for misspecification of the mean function.

Interpretations of the IM test have ignored the first component of the IM test because they have focused on the linear model where $\mu_i = \mathbf{x}_i'\boldsymbol{\beta}$, in which case $\partial^2\mu_i/\partial\boldsymbol{\beta}\partial\boldsymbol{\beta}' = \mathbf{0}$. In general the components can be negative or positive and so may be offsetting. So even if the first component is large in magnitude, indicating a fundamental misspecification, a model may pass the IM test. This indicates the usefulness, in nonlinear settings, of determining the moment conditions being tested by the IM test.

5.6.6 *Hausman Tests*

One way to test for simultaneity in a single linear regression equation with iid errors is to compare the OLS and two-stage least-squares estimators. If there is simultaneity the two estimators differ in probability limit, because OLS is inconsistent. If there is no simultaneity the two estimators have the same probability limit, because both are consistent. Tests based on such comparisons between two different estimators are called Hausman tests, after Hausman (1978), or Wu-Hausman tests or even Durbin-Wu-Hausman tests, after Wu (1973) and Durbin (1954) who also proposed such tests.

Consider two estimators $\tilde{\boldsymbol{\theta}}$ and $\hat{\boldsymbol{\theta}}$ where

$$\begin{aligned} H_0 &: \text{plim}(\tilde{\boldsymbol{\theta}} - \hat{\boldsymbol{\theta}}) = \mathbf{0} \\ H_a &: \text{plim}(\tilde{\boldsymbol{\theta}} - \hat{\boldsymbol{\theta}}) \neq \mathbf{0}. \end{aligned} \tag{5.100}$$

The *Hausman test statistic* of H_0 is

$$\mathsf{T_H} = n\,(\tilde{\boldsymbol\theta} - \hat{\boldsymbol\theta})'\mathbf{V}^{-1}_{\tilde\theta-\hat\theta}(\tilde{\boldsymbol\theta} - \hat{\boldsymbol\theta}), \tag{5.101}$$

which is $\chi^2(q)$ under H_0, where it is assumed that $\sqrt{n}(\tilde{\boldsymbol\theta} - \hat{\boldsymbol\theta}) \xrightarrow{d} \mathsf{N}[\mathbf{0}, \mathbf{V}_{\tilde\theta-\hat\theta}]$, under H_0. In some applications $\mathbf{V}_{\tilde\theta-\hat\theta}$ is of less than full rank, in which case $\mathbf{V}^{-1}_{\tilde\theta-\hat\theta}$ is replaced by the generalized inverse of $\mathbf{V}_{\tilde\theta-\hat\theta}$ and the degrees of freedom are $\mathsf{rank}[\mathbf{V}_{\tilde\theta-\hat\theta}]$. We reject H_0 if $\mathsf{T_H}$ exceeds the chi-square critical value.

The Hausman test is easy in principle but difficult in practice due to the need to obtain a consistent estimate of the variance matrix $\mathbf{V}_{\tilde\theta-\hat\theta}$. In the special case in which $\tilde{\boldsymbol\theta}$ is the fully efficient estimator under the null, $\mathbf{V}_{\tilde\theta-\hat\theta} = \mathbf{V}_{\hat\theta} - \mathbf{V}_{\tilde\theta}$. Therefore it is easily computed as the difference between the variance matrices of the two estimators (see Hausman, 1978, or Amemiya, 1985, p. 146). An example is linear regression with possible correlation between regressors and the error, with $\tilde{\boldsymbol\theta}$ the OLS estimator, which is the efficient estimator under the null of no correlation, while $\hat{\boldsymbol\theta}$ is the two-stage least squares estimator, which maintains consistency under the alternative. Hausman (1978) gives examples in which the Hausman test can be computed by a standard test for the significance of regressors in an augmented regression, but these results are confined to linear models.

Holly (1982) considered Hausman tests for nonlinear models in the likelihood framework and compared the Hausman test with standard likelihood-based hypothesis tests such as the LM test. Partition the parameter vector as $\boldsymbol\theta = (\boldsymbol\theta_1', \boldsymbol\theta_2')'$, where the null hypothesis $H_0 : \boldsymbol\theta_1 = \boldsymbol\theta_{10}$ applies to the first component of $\boldsymbol\theta$, and the second component $\boldsymbol\theta_2$ is a nuisance parameter vector. Restricted and unrestricted maximum likelihood estimation of $\boldsymbol\theta$ provides two estimates $\tilde{\boldsymbol\theta}_2$ and $\hat{\boldsymbol\theta}_2$ of the nuisance parameter. Suppose the alternative hypothesis is $H_0 : \boldsymbol\theta_1 = \boldsymbol\theta_{10} + \boldsymbol\delta$, in which case classical hypothesis tests are tests of $H_0 : \boldsymbol\delta = \mathbf{0}$. Holly (1982) showed that by comparison the Hausman test based on the difference $\tilde{\boldsymbol\theta}_2 - \hat{\boldsymbol\theta}_2$ is a test of $H_0 : \mathcal{I}_{22}^{-1}\mathcal{I}_{21}\boldsymbol\delta = \mathbf{0}$, where $\mathcal{I}_{ij} = \mathsf{E}[\partial^2\mathcal{L}(\boldsymbol\theta_1, \boldsymbol\theta_2)/\partial\boldsymbol\theta_i\partial\boldsymbol\theta_j]$. Holly (1987) extended analysis to nonlinear hypothesis $\mathbf{h}(\boldsymbol\theta_1) = \mathbf{0}$, with Hausman tests based on linear combinations $\mathbf{D}(\tilde{\boldsymbol\theta} - \hat{\boldsymbol\theta})$ rather than just the subcomponent $(\tilde{\boldsymbol\theta}_2 - \hat{\boldsymbol\theta}_2)$. Furthermore, the model under consideration may be potentially misspecified, covering the PMLE based on an exponential family density.

The Hausman test can potentially be used in many count applications, particularly ones analogous to those in the linear setting such as testing for endogeneity. It should be kept in mind, however, that the test is designed for situations in which at least one of the estimators is inconsistent under the alternative. Consider a Hausman test of Poisson against the NB2 model, where in the latter model the conditional mean is correctly specified although there is overdispersion ($\alpha \neq 0$). The Poisson MLE is fully efficient under the null hypothesis. Because the Poisson regression coefficients $\boldsymbol\beta$ maintain their consistency under the alternative hypothesis, however, common sense suggests that a Hausman test of the difference between NB2 and Poisson estimates of $\boldsymbol\beta$ will have no power. In terms of Holly's framework, $\theta_1 = \alpha$, $\boldsymbol{\theta}_2 = \boldsymbol{\beta}$, and the Hausman test is a test of $H_0 : \mathcal{I}_{22}^{-1}\mathcal{I}_{21}\boldsymbol{\delta} = \mathbf{0}$. But here $\mathcal{I}_{21} = \mathbf{0}$ from Chapter 3.2. In fact, if the Poisson and NB2 estimates of $\boldsymbol{\beta}$ are compared, then large values of the Hausman test statistic reflect more fundamental misspecification, that of the conditional mean.

5.7 Discriminating among Nonnested Models

Two models are *nonnested models* if neither model can be represented as a special case of the other. Further distinction can be made between models that are *overlapping*, in which case some specializations of the two models are equal, and models that are *strictly nonnested*, in which case there is no overlap at all. Models based on the same distribution that have some regressors in common and some regressors not in common are overlapping models. Models with different nonnested distributions and models with different nonnested functional forms for the conditional mean are strictly nonnested. Formal definitions are given in Pesaran (1987) and Vuong (1989).

The usual method of discriminating among models by hypothesis test of the parameter restrictions that specialize one model to the other, for example whether the dispersion parameter is zero in moving from the negative binomial to Poisson, is no longer available. Instead, beginning with Akaike (1973), models are compared on the basis of the fitted log-likelihood with penalty given for lack of parsimony. Or, beginning with Cox (1961, 1962a), hypothesis testing is performed in a nonstandard framework. These likelihood-based approaches are presented here.

The Cox approach has spawned a variety of related procedures, some not restricted to the likelihood framework. These are not presented here, for brevity and because most applications have been to linear models. A brief review is given in Davidson and MacKinnon (1993, chapter 11). Artificial nesting, proposed by Davidson and MacKinnon (1981), leads to J tests and related tests. The encompassing principle, proposed by Mizon and Richard (1986), leads to a quite general framework for testing one model against a competing nonnested model. White (1994) and Lu and Mizon (1996) link this approach with CM tests. Wooldridge (1990b) derived encompassing tests for the conditional mean in nonlinear regression models with heteroskedasticity, including GLMs such as the Poisson estimated by PML.

5.7.1 *Information Criteria*

For comparison of nonnested models based on maximum likelihood, several authors beginning with Akaike (1973) have proposed model selection criteria based on the fitted log-likelihood function. Because we expect the log-likelihood to increase as parameters are added to a model, these criteria penalize models with larger k, the number of parameters in the model. This penalty function may also be a function of n, the number of observations.

Akaike (1973) proposed the *Akaike information criterion*

$$\mathsf{AIC} = -2\ln \mathsf{L} + k, \tag{5.102}$$

with the model with lowest AIC preferred. The term *information criterion* is used because the log-likelihood is closely related to the Kullback-Liebler information criterion. Modifications to AIC include the *Bayesian information criterion*

$$\mathsf{BIC} = -2\ln \mathsf{L} + (\ln n)\, k, \tag{5.103}$$

proposed by Schwarz (1978) and the *consistent Akaike information criterion*

$$\mathsf{CAIC} = -2\ln \mathsf{L} + (1 + \ln n)\, k. \tag{5.104}$$

These three criteria give increasingly large penalties in k and n. As an example, suppose we wish to compare two models where one model has one more parameter than the other, so $\Delta k = 1$, and the sample size is $n = 1000$, so $\ln n = 6.9$. For the larger model to be preferred it needs to increase $2\ln \mathsf{L}$ by 1.0 if one uses AIC, 6.9 if BIC is used, and 7.9 if CAIC is used. By comparison if the two models were nested and a likelihood ratio test was formed, the larger model is preferred at significance level 5% if $2\ln \mathsf{L}$ increases by 3.84. The AIC, BIC, and CAIC in this example correspond to p-values of, respectively, .317, .009 and .005.

5.7.2 *Tests of Nonnested Models*

There is a substantial literature on discrimination among nonnested models on the basis of hypothesis tests, albeit nonstandard tests. Consider choosing between two nonnested models – model F_θ with density $f(y_i \mid \mathbf{x}_i, \boldsymbol{\theta})$ and model G_γ with density $g(y_i \mid \mathbf{x}_i, \gamma)$.

The LR statistic for the model F_θ against G_γ is

$$\mathsf{LR}(\hat{\boldsymbol{\theta}}, \hat{\gamma}) \equiv \mathcal{L}_f(\hat{\boldsymbol{\theta}}) - \mathcal{L}_g(\hat{\gamma}) = \sum_{i=1}^{n} \ln \frac{f(y_i \mid \mathbf{x}_i, \hat{\boldsymbol{\theta}})}{g(y_i \mid \mathbf{x}_i, \hat{\gamma})}. \tag{5.105}$$

In the special case where the models are nested, $F_\theta \subset G_\gamma$, we get the usual result that 2 times $\mathsf{LR}(\hat{\boldsymbol{\theta}}, \hat{\gamma})$ is chi-square distributed under the null hypothesis that $G_\gamma = F_\theta$. Here we consider the case of nonnested models in which $F_\theta \not\subseteq G_\gamma$ and $G_\gamma \not\subseteq F_\theta$. Then the chi-square distribution is no longer appropriate.

Cox (1961, 1962a) proposed solving this problem by applying a central limit theorem under the assumption that F_θ is the true model. This approach is difficult to implement as it requires analytically obtaining $\mathsf{E}_f[\ln(f(y_i \mid \mathbf{x}_i, \boldsymbol{\theta})/g(y_i \mid \mathbf{x}_i, \gamma))]$, where E_f denotes expectation with respect to the density $f_i(y_i \mid \mathbf{x}_i, \theta)$. Furthermore, if a similar test statistic is obtained with the roles of F_θ and G_γ reversed it is possible to find both that model F_θ is rejected in favor of G_γ and that model G_γ is rejected in favor of F_θ.

Vuong (1989) instead discriminated between models on the basis of their distance from the true data-generating process, which has density $h_0(y_i \mid X_i)$, where distance is measured using the Kullback-Liebler information criterion. He proposed use of the statistic

$$\begin{aligned}\mathsf{T}_{\mathsf{LR,NN}} &= \frac{1}{\sqrt{n}} \sum_{i=1}^{n} \ln \frac{f(y_i \mid \mathbf{x}_i, \hat{\boldsymbol{\theta}})}{g(y_i \mid \mathbf{x}_i, \hat{\gamma})} \\ &\quad \div \left\{ \frac{1}{n} \sum_{i=1}^{n} \left(\ln \frac{f(y_i \mid \mathbf{x}_i, \hat{\boldsymbol{\theta}})}{g(y_i \mid \mathbf{x}_i, \hat{\gamma})} \right)^2 - \left(\frac{1}{n} \sum_{i=1}^{n} \ln \frac{f(y_i \mid \mathbf{x}_i, \hat{\boldsymbol{\theta}})}{g(y_i \mid \mathbf{x}_i, \hat{\gamma})} \right)^2 \right\} \\ &= \frac{1}{\sqrt{n}} \mathsf{LR}(\hat{\boldsymbol{\theta}}, \hat{\gamma}) \Big/ \hat{\omega}^2, \end{aligned} \tag{5.106}$$

where

$$\hat{\omega}^2 = \frac{1}{n} \sum_{i=1}^{n} \left(\ln \frac{f(y_i \mid \mathbf{x}_i, \hat{\boldsymbol{\theta}})}{g(y_i \mid \mathbf{x}_i, \hat{\gamma})} \right)^2 - \left(\frac{1}{n} \sum_{i=1}^{n} \ln \frac{f(y_i \mid \mathbf{x}_i, \hat{\boldsymbol{\theta}})}{g(y_i \mid \mathbf{x}_i, \hat{\gamma})} \right)^2 \tag{5.107}$$

is an estimate of the variance of $\frac{1}{\sqrt{n}}\mathsf{LR}(\hat{\boldsymbol{\theta}}, \hat{\gamma})$. Alternative asymptotically equivalent statistics to (5.106) and (5.107) use $\tilde{\omega}^2 = \frac{1}{n}\sum_{i=1}^{n}(\ln(f(y_i \mid \mathbf{x}_i, \hat{\boldsymbol{\theta}})/ g(y_i \mid \mathbf{x}_i, \hat{\gamma})))^2$.

For strictly nonnested models

$$\mathsf{T}_{\mathsf{LR,NN}} \overset{d}{\to} \mathsf{N}[0, 1] \tag{5.108}$$

under

$$H_0 : \mathsf{E}_h\left[\ln \frac{f(y_i \mid \mathbf{x}_i, \boldsymbol{\theta})}{g(y_i \mid \mathbf{x}_i, \boldsymbol{\gamma})} \right] = 0, \tag{5.109}$$

where E_h denotes expectation with respect to the (unknown) dgp $h(y_i \mid \mathbf{x}_i)$. One therefore rejects at significance level .05 the null hypothesis of equivalence of the models in favor of F_θ being better (or worse) than G_γ if $\mathsf{T}_{\mathsf{LR,NN}} > z_{.05}$ (or if $\mathsf{T}_{\mathsf{LR,NN}} < -z_{.05}$). The null hypothesis is not rejected if $|\mathsf{T}_{\mathsf{LR,NN}}| \leq z_{.025}$.

Tests of overlapping models are more difficult to implement than tests of strictly nonnested models because there is a possibility that $f(y_i \mid \mathbf{x}_i, \boldsymbol{\theta}_*) = g(y_i \mid \mathbf{x}_i, \boldsymbol{\gamma}_*)$, where $\boldsymbol{\theta}_*$ and $\boldsymbol{\gamma}_*$ are the pseudotrue values of $\boldsymbol{\theta}$ and $\boldsymbol{\gamma}$. To eliminate the possibility of equality, Vuong (1989) shows that

$$\Pr[n\hat{\omega}^2 \leq x] - M_{p+q}(x; \hat{\lambda}^2) \overset{as}{\to} 0, \tag{5.110}$$

for any $x > 0$, under

$$H_0^\omega : \mathsf{V}_0\left[\ln \frac{f(y_i \mid \mathbf{x}_i, \boldsymbol{\theta})}{g(y_i \mid \mathbf{x}_i, \boldsymbol{\gamma})} \right] = 0, \tag{5.111}$$

where E_h denotes expectation with respect to the (unknown) dgp $h(y_i \mid \mathbf{x}_i)$ and $\boldsymbol{\theta}$ and $\boldsymbol{\gamma}$ have dimensions p and q. $M_{p+q}(x; \hat{\lambda}^2)$ denotes the cdf of the weighted sum of chi-squared variables $\sum_{j=1}^{p+q} \hat{\lambda}_j^2 Z_j^2$, where Z_j^2 are iid $\chi^2(1)$ and $\hat{\lambda}_j^2$ are the squares of the eigenvalues of the sample analog of the matrix $\mathbf{W}$ defined in Vuong (1989, p. 313). One therefore rejects H_0^ω if $n\hat{\omega}^2$ exceeds the critical value obtained using (5.110). If H_0^ω is not rejected it is concluded that the data cannot discriminate between F_θ and G_γ. If H_0^ω is rejected then proceed to discriminate between F_θ and G_γ on the basis of the same test of H_0 as used in the case of strictly nested models.

Vuong (1989, p. 322) also considers the case in which one of the overlapping models is assumed to be correctly specified, an approach qualitatively similar to Cox (1961, 1962a), in which case

$$\Pr[n\hat{\omega}^2 \leq x] - M_{p+q}(x; \hat{\lambda}) \stackrel{as}{\rightarrow} 0, \qquad (5.112)$$

can be used as the basis for a two-sided test.

5.8 Derivations

5.8.1 *Test of Poisson Against Katz System*

The Katz system density with mean μ and variance $\mu + \alpha g(\mu)$ can be written as

$$f(y) = f(0) \prod_{l=1}^{y} \frac{\mu + \alpha\mu^{-1}g(\mu)(y-l)}{[1 + \alpha\mu^{-1}g(\mu)](y-l+1)}, \qquad \text{for } y = 1, 2, \ldots, \qquad (5.113)$$

where $f(0)$ is the density for $y = 0$. This density generalizes slightly the Chapter 4 density, which sets $g(\mu) = \mu\mu^{k_2}$ and changes the index from j to $l = y - j + 1$. The log-density is

$$\ln f(y) = \sum_{l=1}^{y} \ln(\mu + \alpha\mu^{-1}g(\mu)(y-l)) - \ln(1 + \alpha\mu^{-1}g(\mu)) - \ln(y - l + 1) + \ln f(0). \qquad (5.114)$$

Then

$$\frac{\partial \ln f(y)}{\partial \alpha} = \left\{ \sum_{l=1}^{y} \frac{\mu^{-1}g(\mu)(y-l)}{\mu + \alpha\mu^{-1}g(\mu)(y-l)} - \frac{\mu^{-1}g(\mu)}{\mu + \alpha\mu^{-1}g(\mu)} \right\} + \frac{\partial \ln f(0)}{\partial \alpha}.$$

Specializing to $H_0 : \alpha = 0$

$$\left.\frac{\partial \ln f(y)}{\partial \alpha}\right|_{\alpha=0} = \left\{ \sum_{l=1}^{y} \mu^{-2} g(\mu)(y-l) - \mu^{-1} g(\mu) \right\} + \left.\frac{\partial \ln f(0)}{\partial \alpha}\right|_{\alpha=0}$$

$$= \mu^{-2} g(\mu)\{y(y-1)/2 - \mu y\} + \left.\frac{\partial \ln f(0)}{\partial \alpha}\right|_{\alpha=0},$$

using $\sum_{l=1}^{y}(y-l) = y(y-1)/2$. Because $\mathsf{E}[\partial \ln f(y)/\partial \alpha] = 0$ under the usual maximum likelihood regularity conditions, a derivative of the form $\partial \ln f(y)/\partial \alpha = h(y) + \partial \ln f(0)/\partial \alpha$ implies $\mathsf{E}[\partial \ln f(0)/\partial \alpha] = -\mathsf{E}[h(y)]$. Therefore

$$\left.\frac{\partial \ln f(y)}{\partial \alpha}\right|_{\alpha=0} = \mu^{-2} g(\mu)\{y(y-1)/2 - \mu y - \mathsf{E}[y(y-l)/2 - \mu y]\}$$

$$= \mu^{-2} g(\mu)\{y(y-1)/2 - \mu y - (\mu^2/2 - \mu^2)\}$$

$$= \mu^{-2} g(\mu)\frac{1}{2}\{(y-\mu)^2 - y\}.$$

Similar manipulations lead to

$$\left.\frac{\partial \ln f(y)}{\partial \beta}\right|_{\alpha=0} = \mu^{-1}(y-\mu)\frac{\partial \mu}{\partial \beta}.$$

Using $\mathcal{L} = \sum_{i=1}^{n} \ln f(y_i)$ leads directly to (5.38).

5.8.2 *LM Test Against Local Alternatives*

We begin with

$$h(y \mid \mu, \tau) = \int \{f(y \mid \mu) + f'(y \mid \mu)(\lambda - \mu) + \frac{1}{2} f''(y \mid \mu)(\lambda - \mu)^2 + R\} p(\lambda \mid \mu, \tau)\, d\lambda.$$

Because λ has mean μ and variance τ this implies

$$h(y \mid \mu, \tau) = f(y \mid \mu) + 0 + \frac{1}{2} f''(y \mid \mu)\tau + O(n^{-1}).$$

Now

$$\frac{\partial \ln f(y \mid \mu)}{\partial \mu} = \frac{f'(y \mid \mu)}{f(y \mid \mu)},$$

and

$$\frac{\partial^2 \ln f(y \mid \mu)}{\partial \mu^2} = \frac{f''(y \mid \mu)}{f(y \mid \mu)} - \frac{f'(y \mid \mu)^2}{f(y \mid \mu)^2}$$

$$= \frac{f''(y \mid \mu)}{f(y \mid \mu)} - \left(\frac{\partial \ln f(y \mid \mu)}{\partial \mu}\right)^2,$$

which implies

$$f''(y \mid \mu) = f(y \mid \mu)\left\{\frac{\partial^2 \ln f(y \mid \mu)}{\partial \mu^2} + \left(\frac{\partial \ln f(y \mid \mu)}{\partial \mu}\right)^2\right\}.$$

Making this substitution yields

$$h(y \mid \mu, \tau) = f(y \mid \mu)\left[1 + \frac{1}{2}\tau\left\{\frac{\partial^2 \ln f(y \mid \mu)}{\partial \mu^2} + \left(\frac{\partial \ln f(y \mid \mu)}{\partial \mu}\right)^2\right\} + O(n^{-1})\right],$$

and using $\exp[x] \simeq 1 + x$ for small x,

$$h(y \mid \mu, \tau) = f(y \mid \mu)\exp\left[\frac{1}{2}\tau\left\{\frac{\partial^2 \ln f(y \mid \mu)}{\partial \mu^2} + \left(\frac{\partial \ln f(y \mid \mu)}{\partial \mu}\right)^2\right\}\right] + O(n^{-1}).$$

5.9 Bibliographic Notes

Key references on residuals include Cox and Snell (1968), who considered a very general definition of residuals; Pregibon (1981), who extended many of the techniques for normal model residuals to logit model residuals; McCullagh and Nelder (1989, chapter 12), who summarize extensions and refinements of Pregibon's work to GLMs; and Davison and Snell (1991), who consider both GLMs and more general models. Discussion of the Pearson and deviance statistics is given in any GLM review, such as McCullagh and Nelder (1989) or Firth (1991). In the econometrics literature, generalized residuals and simulated residuals were proposed by Gourieroux, Monfort, Renault, and Trognon (1987a, 1987b) and are summarized in Gourieroux and Monfort (1995). The material on R-squared measures is based on Cameron and Windmeijer (1996, 1997). A comprehensive treatment of the chi-square goodness-of-fit test is given in Andrews (1988a, 1988b), with the latter of these providing the more accessible treatment.

There is a long literature on overdispersion tests. Attention has focused on the LM test of Poisson against negative binomial, introduced in the iid case by Collings and Margolin (1985) and in the regression case by Lee (1986) and Cameron and Trivedi (1986). Small-sample corrections were proposed by Dean and Lawless (1989a). A more modern approach is to use the bootstrap. Efron and Tibsharani (1993) provide an introduction, and Horowitz (1997) covers the regression case in considerable detail. Treatments of overdispersion tests under weaker stochastic assumptions are given by Cox (1983), Cameron and Trivedi (1985, 1990a), Breslow (1990), and Wooldridge (1991a, 1991b). White (1994) considers various specializations that arise for statistical inference with LEF densities. White also covers the CM test framework in considerable detail.

5.10 Exercises

5.1 Show that if $y_i \sim \mathsf{P}[\mu_i]$ the log-density of y_i is maximized with respect to μ_i by $\mu_i = y_i$. Conclude that $\mathbf{y}$ maximizes $\mathcal{L}(\boldsymbol{\mu})$ for the Poisson. Hence, show that for the Poisson the deviance statistic defined in (5.18) specializes to (5.21), and the deviance residual is (5.3).

5.2 Show that if y_i has the LEF density defined in chapter 2.4.2 then the log-density of y_i is maximized with respect to μ_i by $\mu_i = y_i$. Conclude that $\mathbf{y}$ maximizes $\mathcal{L}(\boldsymbol{\mu})$ for LEF densities. Hence, obtain (5.22) for the deviance of the NB2 density with α known, using the result in section 3.3.2 that this density is a particular LEF density.

5.3 For discrete data y_i that takes only two values, 0 or 1, the appropriate model is a binary choice model with $\Pr[y_i = 1] = \mu_i$ and $\Pr[y_i = 0] = 1 - \mu_i$. The density $f(y_i) = \mu_i^{y_i}(1 - \mu_i)^{y_i}$ is an LEF density. Show that the deviance R^2 in this case simplifies to $R^2 = 1 - (\mathcal{L}_{\text{fit}}/\mathcal{L}_0)$ rather than the more general form (5.28).

5.4 Show that Pearson's chi-square test statistic given in (5.34) can be rewritten using the notation of section 5.3.4 as

$$\left(\sum_{i=1}^{n}(\mathbf{d}_i(y_i) - \mathbf{p}_i(\mathbf{x}_i, \hat{\theta}))\right)' \mathbf{D}\left(\sum_{i=1}^{n}(\mathbf{d}_i(y_i) - \mathbf{p}_i(\mathbf{x}_i, \hat{\theta}))\right).$$

Conclude that the test statistic (5.34) is only chi-square distributed in the special case in which $\mathbf{V}_m^-$ in (5.33) equals $\mathbf{D}$. Hint: $\sum_{i=1}^n d_{ij}(y_i) = n\bar{p}_j$ and $\sum_{i=1}^n p_{ij}(\mathbf{x}_i, \hat{\theta}) = n\hat{p}_j$, where $\mathbf{D}$ is a diagonal matrix with i^{th} entry $(\sum_{i=1}^n p_{ij}(\mathbf{x}_i, \hat{\theta}))^{-1}$.

5.5 Obtain the general formula for the t statistic for $\alpha = 0$ in the linear regression $y_i^* = \alpha x_i + u_i$, where x_i is a scalar and an intercept is not included. Hence, obtain the regression-based overdispersion test statistic given in (5.71).

5.6 Consider testing whether $\boldsymbol{\beta}_2 = \mathbf{0}$ in the regression model $\mathsf{E}[y_i \mid \mathbf{x}_i] = \exp(\mathbf{x}_{1i}'\boldsymbol{\beta}_1 + \mathbf{x}_{2i}'\boldsymbol{\beta}_2)$. Show that a first-order Taylor series expansion around $\boldsymbol{\beta}_2 = \mathbf{0}$ yields $\mathsf{E}[y_i] = \mu_{1i} + \mu_{1i}\mathbf{x}_{2i}'\boldsymbol{\beta}_2$, where $\mu_{1i} = \exp(\mathbf{x}_{1i}'\boldsymbol{\beta}_1)$ and for small $\boldsymbol{\beta}_2$ the remainder term is ignored. Hence, test $\boldsymbol{\beta}_2 = \mathbf{0}$ using (5.85) for the regression-based CM test of $H_0 : \mathsf{E}[y_i - \mu_{1i} \mid \mathbf{x}_i] = 0$ against $H_a : \mathsf{E}[y_i - \mu_{1i} \mid \mathbf{x}_i] = \mu_{1i}\mathbf{x}_{2i}'\boldsymbol{\beta}_2$. Show that when $y_i \sim \mathsf{P}[\mu_{1i}]$ under H_0, (5.85) is the same as (5.63), the moment condition for the LM test of exclusion restrictions.

5.7 For $y_i \sim \mathsf{P}[\mu_i = \mu(\mathbf{x}_i'\boldsymbol{\beta})]$ show that the IM test is a test of moment condition (5.98) and specializes to (5.97) if $\mu_i = \exp(\mathbf{x}_i'\boldsymbol{\beta})$.

CHAPTER 6

Empirical Illustrations

6.1 Introduction

In this chapter we provide a detailed discussion of empirical models based on two cross-sectional data sets. The first of these analyzes the demand for medical care by the elderly in the United States. This data set shares many features of health utilization studies based on cross-section data. The second is an analysis of recreational trips.

Section 6.2 extends the introduction by surveying two general modeling issues. The first is the decision to model only the conditional mean versus the full distribution of counts. The second issue concerns behavioral interpretation of count models, an issue of importance to econometricians who emphasize the distinction between reduced form and structural models. Sections 6.3 and 6.4 deal in turn with each of the two empirical applications. Each has several subsections that deal with details. The health care example in section 6.3 is intended to illustrate in detail the methodology for fitting a finite mixture model. There are relatively few econometric examples that discuss at length the implementation of the finite mixture model and the interpretation of the results. The example is intended to fill this gap. Section 6.5 pursues a methodological question concerning the distribution of the LR test under nonstandard conditions, previously raised in section 4.8.5. The final two sections provide concluding remarks and bibliographic notes.

The emphasis of this chapter is on practical aspects of modeling. Each application involves several competing models which are compared and evaluated using model diagnostics and goodness-of-fit measures. Although the Poisson regression model is the most common starting point in count data analysis, it is usually abandoned in favor of a more general mixed Poisson model. This usually occurs after diagnostic tests reveal overdispersion. But in many cases this mechanical approach can produce misleading results. Overdispersion may be a consequence of many diverse factors. An empirical model that simply controls for overdispersion does not shed any light on its source. Tests of overdispersion do not unambiguously suggest remedies. This is because they may have power against many commonplace misspecifications. Rejection of the null against a specific alternative does not imply that the alternative itself is valid. Hence misspecifications and directions for model revision should be explored with care.

6.2 Background

6.2.1 *Fully Parametric Estimation*

Event count models may have two different uses. In some cases, the main interest is in modeling the conditional expectation of the count and in making inferences about key parameters, such as price elasticity. Different models and estimation methods may yield similar results with respect to the conditional mean, even though they differ in the goodness of fit.

In other cases, the entire frequency distribution of events is relevant. An interesting example is Dionne and Vanasse (1992), where the entire distribution of auto accidents is used to derive insurance-premium tables as a function of accident history and individual characteristics. Another example is the probability distribution of number of patient days in hospital as a function of patient characteristics. These probabilities might be needed to generate the expected costs of hospital stays.

If the objective is to make conditional predictions about the expected number of events, the focus is on the conditional mean function. But if the focus is on the conditional probability of a given number of events, the frequency distribution itself is relevant. In the former case, features such as overdispersion may affect the prediction intervals but not mean prediction. In the latter case overdispersion will affect the estimated cell probability. Hence, parametric methods are attractive in the latter case, whereas robustness of the estimate is more important in the former.

This neat separation of modeling issues is not possible, however, if consistent estimation of the conditional expectation also requires fully parametric models. For example, the conditional mean may correspond to that for the ZIP or Poisson hurdle model, in which case one needs to model the probabilities. Chapter 3 focused on methods by which other aspects of the distribution, notably the variance, are modeled to improve efficiency. Chapter 4, in contrast, presents many parametric models in which consistent estimation of the conditional mean parameters requires fully parametric methods. The attention given to features such as variance function modeling varies on a case-by-case basis.

To make the foregoing discussion concrete, consider the issue of how to treat the joint presence of excess zero observations and long right tails relative to the Poisson regression. One interpretation of this condition is that it indicates unobserved heterogeneity. Hence, it is a problem of modeling the variance function. The Two-Crossings Theorem supports this interpretation. An alternative interpretation is that the excess zeros reflect behavior. Many individuals do not record (experience) positive counts because they do not "participate" in a relevant activity. That is, optimizing behavior generates corner solutions. On this interpretation, the presence of excess zeros may well be a feature of the conditional mean function, not the variance function. If one adds to this the presence of unobserved heterogeneity, it is concluded that both the conditional expectation and variance function are involved. So the use of an overdispersed Poisson model, such as the negative binomial, without also allowing for the additional nonlinearity generated by an excess of corner solutions, yields inconsistent estimates of the parameters.

6.2.2 *Repeated Events*

Consider a single probabilistic event such as the desire for a recreational trip or the number of spells of sickness. That may or may not lead to the outcome of interest, such as a doctor visit or a recreational trip. If the outcome reflects individual decision making, it may be analyzed within the random utility framework used in binary choice models. Suppose we consider a doctor consultation. Denote by U_0 the utility of not seeking care and by U_1 the utility of seeking care. Both U_0 and U_1 are latent variables. Let

$$U_{1i} = \mathbf{x}_i'\boldsymbol{\beta}_1 + \varepsilon_{1i}$$

$$U_{0i} = \mathbf{x}_i'\boldsymbol{\beta}_0 + \varepsilon_{0i},$$

where $\mathbf{x}_i$ is the vector of individual attributes, and ε_{1i} and ε_{0i} are random errors. Then for individual i who seeks care, we have

$$U_{1i} > U_{0i} \Rightarrow \varepsilon_{0i} - \varepsilon_{1i} < \mathbf{x}_i'(\boldsymbol{\beta}_1 - \boldsymbol{\beta}_0).$$

Thus, the probability of the decision to seek care is characterized by the standard binary outcome model. The individual i seeks care if $U_{1i} > U_{0i}$, and we observe $y = 1$. Otherwise we observe $y = 0$. The probability of $y = 1$, denoted π, is given by $\Pr[\varepsilon_{0i} - \varepsilon_{1i} < \mathbf{x}_i'(\boldsymbol{\beta}_1 - \boldsymbol{\beta}_0)]$.

Next consider repeated events of the same kind. If there is a fixed number, N, of repetitions, the event distribution is binomial $\mathsf{B}(N, p)$. Suppose, however, that N is random and follows Poisson distribution. For simplicity treat the events as N independent Bernoulli trials occurring over some time interval. By the application of the Poisson-stopped binomial result, the number of successes is Poisson-distributed (see Chapter 1). This argument justifies the framework of count-data models for the study of repeated events based on event counts.

This argument can be generalized in a straightforward manner to allow for serial correlation of events or unobserved heterogeneity, both of which imply overdispersion. The framework also generalizes to the multinomial case in which the observed event is one of k outcomes. For example, the individual may choose to visit any one of k possible recreational sites, and such a choice outcome may be repeated a random number of times.

6.3 Analysis of Demand for Health Services

Count models are extensively used in modeling healthcare utilization. Discrete measures of units of healthcare use are often more easily available than data on expenditures. They are usually obtained from national health or health expenditure surveys, which also provide information on key covariates such as measures of health insurance, health status, income, education, and many sociodemographic variables.

This example draws on Deb and Trivedi (1997), which deals with counts of medical care utilization. The article compares the performance of a negative binomial (NB), two-part hurdles negative binomial (NBH), and finite mixture negative binomial (FMNB) in a study of the demand for medical care by the elderly aged 66 years and over in the United States, using six mutually exclusive measures of utilization.

6.3.1 *Health Service Data*

A sample of 4406 cases was obtained from the National Medical Expenditure Survey conducted in 1987 and 1988 (NMES). The data provide a comprehensive picture of how Americans use and pay for health services. Here only one of these six measures, that dealing with the office visits to physicians (*OFP*), is considered. A feature of these data is that they do not include a high proportion of zero counts but do reflect a high degree of unconditional overdispersion.

The NMES is based on a representative, national probability sample of the civilian, noninstitutionalized population and individuals admitted to long-term care facilities during 1987. Under the household survey of the NMES, more than 38,000 individuals in 15,000 households across the United States were interviewed quarterly about their health insurance coverage, the services they used, and the cost and source of payments of those services. In addition to healthcare data, NMES provides information on health status, employment, sociodemographic characteristics, and economic status.

An important issue in healthcare modeling is endogeneity of health insurance. If consumers make their decisions on health insurance and healthcare utilization jointly, then the two are stochastically dependent. Hence, health insurance status should not be treated as a valid exogenous variable. We first consider the argument of Deb and Trivedi (1997) that for the elderly U.S. population it is reasonable to take health insurance status as an exogenous covariate.

All cases in the sample were covered by Medicare, a public insurance program that offers substantial protection against healthcare costs. Residents of the United States are eligible for Medicare coverage at age 65 years. Some individuals start receiving Medicare benefits a few months into their 65th year primarily because they fail to apply for coverage at the appropriate time. Virtually all individuals who are 66 years of age or older are covered by Medicare. In addition, most individuals make a choice of supplemental private insurance coverage shortly before or in their 65th year because the price of such insurance

Table 6.1. *OFP visits: actual frequency distribution*

Number of visits	0	1	2	3	4	5	6	7	8	9	10	11	12	13+
Frequency	683	481	428	420	383	338	268	217	188	171	128	115	86	500

rises sharply with age and coverage becomes more restrictive. Therefore, given the choice of sample, the treatment of private insurance status as predetermined, rather than endogenous, is justified. On the other hand, to the extent that private insurance purchase is in anticipation of required healthcare, given health status, private insurance status may be treated as endogenous. Because the specification controls for health status by including several health status variables, the force of this argument is reduced. Exogeneity of insurance is a major econometric simplification.

The frequency distribution of physician office visits is given in Table 6.1. The zero counts account for only about 15% of the visits. There is a long right tail. Around 11% of the patients have 13 or more visits. Definitions and summary statistics for the explanatory variables are presented in Table 6.2. The health measures include self-perceived measures of health (*EXCLHLTH* and *POORHLTH*), the number of chronic diseases and conditions (*NUMCHRON*) and a measure of disability status (*ADLDIFF*). In order to control for regional differences we use *NOREAST*, *MIDWEST*, and *WEST*. The demographic variables include *AGE*, race (*BLACK*), sex (*MALE*), marital status (*MARRIED*), and education (*SCHOOL*). Finally, the economic variables are family income (*FAMINC*), employment status (*EMPLOY*), supplementary private insurance status (*PRIVINS*), and public insurance status (*MEDICAID*). Medicaid, which should not be confused with Medicare, is available to low-income individuals only. Both *PRIVINS* and *MEDICAID* serve as indicators of the price of service.

6.3.2 *Demand for Medical Care*

Beginning with the obvious starting point of the Poisson regression is unnecessary. The data display a high degree of overdispersion, leading to the rejection of the Poisson model. Even the NB1 and NB2 models are easily rejected by the chi-squared goodness-of-fit test, suggesting that the conditional mean may be misspecified.

Several recent studies have suggested that the two-part hurdle model provides a better starting point than the NB class. The two-part hurdle model has performed satisfactorily in several empirical studies (Pohlmeier and Ulrich, 1995; Gurmu, 1997; Geil et al., 1997) of health utilization. It is typically superior to specifications in which the two separate origins of zero observations are not recognized. It may be interpreted as a principal-agent type model in which the first part specifies the decision to seek care as a binary outcome process,

Table 6.2. *OFP visits: variable definitions and summary statistics*

Variable	Definition	Mean	Standard deviation
OFP	Number of physician office visits	5.77	6.76
OFNP	Number of nonphysician office visits	1.62	5.32
OPP	Number of physician outpatient visits	0.75	3.65
OPNP	Number of nonphysician outpatient visits	0.54	3.88
EMR	Number of emergency room visits	0.26	0.70
HOSP	Number of hospitalizations	0.30	0.75
EXCLHLTH	Equals 1 if self-perceived health is excellent	0.08	0.27
POORHLTH	Equals 1 if self-perceived health is poor	0.13	0.33
NUMCHRON	Number of chronic conditions	1.54	1.35
ADLDIFF	Equals 1 if the person has a condition that limits activities of daily living	0.20	0.40
NOREAST	Equals 1 if the person lives in northeastern U.S.	0.19	0.39
MIDWEST	Equals 1 if the person lives in the midwestern U.S.	0.26	0.44
WEST	Equals 1 if the person lives in the western U.S.	0.18	0.39
AGE	Age in years (divided by 10)	7.40	0.63
BLACK	Equals 1 if the person is African-American	0.12	0.32
MALE	Equals 1 if the person is male	0.40	0.49
MARRIED	Equals 1 if the person is married	0.55	0.50
SCHOOL	Number of years of education	10.30	3.74
FAMINC	Equals family income in $10,000	2.53	2.92
EMPLOYED	Equals 1 if the person is employed	0.10	0.30
PRIVINS	Equals 1 if the person is covered by private health insurance	0.78	0.42
MEDICAID	Equals 1 if the person is covered by Medicaid	0.09	0.29

and the second part models the number of visits for the individuals who receive some care. The second part allows for population heterogeneity among the users of health care.

A finite mixture model, as a competing model, has several additional attractive features. The finite mixture model allows for additional population heterogeneity but avoids the sharp dichotomy between the populations of "users" and "nonusers." In the finite mixture ("latent class") formulation of unobserved heterogeneity the factor that splits the population into latent classes is assumed to be based on the person's latent long-term health status, which may not be well captured by proxy variables such as self-perceived health status and chronic health conditions. In the case of a two-point finite mixture model, a dichotomy between the "healthy" and the "ill" groups, whose demands for health care are characterized by, respectively, low mean and low variance and high mean and high variance may be suggested. Although the two-step model captures an important feature of the data that the one-step model does not, the finite mixture model has greater flexibility of functional form because it incorporates a combination of discrete and continuous representation of population heterogeneity. An example is a two-point finite mixture of NB models – within its framework, one might view a population of healthcare consumers as consisting of discrete "types" (ill and healthy) and yet allow for heterogeneity within each type.

6.3.3 *Competing Models*

Three models are compared. The first is the NB model with mean $\mathsf{E}[y_i \mid \mathbf{x}_i] = \mu_i = \exp(\mathbf{x}_i'\beta)$ and variance $\mathsf{V}[y_i \mid \mathbf{x}_i] = \mu_i + \alpha\mu_i^p$ where $\alpha > 0$ is an overdispersion parameter. The NB1 model is obtained by specifying $p = 1$; NB2 is obtained by setting $p = 2$.*

The second is the NBH, which has the following components:

$$\mathsf{Pr}_h[y_i = 0 \mid \mathbf{x}_i] = \left(\frac{\psi_{h,i}}{\mu_{h,i} + \psi_{h,i}}\right)^{\psi_{h,i}}, \tag{6.1}$$

$$\mathsf{Pr}\,[y_i > 0 \mid \mathbf{x}_i] = 1 - \left(\frac{\psi_i}{\mu_i + \psi_i}\right)^{\psi_i}, \tag{6.2}$$

where the subscript h refers to the hurdle distribution and $\psi_i = (1/\alpha)\mu_i^{2-p}$. This is introduced in section 4.7. In the NBH model, the mean of the count variable is given by

$$\mathsf{E}[y_i \mid \mathbf{x}_i] = \frac{\mathsf{Pr}_h[y_i > 0 \mid \mathbf{x}_i]}{\mathsf{Pr}\,[y_i > 0 \mid \mathbf{x}_i]}\mu_i \tag{6.3}$$

and the variance by

$$\mathsf{V}[y_i \mid \mathbf{x}_i] = \frac{\mathsf{Pr}_h[y_i > 0 \mid \mathbf{x}_i]}{\mathsf{Pr}\,[y_i > 0 \mid \mathbf{x}_i]}\left[\mu_i + \alpha\mu_i^p + \left(1 - \frac{\mathsf{Pr}_h[y_i > 0 \mid \mathbf{x}_i]}{\mathsf{Pr}\,[y_i > 0 \mid \mathbf{x}_i]}\right)\mu_i^2\right]. \tag{6.4}$$

The third model is the C-component finite mixture density specified as follows:

$$f(y_i \mid \Theta) = \sum_{j=1}^{C-1} \pi_j f_j(y_i \mid \theta_j) + \pi_C f_C(y_i \mid \theta_C), \tag{6.5}$$

where $\pi_1 \geq \pi_2 \geq \cdots \geq \pi_C, \pi_C = (1 - \sum_{j=1}^{C-1} \pi_j)$ are the mixing probabilities (proportions of the sampled latent subpopulations) estimated along with all other parameters, all collectively denoted by Θ; see section 4.8. The component distributions in a C-point FMNB model (FMNB-C) are specified as

$$f_j(y_i) = \frac{\Gamma(y_i + \psi_{j,i})}{\Gamma(\psi_{j,i})\Gamma(y_i + 1)}\left(\frac{\psi_{j,i}}{\mu_{j,i} + \psi_{j,i}}\right)^{\psi_{j,i}}\left(\frac{\mu_{j,i}}{\mu_{j,i} + \psi_{j,i}}\right)^{y_i}. \tag{6.6}$$

* This notation is slightly different from Chapter 3, where the notation is $\mathsf{V}[y_i \mid \mathbf{x}_i] = \mu_i + \alpha\mu_i^p$, with $p = 1$ yielding NB1 and $p = 2$ yielding NB2.

A variant of the third model constrains slope coefficients to be equal. If $\dim[\boldsymbol{\beta}_j] = k$, then the fully unconstrained C component mixture has dimension $C(k+1) - 1$. The models in the current application become possibly overparameterized when k is around 10. Hence considerations of parsimonious parameterization motivate restrictions across the component densities. Therefore Deb and Trivedi (1997) also considered a constrained FMNB-C (CFMNB-C) in which all slope parameters in β_j were restricted to be equal across all C components. The differences between component distributions then arise only from intercept differences.

The slope-constrained, or random intercept, model is the same as the discrete specification of heterogeneity used in Simar (1976), Laird (1978), Lindsay (1995), and Heckman and Singer (1984). This specification is relatively parsimonious and, as discussed in Chapter 4, may provide an adequate semi- or nonparametric representation of the possibly continuous distribution of unobserved heterogeneity.

It is interesting that the CFMNB-C may be consistently estimated, up to the intercept, by Poisson maximum likelihood. This follows from the exponential mean function $\mathsf{E}[y_i \mid \mathbf{x}_i]$. For example, with $C = 2$,

$$\mathsf{E}[y_i \mid \mathbf{x}_i] = \exp\left[\pi\beta_{01} + (1-\pi)\beta_{02} + \mathbf{x}_i'\beta\right].$$

The intercept of the constrained finite mixture is a weighted sum of the intercepts in the components, with weights being the population proportions π and $1-\pi$. Hence, Poisson maximum likelihood yields only an estimate of the weighted sum of the intercepts and not the individual components that we need in order to estimate subpopulation means.

6.3.4 *Is There a Mixture?*

There are two important issues in evaluating fitted finite mixture models. First, is there evidence for the presence of more than one components? That is, is mixing present? Second, is a global maximum attained in estimation?

Lindsay and Roeder (1992) have developed diagnostic tools for checking these properties for the case of exponential mixtures. The key idea behind the diagnostic for the presence of a mixture component is the Two Crossings Theorem given in section 4.2. Let $\hat{p}(y;\boldsymbol{\theta}^*)$ denote fitted-cell probabilities calculated under the assumption that the data are generated by a one-component model, and let $\hat{p}(y;\hat{C})$ denote the fitted probability based on the assumption that the sample comes from a C-component mixture distribution. Then by an extension of Shaked's Two Crossings Theorem, the differences $(\hat{p}(y;\boldsymbol{\theta}^*) - \hat{p}(y;\hat{C}))$ show a $\{+,-,+\}$ sign pattern. This is the basis of the first of two diagnostic tools developed by Lindsay and Roeder. Their *directional gradient function* is

$$d(y, \hat{C}, \boldsymbol{\theta}^*) = \left(\frac{\hat{p}(y;\boldsymbol{\theta}^*)}{\hat{p}(y;\hat{C})} - 1\right), \qquad y = 0, 1, 2, \ldots, \tag{6.7}$$

where $\boldsymbol{\theta}^*$ is the unicomponent MLE and $\hat{C}$ is the C-component MLE. To calculate $d(y, \hat{C}, \boldsymbol{\theta}^*)$ we first calculate $d(y_i, \hat{C}, \boldsymbol{\theta}^* \mid \mathbf{x}_i)$ and then average across all observations. The convexity of the graph of $d(y, \hat{C}, \boldsymbol{\theta}^*)$ against y is interpreted as evidence in favor of a mixture. However, note that such convexity may be observed for more than one value of C, leaving open the issue of which value to select for C.

Lindsay and Roeder also suggest the use of the weighted sum measure

$$D(\hat{C}, \boldsymbol{\theta}^*) = \sum_{y \in S} d(y, \hat{C}, \boldsymbol{\theta}^*) p(y) \tag{6.8}$$

as an additional diagnostic. This can be interpreted as a quantitative measure of the deviation in fitted cell probabilities induced by the mixture. A limitation of this statistic is that in the event of a long right tail, the contribution of high values of y may be large. This tends to make the components of $D(\hat{C}, \boldsymbol{\theta}^*)$ erratic, and the statistic itself may be hard to interpret. Recognizing this feature, Lindsay and Roeder suggest that a truncated gradient statistic is preferred for unbounded densities. However, currently there is little guidance on how the statistic should be truncated.

The diagnostic tools of Lindsay and Roeder are intended for exponential mixtures. Strictly speaking, they should not be used for the negative binomial mixture.* In this chapter these tools are applied in a heuristic and exploratory fashion to the FMNB-C model.

6.3.5 *Model Comparison and Selection*

Given the presence of mixture, one may either sequentially compare models with different values of C or compare unconstrained and constrained models for a given C. Although these are both nested hypotheses, the use of the LR test is only appropriate for the latter simplification, not the former in which the hypothesis is on the boundary of the parameter space. This violates the standard regularity conditions for maximum likelihood. For example, in a model with no component-density parameters estimated, the LR test of the null hypothesis $H_0 : \pi_C = 0$ versus $H_a : \pi_C \neq 0$ does not have the usual null $\chi^2(1)$ distribution. Instead, the asymptotic distribution of the likelihood ratio is a weighted chi-square.

Böhning et al. (1994) have used simulation analysis to examine the distribution of the LR test for several distributions involving a boundary hypothesis. This showed that the use of the nominal $\chi^2(1)$ test is likely to underreject the false null. Therefore, systematic reliance on the LR test may cause an investigator to choose a value of C that is too small. However, the use of information criteria – we use the AIC and the BIC – for model selection has formal justification. Leroux (1992) proves that under regularity conditions the maximum penalized

* Note, however, that the two-crossings result is extended to two-parameter exponential families by Gelfand and Dalal (1990).

likelihood approach, for example the use of the AIC-BIC, leads to a consistent estimator of the true finite-mixture model (Leroux, 1992, section 3.3). Section 6.4 provides a further discussion of these issues using simulation evidence.

Model simplification in going from NBH to NB involves a standard nested hypothesis; therefore, it may be based on the LR test. Finally, if FMNB-C, $C > 1$, and NBH are the preferred models after initial tests, one should select between these two. Note that FMNB-1 means NB and NB may refer to either NB1 or NB2. Again this involves nonnested comparisons, for which we use information criteria to choose between them.

A possible strategy for model selection can be summarized as follows:

- Fix maximum $C = C^*$. Use information criteria to compare the sequence of models FMNB-C*, ..., FMNB-1.
- Use the LR test to compare FMNB-C and CFMNB-C.
- Use the LR test to compare NBH and NB.
- Use information criteria to compare FMNB-C (or CFMNB-C) and NBH.

Finally, to evaluate the goodness of fit of the model selected after this multilevel comparison of models, one may use the chi-square diagnostic test introduced in section 5.3.4. This compares actual and fitted cell frequencies of events for which cells are centered on integer values. The fitted cell frequencies are calculated as follows. Let $\hat{p}_{ij}$, $i = 1, 2, \ldots, N$; $y = 0, 1, 2, \ldots,$ denote the fitted probability that individual i experiences j events. Then the fitted frequency in cell j is calculated as $n\hat{p}_j$, where

$$\hat{p}_j = \frac{1}{n}\sum_i \hat{p}_{ij}, \qquad j = 0, 1, 2, \ldots. \tag{6.9}$$

In the present case, the chi-square goodness-of-fit statistic is

$$\mathsf{T}_{\mathsf{GoF}} = (\bar{\mathbf{f}} - \hat{\mathbf{f}})'\hat{\mathbf{V}}^{-1}(\bar{\mathbf{f}} - \hat{\mathbf{f}}) \tag{6.10}$$

where $\bar{\mathbf{f}} - \hat{\mathbf{f}}$ is the q dimensional vector of difference between sample and fitted cell frequencies, q is the number of cells used in the test, and $\hat{\mathbf{V}}$ is the estimated variance matrix of the difference; see Chapter 5.3. Under the null hypothesis of no misspecification the test has an asymptotic $\chi^2(q - 1)$ distribution. In most cases the last cell aggregates over several sample support points. If the sample mean is low, then fewer support points are used than if the value is large. For computational simplicity, the covariance matrix of $\bar{\mathbf{f}} - \hat{\mathbf{f}}$ is estimated by an auxiliary regression based on the outer product of gradients as discussed in Andrews (1988b, Appendix 5).

Be aware that the proposed model comparison and selection approach is subject to the usual criticism that there will be pre-test bias resulting from the choices. Hence, if the data availability permits, the above approach should be used on a training sample and the selected model should be reestimated using new data.

Table 6.3. *OFP visits: likelihood ratio tests*

Null model	Alternative	NB1	NB2	χ^2 degrees of freedom
NB	NBH	59.8	183.4	17
NB	CFMNB-2	116.7	106.7	3
NB	FMNB-2	166.9	136.0	19
CFMNB-2	FMNB-2	50.2	29.2	16
CFMNB-2	CFMNB-3	0.002	0.003	3
FMNB-2	FMNB-3	11.3	0.002	19

Note: The LR test statistic of the null against the alternative is shown.

6.3.6 *Evaluation of Fitted Models*

Models can be compared and evaluated at two levels. First, model selection criteria may be used to choose among competing models. Next, a goodness-of-fit criterion can be used to evaluate whether the preferred model provides a good fit to the data.

Table 6.3 presents LR tests of NB versus NBH, the unicomponent model versus the two-component models (CFMNB-2 and FMNB-2), and the two-component models versus the corresponding three-component models. The NB model is rejected in favor of NBH in every case. The NB model is also rejected in favor of two-component mixture models, notwithstanding the fact that we have used conservative critical values.

Although there are problems with the LR test for choosing between two- and three-component mixtures, it is interesting to note that we do not get a significant LR statistic for any pairwise comparison between two- and three-component finite mixture, regardless of whether the NB1 or NB2 mixtures are used. Finally, within the two-component models, the evidence in favor of the constrained model is mixed. The LR test of CFMNB-2 against FMNB-2, based on the NB1 specification, rejects the null model, but if comparison is based on the NB2 specification, the null model is not rejected at a 5% significance level. This evidence is corroborated by the directional gradient function evaluated against FMNB-2, which is presented in Figure 6.1 for the NB1 specification. This appears to satisfy the convexity requirement.

Table 6.4 presents values of the AIC, BIC, and T_{GoF}. These show that CFMNB-2 and FMNB-2, based on the NB1 specifications, are the preferred models overall. The AIC criterion favors the latter; the BIC criterion favors the more parsimonious constrained specification based on the NB1 specification. To emphasize, neither NBH nor FMNB-3 are preferred to the FMNB-2 model.

Taking together the evidence that has been described, the conclusion is that the FMNB-2 model is best within each density class and that models based on NB1 specifications perform better overall than those based on NB2 specifications. This evidence in favor of a two-component mixture also allows us to interpret the two populations as being healthy and ill.

Table 6.4. *OFP visits: information criteria (AIC and BIC)*

		NB1	NB2
NB	AIC	24348	24440
	BIC	24463	24555
	T_{GoF}	32.3	58.0
NBH	AIC	24323	24291[a]
	BIC	24546	24515
	T_{GoF}	37.4	21.8
CFMNB-2	AIC	24238	24340
	BIC	24372[c,d]	24474[c]
	T_{GoF}	6.0	98.0
FMNB-2	AIC	24220[a,b]	24342
	BIC	24456	24579
	T_{GoF}	11.2	123.8
CFMNB-3	AIC	24244	24346
	BIC	24397	24499
	T_{GoF}	2666	2946
FMNB-3	AIC	24246	24380
	BIC	24604	24738
	T_{GoF}	74.3	137

Note: $\text{AIC} = -2\ln \text{L} + 2k$, $\text{BIC} = -2\ln \text{L} + k\ln n$, where L, k, and n are the maximized log likelihood, number of parameters, and observations, respectively. T_{GoF} is the $\chi^2(5)$ goodness-of-fit test.
[a] Model preferred by the AIC within the negative binomial-i class.
[b] Model preferred by the AIC overall.
[c] Model preferred by the BIC within the negative binomial-i class.
[d] Model preferred by the BIC overall.

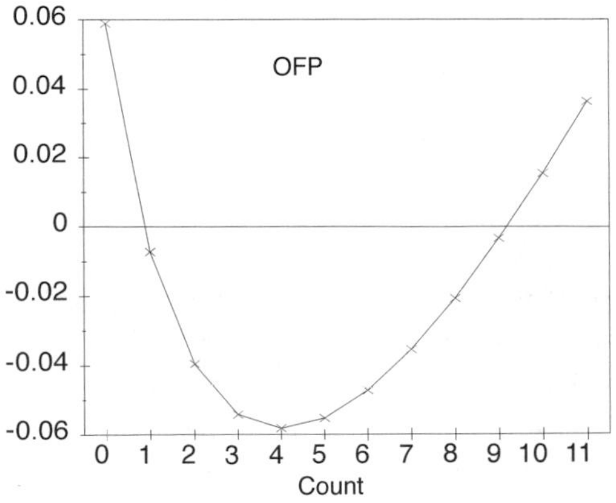

Figure 6.1. OFP visits: directional gradients.

Table 6.5. *OFP visits: FMNB2 NB1 model, actual, fitted distributions and goodness-of-fit tests*

Count	0	1	2	3	4	5	6+
Actual	15.5	10.9	9.7	9.5	8.7	7.7	38.0
Fitted	15.1	11.5	10.5	9.4	8.2	7.0	38.3
T_{GoF}				14.80			

Note: The fitted frequencies are the sample averages of the cell frequencies estimated from the FMNB2 NB1 models. T_{GoF} is the $\chi^2(13)$ goodness-of-fit test.

Table 6.6. *OFP visits: FMNB2 NB1 model estimates and standard errors*

	OFP			OFP	
Variable	High users	Low users	Variable (cont.)	High users	Low users
EXCLHLTH	−0.25	−0.77	*MARRIED*	0.04	−0.44
	(0.06)	(0.57)		(0.04)	(0.38)
POORHLTH	0.24	0.06	*SCHOOL*	0.01	0.15
	(0.07)	(0.89)		(0.00)	(0.05)
NUMCHRON	0.20	0.14	*FAMINC*	−0.00	−0.00
	(0.01)	(0.11)		(0.01)	(0.01)
ADLDIFF	0.01	0.58	*EMPLOYED*	−0.06	0.39
	(0.04)	(0.39)		(0.05)	(0.52)
NOREAST	0.08	0.21	*PRIVINS*	0.25	2.89
	(0.05)	(0.44)		(0.05)	(1.84)
MIDWEST	0.01	0.09	*MEDICAID*	0.34	−2.44
	(0.04)	(0.33)		(0.06)	(0.99)
WEST	0.09	0.23	*ONE*	0.78	1.71
	(0.05)	(0.44)		(0.18)	(0.63)
AGE	0.03	−0.57	α_1	3.45	18.82
	(0.02)	(0.20)		(0.19)	(0.58)
BLACK	−0.07	−1.16	π_1	0.91	
	(0.06)	(1.10)		(0.02)	
MALE	−0.12	0.06			
	(0.04)	(0.28)	$-\ln L$	12072.8	

6.3.7 *Assessing the Preferred Model*

Having selected the model we shall now evaluate it in terms of statistical criteria such as goodness of fit and its economic implications.

Table 6.5 presents the sample frequency distribution of the count variable along with the sample averages of the estimated cell frequencies from the selected model. We then present two views of the differences between the two populations that compose the mixture. Table 6.6 contains parameter estimates for the FMNB-2 models estimated using NB1 specifications. Finally, Table 6.7

Table 6.7. *OFP visits: FMNB2 NB1 model fitted means and variances*

	Mean	Variance
Low-use group	5.55	24.69
High-use group	8.17	161.93
Mixture	5.78	42.82

Note: The fitted means and variance for the two components are calculated using Eqs. (6.10) and (6.11), respectively.

reports the fitted mean and variances for the fitted component densities. The first component corresponds to the healthy population; the second component corresponds to the ill population. Figure 6.2 presents the fitted frequency distributions for the two subpopulations. The darker histogram shows the fitted frequency distribution for low users, while the lighter histogram shows the same for heavy users.

Goodness of fit: A comparison of sample and fitted frequency distributions in Table 6.5 shows a good fit over the entire range of the distribution. The discrepancy between the actual and fitted cell frequencies is never greater than 1%. Discrepancies between actual and predicted frequencies based on NB and NBH models (not presented) are usually much larger.

The $\chi^2(5)$ goodness-of-fit statistics are shown in Table 6.4 only for several models. The CFMNB-2 and FMNB-2 models are not rejected by the test. The NBH model based on the NB2 specification also provides a good fit to the data, although that model is formally rejected. This suggests that the test may be too stringent, an issue that is followed up further in section 6.4. The finite mixture models do considerably better in relative terms.

Estimates of π, component means, and densities: The estimate of the π component is 0.91 for *OFP*, large relative to its estimated standard errors. This reinforces the evidence supporting the two-population hypothesis.

The sample moments for the high-use and low-use subpopulations, are shown in Table 6.7. These are based on the formulae

$$\mathsf{E}(y_i \mid \mathbf{x}_i) = \bar{\mu}_i = \sum_{j=1}^{2} \pi_j \mu_{j,i}, \tag{6.11}$$

and

$$\mathsf{V}(y_i \mid \mathbf{x}_i) = \sum_{j=1}^{2} \left(\pi_j \mu_{j,i}^2 \left[1 + \alpha_j \mu_{j,i}^{p-2}\right]\right) + \bar{\mu}_i - \bar{\mu}_i^2. \tag{6.12}$$

Healthy individuals who comprise 91% of the population have on average 5.6 visits to a physician; the remaining ill individuals seek care 8.2 times. The component distributions shown in Figure 6.2 suggest that this difference in

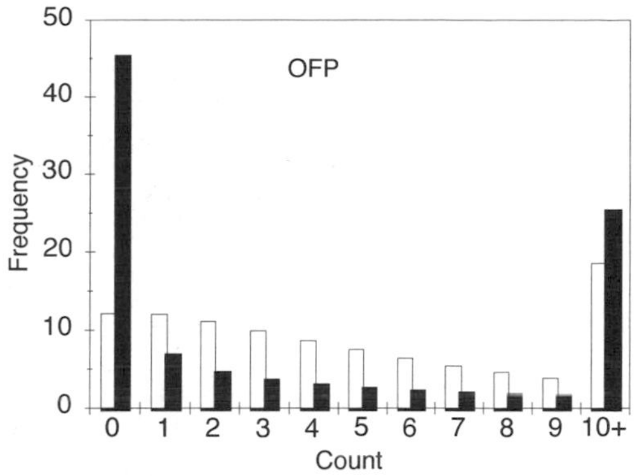

Figure 6.2. OFP visits: component densities from the FMNB2 NB1 model.

means is caused by a greater proportion of zeros and high values for the ill population. It appears that, although most healthy individuals see a doctor a few times a year for health maintenance and minor illnesses, a larger fraction of the ill do not seek any (preventive?) care. Those ill individuals who do see a doctor (these individuals have sickness events) do so much more often than healthy individuals. Because preventive care usually takes the form of a visit to a doctor in an office setting, one would not expect such a pattern of differences between the healthy and ill to arise for the other measures of utilization.

6.3.8 *Interpreting the Coefficients*

In this section we highlight selected aspects of our results. We also interpret some implications of the estimates given in Table 6.8. The following features of the results underscore the advantage of a finite-mixture formulation. These concern the differential response of different groups to changes in covariates.

- Consistent with previous studies, both the number of chronic conditions (*NUMCHRON*) and self-perceived health status (*EXCLHLTH* and *POORHLTH*) are important determinants of *OFP*. An additional chronic condition increases the office visits by 20% in the low-use (healthy) group and by 14% in the low-use (ill) group, but the latter estimate is less precise than the former. The presence of *EXCLHLTH* reduces *OFP* by around 75% in the high-use group and only 25% in the low-use group.
- Medicaid coverage is a significant determinant of the number of doctor visits. In both cases, the coefficient is significantly positive in the component density for the high-use group and is significantly negative in the component density for the low-use group. This is an intriguing result that requires an explanation. For the healthy group, the price (insurance) effect of the *MEDICAID* dummy outweighs the income

Table 6.8. *OFP visits: NB2 hurdle model estimates and t ratios*

	Zeros		Positives	
Variable	Coefficient	$\|t\|$	Coefficient	$\|t\|$
EXCLHLTH	−0.330	2.36	0.377	4.32
POORHLTH	0.070	0.40	0.331	5.79
NUMCHRON	0.556	10.43	0.143	10.51
ALDIFF	−0.187	−1.35	0.129	2.44
NOREAST	0.130	1.03	0.103	1.96
MIDWEST	0.102	0.86	−0.015	0.32
WEST	0.204	1.49	0.123	2.42
AGE	0.190	2.02	−0.075	1.61
BLACK	−0.326	2.36	0.001	0.01
MALE	−0.464	4.54	0.004	0.09
MARRIED	0.247	2.18	−0.092	1.99
SCHOOL	0.054	4.08	0.021	3.66
FAMINC	0.006	0.36	−0.002	−0.37
EMPLOYED	−0.011	−0.07	0.029	0.39
PRIVINS	0.761	6.14	0.221	3.82
MEDICAID	0.550	2.96	0.184	2.69
ONE	−1.471	1.92	1.630	4.07
α			0.743	18.40
$-\ln L$	12110			
T_{GoF}	21.86			

effect because Medicaid is a health insurance plan for the poor. But for poor individuals within the low-use group the opportunity cost of seeking care is disproportionately large relative to the money price of care. This may induce them to seek care less often even though they have Medicaid insurance coverage.

- Persons with supplementary private insurance seek care from physicians in office more often than individuals without supplementary coverage. The usage for *OFP* is estimated to be nearly 10 times higher for the high-use group than the low-use group. For the former, *PRIVINS* has a coefficient of 2.89 as compared with only 0.25 for the low-use group. *OFP* is insensitive to marginal changes in price given the small baseline price levels.
- Income effect on *OFP* usage is negligible. The family income variable (*FAMINC*) does not affect *OFP*. Furthermore, *EMPLOYED*, which may capture income effects also, is never significant. One explanation for the negligible income effect is that the overall generosity of Medicare irrespective of family income, combined with Social Security income, which guarantees a certain level of income, makes utilization insensitive to marginal changes in income.

The above results may be compared with the more commonly used NBH model. We indicate some of the ways in which a comparison between the NBH and FMNB models may be carried out but do not implement these ideas numerically. One suitable measure is $\partial \mathsf{E}[y_i \mid \mathbf{x}_i]/\partial x_{i,j}$, the change in the mean number of events due to a unit change in a variable x_j, which for simplicity is assumed to be continuous. Some users may prefer elasticity measures $\partial \ln \mathsf{E}[y_i \mid \mathbf{x}_i]/\partial \ln x_{i,j}$. Suppressing the individual subscript, this effect in the NB version of the hurdle model is calculated as follows:

$$\frac{\partial \mathsf{E}[y \mid \mathbf{x}]}{\partial x_j} = \frac{\partial [\Pr[y > 0 \mid \mathbf{x}] \mathsf{E}[y \mid \mathbf{x}, y > 0]]}{\partial x_j}$$

$$= \mu_\tau \frac{\partial (1 - F_{\mathsf{NB}}(0 \mid \mathbf{x}))}{\partial x_j} + (1 - F_{\mathsf{NB}}(0 \mid \mathbf{x})) \frac{\partial \mu_\tau}{\partial x_j}, \qquad (6.13)$$

where μ_τ denotes the mean of the zero truncated NB model (see section 4.5.1) and $1 - F_{\mathsf{NB}}(0 \mid \mathbf{x})$ denotes the truncation probability $\Pr[y > 0 \mid \mathbf{x}]$. The two terms in the third line reflect, respectively, the direct effect due to an individual moving from the nonuser to user category and the indirect effect on the usage of those already in the user category. Note that the calculation of this expression involves both parts of the hurdle model. The truncation probability is given by the binary ("zero") part of the model, and the truncated mean by the "positive" part of the model. Every term in the expression is conditioned on $\mathbf{x}$. Using the standard functional forms for F and μ, the expression given above can be readily calculated for each $\mathbf{x}_i$. A suitable overall measure of partial response is the sample average $n^{-1} \sum_i \partial \mathsf{E}[y_i \mid \mathbf{x}_i]/\partial x_{i,j}$.

The corresponding expression for $\partial \mathsf{E}[y_i | \mathbf{x}_i]/\partial x_{i,j}$ from the FMNB-2 model is relatively simple:

$$\frac{\partial \mathsf{E}[y_i \mid \mathbf{x}_i]}{\partial x_{i,j}} = \pi_1 \mu_{1,i} \beta_j^{(1)} + (1 - \pi_1) \mu_{2,i} \beta_j^{(2)},$$

where $\beta_j^{(1)}$ and $\beta_j^{(2)}$ are the response coefficients for the regressor x_j from each of the two components. Here the partial response is a weighted sum of the partial responses in the two subpopulations. Because the sampling fractions are treated as constants, the resulting expression is simpler than in the NBH model.

6.3.9 *Economic Significance*

Once a finite mixture model has been estimated, the posterior probability that observation i belongs to category j can be calculated for all (i, j) pairs using (4.64). Each observation may then be assigned to the highest probability class. The crispness of the resulting classification by "types" or "groups" varies in practice depending on the differences between the respective mean rates of utilization. Large and significant differences induce a crisp classification of data.

We can then obtain further insights into the data by examining the distribution of related variables in different categories. These variables may be explanatory variables already included in the regression, or other variables that are analyzed separately. For example, we could make useful summary statements about the sociodemographic characteristics of the identified groups. An example is from marketing. One might wish to identify the characeristics of the group of frequent purchasers of some item.

Such an ex-post analysis was applied to the data used in the present illustration. We augmented the data used here with information derived from similar analyses of five additional count measures of healthcare utilization from the same NMES data source (Deb and Trivedi, 1997). These measures are number of nonphysician office visits (*OFNP*), number of physician hospital outpatient visits (*OPP*), number of nonphysician hospital outpatient visits (*OPNP*), number of emergency room visits (*EMR*), and number of hospital stays (*HOSP*). Separate models were specified and estimated for each utilization measure. Finally, a preferred specification of the model was determined using the criteria presented in this chapter.

One interesting issue concerns the frequency with which individuals who are assigned to the high-use group on one measure, such as *OFP*, get classified similarly on a different measure, such as *OFNP*. A second issue is whether high users are concentrated in particular sociodemographic groups.

According to our analysis of *OFP*, 91% of the sample falls in the low-utilization category and the remaining 9% in the high-utilization category. Using posterior probability calculation we have assigned every individual in our sample of 4406 to one of these two categories. Similar assignment was also made using the finite mixture models for the other five variables. It is interesting to find out whether the same individuals fall into the high- or low-use categories with respect to different measures of utilization. This only requires simple two-way frequency tables. Of the 99 users classified as high users of *OFP*, 66 (67%) are also classified as high users of *OFNP*, and 77 (78%) as high users of *OPNP*. However, less than 10 (10%) of these 99 are classified as high users of *EMR* or *HOSP*. These intuitively sensible results suggest that *OFP*, *OPNP*, and *OFNP* are closely related. Hence a joint analysis of these measures may be worthwhile.

Next we ask whether high usage is concentrated in particular demographic groups. Here it is found that of the 516 black members of the sample, 416 (81%) are classified as high users of *OFNP* and 462 (90%) are classified as high users of *OPNP*. With respect to *OFP*, however, only 14 (14%) of the 99 high users are black. Two-way frequency tables were also calculated for the high users of *OPP* and *OPNP* against *MEDICAID*. Interestingly, these showed that of the 402 individuals on Medicaid, 271 (67%) were classified as high users of *OFNP* and 364 (91%) as high users of *OPNP*. Of the 402 on Medicaid, 142 (35%) are black, so these results seem internally coherent.

We end this discussion here. Those interested in detailed results and interpretations should see Deb and Trivedi (1997). This illustration has shown that the latent-class framework may be more realistic and fruitful than the hurdles framework, mainly because the dichotomy between one population at risk and the other not so may be too extreme. At the same time caution should be exercised to avoid overfitting the data. For example, if measurement errors raise the proportion of high counts there is a tendency to overestimate the number of categories. Moment-type estimators may be devised to downweigh these high counts.

Our next example deals with modeling of recreational trips. In this case we have found that the hurdle model seems empirically more appropriate than the latent-class model.

6.4 Analysis of Recreational Trips

In the literature on environmental and resource economics, count models have been widely used to model recreational trips. A readily available measure of an individual's demand for some recreational activity is the frequency with which a particular activity, such as boating, fishing, or hiking, was undertaken. An important issue in these studies is the sensitivity of resource usage to entrance charges and travel costs. The latter are inputs into calculations of the changes in consumer welfare resulting from reduced access or higher costs.

The data used in analyses of trips are often derived from sample surveys of potential users of such resources who are asked to recall their usage in some past period. Sometimes, however, the data are derived from on-site surveys of those who actually used the resource or facility during some time period. They are not a random sample from the population. The resulting complications are discussed in Chapter 11.

In this section we consider a case study based on data that come from a survey that covers actual and potential users of the resource. This illustration draws heavily from an article by Gurmu and Trivedi (1996), which provides further details about several aspects that are dealt with briefly here. This illustration considers a broader range of econometric specifications than is the case for the NMES data.

6.4.1 *Recreational Trips Data*

The ideas and techniques of earlier chapters are illustrated by estimating a recreation demand function, due to Ozuna and Gomaz (1995), based on survey data on the number of recreational boating trips to Lake Somerville, Texas, in 1980, denoted by *TRIPS*. The data are a subset of that collected by Sellar, Stoll, and Chavas (1985) through a survey administered to 2000 registered leisure boat owners in 23 counties in eastern Texas. All subsequent analyses are based on a sample of 659 observations. Their descriptive features and data definitions are shown in Tables 6.9 and 6.10. For a more comprehensive description of the data and the method used for calculating the costs of the visit, the reader is referred to Sellar et al. (1985). Two noteworthy features of Table 6.9 are the relatively long tail – 50 respondents reported taking 10 or more trips – and

Table 6.9. *Recreational trips: actual frequency distribution*

Number of Trips	0	1	2	3	4	5	6	7	8	9	10	11	12	15	16	20	25	26	30	40	50	88
Frequency	417	68	38	34	17	13	11	2	8	1	13	2	5	14	1	3	3	1	3	3	1	1

Table 6.10. *Recreational trips: variable definitions and summary statistics*

Variable	Definition	Mean	Standard deviation
TRIPS	Number of recreational boating trips in 1980 by a sampled group	2.244	6.292
SO	Facility's subjective quality ranking on a scale of 1 to 5	1.419	1.812
SKI	Equal 1 if engaged in water-skiing at the lake	0.367	0.482
I	Household income of the head of the group ($1,000/year)	3.853	1.851
FC3	Equal 1 if user's fee paid at Lake Somerville	0.019	0.139
C1	Dollar expenditure when visiting Lake Conroe	55.42	46.68
C3	Dollar expenditure when visiting Lake Somerville	59.93	48.77
C4	Dollar expenditure when visiting Lake Houston	55.99	46.13

the high proportion of zero observations. More than 65% of the respondents reported taking no trips in the survey period. There is also some clustering at 10 and 15 trips, creating a rough impression of multimodality. Further, the presence of responses in "rounded" categories like 20, 25, 30, 40, and 50 raises a suspicion that the respondents in these categories may not accurately recall the frequency of their visits.

6.4.2 *Initial Specifications*

The models and methods of Chapter 3 provide a starting point. In modeling this data set, we focus on the choice of the parametric family and estimation method, representation of unobserved heterogeneity in the sample, and evaluation of the fitted model. Our example is intended to provide alternatives to the commonly followed approach in which one settles on the NB model after pretesting for overdispersion.

As a first approximation, one may begin, following Ozuna and Gomaz (1995), with the Poisson regression based on the conditional mean function

$$\mu_i \equiv \mathsf{E}[TRIPS_i] = \exp\left(\beta_0 + \sum_{j=1}^{7} \beta_i x_{ij}\right), \tag{6.14}$$

Table 6.11. *Recreational trips: Poisson, NB2, and ZIP model estimates and t ratios*

	Poisson			NB2		ZIP	
Variable	Coefficient	$\lvert t \rvert$	$\lvert t \rvert^{EW}$	Coefficient	$\lvert t \rvert$	Coefficient	$\lvert t \rvert$
ONE	.264	2.82	0.61	−1.12	5.04	1.964	3.76
SO	.471	27.60	9.66	.722	16.45	.046	0.53
SKI	.418	7.31	2.15	.621	4.38	.445	2.54
I	−.111	5.68	2.21	−.026	0.64	−.1078	2.33
FC3	.898	11.37	3.64	.669	1.48	.656	2.67
C1	−.003	1.10	0.23	.048	4.62	.003	0.23
C3	−.042	25.4	3.62	−.092	15.3	−.040	3.69
C4	.036	13.3	3.85	.038	4.43	.028	3.33
α	—			1.37	9.24	—	—
R_P^2		.65		—	—	—	—
$-\ln$ L		1529		825		1338	
CAIC		2998		1582		2616	
T_Z		6.87		—		—	
T_{GoF}		252.57		23.52			

where the vector $\mathbf{x} = (SO, SKI, I, FC3, C1, C3, C4)$. The Poisson regression results are given in column 2 of Table 6.11. Also provided are absolute t ratios, and the second t ratio in the Poisson column is the "robust" Eicker-White t ratio. The t statistics of all coefficients except that of *C1* are significant. However, the robust versions of the t ratios are much smaller, reflecting how the neglect of overdispersion inflates the Poisson t ratios.

Three measures of goodness of fit are also included. The first is the deviance measure presented in section 5.3.2. For the Poisson family, the deviance measure is also called the G^2 statistic.

A second measure presented is a pseudo-R^2 measure based on Pearson residuals (see section 5.3.3). Table 6.11 shows a relatively high Pearson-based R_P^2 value of 0.65, suggesting a good fit. One could instead use a pseudo-R^2 based on deviance residuals also presented in section 5.3.3.

The third indicator of the goodness of fit of the Poisson model is based on a comparison of observed zero outcomes and the proportion expected in the zero cell under the null model. This is a special case of the chi-square goodness-of-fit test based on several cell frequencies. A formal test approach, proposed by Mullahy (1997b), relies on the fact that the actual proportion of zero outcomes in an arbitrarily overdispersed Poisson model tends to exceed the proportion expected under the Poisson null. Letting $\mathbf{1}(\cdot)$ be the 0/1 indicator function and $y = TRIPS$, Mullahy's test is based on

$$\hat{m} = n^{-1}\sum_{i=1}^{N}[\mathbf{1}(y_i = 0) - \exp(-\hat{\mu})] \equiv n^{-1}\sum_{i}\delta_i. \tag{6.15}$$

Let $\hat{\varepsilon}_i = y_i - \hat{f}_i$ and $\mathbf{x}_i$ denote a column vector of explanatory variables. The computationally tractable version of the test, which is asymptotically distributed as N[0, 1], may be implemented using the statistic:

$$\mathsf{T}_\mathsf{Z} = \frac{\sqrt{n}\hat{m}}{\sqrt{\hat{V}}}, \tag{6.16}$$

where $\hat{V} = n^{-1} \sum_i v_i^2$ where

$$v_i = \delta_i - \left[n^{-1} \sum_i \mathbf{1}(y_i = 0) \hat{\varepsilon}_i \mathbf{x}_i' \right] \left[\left(- \sum_i \hat{\theta}_i \mathbf{x}_i \mathbf{x}_i' \right)^{-1} \mathbf{x}_i \hat{\varepsilon}_i \right]. \tag{6.17}$$

The excess zero test statistic for the trip data is $\mathsf{T}_\mathsf{Z} = 6.87$, which is statistically significant, suggesting that the Poisson null be rejected. Actually the rejection is even stronger if a more general chi-square goodness-of-fit test is used. A five-degrees-of-freedom test based on (6.10) has a value of 252.6, indicating a poor fit to the data.

The deficiencies in the fitted (Poisson) model are obvious in the comparison of the actual and fitted frequency distributions of trips. The actual frequency of zeros (417) is considerably higher than the fitted value of 276. Second, the fitted model overpredicts the observed frequencies between 1 and 14 trips. Finally, the fitted model underpredicts the high counts, perhaps because of the curious clumping of the actual frequency distribution. This lack of fit could be reflected in significant values of specification test statistics. Consider for example, the regression-based score tests of the null hypothesis of zero overdispersion. Following section 3.4, regress the moment function $(\hat{\varepsilon}_i^2 - TRIPS_i)$ on $\hat{\mu}_i$ and $(\hat{\varepsilon}_i^2 - TRIPS_i)$ on $\hat{\mu}_i^2$, where $\hat{\varepsilon}_i = TRIPS_i - \hat{f}_i$. The results, with heteroskedasticity robust t ratios shown in parentheses, are as follows:

$$\hat{\varepsilon}_i^2 - TRIPS_i = \underset{(2.09)}{5.44}\,\hat{\mu}_i, \qquad \hat{\varepsilon}_i^2 - TRIPS_i = \underset{(3.03)}{1.45}\hat{\mu}_i^2.$$

There is clearly evidence of overdispersion in the data; the Poisson regression model is rejected against both the NB1 and the NB2 alternatives. The five-degrees-of-freedom chi-square goodness-of-fit test has a value of more than 250, leading to the rejection of the model.

The model was then reestimated using the NB2 specification; Table 6.11 shows the result. Observe that allowing for overdispersion greatly increases the log-likelihood; the log-likelihood of the Poisson model was −1529; that of the NB model is −825, which reflects the importance of modeling overdispersion. Similarly, there is a substantial reduction in the Akaike information criterion; CAIC values for Poisson and NB2 are 2998 and 1582, respectively. There are also sizeable shifts in the size and the significance of several coefficients, a fact that is not easily reconciled with the idea that the conditional mean of the Poisson model is correctly specified. The income variable, I, and the cost variable *FC3* become "insignificant" once overdispersion is allowed for, and the coefficient of *C1* changed sign from negative to (a priori correct) positive and becomes "significant". The NB estimates are plausible in that they indicate substitution from other sites toward Lake Somerville as travel costs rise and away from Lake Somerville as its own travel costs rise. *SO* and *SKI* also have the a priori expected positive sign.

The presence of overdispersion, although consistent with the NB specification, does not in itself imply that the NB specification is adequate; rejection of the null against a specified alternative does not necessarily imply that the alternative is the correct one. Further examination of the fit of the model (Table 6.11) shows that the predicted values of high counts are generally higher than the actual values. The statistic $\mathsf{T}_{\mathsf{GoF}}$, although much smaller at 23.5, still rejects the model. The deficiencies of the model, including the poor fit particularly in the right tail of the observed distribution, can be interpreted in several different ways including the following: The conditional mean function is misspecified; the unobserved heterogeneity distribution is misspecified; or the high counts reflect measurement errors. We consider alternative approaches for obtaining improvements based on these considerations.

The failure to account for high counts could reflect the need for additional nonlinearities in the conditional mean function. These can be introduced by including quadratic cost and income terms in the conditional mean function. Accordingly, three squared-cost variables, $C1SQ$, $C3SQ$, $C4SQ$, and three cross-product variables, $C1C3$, $C1C4$, $C3C4$, were introduced into the conditional mean function for NB2. This can be justified by appealing to the possible presence of nonlinearities in the budget constraint, or simply in terms of a better approximation to the functional form. They produced a significant increase in the log-likelihood, but there was no significant improvement using the AIC. The correspondence between actual and observed frequencies now deteriorates; low counts are underpredicted, and the very high counts are overpredicted.

6.4.3 *Modified Poisson Models*

Plausible alternatives to the models considered above are the ZIP model or the hurdle-type model; they lead to changes in the conditional mean and the conditional variance specification.

Consider the possibility that the sample under analysis may represent a mixture of at least two types, those who never choose boating as recreation and those that do, but some of the latter simply might not have had a positive number of boating trips in the sample period. The "non-Poissonness" in the sample arises because the zeros come from two sources, not one; this is the ZIP model.

In Table 6.11 we also include an estimate of the ZIP model in which the probability of a nonzero count is further modeled as a logit function ($e^{\mathbf{z}'\gamma}/(1 + e^{\mathbf{z}'\gamma})$) where $\mathbf{z}$ denotes the three variables, an intercept (*ONE*), quality ranking

Table 6.12. *Recreational trips: finite mixture estimates and t ratios*

	FMP2				FMNB-2			
	High users		Low users		High users		Low users	
Variable	Coefficient	$\lvert t \rvert$	Coefficient	$\lvert t \rvert$	Coefficient	$\lvert t \rvert$	Coefficient	$\lvert t \rvert$
ONE	1.22	2.19	−1.865	6.00	1.006	1.01	−1.876	9.11
SO	.281	2.91	.659	15.47	−.09	5.43	.889	19.92
SKI	.852	5.97	.557	3.05	1.369	3.58	.449	2.51
I	.092	1.28	−.097	0.43	−.03	2.24	−.048	1.02
FC3	.158	.84	.970	3.43	−.12	9.43	1.069	2.98
C1	.054	4.40	.0003	.03	.186	7.52	−0.00	0.00
C3	−.064	7.91	−.064	7.85	−.258	9.47	−.050	5.24
C4	.002	.24	.057	4.50	.049	3.41	.047	3.11
α					.192	1.88	.825	7.58
π	.113	5.04			.124	2.55		
Fitted mean	10.11		1.55					
−ln L		916.63				786.01		
CAIC		1953.11				1706.85		
T_{GoF}		43.7				20.6		

of the facility (*SO*) and income (*I*).* The results are once again plausible in that they suggest that the higher the subjective ranking of Lake Somerville as a water-skiing facility, the greater the probability of a positive number of visits. The variable *I* does not seem to significantly affect that probability. The coefficients in the conditional-mean part of the model are similar to those found earlier. The fit of the ZIP model showed that it seriously overpredicts the zero counts – the actual frequency of zeros is 417, the fitted frequency is 528. As a result the remaining counts are largely underpredicted. Clearly, in terms of both the maximized log-likelihood and the CAIC, the ZIP model is dominated by NB2.

As in the case of NMES data, finite mixtures of Poisson or NB and the NBH model are plausible alternatives. Although the ZIP model fits poorly, a two-component finite mixture Poisson (FMP-2) model, or FMNB2, especially the latter, are likely to do better. Table 6.12 shows estimates of the two-component Poisson and NB mixtures. Although the latter clearly dominates the former, the FMNB is still rejected by the chi-square goodness-of-fit test. We interpret this result to mean that the characterization of the dgp as a mechanism that samples two subpopulations, one of relatively high users and the other of low users of the recreational site, leaves some features of the data unexplained. Therefore, we consider the NBH model.

In the hurdle model the conditional means for the zero and nonzero observations are different. If this were an important feature, the choice of the Poisson

* The *t* ratios for the constant term and for *SO* in the logit specification were significant at 1%. Results from the logit specification are not given in the table.

or the NB hurdle model would lead to an improved fit. Regression results for the Poisson hurdle and NB2 hurdle are given in Table 6.13. For the Poisson hurdle model, the parameter estimates for the two parts are significantly different; the log-likelihood is now -1291 $(-277 - 1014)$, significantly higher than -1529 for the Poisson model, although not as high as for the NB model. The CAIC criterion and the distribution of the fitted frequency also revealed similar ranking. This suggests that a hurdle specification that also models overdispersion could be an improvement. Accordingly, the last columns of Table 6.13 provide estimates based on NB2 hurdles. For the zero part of the model there are two sets of estimates, one with a free dispersion parameter and the other with the parameter value constrained to unity. The latter have smaller standard errors and may be preferred if the zero part cannot identify the overdispersion parameter. Again, the parameter estimates for the zeros and the positives are significantly different; the log-likelihood is now -725 and the CAIC is 1321. However, few of the variables for the zeros part of the model are significant, which suggests that most of the explanatory power of the covariates derives from their impact on positive counts. In terms of fitted frequency distribution (Table 6.14), the NBH model does extremely well, for zero counts and high counts. Indeed, NBH is the only model that is not rejected by the goodness-of-fit test. This result is especially interesting because the difference between NBH and FMNB is quantitative rather than qualitative – NBH views the data a mixture with respect to zeros only, but FMNB views the data as a mixture with respect to zeros and positives. The opposite conclusion was reached in regard to the NMES data. Finally, the NBH model is also superior to some flexible parametric or "semi-parametric" models based on series-expansion methods; these are developed and discussed further in Chapter 12.

In terms of goodness of fit, measured by either log-likelihood or the AIC, NBH is the best, followed by FMNB2. This result can be interpreted as follows: Although there is considerable unobserved heterogeneity among those who use recreational facility, there is also a significant proportion in the population for whom the "optimal" solution is a corner solution. That is, they may consistently have a zero demand for recreational boating. Because no theoretical model is provided for explaining zero demand for recreational boating, the potential importance of excess zeros is not emphasized. Consumer choice theory (and common sense) predicts the occurrence of zero solutions (see Pudney, 1989, section 4.3). However, a priori reasoning cannot in itself predict whether their relative frequency is greater or less than that implied by the Poisson model. This is an empirical issue, whose resolution depends also on how the sample data were obtained. However, theory may still help in suggesting variables that explain the proportion of such corner solutions.

As in the case of the NMES data, several other finite mixture models were also estimated. The diagnostic tests and the CAIC criteria show all finite mixture models to be inferior to the NBH model. Thus, in contrast to the NMES data, the outcome supports the idea that the sample is drawn from two subpopulations of nonusers and users, rather than two subpopulations of low and high users.

Table 6.13. *Recreational trips: hurdle model estimates and t ratios*

	Poisson hurdle				NB hurdle					
	Zeros		Positives		Zeros-1		Zeros-2		Positives	
Variable	Coefficient	$\|t\|$	Coefficient	$\|t\|$	Coefficient	$\|t\|$	Coefficient	$\|t\|$	Coefficient	$\|t\|$
ONE	−1.88	9.30	2.15	19.2	−3.046	2.52	−2.88	6.80	.841	1.97
SO	.815	20.76	.044	1.86	4.638	2.43	1.44	12.68	.172	2.25
SKI	.403	2.97	.467	7.94	−.025	.02	0.40	1.24	.622	3.14
I	.010	.27	−.097	4.75	.026	.11	0.03	0.30	−.057	0.78
FC3	2.95	.19	.601	7.55	16.203	.97	9.43	16.17	.576	0.87
C1	.006	.51	.002	0.35	.030	.28	0.01	0.42	.057	2.89
C3	−.052	7.58	−.036	−17.9	−.156	1.62	−.080	4.65	−.078	7.07
C4	.046	4.66	.024	6.87	.117	1.40	.071	3.70	.012	0.84
α	—		—		5.609	1.81	1(fixed)		1.70	3.87
$-\ln L$	277		1014		134		150		591	
CAIC	3016				1321					
T_{GoF}					2.25					

Table 6.14. *Recreational boating trips: actual and fitted cumulative frequencies*

Frequency	0	1	2	3	4	5	6–8	9–11	12–14	15–17	18–62	63+
Observed	417	68	38	34	17	13	21	16	5	15	14	1
Cumulative	.632	.736	.794	.845	.871	.891	.923	.947	.954	.977	.998	1
Poisson	276	145	68	41	30	23	40	17	8	4	6	1
Cumulative	.420	.640	.744	.805	.850	.885	.945	.971	.983	.988	.998	1
Negbin	422	81	33	20	14	11	22	13	9	6	22	6
Cumulative	.642	.764	.815	.845	.866	.883	.915	.935	.948	.958	.992	1
ZIP	528	15	18	18	16	14	27	12	5	3	3	0
Cumulative	.801	.823	.850	.878	.902	.923	.964	.983	.991	.995	1	1
Poisson-H	376	31	35	36	34	30	61	29	13	6	8	0
Cumulative	.570	.617	.671	.725	.776	.821	.914	.959	.979	.988	1	1
Negbin-H	410	71	42	28	20	15	27	14	9	6	15	2
Cumulative	.623	.730	.793	.836	.866	.889	.930	.952	.965	.974	.997	1

6.4.4 *Economic Implications*

The model discrimination and selection exercise rely heavily on statistical criteria in both applications. Are we simply fine-tuning the model, or are the resulting changes economically meaningful? Only a partial answer can be given here. In the modeling of recreational trips it is reasonable to suppose that a random sample includes nonparticipants because of taste differences among individuals. A hurdles-type model is worthwhile in this case because parameter estimates and welfare analysis should be based only on the participant's responses. In the case of NMES data on the elderly, the notion of nonparticipants is implausible. However, given differences in health status of individuals as well as other types of unobserved heterogeneity, the distinction between high users and low users is reasonable. This feature can explain the superior performance of the finite mixture NB model.

6.5 LR Test: A Digression

The two examples in this chapter illustrate alternative ways of handling "non-Poisson" features of two data sets. The hurdles version provides a good fit to the recreational trips data, and the latent-class approach a good fit to the doctor visits data. These outcomes can also be rationalized in terms of a priori reasoning. Distinguishing between hurdles and finite-mixture models may be difficult in many situations, in which neither formulation may be a priori unacceptable. Furthermore, one might also construct finite mixtures based on hurdles, which would involve finite mixtures of binomials for the zero outcome, and finite mixtures of truncated counts for the positives. Identification and estimation of such models is likely to prove challenging.

6.5.1 *Simulation Analysis of Model Selection Criteria*

This section reports the results of a small simulation experiment designed to throw light on the properties of model evaluation criteria used in this chapter.

Simulation Design

Data were generated using, respectively, the Poisson, Poisson hurdles, and FMP2 structures. The conditional mean in each case was specified thus:

Poisson: $\mu_i = \exp[-1.445 + 3.0x_i]$
PH: Zeros part: $\mu_i = \exp[-1.6 + 3.0x_i]$;
positives: $\mu_i = \exp[-1.35 + 3.0x_i]$
FMP2: $\mu_1 = \exp[-1.225 + 3.0x_i]$; $\mu_2 = \exp[-1.5 + .75x_i]$;
$\pi = 0.75$

The dgp was calibrated in each case to mimic the excess zeros situation. The zeros accounted for about 40% of the observations. We examine the frequency

Table 6.15. *Rejection frequencies at nominal 10% significance level*

	dgp		
Test/criterion	Poisson	Hurdle (PH)	Finite mixture (FMP)
LR-PH	.100	.926	.990
LR-FMP	.092	.880	1.000
GoF-P	.126	.740	.988
GoF-H	.244	.100	.530
GoF-FM	.142	.346	.118
AIC-P	.822	.050	.000
AIC-PH	.146	.800	.066
AIC-FMP	.032	.148	.934
BIC-P	.998	.544	.060
BIC-PH	.002	.400	.050
BIC-FMP	.000	.050	.890

of rejection at nominal significance level of 10% using the likelihood ratio, the chi-square goodness of fit, and the information criteria. The reported goodness-of-fit test is based on five cell frequencies. The rejection frequencies based on 500 replications are shown in Table 6.15.

Simulation Outcomes

The $\chi^2(1)$ LR test of Poisson null against PH alternative, LR-PH in Table 6.15, has a rejection frequency of 10%, equal to the nominal significance level. Against the FMP2 alternative, the test (LR-FMP) appears to be undersized. This confirms that the nominal critical value is not appropriate. The size of the goodness-of-fit test appears to be roughly correct, with perhaps a slight tendency toward overrejection of the true null.

The performance of the information criteria is shown in the lower part of Table 6.15. The interpretation of the "rejection frequency" here is somewhat different because the reported figure shows the proportion of times the model had the smallest value of the criterion. For example, if the true model is Poisson, the AIC selects Poisson as the best model in 81% to 82% of the cases, whereas BIC does so in almost every case. If the true model is the PH, the AIC selects it as the best model in around 80% of the cases, whereas BIC does so in only 40% of the cases; it picks the Poisson model as the best more frequently, in about 54% of the cases. BIC favors a more parsimoniously parameterized model. Finally, if the true model is the FMP2, the AIC and the BIC pick it as the best in 93.4% and 89% of the cases, respectively.

Finally consider the power of the LR and goodness-of-fit tests. If the dgp is FMP2, the LR test has high power. Under the PH dgp, the goodness-of-fit-P test rejects the Poisson model in 74% of the cases, and goodness-of-fit-FM rejects the FMP model in only 34.6% of the cases. In the converse case in which the dgp is the FMP model, the goodness-of-fit-P test rejects the Poisson in 98.8% of the cases, and goodness-of-fit-H rejects the hurdle model in only 53.3% of the cases. Of course, these results are affected by the choice of parameter values. However, these results indicate that the discrimination between the hurdles and the finite mixture models using the goodness-of-fit test may be more difficult than the discrimination between the one-component model and a mixture alternative.

To summarize, collectively, the goodness-of-fit tests and the information criteria are useful in evaluating models. Rejection of the null by the LR, goodness-of-fit, or the AIC would seem to indicate a deficiency of the model. Thus, despite its theoretical limitations, the standard LR test of the one-component model against the mixture alternative may have useful power.

6.5.2 *Bootstrapping the LR Test*

If computational cost is not an important consideration, a parametric bootstrap of the LR test provides another way to obtain better critical values for the test. Feng and McCulloch (1996) suggested and analyzed a bootstrap LR test for the null that the number of components in the mixture is $C - 1$ against the alternative that it is C. Their examples are in a univariate iid setting. Hence their procedure must be adapted to the non-iid regression case, as discussed in section 5.5. As an illustration we consider the case $C = 2$.

1. Estimate the one-component model and the two-component mixture model by MLE. Form the LR statistic, denoted LR^*.
2. Draw a bootstrap pseudosample $(y_i^*, \mathbf{x}_i^*)$ by sampling with replacement from the original sample $(y_i, \mathbf{x}_i)$, $i = 1, \ldots, n$. Estimate the null model and construct the LR statistic.
3. Repeat steps 1 and 2 B times, giving B values of the LR statistic, denoted $\widehat{LR}_i$, $i = 1, \ldots, B$.
4. Using the bootstrap distribution of the LR statistic, determine the $(1 - \alpha)$ percent quantile as the critical value, denoted LR_B.
5. Reject H_0 if $LR^* > LR_B$.

The procedure generalizes to other null and alternative models. Application of this procedure to the NMES sample would have been prohibitively expensive if we had set $B = 100$ or more.

6.6 Concluding Remarks

Most empirical studies generate substantive and methodological questions that motivate subsequent investigations. We conclude by mentioning two issues and lines of investigation worth pursuing. First, in the context of the recreational trips example, one might question the assumption of independence of sample observations. This is standard in cross-section analysis. However, our data also have a spatial dimension. Even after conditioning, observations may be spatially correlated. This feature will affect the estimated variances of the parameters. Essentially, the assumption of independent observations implies that our sample is more informative than might actually be the case.

A related issue concerns the stochastic process for events. Many events may belong to a spell of events, and each spell may constitute several correlated events. The spells themselves may follow some stochastic process and may in fact be observable. One might then consider whether to analyze pooled data or to analyze events grouped by spells. An example is the number of doctor visits within a spell of illness (Newhouse, 1993). In many data situations one is uncertain whether the observed events are a part of the same spell or different spells.

Another issue is joint modeling of several types of events. The empirical examples considered in this chapter involve conditional models for individual events, not joint models for several events. This may be restrictive. In some studies the event of interest generates multiple observations on several counts. A health event, for instance, may lead to hospitalization, doctor consultations, and usage of prescribed medicines, all three being interrelated. The analysis described in the previous paragraph can be extended to this type of situation by considering a mixture of multinomial and count models, which leads to multivariate count models, a topic that is discussed in Chapter 8.

6.7 Bibliographic Notes

Applications of single-equation count data models in economics, especially in accident analysis, insurance, health, labor, and resource and environmental economics, are now standard; examples are Johansson and Palme (1996), Pohlmeier and Ulrich (1995), Gurmu and Trivedi (1996), and Grogger and Carson (1991). Rose (1990) uses Poisson models to evaluate the effect of regulation on airline safety record. Dionne and Vanasse (1992) use a sample of about 19,000 Quebec drivers to estimate an NB2 model that is used to derive predicted claims frequencies, and hence insurance premia, from data on different individuals with different characteristics and records. Schwartz and Torous (1993) combine the Poisson regression approach with the proportional hazard structure. They separately model monthly grouped data on mortgage prepayments and defaults, the two being modeled separately. Lambert (1992) provides an interesting analysis of the number of defects in a manufacturing process using the Poisson regression with "excess zeros." Cameron and Trivedi (1996) survey this and a number of other count data applications in financial economics. Nagin and Land (1993) use the Heckman-Singer–type nonparametric approach in their mixed Poisson longitudinal data model of criminal careers. Their model is essentially a hurdles-type Poisson model with nonparametric treatment of heterogeneity. After estimation, they classify observations into groups according to criminal propensity, in a manner analogous to that used in the health utilization example. Cameron and Windmeijer (1996) consider pseudo-R^2–type goodness-of-fit measures for Poisson and NB models. Panel data applications are featured in Chapter 9. Two interesting marketing applications of latent class (finite mixture) count models are Wedel et al. (1993) and Ramaswamy, Anderson, and DeSarbo (1994). Wang, Cockburn, and Puterman (1998) apply the finite mixture model to patent data; they also parameterize the sampling fractions as functions of covariates. Haab and McConnell (1996) discuss estimation of consumer surplus measures in the presence of excess zeros.

6.8 Exercises

6.1 Using the estimated mixing proportion π_1 in Table 6.6, and the estimated component means in Table 6.7, check whether the sample mean of *OFP* given in Table 6.2 coincides with the fitted mean. Using the first-order conditions for maximum likelihood estimation of NB2, consider whether a two-component finite mixture of the NB2 model will display an analogous property.

6.2 Suppose the dgp is a two-component CFMNB family, with the slope parameters of the conditional mean functions equal but intercepts left free. An investigator misspecifies the model and estimates a unicomponent Poisson regression model instead. Show that the Poisson MLE consistently estimates the slope parameters.

6.3 In the context of the modeling the zeros/positives binary outcome using the NBH specification, compare the following two alternatives from the viewpoint of identifiability of the parameters $(\boldsymbol{\beta}, \alpha_1)$,

$$\Pr[y_i = 0 \mid \mathbf{x}_i] = \begin{cases} 1/(1+\alpha_1\mu_i)^{1/\alpha_1}, \text{ or} \\ 1/(1+\mu_i), \end{cases}$$

where $\mu_i = \exp(\mathbf{x}_i'\boldsymbol{\beta})$.

6.4 Consider how to specify and estimate a two-component finite mixture of the NBH model. Show that this involves a mixture of binomials as well as a mixture of NB families.

6.5 Consider whether the alternative definitions of residuals in Chapter 5 can be extended to finite mixtures of Poisson components.

6.6 Verify the result given in (6.12). To do so, first derive (4.62) for $r = 2$, then derive the central second moment by subtracting off $\bar{\mu}^2$.

CHAPTER 7

Time Series Data

7.1 Introduction

The previous chapters have focused on models for cross-section regression on a single count dependent variable. We now turn to models for more general types of data – univariate time series data in this chapter, multivariate cross-section data in Chapter 8, and longitudinal or panel data in Chapter 9.

Count data introduce complications of discreteness and heteroskedasticity. For cross-section data, this leads to moving from the linear model to the Poisson regression model. This model is often too restrictive for real data, which are typically overdispersed. With cross-section data, overdispersion is most frequently handled by leaving the conditional mean unchanged and rescaling the conditional variance. The same adjustment is made regardless of whether the underlying cause of overdispersion is unobserved heterogeneity in a Poisson point process or true contagion leading to dependence in the process.

For time series count data, one can again begin with the Poisson regression model. In this case, however, it is not clear how to proceed if dependence is present. For example, developing even a pure time series count model in which the count in period t, y_t, depends only on the count in the previous period, y_{t-1}, is not straightforward, and there are many possible ways to proceed. Even restricting attention to a fully parametric approach, one can specify distributions for y_t either conditional on y_{t-1} or unconditional on y_{t-1}. For count data this leads to quite different models, whereas for continuous data the assumption of joint normality leads to both conditional and marginal distributions that are also normal.

Time series models for count data are in their infancy, yet remarkably many models have been developed. These models, although conceptually and in some cases mathematically innovative, are generally restrictive. For example, some models restrict serial correlation to being positive. At this stage it is not clear which, if any, of the current models will become the dominant model for time series count data.

A review of linear time series models is given in section 7.2, along with a brief summary of six different classes of count time series models. In section 7.3

we consider estimation of static regression models and residual-based tests for serial correlation. In sections 7.4 through 7.9 each of the six models is presented in detail. In section 7.10 some of these models are applied to monthly time series data on the number of contract strikes in U.S. manufacturing, first introduced in section 7.3.4.

Estimators for basic static and dynamic regression models, controlling for both autocorrelation and heteroskedasticity present in time series data, are detailed in sections 7.3 to 7.6. The simplest, although not necessarily fully efficient, estimators for these models are relatively straightforward to implement. For many applied studies this is sufficient. For a more detailed analysis of data, the models of sections 7.4, 7.7, and 7.8 are particularly appealing. Estimation (efficient estimation in the case of section 7.4) of these models entails complex methods. Implementation requires reading the original papers.

7.2 Models for Time Series Data

7.2.1 *Linear Models*

For a continuous dependent variable, the standard models are well established. For *pure time series*, where the only explanatory variables are lagged values of the dependent variable, the standard class of linear models is the *autoregressive moving average* model of orders p and q, or ARMA(p, q), model. In the ARMA(p, q) model, the current value of y is the weighted sum of the past p values of y and the current and past q values of an iid error

$$y_t = \rho_1 y_{t-1} + \cdots + \rho_p y_{t-p} + \varepsilon_t + \gamma_1 \varepsilon_{t-1} + \cdots + \gamma_q \varepsilon_{t-q},$$
$$t = p+1, \ldots, T, \tag{7.1}$$

where ε_t is iid $(0, \sigma^2)$.

For linear *time series regression* the explanatory variables include exogenous regressors. The *autoregressive* or *dynamic* model includes exogenous regressors and lagged dependent variables in the regression function. An example is

$$y_t = \rho y_{t-1} + \mathbf{x}_t'\boldsymbol{\beta} + \varepsilon_t, \tag{7.2}$$

where the error term ε_t is iid $(0, \sigma^2)$. Note that this model is equivalent to assuming that

$$y_t \mid y_{t-1} \sim \mathsf{D}\left[\rho y_{t-1} + \mathbf{x}_t'\boldsymbol{\beta}, \sigma^2\right], \tag{7.3}$$

that is, y_t conditional on y_{t-1} and $\mathbf{x}_t$ is distributed with mean $\rho y_{t-1} + \mathbf{x}_t'\boldsymbol{\beta}$ and variance σ^2. More generally, additional lags of y and $\mathbf{x}$ may appear as regressors. If only $\mathbf{x}_t$ and lags of $\mathbf{x}_t$ appear, the model is instead called a *distributed lag* model. If $\mathbf{x}_t$ alone appears as a regressor, the model is called a *static* model.

An alternative time series regression model is the *serially correlated error* model. This starts with a static regression function

$$y_t = \mathbf{x}_t'\beta + u_t, \tag{7.4}$$

but then assumes that the error term u_t is serially correlated, following for example an ARMA process. The simplest case is an autoregressive error of order one (AR[1]) error

$$u_t = \rho u_{t-1} + \varepsilon_t, \tag{7.5}$$

where ε_t is iid $(0, \sigma^2)$. Then the model can be rewritten as

$$y_t = \rho y_{t-1} + \mathbf{x}_t'\beta - \mathbf{x}_{t-1}'\beta\rho + \varepsilon_t, \tag{7.6}$$

which is an autoregressive model with nonlinear restrictions imposed on the parameters.

The autoregressive and serial correlation models can be combined, to yield an autoregressive model with serially correlated error.

Estimation for these models is by NLS, or by maximum likelihood if a distribution is specified for ε_t. For models with autoregressive errors of order p, specification of a normal distribution for ε_t leads by change of variable techniques to a joint density for $y_{p+1}, \ldots, y_T$, given $y_1, \ldots, y_p$, which is maximized by the MLE. Alternatively, the NLS estimator minimizes the sum of squared residuals, $\sum_{t=p+1}^{T} \varepsilon_t^2$. For example the model in (7.4) and (7.5) leads to ε_t defined implicitly in (7.6), which leads to first-order conditions that are nonlinear in parameters. Because ε_t is homoskedastic and uncorrelated, inference for the NLS estimator is the same as in the non–time series case. Note that if u_t is serially correlated, it is $\sum_t \varepsilon_t^2$ rather than $\sum_t u_t^2$ that is minimized. Minimizing the latter would lead to estimates that are inefficient and even inconsistent if lagged dependent variables appear as regressors. The MLE and NLS estimator are asymptotically equivalent, although they differ in small samples due to different treatment of the first observation y_1. For models with a moving average component in the error, estimation is more complicated but covered in standard time series texts.

Recent econometrics literature on linear models for continuous data has focused on models with unit roots, where ρ in (7.2) or (7.5) takes the value $\rho = 1$, and the related analysis of cointegrated time series. Then y_t is nonstationary, due to a nonstationary stochastic trend, and the usual asymptotic normal theory for estimators no longer applies. Nonstationary stochastic trends have not been studied for count regression. Nonstationarity is instead accommodated by deterministic trends, in which case the usual asymptotic theory still applies.

The preceding models are only those most commonly used for continuous data. There are many extensions, two of which are now presented and also considered subsequently in the count context.

The *state-space* or *time-varying parameter model* is a modification of (7.4) that introduces dependence through parameters that vary over time rather than through the error term. An example is

$$\begin{aligned} y_t &= \mathbf{x}_t'\boldsymbol{\beta}_t + \varepsilon_t \\ \boldsymbol{\beta}_t - \bar{\boldsymbol{\beta}} &= \boldsymbol{\Phi}(\boldsymbol{\beta}_{t-1} - \bar{\boldsymbol{\beta}}) + \boldsymbol{v}_t, \end{aligned} \tag{7.7}$$

where ε_t is iid $(0, \sigma^2)$, $\boldsymbol{\Phi}$ is a $k \times k$ matrix, and $\boldsymbol{v}_t$ is a $k \times 1$ iid $(\mathbf{0}, \boldsymbol{\Sigma})$ error vector. If the roots of $\boldsymbol{\Phi}$ lie inside the unit circle this model is stationary. The model is estimated by reexpressing it in state space form and using the Kalman filter (Harvey, 1989). This model is also widely used in Bayesian analysis of time series, where it is called the *dynamic linear* model. A detailed treatment is given in West and Harrison (1997).

The *hidden Markov* model, or *regime shift* model, is an extension of the preceding models that additionally allows the parameters to differ according to which of a finite number of regimes is currently in effect. The unobserved regimes evolve over time according to a Markov chain – hence the term *hidden Markov* models. These models were popularized in economics by Hamilton (1989), who considered a two-regime Markov trend model

$$y_t^* = \alpha_1 d_{t1} + \alpha_2 d_{t2} + y_{t-1}^*, \tag{7.8}$$

where y_t^* is the trend component of y_t, and d_{tj} are indicator variables for whether or not in regime j, $j = 1$ or 2. The transitions between the two regimes are determined by realization c_t of the first-order Markov chain C_t with transition probabilities

$$\gamma_{ij} = \Pr\left[C_t = j \mid C_{t-1} = i\right], \qquad i, j = 1, 2, \tag{7.9}$$

where $\gamma_{1i} + \gamma_{2i} = 1$. Then

$$d_{tj} = \begin{cases} 1 & \text{if } c_t = j \\ 0 & \text{otherwise} \end{cases} \qquad j = 1, 2. \tag{7.10}$$

Parameters to be estimated are the intercepts α_1 and α_2, the transition probabilities γ_{11} and γ_{21}, and the parameters in the model for the trend component y_t^* of the actual data y_t. An even simpler example sets $y_t^* = y_t$ and omits y_{t-1}^* from (7.8), in which case dynamics are introduced solely via the Markov chain determining the regime switches.

7.2.2 *Count Models*

There are many possible time series models for count data. Different models arise through different models of the dependency of y_t on past y, current and past $\mathbf{x}$, and the latent process or error process ε_t; through different models of the latent process; and through different extensions of basic models.

Before presenting the various count models in detail, it is helpful to provide a summary. For simplicity the role of regressors other than lagged dependent variables is suppressed.

1. Integer-valued ARMA (or INARMA) models specify y_t to be the sum of an integer whose value is determined by past y_t and an independent innovation. Appropriate distributional assumptions lead to a count marginal distribution of y_t such as Poisson or NB2. This is a generalization of the autoregressive model (7.2).
2. Autoregressive models or Markov models specify the conditional distribution of y_t to be a count distribution such as Poisson or NB2, with mean parameter that is a function of lagged values of y_t. This is an extension of (7.3), and hence also the autoregressive model (7.2). Here the conditional distribution of y_t is specified, whereas the INARMA model specifies the marginal distribution of y_t.
3. Serially correlated error models or latent variable models let y_t depend on a static component and a serially correlated latent variable. This is an extension of the serially correlated error model in (7.4) and (7.5).
4. State-space models or time-varying parameter models specify the distribution of y_t to be a count distribution such as Poisson or NB2, with conditional mean or parameters of the conditional mean that depend on their values in previous periods. This is an extension of the state-space model (7.7).
5. Hidden Markov models or regime shift models specify the distribution of y_t to be a count distribution such as Poisson or NB2, with parameters that vary according to which of a finite number of regimes is currently in effect. The unobserved regimes evolve over time according to a Markov chain. This is an extension of (7.8) and (7.9).
6. Discrete ARMA (DARMA) models introduce time dependency through a mixture process.

Attempts have been made to separate these models into classes of models, but there is no simple classification system that nests all models. Some authors follow Cox (1981) and refer to models as either *observation-driven*, with time series dependence introduced by specifying conditional moments or densities as explicit functions of past outcomes, or *parameter-driven*, with dependence induced by a latent variable process.

Others distinguish between *conditional* models, where the moments or density are conditional on both $\mathbf{x}_t$ and past outcomes of y_t, and *marginal* models, where conditioning is only on $\mathbf{x}_t$ and not on past outcomes of y_t. This is most useful for distinguishing between models 1 and 2.

Once a model is specified, maximum likelihood estimation is generally not as straightforward as in the normal case. NLS estimation is usually possible but may be inefficient, as the error term may be heteroskedastic or autocorrelated. Estimation is often by nonlinear feasible GLS or by GMM.

Criteria for choosing among various models include ease of estimation – models 1 through 3 are best – and similarity to standard time series models such as having a serial correlation structure similar to ARMA models – models 1 and 6 are best. One should also consider the appropriateness of models to count data typically encountered and the problem at hand. If interest lies in the role of regressor variables, a static model of $\mathsf{E}[y_t \mid \mathbf{x}_t]$ may be sufficient. For forecasting, a conditional model of $\mathsf{E}[y_t \mid \mathbf{x}_t, y_{t-1}, y_{t-2}, \ldots]$ may be more useful.

7.3 Static Regression

Before studying in detail various time series count models, we consider static regression, such as Poisson regression of y_t on $\mathbf{x}_t$, and some simple extensions. We present a method for valid statistical inference in the presence of serial correlation. Residual-based tests for serial correlation are also presented, with implementation easiest if standardized residuals are used.

Sometimes a static regression may be sufficient. Several regression applications of time series of counts, cited here, find little or no serial correlation. Then there is no need to use the models presented in this chapter. This may seem surprising, but it should be recalled that a pure Poisson point process generates a time series of independent counts.

7.3.1 *Estimation*

We consider estimation of a static regression model, with exponential conditional mean

$$\mathsf{E}[y_t \mid \mathbf{x}_t] = \exp(\mathbf{x}_t'\boldsymbol{\beta}). \tag{7.11}$$

Conditional on static regressors $\mathbf{x}_t$, the dependent variable y_t may be heteroskedastic, as is common for count data, and serially correlated, as is common for time series data. It is relatively easy to obtain a consistent estimator of $\boldsymbol{\beta}$. Both NLS and the Poisson PMLE maintain their consistency in the presence of autocorrelation, if (7.11) still holds. More difficult is obtaining a consistent estimator of the variance matrix of these estimators, which is necessary for statistical inference. We assume that autocorrelation is present to lag l, and define

$$\omega_{tj} = \mathsf{E}[(y_t - \mu_t)(y_{t-j} - \mu_{t-j}) \mid \mathbf{x}_1, \ldots, \mathbf{x}_T], \qquad j = 0, \ldots, l, \tag{7.12}$$

where $\mu_t = \exp(\mathbf{x}_t'\beta)$.

The NLS estimator, $\hat{\boldsymbol{\beta}}_{\mathsf{NLS}}$, minimizes $\sum_{t=1}^{T}(y_t - \exp(\mathbf{x}_t'\boldsymbol{\beta}))^2$. Applying to (7.11) results in White and Domowitz (1984), who considered general regression function $g(\mathbf{x}_t, \boldsymbol{\beta})$, $\hat{\boldsymbol{\beta}}_{\mathsf{NLS}}$ is asymptotically normal with mean $\boldsymbol{\beta}$ and variance matrix

$$\mathsf{V}[\hat{\boldsymbol{\beta}}_{\mathsf{NLS}}] = \left(\sum_{t=1}^{T} \mu_t^2 \mathbf{x}_t \mathbf{x}_t'\right)^{-1} \mathbf{B}_{\mathsf{NLS}} \left(\sum_{t=1}^{T} \mu_t^2 \mathbf{x}_t \mathbf{x}_t'\right)^{-1}, \tag{7.13}$$

where

$$\mathbf{B}_{\mathsf{NLS}} = \sum_{t=1}^{T} \omega_{t0}\mu_t^2 \mathbf{x}_t\mathbf{x}_t' + \sum_{j=1}^{l}\sum_{t=l}^{T} \omega_{tj}\mu_t\mu_{t-j}\left(\mathbf{x}_t\mathbf{x}_{t-j}' + \mathbf{x}_{t-j}\mathbf{x}_t'\right). \tag{7.14}$$

Note that if there is no autocorrelation at all in y_t, so $\omega_{tj}=0$ for $j\neq 0$, the variance matrix simplifies to that for the cross-section case given in section 3.7.3.

A similar result holds if instead one uses the Poisson PMLE, $\hat{\boldsymbol{\beta}}_{\mathsf{P}}$, presented in section 3.2.3. Then $\hat{\boldsymbol{\beta}}_{\mathsf{P}}$ is asymptotically normal with mean $\boldsymbol{\beta}$ and variance matrix

$$\mathsf{V}[\hat{\boldsymbol{\beta}}_{\mathsf{P}}] = \left(\sum_{t=1}^{T} \mu_t\mathbf{x}_t\mathbf{x}_t'\right)^{-1} \mathbf{B}_{\mathsf{P}} \left(\sum_{t=1}^{T} \mu_t\mathbf{x}_t\mathbf{x}_t'\right)^{-1}, \tag{7.15}$$

where

$$\mathbf{B}_{\mathsf{P}} = \sum_{t=1}^{T} \omega_{t0}\mathbf{x}_t\mathbf{x}_t' + \sum_{j=1}^{l}\sum_{t=l}^{T} \omega_{tj}\left(\mathbf{x}_t\mathbf{x}_{t-j}' + \mathbf{x}_{t-j}\mathbf{x}_t'\right). \tag{7.16}$$

See exercise 7.1 for a way to derive this result. It is expected but not guaranteed that the Poisson PMLE will lead to more efficient estimates than NLS, because the Poisson PMLE uses a working matrix that allows for heteroskedasticity.

The robust sandwich estimate of these variance matrices replaces μ_t by $\hat{\mu}_t = \exp(\mathbf{x}_t'\hat{\boldsymbol{\beta}})$ and ω_{tj} by $(y_t - \hat{\mu}_t)(y_{t-j} - \hat{\mu}_{t-j})$. Some models presented below place more structure on variances and autocovariances, that is, on ω_{tj}. In particular, we expect ω_{tj} to be a function of μ_t and μ_{t-j}. Then consistent estimates $\hat{\omega}_{tj}$ of ω_{tj} may be used in (7.14) or (7.16). In these cases it is better, of course, to use estimators of $\boldsymbol{\beta}$ that use this knowledge of ω_{tj}, as they generally are more efficient than NLS or the Poisson PMLE.

The results (7.13) and (7.15) extend immediately to distributed lag models. Then interpret $\mathbf{x}_t$ as including lagged exogenous variables as well as contemporaneous exogenous variables. The results also extend to dynamic models with lagged dependent variables as regressors, provided enough lags are included to ensure that there is no serial correlation in y_t after controlling for regressors, so $\omega_{tj} = 0$ for $j \neq 0$.

The results do not apply if lagged dependent variables are regressors and there is serial correlation in y_t after controlling for regressors. Then the NLS and Poisson PML estimators are inconsistent, just as the OLS estimator is inconsistent in similar circumstances in the linear model.

7.3.2 *Tests of Serial Correlation*

Serial correlation tests are useful for several reasons. Tests based on residuals from static regressions can indicate if any time series corrections are necessary, or if instead results from the previous chapters can still be used. Tests based on residuals from dynamic regressions can indicate whether, after inclusion of lagged variables, there is still autocorrelation that needs to be controlled for.

Let z_t denote a detrended zero mean time series such as the deviation of the original dependent count from the sample mean, $z_t = y_t - \bar{y}$, or the residual from a regression model such as Poisson, $z_t = y_t - \mu_t$. The standard measure of time series correlation is the autocorrelation at lag k,

$$\rho_k = \frac{\mathsf{E}[z_t z_{t-k}]}{\sqrt{\mathsf{E}[z_t^2]\mathsf{E}[z_{t-k}^2]}}. \tag{7.17}$$

Raw residuals from Poisson regression are nonstationary, with nonconstant variance because the variance equals the mean, which is nonconstant. Thus the raw residuals from count regression need to be standardized before performing the standard tests of serial correlation used in linear time series modeling. Various standardized residuals are defined in section 5.2. Here we focus on the Pearson residual

$$z_t = \frac{y_t - \mu_t}{\sqrt{\omega_t}},$$

where $\mu_t = \mu(\mathbf{x}_t, \boldsymbol{\beta})$,

$$\omega_t = \mathsf{V}[y_t \mid \mathbf{x}_t] = \omega(\mu_t, \boldsymbol{\alpha}),$$

$\boldsymbol{\alpha}$ are parameters in the variance function but not the mean function, and evaluation is at consistent estimates of $\boldsymbol{\alpha}$ and $\boldsymbol{\beta}$. Li (1991) formally obtained the asymptotic distribution of autocorrelations based on Pearson residuals in GLMs, including $z_t = (y_t - \hat{\mu}_t)/\sqrt{\hat{\mu}_t}$ for the Poisson. In this subsection we specialize to the distribution under the null hypothesis that there is no serial correlation.

If z_t is standardized to have constant variance, at least asymptotically, we can follow Box-Jenkins modeling in the continuous case, using the autocorrelation function, which plots the estimated correlations $\hat{\rho}_k$ against k where

$$\hat{\rho}_k = \frac{\sum_{t=k+1}^{T} z_t z_{t-k}}{\sum_{t=1}^{T} z_t^2}. \tag{7.18}$$

If no correlation is present $\hat{\rho}_k \simeq 0$, $k \neq 0$. Formal tests require a distribution for $\hat{\rho}_k$. The standard result is that $\hat{\rho}_k \overset{a}{\sim} \mathsf{N}[0, \frac{1}{T}]$ under the null hypothesis that $\rho_j = 0$, $j = 1, \ldots, k$. This leads to the standard normal distributed test statistic

$$\mathsf{T}_k = \sqrt{T}\hat{\rho}_k. \tag{7.19}$$

Provided z_t has constant variance this result holds here. A related overall test for serial correlation is the Box-Pierce portmanteau statistic, based on the sum of the first l squared sample correlation coefficients

$$\mathsf{T}_{\mathsf{BP}} = T\sum_{k=1}^{l} \hat{\rho}_k^2. \tag{7.20}$$

The standard result is that asymptotically $\mathsf{T_{BP}}$ is $\chi^2(l)$ under the null hypothesis of independence, assuming z_t is normalized to have constant variance. For simplicity we present $\mathsf{T_{BP}}$ rather than its small-sample refinement, the Box-Ljung statistic.

If z_t is not standardized, or z_t is standardized but one wants to guard against incorrect standardization, the correct test statistic to use is

$$\mathsf{T}_\mathsf{k}^* = \frac{\sum_{t=k+1}^{T} z_t z_{t-k}}{\sqrt{\sum_{t=k+1}^{T} z_t^2 z_{t-k}^2}}, \tag{7.21}$$

rather than (7.19). This has an asymptotic $\mathsf{N}[0, 1]$ distribution under the null hypothesis that $\rho_j = 0,\ j = 1, \ldots, k$ (see the derivations section). The statistic (7.21) is the sample analog of ρ_k defined in (7.17), whereas the statistic (7.18) used the simplification that $\mathsf{E}[z_t^2] = \mathsf{E}[z_{t-k}^2]$ under stationarity. An overall chi-square distributed test, analogous to $\mathsf{T_{BP}}$, is

$$\mathsf{T}_\mathsf{BP}^* = \sum_{k=1}^{l} \left(\mathsf{T}_\mathsf{k}^*\right)^2. \tag{7.22}$$

An alternative method, for unstandardized z_t, is to regress z_t on z_{t-k} and use robust sandwich (or Eicker-White) heteroskedastic consistent standard errors for individual t tests, which are asymptotically standard normal if there is no correlation. This latter procedure controls only for heteroskedasticity, but this is sufficient, as under the null hypothesis there is no need to control for serial correlation.

Brännäs and Johansson (1994) find good small-sample performance of serial correlation tests based on T_k for samples of size 40. Cameron and Trivedi (1993) present tests for the stronger condition of independence in count data and argue that it is better to base tests on orthogonal polynomials rather than simply powers of z_t.

Several time series count data applications have found little evidence of serial correlation in residuals, in models with exogenous contemporaneous or lagged regressors. Davutyan (1989) modeled the annual number of bank failures in the United States. He found no serial correlation if attention is confined to the period 1947 through 1981, with serial correlation appearing as data for the 1980s are included. He based correlation tests on raw Poisson residuals and used the Durbin-Watson statistic. This is asymptotically equivalent to a test based on $\hat{\rho}_1$, so the usual Durbin-Watson critical values are not appropriate for the same reason that $\hat{\rho}_1$ is not asymptotically $\mathsf{N}[0, \frac{1}{T}]$. Grogger (1990) estimated a count regression model for daily data on homicides in California and reported no evidence of serial correlation. Unpublished work on another such study, that of Pope, Schwartz, and Ransom (1992), finds no evidence of serial correlation in the daily number of deaths in Salt Lake County.

For continuous time series, such as gross domestic product, the degree of serial correlation can depend on whether first differences or levels are modeled.

The same is true for count data. Consider modeling the number of firms in an industry. Serial correlation is much less for the net change in the number of firms (entry minus exit) than for the total number of firms in the industry (cumulative entry minus exit).

In the continuous case an extensive literature has developed for unit root tests, which are tests of whether the first difference is a random walk. Results exist for heterogeneous processes (for example see Phillips, 1987). To date there has been no application to count data.

7.3.3 *Trends and Seasonality*

Time dependence can be modeled by extending the pure Poisson process of section 1.1.2 to a nonhomogeneous (or nonstationary) Poisson process. For this process the rate parameter μ is replaced by $\mu(t)$, allowing the rate to vary with the time elapsed since the start of the process. Let $N(t, t+h)$ denote the number of events occurring in the interval $(t, t+h]$. For the nonhomogeneous Poisson process, $N(t, t+h)$ has Poisson distribution with mean

$$\mathsf{E}[N(t, t+h)] = \int_t^{t+h} \mu(s)\, ds. \tag{7.23}$$

If $\mu(t) = \lambda \exp(\alpha t)$ and $h = 1$, (7.23) yields

$$\mathsf{E}[N(t, t+1)] = \frac{\lambda(\exp(\alpha) - 1)}{\alpha} \exp(\alpha t),$$

which introduces an exponential time trend to the Poisson mean.

For regression analysis this suggests the model

$$\mathsf{E}[y_t \mid \mathbf{x}_t] = \exp\big(\mathbf{x}_t'\beta + \alpha t\big),$$

ignoring the additional complication introduced by time-varying regressors $\mathbf{x}_t$. This model picks up nonstationarity due to an exponential deterministic time trend.

Seasonality can be modeled in ways similar to those in linear models. For example, consider monthly data with annual seasonal effects. A set of 11 monthly seasonal indicator variables might be included as regressors. It may be more parsimonious to include a mix of sine and cosine terms, $\cos(2\pi jt/12)$ and $\sin(2\pi jt/12)$, $j = 1, \ldots, p$, for some chosen p.

An early and illuminating discussion of trends and seasonality in count data models is given by Cox and Lewis (1966). Estimation of the nonhomogeneous Poisson process is considered by Lawless (1987a).

7.3.4 *Example: Strikes*

We analyze the effect of the level of economic activity on strike frequency, using monthly U.S. data from January 1968 through December 1976. The

Table 7.1. *Strikes: variable definitions and summary statistics*

Variable	Definition	Mean	Standard deviation
STRIKES	Number of strikes commenced each month	5.241	3.751
OUTPUT	Deviation of monthly industrial production from its trend level	−.004	.055

dependent variable *STRIKES* is the number of contract strikes in U.S. manufacturing beginning each month. The one independent variable, *OUTPUT*, is a measure of the cyclical departure of aggregate production from its trend level. High values of *OUTPUT* indicate a boom and low levels a recession. A static model is analyzed here; application of some dynamic models is reported in section 7.10.

The application comes from Kennan (1985) and Jaggia (1991), who analyzed the data using duration models, notably the Weibull, applied to the completed length of each strike that commenced during this period. Here we instead model the number of strikes commencing each month during the period. Time series methods for counts are likely to be needed, because Kennan found evidence of duration dependence. The data are from Table 1 of Kennan (1985). For the 5 months in which there were no strikes ($STRIKES = 0$), the data on *OUTPUT* were not given. We interpolated these data by averaging adjacent observations, giving values of .06356, −.0743, .04591, −.04998, and −.06035 in, respectively, the months 1969(12), 1970(12), 1972(11), 1974(12), and 1975(9).

Summary statistics and variable definitions are given in Table 7.1. The sample mean number of strikes is low enough to warrant treating the data as count data. There is overdispersion in the raw data, with the sample variance 2.68 times the raw mean.

The data on *STRIKES* and *OUTPUT* are plotted in Figure 7.1, where for this figure only *OUTPUT* has been rescaled to have the same mean and variance as *STRIKES*. It appears that strike activity increases with increase in economic activity, although with a considerable lag during the middle of the sample period. The data on *STRIKES* are considerably more variable than the data on *OUTPUT*.

Estimates from static Poisson regression with exponential conditional mean are given in Table 7.2. The standard errors and t statistics assume heteroskedasticity of NB1 form, so $\mathsf{V}[y_t] = \phi\mu_t$. The estimated value of ϕ is 2.59, indicating considerable overdispersion even after inclusion of *OUTPUT* as a regressor. The coefficient of *OUTPUT* indicates that as economic activity increases the number of strikes increases, with a one-standard-deviation change in *OUTPUT* leading to a 17% increase in the mean number of strikes ($.055 \times 3.134 = .172$). The effect appears statistically significant at 5%, but note that the standard errors correct only for heteroskedasticity. If there is positive autocorrelation these

Table 7.2. *Strikes: Poisson PMLE with NB1 standard errors and t ratios*

Variable	Coefficient	Standard error	*t* Statistic
ONE	1.654	.0665	24.90
OUTPUT	3.134	1.264	2.48

Note: Reported standard errors and *t* ratios correct for heteroskedasticity but not for autocorrelation.

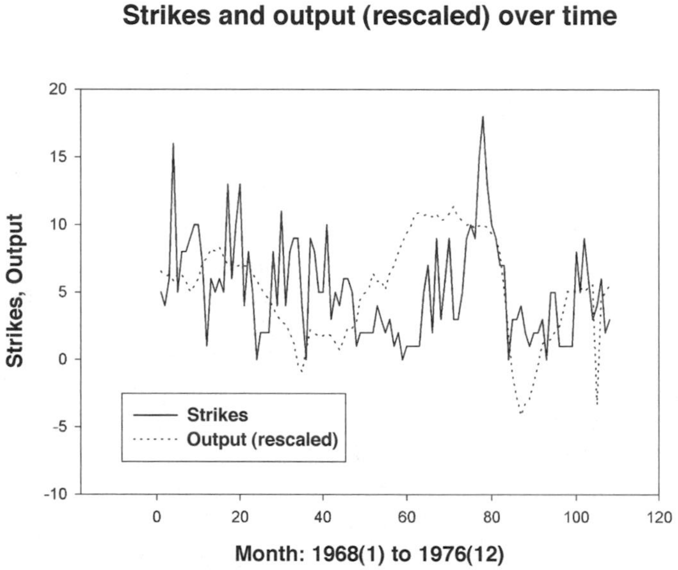

Figure 7.1. Strikes: output (rescaled) and strikes per month.

standard errors will be understated and t statistics overstated. One should instead compute standard errors using (7.15), or use alternative models presented subsequently that eliminate autocorrelation by inclusion of lagged variables. The latter approach is taken here, with results presented in section 7.10.

A plot of the predicted value of *STRIKES* from this static regression, $\exp(1.654 + 3.134 \times OUTPUT)$, is given in Figure 7.2. Clearly, *OUTPUT* explains only a small part of the variation in *STRIKES*. This is also reflected in low R squareds. The Poisson deviance R^2 and Pearson R^2 defined in section 5.3.3 are, respectively, .053 and .060. Considerable improvement occurs with lagged dependent variables included as regressors. This is reported in section 7.10.

Autocorrelation and tests for serial correlation are presented in Table 7.3. The first three columns give autocorrelation coefficients based on various residuals: the raw data y on *STRIKES* or equivalently the residual $y - \bar{y}$ from Poisson regression of *STRIKES* on a constant; the raw residual $r = y - \hat{\mu}$ from Poisson regression of *STRIKES* on a constant and *OUTPUT*; and the Pearson residual

Table 7.3. *Strikes: residuals autocorrelations and serial correlation tests*

	Autocorrelations			z Statistics	
Lag	y	r	p	r	p
1	.53	.50	.47	3.92	4.90
2	.47	.44	.41	4.01	4.08
3	.40	.38	.36	3.52	3.47
4	.23	.20	.21	2.21	2.19
5	.11	.10	.10	1.25	1.17
6	.01	.01	.01	.32	.32
7	−.01	.00	.01		
8	.06	.09	.09		
9	.05	.10	.10		
10	.01	.07	.05		
11	.06	.12	.12		
12	.00	.04	.04		
13	.07	.12	.12		
14	−.15	−.12	−.12		
15	−.17	−.15	−.13		
BP	84.1	77.7	70.1	50.3	62.4

Note: Autocorrelations up to lag 15 are based on three different residuals: the raw data (y) on STRIKES, and the raw residual (r), and the Pearson residual (p) from Poisson regression of STRIKES on OUTPUT. The z statistics to lag 6 use residuals from this same regression. The z statistic r is the heteroskedasticity-corrected statistic T_k based on the raw residual. The z statistic p is the square root of the sample size times the autocorrelation of the Pearson residual. *BP* is the Box-Pierce statistic with degrees of freedom of, respectively, 15, 15, 15, 6, and 6.

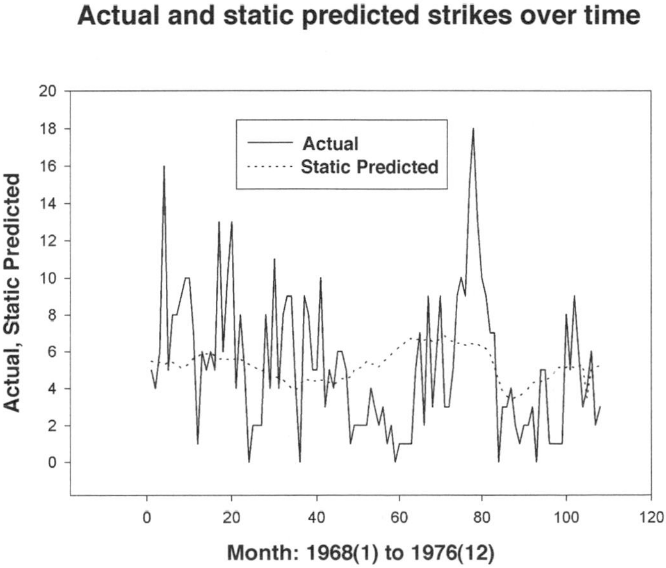

Figure 7.2. Strikes: actual and predicted from a static model.

$p = (y - \mu)/\sqrt{\mu}$ from this regression. Because there is relatively little variability in μ around $\bar{y}$ (see Figure 7.2), in this application we expect the autocorrelations to tell a similar story, even though those based on the Pearson residual are theoretically preferred.

All three indicate autocorrelation that dies out after five lags. Individual test statistics for autocorrelation at each lag are presented in the last two columns of Table 7.3. These are asymptotically N[0, 1] distributed under the null hypothesis of no autocorrelation. The first measure uses the Pearson residuals and the result (7.19) for standardized residuals. The second measure uses the raw residuals and the more general result (7.21). Note that the first measure assumes that the conditional variance is proportional to the conditional mean, while the second measure leaves the conditional variance unspecified. The two lead to very similar conclusions. At the 5% significance level there is statistically significant autocorrelation through the first four lags. This is highly jointly significant, using the Box-Pierce test reported in the last row of Table 7.3. For the first four columns this is T_{BP} in (7.20), which is chi-squared distributed only for column four. For the fifth column this is T^*_{BP} in (7.22). Clearly time series methods are called for.

7.4 Integer-Valued ARMA Models

The preceding section considered static count regression models, where the goal is to perform valid statistical inference and place minimal structure on any serial correlation. In the remainder of this chapter we consider more explicit models of this serial correlation. The first model presented is fully parametric and has the same serial correlation structure as linear ARMA models for continuous data.

INARMA models specify the realized value of y_t to be the sum of a count random variable whose value depends on past outcomes and the realization of an iid count random variable ε_t whose value does not depend on past outcomes. This model is similar to the linear model $y_t = \rho y_{t-1} + \varepsilon_t$, for example, although it explicitly models y_t as a count. Different choices of the distribution for ε_t lead to different marginal distributions for y_t, such as the Poisson. The model has the attraction of having the same serial correlation structure as linear ARMA models for continuous data.

INARMA models were independently proposed by McKenzie (1986) and Al-Osh and Alzaid (1987), for the pure time series case, and extended to the regression case by Brännäs (1995a). They build on earlier work for continuous non-Gaussian time series, specifically exponential and gamma distributions. See Jacobs and Lewis (1977) and further references in Lewis (1985).

7.4.1 *Pure Time Series Models*

We begin with the pure time series case, before introducing other regressors $\mathbf{x}_t$ in the next subsection. Let $\mathbf{Y}^{(t-1)} = (y_{t-1}, y_{t-2}, \ldots, y_0)$. The simplest example is the INAR(1) process

$$y_t = \rho \circ y_{t-1} + \varepsilon_t, \qquad 0 \leq \rho < 1, \tag{7.24}$$

where ε_t is an iid latent count variable independent of $\mathbf{Y}^{(t-1)}$. The symbol $\circ$ denotes the *binomial thinning operator* of Steutel and Van Harn (1979), whereby $\rho \circ y_{t-1}$ is the realized value of a binomial random variable with y_{t-1} trials and probability ρ of success on each trial. More formally $\rho \circ y = \sum_{j=1}^{y} u_j$, where u_j is a sequence of iid binary random variables that take value 1 with probability ρ and value 0 with probability $1-\rho$. Thus each of the y components survives with probability ρ, and dies with probability $1-\rho$.

First consider the unconditional distribution of y. It can be shown that

$$\mu = \mathsf{E}[y] = \frac{\mathsf{E}[\varepsilon]}{1-\rho}, \tag{7.25}$$

and

$$\sigma^2 = \mathsf{V}[y] = \frac{\rho\mathsf{E}[\varepsilon] + \mathsf{V}[\varepsilon]}{1-\rho^2}, \tag{7.26}$$

(see for example Brännäs, 1995a, and exercise 7.3). Given a particular distribution for ε, the unconditional stationary distribution for y can be found by probability generating function techniques; see Steutel and Van Harn (1979) and McKenzie (1986). For example, y is Poisson if ε is Poisson.

For the conditional distribution, taking the conditional expectation of (7.24) yields the conditional mean

$$\mu_{t\,|\,t-1} = \mathsf{E}[y_t \mid y_{t-1}] = \rho y_{t-1} + \mathsf{E}[\varepsilon_t], \tag{7.27}$$

a result similar to that for the Gaussian model. The conditional variance is

$$\sigma^2_{t\,|\,t-1} = \mathsf{V}[y_t \mid y_{t-1}] = \rho(1-\rho)y_{t-1} + \mathsf{V}[\varepsilon_t]. \tag{7.28}$$

The key step in obtaining (7.27) and (7.28) is to note that $\rho \circ y_{t-1}$, conditional on y_{t-1}, has mean ρy_{t-1} and variance $\rho(1-\rho)y_{t-1}$ using standard results on the binomial with y_{t-1} trials.

It can be shown that the autocorrelation at lag k is ρ^k. Thus the INAR(1) model has the same autocorrelation function as the AR(1) model for continuous data. The conditional distribution of y_t given y_{t-1} is that of a Markov chain.

The Poisson INAR(1) model results from specifying the latent variable ε_t in (7.24) to be iid Poisson with parameter λ. Then y_t is unconditionally Poisson with parameter $\lambda/(1-\rho)$. Furthermore, in this case (y_t, y_{t-1}) is bivariate Poisson, defined in Chapter 8. The conditional moments using (7.27) and (7.28) are

$$\begin{aligned} \mu_{t\,|\,t-1} &= \rho y_{t-1} + \lambda \\ \sigma^2_{t\,|\,t-1} &= \rho(1-\rho)y_{t-1} + \lambda, \end{aligned} \tag{7.29}$$

so the Poisson INAR(1) model is conditionally underdispersed. The transition probabilities for the Markov chain conditional distribution are

$$\Pr[y_t \mid y_{t-1}] = \exp(-\lambda) \sum_{j=0}^{\min(y_t, y_{t-1})} \frac{\lambda^{y_t - j}}{(y_t - j)!} \binom{y_{t-1}}{j} \rho^j (1-\rho)^{y_{t-1}-j}. \tag{7.30}$$

Generalizations of Poisson INAR(1) to INAR(p) and INARMA(p, q) models and to marginal distributions other than Poisson are given in various papers by McKenzie and by Al-Osh and Alzaid; Al-Osh and Alzaid additionally considered estimation. See also Jin-Guan and Yuan (1991). McKenzie (1986) obtained an INARMA model with an unconditional NB model distribution for y_t by specifying ε_t to be iid NB. McKenzie (1988) studied the Poisson INARMA model in detail. Al-Osh and Alzaid (1987) considered estimation of the Poisson INAR(1) model and detailed properties of INAR(1) and INAR(p) models in Alzaid and Al-Osh (1988, 1990, respectively). Alzaid and Al-Osh (1993) obtained an INARMA model with an unconditional generalized Poisson distribution (see section 4.4.5), which potentially permits underdispersion. This model specifies ε_t to be generalized Poisson and replaces the binomial thinning operator by quasibinomial thinning. Although the INARMA models have the same autocorrelation function as linear ARMA models, the partial autocorrelation functions differ.

Further models are given by Gauthier and Latour (1994), who define a generalized Steutel–Van Harn operator. Still further generalization may be possible. In the AR(1) case, for example, essentially all that is needed is an operator that yields a discrete value for the first term in the right-hand side of (7.24). For example, there is no reason why the y_{t-1} trials need be independent, and one could, for example, use a correlated binomial model.

Research on INARMA models has focused on stochastic properties. Less attention has been paid to estimation. In the pure time series case exact MLE, as well as conditional MLE which conditions on an initial value y_1, were proposed and investigated by Al-Osh and Alzaid (1987) and Ronning and Jung (1992) for the Poisson INAR(1) model. These estimators can be difficult to implement, especially for models other than the Poisson.

An alternative estimator is conditional least squares. For the Poisson INAR(1) model, $\mathsf{E}[y_t \mid y_{t-1}] = \rho y_{t-1} + \lambda$. This allows simple estimation of ρ and λ by OLS regression of y_t on an intercept and y_{t-1}, a method proposed by Al-Osh and Alzaid (1987). The error in this regression is heteroskedastic, because $\mathsf{V}[y_t \mid y_{t-1}] = \rho(1-\rho)y_{t-1} + \lambda$, so care needs to be taken to obtain the correct variance matrix, and the estimator could potentially be quite inefficient.

Brännäs (1994) proposed and investigated the use of GMM estimators for this model. GMM has the theoretical advantage of incorporating more of the moment restrictions, notably autocovariances, implied by the Poisson INAR(1) model than simply the conditional mean, or conditional mean and variance in the case of conditional WLS.

None of these studies include exogenous regressors, with the exception of McKenzie (1985, p. 649), who briefly considered introduction of trends.

7.4.2 *Regression Models*

Brännäs (1995a) proposed a *Poisson INAR(1) regression* model, with regressors introduced into (7.24) through both the binomial thinning parameter ρ and the latent count variable ε_t. Thus

$$y_t = \rho_t \circ y_{t-1} + \varepsilon_t. \tag{7.31}$$

The latent variable ε_t in (7.31) is assumed to be Poisson-distributed with mean

$$\lambda_t = \exp(\mathbf{x}_t'\beta). \tag{7.32}$$

To ensure $0 < \rho_t < 1$, the logistic function is used

$$\rho_t = \frac{1}{1+\exp(-\mathbf{z}_t'\gamma)}. \tag{7.33}$$

From (7.27) with ρ replaced by ρ_t, the conditional mean for this model is

$$\mu_{t\mid t-1} = \mathsf{E}[y_t \mid \mathbf{x}_t, \mathbf{z}_t, y_{t-1}] = \left(\frac{1}{1+\exp(-\mathbf{z}_t'\gamma)}\right) y_{t-1} + \exp(\mathbf{x}_t'\beta). \tag{7.34}$$

A simpler specification sets $\mathbf{z}_t = 1$, so the parameter ρ is a constant. The conditional variance is

$$\sigma^2_{t\mid t-1} = \mathsf{V}[y_t \mid \mathbf{x}_t, \mathbf{z}_t, y_{t-1}] = \left(\frac{\exp(-\mathbf{z}_t'\gamma)}{[1+\exp(-\mathbf{z}_t'\gamma)]^2}\right) y_{t-1} + \exp(\mathbf{x}_t'\beta), \tag{7.35}$$

from (7.35).

Brännäs proposed estimation of this model by conditional least squares and by GMM. Using (7.34), the conditional NLS estimator minimizes with respect to β and γ

$$S(\beta,\gamma) = \sum_{t=1}^{T} \left\{ y_t - \left(\frac{1}{1+\exp(-\mathbf{z}_t'\gamma)}\right) y_{t-1} - \exp(\mathbf{x}_t'\beta) \right\}^2, \tag{7.36}$$

where the usual standard errors need to be adjusted to allow for heteroskedasticity. This estimator is relatively straightforward to implement given access to a statistical package that includes NLS estimation, although reported standard errors and t statistics may assume a homoskedastic error. An alternative, more efficient estimator is conditional WLS, where the weighting function can be obtained from (7.35).

Brännäs also proposed estimating β and γ by GMM, using knowledge of the functional form for the autocovariances implied by the Poisson INAR(1) model. Details of the GMM procedure, which is considerably more complex to implement than conditional least squares, are given in Brännäs (1995a). He found little gain from performing GMM rather than conditional least squares.

Brännäs additionally considered prediction from this model. In an application to annual Swedish data on the number of paper mills of a particular type, the parameters γ in ρ_t are interpreted as representing the role of regressors in explaining the death of firms; the parameters β of the Poisson density for ε_t represent the role of regressors in explaining the birth of firms.

7.5 Autoregressive Models

The most direct method to specify a time series model is to specify a standard count regression model, where analysis is conditional on past outcomes as well as current and past values of exogenous variables. Thus the conditioning set is now $(\mathbf{X}^{(t)}, \mathbf{Y}^{(t-1)})$ where $\mathbf{X}^{(t)} = (\mathbf{x}_t, \mathbf{x}_{t-1}, \ldots, \mathbf{x}_0)$ and $\mathbf{Y}^{(t-1)} = (y_{t-1}, y_{t-2}, \ldots, y_0)$.

The simplest model specifies an exponential conditional mean, where y_{t-1} additionally appears as a regressor. So the conditional mean is $\exp(\mathbf{x}_t'\beta + \rho y_{t-1})$. This model may not be practically useful, however, as it is explosive for $\rho > 0$. Simulations and discussion are given in Blundell, Griffith, and Windmeijer (1995), who call this model *exponential feedback*. A better and more natural model specifies a multiplicative role for y_{t-1}, i.e.,

$$\begin{aligned}
\mu_{t\,|\,t-1} &= \mathsf{E}[y_t \,|\, \mathbf{X}^{(t)}, \mathbf{Y}^{(t-1)}] \\
&= \exp\big(\mathbf{x}_t'\beta + \rho \ln y_{t-1}^*\big) \\
&= \exp\big(\mathbf{x}_t'\beta\big)\big(y_{t-1}^*\big)^{\rho},
\end{aligned} \tag{7.37}$$

where y_{t-1}^* is a transformation of y_{t-1}, such as (7.38) or (7.39), that is strictly positive. This transformation is needed, as otherwise $y_{t-1} = 0$ is an absorbing state, because then $\mu_{t\,|\,t-1} = 0$ and hence $y_t = 0$ in fully parametric models for y_t such as $\mathsf{P}[\mu_{t\,|\,t-1}]$. Possibilities for y_{t-1}^* include rescaling only the zero values of y_{t-1} to a constant c

$$y_{t-1}^* = \max(c, y_{t-1}), \qquad 0 < c < 1, \tag{7.38}$$

and translating all values of y_{t-1} by the same amount

$$y_{t-1}^* = y_{t-1} + c, \qquad c > 0. \tag{7.39}$$

The model (7.37) can be viewed as a multiplicative AR(1) model, by comparison with the linear AR(1) model in (7.1). We can also consider a multiplicative AR(1) error model

$$\begin{aligned}\mu_{t\,|\,t-1} &= \mathsf{E}[y_t \mid \mathbf{X}^{(t)}, \mathbf{Y}^{(t-1)}] \\ &= \exp\big(\mathbf{x}_t'\boldsymbol{\beta} + \rho\big(\ln y_{t-1}^* - \mathbf{x}_{t-1}'\boldsymbol{\beta}\big)\big) \\ &= \exp\big(\mathbf{x}_t'\boldsymbol{\beta}\big)\left(\frac{y_{t-1}^*}{\mathbf{x}_{t-1}'\boldsymbol{\beta}}\right)^{\rho}. \end{aligned} \tag{7.40}$$

By comparison the linear AR(1) error model from (7.6) implies $\mu_{t\,|\,t-1} = \mathbf{x}_t'\boldsymbol{\beta} + \rho(y_{t-1} - \mathbf{x}_{t-1}'\boldsymbol{\beta})$.

Models (7.37) and (7.40) were proposed by Zeger and Qaqish (1988) for GLM models, with the exponential function more generally replaced by the canonical link function. The model was called a *Markov* model, here Markov model of order 1, because y_{t-1} is the only element of the past history $\mathbf{Y}^{(t-1)}$ that affects the conditional distribution of y_t. An alternative terminology, used here, is to call this model an *autoregressive* model, given its obvious similarity to the linear model (7.2) and to avoid possible confusion with hidden Markov models.

Given the conditional mean specification in (7.37), estimation can be by NLS, the only complication being finding consistent standard errors. Provided there is no serial correlation in the model residual $y_t - \hat{\mu}_{t\,|\,t-1}$, these can be obtained using (7.13) with $\omega_{tj} = 0$ for $j > 0$.

If the conditional density is specified, for example, $f(y_t \mid \mathbf{x}_t, y_{t-1})$ is Poisson, then estimation can be by maximum likelihood, which maximizes

$$\mathcal{L} = \sum_{t=1}^{T} f(y_t \mid \mathbf{x}_t, y_{t-1}). \tag{7.41}$$

Estimation theory is given in Wong (1986) and Fahrmeir and Kaufman (1987). Overdispersion could be handled by instead specifying $f(y_t \mid \mathbf{x}_t, y_{t-1})$ to be the NB2 density.

Zeger and Qaqish (1988) used quasilikelihood methods, an intermediate approach between NLS and maximum likelihood estimation. In particular, obtain the Poisson PMLE assuming that $y_t \mid \mathbf{x}_t, y_{t-1}$ is distributed as $\mathsf{P}[\mu_{t\,|\,t-1}]$, where $\mu_{t\,|\,t-1}$ is given in (7.37). Then if the conditional variance specification is relaxed to the NB1 form $\mathsf{V}[y_t \mid \mathbf{x}_t, y_{t-1}] = \phi\mu_{t\,|\,t-1}$, the computed Poisson maximum likelihood standard errors can be rescaled by $\hat{\phi}^{1/2}$ as in section 3.2.3.

If the constant c in (7.38) or (7.39) is specified, then a standard Poisson program can be used. If instead c is an additional parameter to be estimated, standard Poisson software can still be used for $y_t^* = \max(c, y_{t-1})$ as in (7.38). Rewrite (7.40) as

$$\mu_{t\,|\,t-1} = \exp\big(\mathbf{x}_t'\boldsymbol{\beta} + \rho \ln y_{t-1}^{**} + (\rho \ln c)\, d_t\big)$$

where

$$y_{t-1}^{**} = y_{t-1} \quad \text{and} \quad d_t = 0, \qquad y_{t-1} > 0,$$

$$y_{t-1}^{**} = 1 \qquad \text{and} \quad d_t = 1, \qquad y_{t-1} = 0.$$

Poisson regression of y_t on $\mathbf{x}_t$, y_{t-1}^{**} and d_t yields estimates of $\boldsymbol{\beta}$, ρ, and $\rho \ln c$. Then use $c = \exp[(\rho \ln c)/\rho]$ to obtain an estimate of c. The autoregressive count model is attractive because it is relatively simple to implement.

A weakness of the model is that adjustments such as (7.38) or (7.39) for zero lagged values of y_t are ad hoc. Furthermore, they complicate evaluation of the impact of regressors on the change in the conditional mean. One alternative is to replace (7.37) by

$$\mu_{t\,|\,t-1} = \rho y_{t-1} + \mathbf{x}_t'\boldsymbol{\beta}. \qquad (7.42)$$

This equals the conditional mean (7.34) of the Poisson INAR(1) model if ρ is constant, although other features of the distribution such as the conditional variance (see [7.35]) will differ. A major reason for choosing the exponential conditional mean specification is to ensure a positive mean. This is also the case for $\mu_{t\,|\,t-1}$ in (7.42), provided $\rho > 0$. Another alternative to adjustments such as (7.38) or (7.39), proposed by Shephard (1995), is to develop autoregressive models for a particular transformation of the dependent variable.

Autoregressive models have not been widely applied, especially for data for which some counts are zero. Fahrmeir and Tutz (1994, section 6.1) gave an application to monthly U.S. data on the number of polio cases. Cameron and Leon (1993) applied the model to monthly U.S. data on the number of strikes and give some limited simulations to investigate the properties of both estimators and the time series process itself, because theoretical results on its serial correlation properties are not readily obtained. Leon and Tsai (1998) proposed and investigated by simulation quasilikelihood analogues of LM, Wald, and LR tests, following the earlier study by Li (1991), who considered the LM test.

7.6 Serially Correlated Error Models

The preceding models provide a fairly explicit model for dependence of y_t on past outcomes. Zeger (1988) instead introduced serial correlation in y_t via serial correlation in a multiplicative latent variable. This model is like the static regression model studied in section 7.3. More structure is placed on the model here, however, leading to autocorrelations that are a function of current and lagged values of μ_t. This permits more efficient estimation than in section 7.3, assuming that the autocorrelations are correctly specified.

For counts the Poisson is used as a starting point, with variance equal to the mean. The conditional distribution of the dependent variable y_t is specified to be independent over t with mean $\lambda_t \varepsilon_t$ and variance $\lambda_t \varepsilon_t$, where conditioning is on both regressors, via

$$\lambda_t = \exp(\mathbf{x}_t'\boldsymbol{\beta}),$$

and an unobserved latent variable $\varepsilon_t > 0$. The moments conditional on observation of ε_t are

$$\begin{aligned} \mathsf{E}[y_t \mid \lambda_t, \varepsilon_t] &= \lambda_t \varepsilon_t \\ \mathsf{V}[y_t \mid \lambda_t, \varepsilon_t] &= \lambda_t \varepsilon_t. \end{aligned} \tag{7.43}$$

This setup is similar to the mixture models in Chapter 4. Here, however, the latent variable is not independently distributed across observations and, rather than integrating out to get a density, just the first and second moments are obtained.

The latent variable ε_t is assumed to follow a stationary process with mean normalized to unity, variance σ^2, and covariances $\mathsf{Cov}[\varepsilon_t, \varepsilon_{t-k}] = \rho_{k\varepsilon}\sigma^2$, where

$$\rho_{k\varepsilon} = \mathrm{Cor}[\varepsilon_t, \varepsilon_{t-k}], \qquad k = 1, 2, \ldots \tag{7.44}$$

is the autocorrelation function for ε_t. It follows that the marginal distribution of y_t, marginal with respect to ε_t but still conditional on λ_t, has first two moments

$$\begin{aligned} \mu_t &= \mathsf{E}[y_t \mid \lambda_t] = \lambda_t \\ \sigma_t^2 &= \mathsf{V}[y_t \mid \lambda_t] = \lambda_t + \sigma^2\lambda_t^2. \end{aligned} \tag{7.45}$$

The latter result uses

$$\begin{aligned} \mathsf{V}[y \mid \lambda] &= \mathsf{E}[\mathsf{V}[y \mid \lambda, \varepsilon] \mid \lambda] + \mathsf{V}[\mathsf{E}[y \mid \lambda, \varepsilon] \mid \lambda] \\ &= \mathsf{E}[\lambda\varepsilon \mid \lambda] + \mathsf{V}[\lambda\varepsilon \mid \lambda] \\ &= \lambda\mathsf{E}[\varepsilon] + \lambda^2\mathsf{V}[\varepsilon]. \end{aligned}$$

The covariance between y_t and y_{t-k} can be shown to equal $\rho_{k\varepsilon}\sigma_t^2\lambda_t\lambda_{t-k}$, implying that the autocorrelation function for y_t is

$$\rho_{ky_t} = \frac{\rho_{k\varepsilon}}{\sqrt{\left(1 + \frac{1}{\sigma^2\lambda_t^2}\right)\left(1 + \frac{1}{\sigma^2\lambda_{t-k}^2}\right)}}, \qquad k = 1, 2, \ldots. \tag{7.46}$$

We refer to this model as a *serially correlated error* model because of its obvious connection to the linear model in (7.4) and (7.5). Other authors refer to this as a *marginal* model, because from (7.45) we model $\mu_t = \exp(\mathbf{x}_t'\boldsymbol{\beta})$, which does not condition on lagged y_t.

Maximum likelihood estimation requires specification of both the density for y_t given ε_t, and a multivariate density for $(\varepsilon_1, \ldots, \varepsilon_T)'$. No closed-form solution is possible, except in trivial cases such as ε_t iid gamma if $y_t \mid \varepsilon_t$ iid Poisson, which gives independent NB.

Instead a quasilikelihood approach is taken, using knowledge of the mean, variance, and covariances of y_t. The nonlinear WLS estimator for $\boldsymbol{\beta}$ solves the first-order conditions

$$\mathbf{D}'\mathbf{V}^{-1}(\mathbf{y} - \boldsymbol{\lambda}) = \mathbf{0}, \tag{7.47}$$

where $\mathbf{D}$ is the $T \times k$ matrix with tj^{th} element $\partial\lambda_t/\partial\beta_j$, $\mathbf{V}^{-1}$ is a $T \times T$ weighting matrix, $\mathbf{y}$ is the $T \times 1$ vector with t^{th}entry y_t and $\boldsymbol{\lambda}$ is the $T \times 1$ vector with t^{th} entry λ_t. This is the same as the linear WLS estimator given in section 2.4.1, $\mathbf{X}'\mathbf{V}^{-1}(\mathbf{y} - \mathbf{X}'\boldsymbol{\beta}) = 0$, except that in moving to nonlinear models x_{tj} in $\mathbf{X}$ is replaced by $\partial\lambda_t/\partial\beta_j$ in $\mathbf{D}$ and the mean $\mathbf{X}'\boldsymbol{\beta}$ is replaced by $\boldsymbol{\lambda}$. Then by results similar to section 2.4.1,$\hat{\boldsymbol{\beta}}_{\mathsf{WLS}}$ is asymptotically normal with mean $\boldsymbol{\beta}$ and variance

$$\mathsf{V}[\hat{\boldsymbol{\beta}}_{\mathsf{WLS}}] = (\mathbf{D}'\mathbf{V}^{-1}\mathbf{D})^{-1}\mathbf{D}'\mathbf{V}^{-1}\boldsymbol{\Omega}\mathbf{V}^{-1\prime}\mathbf{D}\,(\mathbf{D}'\mathbf{V}^{-1}\mathbf{D})^{-1}, \tag{7.48}$$

where $\boldsymbol{\Omega} = \boldsymbol{\Omega}(\boldsymbol{\beta}, \gamma, \sigma^2)$ is the covariance matrix of $\mathbf{y}$, and γ are parameters of the autocorrelation function $\rho_{k\varepsilon}$.

The efficient nonlinear WLS estimator is nonlinear feasible GLS where $\mathbf{V}^{-1} = \hat{\boldsymbol{\Omega}}^{-1}$, and $\hat{\boldsymbol{\Omega}}$ is a consistent estimator of $\boldsymbol{\Omega} = \boldsymbol{\Omega}(\boldsymbol{\beta}, \gamma, \sigma^2)$. This entails inversion of the $T \times T$ estimated covariance matrix of y_t, which poses problems for large T. Zeger instead proposed using less efficient WLS, where the working weighting matrix $\mathbf{V}^{-1}$ is chosen to be reasonably close to $\boldsymbol{\Omega}^{-1}$.

Zeger (1988) applied this method to monthly U.S. data on polio cases; Campbell (1994) applied this model to daily U.K. data on sudden infant death syndrome cases and the role of temperature.

Brännäs and Johansson (1994) study the Zeger (1988) model in further detail. In particular, they observe that in this model the usual Poisson PMLE is still consistent. They find that the Poisson PMLE yields quite similar estimates and efficiency to estimates using Zeger's method, once appropriate correction for serial correlation is made to the Poisson PMLE standard errors. Johansson (1995) presents Wald- and LM-type tests based on GMM estimation (see Newey and West, 1987b) for overdispersion and serial correlation in the Zeger model and investigates their small-sample performance by a Monte Carlo study.

7.7 State-Space Models

The INAR and Markov models specify the conditional distribution of y_t to depend on a specified function of $(\mathbf{X}^{(t)}, \mathbf{Y}^{(t-1)})$. The *state-space* model or *time-varying parameters* model instead specifies the conditional distribution of y_t to depend on stochastic parameters that evolve according to a specified distribution whose parameters are determined by $(\mathbf{X}^{(t)}, \mathbf{Y}^{(t-1)})$.

Analytical results are most easily obtained if only the mean parameter evolves over time, with density that is conjugate to the density of y_t. We begin with this case.

More generally the regression coefficients may all evolve over time, in which case a normal distribution is typically chosen. Analytical results are then no longer attainable, but recent advances in computer power and in computational algorithms mean that this is no longer an obstacle to empirical work. Developing these computational algorithms is a very active area, some of which is touched on in this section and in section 9.4, in which Poisson models with Gaussian random effects are discussed.

Much of the work with random coefficient models, such as time-varying parameters, has been done in a Bayesian framework. Then interest lies in obtaining the posterior mean, which in the time series case is used to generate forecasts that incorporate prior information. A standard reference is West and Harrison (1997). The computational methods developed for Bayesian analysis are also widely used in frequentist analyses in which the focus is on parameter estimation, and it is not uncommon to see frequentist analyses take on a Bayesian flavor because of this. We focus on the frequentist interpretation here.

7.7.1 *Conjugate Distributed Mean*

West, Harrison, and Migon (1985) propose Bayesian time series models for regression models with prior density for the conditional mean chosen to be conjugate to an LEF density. These models are presented as an extension of dynamic linear models (see West and Harrison, 1997), to the GLM framework, although this extension is not seamless. The concern is in obtaining the posterior mean and forecasts, given specified values for the prior density parameters.

Harvey and Fernandes (1989) study these models in a non-Bayesian framework and considered parameter estimation. The most tractable model for count data is a Poisson–gamma model.

The starting point is a Poisson regression model, where y_t conditional on μ_t is $\mathsf{P}[\mu_t]$ distributed, so

$$f(y_t \mid \mu_t) = e^{-\mu_t}\mu_t/y_t!. \tag{7.49}$$

In a departure from earlier Poisson models, the mean parameter μ_t is modeled to evolve stochastically over time with distribution determined by past values of y_t. A convenient choice of distribution is the gamma

$$f(\mu_t \mid a_{t\,|\,t-1}, b_{t\,|\,t-1}) = \frac{e^{-b\mu_t}\mu_t^{a-1}}{\Gamma(a)b^{-a}}, \qquad a_{t\,|\,t-1} > 0,\ b_{t\,|\,t-1} > 0, \tag{7.50}$$

where a and b in (7.50) are evaluated at $a = a_{t\,|\,t-1} = \omega a_{t-1}$ and $b = b_{t\,|\,t-1} = \omega b_{t-1}$ and $0 < \omega \leq 1$. The conditional density of y_t given the observables $\mathbf{Y}^{(t-1)}$ is

$$f\left(y_t \mid \mathbf{Y}^{(t-1)}\right) = \int_0^\infty f(y_t \mid \mu_t) f\left(\mu_t \mid \mathbf{Y}^{(t-1)}\right) d\mu_t. \tag{7.51}$$

From Chapter 4, $f(y_t \mid \mathbf{Y}^{(t-1)})$ is the negative binomial with parameters $a_{t \mid t-1}$ and $b_{t \mid t-1}$. Estimation of ω and the parameters of μ_t is by maximum likelihood, where the joint density of $\mathbf{Y}^{(t)}$ is the product of the conditional densities (7.51). The Kalman filter is used to recursively build $a_{t \mid t-1}$ and $b_{t \mid t-1}$.

Harvey and Fernandes (1989) apply this approach to count data on goals scored in soccer matches, purse snatchings in Chicago, and van driver fatalities. They also obtain tractable results for negative binomial with parameters evolving according to the beta distribution and for the binomial model. Singh and Roberts (1992) consider count data models. Harvey and Shephard (1993) consider the general GLM class. Brännäs and Johansson (1994) investigate small-sample performance of estimators. Johansson (1996) gives a substantive regression application to monthly Swedish data on traffic accident fatalities, which additionally uses the model of Zeger (1988) discussed in section 7.6.

7.7.2 *Normally Distributed Parameters*

In these models the starting point can again be the Poisson regression model (7.49), except now $\mu_t = \exp(\mathbf{x}_t' \boldsymbol{\beta}_t)$ where $\boldsymbol{\beta}_t$ evolves according to

$$\boldsymbol{\beta}_t = \mathbf{A}_t \boldsymbol{\beta}_{t-1} + \boldsymbol{v}_t, \tag{7.52}$$

where

$$\boldsymbol{v}_t \sim \mathsf{N}[0, \boldsymbol{\Sigma}_t].$$

For this model there are no closed-form solutions. The development of numerical techniques for these models is an active area of research.

An example is Durbin and Koopman (1997), who model British data on van driver fatalities. They first follow Shephard and Pitt (1997) in developing a Markov chain Monte Carlo method to numerically evaluate the likelihood of the model. Durbin and Koopman (1997) then propose a faster procedure that calculates the likelihood for an approximating linear Gaussian model by Kalman filter techniques for linear models and then computes the true likelihood as an adjustment to this.

7.8 Hidden Markov Models

Hidden Markov time series models specify different parametric models in different regimes, in which the unobserved regimes evolve over time according to a Markov chain. Here we summarize results given in considerably more detail in MacDonald and Zucchini (1997).

For the model with m possible regimes let $C_t, t = 1, \ldots, T$, denote a Markov chain on state-space $\{1, 2, \ldots, m\}$. Thus $C_t = j$ if at time t we are in regime j. In the simplest case, considered here, C_t is an irreducible homogeneous Markov chain, with transition probabilities

$$\gamma_{ij} = \Pr[C_t = j \mid C_{t-1} = i], \qquad i, j = 1, \ldots, m, \tag{7.53}$$

which are time invariant. It is assumed that there exists a unique strictly positive stationary distribution

$$\delta_j = \Pr[C_t = j], \qquad j = 1, \ldots, m, \tag{7.54}$$

where the δ_j are a function of γ_{ij}. For the Poisson hidden Markov model, it is assumed that the count data y_t in each regime are Poisson distributed, with mean parameter that varies with exogenous variables and the regime

$$\mu_{tj} = \exp(\mathbf{x}_t'\beta_j). \tag{7.55}$$

The moments of y_t, unconditional on C_t although still conditional on $\mathbf{x}_t$, can be shown to bc

$$\mathsf{E}[y_t \mid \mathbf{x}_t] = \sum_{j=1}^{m} \delta_j \mu_{tj} \tag{7.56}$$

$$\mathsf{E}[y_t^2 \mid \mathbf{x}_t] = \sum_{j=1}^{m} \delta_j (\mu_{tj} + \mu_{tj}^2) \tag{7.57}$$

$$\mathsf{E}[y_t y_{t+k} \mid \mathbf{x}_t] = \sum_{i=1}^{m} \sum_{j=1}^{m} \delta_i \gamma_{ij}(k) \mu_{ti} \mu_{t+k,j}, \tag{7.58}$$

where $\gamma_{ij}(k) = \Pr[C_{t+k} = j \mid C_{t-1} = i]$ and $t = 1, \ldots, T$. The autocorrelation function of y_t, which follows directly from (7.56) through (7.58), is a function of the Poisson parameters and the transition probabilities.

The parameters to be estimated are the regime-specific parameters β_j, $j = 1, \ldots, m$, and the transition probabilities γ_{ij}. Estimation by maximum likelihood, imposing the constraints that $\gamma_{ij} \geq 0$ and the constraints $\sum_{j \neq i} \gamma_{ij} \leq 1$, $i = 1, \ldots m$, is presented in MacDonald and Zucchini (1997). Applications to count data include the daily number of epileptic seizures by a particular patient, fitted by a two-state hidden Markov Poisson model with $\mu_{tj} = \mu_j$, and the weekly number of firearm homicides in Cape Town, fitted by a two-state hidden Markov Poisson model with $\mu_{tj} = \exp(\alpha_{1j} + \alpha_{2j}t + \alpha_{3j}t^2)$.

Count data can be directly modeled as a Markov chain, rather than via a hidden Markov chain. For counts there are potentially an infinite number of transition parameters, and additional structure is needed. An example of such structure is the Poisson INAR(1) model, whose transition probabilities are given in (7.30).

7.9 Discrete ARMA Models

The first serious attempt to define a time series count model with similar autocorrelation structure to ARMA models was by Jacobs and Lewis (1978a, 1978b, 1983). They defined the class of DARMA models, for which the realized value of y_t is a mixture of past values $\mathbf{Y}^{(t-1)}$ and the current realization of a latent variable ε_t.

The simplest example is the DARMA(1,0) model with

$$y_t = u_t y_{t-1} + (1 - u_t)\varepsilon_t, \tag{7.59}$$

where u_t is a binary mixing random variable that takes value 1 with probability ρ and value 0 with probability $1 - \rho$, and different distributional assumptions can be made for the iid discrete latent random variable ε_t. This model implies

$$\begin{aligned} \Pr[y_t = y_{t-1}] &= \rho \\ \Pr[y_t = \varepsilon_t] &= 1 - \rho. \end{aligned} \tag{7.60}$$

Clearly for this model the autocorrelation at lag k is ρ^k, as in the AR(1) model, and only positive correlation is possible. Extensions can be made to DARMA(p, q) models with correlation structures equal to that of standard linear ARMA(p, q) models, although with greater restrictions on the permissible range of correlation structures.

A major restriction of the model is that for high serial correlation the data will be characterized by a series of runs of a single value. This might be appropriate for some data, for example the number of firms in an industry in which there is very little entry and exit over time. But most time series count data exhibit more variability over time than this. For this reason this class of models is rarely used, and we do not consider estimation or possible extension to the regression case.

7.10 Application

We illustrate some of the preceding models, using the example on strike frequency introduced in section 7.3.4. We begin with a variant of the autoregressive model of Zeger and Qaqish (1988) given by (7.37) through (7.39), with up to three lags of the dependent variable appearing as explanatory variables. A Poisson regression model is estimated with conditional mean

$$\begin{aligned} \mathsf{E}[y_t \mid x_t, y_{t-1}, y_{t-2}, \ldots] = \exp\bigl(&\beta_1 + \beta_2 x_t + \rho_1 \ln y^*_{t-1} \\ &+ \rho_2 \ln y^*_{t-2} + \rho_3 \ln y^*_{t-3}\bigr), \end{aligned} \tag{7.61}$$

where y_t denotes *STRIKES*, x_t denotes *OUTPUT*, and $y^*_t = \max(c, y_t)$, where c is a value between 0 and 1 that prevents potential problems in taking the natural logarithm if $y_t = 0$. This model can be estimated using a standard Poisson regression program, as explained in section 7.5.

In the first four columns of Table 7.4, estimates for the model (7.61) are presented with 0, 1, 2, or 3 lags (models ZQ0 to ZQ3), with c set to the value 0.5. The first column reproduces the static regression estimates given in Table 7.2. Introducing lagged dependent variables, the biggest gain comes from introducing just one lag. The autocorrelations of the Pearson residuals reduce

Table 7.4. *Strikes: Zeger-Qaqish autoregressive model estimates and diagnostics*

	Model					
Variable	ZQ0	ZQ1	ZQ2	ZQ3	ZQ1(*c*)	B1
ONE	1.654	1.060	.911	.846	.896	1.017
OUTPUT	3.134	2.330	2.192	2.187	2.34	3.479
$\ln y^*(-1)$		.396	.295	.267	.482	
$\ln y^*(-2)$			.205	.162		
$\ln y^*(-3)$				.114		
c		.5	.5	.5	3.146	
$y(-1)$						.469
ACF lag 1	.49	−.09	.01	.04	−.11	−.09
ACF lag 2	.40	.14	.03	.05	.17	.17
ACF lag 3	.34	.13	.13	.02	.13	.14
ACF lag 4	.22	.09	.02	.00	.04	.08
ACF lag 5	.12	.04	.02	−.03	.01	.04
ACF lag 6	.03	.01	−.02	−.06	.00	.00
BP	62.40	6.63	1.93	1.00	6.25	6.92
R^2dev	.053	.245	.287	.300	.295	
Observations	108	107	107	106	105	107

Note: ZQ0, static Poisson regression; ZQ1–ZQ3, Zeger-Qaqish autoregressive model defined in Eq. (7.59) with $c = 0.5$; ZQ1(c), ZQ1 model with c estimated; B1, Brannas INAR(1) model defined in Eq. (7.60), estimated by NLS; ACF lags 1–6, autocorrelations to lag six from the Pearson residuals from each model; BP, associated Box-Pierce statistic with six degrees of freedom.

substantially, and the null hypothesis of no serial correlation is not rejected at 5%, using the Box-Pierce statistics based on up to six lags of the Pearson residuals. The fit of the model improves substantially, with the deviance R squared increasing from .053 to .245. Further gains occur in introducing additional lags, but these gains are relatively small and have little impact on the coefficient of *OUTPUT*.

The preferred model is ZQ1. There is still overdispersion, with $\hat{\phi} = 2.09$ when an NB1 variance function is estimated. Adjusting the reported standard errors for this overdispersion, the coefficient of *OUTPUT* has a standard error of 1.195 and a t statistic of 1.95. So *OUTPUT* is significant at 5% using a one-sided test, and borderline insignificant at 5% using a two-tailed test. Even controlling for past strike activity, there is an independent positive effect if output rises above trend.

The model ZQ1(c) in Table 7.4 is the same as the model ZQ1, except that the coefficient of c is estimated rather than being set at 0.5. An indicator variable is constructed, as detailed in section 7.5. The implied estimated value of c is 3.146, with standard error of .71 calculated using the delta method. Thus the estimated value is statistically different from its theoretical bound of unity. This problem arises because relatively few observations (here, five) actually equal zero. Varying c in the range 0 to 1 makes little difference to estimates of other parameters and the residual autocorrelation function, and we use the midpoint 0.5.

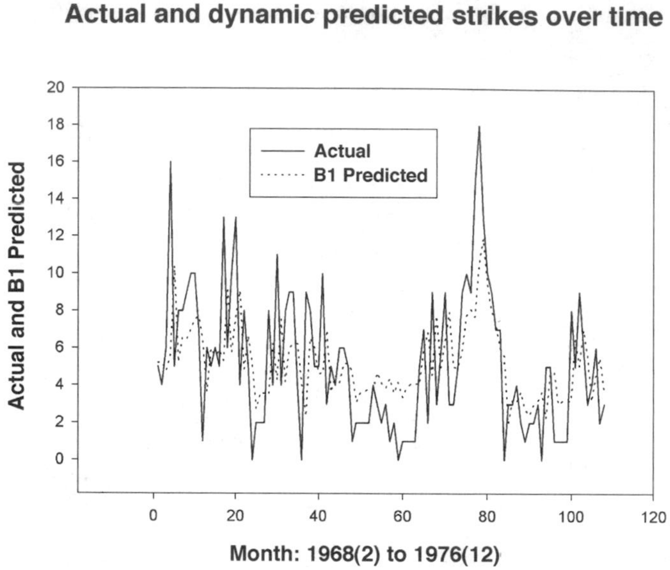

Figure 7.3. Strikes: actual and predicted from a dynamic model.

The final column gives estimates for the Brännäs INAR(1) model, with conditional mean

$$\mathsf{E}[y_t \mid x_t, y_{t-1}, y_{t-2}, \ldots] = \rho_1 y_{t-1} + \exp(\beta_1 + \beta_2 x_t). \tag{7.62}$$

Estimation is by NLS, which is not fully efficient. The estimated model leads to results quite similar to the ZQ1 model, in terms of serial correlation in the residuals and fit of the model.

Neither model is straightforward to analyze for long-run impacts. In the long-run, $y_t = y_{t-1} = y$. The B1 model estimates yield $y = [\exp(1.017 + 3.479x)]/.531$. The ZQ1 model estimates yield $y = [\exp(1.060+2.330x)]^{.604}$.

The predictions of strikes from model B1, plotted in Figure 7.3, fit the data much better than the static regression model presented in Figure 7.2. ZQ1 model predictions are quite similar, with correlation of 0.978 between B1 and ZQ1 predictions.

The application here illustrates a simple way to estimate dynamic count regression models. Richer models such as those in sections 7.8 and 7.9 might then be used. This involves a considerably higher level of complexity, which may require referring to the original sources.

7.11 Derivations

We obtain the section 7.3.2 results on serial correlation tests. Suppose z_t is distributed with mean 0 and is independently distributed, although it is potentially heteroskedastic. Then $\sum_{t=k+1}^{T} z_t z_{t-k}$ has mean

$$\mathsf{E}\left[\sum_{t=k+1}^{T} z_t z_{t-k}\right] = 0,$$

because $\mathsf{E}[z_t z_{t-k}] = 0$, and variance

$$\mathsf{E}\left[\sum_{s=k+1}^{T}\sum_{t=k+1}^{T} z_s z_{s-k} z_t z_{t-k}\right] = \sum_{t=k+1}^{T} \mathsf{E}\left[z_t^2 z_{t-k}^2\right],$$

using $\mathsf{E}[z_t z_u z_v z_w] = \mathsf{E}[z_t]\mathsf{E}[z_u z_v z_w]$ by independence for $t \neq u, v, w$, and $\mathsf{E}[z_t] = 0$. By a law of large numbers

$$\left(\sum_{t=k+1}^{T} \mathsf{E}\left[z_t^2 z_{t-k}^2\right]\right)^{-1/2} \sum_{t=k+1}^{T} z_t z_{t-k} \xrightarrow{d} \mathsf{N}[0, 1], \tag{7.63}$$

which yields (7.21) for tests on unstandardized residuals.

Now specialize to the special case that z_t is scaled to have constant variance, in which case $\mathsf{E}[z_t^2]$ is constant. Then

$$\begin{aligned}\sum_{t=k+1}^{T} \mathsf{E}\left[z_t^2 z_{t-k}^2\right] &= \sum_{t=k+1}^{T} \mathsf{E}\left[z_t^2\right]\mathsf{E}\left[z_{t-k}^2\right] \\ &= \frac{1}{T}\left(\sum_{t=k+1}^{T} \mathsf{E}[z_t^2]\right)\left(\sum_{t=k+1}^{T} \mathsf{E}[z_{t-k}^2]\right) \\ &= \frac{1}{T}\left(\sum_{t=k+1}^{T} \mathsf{E}[z_t^2]\right)\left(\sum_{t=k+1}^{T} \mathsf{E}[z_t^2]\right),\end{aligned}$$

where the first equality uses independence, and the second and third equalities use constancy of $\mathsf{E}[z_t^2]$. It follows that $(\frac{1}{T}\sum_{t=1}^{T} z_t^2)^2$ is consistent for $\frac{1}{T}\sum_{t=k+1}^{T} \mathsf{E}[z_t^2 z_{t-k}^2]$, so

$$\left(\frac{1}{T}\sum_{t=1}^{T} z_t^2\right)^{-1} \sum_{t=k+1}^{T} z_t z_{t-k} \xrightarrow{d} \mathsf{N}[0, 1].$$

This implies $T\hat{\rho}_k \xrightarrow{d} \mathsf{N}[0, 1]$, as in (7.19), or equivalently the usual result that $\hat{\rho}_k \sim \mathsf{N}[0, \frac{1}{T}]$.

If $\mathsf{E}[z_t^2]$ is nonconstant this simplification is not possible. One instead uses $\frac{1}{T}\sum_{t=k+1}^{T} z_t^2 z_{t-k}^2$ as a consistent estimator of $\frac{1}{T}\sum_{t=k+1}^{T} \mathsf{E}[z_t^2 z_{t-k}^2]$, and the more general (7.21).

7.12 Bibliographic Notes

An early treatment is Cox and Lewis (1966). McKenzie (1985) is a stimulating paper that raises, for counts, many standard time series issues, such as trends and seasonality, in the context of hydrological examples. A recent survey of count time series models, which covers many of the models presented in this chapter, is given in Chapter 1 of MacDonald and Zucchini (1997). The best reference for INARMA regression models is Brännäs (1995a). Autoregressive models, serially correlated error models, and state-space models for GLMs are covered in some detail in Fahrmeir and Tutz (1994, chapter 8). State-space models, both linear and nonlinear, are discussed in Harvey (1989) and West and Harrison (1997). Estimation of models with time-varying parameters is an active area of research. Recent summaries of numerical methods include those in Fahrmeir and Tutz (1994) and West and Harrison (1997). The hidden Markov model for count and binomial data is presented in detail by MacDonald and Zucchini (1997).

7.13 Exercises

7.1 The first-order conditions for the Poisson PMLE are $\sum_t \mathbf{g}(y_t, \mathbf{x}_t, \boldsymbol{\beta}) = \mathbf{0}$ where $\mathbf{g}(y_t, \mathbf{x}_t, \boldsymbol{\beta}) = (y_t - \exp(\mathbf{x}_t'\boldsymbol{\beta}))\mathbf{x}_t$. Apply the general result given in section 2.7.1 to obtain (7.15) for y_t heteroskedastic and autocorrelated to lag l.

7.2 Consider OLS regression of y_t on scalar x_t without intercept in the cross-section case. The robust sandwich heteroskedastic consistent estimate of the variance of $\hat{\beta}$ is $[\sum_t x_t^2]^{-1} [\sum_t (y_t - x_t\hat{\beta})^2 x_t^2] [\sum_t x_t^2]^{-1}$. Specialize this formula if there is no relationship between y_t and x_t (so $\beta = 0$), and obtain the resulting formula for $t = \hat{\beta}/\sqrt{\mathsf{V}[\hat{\beta}]}$. Apply this result to the case of regression of z_t on z_{t-k} and compare the formula with (7.21).

7.3 Suppose ε_t in (7.24) is iid. Then y_t is stationary with, say, $\mathsf{E}[y_t] = \mu$ for all t and $\mathsf{V}[y_t] = \sigma^2$ for all t. Using the general result $\mathsf{E}[y] = \mathsf{E}_x[\mathsf{E}[y \mid x]]$, use (7.27) to obtain (7.25). Using the general result $\mathsf{V}[y] = \mathsf{E}_x[\mathsf{V}[y \mid x]] + \mathsf{V}_x[\mathsf{E}[y \mid x]]$, use (7.28) to obtain (7.26).

7.4 For the Poisson INAR(1) model give the objective function for the conditional WLS estimator discussed after (7.36) and obtain the variance matrix for this estimator.

7.5 Show that the binomial thinning operator in section 7.4 implies $0 \circ y = 0$; $1 \circ y = y$; $\mathsf{E}[\alpha \circ y] = \alpha \mathsf{E}[y]$; and $\mathsf{V}[\alpha \circ y] = \alpha^2 \mathsf{V}[y] + \alpha(1-\alpha)\mathsf{E}[y]$; and that for any $\gamma \in [0, 1]$, $\gamma \circ \alpha \circ y = (\gamma\alpha) \circ y$, by definition.

7.6 Given (7.43) and the assumptions on ε_t, obtain (7.45) and (7.46).

CHAPTER 8

Multivariate Data

8.1 Introduction

In this chapter we consider regression models for an m-dimensional vector of jointly distributed, and in general correlated, random variables $\mathbf{y} = (y_1, y_2, \ldots, y_m)$, a subset of which are event counts. A special case is if $m = 2$, y_1 is a count, and y_2 is either discrete or continuous. Multivariate data appear in three contexts in this book. The first is basic cross-section, which is the main subject of this chapter. The second is longitudinal data with repeated measures over time on the same variable, leading to special correlation structure handled in Chapter 9. The third is the context of multivariate cross-section data with endogeneity or feedback from y_j to y_k, dealt with in Chapter 10. There are other forms of multivariate data, such as multivariate time series analogs of Gaussian vector autoregressions, that we do not cover.

Multivariate linear Gaussian models are widely used, but multivariate nonlinear, non-Gaussian models are less common. Fully parametric approaches based on the joint distribution of non-Gaussian vector $\mathbf{y}$, given a set of covariates $\mathbf{x}$, are difficult to apply because analytically and computationally tractable expressions for such joint distributions are available for special cases only. Consequently, it is more convenient to analyze models that are of interest in specific situations.

Multivariate cross-section count models arise in several different settings. The first is that in which several related events are measured as counts and the joint distribution of several counts is required. These models are analogous to the seemingly unrelated regressions model. A second situation is one in which counted events are jointly determined with (but not by) other noncount variables, which may be continuous or discrete. A third situation is one in which the model involves simultaneity between a count variable or variables and another continuous or discrete variable, so the situation is analogous to that in simultaneous equation models.

Empirical examples of each of the three situations are readily found. For example, a model of the frequency of entry and exit of firms to an industry is an example of a bivariate count process (Mayer and Chappell, 1992). A model of healthcare utilization using several measures of healthcare services (hospital admissions, days spent in hospitals, prescribed and nonprescribed medicines) is an example of jointly dependent counts. An example of a joint model of counts and discrete choice variables is a model of the frequency of recreational trips and discrete choice of recreational sites (Terza and Wilson, 1990; Hausman, Leonard, and McFadden, 1995). Examples of joint modeling of counts and continuous variables are provided by Meghir and Robin (1992) and van Praag and Vermeulen (1993), who model frequency of purchase and amount of purchase.

Applications of multivariate count models are relatively uncommon. Practical experience has been restricted to some special computationally tractable cases. Section 8.2 discusses some approaches and general issues relevant to characterizing dependence. Section 8.3 deals with properties and maximum likelihood–based estimation of parametric models, including bivariate Poisson models, without or with unobserved heterogeneity. Section 8.4 considers moment-based estimation of the bivariate and multivariate models with one or more moment restrictions. Section 8.5 considers the orthogonal polynomial series expansions as a way of characterizing and testing for dependence in multivariate models. Section 8.6 considers mixed models with both counts and other continuous or discrete variables.

8.2 Characterizing Dependence

8.2.1 *Some Approaches*

Consider the standard decomposition of the joint distribution of a two-dimensional random variable (Y_1, Y_2), denoted by $f_{Y_1,Y_2}(y_1, y_2 \mid \mathbf{x})$, into conditional and marginal distributions:

$$\begin{aligned} f_{Y_1,Y_2}(y_1, y_2 \mid \mathbf{x}) &= f_{Y_1 \mid Y_2}(y_1 \mid y_2, \mathbf{x}) f_{Y_2}(y_2 \mid \mathbf{x}) \\ &= f_{Y_2 \mid Y_1}(y_2 \mid y_1, \mathbf{x}) f_{Y_1}(y_1 \mid \mathbf{x}), \end{aligned} \tag{8.1}$$

where $\mathbf{x}$ denotes exogenous variables that may have overlapping elements.* The decomposition implies that if these densities exist, the joint distribution can be defined using either product in the decomposition:

$$f_{Y_1 \mid Y_2}(y_1 \mid y_2, \mathbf{x}) f_{Y_2}(y_2 \mid \mathbf{x}) = f_{Y_2 \mid Y_1}(y_2 \mid y_1, \mathbf{x}) f_{Y_1}(y_1 \mid \mathbf{x}). \tag{8.2}$$

The parameters of the joint distribution may be estimated using the joint distribution, if it is available, or by working with the conditional and the marginal distributions, which may be computationally more convenient.

Given conditional specifications $f_{Y_1 \mid Y_2}(y_1 \mid y_2, \mathbf{x})$ and $f_{Y_2 \mid Y_1}(y_2 \mid y_1, \mathbf{x})$, the joint density may be defined if there exist proper marginals that satisfy (8.2). Because not all pairs of conditionals will be coherent in the sense of satisfying

* Elsewhere we have used $f(y)$, $f(y_1, y_2)$, and so forth as generic notation for density. The slightly different notation used here distinguises between random variables and their realizations for additional clarity.

(8.2), they are subject to some restrictions. In econometrics joint distributions are of considerable interest because they have a key role in structural or causal modeling. On the other hand, conditional distributions connect naturally to the regression models that are often a starting point of empirical investigations. In empirical work it is not uncommon to both begin and end with a conditional specification, leaving unresolved the problem of finding a valid joint distribution. Conditional modeling of interdependent variables is justifiable if there is a plausible recursive ordering of outcomes (decisions) that correspond to observed endogenous variables.† It is also a feasible and asymptotically efficient approach in some cases, such as bivariate exponential class if the conditionals are also from a bivariate exponential class (Moschopoulos and Staniswalis, 1994).

The terminology used here is econometric. Some additional clarification may be helpful for those less familiar with it. In this context a definition of *exogeneity*, parallel to that used in time series econometrics (Hendry, 1995), has an important role. Roughly, in modeling y_1 the variables $(y_2, \mathbf{x})$ are exogenous if they are determined without reference to y_1, which rules out contemporaneous or lagged feedback from y_1 to y_2. Because our focus is on cross-section data in this chapter, we are mainly concerned with contemporaneous feedback, or simultaneity and interdependence.

For a more precise definition, first rewrite the conditional-marginal decomposition (8.1) by incorporating parameters as in

$$f_{Y_1,Y_2}(y_1, y_2 \mid \mathbf{x}, \boldsymbol{\theta}) = f_{Y_1 \mid Y_2}(y_1 \mid y_2, \mathbf{x}, \phi_1) f_{Y_2}(y_2 \mid \mathbf{x}, \phi_2),$$

where $\boldsymbol{\theta} \in \Theta \subset \mathcal{R}^k$, $\phi \equiv [\phi_1 \vdots \phi_2] = g(\boldsymbol{\theta})$. If there are constraints connecting elements of $\boldsymbol{\theta}$, they are incorporated in the joint distribution. The function $g(\boldsymbol{\theta})$ is a transformation of the parameters $\boldsymbol{\theta}$, with $\dim(\boldsymbol{\theta}) = \dim(\phi)$. The parameter vector ϕ is partitioned into subsets ϕ_1 and ϕ_2, which appear in the conditional and marginal densities, respectively. Note that association parameters that are included in $\boldsymbol{\theta}$ may not be identified by carrying out conditional or marginal analysis alone.

The conditioning set $(y_2, \mathbf{x})$ is said to be *exogenous* if ϕ_1 is fully informative about $\boldsymbol{\theta}$, or any subset of $\boldsymbol{\theta}$. In this case ϕ_2 does not depend on ϕ_1. Under this condition, it is valid to make inferences about ϕ_1, or the relevant subset of $\boldsymbol{\theta}$, using the conditional model alone. No separate statistical modeling of y_2 is necessary.

If (y_1, y_2) are mutually dependent, as in the simultaneous equations models of economics, there is feedback from y_2 to y_1. In this case inferences about the change in y_1 induced by changes in y_2, based on the conditional model alone, have limited validity. Modeling interdependent variables can be carried out in different ways; a full specification and analysis of a joint distribution is

† The plausibility of recursivity as a justification for conditioning is not always obvious. For example: Does a rational household first determine the number of shoping trips and then the amount spent in each trip, or does it do so jointly?

one approach. Analyses of interdependent variables may be carried out using a fully parametric specification of the joint distribution. This is called a *full information* (maximum likelihood) approach. Interdependent variables may also be analyzed using a moment-based approach such as GMM. If dealing with the statistical implications of stochastic dependence between variables, this approach does not require or use a full parametric specification of the joint distribution and does not permit inferences about all parameters. Hence it is a *limited information* approach.

Models based on joint distributions or joint moments are said to be *structural* if they correspond to autonomous behavioral relationships and incorporate relevant parametric constraints. Univariate and multivariate marginal models may not permit identification of parameters $\boldsymbol{\theta}$. So a statistical analysis may be restricted to ϕ_2 only.

A full information analysis requires a flexible joint distribution. This is often not feasible for general multivariate models with interdependent discrete and continuous variables. Even in special bivariate cases, parametric closed form joint distributions may be obtainable only under restrictive conditions. In section 8.3 we consider some leading bivariate cases. If less restrictive situations are considered, closed-form joint densities are often not available, and consequently the construction of a joint likelihood may proceed on a case-by-case basis with many context-specific assumptions.

In marginal models, the dependence on covariates and the association between the endogenous variables are modeled separately, not jointly. Modeling based on marginal distributions may be handled using the methods developed in Chapters 3, 4, and 5, supplemented by methods for measuring association among jointly dependent variables, which are developed in this chapter. In empirical work, however, the choice of marginal distributions may be more or less arbitrary, and the investigation may not proceed to the derivation of the underlying joint distribution, if it exists.

8.2.2 *Example*

We illustrate the issues raised in the preceding discussion of dependence characterization by reference to a specific example. A useful technique for inducing dependence is to introduce correlated unobserved heterogeneity in marginal distributions. This approach has been used widely in bivariate LEF models. For concreteness, we consider an example that is empirically important and that recurs in Chapter 11. The discussion draws on Terza (1998) and Weiss (1995).

Consider two random variables (y_1, y_2^*) where y_1 is a count variable. Suppose, conditionally on $\mathbf{x}_i$ and ν_i, y_{1i} is distributed $\mathsf{P}[\mu_i]$, and $\mu_i = \exp[\mathbf{x}_i'\beta + \nu_i]$. Here ν_i represents unmeasured heterogeneity. It is an iid random variable independent of $\mathbf{x}_i$. Suppose that y_2^* is a normally distributed unobserved latent variable,

$$y_{2i}^* = \mathbf{z}_i'\delta + \varepsilon_i,$$

where $\varepsilon_i \sim \mathsf{N}[0, \sigma_2^2]$, which is related to an observable binomial variable y_2 in the following way:

$$y_2 = \begin{cases} 0 & \text{if } y_{2i}^* < 0 \\ 1 & \text{if } y_{2i}^* \geq 0. \end{cases}$$

Then an association between y_1 and y_2 is induced by association (correlation) between ν and ε. That is, the joint probability distribution of ν and ε determines in part the joint probability distribution of y_1 and y_2.

The joint probability distribution of y_1 and y_2 is related to the joint probability distribution of ν and ε. Suppose that this distribution is bivariate normal with correlation parameter ρ, and covariance matrix

$$\Sigma = \begin{pmatrix} 1 & \rho\sigma_2 \\ \rho\sigma_2 & \sigma_2^2 \end{pmatrix}$$

where the variance σ_1^2 has been normalized to unity. The association between ε and ν is characterized by

$$\nu = \rho\varepsilon + \eta, \tag{8.3}$$

where η is normally and independently distributed. Then the marginal density of y_1 is a Poisson–normal mixture, $\int f[y_1 \mid X, \nu]g(\nu)d\nu$, which cannot be expressed in a closed form.

First we consider a full information approach based on the joint distribution. Suppose y_2 has a binomial distribution, then the likelihood function is given by

$$\begin{aligned} \mathsf{L}(\boldsymbol{\Theta}) &= \prod_{i=1}^{n} f(y_{1i}, y_{2i}) \\ &= \prod_{i=1}^{n} f(y_{1i}, y_{2i} = 1)^{y_{2i}} \Pr[y_{1i}, y_{2i} = 0]^{1-y_{2i}}, \end{aligned} \tag{8.4}$$

where $\boldsymbol{\Theta}$ contains all the parameters in the joint distribution.

The expressions for probability on the right-hand side can be expressed as integrals over the variable ν. Maximization of such a likelihood requires numerically intensive methods of computation. This is an obstacle to full information analysis. It is computationally more convenient to consider estimation based on the decomposition given in (8.1).

We next consider a limited information approach based on specification of conditional moments using the specification

$$\begin{aligned} y_{1i} &= \exp\left[\mathbf{x}_i'\boldsymbol{\beta} + \alpha y_{2i}\right]\nu_i \\ y_{2i} &= \mathsf{E}[y_{2i} \mid \mathbf{z}_i] + \varepsilon_i, \end{aligned} \tag{8.5}$$

where y_2 in the first equation must be regarded as an endogenous variable correlated with ν. A sequential two-step estimator estimates the first of the above equations after replacing y_2 by an estimate of $\mathsf{E}[y_2 \mid \mathbf{x}]$, which is uncorrelated with ν. But computing this expectation requires the marginal density of y_2, which is often not available. In practice, therefore, the step may be implemented by an ad hoc procedure that uses "an" estimate (rather than "the" estimate) of conditional expectation, calculated by a first-step regression on variables assumed uncorrelated with ν, which amounts to an instrumental variable procedure. Thus the equation of interest becomes

$$y_{1i} = \exp\left[\mathbf{x}_i'\beta + \alpha \widehat{\mathsf{E}[y_{2i} \mid \mathbf{z}_i]} - \alpha(\widehat{\mathsf{E}[y_{2i} \mid \mathbf{z}_i]} - \mathsf{E}[y_{2i} \mid \mathbf{z}_i])\right]\nu_i.$$

For example, for the binary y_2 variable, the first stage could generate the fitted probability, a proxy for $\widehat{\mathsf{E}[y_{2i} \mid \mathbf{z}_i]}$, from a probit regression. The analysis of y_{1i} would be conditional on stage-one estimates. This problem is further analyzed in Chapter 11.

8.3 Parametric Models

8.3.1 *Bivariate Poisson*

Unlike the case of the normal distribution, there is no unique multivariate Poisson. There are several ways in which a model with Poisson marginals can be derived. Often any distribution that leads to Poisson marginals is referred to as a multivariate Poisson.

A well-established technique for deriving multivariate (especially bivariate) count distributions is the method of mixtures and convolutions. The oldest and the most studied special case is the bivariate Poisson model, which can be generated by sums of independent random counts with common components in the sums, also called the *trivariate reduction* technique (Kocherlakota and Kocherlakota, 1993). Suppose count variables y_1 and y_2 are defined as

$$y_1 = u + w, \tag{8.6}$$

$$y_2 = v + w, \tag{8.7}$$

and u, v, and w are independently distributed as Poisson variables with parameters μ_1, μ_2, and μ_3, respectively, $\mu_j > 0$, $j = 1, 2, 3$. Then the joint frequency distribution, which is derived in section 8.7, is given by

$$f(y_1 = r, y_2 = s) = \exp(\mu_1 + \mu_2 + \mu_3) \sum_{l=0}^{\min(r,s)} \frac{\mu_1^{r-l} \mu_2^{s-l} \mu_3^l}{(r-l)!(s-l)!l!}. \tag{8.8}$$

The marginals are, respectively,

$$y_1 \sim \mathsf{P}[\mu_1 + \mu_3], \tag{8.9}$$

and

$$y_2 \sim \mathsf{P}[\mu_2 + \mu_3], \tag{8.10}$$

with the squared correlation given by

$$\rho^2 = \frac{\mu_3^2}{(\mu_1 + \mu_3)(\mu_2 + \mu_3)}, \tag{8.11}$$

(see Johnson and Kotz, 1969). Allowing for heterogeneity by allowing the parameters to vary across individuals implies that the correlation between events also varies across individuals. However, maximum correlation between y_1 and y_2 is given by $\mu_3/[\mu_3 + \min(\mu_1, \mu_2)]$. Gourieroux et al. (1984b) present a different derivation of the bivariate Poisson.

The use of trivariate reduction technique leads to the following properties:

1. In general, in multivariate nonnormal distributions the correlation does not fully describe the dependence structure of variables. However, in this special case the correlation coefficient fully characterizes dependence, and no additional measures of dependence are needed.
2. The marginal distributions for y_1 and y_2 are both Poisson. Hence, with a correctly specified conditional mean function the marginal models can be estimated consistently, but not efficiently, by maximum likelihood. Joint estimation is more efficient even if the two mean functions depend on the same covariates.
3. This model only permits positive correlation between counts.

Then the log-likelihood for the model is

$$\mathcal{L}(\mu_1, \mu_2, \mu_3 \mid y_1, y_2, \mathbf{x}) = \sum_{i=1}^{n} \mu_{3i} - \sum_{i=1}^{n} (\mu_{1i} + \mu_{2i}) + \sum_{i=1}^{n} \ln S_i,$$

where

$$S_i = \sum_{l=0}^{\min(y_{1i}, y_{2i})} \frac{\mu_1^{y_{1i}-l} \mu_2^{y_{2i}-l} \mu_3^{l}}{(y_{1i} - l)!(y_{2i} - l)!l!}.$$

At this stage there are two ways to proceed. One approach parameterizes the sum $\mu_{1i} + \mu_{2i}$ as an (exponential) function of $\mathbf{x}_i$. A second approach parameterizes μ_{1i} and μ_{2i} individually in terms of same or different covariates. The two approaches imply different specifications of the conditional means. Taking the second approach, assume that $\mu_{3i} = \mu_3$, $\mu_{1i} = \exp(\mathbf{x}_i'\beta)$ and $\mu_{2i} = \exp(\mathbf{x}_i'\gamma)$. This leads to the log-likelihood

$$\mathcal{L}(\beta, \gamma, \mu_3 \mid y_1, y_2, \mathbf{x}) = n\mu_3 - \sum_{i=1}^{n} \left(\exp(\mathbf{x}_i'\beta) + \exp(\mathbf{x}_i'\gamma)\right) + \sum_{i=1}^{n} \ln S_i.$$

King (1989a) calls this *seemingly unrelated Poisson regression maximum likelihood estimator* (SUPREME) by analogy with the well-known seemingly unrelated least squares model. Jung and Winkelmann (1993), in their application of the bivariate Poisson to the number of voluntary and involuntary job changes, assume a *constant covariance* and exponential mean parameterization for the marginal means so that $\mu_j + \mu_3 = \exp(\mathbf{x}_j'\boldsymbol{\beta}_j)$, $j = 1, 2$; this allows the two means to depend on separate or common sets of covariates. This assumption substituted into (8.8) provides the basis for deriving the joint likelihood of the unknown parameters.

Bivariate Poisson is a special case of the generalized exponential family (Jupp and Mardia, 1980; Kocherlakota and Kocherlakota, 1993)

$$f(y_1, y_2 \mid \mu_1, \mu_2, \rho) = \exp\{\mu_1' v(y_1) + v(y_1)' \rho w(y_2) + \mu_2' w(y_2) \\ - c(\mu_1, \mu_2, \rho) + d_1(y_1) + d_2(y_2)\} \quad (8.12)$$

where $v(\cdot)$, $w(\cdot)$, $d_1(\cdot)$ and $d_2(\cdot)$ are functions, and $c(\mu_1, \mu_2, 0) = c_1(\mu_1)c_2(\mu_2)$. Under independence, $\rho = 0$, in which case the right-hand side is a product of two exponential families. In this family $\rho = 0$ is a necessary and sufficient condition for independence. The correlation coefficient is increasing in μ_3 and decreasing steeply in both μ_1 and μ_2.

8.3.2 *Other Fully Parametric Models*

The bivariate Poisson can be generalized and extended to allow for unobserved heterogeneity and overdispersion in the respective marginal distributions using mixtures and convolutions as in the univariate case.

Marshall and Olkin (1990) generate multivariate distributions from mixtures and convolutions of product families in a manner analogous to equation (4.10), which leads to compound marginal distributions. Consider the bivariate distribution

$$f(y_1, y_2 \mid x_1, x_2) = \int_0^\infty f_1(y_1 \mid x_1, \nu) f_2(y_2 \mid x_2, \nu) g(\nu)\, d\nu, \qquad (8.13)$$

where f_1, f_2, and g are univariate densities, and ν may be interpreted as common unobserved heterogeneity affecting both counts. Multivariate distributions generated in this way have univariate marginals in the same family (Kocherlakota and Kocherlakota, 1993). Thus, a bivariate negative binomial mixture generated in this way will have univariate negative binomial mixture densities. This approach suggests a way of specifying or justifying overdispersed and correlated count models, based on a suitable choice of $g(\cdot)$, more general than in the example given above. Marshall and Olkin (1990) generate a bivariate negative binomial distribution beginning with $f(y_1)$ and $f(y_2)$, which are Poisson with parameters $\mu_1\nu$ and $\mu_2\nu$, respectively; ν has gamma distribution with parameter α^{-1}. That is,

$$h(y_1, y_2 \mid \mu_1, \mu_2, \alpha^{-1}) = \int_0^{\infty} [(\mu_1 \nu)^{y_1} \exp(-\mu_1 \nu)/y_1!]$$

$$\times \left[(\mu_2 \nu)^{y_2} \exp(-\mu_2 \nu)/y_2!\right]\left[\nu^{\alpha^{-1}-1} \exp(-\nu)/\Gamma(\alpha^{-1})\right] d\nu$$

$$= \frac{\Gamma\left(y_1 + y_2 + \alpha^{-1}\right)}{y_1! y_2! \Gamma(\alpha^{-1})} \left[\frac{\mu_1}{\mu_1 + \mu_2 + 1}\right]^{y_1} \left[\frac{\mu_2}{\mu_1 + \mu_2 + 1}\right]^{y_2}$$

$$\times \left[\frac{1}{\mu_1 + \mu_2 + 1}\right]^{\alpha^{-1}}. \tag{8.14}$$

The marginals are again univariate negative binomial and the correlation is positive. After parameterizing (μ_1, μ_2) maximum likelihood estimation appears feasible, but to date there do not appear to have been applications or documented computational experience. Note that a result of Lindeboom and van den Berg (1994) for bivariate survival models indicates that it is hazardous to estimate bivariate models in which mutual dependence survival times arise purely from unobserved heterogeneity characterized as a univariate random variable. This result is also likely to apply to bivariate count models, and it suggests the desirability of flexible handling of the correlation structure between counts.

More flexible bivariate and multivariate parametric count data models can be constructed by introducing correlated, rather than identical, unobserved heterogeneity components in models. For example, suppose y_1 and y_2 are, respectively, $\mathsf{P}[\mu_1 \mid \nu_1]$ and $\mathsf{P}[\mu_2 \mid \nu_2]$ with $\mathsf{E}[\nu_1] = \mathsf{E}[\nu_2] = 1$, and

$$\mu_1 = \exp(\beta_0 + \nu_1 + \mathbf{x}'\beta_1) \tag{8.15}$$

and

$$\mu_2 = \exp(\beta_0 + \nu_2 + \mathbf{x}'\beta_2), \tag{8.16}$$

where ν_1 and ν_2 represent unobserved heterogeneity; their presence induces overdispersion in the marginal distributions of y_1 and y_2. Dependence between y_1 and y_2 is induced if ν_1 and ν_2 are correlated. In these cases the marginal distributions for y_1 and y_2 exhibit both overdispersion and dependence, but in general in such cases neither the joint nor the marginal distributions have closed-form expressions. The joint distribution can be derived by extending the approach based on (8.13). For example, the assumption of common heterogeneity may be replaced by a bivariate normal distribution of (ν_1, ν_2). Maximum likelihood estimation of such models requires numerically intensive methods, such as numerical or Monte Carlo integration.

8.4 Moment-Based Estimation

8.4.1 *Bivariate Poisson with Heterogeneity*

We wish to allow jointly for departures from equidispersion and a flexible pattern of correlation between counts. But we also want a tractable estimation procedure. With these motivations, Gourieroux et al. (1984b, pp. 716–717) propose a sequential moment-based procedure for a bivariate count model. Their model is more general than the bivariate Poisson because it permits overdispersion in the conditional distributions.

The pair (y_1, y_2) have a common additive stochastic component v as in

$$\begin{aligned} y_1 &= u + v \\ y_2 &= w + v, \end{aligned} \tag{8.17}$$

conditional on an unobserved component, respectively ν_1, ν_2, ν_3, the component random variables u, v and w are each Poisson distributed. The conditional means and variances, suppressing the conditioning on $\mathbf{x}$ for notational simplicity, are as follows:

$$\begin{aligned} \mathsf{E}[u \mid \nu_1] &= \exp(\mathbf{x}_1'\boldsymbol{\beta}_1 + \nu_1) \\ \mathsf{E}[v \mid \nu_2] &= \exp(\mathbf{x}_2'\boldsymbol{\beta}_2 + \nu_2) \\ \mathsf{E}[w \mid \nu_3] &= \exp(\mathbf{x}_3'\boldsymbol{\beta}_3 + \nu_3), \end{aligned} \tag{8.18}$$

$$\begin{aligned} \mathsf{E}[\mathbf{y}_i \mid \boldsymbol{\nu}_i] &= \begin{bmatrix} \mathsf{E}[y_{1i} \mid \nu_{1i}, v_{2i}] \\ \mathsf{E}[y_{2i} \mid \nu_{2i}, v_{3i}] \end{bmatrix} \\ &= \begin{bmatrix} \exp(\mathbf{x}_{1i}'\boldsymbol{\beta}_1 + \nu_{1i}) + \exp(\mathbf{x}_{2i}'\boldsymbol{\beta}_2 + \nu_{2i}) \\ \exp(\mathbf{x}_{2i}'\boldsymbol{\beta}_2 + \nu_{2i}) + \exp(\mathbf{x}_{3i}'\boldsymbol{\beta}_3 + \nu_{3i}) \end{bmatrix}, \end{aligned} \tag{8.19}$$

where, the unobserved components ν_i are assumed to have moments

$$\mathsf{E}[\boldsymbol{\nu}_i] = \mathsf{E}\begin{bmatrix} \nu_{1i} \\ \nu_{2i} \\ \nu_{3i} \end{bmatrix} = \begin{bmatrix} 1 \\ 1 \\ 1 \end{bmatrix}; \ \mathsf{V}[\boldsymbol{\nu}_i] = \boldsymbol{\Omega}; \quad i = 1, \ldots, n. \tag{8.20}$$

Define the (2×1) row vector $\mathbf{y}_i' = (y_{1i}, y_{2i})$, $i = 1, \ldots, n$, and (2×3) matrix

$$\mathbf{M}_i = \begin{bmatrix} \exp(\mathbf{x}_{1i}'\boldsymbol{\beta}_1) & \exp(\mathbf{x}_{2i}'\boldsymbol{\beta}_2) & 0 \\ 0 & \exp(\mathbf{x}_{2i}'\boldsymbol{\beta}_2) & \exp(\mathbf{x}_{3i}'\boldsymbol{\beta}_3) \end{bmatrix}. \tag{8.21}$$

Further,

$$\mathsf{V}[\mathbf{y}_i \mid \boldsymbol{\nu}_i] = \begin{bmatrix} \exp(\mathbf{x}_{1i}'\boldsymbol{\beta}_1) + \exp(\mathbf{x}_{2i}'\boldsymbol{\beta}_2) & \exp(\mathbf{x}_{2i}'\boldsymbol{\beta}_2) \\ \exp(\mathbf{x}_{2i}'\boldsymbol{\beta}_2) & \exp(\mathbf{x}_{2i}'\boldsymbol{\beta}_2) + \exp(\mathbf{x}_{3i}'\boldsymbol{\beta}_3) \end{bmatrix}. \tag{8.22}$$

Unconditionally, the first two moments of $\mathbf{y}$ are, respectively,

$$\mathsf{E}[\mathbf{y}_i] = \begin{bmatrix} \mathsf{E}[y_{1i}] \\ \mathsf{E}[y_{2i}] \end{bmatrix} = \begin{bmatrix} \exp(\mathbf{x}'_{1i}\boldsymbol{\beta}_1) + \exp(\mathbf{x}'_{2i}\boldsymbol{\beta}_2) \\ \exp(\mathbf{x}'_{2i}\boldsymbol{\beta}_2) + \exp(\mathbf{x}'_{3i}\boldsymbol{\beta}_3) \end{bmatrix} \tag{8.23}$$

and

$$\mathsf{V}[\mathbf{y}_i] = \mathbf{V}_i = \mathbf{V}_{1i} + \mathbf{M}_i \boldsymbol{\Omega} \mathbf{M}'_i, \tag{8.24}$$

where

$$\mathbf{V}_{1i} = \begin{bmatrix} \exp(\mathbf{x}'_{1i}\boldsymbol{\beta}_1) + \exp(\mathbf{x}'_{2i}\boldsymbol{\beta}_2) & \exp(\mathbf{x}'_{2i}\boldsymbol{\beta}_2) \\ \exp(\mathbf{x}'_{2i}\boldsymbol{\beta}_2) & \exp(\mathbf{x}'_{3i}\boldsymbol{\beta}_3) + \exp(\mathbf{x}'_{2i}\boldsymbol{\beta}_2) \end{bmatrix},$$

and

$$\mathbf{M}_i \boldsymbol{\Omega} \mathbf{M}'_i = \begin{bmatrix} a^2\omega_{11} + ab\omega_{21} + ba\omega_{12} + b^2\omega_{22} & ba\omega_{12} + b^2\omega_{22} + ca\omega_{13} + cb\omega_{23} \\ ab\omega_{21} + ac\omega_{31} + b^2\omega_{22} + bc\omega_{32} & b^2\omega_{22} + bc\omega_{32} + cb\omega_{23} + c^2\omega_{33} \end{bmatrix},$$

where $a = \exp(\mathbf{x}'_{1i}\boldsymbol{\beta}_1)$, $b = \exp(\mathbf{x}'_{2i}\boldsymbol{\beta}_2)$, and $c = \exp(\mathbf{x}'_{3i}\boldsymbol{\beta}_3)$ and ω_{jk} is the jk^{th} entry of Ω. This result is obtained by applying (4.4).

Then the QGPML estimator of $(\boldsymbol{\beta}_1, \boldsymbol{\beta}_2, \boldsymbol{\beta}_3)$ may be obtained by minimizing

$$\sum_{i=1}^{n} (\mathbf{y}_i - \mathsf{E}[\mathbf{y}_i])' \hat{\mathbf{V}}_i^{-1} (\mathbf{y}_i - \mathsf{E}[\mathbf{y}_i]), \tag{8.25}$$

where $\hat{\mathbf{V}}_i$ is a consistent estimator of the variance of $\mathbf{y}_i$, denoted $\mathbf{V}_i$.

The two-step QGPML estimator can be computed by the following algorithm:

1. Obtain consistent estimates of $(\boldsymbol{\beta}_1, \boldsymbol{\beta}_2, \boldsymbol{\beta}_3)$ using a method such as NLS, based on the conditional means given in (8.23). Use them to obtain consistent estimates $(\hat{a}, \hat{b}, \hat{c})$.
2. Obtain a consistent estimator of the elements of $\boldsymbol{\Omega}$ by auxiliary linear regressions of the distinct elements of the (2×2) matrix $(\hat{\mathbf{V}}_i - \hat{\mathbf{V}}_{1i})$ on the corresponding elements of the (2×2) matrix $\hat{\mathbf{M}}_i \boldsymbol{\Omega} \hat{\mathbf{M}}'_i$ (the elements of $\hat{\mathbf{V}}_i$ are squares or cross-products of raw residuals from step 1). This step is suggested by the structure of the variance matrix as given in equation (8.24). For example, the regression of the (1, 1) element of $(\hat{\mathbf{V}}_i - \hat{\mathbf{V}}_{1i})$ on $(\hat{a}^2, 2\hat{a}\hat{b}, \hat{b}^2)$ will yield estimates of ω_{11}, $\omega_{21} (= \omega_{12})$, and ω_{22}.
3. Obtain an estimate of $\mathbf{V}_i$ by substituting $(\hat{\boldsymbol{\beta}}_1, \hat{\boldsymbol{\beta}}_2, \hat{\boldsymbol{\beta}}_3, \hat{\boldsymbol{\Omega}})$ into the expression (8.24) for $\mathbf{V}_i$.
4. Minimize the objective function (8.25) and obtain the asymptotic covariance matrix by specializing the result (2.76) in Chapter 2.

This moment-based estimator is not entirely without problems. Note that because the three regressions yield nine estimates of six distinct elements of $\boldsymbol{\Omega}$, there is a problem of nonuniqueness. Further, the consistent estimates need not lead to a symmetric positive definite $\hat{\Omega}$ required for second-stage estimation. The nonuniqueness problem can be tackled by estimating the auxiliary regressions as a system of three linear regressions constrained to yield a symmetric $\hat{\Omega}$, but the lack of positive definiteness may remain a problem in small samples.

8.4.2 *Seemingly Unrelated Regressions*

Consider a multivariate nonlinear heteroskedastic regression model of the form

$$\mathbf{y}_j = \exp(\mathbf{x}_j'\beta_j) + \mathbf{u}_j,\ j = 1, 2, \ldots, m,$$

where $\mathbf{y}_j$ is an $n \times 1$ vector on the jth component of the regression and $\mathsf{E}[\mathbf{u}_j\mathbf{u}_k'] = \sigma(\mathbf{x}_j, \mathbf{x}_k)$. Define the following stacked $(nm \times 1)$ vectors $\mathbf{y}$ and $\mathbf{u}$, $(nm \times 1)$ vector $\mu(\beta)$, $(km \times 1)$ vector β, and $(nm \times nm)$ matrix $\Sigma(\mathbf{X})$:

$$\mathbf{y} = \begin{bmatrix} \mathbf{y}_1 \\ \cdots \\ \cdots \\ \mathbf{y}_m \end{bmatrix}, \quad \mu(\beta) = \begin{bmatrix} \exp(\mathbf{x}_1'\beta_1) \\ \cdots \\ \cdots \\ \exp(\mathbf{x}_m'\beta_m) \end{bmatrix}, \quad \beta = \begin{bmatrix} \beta_1 \\ \cdots \\ \cdots \\ \beta_m \end{bmatrix}, \quad \mathbf{u} = \begin{bmatrix} \mathbf{u}_1 \\ \cdots \\ \cdots \\ \mathbf{u}_m \end{bmatrix}.$$

$$\Sigma(\mathbf{X}) = \begin{bmatrix} \sigma(\mathbf{X}_1) & \ldots & \sigma(\mathbf{X}_1, \mathbf{X}_m) \\ \cdots & & \cdots \\ \cdots & & \cdots \\ \sigma(\mathbf{X}_1, \mathbf{X}_m) & \ldots & \sigma(\mathbf{X}_m) \end{bmatrix}.$$

In this case association between elements of $\mathbf{y}$ arises only through the covariance matrix Σ. If Σ is diagonal then conditional modeling of each component of $\mathbf{y}$ is simpler and equivalent to joint modeling. The above formulation does not specify the functional form of the elements in the $\Sigma(\mathbf{X})$ matrix, but the general notation is intended to imply that there is heteroskedasticity within each equation. At this level of generality the problem of consistent estimation and inference of parameters β is difficult.

An important difference between the above formulation and that given in the preceding section lies in the treatment of the variances. The marginal means in the two models are the same.

In the context of a linear multiple regression with a linear conditional expectation $\mathsf{E}[y_i \mid \mathbf{x}_i] = \mathbf{x}_i'\beta$, Robinson (1987) gives conditions under which asymptotically efficient estimation is possible in a model in which the variance function $\sigma_i(\mathbf{x})$ has an unknown form. His technique is to estimate a variance function $\mathsf{V}[y_i \mid \mathbf{x}] = \sigma_i(\mathbf{x})$ by kernel estimators of $\mathsf{E}[y_i \mid \mathbf{x}]$ and $\mathsf{E}[y_i^2 \mid \mathbf{x}]$, and then estimate β using the WLS estimator

$$\tilde{\beta} = \left[\sum_{i=1}^{n} \mathbf{x}_i\mathbf{x}_i'\hat{\sigma}_i^{-2}\right]^{-1} \sum_{i=1}^{n} \mathbf{x}_i\mathbf{y}_i\hat{\sigma}_i^{-2}$$

and its asymptotic covariance by

$$\mathsf{V}[\tilde{\beta}] = \left[\sum_{i=1}^{n} \mathbf{x}_i \mathbf{x}_i' \hat{\sigma}_i^{-2} \right]^{-1}.$$

Specifically, Robinson suggested using the k nearest neighbor method. We refer to this technique as *semiparametric generalized least squares* (SPGLS). Section 12.5 provides additional details of the implementation of this approach to a single equation count model.

Delgado (1992) extended the SPGLS to multivariate nonlinear models, which include the type considered previously. This technique amounts to nonlinear GLS estimation, based on a first-step consistent estimate of a $\mathbf{\Sigma}(\mathbf{X})$ matrix using the k nearest neighbor method and then minimizing the quadratic form

$$\mathbf{u}(\beta)'[\hat{\mathbf{\Sigma}}(\mathbf{X})]^{-1}\mathbf{u}(\beta),$$

where $\hat{\mathbf{\Sigma}}(\mathbf{X})$ denotes the consistent first-step estimator based on nonlinear seemingly unrelated regression estimates of β. Practical experience with the multivariate SPGLS estimator is limited, but Delgado provides some simulation results. The efficiency of such estimators is a complex issue (Newey, 1990b; Chamberlain, 1992a).

8.5 Orthogonal Polynomial Series Expansions

8.5.1 *Definitions and Conditions*

A useful (but not widely used) technique for generating and approximating multivariate discrete distributions is via a sequence of orthogonal or orthonormal polynomial expansions for the unknown joint density. For example, the bivariate density $f(y_1, y_2)$ may be approximated by a series expansion in which the terms are orthonormal polynomials of the univariate marginal densities $f(y_1)$ and $f(y_2)$. A required condition for the validity of the expansion is the existence of finite moments of all orders, denoted $\mu^{(k)}$, $k = 1, 2, \ldots$.

Begin by considering an important definition in a univariate context.

Definition (Orthogonality). An *orthogonal* polynomial of integer order j, denoted by $Q_j(y_i)$, $j = 1, \ldots, K$, or more compactly just $Q_j(y)$, has the property that

$$\int Q_j(y) Q_k(y) f(y) dy = \delta_{jk}\sigma_{jj}, \tag{8.26}$$

where δ_{jk} is the Kronecker delta, which equals zero if $j \neq k$ and one otherwise, and σ_{jj} denotes the variance of $Q_j(y)$. That is,

$$\mathsf{E}_f \left[Q_j(y_i) Q_k(y_i) \right] = \delta_{jk}\sigma_{jj}. \tag{8.27}$$

An orthogonal polynomial obtained by a scale transformation of $Q_j(y)$ such that it has unit variance is referred to as *orthonormal* polynomial of degree j. Thus $Q_j(y)/\sqrt{\sigma_{jj}}$ is an orthonormal polynomial; it has zero mean and unit variance. For convenience we use the notation $P_j(y)$ to denote a jth order orthonormal polynomial.

Let $\boldsymbol{\Delta}$ be a matrix whose ij^{th} element is $\mu^{(i+j-2)}(i \geq 1, j \geq 1)$. Then the neccssary and sufficient condition for an arbitrary sequence $\{\mu^{(k)}\}$ to give rise to a sequence of orthogonal polynomials, unique up to an arbitrary constant, is that $\boldsymbol{\Delta}$ should be positive definite (Cramer, 1946). An orthonormal sequence $P_j(y)$ is complete if, for every function $R(y)$ with finite variance, $\mathsf{V}[R(y)] = \sum_{j=0}^{\infty} a_j^2$, where $a_j = \mathsf{E}[R(y)P_j(y)]$.

8.5.2 *Univariate Expansion*

A well-behaved or regular pdf has a series representation in terms of orthogonal polynomials with respect to that density (Cramer, 1946, chapter 12; Lancaster, 1969). Let $\{Q_j(y), j=0, 1, 2, \ldots; Q_0(y) = 1\}$ be a sequence of orthogonal polynomials for $f(y)$. Let $H(y)$ denote the true but unknown distribution function and $h(y)$ denote a data density that satisfies regularity conditions (Lancaster, 1969). Then the following series expansion of $h(y)$ around a baseline density $f(y)$ is available:

$$h(y) = f(y)\left[1 + \sum_{j=1}^{\infty} a_j Q_j(y)\right]. \tag{8.28}$$

Multiplying both sides of (8.28) by $Q_j(y)$ and integrating shows that the coefficients in the expansion are defined by

$$a_j = \int Q_j(y)h(y)dy = \mathsf{E}_h[Q_j(y)], \tag{8.29}$$

which are identically zero if $h(y) = f(y)$. The terms in the series expansion reflect the divergence between the true but unknown pdf $h(y)$ and the assumed (baseline) pdf $f(y)$. A significant deviation implies that these coefficients are significantly different from zero. The orthogonal polynomials $Q_j(y)$ have a zero mean property, that is,

$$\mathsf{E}[Q_j(y)] = 0. \tag{8.30}$$

Further, the variance of $Q_j(y)$, evaluated under $f(y)$, is given by $\mathsf{E}[Q_j^2(y)]$.

A general procedure for deriving orthogonal polynomials is discussed in Cameron and Trivedi (1990b). For selected densities the orthogonal polynomials can also be derived using generating functions. These generating functions are known for the classical cases and for the Meixner class of distributions, which includes the normal, binomial, negative binomial, gamma, and Poisson densities (Cameron and Trivedi, 1993). For ease of later reference we also note the following expressions for $Q_j(y)$, $j=0, 1, 2$;

$$\begin{aligned}
Q_0(y) &= 1\\
Q_1(y) &= y - \mu\\
Q_2(y) &= (y-\mu)^2 - (\mu_3/\mu_2)(y-\mu) - \mu_2,
\end{aligned}$$

where μ_k, $k=1, 2$, and 3 denote, respectively, the first, second, and third central moments of y. Hence, it is seen that the orthogonal polynomials are functions of the "raw" residuals $(y-\mu)$.

8.5.3 *Multivariate Expansions*

We first consider the bivariate case. Let $f(y_1, y_2)$ be a bivariate pdf of random variables y_1 and y_2 with marginal distributions $f_1(y)$ and $f_2(y)$ whose corresponding orthogonal polynomial sequences (OPSs), are $Q_j(y)$ and $R_j(y)$, $j=0, 1, 2, \ldots$. If $h(\cdot)$ satisfies regularity conditions then the following expansion is formally valid:

$$f(y_1, y_2) = f_1(y_1)f_2(y_2)\left[1 + \sum_{j=1}^{\infty}\sum_{k=1}^{\infty} \rho_{jk} Q_j(y_1)R_k(y_2)\right] \tag{8.31}$$

where

$$\begin{aligned}
\rho_{jk} &= \mathsf{E}[Q_j(y_1)R_k(y_2)]\\
&= \int\!\!\int Q_j(y_1)R_k(y_2)f(y_1, y_2)\,dy_1\,dy_2.
\end{aligned}$$

The derivation of this result is similar to that given earlier for the a_j coefficients (Lancaster, 1969, p. 97).

The general multivariate treatment has close parallels with the bivariate case. Consider r random variables $(y_1, \ldots, y_r)$ with joint density $f(y_1, \ldots, y_r)$ and r marginals $f_1(y_1), f_2(y_2), \ldots, f_r(y_r)$ whose respective OPSs are denoted by $Q_s^i(y)$, $s=0, 1, \ldots, \infty$; $i=1, 2, \ldots, r$. Under regularity conditions the joint pdf admits a series expansion of the same type as that given in equation (8.31); that is,

$$\begin{aligned}
f(y_1, \ldots, y_r) &= f_1(y_1)f_2(y_2)\cdots f_r(y_r)\left[1 + \sum_{i<j}^{r}\sum_{j}^{r}\sum_{s}^{\infty}\sum_{t}^{\infty}\rho_{st}^{ij} Q_s^i(y_i)Q_t^j(y_j)\right.\\
&\left. + \sum_{i<j}^{r}\sum_{j<k}^{r}\sum_{k}^{r}\sum_{s}^{\infty}\sum_{t}^{\infty}\sum_{o}^{\infty}\rho_{sto}^{ijk} Q_s^i(y_i)Q_t^j(y_j)Q_o^k(y_k)\right],
\end{aligned} \tag{8.32}$$

where ρ_{st}^{ij} denotes the correlation coefficient between $Q_s^i(y_i)$ and $Q_t^j(y_j)$.

8.5.4 *Tests of Independence*

Series expansions can be used to generate and estimate approximations to unknown joint densities in a manner similar to the "seminonparametric" approach of Gallant and Tauchen (1989), adapted and applied to univariate count data by Cameron and Johansson (1997). Section 12.3 provides details of implementing this approach using nonorthogonal polynomial expansions. The objective is estimation of flexible parametric forms. The approach has not yet been systematically applied to multivariate count models.

In this section we present applications of series expansions only to tests of independence in a multivariate framework assuming given marginals, leaving the estimation problem to a later section. A complication in estimation, not present in testing, is the need to ensure the more general series-expansion density is properly defined. This leads to replacing the term in square brackets in (8.28) by its square, requiring the introduction of a normalizing constant. Also the order of the polynomial is truncated at less than infinity. Our treatment of testing follows the developments in Cameron and Trivedi (1990b, 1993).

Unfortunately, except in special cases such as the bivariate Poisson or the negative binomial, it is often not possible to express bivariate distributions in a flexible closed form. Wald and LR procedures are then not feasible for testing either the hypothesis of independence or the restricted hypothesis of zero correlation. In contrast, score and CM tests based on estimation under the null of independence are appealing. The null of zero correlation is the usual starting point for testing independence, but in non-Gaussian models this is, in general, only a necessary, not sufficient, condition for independence.

Using the key idea that under independence the joint pdf factorizes into a product of marginals, Cameron and Trivedi (1993) developed score-type tests of independence based on a series expansion of the type given in (8.31). The leading term in the series is the product of the marginals; the remaining terms in the expansion are orthonormal polynomials of the univariate marginal densities. The idea behind the test is to measure the significance of the higher-order terms in the expansion using estimates of the marginal models only. The conditional moment test of independence consists of testing for zero correlation between all pairs of orthonormal polynomials. The steps are: First, specify the marginals and estimate their parameters. Then, evaluate the orthogonal or orthonormal polynomials at the estimated parameter values. Finally, calculate the tests.

Given the marginals and corresponding orthogonal polynomials, the tests can be developed as follows. Using equation (8.31), the test of independence in the bivariate case requires us to test $H_0: \rho_{jk} = 0$ (all j, k). This onerous task may be simplified in one of two ways. The null may be tested against an alternative in which dependence is restricted to be a function of a small number of parameters, usually just one. Or we may approximate the bivariate distribution by a series expansion with a smaller number of terms and then derive a score (LM) test of the null hypothesis $H_0: \rho_{jk} = 0$ (some j, k). For independence we require $\rho_{jk} = 0$ for all j and k. By testing only a subset of the restrictions, the hypothesis of approximate independence is tested. If $p=2$, this is equivalent to the null hypothesis H_0: $\rho_{11}=\rho_{22}=\rho_{12}=\rho_{21}=0$. For general p, the appropriate moment restriction is: $\mathsf{E}_0[Q_j(y_1)R_k(y_2)]=0$, $j,k=1,2,\ldots,p$, where E_0 denotes expectation under the null hypothesis of independence of y_1 and y_2.

The key moment restriction is

$$\mathsf{E}_0[S_{jk}(\mathbf{y},\mathbf{x},\boldsymbol{\theta})]=0,$$

where $S_{jk}(\mathbf{y},\mathbf{x},\boldsymbol{\theta}) = Q_j(y_1 \mid \mathbf{x}_1,\boldsymbol{\theta}_1)R_k(y_2 \mid \mathbf{x}_2,\boldsymbol{\theta}_2)$. The conditioning operator is used to make explicit the presence of subsets of regressors $\mathbf{x}$ in the model. By independence of Q_j and R_k, and using the property that $\mathsf{E}_0[R_j(\cdot)]=\mathsf{E}_0[Q_k(\cdot)]=0$, and conditional on $\mathbf{x}$,

$$\begin{aligned}\mathsf{V}_0[S_{jk}(\cdot)] &= (\,\mathsf{E}_0[R_j(\cdot)])^2\,\mathsf{V}_0[Q_k(\cdot)] + (\,\mathsf{E}_0[Q_k(\cdot)])^2\,\mathsf{V}_0[R_j(\cdot)]\\ &\quad + \mathsf{V}_0[Q_k(\cdot)]\,\mathsf{V}_0[R_j(\cdot)] = \mathsf{V}_0[Q_k(\cdot)]\,\mathsf{V}_0[R_j(\cdot)].\end{aligned}$$

Assume initially that the parameters of the marginal distributions are known. By application of a central limit theorem for orthogonal polynomials $Q_{j,i}$ and $R_{k,i}$, which have zero mean by construction, we can obtain the following test statistic for the null hypothesis of $H_0:\rho_{jk}=0$:

$$\mathsf{r}^2_{jk} = \left(\sum_{i=1}^{n} Q_{j,i}R_{k,i}\right)\left[\sum_{i=1}^{n}(Q_{j,i}R_{k,i})^2\right]^{-1}\left(\sum_{i=1}^{n} Q_{j,i}R_{k,i}\right) \overset{a}{\sim} \chi^2(1) \tag{8.33}$$

Note that r^2_{jk} can be computed as n times the uncentered R^2_U (equals the proportion of the uncentered explained sum of squares) from the auxiliary regression of 1 on $Q_{j,i}R_{k,i}$.

For orthonormal polynomials, distinguished by an asterisk, we have the result that

$$\mathsf{E}_0\left(\sum_{i=1}^{n} Q^{*2}_{j,i}\right)\left(\sum_{i=1}^{n} R^{*2}_{k,i}\right) = n^{-1}\,\mathsf{E}_0\left(\sum_{i=1}^{n}(Q^*_{t,i}R^*_{s,i})^2\right),$$

by the properties of homoskedasticity and independence of $Q^*_{t,i}$ and $R^*_{s,i}$. A test of the null hypothesis of $H_0:\rho_{ts}=0$ is

$$\begin{aligned}\mathsf{r}^2_{jk} &= n\left(\sum_{i=1}^{n} Q^*_{j,i}R^*_{k,i}\right)\left(\left(\sum_{i=1}^{n} Q^{*2}_{j,i}\right)\left(\sum_{i=1}^{n} R^{*2}_{k,i}\right)\right)^{-1}\\ &\quad\times\left(\sum_{i=1}^{n} Q^*_{j,i}R^*_{k,i}\right) \overset{a}{\sim} \chi^2(1).\end{aligned} \tag{8.34}$$

These polynomials are functions of parameters $\boldsymbol{\theta}$. To implement the tests they are evaluated at the maximum likelihood estimates. Consider the effect of substituting the estimated parameters $\hat{\boldsymbol{\theta}}_1$ for $\boldsymbol{\theta}_1$ and $\hat{\boldsymbol{\theta}}_2$ for $\boldsymbol{\theta}_2$ in the test statistics. Using the general theory of conditional moment tests given in Chapter 2.6, and specifically noting that the derivative condition (5.59)

$$\mathsf{E}_0[\nabla_{\boldsymbol{\theta}} S_{jk,i}(\mathbf{y}, \mathbf{x}, \hat{\boldsymbol{\theta}} \mid \mathbf{x})] = \mathbf{0}$$

is satisfied, it follows that the asymptotic distribution of the test statistics (8.33) and (8.34) is not affected by the replacement of $\boldsymbol{\theta}$ by $\hat{\boldsymbol{\theta}}$.

The application of these ideas to the multivariate case is potentially burdensome because it involves all unique combinations of the polynomials of all marginal distributions. If the dimension of the $\mathbf{y}$ vector is large, it would seem sensible to exploit prior information on the structure of dependence in constructing a test. It is simpler to test for zero correlation between two subsets of $\mathbf{y}$, denoted $\mathbf{y}_1$ and $\mathbf{y}_2$, of dimensions r_1 and r_2, respectively, with the covariance matrix $\boldsymbol{\Sigma} = [\boldsymbol{\Sigma}_{jk}]$, $j, k = 1, 2$. Define the squared canonical correlation coefficient

$$\begin{aligned}\rho_c^2 &= (\text{vec}\boldsymbol{\Sigma}_{21})' \left(\boldsymbol{\Sigma}_{11}^{-1} \otimes \boldsymbol{\Sigma}_{22}^{-1}\right) (\text{vec}\boldsymbol{\Sigma}_{21}) \\ &= tr\left(\boldsymbol{\Sigma}_{11}^{-1}\boldsymbol{\Sigma}_{12}\boldsymbol{\Sigma}_{22}^{-1}\boldsymbol{\Sigma}_{21}\right), \end{aligned} \tag{8.35}$$

which equals zero under the null hypothesis of independence of $\mathbf{y}_1$ and $\mathbf{y}_2$. Let r_c^2 denote the sample estimate of ρ_c^2. Then, analogous to the test in (8.34) we have the result that

$$n\,\mathrm{r}_c^2 \overset{d}{\rightarrow} \chi^2(r_1 r_2). \tag{8.36}$$

See Jupp and Mardia (1980) and Shiba and Tsurumi (1988) for related results.

In practice tests of independence may simply turn out to be misspecification tests of misspecified marginals. The tests may be significant because the baseline marginals are misspecified, not necessarily because the variables are dependent. However, rather remarkably, in the bivariate case if only one marginal is misspecified, the tests retain validity as tests of independence. See Cameron and Trivedi (1993, pp. 34–35), who also investigate properties of the tests in Monte Carlo experiments. The investigations of these tests for bivariate count regression models show that the tests have the correct size and high power if the marginals are correctly specified, but they overreject if the marginals are misspecified.

8.5.5 *Example: Medical Services*

Table 8.1 shows first- and second-order polynomials for the specific cases of Poisson, NB1 (with overdispersion parameter α_1), and NB2 (with overdispersion parameter α_2).

Data on Australian healthcare utilization, which were introduced in section 1.4, were used to calculate tests of independence among six possible bivariate pairs using data on hospital admissions (*HOSPADM*), the number of

Table 8.1. *Orthogonal polynomials: first and second order*

Density	$Q_1(y)$	$Q_2(y)$
Poisson	$y-\mu$	$(y-\mu)^2-y$
NB1	$y-\mu$	$(y-\mu)^2-(2\alpha_1-1)(y-\mu)-\alpha_1\mu$
NB2	$y-\mu$	$(y-\mu)^2-(1+2\alpha_2\mu)(y-\mu)-(1+\alpha_2\mu)\mu$

Table 8.2. *Health services: pairwise independence tests*

Pair	(1)	(2)	(3)	(4)
HOSPADM, HOSPDAYS	189.6	72.43	275.2	94.7
HOSPADM, PRESC	20.28	22.88	4.82	.18
HOSPADM, NONPRESC	.20	16.26	.82	.05
HOSPDAYS, PRESC	.18	10.06	1.09	9.23
HOSPDAYS,NONPRESC	.01	1.91	.55	.16
PRESC, NONPRESC	9.20	9.85	4.35	4.07

Note: This table gives the test statistic (8.33); $j, k = 1$ in column (1); $j, k = 2$ in column (2); $j = 1, k = 2$ in column (3); $j = 2, k = 1$ in column (4).

days spent in hospital (*HOSPDAYS*), and the number of prescribed (*PRESC*) and nonprescribed (*NONPRESC*) medicines taken. NB1 specifications were estimated using the specification in Cameron et al. (1988). Table 8.2 gives the values of the test statistic (8.33) using four combinations with $j = 1, 2$, and $k = 1, 2$. For approximate independence, it is required that all statistics in each row should be small. There is strong evidence that (*HOSPADM*, *HOSPDAYS*), (*PRESC*, *NONPRESC*), and (*HOSPADM*, *PRESC*) are dependent pairs. This finding is plausible. All equations display overdispersion, which may be due to unobserved heterogeneity. Consequently NB1 is preferred to the Poisson. Because the explanatory variable in all the equations is the same, it seems plausible that the unobserved heterogeneity in different equations is correlated.

8.6 Mixed Multivariate Models

8.6.1 *Discrete Choice and Counts*

In some studies the objective is to analyze several types of events that are mutually exclusive and collectively exhaustive. Such models involve two types of discrete outcomes. An example is the frequency of visits to alternative recreational sites. Typically one observes $(y_{ij}, \mathbf{x}_{ij};\ i = 1, \ldots, n;\ j = 1, \ldots, M)$ where i is the individual subscript and j is the destination subscript. The variable y measures trip frequency and $\mathbf{x}$ refers to covariates. In this section we consider a framework for modeling such data. For simplicity we suppress the subscript i.

The starting point in such an analysis is to condition on the total number of events across all types, using the multinomial distribution,

$$f(\mathbf{y} \mid N) = N! \frac{\prod_{j=1}^{M} p_j^{y_j}}{\prod_{j=1}^{M} y_j!}, \tag{8.37}$$

where $\mathbf{y} = (y_1, \ldots, y_M)$, $y_j \in \{0, 1, 2, \ldots; j = 1, \ldots, M\}$ where p_j denotes the probability of jth type of event, so that $\sum p_j = 1$, y_j denotes the frequency of the jth event, and $\sum y_j = N$ denotes the total number of outcomes across the alternatives. The multinomial distribution is conditional on the total number of all types of events, N. This is a useful specification for analyzing if N is given.

If it is assumed that each event frequency type has the Poisson density

$$f(y_j = r_j) = \frac{e^{-\mu_j} \mu_j^{r_j}}{r_j!}, \qquad y_j \in \{0, 1, 2, \ldots, \ j = 1, \ldots, M\},$$

then the frequencies of different events may be written as

$$f^*(y_1, \ldots, y_J) = \prod_{j=1}^{M} \frac{e^{-\mu_j} \mu_j^{r_j}}{r_j!}. \tag{8.38}$$

In this approach one simply estimates the Poisson regression for each type of event.

An alternative approach combines the conditional multinomial probability with the probability of the total number of events,

$$\Pr[\mathbf{y}] = \Pr\left[\sum y_j = N\right] \Pr[\mathbf{y} \mid N],$$

where the probability function $\Pr[\mathbf{y} \mid N]$ is sometimes based on the multinomial logit (Hausman, Leonard, and McFadden, 1995) or the conditional logit. Although in principle a more flexible specification such as the multinomial probit may be used, the choice of the multinomial logit is computationally more tractable when $M \geqq 3$.

Terza and Wilson (1990) propose a mixed multinomial (logit) Poisson model which is specified as

$$f^{MP}(\mathbf{y}) = \left(\prod_{j=1}^{M} p_j^{y_j}\right) \left(\frac{e^{-\mu} \mu^{\left[\sum_{j=1}^{M} y_j\right]}}{\prod_{j=1}^{M} y_j!}\right),$$

where

$$p_j = \frac{\exp[\mathbf{x}_j' \boldsymbol{\beta}_j]}{\sum_{j=1}^{M} \exp[\mathbf{x}_j' \boldsymbol{\beta}_j]}$$

$$\mu = \sum_{j=1}^{M} \mu_j,$$

$$\mu_j = p_j \mu.$$

Combining these equations with the (8.38) specification, it is seen that the mixed multinomial Poisson and the M individual Poisson specifications are equivalent.

The estimation of the mixed model by maximum likelihood is simplified on noting that the log-likelihood is additive in the parameters $(\boldsymbol{\beta}_1, \ldots, \boldsymbol{\beta}_M)$ and μ. Hence, to maximize the likelihood one can *sequentially* estimate the sublikelihoods for the Poisson model for the total number of events, N, and for the multinomial model for the choice probabilities, although not necessarily in that order.

This analysis remains valid if the Poisson specification is replaced by one of the modified or generalized variants discussed in Chapter 4, and the multinomial logit is replaced by a nested multinomial logit. For example, Terza and Wilson (1990) use a mixed multinomial logit and Poisson hurdles specification.

Hausman, Leonard, and McFadden (1995) develop a joint model of choice of recreational sites and number of recreational trips. They use panel data from a large-scale telephone survey of Alaskan residents. Although there are similarities with Terza and Wilson (1990), their model explicitly incorporates restrictions from utility theory. The model conforms to a two-stage budgeting process. First a multinomial model is specified and estimated for explaining the choice of recreational sites in Alaska. Explanatory variables $\mathbf{x}$ include the prices associated with the choice of sites. The estimates from this model are used to construct a price index for recreational trips. This price index subsequently becomes an explanatory variable in the count model for total number of trips, which the authors specify as a fixed-effects Poisson (see Chapter 9). The two-step modeling approach is described as *utility consistent* in the sense that it is consistent with two-stage consumer budgeting. At step one the consuming unit allocates a utility-maximizing expenditure on the total number of trips. At the second stage this amount is optimally allocated across trips to alternative sites.

8.6.2 *Counts and Continuous Variables*

We begin with an example (van Praag and Vermeulen, 1993) in which the data consist of number of events (shopping trips or number of plane trips), denoted by y_1, and the vector of outcomes (recorded expenditures), denoted by $\mathbf{y}_2' = (y_{21}, \ldots, y_{2k})$ where k refers to the number of events, $y_1 = k$. The objective is to formulate a joint probability model

$$f(y_1 \mid \boldsymbol{\theta}_1) g(\mathbf{y}_2 \mid \boldsymbol{\theta}_2, y_1) = \Pr[y_1 = k] \Pr\left[\mathbf{y}_2' = (y_{21}, \ldots, y_{2k})\right],$$

where $(\boldsymbol{\theta}_1, \boldsymbol{\theta}_2)$ are unknown parameters, and $\mathbf{x}$ is a set of explanatory variables.

In one formulation the joint modeling is accomplished by assuming that conditional on $\mathbf{x}$ the variables y_1 and $\mathbf{y}_2$ are stochastically independent. One could interpret this to mean that the dependency is captured through $\mathbf{x}$. Under this assumption the joint log-likelihood $\mathcal{L}(\boldsymbol{\theta}_1, \boldsymbol{\theta}_2)$ factors into a component for count and another component for the amount, which may be estimated separately. The assumptions permit one to specify a flexible model for the counts, accounting for example for the presence of excess of zero counts due to taste differences in the population, and possible truncation of expenditures due to, for example, expenditures smaller than a specified amount, say $y_{2,\min}$, not being recorded. van Praag and Vermeulen (1993) estimate a count–amount model for tobacco, bakery, and aggregate food expenditures in which the frequencies are modeled by a zero-inflated NB model and the amounts are modeled by a truncated normal.

The assumption of stochastic independence is convenient because it simplifies maximum likelihood estimation by making the log-likelihood functionally separable in the components $\boldsymbol{\theta}_1$ and $\boldsymbol{\theta}_2$, but in certain cases the assumption may be tenuous. For example, in the above case of the count–amount model, consider the availability of bulk discounts in shopping, which may provide an incentive for larger but fewer transactions. This dependency might be captured by using bulk discount as an explanatory variable.

Maximum likelihood modeling of counts and amounts, or counts and other discrete variables, allowing for stochastic dependencies, is problematic because of the obvious difficulty of formulating suitable joint probability distributions. In such cases moment-based estimators have a greater appeal.

8.7 Derivations

Kocherlakota and Kocherlakota (1993) show several ways in which the bivariate Poisson distribution may arise. The method of trivariate reduction is one that is commonly used. The joint pgf of y_1 and y_2 defined at (8.6) and (8.7) is

$$\begin{aligned} P(z_1, z_2) &= \mathsf{E}\left[z_1^{y_1} z_2^{y_2}\right] \\ &= \mathsf{E}\left[z_1^{u} z_2^{v} (z_1 z_2)^{w}\right] \\ &= \exp[\mu_1(z_1 - 1) + \mu_2(z_2 - 1) + \mu_3(z_1 z_2 - 1)] \\ &= \exp[(\mu_1 + \mu_3)(z_1 - 1) + (\mu_2 + \mu_3)(z_2 - 1) \\ &\qquad + \mu_3(z_1 - 1)(z_2 - 1)]. \end{aligned} \tag{8.39}$$

The marginal pgf are

$$P_j(z) = \exp[(\mu_j + \mu_3)(z - 1)], \quad j = 1, 2, \tag{8.40}$$

whence the marginal distributions are $y_1 \sim \mathsf{P}[\mu_1 + \mu_3]$ and $y_2 \sim \mathsf{P}[\mu_2 + \mu_3]$. The condition for the independence of y_1 and y_2 is that the joint pgf is the product of the two marginals, which is true iff $\mu_3 = 0$.

To derive the joint probability function expand (8.39) in powers of z_1 and z_2 as

$$P[z_1, z_2] = \exp[\mu_1 + \mu_2 + \mu_3] \sum_{i=0}^{\infty} \frac{\mu_1^i z_1^i}{i!} \sum_{j=0}^{\infty} \frac{\mu_2^j z_2^j}{j!} \sum_{k=0}^{\infty} \frac{\mu_3^k z_1^k z_2^k}{k!}, \tag{8.41}$$

which yields the joint frequency distribution as the coefficient of $z_1^r z_2^s$:

$$f(y_1 = r, y_2 = s) = \exp[\mu_1 + \mu_2 + \mu_3] \sum_{i=0}^{\min(r,s)} \frac{\mu_1^{r-i} \mu_2^{s-i} \mu_3^i}{(r-i)!(s-i)!i!}. \tag{8.42}$$

The covariance between y_1 and y_2, using the independence of u, v, w, is given by

$$\begin{aligned} \mathsf{Cov}[y_1, y_2] &= \mathsf{Cov}[u + w, v + w] \\ &= \mathsf{V}[w] \\ &= \mu_3, \end{aligned}$$

and the correlation is given by

$$\mathsf{Cov}[y_1, y_2]/\sqrt{\mathsf{V}[y_1]\,\mathsf{V}[y_2]} = \mu_3/\sqrt{(\mu_1 + \mu_3)(\mu_2 + \mu_3)}.$$

Jung and Winkelmann (1993, pp. 555–556) provide first and second derivatives of the log-likelihood.

If the method of trivariate reduction is used, zero correlation between any pair implies independence.

8.8 Bibliographic Notes

An introductory survey of multivariate extensions of GLMs is given in Fahrmeier and Tutz (1994); see especially their treatment of multivariate models with correlated responses. Formal statistical properties of bivariate discrete models are found in Kocherlakota and Kocherlakota (1993) and Johnson, Kotz, and Balakrishnan (1997). Aitchison and Ho (1989) study a multivariate Poisson with log-normal heterogeneity. Lindeboom and van den Berg (1994) analyze the impact of heterogeneity on correlation between survival times in bivariate survival models; their results are suggestive of consequences to be expected in bivariate count models. Arnold and Strauss (1988, 1992) and Moschopoulos and Staniswalis (1994) have considered the problem of estimating the parameters of bivariate exponential family distributions with given conditionals. The econometric literature on estimation of multivariate models under conditional moment restrictions is relevant if the nonlinear generalized least squares or SPGLS approach is followed. But only some of this relates easily to count models; see Newey (1990a) and Chamberlain (1992a). Jung and Winkelmann (1993) consider the number of voluntary and involuntary job changes as a bivariate Poisson process; Mayer and Chappell (1992) apply it to study determinants of entry and exit of firms. Bivariate count models have also been used in sociology and political science. For example, Good and Pirog-Good (1989) consider several bivariate count models for teenage delinquency and paternity, but without the regression component. King (1989a) presented a bivariate model of U.S. presidential vetoes of social welfare and defense policy legislation with a regression component. Meghir and Robin (1992) develop and estimate a joint model of frequency of purchase and a consumer demand system for eight types of foodstuffs using French data on households that were observed to purchase all eight foodstuffs over the survey period. They show that consistent estimation of the demand system may require data on frequency of purchase. They adopt a sequential approach in which a frequency-of-purchase equation is estimated by NLS, and the ratio of the fitted mean to actual frequency of purchase is used to weight all observed expenditures. A system of demand equations is fitted using these reweighted expenditures.

CHAPTER 9

Longitudinal Data

9.1 Introduction

Longitudinal data or *panel data* are observations on a cross-section of individual units such as persons, households, firms, and regions that are observed over several time periods. The data structure is similar to that of multivariate data considered in Chapter 8. Analysis is simpler than for multivariate data because for each individual unit the same outcome variable is observed, rather than several different outcome variables. Analysis is more complex because this same outcome variable is observed at different points in time, introducing time series data considerations presented in Chapter 7.

In this chapter we consider longitudinal data analysis if the dependent variable is a count variable. Remarkably, many count regression applications are to longitudinal data rather than simpler cross-section data. Econometrics examples include the number of patents awarded to each of many individual firms over several years, the number of accidents in each of several regions, and the number of days of absence for each of many persons over several years. A political science example is the number of protests in each of several different countries over many years. A biological and health science example is the number of occurrences of a specific health event, such as seizure, for each of many patients in each of several time periods.

A key advantage of longitudinal data over cross-section data is that they permit more general types of individual heterogeneity. Excellent motivation was provided by Neyman (1965), who pointed out that panel data enable one to control for heterogeneity and thereby distinguish between true and apparent contagion. For example, consider estimating the impact of research and development expenditures on the number of patent applications by a firm, controlling for individual firm-specific propensity to patent. For a single cross-section these controls can only depend on observed firm-specific attributes such as industry, and estimates may be inconsistent if there is additionally an unobserved component to individual firm-specific propensity to patent. With longitudinal data one can additionally include a firm-specific term for unobserved firm-specific propensity to patent.

The simplest longitudinal count data regression models are standard count models, with the addition of an individual specific term reflecting individual heterogeneity. In a *fixed effects* model this is a separate parameter for each individual. Creative estimation methods are needed if there are many individuals and hence parameters in the sample. In a *random effects* model this individual specific term is instead drawn from a specified distribution. Then creativity is required either in choosing a distribution that leads to tractable analytical results or in obtaining estimates if results are not tractable.

Asymptotic theory requires that the number of observations, here the number of individual units times the number of time periods, goes to infinity. We focus on the most common case of a *short panel*, in which only a few time periods are observed and the number of cross-sectional units goes to infinity. We also consider briefly the case in which the number of cross-sectional units is small but is observed for a large number of periods, as can be the case for cross-country studies. Then the earlier discussion for handling individual specific terms is mirrored in a similar discussion for time-specific effects. It is important to realize that the distribution of estimators, and which estimators are preferred, varies according to the type of sampling scheme.

In longitudinal data analysis the data are assumed to be independent over individual units for a given year but are permitted to be correlated over time for a given individual unit. In the simplest models this correlation over time is assumed to be adequately controlled for by individual-specific effects. In more general models *correlation* over time is additionally introduced in ways similar to those used in time series analysis. Finally, as in time series models, one can consider *dynamic models* or *transition models* that add a dynamic component to the regression function, allowing the dependent variable this year to depend on its own value in previous years.

A review of the standard linear models for longitudinal data, with fixed effects and random effects, is given in section 9.2, along with a statement of the analogous models for count data. In section 9.3 fixed effects models for count data are presented, along with application to data on the number of patents awarded to each of 346 firms in each of the years 1975 through 1979. Random effects models are studied in section 9.4. In sections 9.3 and 9.4 both MLEs and moment-based estimators are detailed. A discussion of applications and of the relative merits of fixed effects and random effects approaches is given in section 9.5. Model specification tests are presented in section 9.6. Dynamic models, in which the regressors include lagged dependent variables, are studied in section 9.7.

9.2 Models for Longitudinal Data

In this chapter we consider almost exclusively models that include fixed or random individual-specific effects. Even simpler models ignore such effects, assuming that the variation in regressors across individuals is sufficient to capture the differences in the dependent variable across individuals. We give little attention to these simpler models, as they do not exploit the advantage of longitudinal data over cross-section data.

9.2.1 *Linear Models*

Standard references for linear models for longitudinal data include Hsiao (1986), Diggle, Liang, and Zeger (1994), and Baltagi (1995). We give a brief review.

A quite general linear model for longitudinal data is

$$y_{it} = \alpha_{it} + \mathbf{x}_{it}'\boldsymbol{\beta}_{it} + u_{it}, \qquad i = 1, \ldots, n, \quad t = 1, \ldots, T, \tag{9.1}$$

where y_{it} is a scalar dependent variable, $\mathbf{x}_{it}$ is a $k \times 1$ vector of independent variables and u_{it} is a scalar disturbance term. The subscript i indexes an individual person, firm, or country in a cross-section, and the subscript t indexes time. The distinguishing feature of longitudinal data models is that the intercept α_{it} and regressor coefficients $\boldsymbol{\beta}_{it}$ may differ across individuals or time. Such variation in coefficients reflects individual and time-specific effects. But the model (9.1) is too general and is not estimable. Further restrictions need to be placed on the extent to which α_{it} and $\boldsymbol{\beta}_{it}$ vary with i and t, and on the behavior of the error u_{it}.

The simplest linear model is the *one-way individual-specific effect* model

$$y_{it} = \alpha_i + \mathbf{x}_{it}'\boldsymbol{\beta} + u_{it}, \qquad i = 1, \ldots, n, \quad t = 1, \ldots, T, \tag{9.2}$$

where u_{it} is iid with mean 0 and variance σ_u^2. This is the standard linear regression model, except that rather than one intercept α there are n individual specific intercepts $\alpha_1, \ldots, \alpha_n$. The two standard models based on (9.2) are the *fixed effects linear* model, which treats α_i as a parameter to be estimated and excludes an intercept from $\mathbf{x}_{it}$, and the *random effects linear* model, which treats α_i as an iid random variable with mean 0 and variance σ_α^2 and includes an intercept in $\mathbf{x}_{it}$.

For the fixed effects linear model the estimator of the slope coefficients is

$$\hat{\boldsymbol{\beta}}_{\mathsf{LFE}} = \left[\sum_{i=1}^{n}\sum_{t=1}^{T}(\mathbf{x}_{it} - \bar{\mathbf{x}}_i)(\mathbf{x}_{it} - \bar{\mathbf{x}}_i)'\right]^{-1} \sum_{i=1}^{n}\sum_{t=1}^{T}(\mathbf{x}_{it} - \bar{\mathbf{x}}_i)(y_{it} - \bar{y}_i), \tag{9.3}$$

where $\bar{\mathbf{x}}_i = \frac{1}{T}\sum_{t=1}^{T}\mathbf{x}_{it}$ and $\bar{y}_i = \frac{1}{T}\sum_{t=1}^{T}y_{it}$ are individual-specific averages over time. The individual-specific fixed effects can be estimated by $\hat{\alpha}_i = \bar{y}_i - \bar{\mathbf{x}}_i'\hat{\boldsymbol{\beta}}_{\mathsf{LFE}}$. For a short panel, that is, $n \to \infty$ and T is fixed, $\hat{\boldsymbol{\beta}}_{\mathsf{FE}}$ is consistent for $\boldsymbol{\beta}$, while $\hat{\alpha}_i$ is not consistent for α_i as only T observations are used in estimating each α_i.

The linear fixed effects estimator $\hat{\boldsymbol{\beta}}_{\mathsf{LFE}}$ can be motivated in several ways. First, joint estimation of α and $\boldsymbol{\beta}$ in (9.2) by OLS yields (9.3) for $\boldsymbol{\beta}$. Second, if ε_{it} is assumed to be normally distributed, then (9.3) is obtained by maximizing with respect to $\boldsymbol{\beta}$ the conditional likelihood function given $\sum_{t=1}^{T} y_{it}$,

$i = 1, \ldots, n$, where $\sum_{t=1}^{T} y_{it}$ can be shown to be the sufficient statistic for α_i. Third, (9.2) implies

$$(y_{it} - \bar{y}_i) = (\mathbf{x}_{it} - \bar{\mathbf{x}}_i)'\boldsymbol{\beta} + (u_{it} - \bar{u}_i), \tag{9.4}$$

meaning that differencing around the mean eliminates α_i. The GLS estimator of this equation can be shown to be OLS, and OLS of $(y_{it} - \bar{x}_i)$ on $(\mathbf{x}_{it} - \bar{\mathbf{x}}_i)$ yields (9.3). Using this interpretation $\hat{\boldsymbol{\beta}}_{\mathsf{LFE}}$ is called the *within estimator* as it explains variation in y_{it} around $\bar{y}_i$ by variation in $\mathbf{x}_{it}$ around $\bar{\mathbf{x}}_i$ – only variation within each individual is used.

For the random effects linear model the estimator of the slope coefficient estimator $\hat{\boldsymbol{\beta}}_{\mathsf{LRE}}$ can be shown to be a matrix-weighted average of $\hat{\boldsymbol{\beta}}_{\mathsf{LFE}}$, defined in (9.3), and $\hat{\boldsymbol{\beta}}_{\mathsf{LB}}$ obtained from the OLS regression

$$(\bar{y}_i - \bar{y}) = (\bar{\mathbf{x}}_i - \bar{\mathbf{x}})'\boldsymbol{\beta} + (\bar{u}_i - \bar{u}),$$

where $\bar{\mathbf{x}} = \frac{1}{n}\sum_{i=1}^{n} \bar{\mathbf{x}}_i$ and $\bar{y} = \frac{1}{n}\sum_{i=1}^{n} \bar{y}_i$. The estimator $\hat{\boldsymbol{\beta}}_{\mathsf{LB}}$ is called the *between estimator* as it uses only variation between individuals, essentially ignoring the additional information available in a panel compared with a single cross-section. The weights used to form $\hat{\boldsymbol{\beta}}_{\mathsf{LRE}}$ from $\hat{\boldsymbol{\beta}}_{\mathsf{LFE}}$ and $\hat{\boldsymbol{\beta}}_{\mathsf{LB}}$ depend on the variances σ_u^2 and σ_α^2. See basic treatments of this model.

The random effects estimator can be obtained in several ways. First, given the assumptions on the means and variances of u_{it} and α_i, it is the GLS estimator from estimation of (9.2). Second, it is asymptotically equivalent to the MLE, which additionally assumes that u_{it} and α_i are normally distributed. The MLE in practice leads in small samples to different estimates of the variances σ_u^2 and σ_α^2, and hence a different estimator of $\boldsymbol{\beta}$, and is more difficult to estimate, as the log-likelihood is nonlinear in the parameters. A third method, which provides better small-sample estimates of σ_u^2 and σ_α^2, is the restricted MLE method of Patterson and Thompson (1971) and Harville (1977), reviewed in Diggle, Liang, and Zeger (1994, pp. 65–68).

The random and fixed effects linear models are compared by, for example, Hsiao (1986, pp. 41–47). The models are conceptually different, with the fixed effects analysis being conditional on the effects for individuals in the sample; random effects is an unconditional or marginal analysis with respect to the population. A major practical difference is that the fixed effects analysis provides only estimates of time-varying regressors. Thus, for example, it does not allow estimation of an indicator variable for whether or not a patient in a clinical trial was taking the drug under investigation (rather than a placebo). Another major difference is that the random effects model assumption that individual effects are iid implies that individual effects are uncorrelated with the regressors. If, instead, unobserved individual effects are correlated with observed effects, the random effects estimator is inconsistent. Many econometrics studies in particular prefer fixed effects estimators because of this potential problem.

Standard extensions to the linear model (9.2) are serial correlation in the error, for example, $u_{it} = \rho u_{it-1} + \varepsilon_{it}$; dynamic models, for example, $\mathbf{x}_{it}$ including

$y_{i,t-1}$; and more general random effects models with random slope coefficients in addition to random intercepts, for example, $\mathbf{x}'_{it}\boldsymbol{\beta}$ is replaced by $\mathbf{x}'_{1it}\boldsymbol{\beta}_1 + \mathbf{x}'_{2it}\boldsymbol{\beta}_{2i}$ where $\boldsymbol{\beta}_{2i}$ is iid with mean $\boldsymbol{\beta}_2$ and variance $\boldsymbol{\Sigma}_{\beta_2}$.

9.2.2 *Count Models*

For count models for longitudinal data, the starting point is the Poisson regression model with exponential mean function and multiplicative individual specific term

$$\begin{aligned} y_{it} &\sim \mathsf{P}[\mu_{it} = \alpha_i \lambda_{it}] \\ \lambda_{it} &= \exp(\mathbf{x}'_{it}\boldsymbol{\beta}), \qquad i = 1, \ldots, n, \quad t = 1, \ldots, T. \end{aligned} \tag{9.5}$$

Note that α used here refers to the individual effect and is not used in the same way as in previous chapters, where it was an overdispersion parameter.

In the fixed effects model the α_i are unknown parameters. Like the linear model, estimation is possible by eliminating α_i, either by conditioning on $\sum_{t=1}^{T} y_{it}$, which requires fully parametric assumptions, or by using a quasi-differencing procedure that requires only first-moment assumptions.

In the random effects model the α_i are instead iid random variables. As in the linear model, estimation is possible either by assuming a distribution for α_i or by making second-moment assumptions, although unlike in the linear model under normality these can lead to quite different estimators.

A key departure from the linear model is that the individual specific effects in (9.5) are multiplicative, rather than additive as in the linear model (9.2). Given the exponential form for λ_{it}, the multiplicative effects can still be interpreted as a shift in the intercept because

$$\begin{aligned} \mathsf{E}[y_{it} \mid \mathbf{x}_{it}, \alpha_i] &= \mu_{it} \\ &= \alpha_i \exp(\mathbf{x}'_{it}\boldsymbol{\beta}) \\ &= \exp(\delta_i + \mathbf{x}'_{it}\boldsymbol{\beta}), \end{aligned} \tag{9.6}$$

where $\delta_i = \ln \alpha_i$.

Note that this equality between multiplicative effects and intercept shift does not hold in some count data models, nor does it hold in noncount models such as binary models to which similar longitudinal methods might be applied. Suppose the starting point is a more general conditional mean function $g(\mathbf{x}'_{it}\boldsymbol{\beta})$. Then some models and estimation methods continue with multiplicative effects, so

$$\mathsf{E}[y_{it} \mid \mathbf{x}_{it}, \alpha_i] = \mu_{it} = \alpha_i g(\mathbf{x}'_{it}\boldsymbol{\beta}), \tag{9.7}$$

while other methods use a shift in the intercept

$$\mathsf{E}[y_{it} \mid \mathbf{x}_{it}, \alpha_i] = \mu_{it} = g(\delta_i + \mathbf{x}'_{it}\boldsymbol{\beta}). \tag{9.8}$$

Results are most easily obtained for the Poisson. Extensions to the negative binomial do not always work, and when they do work they do so for some methods for the NB1 model and in other cases for the NB2 model. It should be kept in mind, however, that a common reason for such extensions in using cross-section data is to control for unobserved heterogeneity. The longitudinal data methods already control for heterogeneity, and Poisson longitudinal models may be sufficient.

The following sections begin with fixed effects and random effects models, with no consideration to either serial correlation and dynamics. In particular, for multiplicative effects models the regressors $\mathbf{x}_{it}$ are initially assumed to be *strictly exogenous*, so that

$$\mathsf{E}[y_{it} \mid \mathbf{x}_{i1}, \ldots, \mathbf{x}_{iT}, \alpha_i] = \alpha_i \lambda_{it}. \tag{9.9}$$

This is a stronger condition than $\mathsf{E}[y_{it} \mid \mathbf{x}_{it}, \alpha_i] = \alpha_i \lambda_{it}$. This condition is relaxed when time series models are presented in section 9.7.

9.3 Fixed Effects Models

We consider three approaches to estimation of fixed effect count data models. First, we consider direct estimation by maximum likelihood, which may not necessarily lead to consistent estimates for the common case in which T is fixed and $n \to \infty$. Second, we present conditional maximum likelihood, which does analysis conditional on sufficient statistics for the individual effects. This works for NB1 models in addition to Poisson. Third, we consider a moment-based approach that bases estimation on a differencing transformation, which differs from that in the linear model, as here the effects are multiplicative, not additive.

9.3.1 *Maximum Likelihood*

The simplest fixed effects model for count data is the *Poisson fixed effects* model (9.5) where, conditional on λ_{it} and parameters α_i, y_{it} is iid $\mathsf{P}[\mu_{it} = \alpha_i \lambda_{it}]$, λ_{it} is a specified function of $\mathbf{x}_{it}$ and $\boldsymbol{\beta}$, and $\mathbf{x}_{it}$ excludes an intercept. At times we specialize to the exponential form (9.6).

If n is small this model is easily estimated. In particular, the exponential mean specification (9.6) can be rewritten as $\exp(\sum_{j=1}^{n} \delta_j d_{jit} + \mathbf{x}_{it}'\boldsymbol{\beta})$, where d_{jit} is an indicator variable equal to one if the it^{th} observation is for individual j and zero otherwise. Thus we can use standard Poisson software to regress y_{it} on $d_{1it}, d_{2it}, \ldots, d_{nit}$ and $\mathbf{x}_{it}$.

This is impractical, however, if n is so large that $(n + \dim(\boldsymbol{\beta}))$ exceeds software restrictions on the maximum number of regressors. In this chapter we focus on the case in which n is large and T is small, in which case this barrier is likely to be encountered. Then analytical expressions for estimators of $\boldsymbol{\beta}$ and the α_i are needed, analogous to those obtained for the linear model by partitioning of the OLS estimator.

A potentially more serious problem is possible inconsistency of parameter estimates if T is small and $n \to \infty$. This possibility arises because as $n \to \infty$ the number of parameters, $n + \dim(\boldsymbol{\beta})$, to be estimated goes to infinity, possibly negating the benefit of a larger sample size, nT. The individual fixed effects can be viewed as *incidental parameters*, because real interest lies in the slope coefficients. For some fixed effects panel data models, too many incidental parameters lead to inconsistent parameter estimates of $\boldsymbol{\beta}$, in addition to α_i. A leading example is the logit model with fixed effects, with

$$\Pr[y_{it}=1]=\left[\alpha_i+\exp\left(\mathbf{x}_{it}'\boldsymbol{\beta}\right)\right]/\left[1+\alpha_i+\exp\left(\mathbf{x}_{it}'\boldsymbol{\beta}\right)\right].$$

Hsiao (1986, section 7.3.1) demonstrates the inconsistency of the MLE for $\boldsymbol{\beta}$ in this case, for fixed T and $n \to \infty$. This inconsistency disappears, of course, if $T \to \infty$. In the case of the linear model, however, there is no such incidental parameters problem.

An interesting question therefore is whether there is an incidental parameters problem for the Poisson fixed effects model. The literature has generally not directly addressed this issue, although it has suggested that there is a problem.* For y_{it} iid $\mathsf{P}[\alpha_i\lambda_{it}]$, the conditional joint density for the ith observation is

$$\begin{aligned}\Pr\left[y_{i1},\ldots,y_{iT}\mid\alpha_i,\boldsymbol{\beta}\right] &= \prod_t\left[\exp(-\alpha_i\lambda_{it})\,(\alpha_i\lambda_{it})^{y_{it}}/y_{it}!\right]\\ &= \exp\left(-\alpha_i\sum_t\lambda_{it}\right)\prod_t\alpha_i^{y_{it}}\prod_t\lambda_{it}^{y_{it}}\Big/\prod_t y_{it}!.\end{aligned} \tag{9.10}$$

The corresponding log-density is

$$\begin{aligned}\ln\Pr\left[y_{i1},\ldots,y_{iT}\mid\alpha_i,\boldsymbol{\beta}\right] = -\alpha_i\sum_t\lambda_{it} + \ln\alpha_i\sum_t y_{it}\\ +\sum_t y_{it}\ln\lambda_{it}-\sum_t\ln y_{it}!.\end{aligned}$$

Differentiating with respect to α_i and setting to zero yields

$$\hat{\alpha}_i=\frac{\sum_t y_{it}}{\sum_t\lambda_{it}}. \tag{9.11}$$

Substituting this back into (9.10), simplifying and considering all n observations yields the concentrated likelihood function,

$$\begin{aligned}\mathsf{L}_{\text{conc}}(\boldsymbol{\beta}) &= \prod_i\left[\exp\left(-\sum_t y_{it}\right)\prod_t\left(\frac{\sum_t y_{it}}{\sum_t\lambda_{it}}\right)^{y_{it}}\prod_t\lambda_{it}^{y_{it}}\Big/\prod_t y_{it}!\right]\\ &\propto \prod_i\left[\prod_t\left(\frac{\lambda_{it}}{\sum_s\lambda_{is}}\right)^{y_{it}}\right].\end{aligned} \tag{9.12}$$

* We thank Frank Windmeijer and Tony Lancaster for pointing out that there is no incidental parameters problem here. The proof given here is due to Tony Lancaster.

This is the likelihood for n independent observations on a T-dimensional multinomial variable with cell probabilities

$$p_{it} = \frac{\lambda_{it}}{\sum_s \lambda_{is}} = \frac{\exp(\mathbf{x}'_{it}\boldsymbol{\beta})}{\sum_s \exp(\mathbf{x}'_{is}\boldsymbol{\beta})}.$$

It follows that for the Poisson fixed effects model there is no incidental parameters problem. Estimates of $\boldsymbol{\beta}$ that are consistent for fixed T and $n \rightarrow \infty$ can be obtained by maximization of $\ln \mathsf{L}_{\text{conc}}(\boldsymbol{\beta})$ in (9.12). The first-order conditions for this estimator are given in section 9.3.2, and its distribution is given in section 9.3.3 under much weaker conditions than those assumed here. Estimates of α_i can then be obtained from (9.11) and are consistent if in fact $T \rightarrow \infty$.

This consistency of the MLE for $\boldsymbol{\beta}$ despite the presence of incidental parameters is a special result that holds for the Poisson multiplicative fixed effects and, for continuous data, linear additive fixed effects. It holds in few other models, if any, in which case we need to transform the model into one in which the individual effects do not appear. The next two subsections present different ways to do this. We begin with the simplest case, the Poisson, even though as already noted there is no incidental parameters problem in this case.

9.3.2 *Conditional Maximum Likelihood*

The *conditional maximum likelihood* approach of Andersen (1970) performs inference conditional on the sufficient statistics for $\alpha_1, \ldots, \alpha_n$, which for LEF densities such as the Poisson are the individual-specific totals $T\bar{y}_i = \sum_{t=1}^{T} y_{it}$. In section 9.8.1 it is shown that for y_{it} iid $\mathsf{P}[\mu_{it}]$, the conditional joint density for the ith observation is

$$\Pr\left[y_{i1}, \ldots, y_{iT} \,\middle|\, \sum_{t=1}^{T} y_{it}\right] = \frac{\left(\sum_t y_{it}\right)!}{\prod_t y_{it}!} \times \prod_t \left(\frac{\mu_{it}}{\sum_s \mu_{is}}\right)^{y_{it}}. \tag{9.13}$$

This is a multinomial distribution, with probabilities $p_{it} = \mu_{it}/\sum_t \mu_{it}$, $t = 1, \ldots, T$, which has already been used in section 8.6.

Models with multiplicative effects set $\mu_{it} = \alpha_i \lambda_{it}$. This has the advantage that simplification occurs as α_i cancels in the ratio $\mu_{it}/\sum_s \mu_{is}$. Then (9.13) becomes

$$\Pr\left[y_{i1}, \ldots, y_{iT} \,\middle|\, \sum_{t=1}^{T} y_{it}\right] = \frac{\left(\sum_t y_{it}\right)!}{\prod_t y_{it}!} \times \prod_t \left(\frac{\lambda_{it}}{\sum_s \lambda_{is}}\right)^{y_{it}}. \tag{9.14}$$

Because $y_{i1}, \ldots, y_{iT} \mid \sum_t y_{it}$ is multinomial distributed with probabilities $p_{i1}, \ldots, p_{iT}$, where $p_{it} = \lambda_{it}/\sum_s \lambda_{is}$, it follows that y_{it} has mean $p_{it} \sum_s y_{is}$. Given (9.6) this implies that we are essentially estimating the fixed effects α_i by $\sum_s y_{is}/\sum_s \lambda_{is}$.

In the special case $\lambda_{it} = \exp(\mathbf{x}'_{it}\boldsymbol{\beta})$ this becomes

$$\Pr\left[y_{i1},\ldots,y_{iT}\,\middle|\,\sum_{t=1}^{T} y_{it}\right] = \frac{(\sum_t y_{it})!}{\prod_t y_{it}!} \times \prod_t \left(\frac{\exp(\mathbf{x}'_{it}\boldsymbol{\beta})}{\sum_s \exp(\mathbf{x}'_{is}\boldsymbol{\beta})}\right)^{y_{it}}. \tag{9.15}$$

The *conditional* MLE of the *Poisson fixed effects model* $\hat{\boldsymbol{\beta}}_{\mathsf{PFE}}$ therefore maximizes the conditional log-likelihood function

$$\mathcal{L}_c(\boldsymbol{\beta}) = \sum_{i=1}^{n}\left[\ln\left(\sum_{t=1}^{T} y_{it}\right)! - \sum_{t=1}^{T}\ln(y_{it}!) + \sum_{t=1}^{T} y_{it}\ln\left(\frac{\exp(\mathbf{x}'_{it}\boldsymbol{\beta})}{\sum_{s=1}^{T}\exp(\mathbf{x}'_{is}\boldsymbol{\beta})}\right)\right]. \tag{9.16}$$

Note that this is proportional to the natural logarithm of $\mathsf{L}_{\text{conc}}(\boldsymbol{\beta})$ given in (9.12), and therefore here the concentrated MLE equals the MLE.

Differentiation of (9.16), or equivalently (9.12), with respect to $\boldsymbol{\beta}$ yields first-order conditions for $\hat{\boldsymbol{\beta}}_{\mathsf{PFE}}$ that can be reexpressed as

$$\sum_{i=1}^{n}\sum_{t=1}^{T}\mathbf{x}_{it}\left(y_{it} - \lambda_{it}\frac{\bar{y}_i}{\bar{\lambda}_i}\right) = \mathbf{0}, \tag{9.17}$$

where $\bar{y}_i = \frac{1}{T}\sum_t y_{it}$ and $\bar{\lambda}_i = \frac{1}{T}\sum_t \lambda_{it}$ and $\lambda_{it} = \exp(\mathbf{x}'_{it}\boldsymbol{\beta})$; see Blundell, Griffith, and Windmeijer (1995). The distribution of the resulting estimator can be obtained using standard maximum likelihood theory. In practice it is better to use results, given in the next subsection, obtained under weaker assumptions than y_{it} iid $\mathsf{P}[\alpha_i\lambda_{it}]$.

The log-likelihood function (9.16) is similar to that of the multinomial logit model, except that y_{it} is not restricted to taking only values zero or one and to sum over t to unity. Also the most standard form of a multinomial logit model with T outcomes has regressors fixed and parameters varying over the choices: $p_{it} = \exp(\mathbf{x}'_i\boldsymbol{\beta}_t)/\sum_{s=1}^{T}\exp(\mathbf{x}'_i\boldsymbol{\beta}_s)$. Here instead the parameters $\boldsymbol{\beta}$ are constant and the regressors $\mathbf{x}_{it}$ are time-varying.

The Poisson fixed effects model was proposed by Palmgren (1981) and Hausman, Hall, and Griliches (1984). The latter authors additionally presented a *negative binomial fixed effects* model. Then y_{it} is iid NB1 with parameters $\alpha_i\lambda_{it}$ and ϕ_i, where $\lambda_{it} = \exp(\mathbf{x}'_{it}\boldsymbol{\beta})$, so y_{it} has mean $\alpha_i\lambda_{it}/\phi_i$ and variance $(\alpha_i\lambda_{it}/\phi_i)\times(1+\alpha_i/\phi_i)$.

This negative binomial model is of the less common NB1 form, with the variance a multiple of the mean. The parameter α_i is the individual-specific fixed effect; the parameter ϕ_i is the negative binomial overdispersion parameter, which is permitted to vary across individuals. Clearly α_i and ϕ_i can only be identified to the ratio α_i/ϕ_i, and even this ratio drops out for conditional maximum likelihood.

Some considerable algebra yields the conditional joint density for the ith observation

$$\Pr\left[y_{i1}, \ldots, y_{iT} \,\middle|\, \sum_{t=1}^{T} y_{it} \right] = \left(\prod_t \frac{\Gamma(\lambda_{it} + y_{it})}{\Gamma(\lambda_{it})\Gamma(y_{it} + 1)} \right) \times \frac{\Gamma\left(\sum_t \lambda_{it}\right) \Gamma\left(\sum_t y_{it} + 1\right)}{\Gamma\left(\sum_t \lambda_{it} + \sum_t y_{it}\right)}, \tag{9.18}$$

which involves $\boldsymbol{\beta}$ through λ_{it} but does not involve α_i and ϕ_i. This distribution for integer λ_{it} is the negative hypergeometric distribution. The log-likelihood function follows from this density and the MLE $\hat{\boldsymbol{\beta}}_{\mathsf{NB1FE}}$ is obtained in the usual way.

McCullagh and Nelder (1989, section 7.2) consider the conditional maximum likelihood method in a quite general setting. Diggle, Liang, and Zeger (1994, section 9.2) specialize to GLMs with canonical link function (see section 2.4.4), in which case we again obtain the multinomial form (9.14). They also consider more general fixed effects in which the conditional mean function is of the form $g(\mathbf{x}_{it}'\boldsymbol{\beta} + \mathbf{d}_{it}'\boldsymbol{\alpha}_i)$ where $\mathbf{d}_{it}$ takes a finite number of values and $\boldsymbol{\alpha}_i$ is now a vector. Hsiao (1986) specializes to binary models and finds that the conditional maximum likelihood approach is tractable for the logit model but not the probit model; that is, the method is tractable for individual intercepts if the canonical link function is used.

9.3.3 *Moment-Based Methods*

In the linear model (9.2) with additive fixed effects, there are several ways to transform the model to eliminate the fixed effects and hence obtain a consistent estimator of $\boldsymbol{\beta}$. Examples are subtraction from y_{it} of the observation in another time period, say y_{i2}, or subtraction from y_{it} of the average over all time periods $\bar{y}_i$. The latter transformation, given in (9.4), yields the fixed effects estimator $\hat{\boldsymbol{\beta}}_{\mathsf{LFE}}$.

Similarly in the Poisson model (9.5) with multiplicative effects, there are several ways to transform the model to eliminate the multiplicative effect. One example is subtraction from y_{it} of the observation in another time period, say y_{i2}, where y_{i2} is scaled to have the same mean as y_{it}. Thus we consider $(y_{it} - (\lambda_{it}/\lambda_{i2})y_{i2})$. Alternatively we could subtract the average over all time periods, appropriately rescaled, and consider $(y_{it} - (\lambda_{it}/\bar{\lambda}_i)\bar{y}_i)$. Then given (9.9) it follows that

$$\mathsf{E}[(y_{it} - (\lambda_{it}/\bar{\lambda}_i)\bar{y}_i) \,|\, \mathbf{x}_{i1}, \ldots, \mathbf{x}_{iT}] = 0,$$

and hence

$$\mathsf{E}\left[\mathbf{x}_{it} \left(y_{it} - \frac{\lambda_{it}}{\bar{\lambda}_i} \bar{y}_i \right) \right] = \mathbf{0}. \tag{9.19}$$

This suggests method of moments estimation of β by solving the corresponding sample moment conditions

$$\sum_{i=1}^{n}\sum_{t=1}^{T}\mathbf{x}_{it}\left(y_{it}-\frac{\bar{y}_i}{\bar{\lambda}_i}\lambda_{it}\right)=\mathbf{0}. \tag{9.20}$$

These are the first-order conditions (9.17) of both the Poisson fixed effects conditional MLE $\hat{\beta}_{\mathsf{PFE}}$ and the Poisson fixed effects MLE from section 9.3.1. Thus, the essential requirement for consistency of $\hat{\beta}_{\mathsf{PFE}}$ is that (9.9) is the correct specification for the conditional mean. For example, $\hat{\beta}_{\mathsf{PFE}}$ is also a consistent estimate of β in the negative binomial fixed effects model. Furthermore, the distribution of $\hat{\beta}_{\mathsf{PFE}}$ can be obtained under weaker second-moment assumptions than variance–mean equality for y_{it}, or equivalently weaker than those imposed by the multinomial conditional distribution (9.15) for $y_{i1},\ldots,y_{iT}\mid\sum_t y_{it}$. The discussion is similar to that in section 3.2 for the cross-section Poisson model.

The first-order conditions (9.20) have first-derivative matrix with respect to β

$$\mathbf{A}_n=\sum_{i=1}^{n}\left[\sum_{t=1}^{T}\mathbf{x}_{it}\mathbf{x}_{it}'\frac{\bar{y}_i}{\bar{\lambda}_i}\lambda_{it}-\frac{1}{T}\sum_{t=1}^{T}\sum_{s=1}^{T}\mathbf{x}_{it}\mathbf{x}_{is}'\frac{\bar{y}_i}{\bar{\lambda}_i}\lambda_{it}\lambda_{is}\right], \tag{9.21}$$

for $\lambda_{it}=\exp(\mathbf{x}_{it}'\beta)$, while the outer product on taking expectations and eliminating cross-products in i and $j\neq i$ due to independence is

$$\mathbf{B}_n=\sum_{i=1}^{n}\sum_{t=1}^{T}\sum_{s=1}^{T}\mathbf{x}_{it}\mathbf{x}_{is}'\left(y_{it}-\frac{\bar{y}_i}{\bar{\lambda}_i}\lambda_{it}\right)\left(y_{is}-\frac{\bar{y}_i}{\bar{\lambda}_i}\lambda_{is}\right)'. \tag{9.22}$$

Using the general result in section 2.5.1, an estimator of $\mathsf{V}[\hat{\beta}_{\mathsf{PFE}}]$ that requires only first-moment assumptions, that is, the robust sandwich estimate, is

$$\mathsf{V}_{\mathsf{RS}}[\hat{\beta}_{\mathsf{PFE}}]=\hat{\mathbf{A}}_n^{-1}\hat{\mathbf{B}}_n\hat{\mathbf{A}}_n^{-1}, \tag{9.23}$$

where $\hat{\mathbf{A}}_n$ and $\hat{\mathbf{B}}_n$ are $\mathbf{A}_n$ and $\mathbf{B}_n$ evaluated at $\hat{\beta}_{\mathsf{PFE}}$. By contrast, usual maximum likelihood estimates of the standard error are $\hat{\mathbf{A}}_n^{-1}$, using minus the inverse of the second derivatives of the log-likelihood function, or $\hat{\mathbf{B}}_n^{-1}$ using the BHHH estimate. These MLEs of $\mathsf{V}[\hat{\beta}_{\mathsf{PFE}}]$ are inconsistent if the conditional variance does not equal the conditional mean $\alpha_i\mu_{it}$. If the conditional variance equals a constant γ times $\alpha_i\mu_{it}$, however, then a consistent estimate of $\mathsf{V}[\hat{\beta}_{\mathsf{PFE}}]$ is γ times $\hat{\mathbf{A}}_n^{-1}$ or $\hat{\mathbf{B}}_n^{-1}$.

A quite general treatment of the distribution of the multinomial conditional MLE is given by Wooldridge (1990c), who considers a multiplicative fixed effect for general specifications of $\lambda_{it}=g(\mathbf{x}_{it}'\beta)$. In addition to giving robust variance matrix estimates, he gives more efficient GMM estimators if the conditional mean is specified to be of form $\alpha_i\lambda_{it}$ with other moments not specified, and when additionally the variance is specified to be of the form $\psi_i\alpha_i\lambda_{it}$. Chamberlain (1992a) gives semiparametric efficiency bounds for models using only specified first moment of form (9.6). Attainment of these bounds is theoretically

Table 9.1. *Patents: Poisson PMLE with NB1 standard errors*

	Poisson PMLE		Poisson fixed effects CMLE		NB1 fixed effects CMLE	
Variable	Coefficient	Standard error	Coefficient	Standard error	Coefficient	Standard error
ln R_0	.19	.16	.32	.07	.32	.07
ln R_{-1}	−.07	.10	−.09	.10	−.08	.09
ln R_{-2}	.07	.10	.08	.09	.06	.09
ln R_{-3}	.06	.09	−.01	.08	−.01	.01
ln R_{-4}	.16	.08	−.01	.08	.04	.07
ln R_{-5}	.17	.12	−.03	.06	.01	.05
ln SIZE	.59	.07				
DSCI	.30	.13				
Sum ln R	.58		.32		.33	

Note: Poisson fixed effects conditional MLE with NB1 standard errors. NB1 fixed effects conditional MLE with MLE standard errors. All models include four time dummies for years 1976 to 1979.

possible but practically difficult, as it requires high-dimensional nonparametric regressions.

9.3.4 *Example: Patents*

Many longitudinal count-data studies, beginning with Hausman, Hall, and Griliches (1984), consider the relationship between past research and development (R&D) expenditures and the number of patents y_{it} awarded to the ith firm in the tth year, using data in a short panel. Here we consider data used by Hall, Griliches, and Hausman (1986) on 346 firms for 5 years' 1975 through 1979. Regression results are given in Table 9.1.

The Poisson PMLE estimates treat the data as one long cross-section, with y_{it} having conditional mean $\exp(\mathbf{x}_{it}'\beta)$. The reported standard errors are corrected for the considerable overdispersion in the data. The regressors of interest are $\ln R_0, \ldots, \ln R_{-5}$, the logarithm of current and up to 5 past years' research and development expenditures. Given the logarithmic transformation and the exponential conditional mean, the coefficient of $\ln R_{-j}$ is an elasticity, so that the coefficients of $\ln R_0, \ldots, \ln R_{-5}$ should sum to unity if a doubling of R&D expenditures leads to a doubling of patents. To control for firm-specific effects, the estimated model includes two time-invariant regressors, *SIZE*, the logarithm of firm book value in 1972 which is a measure of firm size, and *DSCI*, an indicator variable equal to one if the firm is in the science sector. If firm size doubles the number of patents increases by 59%.

The key empirical result for the Poisson PMLE estimates is that the coefficients of current and lagged R&D expenditures, $\ln R_{-j}$, sum to 0.58, which is considerably less than one, statistically so at conventional levels of significance. One possible explanation is that this is an artifact of failure to control adequately for firm-specific effects. However, the Poisson and NB1 fixed effects estimators, also given in Table 9.1, are even further away from one. (Estimated coefficients for ln *SIZE* and *DSCI* are not given, because the coefficients of time-invariant regressors are not identified in a fixed effects model.) These longitudinal estimators imply that in the long run a doubling of R&D expenditures leads to only a 33% increase in the number of patents. Qualitatively similar results have been found with other data sets and estimators, leading to a large literature on alternative estimators that may lead to results closer to a priori beliefs.

9.4 Random Effects Models

The simplest random effects model for count data is the *Poisson random effects* model. This model is given by (9.5), that is, y_{it} conditional on α_i and λ_{it} is iid Poisson ($\mu_{it} = \alpha_i \lambda_{it}$) and λ_{it} is a function of $\mathbf{x}_{it}$ and parameters $\boldsymbol{\beta}$. But in a departure from the fixed effects model, the α_i are iid random variables.

One approach is to specify the density $f(\alpha_i)$ of α_i and then integrate out α_i to obtain the joint density of $y_{i1}, \ldots, y_{iT}$ conditional on just $\lambda_{i1}, \ldots, \lambda_{iT}$. Then

$$\begin{aligned}\Pr[y_{i1}, \ldots, y_{iT}] &= \int_0^\infty \Pr[y_{i1}, \ldots, y_{iT} \mid \alpha_i] f(\alpha_i)\, d\alpha_i \\ &= \int_0^\infty \left[\prod_t \Pr[y_{it} \mid \alpha_i]\right] f(\alpha_i)\, d\alpha_i, \qquad (9.24)\end{aligned}$$

where for notational simplicity dependence on $\lambda_{i1}, \ldots, \lambda_{iT}$ is suppressed as in the fixed effects case. This integral appears similar to those in Chapter 4, except that here there is only one draw of α_i for the T random variables $y_{i1}, \ldots, y_{iT}$, so that this integral does not equal the product $\prod_t [\int_0^\infty \Pr[y_{it} \mid \alpha_i] f(\alpha_i)\, d\alpha_i]$ of mixtures considered in Chapter 4.

Different distributions for α_i lead to different distributions for $y_{i1}, \ldots, y_{iT}$. Analytical results can be obtained as they would be obtained in a similar Bayesian setting: by choosing $f(\alpha_i)$ to be conjugate to $\prod_t \Pr[y_{it} \mid \alpha_i]$. Conjugate densities exist for Poisson and NB2. In these standard count models the conjugate density is not the normal. Nonetheless there is considerable interest in results if $f(\alpha_i)$ is the normal density, because if results can be obtained for scalar α_i then they can be extended to random effects in slope coefficients. A number of methods have been proposed. Another solution if analytical results for the distribution are not available is to use moment methods if at least an analytical expression for the mean is available.

9.4.1 *Conjugate-Distributed Random Effects*

The gamma density is conjugate to the Poisson. In the pure cross-section case a Poisson–gamma mixture leads to the negative binomial; see section 4.2.2.

A similar result is obtained in the longitudinal setting. In section 9.8.2 it is shown that for y_{it} iid $\mathsf{P}[\alpha_i\lambda_{it}]$, where α_i is iid gamma(δ, δ) so that $\mathsf{E}[\alpha_i]=1$ and $\mathsf{V}[\alpha_i]=1/\delta$, integration with respect to α_i leads to the joint density for the ith individual

$$\Pr[y_{i1}, \ldots, y_{iT}] = \left[\prod_t \frac{\lambda_{it}{}^{y_{it}}}{y_{it}!}\right] \times \left(\frac{\delta}{\sum_t \lambda_{it} + \delta}\right)^{\delta} \times \left(\sum_t \lambda_{it} + \delta\right)^{-\sum_t y_{it}} \frac{\Gamma\left(\sum_t y_{it} + \delta\right)}{\Gamma(\delta)}. \tag{9.25}$$

This is the density of the Poisson random effects model (with gamma-distributed random effects). For this distribution $\mathsf{E}[y_{it}]=\lambda_{it}$ and $\mathsf{V}[y_{it}]=\lambda_{it}+\lambda_{it}^2/\delta$ so that overdispersion is of the NB2 form. Maximum likelihood estimation of β and δ is straightforward. For $\lambda_{it} = \exp(\mathbf{x}_{it}'\beta)$, the first-order conditions for $\hat{\beta}_{\mathsf{PRE}}$ can be expressed as

$$\sum_{i=1}^{n}\sum_{t=1}^{T} \mathbf{x}_{it}\left(y_{it} - \lambda_{it}\frac{\bar{y}_i + \delta/T}{\bar{\lambda}_i + \delta/T}\right) = \mathbf{0}; \tag{9.26}$$

see exercise 9.3. Thus this estimator, like the Poisson fixed effects estimator, can be interpreted as being based on a transformation of y_{it} to eliminate the individual effects, and consistency essentially requires correct specification of the conditional mean of y_{it}. As for NB2 in the cross-section case the information matrix is block-diagonal and the first-order conditions for δ are quite complicated.

Hausman, Hall, and Griliches (1984) proposed this model and additionally considered the negative binomial case. Then y_{it} is iid NB2 with parameters $\alpha_i\lambda_{it}$ and ϕ_i, where $\lambda_{it} = \exp(\mathbf{x}_{it}'\beta)$, and hence y_{it} has mean $\alpha_i\lambda_{it}/\phi_i$ and variance $(\alpha_i\lambda_{it}/\phi_i) \times (1+\alpha_i/\phi_i)$. It is assumed that $(1+\alpha_i/\phi_i)^{-1}$ is a beta-distributed random variable with parameters (a, b).

Hausman, Hall, and Griliches show after considerable algebra that the *negative binomial random effects* model (with beta-distributed random effects) has joint density for the ith individual

$$\Pr[y_{i1}, \ldots, y_{iT}] = \left(\prod_t \frac{\Gamma(\lambda_{it} + y_{it})!}{\Gamma(\lambda_{it})!\Gamma(y_{it}+1)!}\right) \times \frac{\Gamma(a+b)\,\Gamma\left(a + \sum_t \lambda_{it}\right)\Gamma\left(b + \sum_t y_{it}\right)}{\Gamma(a)\,\Gamma(b)\,\Gamma\left(a + b + \sum_t \lambda_{it} + \sum_t y_{it}\right)}. \tag{9.27}$$

This is the basis for maximum likelihood estimation of β, a, and b.

9.4.2 *Gaussian Random Effects*

An alternative random effects model is to allow the random effects to be normally distributed. In these models it is standard to assume an exponential mean function. Thus for the Poisson model the data y_{it} are assumed to be iid $\mathsf{P}[\exp(\delta_i + \mathbf{x}'_{it}\boldsymbol{\beta})]$, where the random effect δ_i is iid $\mathsf{N}[0, \sigma_\delta^2]$. From (9.6) this model can be rewritten as $y_{it} \sim \mathsf{P}[\alpha_i \exp(\mathbf{x}'_{it}\boldsymbol{\beta})]$, where $\alpha_i = \exp \delta_i$, and is therefore the preceding model where the random effects are log-normally distributed.

Unfortunately there is no analytical expression for the unconditional density (9.24) in this case. Development of estimation methods for such problems is an active area of research in generalized linear models. One solution (Schall, 1991; McGilchrist, 1994) is to linearize the model and use linear model techniques. An alternative is to directly compute the unconditional density by numerical integration or using simulation methods (Fahrmeir and Tutz, 1994, chapter 7). A recent example, using a Markov-chain Monte Carlo scheme to simulate, is Chib, Greenberg, and Winkelmann (1998). They apply their methods to epilepsy data from Diggle et al. (1994), patent data from Hall et al. (1986), and German work absence data.

9.4.3 *Moment-Based Methods*

In the linear random effects model (9.2) the OLS estimator from regression of y_{it} on $\mathbf{x}_{it}$ is still consistent. This is because if α_i is iid with zero mean the marginal mean of y_{it}, i.e., the mean conditional on $\mathbf{x}_{it}$ but marginal with respect to α_i, is $\mathbf{x}'_{it}\boldsymbol{\beta}$. The OLS standard errors need to be corrected for the correlation induced by the random effects α_i, however, and it is more efficient to use the GLS estimator discussed in section 9.2.1.

Zeger and Liang (1986) carried this idea over to random effects in GLMs. Ideally, one would estimate by nonlinear feasible GLS, but this is not practical because unlike the linear case there is no simple analytical way to invert the covariance matrix of $\mathbf{y}$ conditional on $\mathbf{x}$. Instead, following a similar approach to that of Zeger (1988) for serially correlated error time series models presented in section 7.6, Zeger and Liang proposed estimation by nonlinear WLS, with corrections made to standard errors to ensure that they are consistently estimated.

For count data it is assumed that the marginal distribution of y_{it}, that is conditional on $\mathbf{x}_{it}$ but marginal on α_i, has first two moments

$$\begin{aligned} \mu_{it} = \mathsf{E}[y_{it} \,|\, \mathbf{x}_{it}] &= \exp(\mathbf{x}'_{it}\boldsymbol{\beta}) \\ \sigma_{it}^2 = \mathsf{Var}[y_{it} \,|\, \mathbf{x}_{it}] &= \phi \exp(\mathbf{x}'_{it}\boldsymbol{\beta}), \end{aligned} \tag{9.28}$$

where the multiplicative scalar ϕ implies that the random effects induce heteroskedasticity of NB1 form. The random effects additionally induce correlation between y_{it} and y_{is}, but this correlation is ignored. A consistent estimator for $\boldsymbol{\beta}$ is the generalized estimating equations estimator or nonlinear WLS estimator

$\hat{\beta}_{\mathsf{WLS}}$, with first-order conditions

$$\sum_{i=1}^{n} \mathbf{D}_i' \hat{\mathbf{V}}_i (\mathbf{y}_i - \boldsymbol{\mu}_i) = \mathbf{0}, \tag{9.29}$$

where $\mathbf{D}_i$ is the $T \times k$ matrix with tj^{th} element $\partial \mu_{it} / \partial \beta_j$, $\mathbf{V}_i$ is a $T \times T$ diagonal weighting matrix with t^{th} entry $[1/\sigma_{it}^2]$ or equivalently for this model $[1/\mu_{it}]$, $\mathbf{y}_i$ is the $T \times 1$ vector with t^{th} entry y_{it} and $\boldsymbol{\mu}_i$ is the $T \times 1$ vector with t^{th} entry μ_{it}. This is similar to the linear WLS estimator given in section 2.4.1 (see also section 7.6), and $\hat{\beta}_{\mathsf{WLS}}$ is asymptotically normal with mean β and variance

$$\begin{aligned} \mathsf{V}[\hat{\beta}_{\mathsf{WLS}}] = & \left[\sum_{i=1}^{n} \mathbf{D}_i' \mathbf{V}_i \mathbf{D}_i \right]^{-1} \times \sum_{i=1}^{n} \mathbf{D}_i' \mathbf{V}_i \boldsymbol{\Omega}_i \mathbf{V}_i \mathbf{D}_i \\ & \times \left[\sum_{i=1}^{n} \mathbf{D}_i' \mathbf{V}_i \mathbf{D}_i \right]^{-1}, \end{aligned} \tag{9.30}$$

where $\boldsymbol{\Omega}_i$ is the covariance matrix of $\mathbf{y}_i$. In practice $\boldsymbol{\Omega}_i$ is left unspecified and $\mathsf{V}[\hat{\beta}_{\mathsf{WLS}}]$ is consistently estimated by (9.30) with $\boldsymbol{\Omega}_i$ replaced by $(\mathbf{y}_i - \boldsymbol{\mu}_i)(\mathbf{y}_i - \boldsymbol{\mu}_i)'$.

Zeger and Liang (1986) and Liang and Zeger (1986) call this approach *marginal analysis*, as estimation is based on moments of the distribution marginal to the random effects. Zeger, Liang, and Albert (1988) consider mixed GLMs in which the random effects may interact with regressors. They call the approach *population-averaged*, as the random effects are averaged out, and contrast this with subject-specific models that explicitly model the individual effects. These papers present estimating equations of the form (9.29) with little explicit discussion of the random effects and the precise form of the correlation and modified heteroskedasticity that they induce. More formal treatment of random effects using this approach is given in Thall and Vail (1990).

Brännäs and Johansson (1996) consider a more tightly specified model than Zeger and Liang (1986), the Poisson model with multiplicative random effects in which the random effects are also time varying, that is, α_{it} replaces α_i in (9.6). They generalize (9.29) so that the weighting matrix has nonzero off-diagonal entries, reflecting correlation induced by the random effects. In addition they consider estimation by GMM, which exploits more of the moment conditions implied by the model. They apply these estimation methods to data on number of days absent from work for 895 Swedish workers in each of 11 years.

9.5 Discussion

The fixed effects model can be generalized from linear models to count data models. The conditional maximum likelihood approach leads to tractable results for some count models – for example, for the Poisson (9.13) simplifies to

(9.14) – but not for all count data models. Moment-based methods can more generally be used for all models with multiplicative individual effects as in (9.7).

The random effects model can also be used in a wide range of settings. The maximum likelihood approach is generally computationally difficult, unless a model with conjugate density for the random effects, such as Poisson-gamma, is used. Moment-based methods can again be used in a much wider range of settings.

The strengths and weaknesses of fixed effects versus random effects models in the linear case carry over to nonlinear models. For the linear model a considerable literature exists on the difference between fixed and random effects, see especially Mundlak (1978) and a summary by Hsiao (1986). The random effects model is appropriate if the sample is drawn from a population and one wants to do inference on the population; the fixed effects model is appropriate if one wishes to confine oneself to explaining the sample. The random effects model more easily accommodates random slope parameters as well as random intercepts. For the fixed effects model, coefficients of time-invariant regressors are absorbed into the individual-specific effect α_i and are not identified. For the random effects model, coefficient estimates may be inconsistent if the random effects are correlated with regressors. A test of correlation with regressors is presented in the next subsection.

We have focused on individual fixed effects in a short panel. Time specific effects can additionally be included to form a two-way fixed effects error-component model. This can be estimated using conditional maximum likelihood as outlined previously, where the regressors $\mathbf{x}_{it}$ include time dummies. The results can clearly be modified to apply to a long panel with few individuals. Conditional maximum likelihood would then condition on $\sum_i y_{it}$ where, for example, y_{it} is iid $\mathsf{P}[\alpha_t \lambda_{it}]$.

In the linear model the total sample variability is split into between-group variability and within-group variability, where variability is measured by sums of squares. Hausman, Hall, and Griliches (1984) attempt a similar decomposition for count data models, where sample variability is measured by the log-likelihood function. For the Poisson model with gamma-distributed random effects, the log-likelihood of the iid $\mathsf{P}[\mu_{it}]$ can be decomposed as the sum of the conditional (on $\sum_t y_{it}$) log-likelihood and a marginal (for $\sum_t y_{it}$) log-likelihood. The conditional log-likelihood is naturally interpreted as measuring within variation; the marginal log-likelihood can be interpreted as between variation, although it depends on $\sum_t \lambda_{it}$, which depends on $\boldsymbol{\beta}$, rather than $\bar{\mathbf{x}}_i$ alone. A similar decomposition for negative binomial is not as neat.

References to count applications outside economics are given in Diggle, Liang, and Zeger (1994) and Fahrmeir and Tutz (1994). Many of these applications use random effects models with Gaussian effects or use the generalized estimating equations approach of Liang and Zeger (1986). Here we focus on economics applications, which generally use the fixed effects models or random effects models with conjugate density for the random effects.

The paper by Hausman, Hall, and Griliches (1984) includes a substantial application to number of patents for 121 U.S. firms observed from 1968 through 1975. This paper estimates Poisson and NB models with both fixed and random effects. Other studies using patent data are discussed in section 9.7.

Ruser (1991) studies the number of workdays lost at 2788 manufacturing establishments from 1979 through 1984. He uses the NB fixed effects estimator and finds that workdays lost increase with higher workers' compensation benefits, with most of the effect occurring in smaller establishments whose workers' compensation insurance premiums are less experience-rated.

Blonigen (1997) applies the NB2 random effects model to data on the number of Japanese acquisitions in the United States across 365 three-digit Standard Industry Classification industries from 1975 through 1992. The paper finds that if the U.S. dollar is weak relative to the Japanese yen, Japanese acquisitions increase in industries more likely to involve firm-specific assets, notably high R&D manufacturing sectors, which can generate a return in yen without involving a currency transaction.

In a novel application, Page (1995) applies the Poisson fixed effects model to data on the number of housing units shown by housing agents to each of two paired auditors, where the two auditors are as much as possible identical except that one auditor is from a minority group and the other is not. Specifically black/white pairs and Hispanic/Anglo pairs are considered. Here the subscript i refers to a specific auditor pair, $i = 1, \ldots, n$; subscript $t = 1, 2$ refers to whether the auditor is minority (say $t = 1$) or nonminority (say $t = 2$). A simple model without covariates is that $\mathsf{E}[y_{it}] = \alpha_i \exp(\beta d_{it})$, where $d_{it} = 1$ if minority and equals 0 otherwise. Then $\exp(\beta)$ equals the ratio of population-mean housing units shown to minority auditors to those shown to nonminority, and $\exp(\beta) < 1$ indicates discrimination is present. Page shows that in this case the Poisson fixed effects conditional MLE has explicit solution $\exp(\hat{\beta}) = \bar{y}_1/\bar{y}_2$. For the data studied by Page (1995) $\exp(\hat{\beta})$ lies between 0.82 and 0.91, with robust standard errors using (9.23) of between 0.022 and 0.028. Thus discrimination is present. Further analysis includes regressors that might explain the aggregate difference in number of housing units shown.

Van Duijn and Böckenholt (1995) analyze the number of spelling errors by 721 first-grade pupils on each of four dictation tests. They consider a Poisson–gamma mixture model that leads to a conditional multinomial distribution. This does not adequately model overdispersion, so they consider a finite mixtures version of this model using the methods of section 4.8. On the basis of chi-square goodness-of-fit tests they prefer a model with two classes, essentially good spellers and poor spellers.

Pinquet (1997) uses estimates of individual effects from longitudinal models of the number and severity of insurance claims to determine "bonus-malus" coefficients used in experience-rated insurance. In addition to an application to an unbalanced panel of over 100,000 policyholders, the paper gives considerable discussion of discrimination between true and apparent contagion. A range of models, including the random effects model of section 9.4, is considered.

9.6 Specification Tests

9.6.1 *Fixed Versus Random Effects*

The random effects estimator assumes that α_i is iid distributed, which in particular implies that the random effects are uncorrelated with the regressors. Thus it is assumed that individual specific unobservables are uncorrelated with individual specific observables, a strong assumption. The fixed effects model makes no such assumption – α_i could be determined by individual-specific time-invariant regressors.

If the random effects model is correctly specified, then both fixed- and random effects models are consistent, while if the random effects are correlated with regressors the random effects estimator loses its consistency. The difference between the two estimators can therefore be used as the basis for a Hausman test, introduced in section 5.6.6. This test is easily implemented because the random effects estimator is fully efficient, so the covariance matrix of the difference between estimators equals the difference in covariance matrices.

Thus form

$$\mathsf{T}_{\mathsf{H}} = (\hat{\beta}_{\mathsf{RE}} - \tilde{\beta}_{\mathsf{FE}})'[\mathsf{V}[\tilde{\beta}_{\mathsf{FE}}] - \mathsf{V}_{\mathsf{ML}}[\hat{\beta}_{\mathsf{RE}}]]^{-1}(\hat{\beta}_{\mathsf{RE}} - \tilde{\beta}_{\mathsf{FE}}). \qquad (9.31)$$

If $\mathsf{T}_{\mathsf{H}} < \chi^2_\alpha(\dim(\beta))$ then at significance level α we do not reject the null hypothesis that the individual specific effects are uncorrelated with regressors. This test is used in Hausman, Hall, and Griliches (1984, pp. 921 and 928) and leads to rejection of the random effects model in their application.

9.6.2 *Tests for Serial Correlation*

Tests for serial correlation are considered by Hausman, Hall, and Griliches (1984). If individual effects are present, then models that ignore such effects will have residuals that are serially correlated. If this serial correlation disappears after controlling for individual effects, then time series methods introduced in section 9.7 are not needed. We consider in turn tests for these two situations.

The natural model for initial analysis of count longitudinal data is Poisson regression of y_{it} on λ_{it} where independence is assumed over both i and t. Residuals from this regression are serially correlated if in fact individual effects α_i are present. Furthermore, the serial correlation between residuals from periods t and s is approximately constant in $(t - s)$, because it is induced by α_i, which is constant over time. It is natural to base tests on standardized residuals such as the Pearson residual $\varepsilon_{it} = (y_{it} - \lambda_{it})/\sqrt{\lambda_{it}}$. Then we expect the correlation coefficient between ε_{it} and ε_{is}, estimated as $\sum_i \varepsilon_{it}\varepsilon_{is}/\sqrt{\sum_i \varepsilon_{it}^2}\sqrt{\sum_i \varepsilon_{is}^2}$, to equal zero, $t \neq s$, if individual effects are not present. In practice these correlations are often sufficiently large that a formal test is unnecessary.

If models with individual effects are estimated, the methods yield consistent estimates of β but not α_i. Thus residuals $y_{it} - \alpha_i\lambda_{it}$ cannot be readily computed and tested for lack of serial correlation. For the fixed effects Poisson,

$y_{i1}, \ldots, y_{iT} \mid \sum_t y_{it}$ is multinomial-distributed with probability $p_{it} = \lambda_{it} / \sum_s \lambda_{is}$. It follows that y_{it} has mean $p_{it} \sum_s y_{is}$ and variance $p_{it}(1 - p_{it}) \sum_s y_{is}$, and the covariance between y_{it} and y_{is} is $-p_{it} p_{is} \sum_s y_{it}$. The residual $u_{it} = (y_{it} - p_{it} \sum_s y_{is}) / \sqrt{\sum_s y_{is}}$ therefore satisfies $\mathsf{E}[u_{it}^2] = (1 - p_{it}) p_{it}$ and $\mathsf{E}[u_{it} u_{is}] = -p_{it} p_{is}, t \neq s$. Hausman, Hall, and Griliches (1984) propose a conditional moment test based on these moment conditions, where one of the residuals is dropped because predicted probabilities sum to one.

The dynamic longitudinal model applications discussed in section 9.7 generally implement tests of serial correlation. Blundell, Griffith, and Windmeijer (1995) adapt serial correlation tests proposed by Arellano and Bond (1991) for the linear model. Crepon and Duguet (1997a) and Brännäs and Johansson (1996) apply serial correlation tests in the GMM framework.

9.7 Dynamic and Transition Models

9.7.1 *Some Approaches*

Dynamic or transition longitudinal models allow current realizations of the count y_{it} to depend on past realizations $y_{i,t-k}$, $k > 0$, where $y_{i,t-k}$ defines individual i in period $t - k$.

One approach is to ignore the panel nature of the data. Simply assume that all regression coefficients are the same across individuals, so that there are no individual-specific fixed or random effects. Then one can directly apply the time series methods presented in Chapter 7, even for small T provided $n \to \infty$. This approach is given in Diggle, Liang, and Zeger (1994, chapter 10), who usc autoregressive models that directly include $y_{i,t-k}$ as regressors. Also Brännäs (1995a) briefly discusses a generalization of the INAR(1) time series model to longitudinal data.

This approach may be adequate if there is considerable serial correlation in the data, because then lagged values of the dependent variable might be an excellent control for an individual effect. There may be no need to additionally include fixed or random effects. For example, firm-specific propensity to patent might be adequately controlled for simply by including patents last year as a regressor. A refinement is to consider a finite mixtures model with, say, two or three different types of firm, constant parameters for all firms of the same type, and firm type determined by the methods presented in Chapter 4.

Analysis becomes considerably more complicated if individual specific effects are introduced. In this case many of the preceding methods for panel count data are no longer appropriate, especially for short panels where $n \to \infty$ but T is fixed.

A similar complication arises for linear models, and is discussed for example in Nickell (1981), Hsiao (1986), and Baltagi (1995). In the simplest case of a fixed effects linear model with $y_{i,t-1}$ the only regressor, that is, $y_{it} = \beta y_{i,t-1} + u_{it}$, the differenced model (9.4) is

$$(y_{it} - \bar{y}_i) = \beta(y_{i,t-1} - \bar{y}_{i,-1}) + (u_{it} - \bar{u}_i), \qquad t = 2, \ldots, T,$$

where $\bar{y}_{i,-1} = \frac{1}{T-1}\sum_{t=2}^{T} y_{i,t-1}$. OLS estimation for finite T leads to an inconsistent estimate of β because the regressor $(y_{i,t-1} - \bar{y}_{i,-1})$ is correlated with $\bar{u}_i$; to see this, lag the above equation by one period – hence, the regressor is correlated with the error term.

For linear models, one solution is to restrict attention to the case $T \rightarrow \infty$. Then the problem disappears because $\bar{u}_i$ is then a small component of $u_{it} - \bar{u}_i$. A second solution, for finite T, is to use an alternative differenced model that subtracts the lagged value of y_{it}, so

$$(y_{it} - y_{i,t-1}) = \beta(y_{i,t-1} - y_{i,t-2}) + (u_{it} - u_{it-1}), \qquad t = 2, \ldots, T.$$

A consistent estimate of β can be obtained by instrumental variables methods, using for example $(y_{i,t-2} - y_{i,t-3})$ as an instrument. A considerable literature has developed on increasing the efficiency of such moment-based estimators. A third solution is to use MLEs of random effects models, in which case consistency depends crucially on assumptions regarding starting values.

For dynamic count models with individual-specific effects, qualitatively similar solutions to the above for linear models can be used.

An example of the first solution is Hill, Rothchild, and Cameron (1998), who model the monthly incidence of protests using data from 17 western countries for 35 years. To control for overdispersion and dynamics they use a negative binomial model with lagged y_{it} appearing as $\ln(y_{i,t-1} + c)$, where c is a constant whose role was explained in section 7.5. Country-specific effects are additionally controlled for by inclusion of country-specific indicator variables, which poses no consistency problems because in this example $T \rightarrow \infty$ while $n = 17$ is small.

In this section we concentrate on applying the second solution to dynamic count panel data models with fixed effects. Moment-based methods have already been presented for nondynamic models with multiplicative fixed effects in section 9.3.2. Here we present extension of these moment methods to the dynamic case. This is an active area of research, with most applications being to count data on patents.

9.7.2 *Fixed Effects Models*

The methods in preceding sections have implicitly assumed that regressors are strictly exogenous, that is,

$$\mathsf{E}[y_{it} \mid \mathbf{x}_{it}] = \mathsf{E}[y_{it} \mid \mathbf{x}_{iT}, \ldots, \mathbf{x}_{i1}] = \alpha_i \lambda_{it}. \tag{9.32}$$

This rules out cases in which regressors are *weakly exogenous*, or

$$\mathsf{E}[y_{it} \mid \mathbf{x}_{it}] = \mathsf{E}[y_{it} \mid \mathbf{x}_{it}, \ldots, \mathbf{x}_{i1}] = \alpha_i \lambda_{it}, \tag{9.33}$$

as in dynamic models in which lagged dependent variables appear as regressors. In this section we present results to estimate dynamic longitudinal data models using first-moment conditions.

We begin by considering the Poisson fixed effects estimator introduced in section 9.3. Given independence over i, the first-order conditions for $\boldsymbol{\beta}$ given in (9.17) have expected value zero if

$$\mathsf{E}\left[\sum_{t=1}^{T}\mathbf{x}_{it}\left(y_{it}-\frac{\bar{y}_i}{\bar{\lambda}_i}\lambda_{it}\right)\right]=\mathbf{0}. \tag{9.34}$$

The presence of the average $\bar{y}_i$, introduced to eliminate the fixed effects, in these moment conditions limits application of this estimator to strictly exogenous regressors. To see this, consider the tth term in the sum and assume $\mathsf{E}[y_{it}\,|\,\mathbf{x}_{i1},\ldots,\mathbf{x}_{iT}]=\alpha_i\lambda_{it}$ as in (9.32). Then $\mathsf{E}[\bar{y}_i\,|\,\mathbf{x}_{i1},\ldots,\mathbf{x}_{iT}]=\alpha_i\bar{\lambda}_i$ and

$$\begin{aligned}\mathsf{E}\left[\mathbf{x}_{it}\left(y_{it}-\frac{\bar{y}_i}{\bar{\lambda}_i}\lambda_{it}\right)\right] &= \mathsf{E}_{\mathbf{x}_{i1},\ldots,\mathbf{x}_{iT}}\left[\mathbf{x}_{it}\mathsf{E}\left[y_{it}-\frac{\bar{y}_i}{\bar{\lambda}_i}\lambda_{it}\,|\,\mathbf{x}_{i1},\ldots,\mathbf{x}_{iT}\right]\right]\\ &= \mathsf{E}_{\mathbf{x}_{i1},\ldots,\mathbf{x}_{iT}}\left[\mathbf{x}_{it}\left(\alpha_i\lambda_{it}-\frac{\alpha_i\bar{\lambda}_i}{\bar{\lambda}_i}\lambda_{it}\right)\right]\\ &= \mathbf{0}.\end{aligned}$$

Note that it is not enough to assume $\mathsf{E}[y_{it}\,|\,\mathbf{x}_{it}]=\alpha_i\lambda_{it}$, because this does not necessarily imply $\mathsf{E}[\bar{y}_i\,|\,\mathbf{x}_{it}]=\alpha_i\bar{\lambda}_i$. For example, suppose $\mathbf{x}_{it}=y_{it-1}$ and $\mathsf{E}[y_{it}\,|\,y_{it-1}]=\alpha_i\rho y_{it-1}$, or $\lambda_{it}=\rho y_{it-1}$. Then

$$\mathsf{E}\left[\bar{y}_i\,|\,y_{it-1}\right]=\mathsf{E}\left[\frac{1}{T}(y_{i1}+\cdots+y_{iT})\,|\,y_{it-1}\right]$$

while

$$\alpha_i\bar{\lambda}_i=\frac{1}{T}\alpha_i\rho(y_{i0}+\cdots+y_{iT-1}).$$

Equality of the two requires $\mathsf{E}[y_{is}\,|\,y_{it-1}]=\alpha_i\rho y_{is-1}$ for $s\neq t$, which is clearly not the case. Similar problems arise if we assume $\mathsf{E}[y_{it}\,|\,\mathbf{x}_{it},\ldots,\mathbf{x}_{i1}]=\alpha_i\lambda_{it}$, because again this does not imply $\mathsf{E}[\bar{y}_i\,|\,\mathbf{x}_{it},\ldots,\mathbf{x}_{i1}]=\alpha_i\bar{\lambda}_i$.

One could instead eliminate fixed effects by quasidifferencing, as noted at the beginning of section 9.3.2. For weakly exogenous regressors, Chamberlain (1992b) proposes eliminating the fixed effects by the transformation

$$q_{it}=y_{it}-\frac{\lambda_{it}}{\lambda_{it+1}}y_{it+1}. \tag{9.35}$$

Suppose instruments $\mathbf{z}_{it}$ exist such that

$$\mathsf{E}[y_{it}-\alpha_i\lambda_{it}\,|\,\mathbf{z}_{it},\ldots,\mathbf{z}_{i1}]=0. \tag{9.36}$$

Then

$$\begin{aligned}&\mathsf{E}[y_{it+1}-\alpha_i\lambda_{it+1}\,|\,\mathbf{z}_{it},\ldots,\mathbf{z}_{i1}]\\ &\quad=\mathsf{E}_{\mathbf{z}_{it+1}}[\mathsf{E}[y_{it+1}-\alpha_i\lambda_{it+1}\,|\,\mathbf{z}_{it+1},\mathbf{z}_{it},\ldots,\mathbf{z}_{i1}]]\\ &\quad=\mathsf{E}_{\mathbf{z}_{it+1}}[0]\\ &\quad=0.\end{aligned}$$

It follows that

$$\mathsf{E}\left[y_{it} - \frac{\lambda_{it}}{\lambda_{it+1}} y_{it+1} \mid \mathbf{z}_{it}, \ldots, \mathbf{z}_{i1}\right] = \alpha_i \lambda_{it} - \frac{\lambda_{it}}{\lambda_{it+1}} \alpha_i \lambda_{it+1}$$
$$= 0.$$

In the case in which there are as many instruments as parameters one solves

$$\sum_{t=1}^{T} \mathbf{z}_{it} \left(y_{it} - \frac{\lambda_{it}}{\lambda_{is}} y_{is} \right) = \mathbf{0}. \tag{9.37}$$

As an example, suppose

$$\mathsf{E}[y_{it} \mid y_{it-1}, \ldots, \mathbf{x}_{it}, \ldots] = \alpha_i \lambda_{it} = \alpha_i \left(\rho y_{it-1} + \exp\left(\mathbf{x}_{it}' \boldsymbol{\beta}\right)\right).$$

Then the natural choice of instruments is $\mathbf{z}_{it} = (y_{it-1}, \mathbf{x}_{it})$.

If there are more instruments $\mathbf{z}_{it}$ than regressors, such as through adding additional lags of regressors into the instrument set, one can consistently estimate $\boldsymbol{\beta}$ by the GMM estimator, which minimizes

$$\frac{1}{n} \left(\sum_{i=1}^{n} \mathbf{q}_i(\boldsymbol{\beta})' \mathbf{z}_i \right) \mathbf{W}_n^{-1} \left(\sum_{i=1}^{n} \mathbf{z}_i' \mathbf{q}_i(\boldsymbol{\beta}) \right), \tag{9.38}$$

where $\mathbf{q}_i(\boldsymbol{\beta}) = (q_{i1} \cdots q_{iT})'$, $\mathbf{z}_i = \left(\mathbf{z}_{i1}' \cdots \mathbf{z}_{iT}'\right)'$, $\mathbf{W}_n^{-1}$ is a weighting matrix, and, given specification of $\mathbf{q}_i$ and $\mathbf{z}_i$, the optimal choice of $\mathbf{W}_n$ is $\mathbf{W}_n = \sum_{i=1}^{n} \mathbf{z}_i' \tilde{\mathbf{q}}_i \tilde{\mathbf{q}}_i' \mathbf{z}_i$ where $\tilde{\mathbf{q}}_i = \mathbf{q}_i(\tilde{\boldsymbol{\beta}})$ and $\tilde{\boldsymbol{\beta}}$ is an initial consistent estimate obtained for example by minimizing (9.38) with $\mathbf{W}_n = \mathbf{I}_n$.

An alternative transformation to eliminate the fixed effects is

$$q_{it} = \frac{y_{it}}{\lambda_{it}} - \frac{y_{it+1}}{\lambda_{it+1}}, \tag{9.39}$$

proposed by Wooldridge (1997), which is simply the earlier choice divided by λ_{it}. Yet another possibility is the mean scaling transformation

$$q_{it} = y_{it} - \frac{\bar{y}_{i0}}{\lambda_{i0}} \lambda_{it}, \tag{9.40}$$

proposed by Blundell, Griffith, and Windmeijer (1995), where $\bar{y}_{i0}$ is the presample mean value of y_i and the instruments are $(\mathbf{x}_{it} - \mathbf{x}_{i0})$. The latter estimator leads to estimates that are inconsistent, but in a simulation this inconsistency is shown to be small, and efficiency is considerably improved. This estimator is especially useful if data on the dependent variable go back farther in time than data on the explanatory variables.

These methods are applicable to quite general models with multiplicative fixed effects. Several studies, beginning with Montalvo (1997), have refined and applied these methods, mostly to count data on patents. Application to patents is of particular interest for several reasons. There are few ways to measure innovation aside from patents, which are intrinsically a count. R&D expenditures affect patents with a considerable lag, so there is potentially parsimony and elimination of multicollinearity in having patents depend on lagged patents rather than a long-distributed lag in R&D expenditures. And, as noted in the example earlier, most studies using distributed lags on R&D expenditure find the R&D expenditure elasticity of patents to be much less than unity.

Blundell, Griffith, and Windmeijer (1995) model the U.S. patents data of Hall, Griliches, and Hausman (1986). They pay particular attention to the functional form for dynamics and the time series implications of various functional forms. The lagged dependent variable is introduced in either multiplicative fashion as

$$\mu_{it} = \alpha_i \exp\left(\rho \ln y^*_{it-1} + \mathbf{x}'_{it}\boldsymbol{\beta}\right)$$

where $y^*_{it-1} = y_{it-1}$ unless $y_{it-1} = 0$ in which case $y^*_{it-1} = c$, or additive fashion as

$$\mu_{it} = \rho y_{it-1} + \alpha_i \exp\left(\mathbf{x}'_{it}\boldsymbol{\beta}\right),$$

where $\rho > 0$. Another variant of the additive model, not considered, is

$$\mu_{it} = \alpha_i \left(\rho y_{it-1} + \exp\left(\mathbf{x}'_{it}\boldsymbol{\beta}\right)\right).$$

In their application up to two lags of patents and three lags of R&D expenditures appear as regressors. The estimates indicate long lags in the response of patents to R&D expenditures.

Related studies by Blundell, Griffith, and Van Reenen (1995a, b) model the number of "technologically significant and commercially important" innovations commercialized by British firms. Dynamics are introduced more simply by including the lagged value of the knowledge stock, an exponentially weighted sum of past innovations.

Montalvo (1997) uses the Chamberlain (1992b) transformation to model the number of licensing agreements by individual Japanese firms and the Hall et al. (1986) data. Lagged dependent variables do not appear as regressors. Instead Montalvo argues that current R&D expenditures cannot be assumed to be strictly exogenous because patents depend on additional R&D expenditures for their full development. So there is still a need for quasidifferenced estimators.

Crepon and Duguet (1997a) apply GMM methods to French patents data. They also use a relatively simple functional form for dynamics. First, as regressor they use a measure of R&D capital. This capital measure is calculated as the weighted sum of current and past depreciated R&D expenditure and can be viewed as imposing constraints on R&D coefficients in a distributed lag model. Dynamics in patents are introduced by including indicator variables for whether y_{it-1} is in the ranges 1 to 5, 6 to 10, or 11 or more. Particular attention is paid to model specification testing and the impact of increasing the size of the instrument set $\mathbf{z}_i$ in (9.38).

In a more applied study, Cincera (1997) includes not only a distributed lag in firm R&D expenditures but also a distributed lag in R&D expenditures by other firms in the same sector to capture spillover effects. Application is to a panel of 181 manufacturing firms from six countries.

9.8 Derivations

9.8.1 *Conditional Density for Poisson Fixed Effects*

Consider the conditional joint density for observations in all time periods for a given individual, where for simplicity the individual subscript i is dropped. In general the density of $y_1, \ldots, y_T$ given $\sum_t y_t$ is

$$\Pr\left[y_1, \ldots, y_T \,\middle|\, \sum_t y_t\right] = \Pr\left[y_1, \ldots, y_T, \sum_t y_t\right] \Big/ \Pr\left[\sum_t y_t\right]$$
$$= \Pr\left[y_1, \ldots, y_T\right] \Big/ \Pr\left[\sum_t y_t\right],$$

where the last equality arises because knowledge of $\sum_t y_t$ adds nothing given knowledge of $y_1, \ldots, y_T$.

Now specialize to y_t iid Poisson (μ_t). Then $\Pr[y_1, \ldots, y_T]$ is the product of T Poisson densities, and $\sum_t y_t$ is Poisson ($\sum_t \mu_t$). It follows that

$$\Pr\left[y_1, \ldots, y_T \,\middle|\, \sum_t y_t\right] = \frac{\prod_t \left(\exp(-\mu_t)\mu_t^{y_t}/y_t!\right)}{\exp(-\sum_t \mu_t)(\sum_t \mu_t)^{\sum_t y_t}/(\sum_t y_t)!}$$
$$= \frac{\exp(-\sum_t \mu_t)\prod_t \mu_t^{y_t}/\prod_t y_t!}{\exp(-\sum_t \mu_t)\prod_t (\sum_s \mu_s)^{y_t}/(\sum_t y_t)!}$$
$$= \frac{(\sum_t y_t)!}{\prod_t y_t!} \times \prod_t \left(\frac{\mu_t}{\sum_s \mu_s}\right)^{y_t}.$$

Introducing the subscript i yields (9.13) for $\Pr[y_{i1}, \ldots, y_{iT} \mid \sum_t y_{it}]$.

9.8.2 *Density for Poisson with Gamma Random Effects*

Consider the joint density for observations in all time periods for a given individual, where for simplicity the individual subscript i is dropped. From (9.13) the joint density of $y_1, \ldots, y_T$ if $y_t \mid \alpha$ is $\mathsf{P}[\alpha\lambda_t]$ is

$$\Pr[y_1, \ldots, y_T] = \int_0^\infty \left[\prod_t \left(e^{-\alpha\lambda_t}(\alpha\lambda_t)^{y_t}/y_t!\right)\right] f(\alpha)\, d\alpha$$
$$= \int_0^\infty \left[\prod_t \lambda_t^{y_t}/y_t!\right]\left(e^{-\alpha\sum_t \lambda_t} \cdot \alpha^{\sum_t y_t}\right) f(\alpha)\, d\alpha$$
$$= \left[\prod_t \lambda_t^{y_t}/y_t!\right] \times \int_0^\infty \left(e^{-\alpha\sum_t \lambda_t} \cdot \alpha^{\sum_t y_t}\right) f(\alpha)\, d\alpha.$$

Now let $f(\alpha)$ be the gamma density with parameters density. Similar algebra to that in section 4.2.2 yields the Poisson random effects density given in (9.25).

9.9 Bibliographic Notes

Longitudinal data models fall in the class of multilevel models, surveyed by Goldstein (1995), who includes a brief treatment of Poisson. Standard references for linear models for longitudinal data include Hsiao (1986), Diggle, Liang, and Zeger (1994), and Baltagi (1995). Diggle et al. (1994) and Fahrmeir and Tutz (1994) consider generalized linear models in detail. A useful reference for general nonlinear longitudinal data models is Mátyás and Sevestre (1995).

There are remarkably many different approaches to nonlinear models, and many complications including serial correlation, dynamics and unbalanced panels. The treatment here is comprehensive for models used in econometrics and covers many of the approaches used in other areas of statistics. Additional statistical references can be found in Diggle et al. (1994) and Fahrmeir and Tutz (1994). Lawless (1995) considers both duration and count models for longitudinal data for recurrent events. For dynamic models the GMM fixed effects approach is particularly promising. In addition to the count references given in section 9.7, it is useful to refer to earlier work for the linear model by Arellano and Bond (1991) and Keane and Runkle (1992).

9.10 Exercises

9.1 Show that the Poisson fixed effects conditional MLE of β that maximizes the log-likelihood function given in (9.16) is the solution to the first-order conditions (9.17).

9.2 Find the first-order conditions for the negative binomial fixed effects conditional MLE of β that maximizes the log-likelihood function based on the density (9.18). (Hint: Use the gamma recursion as in section 3.3.) Do these first-order conditions have a simple interpretation, like those for the Poisson fixed effect conditional MLE?

9.3 Verify that the first-order conditions for the Poisson random effects MLE for β can be expressed as (9.26).

9.4 Show that the Poisson fixed effects conditional MLE that solves (9.17) reduces to $\exp(\hat{\beta}) = \bar{y}_1/\bar{y}_2$ in the application by Page (1995) discussed at the end of section 9.5.

CHAPTER 10

Measurement Errors

10.1 Introduction

The well-known bivariate linear errors-in-variables regression model with additive measurement errors in both variables provides one benchmark for nonlinear errors-in-variables models. The standard textbook treatment of the errors-in-variables case emphasizes the attenuation result, which says that the estimated least squares estimate of the slope parameter is downward-biased if both variables are subject to measurement error. The essential problem lies in the correlation between the observed explanatory variable and the measurement error. This leads to distorted inferences about the role of the covariate. Although this result does not always extend to general cases, such as a linear model with two or more covariates measured with error, it is usually of interest to consider whether a similar attenuation bias exists generally in nonlinear models (Carroll et al., 1995).

There are important similarities and differences between measurement errors in nonlinear and linear models. First, in nonlinear models it may be more natural to allow measurement errors to enter multiplicatively rather than additively. Second, models in which the measurement errors are confined to the count variable, rather than covariates, are of considerable interest. Third, the direction of measurement errors in count models is sometimes strongly suspected from a priori analysis, which permits stronger conclusions.

Given these motivations, this chapter considers estimation and inference in the presence of measurement errors in exposure time, errors due to underreporting and misclassification of events. Such errors are shown to have important consequences for model identification, specification, estimation, and testing. One way to analyze the impact of measurement errors is to consider what impact they have on the properties of a particular estimator that might be otherwise optimal. We also emphasize the effect of the measurement error on the observed distribution of counts, and the consequences of the choice of modeling approaches for such data.

A general approach is to introduce measurement errors in the counts and the covariates, together with assumptions about the joint distribution of errors. Although this case is of major interest, we shall begin with a slightly simpler case in which the measurement error affects only the count variable. We then focus on its effect on the distribution of the response variable.

We follow this discussion with an analysis of measurement errors in the covariates, without being specific about their origin. In an important class of cases, measurement errors are shown to lead to overdispersion.

There are two other cases in which the appropriate method of inference is of special interest. In the first case, we are interested in event counts that are underreported. For example, certain types of crime, accidents, and absences at the place of work may be underreported because of random failures in the mechanism for recording those events. How should estimation and inference be carried out in such cases?

There is a closely related second case if one is interested in the frequency distribution of a subset of several related types of events, for example, the frequency of industrial accidents in some particular category. However, the events may be occasionally misclassified, sometimes because of lack of clarity in the definition of the event, and sometimes to understate the relative frequency of one type of event. Whittemore and Gong (1991) analyze data on cervical cancer mortality rates using mortality data for several European countries coded into international classification of disease categories. They point out that there are several potential sources of error and systematic intercountry differences in the designation of the code, leading to misclassification errors. As in the case of underreported counts, the main interest is in various approaches to modeling such data.

Section 10.2 examines the impact of measurement errors in counts due to the incorrectly measured exposure. The emphasis is on overdispersion. Section 10.3 concentrates on the case of additive or multiplicative measurement errors in the regressors, ignoring the errors in counts. Section 10.4 studies measurement errors in counts that do not necessarily arise from mismeasured exposure, including the practically important case of misclassified counts. Section 10.5 analyzes estimation and inference for underreported counts, which arise in many commonly occurring situations.

10.2 Measurement Errors in Exposure

It useful to distinguish between separate measurement errors in *exposure* (period of occurrence) and *intensity* (rate of occurrence). For example, in analyzing the number of insurance claims for auto accidents, an error arises if it is assumed that all cases in the sample were covered by insurance for the whole of the period under study, if in truth some members were only covered for some part of the period. This is an example of measurement error in exposure. Suppose the model calls for a variable reflecting driving experience, but the only measure available is the number of years a driving license has been held, which is an imperfect measure of driving experience. This is an example of measurement error in the intensity component. These are considered first.

Let us begin with the initial specification of the Poisson density in Chapter 1

$$f(y_i \mid \mu_i t_i) = \frac{e^{-\mu_i t_i}(\mu_i t_i)^{y_i}}{y_i!}, \qquad y_i = 0, 1, \ldots. \tag{10.1}$$

Compactly, we refer to this density as $\mathsf{P}[\mu_i t_i]$. This is written to emphasize the distinction between the intensity parameter μ_i and the exposure period t_i, defined as the period during which the subject is at "risk" of experiencing the event. Under the assumption that the exposure period is correctly measured and of unit length for all subjects, $\mathsf{E}[y_i] = \mu_i t_i = \mu_i$. Then the density may be written without the exposure period, thus $f(y_i \mid \mu_i) = \exp(-\mu_i)\mu_i^{y_i}/y_i!$.

Again we assume $\mu_i = \mu(\mathbf{x}_i, \boldsymbol{\beta})$ for convenience. It is of interest to consider the consequences of measurement errors for the MLE. Measurement errors in y_i, $\mathbf{x}_i$, and t_i are relevant, those in $\mathbf{x}_i$ for obvious reasons and those in t_i because it is a likely source of measurement error in cases in which the sample data are based on the subject's possibly faulty recall of events experienced in the past. Exposure need not necessarily be just time, because other variables such as population, distance, and so forth may also be relevant. Measurement errors from exposures in the general case have been considered by Brännäs (1996) and Alcañiz (1996).

In analyzing the consequences of measurement errors one may either focus on the properties of a particular estimator, such as inconsistency, or study the effect on the entire distribution of the observed random variable. The first approach is widely used in the analysis of linear errors-in-variables models. The main technique in the latter case involves considering a small-variance local Taylor expansion around the true density (Cox, 1983) and studying the properties of the resulting approximate density.

In relation to exposures, three separate cases are considered. The first is the case of known but unequal exposures, which can be handled in a relatively straightforward manner. The second situation is that in which the exposure variable is not directly observed but there is information on observable factors that affect it. The third case is one in which the exposure period is not observed and is incorrectly assumed to be the same for all subjects, giving rise to measurement errors. A potential advantage of specifying exposure explicitly is to permit separate identification of factors that affect exposure rather than the intensity parameter.

10.2.1 *Correctly Observed Exposure*

Using the exponential mean specification we have

$$\begin{aligned}\mu_i t_i &= \exp(\mathbf{x}_i'\boldsymbol{\beta})t_i \\ &= \exp(\mathbf{x}_i'\boldsymbol{\beta} + \ln t_i) \\ &= \exp\left[\begin{pmatrix}\mathbf{x}_i' & \ln t_i\end{pmatrix}\begin{pmatrix}\boldsymbol{\beta} \\ 1\end{pmatrix}\right] \\ &= \exp\left[\mathbf{x}_i'\boldsymbol{\beta}^{(a)}\right], \qquad (10.2)\end{aligned}$$

where $\mathbf{x}_i' = (\mathbf{x}_i \;\; \ln t_i)$ and $\boldsymbol{\beta}^{(a)\prime} = (\boldsymbol{\beta}' \;\; \beta_{k+1}) = (\boldsymbol{\beta}' \;\; 1)$. With this specification substituted in the usual expression for log-likelihood, estimation can proceed via constrained maximum likelihood, with the coefficient of $\ln t_i$ being restricted to unity. This constraint can be imposed directly by substitution into the likelihood. Another alternative is to estimate β_{k+1} freely and then use the test of the null hypothesis that $\beta_{k+1} = 1$ as a model specification test.

10.2.2 *Multiplicative Error in Exposure*

In this section we show that a measurement error in exposure is analogous to a measurement error in the dependent variable in the linear regression. A consequence is to inflate the variance through overdispersion. Under appropriate assumptions we find strong parallels between measurement errors and unobserved heterogeneity. Both lead to overdispersion, and in both cases, provided there is no dependence with explanatory variables, maximum likelihood is a consistent estimator. There are also strong parallels in the algebraic analysis of the two problems.

Assume that $\mu_i(\cdot)$ is correctly specified, but t_i is measured with error. Also assume that the measurement error is uncorrelated with the explanatory variables $\mathbf{x}_i$. Suppose the model is estimated by Poisson maximum likelihood.

In considering the impact of measurement error on the properties of the estimator, notice that the model set-up is exactly analogous to the case of multiplicative heterogeneity considered in earlier chapters. The variable t_i replaces the term ν_i. Consequently, in the presence of random measurement errors in t_i, the mixed Poisson model emerges. If t_i is gamma-distributed, for example, the resulting marginal distribution of y_i is the NB2. Formally, we have

$$\begin{aligned} f(y_i \mid \mu_i t_i) &= \frac{\mu_i^{y_i}}{y_i!}\frac{t_i^{y_i}}{e^{\mu_i t_i}} \\ &= \mathsf{P}[\mu_i] \times e^{-t_i} t_i^{y_i}. \end{aligned} \tag{10.3}$$

To handle the problem without an explicit parametric assumption regarding the distribution of t_i, we follow the approach of Gurmu, Rilstone, and Stern (1995):

$$\begin{aligned} h(y_i \mid \mu_i) &= \int f(y_i \mid \mu_i, t_i) g(t_i)\, dt_i \\ &= \frac{\mu_i^{y_i}}{y_i!} \int t_i^{y_i} e^{-(\mu_i t_i)} g(t_i)\, dt_i \\ &= \frac{\mu_i^{y_i}}{y_i!} \mathsf{M}_t^{(y)}(-\mu_i), \end{aligned} \tag{10.4}$$

where $\mathsf{M}_t(-\mu_i) = \mathsf{E}_t[e^{-\mu_i t_i}]$ denotes the moment generating function for t_i and

$$\mathsf{M}_t^{(y)}(-\mu_i) = \mathsf{E}_t\left[t_i^{y_i} e^{-(\mu_i t_i)}\right] \tag{10.5}$$

is the y_i^{th} order derivative of $\mathsf{M}_t(-\mu_i)$ with respect to $-\mu_i$; E_t denotes expectation with respect to the mixing distribution. Essentially (10.4) gives the arbitrary, and hence flexible, mixed Poisson density, which can be analyzed after choosing a suitable $g(t)$ density and then doing the necessary algebra to derive the term $\mathsf{M}_t^{(y)}(-\mu_i)$. Although this approach is quite general, it generates formidable algebraic and computational detail, as shown in section 12.5.

Continuing with the assumption that the intensity function $\mu(\cdot)$ is correctly specified, the assumption of a multiplicative measurement error with a specified parametric distribution leads to a mixed (overdispersed) Poisson model. Interestingly, this implies that overdispersion in a count model may reflect measurement errors. For example, the assumption that t_i in (10.3) has gamma distribution leads to the marginal distribution of y_i being the negative binomial distribution.

We say the measurement errors are exogenous if they are uncorrelated with the covariates $\mathbf{x}_i$. Under the assumption of exogenous measurement errors, it follows that the random measurement errors in exposures do not affect the consistency property of the Poisson maximum likelihood. Furthermore, if the variance of the measurement errors is $O(n^{-1/2})$ (a case of "modest overdispersion" in Cox's [1983] terminology), then the estimator is also asymptotically efficient. A heuristic demonstration of this point follows from a second-order Taylor expansion of (10.1) around $(t_i - 1)$. In general, however, the standard errors of the PML estimator will be incorrect and should be adjusted.

First it is assumed that the true exposure period is of unit length, and the measurement error, $t_i - 1$, is zero mean, finite variance, and uncorrelated with $y_i - \mu_i$:

$$\begin{aligned} &\mathsf{E}_t[t_i - 1] = 0, \\ &\mathsf{E}_t[(t_i - 1)(y_i - \mu_i)] = 0, \\ &\mathsf{E}_t[(t_i - 1)^2] = \sigma_i^2. \end{aligned} \tag{10.6}$$

The second-order Taylor expansion around $\mathsf{P}[\mu_i]$ yields

$$\begin{aligned} \frac{e^{-\mu_i t_i}(\mu_i t_i)^{y_i}}{y_i!} = \mathsf{P}[\mu_i]\big[1 &+ (y_i - \mu_i)(t_i - 1) \\ &+ \frac{1}{2}((y_i - \mu_i)^2 - y_i)(t_i - 1)^2 + O(t_i - 1)^3\big]. \end{aligned}$$

Then

$$\mathsf{E}_t\left[\frac{e^{-\mu_i t_i}(\mu_i t_i)^{y_i}}{y_i!}\right] \approx \mathsf{P}[\mu_i]\left[1 + \frac{1}{2}((y_i - \mu_i)^2 - y_i)\sigma_i^2\right] \Big/ a\big(\mu_i, \sigma_i^2\big) \tag{10.7}$$

where $a(\mu_i, \sigma_i^2)$ is a normalizing constant.

From (10.7) it can be seen that, under the assumption that measurement errors are $O(n^{-1/2})$, the neglect of overdispersion is not asymptotically a serious misspecification, although it affects the estimates of the sample covariance matrix of β. We can also interpret this result to mean that the use of mixed Poisson models may be justified by the presence of particular types of measurement errors.

Suppose $(y_i - \mu_i)$ and $(t_i - 1)$ are correlated, and

$$\mathsf{E}_t[(y_i - \mu_i)(t_i - 1)] \equiv \sigma_i(\mathbf{x}_i, t_i).$$

Then

$$\mathsf{E}_t\left[\frac{e^{-\mu_i t_i}(\mu_i t_i)^{y_i}}{y_i!}\right]$$
$$\approx \mathsf{P}[\mu_i]\left[1 + \sigma_i(\mathbf{x}_i, t_i) + \frac{\sigma_i^2}{2}[(y_i - \mu_i)^2 - y_i]\right] \Big/ a\left(\mu_i, \sigma_i^2\right).$$

Unlike the previous case, the moments of this distribution depend on the distribution of t_i through the covariance $\sigma_i(\mathbf{x}_i, t_i)$. Consequently, as the first moment of the distribution is no longer μ_i, estimators based on the Poisson mean specification will be inconsistent. In general, the entire distribution of y_i, not just the variance, is affected by this type of measurement error. Heuristically, the inclusion in the conditional mean function of variables correlated with t_i should reduce the extent of misspecification. This provides a motivation for using proxy variables for exposure.

10.2.3 *Proxy Variables for Exposure*

In some cases the exposure is more realistically specified as a function of a set of observables. For example, Dionne, Desjardins, Laberque-Nadeau, and Maag (1995) estimate the effect of different medical conditions on truck drivers' distribution of accidents, including exposure factors measured by hours behind the wheel, kilometers driven, and other qualitative factors. The conditional mean function is specified as a function of variables that affect the intensity of the process ($\mathbf{x}_1$) and those that affect the exposure ($\mathbf{x}_2$); thus

$$\begin{aligned} \mu_i t_i \mid \mathbf{x}_{1i}, \mathbf{x}_{2i} &= \exp\left(\mathbf{x}_{1i}'\boldsymbol{\beta}_1 + \ln t_i\right) \\ &= \exp\left[\left(\mathbf{x}_{1i}' \; \mathbf{x}_{2i}'\right)\begin{pmatrix}\boldsymbol{\beta}_1 \\ \boldsymbol{\beta}_2\end{pmatrix}\right], \end{aligned} \qquad (10.8)$$

which does not require constrained estimation. A random error may also be included in the conditional mean. For example, if

$$t_i = \exp\left(\mathbf{x}_{2i}'\boldsymbol{\beta}_2\right)u_i,$$

where u denotes an error with unit mean, then one will get results similar to those in the previous subsection.

10.3 Measurement Errors in Regressors

10.3.1 *Additive Measurement Errors*

Some data sets have two features. First, the assumption that covariates are measured with additive Gaussian errors is reasonable. Second, one has access to replicated data sets that make it feasible to estimate moments of the error distribution. In such cases the approach of Carroll et al. (1995) may be applied.

Consider the case in which the true regressors $\mathbf{X}$ in the conditional mean function are not observed, but a proxy, $\mathbf{W}$, where $\mathbf{W} = \mathbf{X} + \mathbf{U}$, is observed; the additive measurement error $\mathbf{U}$ is assumed to be distributed $\mathsf{N}[\mathbf{0}, \Sigma_{uu}]$. The analysis is based on the conditional distribution of $\mathbf{Y}$ given the error-contaminated variable $\mathbf{W}$, although the main interest is in the conditional distribution of $\mathbf{Y}$ given $\mathbf{X}$. Carroll et al. propose two "functional methods" for generalized linear models, which, unlike "structural methods," make minimal assumptions about the distribution of regressors. The analysis is specialized to the Poisson regression. They suggest two methods, the "conditional-score" and the "corrected-score" methods. The first step in applying these methods is to obtain an estimate of the sufficient statistic for $\mathbf{X}$. The standard estimating equations for the Poisson model can then be modified by replacing the term in the score function involving $\mathbf{X}$ by the sufficient statistic. Assuming that an estimate of Σ_{uu} is available, the adjusted estimating equations still cannot be written in a closed form for the Poisson regression; summation of an infinite series is necessary. Second, estimation of Σ_{uu} requires additional data; this step may be feasible if replicates of $\mathbf{W}$ are available, which may be the case in some disciplines. Finally, the calculation of sampling variances is implemented using bootstrap-type methods. In short, this method of dealing with measurement errors is quite computer-intensive. For further details the reader is referred to the original sources. Jordan, Brubacher, Tsugane, Tsubono, Gey, and Moser (1997) consider a similar model that does not require replicated data. Their estimation procedure is Bayesian and simulation-based.

The analysis does not shed any direct light on the existence of attenuation bias. A heuristic qualitative argument suggests that a downward bias is expected. Measurement errors in covariates increase the range of variation of the explanatory variables without a corresponding effect on the range of the response variable. Consequently unit variation in $\mathbf{W}$ elicits a smaller response than unit variation in $\mathbf{X}$. The quantitative impact of attenuation can be expected to vary depending on the nonlinearity of the conditional mean.

10.3.2 *Multiplicative Error in Regressors*

In this subsection we consider the case of multiplicative measurement errors. With the exponential specification for the conditional mean, the multiplicative error model, the additive error model, and the unobserved heterogeneity models can be shown to be algebraically similar. Hence, under certain assumptions some of the effects of additive or multiplicative errors turn out to be very similar. Different implications can be generated, however, by changes in those assumptions.

Consider the exponential mean model with multiplicative heterogeneity. Specifically, let

$$y_i \mid \mu_i, \nu_i \sim \mathsf{P}[\mu_i \nu_i],$$

where

$$\begin{aligned} \mu_i \nu_i &= \exp(\mathbf{x}_i'\boldsymbol{\beta})\nu_i \\ &= \exp(\mathbf{x}_i'\boldsymbol{\beta} + \varepsilon_i), \end{aligned} \tag{10.9}$$

where $\exp(\varepsilon_i) = \nu_i$.

Now let us compare this with the additive measurement error model in which

$$y_i \mid \mu_i \sim \mathsf{P}[\mu_i],$$

where

$$\mu_i = \exp(\mathbf{x}_i^{*\prime}\boldsymbol{\beta}), \tag{10.10}$$

where $\mathbf{x}^*$ is the vector of unobserved true values of explanatory variables. Assume that $\mathbf{x}^* = \mathbf{x} + \boldsymbol{\eta}$, which has an additive measurement error η, so that

$$\begin{aligned} \mathsf{E}[\mathbf{y}_i \mid \mathbf{x}_i, \boldsymbol{\eta}_i] &= \exp[(\mathbf{x}_i + \boldsymbol{\eta}_i)'\boldsymbol{\beta}] \\ &= \exp(\mathbf{x}_i'\boldsymbol{\beta})\exp(\boldsymbol{\eta}_i'\boldsymbol{\beta}) \\ &= \exp(\mathbf{x}_i'\boldsymbol{\beta})w_i, \end{aligned} \tag{10.11}$$

where $w_i = \exp(\boldsymbol{\eta}_i'\boldsymbol{\beta})$. This formulation has an obvious parallel with unobserved heterogeneity. Clearly one might interpret the unobserved heterogeneity term in (10.9) as a measurement error. One may also interpret it as reflecting omitted regressors $\mathbf{z}$ as in

$$\begin{aligned} \mu_i \mid \mathbf{x}_i, \mathbf{z}_i &= \exp(\mathbf{x}_i'\boldsymbol{\beta} + \mathbf{z}_i'\gamma) \\ &= \exp(\mathbf{x}_i'\boldsymbol{\beta})\exp(\mathbf{z}_i'\gamma) \\ &= \exp(\mathbf{x}_i'\boldsymbol{\beta})u_i, \end{aligned} \tag{10.12}$$

where $u_i = \exp(\mathbf{z}_i'\gamma)$, which is again algebraically similar to the preceding measurement error and heterogeneity models.

These similarities can be exploited by reinterpreting the analysis of the previous subsection. For example, parallel to (10.6), we may specify

$$\mathsf{E}_w[w_i - 1] = 0; \qquad \mathsf{E}_w[(w_i - 1)^2] = \sigma_{w,i}^2;$$
$$\mathsf{E}_w[(w_i - 1)(y_i - \mu_i)] \equiv \sigma_i(\mathbf{x}_i, w_i).$$

Further, parallel to (10.7) we can derive

$$\mathsf{E}_w\left[\frac{e^{-\mu_i w_i}(\mu_i w_i)^{y_i}}{y_i!}\right]$$
$$\approx \mathsf{P}[\mu_i]\left[1+\sigma_i(\mathbf{x}_i, w_i)+\frac{\sigma_{w,i}^2}{2}[(y_i-\mu_i)^2-y_i]\right]\Big/ a\left(\mu_i, \sigma_{w,i}^2\right).$$

So the effects of additive measurement are qualitatively similar to those due to omitted heterogeneity, errors in exposure, or omitted regressors from the conditional mean. If the measurement errors are uncorrelated with the regressors $\mathbf{x}$, then $\mathsf{E}[\eta\,|\,\mathbf{x}]=\mathsf{E}[\eta]$ and w_i has unit mean and finite variance. Then the consequences of measurement error are essentially the same as those due to unobserved heterogeneity, namely overdispersion and loss of efficiency of the PML estimator.

An alternative assumption allows for possible correlation between $\mathbf{x}$ and η. Mullahy (1997a) has argued by reference to the omitted variable case that nonzero correlation is more realistic. That is, one or more of the omitted regressors are likely to be correlated with the included variables. Then the standard PMLE is also inconsistent.

Under certain assumptions, the nonlinear instrumental variable estimator provides consistent estimates of the parameters of the model. Write the model in matrix notation as a nonlinear regression,

$$\mathbf{y}=\exp(\mathbf{X}\beta)+\varepsilon, \tag{10.13}$$

where it is assumed that $\mathsf{E}[\varepsilon\,|\,\mathbf{X}]\neq\mathbf{0}$, $\mathsf{V}[\varepsilon\,|\,\mathbf{X}]=\mathbf{\Omega}$. Assume that we have available $\mathbf{w}_i$, a set of g, $g\geq k+m$ instrumental variables that are asymptotically uncorrelated with ε_i and correlated with $\mathbf{x}_i$. The set of instruments may include a subset of $\mathbf{x}_i$. The NLIV estimator, denoted $\hat{\beta}_{\mathsf{NLIV}}$, minimizes

$$(\mathbf{y}-\exp(\mathbf{X}\beta))'\mathbf{W}(\mathbf{W}'\mathbf{\Omega}\mathbf{W})^{-1}\mathbf{W}'(\mathbf{y}-\exp(\mathbf{X}\beta)),$$

for a given $\mathbf{\Omega}$. Two points to note are that the nonlinear regression has an additive, not multiplicative, error, and that the specification and estimation of the (optimal) weighting matrix $\mathbf{\Omega}$ should be considered. These issues are discussed again in Chapter 11.

10.4 Measurement Errors in Counts

10.4.1 *Additive Measurement Errors in Counts*

Suppose that error-contaminated counts, denoted by y^o, are nonnegative and integer-valued. Let y^t denote the true unobserved count and ε the additive measurement error. That is,

$$y^o=y^t+\varepsilon, \quad y^t, \varepsilon \geqq 0. \tag{10.14}$$

One simple model is

$$y^t \mid \mu \sim \mathsf{P}[\mu]$$

$$\varepsilon \mid \gamma \sim \mathsf{P}[\gamma],$$

and y^t and ε are independently distributed. This implies that

$$y^o \mid \mu, \gamma \sim \mathsf{P}[\mu + \gamma].$$

So the measurement error leads to a larger mean and variance relative to the distribution of y^t. This model has a nonnegative measurement error; hence, it is useful only for characterizing count inflation.

More generally we might consider the case where ε is integer-valued but not necessarily nonnegative. This assumption permits both under- and overcounts. But the nonnegativity restriction on y^o implies parallel restrictions on the distribution of ε. It is implausible to expect such restrictions to hold if it is assumed that y^t and ε are independently distributed. A joint distribution for y^t and ε, which admits correlation, may seem more appropriate. The distribution of y^o may be derived by adding a joint distribution to (10.14).

Binomial thinning, considered in section 7.4, is another example of a mechanism for modeling measurement errors in counts. This mechanism operates such that an event that has occurred is not recorded. Such nonrecording then occurs a random number of times and only affects events, not nonevents. However, as its name suggests, this mechanism generates only undercounts – hence its usefulness in modeling underreporting. Binomial thinning is the opposite of the model of count inflation suggested previously. It is used in section 10.5 to model underreported counts.

One may construct a synthetic model that accommodates both under- and overcounts. An example is a finite mixture involving two "pure" types of contamination, one generating only positive and the other generating only negative measurement error. Currently such models remain underdeveloped.

10.4.2 *Misclassified Counts*

Counted events may be categorized by types. Classification into types may itself be subject to error, leading to incorrect total number of events in each category. The basic idea of this subsection is that improvements result from modeling the classification process. This intuitive idea also recurs in section 10.5, in which we consider underrecording.

We shall begin with an example based on Whittemore and Gong (1991), who consider a situation in which the main interest lies in the mortality rate from cervical cancer using cross-country grouped data on deaths and population at risk in different age groups. We change their notation slightly to be consistent with previous notation in this chapter. They assume that the disease may be misclassified as one of several other diseases but that its diagnosis is unlikely to be erroneous. That is, "Process of classifying has perfect specificity, but imperfect sensitivity denoted by π, and the sensitivity π may vary with covariates" (Whittemore and Gong, 1991, p. 83).

Denote by n_{1i} and n_{2i} the number of correct and incorrect disease classifications, respectively; $i = 1, \ldots, G$. Assume (i) $n_{1i} \sim \mathsf{B}(\pi_i, n_{1i} + n_{2i})$; (ii) disease occurs in each population as a Poisson process; and (iii) distinct populations are independent.

Then the Poisson assumption about actual occurrence of the disease implies that observed fallible disease counts y_i^s are mutually independent Poisson variates. That is,

$$\begin{aligned} y_i^s &\sim \mathsf{P}[\mu_i^c] \\ \mu_i^c &= \pi_i \mu_i \\ &= \pi_i \lambda_i L_i, \end{aligned}$$

where μ_i denotes the disease rate and L_i denotes person-years at risk. Because L_i is known, the focus is on modeling the disease rate λ_i. The likelihood for the ith observation is then the product of Poisson and binomial likelihoods

$$\mathsf{L}_i = (\mu_i^c)^{y_i^s} e^{-\mu_i^c} \pi_i^{n_{1i}} (1 - \pi_i)^{n_{2i}} / y_i^s!$$

and the log-likelihood is

$$\begin{aligned} \mathcal{L}(\lambda, \pi \mid \mathbf{X}, \mathbf{Y}^s, \mathbf{L}, \mathbf{Z}, n_1, n_2) = \sum_{i=1}^{G} \{ & y_i^s \ln \pi_i + y_i^s \ln \lambda_i - \pi_i \lambda_i L_i \\ & + n_{1,i} \ln \pi_i + n_{2,i} \ln(1 - \pi_i) \}, \end{aligned} \tag{10.15}$$

where in what follows $\lambda_i = \exp(\mathbf{x}_i'\beta)$, and

$$\pi_i = \exp(\mathbf{z}_i'\delta) / [1 + \exp(\mathbf{z}_i'\delta)] = \Lambda(\mathbf{z}_i'\delta),$$

which allows the covariates in λ and π terms to differ in principle. Let $\dim(\mathbf{x}_i) = k$, $\dim(\mathbf{z}_i) = s$. This specification is slightly different from Whittemore and Gong's example in which exactly the same covariates determine both λ_i and π_i. The likelihood scores are:

$$\begin{aligned} \frac{\partial \mathcal{L}}{\partial \beta} &= \sum (y_i^s - \mu_i^c) \mathbf{x}_i \\ \frac{\partial \mathcal{L}}{\partial \delta} &= \sum ((y_i^s - \mu_i^c)(1 - \Lambda(\mathbf{z}_i'\delta)) + n_{1i} - (n_{1i} + n_{2i}) \Lambda(\mathbf{z}_i'\delta)) \mathbf{z}_i, \end{aligned} \tag{10.16}$$

where the second block of s equations can be interpreted as implying orthogonality between the covariates $\mathbf{z}_i$ and the difference between the actual and expected frequency of disease counts, allowing for misclassification probability. The $(k + s)$-dimensional information matrix is given by

$$\mathcal{I}(\boldsymbol{\beta}, \boldsymbol{\delta}) = \sum_{i=1}^{n} \begin{bmatrix} \mu_i^c \mathbf{x}_i \mathbf{x}_i' & \mathcal{I}_{\beta\delta} \\ \mathcal{I}_{\beta\delta}' & \mu_i^c (1 - \Lambda(\mathbf{z}_i \boldsymbol{\delta})) \mathbf{z}_i \mathbf{z}_i' \end{bmatrix}, \tag{10.17}$$

where

$$\mathcal{I}_{\beta\delta} = \sum \left[n_{1i} + n_{2i} + \mu_i \left(1 - \Lambda\left(\mathbf{z}_i' \boldsymbol{\delta}\right)\right)\right]\left[\Lambda\left(\mathbf{z}_i' \boldsymbol{\delta}\right)(1 - \Lambda(\mathbf{z}_i \boldsymbol{\delta}))\right] \mathbf{x}_i' \mathbf{z}_i .$$

Note that unless the subsets of covariates $\mathbf{x}$ and $\mathbf{z}$ are mutually orthogonal, the information matrix is not block-diagonal. As before, for identifiability we require that *rank* $[\mathcal{I}(\boldsymbol{\beta}, \boldsymbol{\delta})]$ is $k + s$.

The example discussed above is closely related to the work on log-linear models for categorical data with misclassification errors. There are some similarities between this approach and that used in the underrecorded counts problem, especially in relation to modeling the misclassification probability in terms of observed covariates. However, binomial thinning plays a role in underrecording, but not here. Hence, the frequency of observations within the category may be under- or overreported. If one is interested in more than two misclassification categories, a multinomial logit model offers a suitable parameterization. For other possible generalizations, see Whittemore and Gong (1991, pp. 90–91).

10.4.3 *Outlying Counts*

Let us reconsider the data set on recreational trips that was used in Chapter 6. There was a suspicion of measurement errors in this case arising from the curious "rounding" in the number of self-reported boating trips if that number was 10 or higher (see Table 6.9). Some clustering occurs at 10 and 15 trips, and higher counts often occur in rounded categories like 20, 25, 30, 40, and 50.

To avoid distorted inferences from such data, robust estimation based on discarding some proportion of the data is sometimes recommended. However, Christmann (1994, 1996) notes that the finite sample breakdown points of many robust estimators for regressions with discrete responses are not known. He considers the least median of weighted squares estimator for the Poisson regression and shows that it has a high breakdown point and other desirable properties.

More informally, in practice it may be useful to simply form an impression of the impact of the high counts on the estimated model. One way to do this is to "downweight" the higher counts in which we believe the measurement error might be concentrated. For example, we might truncate the sample at 10 visits if we believe that for frequencies larger than this value the measurement error is too large. Then we might estimate a truncated negative binomial model using 10 visits as a truncation point. Another possibility is to use 10, or some other value, as the censoring point in estimating the right censored negative binomial. This procedure also reduces the weight of large frequencies but less drastically than in the truncated case. A limitation of this idea is that it only explores the consequences of suspected measurement errors and lacks formal justification. For example, how should one choose among different censoring values? The robust estimation approach addresses this problem more formally.

10.5 Underreported Counts

In this section we consider how one might model event counts if there is reason to believe that some events that have occurred might not be recorded. It is easy to see that if events are distributed with mean μ, and each event has a constant probability π of being observed, then the observed event count has mean $\pi\mu$. So a count model fitted to observed data yields information about the product $\pi\mu$. This is clearly a downward-biased estimate of μ, the true mean of the event process. This section considers refinements of this model using the basic idea that modeling the recording process may result in improved inference about parameters of interest.

10.5.1 *Mechanism and Examples*

The term *underrecording* refers to that feature of the method of data collection that causes the observed (recorded) count to understate on average the actual number of events. Parametric estimation and inference are to be based on the recorded counts of the event.

Suppose events are generated by a pure count process, but for each event, a Bernoulli process determines whether the event is recorded. This is the binomial thinning mechanism. For a given recording probability for an individual event, the occurrence probability may be either dependent or independent. In either case, the recorded events are shown to follow a mixed binary process. A regression model can be developed by parameterizing the moments of the mixed process. The main idea is to combine a model of underrecording with a model of the count process.

Examples of underrecorded counts may be found in many fields. They include the frequency of absenteeism in workplaces (Barmby, Orme, and Treble, 1991; Johansson and Palme, 1996), the reporting of industrial injuries (Ruser, 1991), the number of violations of safety regulations in nuclear power plants (Feinstein, 1989, 1990), the frequency of criminal victimization (Fienberg, 1981; Schneider, 1981; Yannaros, 1993), hospital medicine (Watermann, Jankowski, and Madan, 1994), and earthquakes and cyclones (Solow, 1993), to mention only a few.

The example of absenteeism in the workplace serves to illustrate certain recurring features of underreported-count models. In some organizations the recorded absences at work reflect the interaction between the actual incidence of absenteeism and the monitoring mechanism for observing those absences. Monitoring mechanisms are usually not perfect because such observation requires resources, whose use may not be economical beyond a certain point, which itself can be expected to vary across organizations. Let y denote the true number of events. Suppose the probability that an event is recorded, conditional on occurrence, is π, $0 \leq \pi \leq 1$. Assume that the recording and occurrence mechanisms are independent. Then the mean number of recorded events, denoted y_s, is

$$\mathsf{E}[y_s \mid \mu, \pi] = \mu\pi,$$

where $\mathsf{E}[y \mid \mu] = \mu$ is the true mean and π is the average recording probability. This argument suggests a simple nonlinear regression approach to estimation based on parameterizing the μ and π components. If, for example, $\mu = \mu(\mathbf{x}, \boldsymbol{\beta})$, and $\pi = \pi(\mathbf{z}, \boldsymbol{\gamma})$, where $\mu(\cdot)$ and $\pi(\cdot)$ are known functions, the approach leads to a nonlinear regression of the form

$$y_s = \mu(\mathbf{x}, \boldsymbol{\beta})\pi(\mathbf{z}, \boldsymbol{\gamma}) + \varepsilon. \tag{10.18}$$

If $(\boldsymbol{\beta}, \boldsymbol{\gamma})$ are identifiable, then a consistent estimation procedure may be devised. If not, then one may estimate a "reduced form" – type regression

$$y_s = m(\mathbf{x}, \mathbf{z} \mid \boldsymbol{\theta}) + \varepsilon, \tag{10.19}$$

where $m(\cdot)$ may be a given function and $\boldsymbol{\theta}$ is some (generally unknown) function of $(\boldsymbol{\beta}, \boldsymbol{\gamma})$. In the subsequent discussion, we take (10.18) as the equation of interest. Although this basic framework is useful in approaching the problem, we begin by considering the more general case in which there is dependence between observation and recording. However, irrespective of whether the two are dependent, the key idea is that recording should be modeled, not ignored.

10.5.2 *Dependence Between Events and Recording*

Consider a bivariate binomial random variable (Y, R) where $Y = 1$ denotes the single occurrence of an event of interest in some specified time interval, and $R = 1$ denotes the recording of that event. The following table establishes the notation for the probabilities associated with the four possible outcomes:

	$R=1$	$R=0$	
$Y=1$	π_{11}	π_{10}	π
$Y=0$	π_{01}	π_{00}	$1-\pi$
	π'	$1-\pi'$	

The recording process is not directly observable. It is assumed that whereas an event that has occurred may not be recorded (observed), the nonoccurrence of an event is always correctly recorded. Thus, there is zero probability of overrecording.

Recording and occurrence may be dependent. For example, if an event is an action of an informed individual, the probability that the event occurs may depend on whether the event will be recorded. A criminal act or an unauthorized absence from work are two examples or situations in which the recording and occurrence are likely to be dependent. In the first, the true occurrence of absences may depend on the probability of the absence being observed (recorded) by the employer. In the second, the commission of the crime could be a function of the probability of detection.

Let N denote the number of trials and Y and R the number of "successes". It is assumed that the components of the joint event (Y, R) are dependent. To allow for the dependence between Y and R, the following orthonormal series expansion representation of the bivariate binomial (a specialization of Chapter 8) is used:

$$\begin{aligned} f(Y, R) &= g(Y \mid \pi, N) g(R \mid \pi', N) \\ &\quad \times \left[1 + \sum_{n=1}^{N} \rho^n Q_n^*(Y \mid N, \pi) Q_n^*(R \mid N, \pi') \right], \end{aligned} \tag{10.20}$$

where $f(Y, R)$ is the joint density,

$$g(Y \mid \pi, N) = \binom{N}{Y} \pi^Y (1-\pi)^{N-Y},$$

$$g(R \mid \pi', N) = \binom{N}{R} \pi'^{Y} (1-\pi')^{N-R},$$

$Q_n^*(Y \mid N, \pi)$ and $Q_n^*(R \mid N, \pi')$ are the orthonormal (Krawtchouk) polynomials with respect to $g(Y \mid \pi, N)$ and $g(R \mid \pi', N)$, respectively, and ρ is the correlation parameter; $\rho = (\pi_{11} - \pi\pi')/\sqrt{\pi(1-\pi)\pi'(1-\pi')}$. The joint density is the product of the marginals if $\rho = 0$; this is the independence case (see Eagleson, 1964, 1969).*

Because initially we are only interested in the single event, set $N = 1$, and the above expressions simplify as follows:

$$f(Y, R) = g(Y \mid \pi) g(R \mid \pi') \left[1 + \rho Q_1^*(Y \mid \pi) Q_1^*(R \mid \pi') \right] \tag{10.21}$$

where $g(Y \mid \pi) = \pi^Y (1-\pi)^{1-Y}$, $g(R \mid \pi') = \pi'^R (1-\pi')^{1-R}$.

The above may be written as follows:

$$\begin{aligned} \pi_{11} &\equiv f(Y=1, R=1) \\ &= \pi\pi' \left[1 + \rho \frac{1-\pi}{\sqrt{\pi(1-\pi)}} \frac{1-\pi'}{\sqrt{\pi'(1-\pi')}} \right]. \end{aligned} \tag{10.22}$$

*The reader should note that in this case the upper limit of the sum in the orthonormal polynomial expansion is N rather than ∞.

By standard methods we can obtain the conditional probability that the event is recorded, given it has occurred; that is,

$$\begin{aligned} f(R=1 \mid Y=1) &= \pi_{11}/\pi \\ &= \pi' \left[1 + \rho \frac{1-\pi}{\sqrt{\pi(1-\pi)}} \frac{1-\pi'}{\sqrt{\pi'(1-\pi')}} \right] \\ &= \pi^{*\prime} \end{aligned} \tag{10.23}$$

where $\pi^{*\prime} \equiv \pi'(1+\rho C)$, and $C \equiv [\pi\pi']^{-1/2}(1-\pi)^{1/2}(1-\pi')^{1/2}$.

In the special case of independence the recording probability does not depend on the event probability π, and we get $\pi' = \pi^{*\prime}$.

10.5.3 *Distribution of Recorded Events*

Poisson Distribution

To proceed to the case of N recorded events we assume a Poisson process for the events; specifically, there is no serial correlation in the event process. Given the conditional probability of recording, the distribution of recorded events, N_i, follows the Poisson distribution by the following lemma, derived in section 10.6.

Lemma. If $\pi^{*\prime}$ is the probability that an event is recorded and the number of events are distributed $\mathsf{P}[\mu]$, then the number of recorded events are distributed $\mathsf{P}[\mu\pi^{*\prime}]$.

It can be seen that:

- The distribution of the recorded events has a smaller mean ($\mu\pi^{*\prime}$) and variance than the distribution of the actual events; the understatement of the Poisson mean is greater if the correlation is negative.
- The understatement is the greatest in the negative correlation case. To see the effect of the correlation (ρ), note that Eagleson (1969, pp. 36–37) has shown that the correlation ρ obeys the bounds (i) $-1-\pi/(1-\pi) \leq \rho \leq 1$ if $\pi \geq \frac{1}{2}$; and (ii) $-\pi/(1-\pi) \leq \rho \leq 1$, if $\pi \leq \frac{1}{2}$, respectively. Hence, $\mu > \mu\pi'(1+\rho C)$ if $\rho > 0$, and $\mu\pi'(1+\rho C) < \mu\pi'$ if $\rho < 0$. Again note that the dependence between Y and R is captured by the probability function $\pi^{*\prime}$. If Y and R are independent, $\pi^{*\prime} = \pi'$.
- Underrecording can be interpreted as a source of excess zeros because it causes the distribution to shift left, reducing both the mean and the mode, and leading to an excess of zeros relative to the parent distribution. This effect, which is similar to the statistical phenomenon of binomial thinning, appears to be a common feature of all underreported-count models considered here.

- Suppose the probability of underrecording for a given individual varies from event to event. In that case the analysis given previously should be interpreted in terms of average recording probability for an event (Feller, 1968, p. 282).

Negative Binomial Distribution

The basic result extends straightforwardly to the negative binomial model, which can allow for the presence of overdispersion, and to the hurdle model.

The model can be motivated as follows. Let the number of recorded events be distributed according to $\mathsf{P}[\mu\pi^{*\prime}\eta]$, given η, where η is interpreted as a random unobserved heterogeneity term distributed across individuals independently of $\mu\pi^{*\prime}$. For example, let η be gamma-distributed with unit mean and variance α; then unconditionally the number of events follows the $\mathsf{NB2}[\mu\pi^{*\prime}, \alpha]$, that is, with mean $\mu\pi^{*\prime}$, and variance $[\mu\pi^{*\prime}(1+\alpha\mu\pi^{*\prime})]$.

Lemma. Let $\pi^{*\prime}$ be the probability that an event is recorded. Let the number of events follow $\mathsf{NB2}[\mu, \alpha]$ distribution. Then the number of recorded events, Y_s, follows $\mathsf{NB2}[\mu\pi^{*\prime}, \alpha]$ distribution.

10.5.4 *Underrecorded-Count Regressions under Independence*

To proceed to parametric regression models, additional functional form assumptions are required. The independence case is relatively easier to handle, so we consider it first. It may be a reasonable assumption in cases in which the observed events (actions) do not adapt to the recording mechanism; for example, see Solow (1993).

Poisson Case

From the first lemma in section 10.5.3, the first two moments in the Poisson case are

$$\mathsf{E}[Y_s] = \mu\pi', \tag{10.24}$$

$$\mathsf{V}[Y_s] = \mu\pi'. \tag{10.25}$$

For a sample of n observations on Y_s, denoted y_i, $i = 1, \dots, n$, the conditional mean μ_i of the actual count process N_i can be parameterized as $g(\mathbf{x}_i, \boldsymbol{\beta})$, where g is a known one-to-one smooth function, $\mathbf{x}_i$ is the vector of k covariates that characterize the dgp, and $\boldsymbol{\beta}$ is the k-dimensional parameter of interest. Let π_i' be the corresponding probability of recording, assumed to vary across i. Let $\pi_i' = F(\mathbf{z}_i, \boldsymbol{\delta})$, where F is a known smooth monotonic function such that $F(-\infty) = 0$, $F(+\infty) = 1$, $\mathbf{z}_i$ is the vector of covariates that represent the observable characteristics of the recording mechanism, which are distinct from $\mathbf{x}_i$, and $\boldsymbol{\delta}$ is an s-dimensional parameter. (The probability parameter π' generally depends on the observational apparatus R. Therefore, it may be helpful to think of π' as a function of the observable traits of the recording mechanism.) This parameterization of π_i' specializes to a probit or logit formulation. By adopting this restrictive specification we avoid the potential complication that μ_i may also depend upon covariates $\mathbf{z}_i$.

Using (10.24) the mean function for the underreported-count process may be parameterized as

$$\mathsf{E}[y_i \mid \mathbf{x}_i, \mathbf{z}_i] = g(\mathbf{x}_i, \boldsymbol{\beta}) F(\mathbf{z}_i, \boldsymbol{\delta}), \tag{10.26}$$

where $\mathbf{x}_i, \mathbf{z}_i$ are the set of covariates and $(\boldsymbol{\beta}', \boldsymbol{\delta}')$ is the $(k+s)$-dimensional parameter vector to be estimated.

The model can be written as a nonlinear regression model of the following form,

$$y_i = \mathsf{E}[y_i \mid \mathbf{x}_i, \mathbf{z}_i] + \epsilon_i = g(\mathbf{x}_i, \boldsymbol{\beta}) F(\mathbf{z}_i, \boldsymbol{\delta}) + \epsilon_i, \quad i = 1, \ldots, n \tag{10.27}$$

where the conditional mean has a *double-index* structure. The primary interest in the regression model (10.27) is to estimate the parameters $\boldsymbol{\theta}' = (\boldsymbol{\beta}', \boldsymbol{\delta}')$ given (i) the functional forms for $g(\mathbf{x}_i, \boldsymbol{\beta})$ and $F(\mathbf{z}_i, \boldsymbol{\delta})$ and (ii) the underlying data generating process for the true counts N_i – for example, the Poisson assumptions. This model could be estimated by NLS, assuming exogeneity of $(\mathbf{x}_i, \mathbf{z}_i)$.

Let $g(\mathbf{x}_i, \boldsymbol{\beta}) = \exp(\mathbf{x}_i'\boldsymbol{\beta})$ and let $F(\mathbf{z}_i, \boldsymbol{\delta})$ be the logistic cdf, so that,

$$F(\mathbf{z}_i, \boldsymbol{\delta}) = \exp\left(\mathbf{z}_i'\boldsymbol{\delta}\right) / \left(1 + \exp\left(\mathbf{z}_i'\boldsymbol{\delta}\right)\right) \equiv \Lambda\left(\mathbf{z}_i'\boldsymbol{\delta}\right).$$

Then the mean specification as in (10.26) can be written as,

$$\mu_i^c \equiv \mathsf{E}(y_i \mid \mathbf{x}_i, \mathbf{z}_i) = \exp\left(\mathbf{x}_i'\boldsymbol{\beta}\right) \Lambda\left(\mathbf{z}_i'\boldsymbol{\delta}\right). \tag{10.28}$$

Defining π_i' to be a function of covariates $\mathbf{z}_i$ allows it to be heterogeneous across observations. But it is important to have sufficient variation in the covariates $\mathbf{z}_i$, that is, in π_i'. If π_i' is constant for all observations, then it cannot be identified. Rewriting (10.26) explicitly as $\mathsf{E}[y_i \mid \mathbf{x}_i, \mathbf{z}_i] = \exp(\beta_0 + \cdots + x_{ik}\beta_k)\pi'$, one can see that constant π_i' enters the model through the intercept term and $\tilde{\beta}_0 = (\beta_0 + \ln \pi')$ and hence both β_0 and π_i' cannot be individually identified from an estimate $\hat{\tilde{\beta}}_0$.*

The choice of $\mathbf{z}_i$ depends on the specific problem at hand and should be determined from the relevant theories but in general is subject to some restrictions.

Example: Safety Violations

An empirical example of the Poisson–binomial model analyzed previously is Feinstein (1989). He used panel data from over 1000 inspections of 17 U.S.

* This is a consequence of the functional form. Under an alternative functional form the problem may be less serious.

commercial nuclear reactors by the Nuclear Regulatory Commission over 3 years to study factors determining the rate of safety violations. The dependent variable is the number of safety violations cited. He reported a finding that economic incentives had a small impact on noncompliance, whereas technological and operating characteristics of the plant had a larger impact. The model he considers has an additional complication. A sampled plant may or may not comply with regulations, with probabilities $1 - F_1(\mathbf{z}'_{1i}\beta_1)$ and $F_1(\mathbf{z}'_{1i}\beta_1)$, respectively. In turn, a violation by a noncompliant plant may or may not be detected, with probabilities $F_2(\mathbf{z}'_{2i}\beta_1)$ and $1 - F_2(\mathbf{z}'_{2i}\beta_2)$, respectively. Reported nonviolations come from both undetected violators and from genuine nonviolators. These formulations lead to a likelihood function for violation and detection,

$$\begin{aligned}\mathcal{L}(\beta_1, \beta_2 \mid \mathbf{z}_1, \mathbf{z}_2) &= \sum_{i\in V}\left[\ln F_1(\mathbf{z}'_{1i}\beta_1)F_2(\mathbf{z}'_{2i}\beta_2)\right]\\ &\quad+\sum_{i\in V^c}\left[(1-\ln F_1(\mathbf{z}'_{1i}\beta_1))F_2(\mathbf{z}'_{2i}\beta_2)\right],\end{aligned}$$

where V is the set of detected violators and V^c its complement. In Feinstein's model the mean number of detected violations is the product of the detection probability and the mean number of violations, $F_2(\mathbf{z}'_{2i}\beta_2)\mu_i$. Feinstein calls his estimator the *detection control estimator*.

Negative Binomial Case

A variant of NB2 can accommodate overdispersion. Substituting $\mu_i^c = \mu_i\pi_i'$ as the mean of the NB2 distribution we can write the expression for the pdf of the recorded events:

$$\Pr[Y_{i,s} = y_i] = \frac{\Gamma(y_i + \alpha^{-1})}{\Gamma(y_i + 1)\Gamma(\alpha^{-1})}\left(\frac{\alpha^{-1}}{\alpha^{-1} + \mu_i^c}\right)^{\alpha^{-1}}\left(\frac{\mu_i^c}{\alpha^{-1} + \mu_i^c}\right)^{y_i}. \tag{10.29}$$

The mean function in (10.26) together with NB2 specification in (10.27) yields an NB2-logistic regression model with overdispersion parameter α in the variance equation $\mathsf{V}[y_i \mid \mathbf{x}_i, \mathbf{z}_i] = \mu_i^c(1 + \alpha\mu_i^c)$.

10.5.5 *Underreported-Count Regressions under Dependence*

Now suppose the observed counts refer to behavioral responses that incorporate knowledge of, or adaptation to, the recording process.

Poisson Case

Assume that ρ is a constant. Then the result of section 10.5.2 implies that $\mathsf{E}[Y_s]$ is given by

$$\mu^c = \mu\pi'(1 + \rho C), \tag{10.30}$$

where C is defined after (10.23).

This may be interpreted to mean that the second term ρC measures the effect of the departure from independence. This suggests that the functions μ, π', and C should be parameterized in such a way as to identify all parameters of interest. This is difficult because the C component depends on all parameters appearing in the model, as, by definition, $C = Q_1^*(Y=1 \mid \pi)Q_1^*(R=1 \mid \pi')$. Explicitly,

$$C = \sqrt{\frac{(1-\pi)(1-\pi')}{\pi\pi'}} > 0.$$

Under the Poisson process assumptions the probability of observing a single event in the time interval $(t, t+h)$ is $\pi = \mu h + o(h)$. Hence the C term depends on both $\mathbf{x}$ variables, through π or μ, and also on the $\mathbf{z}$ variables, through π'. If we substitute known functional forms for all unknown parameters, the resulting expression for μ^c may not be tractable. This provides some motivation for a functional form such as

$$\mu^c = \mu\pi' + g^*(\mathbf{x}, \mathbf{z}), \tag{10.31}$$

where g^* is treated as an unknown function that can be handled by nonparametric methods (see Chapter 12).

To improve tractability, the use of an ad hoc "approximation" may simplify the expression for μ^c. For example, let

$$\mu_i^c = g(\mathbf{x}_i, \boldsymbol{\beta})F(\mathbf{z}_i, \boldsymbol{\delta}) + \gamma h(\mathbf{x}_i, \mathbf{z}_i, \boldsymbol{\theta}),$$

where the function $h(\cdot)$ may be specified to mimic the properties of the term C. If $\gamma = 0$, the model reverts to the independence case.

If the second term in (10.30) is incorrectly ignored, the resulting misspecification generates an equation error correlated with the included variables in the model. Ignoring this correlation produces inconsistent estimates.

To make consistent estimation feasible, weaker distributional assumptions may now be more appropriate in estimation. A suitable estimator for such a model is likely to be an NLIV estimator, discussed in Chapter 11. In the remainder of this section we consider estimation and inference only under the independence assumption.

10.5.6 *MLE under Independence*

We consider maximum likelihood estimation. Quasilikelihood and moment-based procedures are feasible also and are analyzed in Mukhopadhyay and Trivedi (1995).

For conditionally independent observations, and given the $n \times (k+s)$ matrix $[\partial\mu^c/\partial\boldsymbol{\theta}']$, assumed to have column rank $(k+s)$ for $\boldsymbol{\theta} \in \mathcal{R}^{k+s}$, the log-likelihood function for NB2 can be written as,

$$\mathcal{L}(\mu^c, \alpha) = \sum_1^n \big[\ln\Gamma\big(y_i + \alpha^{-1}\big) + \ln y! - \ln\Gamma(\alpha^{-1}) + \alpha^{-1}\ln(\alpha^{-1}) - \alpha^{-1}\ln\big(\alpha^{-1} + \mu_i^c\big) + y_i \ln \mu_i^c - y_i \ln\big(\alpha^{-1} + \mu_i^c\big)\big]. \tag{10.32}$$

Let $\boldsymbol{\xi} = (\boldsymbol{\theta}', \alpha)'$ and $\boldsymbol{\theta}' = (\boldsymbol{\beta}', \boldsymbol{\delta}')$.

The scores are:

$$\mathbf{s}(\boldsymbol{\xi}) = \left(\mathbf{s}_1'\ s_2\right)',$$

$$\mathbf{s}_1 = \sum_{i=1}^n \left[\frac{y_i - \mu_i^c}{1 + \alpha\mu_i^c}\right]\left[\begin{matrix} \mathbf{x}_i \\ (1 - \Lambda(\mathbf{z}_i'\boldsymbol{\delta}))\,\mathbf{z}_i \end{matrix}\right],$$

$$s_2 = \sum_{i=1}^n \left[\psi(y_i + \alpha^{-1}) - \psi(\alpha^{-1}) + 1 + \ln\left(\frac{\alpha^{-1}}{\alpha^{-1} + \mu_i^c}\right) - \frac{\alpha^{-1} + y_i}{\alpha^{-1} + \mu_i^c}\right],$$

where $\psi(x) = \frac{\partial\Gamma(x)}{\partial x} / \Gamma(x)$.

The information matrix is:

$$\mathcal{I}(\boldsymbol{\xi}) = \sum_1^n \left[\frac{\mu_i^c}{1 + \alpha\mu_i^c}\right] \times \left[\begin{matrix} \mathbf{x}_i\mathbf{x}_i' & (1 - \Lambda(\mathbf{z}_i'\boldsymbol{\delta}))\,\mathbf{x}_i\mathbf{z}_i' & \mathbf{0} \\ (1 - \Lambda(\mathbf{z}_i'\boldsymbol{\delta}))\,\mathbf{z}_i'\mathbf{x}_i & (1 - \Lambda(\mathbf{z}_i'\boldsymbol{\delta}))^2\,\mathbf{z}_i\mathbf{z}_i' & \mathbf{0} \\ \mathbf{0} & \mathbf{0} & \mathcal{I}_{\alpha\alpha}(\boldsymbol{\xi}) \end{matrix}\right], \tag{10.33}$$

where

$$\mathcal{I}_{\alpha\alpha}(\boldsymbol{\xi}) = -\mathsf{E}\left[\frac{1 + \alpha\mu_i^c}{\mu_i^c}\left(\psi'(y_i + \alpha^{-1}) - \psi'(\alpha^{-1}) + \alpha - \frac{1 + y_i}{\alpha^{-1} + \mu_i^c} + \frac{\alpha^{-1} + y_i}{\left(\alpha^{-1} + \mu_i^c\right)^2}\right)\right].$$

The block-diagonality property follows from $\mathsf{E}[y_i - \mu_i^c] = 0$ which implies $\mathsf{E}[\partial^2\mathcal{L}/\,\partial\alpha\partial\boldsymbol{\beta}'] = \mathbf{0}$.

Identifiability requires that $\mathcal{I}(\boldsymbol{\xi})$ should be nonsingular. The matrix $\mathcal{I}(\boldsymbol{\xi})$ becomes singular if $\mathbf{x}_i = \mathbf{z}_i$. Computational problems occur if recording probability does not vary sufficiently across observations. It can be shown that the information matrix in (10.33) is nonsingular if and only if either $\mathbf{x}$ or $\mathbf{z}$ does not belong to the column space of the other.

An alternative to the double-index model presented here is a single-index model in which μ_i^c is written in the form $g(\mathbf{x}_i, \mathbf{z}_i)$, where g is treated as a known or unknown function. That is, no attempt might be made to distinguish between the two separate components of μ_i^c. Distinguishing between the double- and single-index models in small samples may be especially difficult, because this distinction relies heavily on functional forms.

10.5.7 *Model with Under- or Overrecording*

The zero-inflated model introduced in section 4.7 has been used if zeros only are overreported, and a zero-deflated distribution has been used if the zeros are underrecorded (Cohen, 1960; Johnson, Kotz, and Kemp, 1992). The model

$$\begin{aligned}
\Pr[y=0] &= \varphi + (1-\varphi)\, e^{-\mu} \\
\Pr[y=r] &= (1-\varphi)e^{-\mu}\, \mu^r/r!, \qquad r=1,2,\ldots
\end{aligned}$$

accommodates overreporting if $0 < \varphi < 1$ and underreporting if $(1-e^{\mu})^{-1} < \varphi < 0$. The case in which both over- and underrecording are present in the same data set is more difficult. A promising approach is to treat it in the finite mixture framework, with the sampling proportions corresponding to the type of measurement error.

10.5.8 *Example: Self-Reported Doctor Visits*

Often the survey data are based on self-reported information that is potentially subject to recall errors whose importance may vary depending on the length of the period to which the information refers. Both under- and overrecording seem possible.

Some evidence from the United States (U.S. National Center for Health Statistics, 1967) for chronic medical conditions suggests that self-reported medical records may understate the degree of health care usage. According to the U.S. National Center for Health Statistics (1965), hospitalizations have also been found to be underreported in the United States.

McCallum, Raymond, and McGilchrist (1995) carry out an interesting study using Australian data in which a comparison is made between self-reported number of doctor visits over a 3-month period and the same usage as measured by the (presumably more accurate) records of the Health Insurance Commission. In a sample of around 500, they find that self-reported estimates were overreported relative to the Health Insurance Commission estimates for small (1 to 4) numbers of visits but generally underreported for higher usage. McCallum et al. analyze the relation between the reporting error and the characteristics of the respondents and conclude with a cautionary note about the use of self-reported data.

The approach of this section has an important potential weakness in regard to the identifiability of the parameters. First, it relies on prior information or theory that sharply distinguishes between the variables that affect the event occurrence probability (**x** variables) and those that affect the recording probability (**z** variables). In practice such a sharp distinction may be difficult, or the **x** and **z** variables may be sufficiently highly correlated as to lead to a loss of identification. Second, in this approach one relies on the exponential and logistic functional forms to distinguish between a theory that assumes no underrecording but postulates that both the **x** and **z** variables enter through a single index function and a theory that postulates that the conditional mean has a double-index structure given in (10.27) or (10.28).

10.6 Derivations

We first consider the derivations of the lemmas in section 10.5.3.

Let $R_1, R_2, \ldots, R_N$ be a sequence of N independent Bernoulli trials, in which each R_j is 1 if the event is recorded (with probability $\pi^{*\prime}$) and 0 otherwise (with probability $1 - \pi^{*\prime}$). The number of recorded events Y_s can be written as $Y_s = R_1 + R_2 + \cdots + R_N$. The resulting distribution of Y_s is a compound Poisson distribution, or a binomial distribution stopped by Poisson distribution. The distribution of Y_s can be derived using the pgf. Let $\varphi(t)$ be the pgf of the Poisson, then

$$\varphi(t) = \exp(-\mu + \mu t) \quad \text{for any real } t.$$

If $\xi(t)$ is the pgf of the Bernoulli trial, then

$$\xi(t) = (1 - \pi^{*\prime}) + \pi^{*\prime} t \quad \text{for any real } t,$$

and the pgf of Y_s is,

$$\begin{aligned} \varphi(\xi(t)) &= \exp(-\mu + \mu\xi(t)) \\ &= \exp(-(\mu\pi^{*\prime}) + (\mu\pi^{*\prime})t) \quad \text{for any real } t. \end{aligned}$$

So, Y_s is Poisson-distributed with parameter $\mu\pi^{*\prime}$. This proves the first lemma.

The proof of the second lemma is similar to the first. The pgf of negative binomial distribution is given as

$$\varphi(t) = (1 + \gamma - \gamma t)^{-\alpha^{-1}} \quad \text{for any real } t,$$

where $\gamma = \alpha\mu$.

Then the pgf of Y_s is

$$\begin{aligned} \varphi(\xi(t)) &= (1 + \gamma - \gamma\xi(t))^{-\alpha^{-1}} \\ &= (1 + (\gamma\pi^{*\prime}) - (\gamma\pi^{*\prime})t)^{-\alpha^{-1}} \quad \text{for any real } t. \end{aligned}$$

So, Y_s follows negative binomial distribution with parameters $\mu\pi^{*\prime}$ and α.

We now present second-order partial derivatives used in deriving the information matrix in section 10.5. These are as follows:

$$\frac{\partial^2 \mathcal{L}}{\partial \beta \partial \beta'} = -\sum_{i=1}^{n} \left[\frac{\alpha^{-1} + y_i}{\alpha^{-1}\left(1 + \alpha\mu_i^c\right)^2} \right] \mu_i^c \mathbf{x}_i \mathbf{x}_i'.$$

$$\frac{\partial^2 \mathcal{L}}{\partial \delta \partial \delta'} = -\sum_{i=1}^{n} \left[\frac{\alpha^{-1} + y_i}{\alpha^{-1}\left(1 + \alpha\mu_i^c\right)^2} + \frac{y_i - \mu_i^c}{1 + \alpha\mu_i^c} \Lambda\left(\mathbf{z}_i'\delta\right) \right] \times \mu_i^c \left[1 - \Lambda\left(\mathbf{z}_i'\delta\right)\right]^2 \mathbf{z}_i \mathbf{z}_i'.$$

$$\frac{\partial^2 \mathcal{L}}{\partial \beta \partial \delta'} = -\sum_{i=1}^{n} \left[\frac{\alpha^{-1} + y_i}{\alpha^{-1}\left(1 + \alpha\mu_i^c\right)^2} \right] \mu_i^c \left[1 - \Lambda\left(\mathbf{z}_i'\delta\right)\right] \mathbf{x}_i \mathbf{z}_i'.$$

$$\frac{\partial^2 \mathcal{L}}{\partial \alpha^2} = \sum_{i=1}^{n} \left[\psi'(y_i + \alpha^{-1}) - \psi'(\alpha^{-1}) + 1/\alpha - \frac{1 + y_i}{\alpha^{-1} + \mu_i^c} + \frac{\alpha^{-1} + y_i}{\left(\alpha^{-1} + \mu_i^c\right)^2} \right].$$

$$\frac{\partial^2 \mathcal{L}}{\partial \alpha \partial \beta'} = -\sum_{i=1}^{n} \frac{y_i - \mu_i^c}{\left(\alpha^{-1} + \mu_i^c\right)^2} \mu_i^c \mathbf{x}_i$$

$$\frac{\partial^2 \mathcal{L}}{\partial \alpha \partial \delta'} = -\sum_{i=1}^{n} \frac{y_i - \mu_i^c}{\left(\alpha + \mu_i^c\right)^2} \mu_i^c \left[1 - \Lambda\left(\mathbf{z}_i'\delta\right)\right] \mathbf{z}_i.$$

10.7 Bibliographic Notes

Carroll et al. (1995) is an up-to-date account of recent research in measurement error in nonlinear models with an emphasis on the GLM literature. The Poisson model with additive normal measurement errors in covariates is discussed in Chapter 6. Jordan et al. (1997) estimate a Poisson regression with overdispersion and normally distributed errors-in-variables for mortality data in a Bayesian framework using Monte Carlo techniques. A general discussion of the effects of measurement error on the distribution of the response variable and in leading to a possible attenuation bias in the LEF and LEFN classes of models is analyzed in Chesher (1991). The proxy variable approach to modeling exposures is illustrated in Dionne et al. (1995). Alcañiz (1996) examines computational algorithms for restricted estimation of Poisson and NB2 models with errors in exposure.

The section on underrecorded counts borrows from Mukhopadhyay and Trivedi (1995). They also develop a score test for underrecording in a negative binomial model. The representation of the bivariate binomial that they use has been studied by Eagleson (1964, 1969). Eagleson's work follows the earlier contributions summarized in Lancaster (1969). Cameron and Trivedi (1993) review some earlier contributions.

Chen (1979) deals with a log-linear model with misclassified data. Whittemore and Gong (1991) provide further references.

10.8 Exercises

10.1 Consider the following sequential estimator: (1) Estimate the Poisson–logistic model by maximum likelihood. Let $\hat{\mu}^c$ denote the MLE. (2) Regress the quantity $(y - \hat{\mu}^c)^2 - \hat{\mu}^c$ on $(\hat{\mu}^c)^2$. (3) Substitute the estimate of α, $\tilde{\alpha}$, into the "score" equations after (10.32) and solve the equations,

$$s(\boldsymbol{\theta}(\tilde{\alpha})) \equiv \sum_{1}^{n} \left(\frac{y_i - \mu_i^c}{1 + \tilde{\alpha}\mu_i^c} \right) \begin{bmatrix} x_i \\ (1 - \Lambda(\mathbf{z}_i'\boldsymbol{\delta}))\mathbf{z}_i \end{bmatrix} = \mathbf{0}.$$

Interpret this sequential estimator as a QGPML estimator. Compare the properties of the estimator with one in which α is estimated using the moment equation

$$\sum_{i=1}^{n} \left[\frac{(y_i - \hat{\mu}_i^c)^2}{\hat{\mu}_i^c(1 + \alpha\hat{\mu}_i^c)} - \frac{n - k - m}{n} \right] = 0.$$

10.2 Consider the recreational trips data from Chapter 6. It was suggested there that the data may be subject to recall or measurement errors. Assuming that these recall errors are potentially concentrated among high counts, reestimate the Poisson and NB2 models after sequentially deleting counts greater than (a) 15, (b) 20, and (c) 25. Which parameters from the estimated model would you expect to be most sensitive to such deletion? Does your expectation match the observed outcome?

10.3 Using the set-up in section 10.5, and assuming independence between event occurrence and event recording, show that the result of lemma 1 also extends to the hurdle count model.

CHAPTER 11

Nonrandom Samples and Simultaneity

11.1 Introduction

This chapter deals with the topic of valid inference about the population given samples that are not simple random samples. There are several well-known ways in which departures from simple random sampling occur. They include choice-based sampling and endogenous stratified sampling, endogenous regressors, and sample selection.

The departure from simple random sampling may cause the sample probability of observations to differ from the corresponding population probabilities. In general such a divergence leads to models in which simple conditioning on exogenous variables does not lead to consistent estimates of the population parameters. These topics have been studied in depth in the discrete choice literature (Manski and McFadden, 1981). The analysis of count data in the presence of such complications is relatively underexplored.

A second topic considered in this chapter is endogenous regressors. Ignoring the feedback from the response variable to the endogenous regressor leads in general to invalid inferences. The estimation procedure should allow for stochastic dependence between the response variable and endogenous regressors. In considering this issue the existing literature on simultaneous equation estimation in nonlinear models is of direct relevance (Amemiya, 1985). This material is a continuation of section 8.2.

The third topic considered is sample selection in count regression, which also is closely related to issues of simultaneity and nonrandom sampling.

Section 11.2 analyzes the consequences of choice-based sampling in general and stratified random sampling with specific reference to standard count models. Section 11.3 is a continuation of section 8.2, in which simultaneity issues in count models and GMM estimation were discussed. The topic of GMM is studied further in section 12.2. Finally, section 11.4 deals with sample selection problems, which is another type of departure from random sampling.

11.2 Alternative Sampling Frames

Simple random samples and exogenous sampling serve as benchmarks for other cases. They are described in sections 11.2.1 and 11.2.2. They generate a likelihood function that we can compare with those that arise in the alternative cases. For example, in section 11.2.3 we show how certain common forms of departures from the random sampling framework arise and affect the likelihood. The resulting likelihood function is a weighted version of that obtained under random sampling. Section 11.2.4 specializes this result to the case of counted data from on-site samples.

11.2.1 *Simple Random Samples*

As a benchmark for subsequent discussion, consider simple random samples for count data. These generally involve a nonnegative integer-valued count variable y and a set of covariates $\mathbf{x}$ whose joint distribution, denoted $f(y, \mathbf{x})$, can be factored as the product of the conditional and marginal distributions thus:

$$f(y, \mathbf{x} \mid \boldsymbol{\theta}) = g(y \mid \mathbf{x}, \boldsymbol{\theta}) h(\mathbf{x}). \tag{11.1}$$

Note that the parameter of interest, $\boldsymbol{\theta}$, does not appear in $h(\mathbf{x})$.

In the preceding chapters the attention has been largely focused on $g(y \mid \mathbf{x}, \boldsymbol{\theta})$, that is, modeling y given $\mathbf{x}$. *Simple random sampling* involves drawing the $(y, \mathbf{x})$ combinations at random from the entire population. A variation of simple random sampling is *stratified random sampling*. This involves partitioning the population into strata defined in terms of $(y, \mathbf{x})$ and making random draws from each stratum. The number of draws from a stratum is some preselected fraction of the total survey sample size. We now consider how departures from simple random sampling arise. Complications arise when the strata are not based on $\mathbf{x}$ alone.

11.2.2 *Exogenous Sampling*

Exogenous sampling from survey data occurs if the analyst segments the available sample into subsamples based only on a set of exogenous variables $\mathbf{x}$, but not on the response variable y, here the number of events. Perhaps it is more accurate to depict this type of sampling as exogenous subsampling because it is done by reference to an existing sample that has already been collected. Segmenting an existing sample by gender, health, or socioeconomic status is very commonplace. For example, in their study of hospitalizations in Germany, Geil et al. (1997) segmented the data into two categories, those with and without chronic conditions. Classification by income categories is also common. Under exogenous sampling the probability distribution of the exogenous variables is independent of y and contains no information about the population parameters of interest, $\boldsymbol{\theta}$. Therefore, one may ignore the marginal distribution of the exogenous variables and simply base estimation on the conditional distribution $g(y \mid \mathbf{x}, \boldsymbol{\theta})$.

11.2.3 *Endogenous or Choice-Based Sampling*

Endogenous or *choice-based sampling* occurs if the probability of an individual being included in the sample depends on the choices made by that individual.

The practical significance of this is that consistent estimation of $\boldsymbol{\theta}$ can no longer be carried out using the conditional population density $g(y \mid \mathbf{x})$ alone. The effect of the sampling scheme must also be taken into account.

In what follows, f denotes the joint, g the conditional, and h the marginal densities. For further analysis we distinguish the sampling probability from the population probability by superscript s on $f(\cdot)$ and $h(\cdot)$. We have

$$f^s(y, \mathbf{x}) = g(\mathbf{x} \mid y) h^s(y),$$

which can be reexpressed using the relations

$$\begin{aligned} f(y, \mathbf{x}) &= g(y \mid \mathbf{x}) h(\mathbf{x}), \\ &= g(\mathbf{x} \mid y) h(y), \end{aligned}$$

where the marginal distributions are $h(\mathbf{x}) = \sum_y f(y, \mathbf{x})$ and $h(y) = \int g(y \mid \mathbf{x}) \times h(\mathbf{x})\, d\mathbf{x}$. Combining the above, we obtain

$$\begin{aligned} f^s(y, \mathbf{x} \mid \boldsymbol{\theta}) &= \frac{f(y, \mathbf{x}) h^s(y)}{h(y)} \\ &= \frac{g(y \mid \mathbf{x}, \boldsymbol{\theta}) h(\mathbf{x}) h^s(y \mid \boldsymbol{\theta})}{\int g(y \mid \mathbf{x}, \boldsymbol{\theta}) h(\mathbf{x})\, d\mathbf{x}} \\ &= g(y \mid \mathbf{x}, \boldsymbol{\theta}) \omega(y, \mathbf{x} \mid \boldsymbol{\theta}), \end{aligned}$$

where

$$\omega(y, \mathbf{x} \mid \boldsymbol{\theta}) = \frac{h(\mathbf{x}) h^s(y \mid \boldsymbol{\theta})}{\int g(y \mid \mathbf{x}, \boldsymbol{\theta}) h(\mathbf{x})\, d\mathbf{x}}.$$

The log-likelihood function based on $f^s(y, \mathbf{x})$ is

$$\mathcal{L}(\boldsymbol{\theta} \mid y, \mathbf{x}) = \sum_{i=1}^{n} \ln g(y_i \mid \mathbf{x}_i, \boldsymbol{\theta}) + \sum_{i=1}^{n} \ln \omega(y_i, \mathbf{x}_i \mid \boldsymbol{\theta}). \tag{11.2}$$

This can be interpreted as weighted log-likelihood, or log-likelihood based on weighted probabilities, where the weights ω_i are ratios of sample and population probabilities and differ from unity (as in simple random samples). If there exists prior information on the weights, then likelihood estimation based on weighted probabilities is straightforward. In the more usual situation in which such information is not available, estimation is difficult because the distribution of $\mathbf{x}$ is involved. The literature on the estimation problem in the context of discrete choice models is extensive (Manski and McFadden, 1981).

Standard conditional estimation considers the case when $f^s(y, \mathbf{x}) = f(y, \mathbf{x})$. Then $\omega(y, \mathbf{x} \mid \boldsymbol{\theta}) = h(\mathbf{x})$, which does not depend on $\boldsymbol{\theta}$, and maximizing $\mathcal{L}(\boldsymbol{\theta} \mid y, \mathbf{x})$ with respect to $\boldsymbol{\theta}$ is the same as just considering the first term in (11.2). If $f^s(y, \mathbf{x}) \neq f(y, \mathbf{x})$, however, analysis using standard conditional estimation, which ignores the last term, leads to inconsistent estimates of $\boldsymbol{\theta}$.

11.2.4 *Counts with Endogenous Stratification*

Count data are sometimes collected by on-site sampling of users. For example, on-site recreational or shopping mall surveys (Shaw, 1988; Englin and Shonkwiler, 1995; Okoruwa, Terza, and Nourse, 1988) may be carried out to study the frequency of use, often using travel-cost models. Such samples involve truncation because only those who use the facility at least once are included in the survey. Furthermore, even among users the likelihood of being included in the sample depends on the frequency of use. The latter feature of the sample is also called *endogenous stratification* or *sampling* because the selection of persons surveyed is based on a stratified sample, with random sampling within each stratum, the latter being defined by the number of events of interest.

Endogenous stratification has some similarities with choice-based sampling. As in that case, lower survey costs provide an important motivation for using stratified samples in preference to simple random samples. It requires a very large random sample to generate enough observations (information) about a relatively rare event, such as visiting a particular recreational site. Hence, it is deemed cheaper to collect an on-site sample. However, the problem is that of making inferences about the population from the sample. To do so we need the relation between the sample frequency function and the population density function (Amemiya, 1985, pp. 319–338; Pudney, 1989, pp. 102–105).

A major objective in the analyses of on-site samples is to estimate the underlying (latent) population demand function for the number of trips. This is usually specified as a function of travel cost to the site j by user i, denoted C_{ij}, and the characteristics of the site j, $\mathbf{z}_j$, and of the user i, $\mathbf{x}_i$. That is, $y_i^* = \phi(C_{ij}, \mathbf{x}_i, \mathbf{z}_j)$, where y_i^* denotes the desired number of trips. The demand (y_i) is only observed if $y^* > 0$, that is, $y = y^*$, if $y^* > 0$. The sample space for the on-site sample is $\{1, 2, \ldots\}$ whereas the sample space for the simple random sample would be $\{0, 1, 2, \ldots\}$. Thus the first consequence of on-site sampling is truncation at zero. If $f(y \mid \mathbf{x})$ denotes the population density of y (the number of trips), then the truncated density is $f(y \mid \mathbf{x})/\Pr[y > 0]$.

To derive a density function suitable for analyzing on-site samples, the joint effect of truncation and stratification has to be considered. Shaw (1988) considered the estimation problem for the choice-based sample. First, assume that in absence of endogenous stratification the probability density of visits by individual i, given characteristics $\mathbf{x}^0$, is $g(y_i \mid \mathbf{x}^0)$. Suppose there are m sampled individuals with $\mathbf{x} = \mathbf{x}^0$. Then the probability that individual i is observed to make y^0 visits is

$$\begin{aligned}\Pr[y_i = y^0 \mid \mathbf{x}^0] &= \Pr[\text{sampled value is } y^0 \text{ and sampled individual is } i] \\ &= \Pr[\text{sampled value is } y^0] \Pr[\text{sampled individual is } i] \\ &= g(y^0 \mid \mathbf{x}^0) \frac{y_i}{y_1 + y_2 + \cdots + y_{i-1} + y_i + \cdots + y_m}.\end{aligned}$$

Next consider the probability of observing y^0 visits across all individuals, not just the ith individual, $\Pr[\mathrm{y} = \mathrm{y}^0 \mid \mathbf{x}^0]$, denoted P_m. This is the weighted sum of probability of y^0 visits, where the weight of individual i ($i = 1, \ldots, m$) is $y^0/(y_1 + y_2 + \cdots + y_{i-1} + y^0 + y_{i+1} + \cdots + y_m)$:

$$
\begin{aligned}
P_m &= g(y^0 \mid \mathbf{x}^0)\left(\frac{y^0}{y^0 + y_2 + \cdots + y_{i-1} + y_i + \cdots + y_m} + \cdots \right.\\
&\quad \left. + \frac{y^0}{y_1 + y_2 + \cdots + y_{i-1} + y_i + \cdots + y^0}\right)\\
&= g(y^0 \mid \mathbf{x}^0)\frac{1}{m}\left(\frac{y^0}{(y^0 + y_2 + \cdots + y_{i-1} + y_i + \cdots + y_m)/m} + \cdots \right.\\
&\quad \left. + \frac{y^0}{(y_1 + y_2 + \cdots + y_{i-1} + y_i + \cdots + y^0)/m}\right).
\end{aligned}
$$

If we let $m \to \infty$, the denominators inside the brackets above approach the population mean value of y, given $\mathbf{x} = \mathbf{x}^0$,

$$
\mathsf{E}[y^0 \mid \mathbf{x}^0] = \sum_{y^0=1}^{\infty} y^0 g(y^0 \mid \mathbf{x}^0).
$$

Then,

$$
\begin{aligned}
\lim_{m\to\infty} P_m &= g(y^0 \mid \mathbf{x}^0)\frac{1}{m}\left(\frac{y^0}{\sum_{y^0=1}^{\infty} y^0 g(y^0 \mid \mathbf{x}^0)} + \cdots + \frac{y^0}{\sum_{y^0=1}^{\infty} y^0 g(y^0 \mid \mathbf{x}^0)}\right)\\
&= \frac{y^0 g(y^0 \mid \mathbf{x}^0)}{\sum_{y^0=1}^{\infty} y^0 g(y^0 \mid \mathbf{x}^0)}.
\end{aligned}
$$

This argument and derivation show that the relation between the conditional density, $g^s(y_i \mid \boldsymbol{\mu}_i)$ for the endogenously stratified sample, and the population conditional density, $g(y_i \mid \mathbf{x}_i)$, is given by

$$
\begin{aligned}
g^s(y_i \mid \boldsymbol{\mu}_i) &= g(y_i \mid \mathbf{x}_i)\frac{y_i}{\sum_{y^0=1}^{\infty} y^0 g(y^0 \mid \mathbf{x}_i)} &\quad (11.3)\\
&= g(y_i \mid \mathbf{x}_i)\omega(y_i, \mu_i), &\quad (11.4)
\end{aligned}
$$

where

$$
\omega(y_i, \mu_i) = \frac{y_i}{\mu_i}.
$$

The key result is (11.4). This expression specializes to the following if the population density is $\mathsf{P}[\mu_i]$:

$$
g^s(y_i \mid \mu_i) = \frac{e^{-\mu_i}\mu_i^{y_i-1}}{(y_i - 1)!}, \quad (11.5)
$$

where

$$\mathsf{E}[y_i \mid \mathbf{x}_i] = \mu_i + 1 \tag{11.6}$$

$$\mathsf{V}[y_i \mid \mathbf{x}_i] = \mu_i. \tag{11.7}$$

Notice that the sample displays underdispersion even though the population shows equidispersion. Maximization of the likelihood based on (11.5) can be interpreted as maximizing a weighted likelihood. The case considered here is a special case of the more general discussion of choice-based sampling in the preceding section.

An interesting implication of the analysis is that there is a computationally simple way of maximizing this particular weighted likelihood. This is achieved by making the transformation $w_i = y_i - 1$, because the resulting sample space for w_i is the same as that for the regular Poisson likelihood for w_i. That is, applying the Poisson model to the original data with 1 subtracted from all y observations yields consistent estimates of the population mean parameter because

$$\frac{e^{-\mu_i}\mu_i^{w_i}}{w_i!} = \frac{e^{-\mu_i}\mu_i^{y_i-1}}{(y_i-1)!}, \qquad y_i = 1, 2, \ldots. \tag{11.8}$$

Hence, estimation can be implemented with the usually available software for Poisson maximum likelihood, whereas maximum likelihood estimation based on (11.5) requires additional (although not difficult) programming.

Although the support for the zero-truncated Poisson (section 4.5) and the choice-based Poisson is the same, the two distributions are different. Specifically, in the truncated Poisson case,

$$\mathsf{E}[y_i \mid y_i \geq 0] = \mu_i/(1 - e^{-\mu_i}) > \mathsf{V}[y_i \mid y_i \geq 0],$$

which implies underdispersion. Choice-based sampling also displays underdispersion, but this arises from a shift in the probability distribution.

The approach developed here can be extended for any parent population density by specializing (11.4). Englin and Shonkwiler (1995) substitute the weighted negative binomial in place of the weighted Poisson and show that the subtraction device shown above for the Poisson also works for the negative binomial. Santos Silva (1997) considers the implications of unobserved heterogeneity in the same model.

11.3 Simultaneity

In this section we consider the application of instrumental variable estimators for dealing with the problem of endogenous regressors. Our treatment explains how the choice of optimal instruments is affected by the way the error term enters the model, and the assumptions about heteroskedasticity. The simplest way to treat the problem is given at the end of section 11.3.2.

11.3.1 *Alternative Approaches*

In Chapter 8 we outlined several empirically interesting cases in which a count variable was jointly determined with another discrete or continuous variable. An example from health economics of a simultaneous model involving counts is the joint model of health-insurance choice, a discrete variable, and a measure of healthcare services utilized, a count variable (Cameron et al., 1988). Another example is a labor supply model with the number of children as an explanatory variable. However, if fertility is treated as endogenous, an equation for the number of children should be a part of the model (Browning, 1992, pp. 1464–1465).

A further motivation for simultaneous equation estimation comes from the correlation between unobserved heterogeneity and included regressors. The common assumption that unobserved heterogeneity is uncorrelated with the regressors is not plausible if it is a consequence of omitted regressors, which are likely to be correlated with the included ones (see section 8.2).

Consider the two-element vector $\mathbf{y} = (y_1, y_2)'$ with joint density $f(\mathbf{y} \mid \mathbf{x}, \boldsymbol{\theta})$, where $\mathbf{x}$ is treated as nonstochastic. It is convenient to treat y_1 as a count; y_2 may be either discrete or continuous. The standard factorization is

$$f(\mathbf{y} \mid \mathbf{x}, \boldsymbol{\theta}) = g(y_1 \mid \mathbf{x}, y_2, \boldsymbol{\theta}_1)h(y_2 \mid \mathbf{x}, \boldsymbol{\theta}_2), \qquad \boldsymbol{\theta} \in \boldsymbol{\Theta}.$$

The standard result is that y_2 and $\mathbf{x}$ may be treated symmetrically if $h(y_2 \mid \mathbf{x})$ does not depend on $\boldsymbol{\theta}_1$. Estimating the parameters $\boldsymbol{\theta}_1$ by conditioning y_1 on y_2 does not yield consistent estimates if the marginal density of y_2 depends on $\boldsymbol{\theta}_1$, in which case y_2 is said to be *endogenous*.

To deal with this case, several approaches have evolved. One approach is to jointly model $(y_1, y_2)'$. This full information approach is reviewed in Chapter 8. A limited information approach is based on specification of one or two moments of $g(y_1 \mid \mathbf{x}, y_2, \boldsymbol{\theta}_1)$. These are extensions of the GMM or instrumental variable methods for linear models. Despite nonlinearity of moment equations, such moment-based methods are attractive. This is because maximum likelihood estimation of $\boldsymbol{\theta}$ is usually computationally cumbersome, as the joint likelihood may not have a closed-form expression. It is often difficult to establish the marginal distribution $h(y_2 \mid \mathbf{x})$, so estimation methods often focus on approaches that do not require this step.

11.3.2 *Additive Errors*

For nonlinear simultaneous equations an instrumental variable procedure was proposed by Amemiya (1974). This approach readily extends to the special case of Poisson-type regression with endogenous regressors. The key step is to specify the conditional mean function with an additive error term.

First we consider estimation of an exponential regression with an additive error that is correlated with the regressors $\mathbf{x}$. Let $\mathbf{X}$ denote $n \times k$ matrix of regressors. Let $\boldsymbol{\mu} = \exp(\mathbf{X}\boldsymbol{\beta})$ and $\mathbf{u} = \mathbf{y} - \exp(\mathbf{X}\boldsymbol{\beta})$, where $\exp(\mathbf{X}\boldsymbol{\beta})$ is an

$(n \times 1)$ vector of n conditional means. With endogenous regressors, $\mathsf{E}[\mathbf{u} \mid \mathbf{x}] \neq \mathbf{0}$, which implies

$$\mathsf{E}[\mathbf{X}'(\mathbf{y} - \exp(\mathbf{X}\beta))] \neq \mathbf{0}. \tag{11.9}$$

Suppose we have available a set of r linearly independent instruments $\mathbf{W}$, where $\mathbf{W}$ is $n \times r$ and may include a subset of $\mathbf{X}$, $r \geq \dim(\beta)$. Assume $\mathbf{W}$, satisfy $\mathsf{E}[(\mathbf{y} - \exp(\mathbf{X}\beta)) \mid \mathbf{W}] = \mathbf{0}$, which implies

$$\mathsf{E}[\mathbf{W}'(\mathbf{y} - \exp(\mathbf{X}'\beta))] = \mathbf{0}. \tag{11.10}$$

Let $\mathbf{P_W} = \mathbf{W}(\mathbf{W}'\mathbf{W})^{-1}\mathbf{W}'$. Then from Chapter 2, the NLIV estimator $\hat{\beta}_{\mathsf{NLIV}}$ minimizes

$$(\mathbf{y} - \boldsymbol{\mu}(\beta))' \, \mathbf{P_W}(\mathbf{y} - \boldsymbol{\mu}(\beta)). \tag{11.11}$$

Under regularity conditions (Amemiya, 1985, p. 246), if $\mathsf{V}[\mathbf{y}] = \sigma^2 \mathbf{I}_n$,

$$\hat{\beta}_{\mathsf{NLIV}} \sim \mathsf{N}\left[\beta, \sigma^2 \left[\left(\frac{\partial \boldsymbol{\mu}'}{\partial \beta}\right) \mathbf{P_W} \left(\frac{\partial \boldsymbol{\mu}}{\partial \beta'}\right)\right]^{-1}\right], \tag{11.12}$$

where a consistent estimator of σ^2 is given by

$$\hat{\sigma}^2 = \frac{1}{n} \sum_{i=1}^{n} \left(y_i - \exp\left(\mathbf{x}_i' \hat{\beta}_{\mathsf{NLIV}}\right)\right)^2.$$

The asymptotic properties of this type of estimator are also studied in Burguette, Gallant, and Souza (1982), Hansen (1982), and Newey (1990a) and are reviewed in Chapter 2 in a slightly different notation.

The preceding results are general. This method is valid for count data but ignores the integer nature of the data and instead models the conditional mean. A refinement needed for count data, however, is to relax the assumption of homoskedastic error. One can either use the estimator in (11.11) with a more general form of the variance matrix than (11.12) or use another more efficient estimator.

Suppose we assume

$$\mathsf{E}[(\mathbf{y} - \boldsymbol{\mu})(\mathbf{y} - \boldsymbol{\mu})' \mid \mathbf{W}] = \boldsymbol{\Omega} = \mathsf{Diag}\left[\sigma_i^2\right].$$

For example, under equidispersion,

$$\boldsymbol{\Omega} = \mathsf{Diag}[\mu_i].$$

Ignoring this information implies that $\hat{\beta}_{\mathsf{NLIV}}$ is consistent but not efficient. A more efficient estimator is obtained if the previous objective function is replaced by

$$(\mathbf{y} - \boldsymbol{\mu}(\beta))' \, \mathbf{P}_{\mathbf{W}\boldsymbol{\Omega}} \, (\mathbf{y} - \boldsymbol{\mu}(\beta)), \tag{11.13}$$

where

$$\mathbf{P}_{\mathbf{W}\Omega} = \mathbf{W}(\mathbf{W}'\Omega\mathbf{W})^{-1}\mathbf{W}'.$$

In implementing this estimator a two-step procedure is used in which a consistent estimator $\hat{\Omega} = \mathsf{Diag}[\hat{\mu}_i]$ is obtained first, and then $\mathbf{P}_{\mathbf{W}\hat{\Omega}}$ is substituted for $\mathbf{P}_{\mathbf{W}\Omega}$ in the objective function. Denote the resulting two-step estimator as $\hat{\beta}_{\mathsf{NLIV2}}$. The previously given distributional result still applies after substituting the above expression for $\mathbf{P}_{\mathbf{W}\Omega}$. That is,

$$\hat{\beta}_{\mathsf{NLIV2}} \sim \mathsf{N}[\beta, [\mathbf{X}'\hat{\Omega}\mathbf{P}_{\mathbf{W}\hat{\Omega}}\hat{\Omega}\mathbf{X}]^{-1}], \tag{11.14}$$

because $\partial\mu/\partial\beta' = -\hat{\Omega}\mathbf{X}$.

Optimal instrumental variables, denoted $\mathbf{W}^*$, are those that yield the smallest asymptotic variances. In the present case the optimal instrumental variable matrix, using the results in section 2.5.3, is

$$\mathbf{W}^* = \mathsf{E}\left[\Omega^{-1}\frac{\partial\mu}{\partial\beta'}\middle|\mathbf{W}\right],$$

which for $\mu = \exp(\mathbf{x}'\beta)$ specializes to just $\mathbf{X}$ if $\mathbf{W} = \mathbf{X}$ (no endogenous regressors). The problem of obtaining an expression for $\mathbf{W}^*$ is compounded further if there is heteroskedasticity of the type commonly assumed in count models, which makes the expression $\Omega^{-1}[\partial\mu/\partial\beta']$ a complicated function of $\mathbf{X}$ and $\mathbf{W}$, some of which are endogenous. The key problem is that an analytical expression for the expectation $\mathsf{E}[\Omega^{-1}\partial\mu/\partial\beta' \mid \mathbf{W}]$ is usually not available if the residual function u is nonlinear in the unknown parameters. In the general case in which $\mathbf{W} \neq \mathbf{X}$, consistent estimation of $\mathbf{W}^*$ is impossible, and one usually has to settle for consistent rather than efficient estimation. If one accepts as a working hypothesis that $\Omega = \mathsf{Diag}[\mu_i]$ or its scalar multiple, then the resulting instruments are $\mathbf{W}^* = \mathsf{E}[\mathbf{X} \mid \mathbf{W}]$. This simple result depends on the assumption that $\mu = \exp(\mathbf{x}'\beta)$. Windmeijer and Santos Silva (1997) suggest that in practice one should use the instrument set $\mathbf{X}_A$, obtained by augmenting $\mathbf{X}$ by variables not collinear with $\mathbf{X}$.

11.3.3 *Multiplicative Errors*

Mullahy (1997b) and Windmeijer and Santos Silva (1997) have discussed the additive versus multiplicative error formulations, and their impact on the choice of optimal instruments. Suppose the conditional mean function is specified as

$$\mathsf{E}[y \mid \mathbf{x}, \eta] = \exp(\mathbf{x}'\beta, \eta), \tag{11.15}$$

where for simplicity the subscript i is suppressed. The regression model with a multiplicative error is

$$y = \exp(\mathbf{x}'\beta + \eta) = \exp(\mathbf{x}'\beta)\exp(\eta) = \exp(\mathbf{x}'\beta)\nu, \tag{11.16}$$

where η is a stochastic error correlated with $\mathbf{x}$. Such an assumption may be rationalized in terms of some relevant but unobserved variables that are omitted from the regression. Endogeneity of some of the regressors implies that $\mathsf{E}[\nu \mid \mathbf{x}] \neq 1$. Though the stochastic error η is not additively separable from $\exp(\mathbf{x}'\boldsymbol{\beta})$, as required for the application of the standard NLIV approach, a transformation can put it in that form. Specifically, the regression model may be written as

$$T(y, \mathbf{x}, \boldsymbol{\beta}) - 1 = \nu - 1, \tag{11.17}$$

where $T(y, \mathbf{x}, \boldsymbol{\beta}) = \exp(-\mathbf{x}'\boldsymbol{\beta})y$. Assume we have instruments $\mathbf{w}$ that satisfy

$$\mathsf{E}[\nu - 1 \mid \mathbf{w}] = \mathbf{0}. \tag{11.18}$$

An NLIV procedure for consistent estimation of $\boldsymbol{\beta}$ is to minimize the objective function $(\boldsymbol{\nu} - 1)'\mathbf{P_W}(\boldsymbol{\nu} - 1)$, or to solve the orthogonality conditions,

$$\mathsf{E}[\mathbf{W}'(\mathbf{T}(y, \mathbf{X}, \boldsymbol{\beta}) - \mathbf{1})] = \mathbf{0}, \tag{11.19}$$

where we have used matrix notation in (11.19).

An important point is that instrumental variables that are orthogonal to a multiplicative error ν are not in general orthogonal to an additive error u. The specification of the error term affects the objective function, the choice of instruments, and the estimates of $\boldsymbol{\beta}$. As before, if $\mathsf{V}[\boldsymbol{\nu}] = \boldsymbol{\Omega} = \mathsf{Diag}[\mu_i]$, the objective function and the orthogonality conditions must be suitably modified. Specifically note that the optimal instruments in the multiplicative case are given by

$$\mathbf{W}^* = \mathsf{E}[\boldsymbol{\Omega}^{-1}\partial\boldsymbol{\nu}/\partial\boldsymbol{\beta}' \mid \mathbf{W}].$$

Because $\partial\boldsymbol{\nu}/\partial\boldsymbol{\beta}' \neq \partial\boldsymbol{\mu}/\partial\boldsymbol{\beta}'$, they differ from those in the additive case. However, this discussion is subject to a caveat. Optimal instruments may have other undesirable properties, motivating one to use a suboptimal set. This issue is analyzed in section 2.5.3.

Finally note that, if the specification of the variance function is ignored, most of the discussion of this section is not tailored to count data models as such. It applies more generally to models with exponential mean. However, heteroskedasticity is a major feature of count data, so customization to count models with given variance functions is useful. For simplicity, the foregoing discussion uses a variance function without a nuisance parameter, but extension is feasible. Consistent estimation of such a nuisance parameter can be based on a sequential two-step procedure. At the first stage NLIV is applied without heteroskedasticity adjustment. At the second stage the nuisance parameter is estimated using methods analogous to those discussed in section 3.2. Finally, although we have emphasized the single-equation NLIV estimation, as pointed out in Chapter 9 the approach can in principle be generalized to dynamic panel data models (Blundell, Griffiths, and Windmeijer, 1995).

11.3.4 *Example*

A two-variable model with interdependent count and binary outcome variables is one of the most relevant. Windmeijer and Santos Silva (1997), for example, consider the following model, in which y_1 is a count and y_2^* is a latent variable,

$$\begin{aligned} y_{1i} &= \exp\left(\alpha y_{2i} + \mathbf{x}_{1i}'\boldsymbol{\beta}\right) + u_{1i} \\ y_{2i}^* &= \gamma y_{1i} + \mathbf{x}_{2i}'\boldsymbol{\delta} + u_{2i}, \end{aligned} \tag{11.20}$$

where

$$\mathsf{Cov}[u_{1i}, u_{2i}] = \begin{bmatrix} \sigma_{1i}^2 & \sigma_{12i} \\ \sigma_{12i} & 1 \end{bmatrix}, \tag{11.21}$$

where $var(u_{2i}) = 1$ is a necessary normalization. The latent variable and the observed variable y_2 are related by

$$y_{2i} = \begin{cases} 1 & \text{if } y_{2i}^* > 0, \\ 0 & \text{otherwise.} \end{cases}$$

This model is logically coherent, in the sense of satisfying the restriction

$$\Pr[y_{2i} = 1] + \Pr[y_{2i} = 0] = 1,$$

only if either $\alpha = 0$ or $\gamma = 0$. Assuming the latter, endogeneity implies $\sigma_{12i} \neq 0$. Suppose, to take account of endogeneity, the y_1 equation is estimated after replacing y_2 by its conditional mean, $F(\mathbf{x}_2'\hat{\boldsymbol{\delta}})$, where $F(\cdot)$ denotes the estimated cdf of y_2. This mimics the logic of instrumental variable estimation in linear simultaneous equations models. In that case the procedure leads to consistent estimates. In the present case,

$$y_{1i} = \exp\left[\alpha F\left(\mathbf{x}_{2i}'\hat{\boldsymbol{\delta}}\right) + \mathbf{x}_{1i}'\boldsymbol{\beta}\right] \exp\left[\alpha\left(y_{2i} - F\left(\mathbf{x}_{2i}'\hat{\boldsymbol{\delta}}\right)\right)\right] + u_{1i};$$

where, ignoring the estimation of $\boldsymbol{\delta}$, the zero mean "error term," $y_2 - F(\mathbf{x}_2'\boldsymbol{\delta})$, depends on $\mathbf{x}_2$ through its variance $F(\mathbf{x}_2'\boldsymbol{\delta})[1 - F(\mathbf{x}_2'\boldsymbol{\delta})]$. Estimation of the y_1 equation with the conditional mean function $\exp[\alpha F(\mathbf{x}_2'\boldsymbol{\delta}) + \mathbf{x}_1'\boldsymbol{\beta}]$ does not yield consistent estimates of the parameters. However, as shown above for the multiplicative error case, the NLIV estimator, with the instrumental variable matrix $\mathbf{W} = [F(\mathbf{x}_2'\hat{\boldsymbol{\delta}})\ \ \mathbf{x}_2]$, is consistent.

11.4 Sample Selection

Sample selection bias, usually induced by a departure from simple random sampling, is an important issue in microeconometrics and may arise in count models. Although the issue is a very general one (Heckman, 1976; Manski, 1995), in econometrics it has usually been discussed in the context of a rather special normal linear model with censoring. The standard formulation of the selection problem in this linear case does not cover three distinguishing features of count regression models: nonnegativity, discreteness of the dependent variable, and the frequently observed high incidence of zero observations. Solutions to these problems have been discussed by Terza (1998) and Weiss (1995). Several of these involve application of numerical methods to overcome analytically intractable expressions in the likelihood. Our exposition focuses on the method, avoiding details of computation that can be found in the cited works. We consider both full information and limited information estimators. We begin by reviewing a commonly used approach in the standard bivariate normal case with the regression/probit structure.

11.4.1 *Normal Linear Case*

In this subsection we sketch the well-known formulation of selection effect in the linear model. Suppose one wants to make inferences about the effectiveness of a treatment, such as a training program for workers. The following two equations describe the decision to participate in the treatment and the outcome measure, for example, post-training wage, y_1:

$$\begin{aligned} y_1 &= \mathbf{x}'\boldsymbol{\beta} + \alpha y_2 + u \\ y_2^* &= \mathbf{z}'\boldsymbol{\gamma} + \varepsilon \\ y_2 &= \begin{cases} 1 & \text{iff } y_2^* > 0 \\ 0 & \text{iff } y_2^* \leq 0, \end{cases} \end{aligned} \qquad (11.22)$$

where $y_2 = 1$ for those who participate and $y_2 = 0$ for those who do not. The variable y_2^* is a latent participation propensity indicator that depends on $\mathbf{z}$. The variable y_2 may also be thought of as a censoring indicator. For $i = 1, \ldots, n$, variables $(\mathbf{x}_i, y_{2i})$ are always observed, but y_{1i} is only observed if $y_{2i} = 1$. If the latent variable is positive the individual participates in the treatment, and otherwise not.

One objective of an empirical investigation may be to make inferences about the average effect of the treatment on the outcome of a randomly selected member of the population, conditional on a given $\mathbf{x}$ vector. However, the partial observability of y_1 makes for a potential identification problem for $\Pr[y_1 \mid \mathbf{x}]$. This is seen from the total probability equation (Manski, 1995)

$$\begin{aligned} \Pr[y_1 \mid \mathbf{x}] = {} & \Pr[y_1 \mid \mathbf{x}, y_2 = 1]\Pr[y_2 = 1 \mid \mathbf{x}] \\ & + \Pr[y_1 \mid \mathbf{x}, y_2 = 0]\Pr[y_2 = 0 \mid \mathbf{x}]. \end{aligned}$$

The sampling process cannot identify the term $\Pr[y_1 \mid \mathbf{x}, y_2 = 0]$. As Manski emphasizes, whenever the censoring probability $\Pr[y_2 = 0 \mid \mathbf{x}]$ is positive, the available empirical evidence places no restrictions on $\Pr[y_1 \mid \mathbf{x}]$. To learn anything about $\mathsf{E}[y_1 \mid \mathbf{x}]$, restrictions must be placed on $\Pr[y_1 \mid \mathbf{x}]$. Frequently, these restrictions are strongly parametric; that is, identification is secured by assuming particular functional forms for moment functions and distributions of random variables, frequently linearity and normality. Given these assumptions, the fully efficient MLE is obtained from the likelihood based on the expression for $\Pr[y_1 \mid \mathbf{x}]$ given above. The alternative is to make weaker assumptions and reach weaker conclusions.

It is assumed that

$$\mathsf{E}[\mathbf{u} \mid \mathbf{X}, \mathbf{y}_2] = \mathbf{0}; \qquad \mathsf{E}[\varepsilon \mid \mathbf{Z}] = \mathbf{0}; \qquad \mathsf{E}[\mathbf{u}\varepsilon' \mid \mathbf{X}, \mathbf{Z}, \mathbf{y}_2] \neq \mathbf{0},$$

and the two disturbances have a joint bivariate normal distribution with covariance matrix $\mathbf{\Sigma} = [\sigma_{jk}]$, $j, k = 1, 2$. If $\mathsf{E}[\mathbf{u}\varepsilon' \mid \mathbf{X}, \mathbf{Z}, \mathbf{y}_2] = \mathbf{0}$, the treatment equation (for y_2) may be estimated by probit MLE, and the outcome equation (for y_1) by linear regression.

Now

$$\begin{aligned}\mathsf{E}[y_{1i} \mid \mathbf{x}_i, y_{2i} = 1] &= \mathbf{x}_i'\boldsymbol{\beta} + \alpha + \mathsf{E}[u_i \mid \mathbf{x}_i, y_{2i} = 1] \\ &= \mathbf{x}_i'\boldsymbol{\beta} + \alpha + \mathsf{E}\big[u_i \mid \varepsilon_i > -\mathbf{z}_i'\gamma\big] \\ &= \mathbf{x}_i'\boldsymbol{\beta} + \alpha + \frac{\sigma_{12}}{\sqrt{\sigma_{22}}} r_{M_i} + u_i, \end{aligned} \tag{11.23}$$

where α is the treatment effect and $\mathsf{E}[u_i \mid \mathbf{x}_i, y_{2i} = 1]$ is the selection effect, $r_{Mi} = \phi_i/(1 - \Phi_i)$ denotes the inverse Mills ratio of standard normal pdf to the cdf, and u_i is a zero mean disturbance.

The estimation of α will be contaminated unless we can control for the selection effect. For example, estimation of $(\boldsymbol{\beta}, \alpha)$ by least squares assuming exogenous y_2 variable yields an inconsistent estimate because of the selection effect. This occurs because y_2 is not exogenous in the outcome equation; that is, $\mathsf{E}[u\varepsilon] \neq 0$. Alternatively, we may think of the inconsistency problem as caused by the omitted "regressor" r_M. Consistent maximum likelihood and sequential estimation procedures have been proposed (Maddala, 1983; Pudney, 1989). An especially popular estimator is the Heckman two-step sequential procedure in which a probit model is fitted first to y_{2i}, and the estimated parameters are used to estimate $r_{M,i}$, denoted $\hat{r}_{M,i}$. The latter is substituted for the true unobserved variable, and the linear regression equation is estimated. The estimator is consistent (Amemiya, 1985); the computation of its variance is complicated and uses the method given in section 2.5.4.

11.4.2 *Selection Effect in a Count Model*

The key feature of data that results in a selectivity bias is that some phenomenon of interest is not fully observed and certain observations are systematically excluded from analysis. In a count model this can arise if the event counts are only observed for a selected subpopulation. An example given by Greene (1994) considers the number of major derogatory reports for a sample of credit-card holders. Suppose this sample were used to make inferences about the probability of loan default of a credit card applicant with specified characteristics. Such an inference would exhibit selectivity bias because it would be based only on major derogatory reports of individuals who have already been issued credit cards. The sample would not be random if some individuals who might otherwise default on payments had their applications for credit cards turned down. Such individuals are underrepresented in the sample of existing card holders. To tackle the task of estimating the count model in the presence of selectivity bias, it is necessary to model both the process of issuing credit cards and the counts of major derogatory reports.

Several authors including Terza (1998) and Greene (1994, 1997b) have developed full maximum likelihood and two-step procedures for a sample-selection model for count data. The model considered has one outcome (count) equation and one selection equation. Although the model can be generalized, in this section we review their approach in the simpler context in which one has two dependent variables, one of which is a binary outcome variable (y_2) and the other a count variable (y_1) that is observed for only one particular realization of the binary variable. The key analytical device for modeling selection effects in such a model is to begin with a parametric count distribution for y_1 conditional on covariates $\mathbf{x}$ and heterogeneity ν, with the assumption that heterogeneity and the disturbance term in the binary outcome model follow a bivariate normal distribution. We observe whether or not $y_2 = 1$ (e.g., whether or not a credit card is issued), and y_1 if $y_2 = 1$ (e.g., number of major derogatory reports given issued credit card).

The observed value of the binary variable y_2, given exogenous variables $\mathbf{z}$, is determined by

$$y_2 = \begin{cases} 1 & \text{if } \mathbf{z}'\boldsymbol{\theta}_2 + \varepsilon > 0 \\ 0 & \text{otherwise.} \end{cases}$$

The count variable y_1 is observed only if $y_2 = 1$. The joint distribution of y_1 and y_2 is denoted $\Pr[y_1, y_2 = 1 \mid \mathbf{x}, \mathbf{z}, \nu]$. The distribution is conditioned on covariates $\mathbf{x}$ and unobserved heterogeneity term ν. The random variables ν and ε are assumed to have a bivariate normal distribution with mean zero and $\text{Cor}[\nu, \varepsilon] = \rho; \mathsf{V}[\nu] = \sigma^2; \mathsf{V}[\varepsilon] = 1$. Then the conditional distribution of ε_i given ν_i is $\mathsf{N}[(\rho/\sigma)\,\nu_i, (1 - \rho^2)]$.

Maximum likelihood estimation is based on the joint density of y_{1i} and $y_{2i} = 1$, and on the probability that $y_{2i} = 0$. Then

$$\mathcal{L}(\boldsymbol{\beta}, \boldsymbol{\theta}_2, \rho, \sigma) = \sum_{i=1}^{n} \ln \Pr[y_{1i}, y_{2i} = 1 \mid \mathbf{x}_i, \mathbf{z}_i, \nu_i] + \ln \Pr[y_{2i} = 0 \mid \mathbf{z}_i]. \tag{11.24}$$

First we need to derive the detailed expressions for the two terms in the log-likelihood. The first term is obtained by integrating out unobserved heterogeneity from the conditional distribution of counts

$$\begin{aligned}\Pr[y_{1i}, y_{2i} = 1 \mid \mathbf{x}_i, \mathbf{z}_i] &= \int_{-\infty}^{\infty} \Pr[y_{1i}, y_{2i} = 1 \mid \mathbf{w}_i, \nu_i]\, g(\nu_i)\, d\nu_i \\ &= \mathsf{E}_\nu\, [\Pr[y_{1i}, y_{2i} = 1 \mid \mathbf{w}_i, \nu_i]] \\ &\approx \frac{1}{S}\sum_{s=1}^{S} \Pr\left[y_{1i}, y_{2i} = 1 \mid \mathbf{w}_i, \nu_i^s\right], \end{aligned} \tag{11.25}$$

where $\mathbf{w}_i = [\mathbf{x}_i, \mathbf{z}_i]$, and the last line is an approximation to $\mathsf{E}_\nu[\cdot]$ based on simulated probability using pseudorandom draws ν_i^s from the distribution of ν, denoted $g(\nu)$. The details of how to draw and use the random numbers efficiently can be found in Gourieroux and Monfort (1997).

Conditional on ν_i, y_{1i} and y_{2i} are independent, hence

$$\Pr[y_{1i}, y_{2i} = 1 \mid \mathbf{w}_i, \nu_i] = \Pr[y_{1i} \mid \mathbf{x}_i, \nu_i]\Pr[y_{2i} = 1 \mid \mathbf{z}_i, \nu_i],$$

where the first term on the right-hand side is the conditional count distribution. The second term is

$$\begin{aligned}&\Pr[y_{2i} = 1 \mid \mathbf{z}_i, \nu_i] \\ &\quad= \Pr\left[\varepsilon_i > -\mathbf{z}_i'\boldsymbol{\theta}_2 \mid \mathbf{z}_i, \nu_i\right] \\ &\quad= \int_{-\mathbf{z}_i'\boldsymbol{\theta}_2}^{\infty} (2\pi)^{-1/2}(1-\rho^2)^{-1/2} \exp\left[-\frac{1}{2(1-\rho^2)}\left(\varepsilon_i - \frac{\rho}{\sigma}\nu_i\right) d\varepsilon_i\right] \\ &\quad= \Phi\left[(1-\rho^2)^{-1/2}\left(\mathbf{z}_i'\boldsymbol{\theta}_2 + \frac{\rho}{\sigma}\nu_i\right)\right].\end{aligned} \tag{11.26}$$

Let $\Pr[y_1, y_2 = 1 \mid \mathbf{w}, \nu, \varepsilon]$ denote the joint distribution of y_1 and y_2, conditional on $\mathbf{w}$, $(= [\mathbf{x}, \mathbf{z}])$, ν, and ε. Integrating out ν we obtain

$$\begin{aligned}&\Pr[y_{1i}, y_{2i} = 1 \mid \mathbf{w}_i] \\ &\quad= \int_{-\infty}^{\infty} \Pr[y_{1i} \mid \mathbf{x}_i, \nu_i]\Phi\left[(1-\rho^2)^{-1/2}\left(\mathbf{z}_i'\boldsymbol{\theta}_2 + \frac{\rho}{\sigma}\nu_i\right)\right] \\ &\qquad\quad \times \frac{1}{\sigma\sqrt{2\pi}}\exp\left(-\frac{\nu_i^2}{2\sigma^2}\right) d\nu_i, \\ &\quad= \frac{1}{\sqrt{\pi}}\int_{-\infty}^{\infty} \exp(-u_i^2)\Pr[y_{1i} \mid \mathbf{x}_i, u_i]\,\Phi\left[\mathbf{z}_i'\boldsymbol{\theta}_2^* + \tau u_i\right] du_i,\end{aligned} \tag{11.27}$$

where the second line is obtained by a change of variable $u = \nu/\sqrt{2\sigma^2}$, $\delta = \sigma/\sqrt{2\sigma^2}$, $\tau = \sqrt{2}\rho/(1-\rho^2)^{1/2}$, $\boldsymbol{\theta}_2^* = \boldsymbol{\theta}_2/(1-\rho^2)^{1/2}$. This expression involves $\Pr[y_{1i} \mid \mathbf{x}_i, u_i]$ which is the heterogeneity-conditional distribution of the counts, specified as Poisson by both Terza and Greene.

Integrating out ν_i from $\Pr[y_{2i} = 0 \mid \mathbf{z}_i, \nu_i]$ in (11.26) yields the expression for the second term in the log-likelihood,

$$\begin{aligned}\Pr[y_{2i} = 0 \mid \mathbf{z}_i] &= \int_{-\infty}^{\infty} \left(1 - \Pr\left[\varepsilon_i > -\mathbf{z}_i'\boldsymbol{\theta}_2 \mid \mathbf{z}_i, \nu_i\right]\right) g(\nu_i)\, d\nu_i \\ &= \frac{1}{\sqrt{2\pi}} \int_{-\infty}^{\infty} \exp(-u_i^2)\Phi\left[-(\mathbf{z}_i'\boldsymbol{\theta}_2^* + \tau u_i)\right] du_i \\ &= \mathsf{E}_\nu \Pr\left[\varepsilon_i < -\mathbf{z}_i'\boldsymbol{\theta}_2 \mid \mathbf{z}_i, \nu_i\right] \\ &\approx \frac{1}{S}\sum_{s=1}^{S} \Pr\left[\varepsilon_i < -\mathbf{z}_i'\boldsymbol{\theta}_2 \mid \mathbf{z}_i, \nu_i^s\right]. \end{aligned} \tag{11.28}$$

The log-likelihood is constructed using the two terms (11.28) and (11.27),

$$\begin{aligned}\mathcal{L}(\boldsymbol{\beta}, \boldsymbol{\theta}_2, \rho, \sigma) &= \sum_{i=1}^{n} \ln \Pr[y_{1i}, y_{2i} = 1 \mid \mathbf{w}_i] \\ &\quad + \sum_{i=1}^{n} \ln \Pr[y_{2i} = 0 \mid \mathbf{z}_i]. \end{aligned} \tag{11.29}$$

The maximization of this likelihood function requires either numerical integration or simulation as illustrated in section 4.9. The SML maximizes

$$\begin{aligned}\mathcal{L}(\boldsymbol{\beta}, \boldsymbol{\theta}_2, \rho, \sigma) &= \sum_{i=1}^{n} \ln\left(\frac{1}{S}\sum_{s=1}^{S} \Pr\left[y_{1i}, y_{2i} = 1 \mid \mathbf{w}_i, \nu_i^s\right]\right) \\ &\quad + \sum_{i=1}^{n} \ln\left(\frac{1}{S}\sum_{s=1}^{S} \Pr\left[\varepsilon_i < -\mathbf{z}_i'\boldsymbol{\theta}_2 \mid \mathbf{z}_i, \nu_i^s\right]\right). \end{aligned} \tag{11.30}$$

The expected values of random functions, expressed as integrals in the log-likelihood, are approximated by a sample mean of S simulated values of these terms based on random draws u_i^s, $s = 1, \ldots, S$. In other words, the probabilities in the log-likelihood, expressed as integrals, are approximated by sample means of their simulated values. The resulting expression is then maximized in the usual way.

Although the method is computationally intensive, Greene's (1997b) illustrative application shows that computation is manageable.

Weiss (1995) proposes an alternative method for modeling sample selection with count data, based on Lee (1983). The marginal distributions of the random variables ν and ε are specified. With known marginals, transformations to convert these random variables to jointly normal variables can be found. Let $G(\nu)$ denote the distribution function cdf of ν, and let there be a function $h(\nu_i)$ such that

$$\varepsilon_i = \rho h(\nu_i) + \xi_i, \tag{11.31}$$

where $\xi_i \mid \nu_i \sim \mathsf{N}[0, \sigma_\xi^2]$. Here ρ is the correlation parameter. For example, assume gamma heterogeneity and consider a transformation of ν_i such that the resulting variable is linearly related to (correlated with) ε_i. That is, the transformation h can be found using

$$\begin{aligned}\Phi\,[h(\nu_i)] &= G(\nu_i)\\ h(\nu_i) &= \Phi^{-1}[G(\nu_i)]\,,\end{aligned} \tag{11.32}$$

then (11.31) may be substituted into the expression for $f(y_1, y_2 \mid w)$. Maximizing the likelihood based on this approach still requires numerical integration (Weiss, 1995).

11.4.3 *Sequential Estimation*

In view of the computational burden of the full information approach, an analog of the Heckman two-step approach (see section 11.4.1) has some appeal. Using essentially the same set-up given previously, the conditional mean of y_1 is given by

$$\begin{aligned}\mathsf{E}[y_{1i} \mid y_{2i} = 1] &= \exp\left[\mathbf{x}_i'\boldsymbol{\beta} + \frac{\sigma^2}{2}\right]\left(\frac{\Phi(\mathbf{z}_i'\boldsymbol{\theta}_2 + \rho\sigma)}{\Phi(\mathbf{z}_i'\boldsymbol{\theta}_2)}\right)\\ &= \exp\left[\mathbf{x}_i'\boldsymbol{\beta}^*\right]\left(\frac{\Phi(\mathbf{z}_i'\boldsymbol{\theta}_2 + \rho\sigma)}{\Phi(\mathbf{z}_i'\boldsymbol{\theta}_2)}\right),\end{aligned} \tag{11.33}$$

where $\boldsymbol{\beta}^*$ is the same as $\boldsymbol{\beta}$ apart from the intercept term, which is shifted by $\sigma^2/2$, (Johnson, Kotz, and Balakrishnan, 1994, p. 241). This regression may be estimated by NLS after substituting in the first stage estimates of $\boldsymbol{\theta}_2$ denoted $\hat{\boldsymbol{\theta}}_2$. This step introduces heteroskedastic errors into the regression and complicates the estimation of the asymptotic covariance matrix as seen in section 2.5.4. If ρ or $\sigma = 0$, the term in the square brackets on the right becomes 1, indicating zero sample selection bias. Thus, the effect of sample selection on the exponential conditional mean of the count equation is multiplicative, not additive as in the normal linear case. This suggests that an ad hoc adjustment based on adding the Mill's ratio to the conditional mean by analogy with the linear case is flawed.

11.4.4 *Two-Part Models*

The preceding analysis can be used to shed additional light on the two-part (hurdle) model discussed in section 4.7.1. Suppose we reinterpret the above model as follows. Let the binary outcome model refer to the outcomes $y_1 = 0$ and $y_1 > 0$. If $y_2 = 1$, we observe $y_1 > 0$, otherwise we observe $y_1 = 0$. Given independence of y_1 and y_2 for positive counts we get

$$\Pr[y_1, y_2 = 1] = \Pr[y_1] \times \Pr[y_2 = 1]\,.$$

For $\Pr[y_1]$ we need a distribution for counts that take values $1, 2, \ldots,$ and in practice we use a truncated Poisson or NB for $\Pr[y_1]$. (This is similar to the Rand two-part model used in modeling expenditures on healthcare in which $\Pr[y_1]$ is lognormal to allow for only positive observations.) Then the log-likelihood for this model is given by

$$\sum_{i=1}^{n} [\ln \Pr[y_{1i} \mid y_{1i} > 0, \mathbf{x}_i] + \ln \Pr[y_{2i} = 1 \mid \mathbf{z}_i]] . \tag{11.34}$$

The log-likelihood is usually maximized by separately maximizing the two terms in the sum, with the first part based on a standard count distribution and the second part on probit or logit model. Although the covariates in the two parts are often the same, this is not necessary. A more general set-up also allows for possible correlation between the two parts, as in the selectivity model, thereby justifying an analysis parallel to that of the selection model. For example, the count distribution could be Poisson conditioned on unobserved heterogeneity ν. The binomial distribution of y_2 could be conditioned on another unobserved heterogeneity term ε, with the (ν, ε) bivariate normal. Likelihood analysis of such a model requires numerical or Monte Carlo integration.

11.5 Bibliographic Notes

Manski and McFadden (1981) survey and discuss choice-based sampling in the context of discrete choice models. Recently the problem has received considerable attention. For example, Imbens and Lancaster (1994) deal with issues that are closely related to those arising in choice-based samples and give many useful references. The optimal instruments problem for heteroskedastic nonlinear models is discussed in Newey (1993).

CHAPTER 12

Flexible Methods for Counts

12.1 Introduction

In this chapter we examine methods for modeling count data that are more flexible than those presented in previous chapters. The focus is on the cross-section case, although some of the methods given here have potential extension to time series, multivariate or longitudinal count data, and treatment of sample selection.

One type of flexible modeling is to specify low-order conditional moments of the dependent variable, rather than the entire distribution. This moment-based approach has already been considered extensively in previous chapters. Here we extend it by considering higher-order moments. The emphasis is on the more difficult question of the most efficient use of the moments, with estimators derived using results on optimal GMM.

The core of the chapter considers two basic types of flexible model. First, we consider a sequence of progressively more flexible parametric models, where the underlying parameters in the sequence are tightly specified, for example, equal to a specified function of a linear combination of regressors and parameters.

Second, we consider models in which part of the distribution or general functional form for the moment is tightly specified, but the remainder is flexibly modeled. For example, the conditional mean may be the exponential of the sum of a linear combination of all but one regressor and a flexible function of the remaining regressor. A second example, in which the conditional mean function is specified but the conditional variance is flexible, has already been considered in earlier chapters but is covered in further depth here.

Some authors call the general approach considered in this chapter *semi-parametric methods* but we prefer the term *flexible methods*. Fully parametric regression methods specify the distribution of y given $\mathbf{x}$, and the estimation problem is finite-dimensional. An example is the NB2 model. Pure nonparametric methods specify no part of the distribution of y given $\mathbf{x}$, leading to an infinite-dimensional estimation problem. Even here some basic assumptions are made. Thus, in kernel regression of y given $\mathbf{x}$ in the continuous data case, it is usually assumed that data are iid and homoskedastic. In principle any method between these extremes is semiparametric. For example, throughout this book we have often considered inference based on specification of only the conditional mean, or on specification of the conditional mean and variance, and these moment methods might be called semiparametric. A tighter definition of semiparametric is that despite specification of part of the model, there is still an infinite-dimensional parameter estimation problem. Using this definition, estimation based on specification of the conditional mean and variance is not semiparametric.

Section 12.2 deals with efficient moment-based estimation. This has been presented in previous studies as an extension of quasilikelihood using the estimating equation approach, presented in Chapter 2. Here we also cast this in the GMM framework. In section 12.3 we consider flexible functional forms for parametric distributions for count data. These include models based on polynomial series expansion, and the family of modified power series distributions. In section 12.4 we consider more flexible models for the conditional mean, focusing on the case in which a functional form is given for part but not all of the conditional mean function. In section 12.5 we consider estimation if a functional form is specified for the conditional mean but not for the conditional variance. Estimators of regression coefficients more efficient than those given in earlier chapters are presented. Section 12.6 presents an application that focuses on some methods presented in sections 12.3 and 12.4.

12.2 Efficient Moment-Based Estimation

Key features of count models may be expressed as conditional mean and variance restrictions, avoiding possible misspecification that may occur in a full parametric specification of the likelihood function. Estimation given correct specification of the conditional mean is done using the GLM and Poisson PML approaches covered extensively in Chapters 2 and 3. Efficiency gains are possible by additionally specifying higher-order conditional moments. In section 12.2.1 we state key results obtained in studies that use estimating equation and QL approaches. These results are then derived in Section 12.2.2, using the GMM approach. This is a good illustration of the usefulness of the GMM framework.

12.2.1 *Estimating Equations and Quasilikelihood*

The extended QL approach is a refinement of the moment-based approach discussed in earlier chapters. The version given here owes much to Crowder (1987) and Godambe and Thompson (1989). In this approach the central focus of estimation is on an estimating equation, whose solution defines an estimator, rather than on an objective function that is maximized or minimized. See section 2.5.1 for the general estimating equation approach. The equations are analogous to the score equations in maximum likelihood theory, leading to the terminology *extended* QL.

We consider models in which functional forms $\mu_i = \mu(\mathbf{x}_i, \boldsymbol{\theta})$ and $\sigma_i^2 = \omega(\mathbf{x}_i, \boldsymbol{\theta})$ are specified for the conditional mean and variance of the scalar dependent variable y_i. Crowder (1987) proposed the following general estimating equation

$$\sum_{i=1}^{n} \left\{ \mathbf{a}(\mathbf{x}_i, \boldsymbol{\theta})(y_i - \mu_i) + \mathbf{b}(\mathbf{x}_i, \boldsymbol{\theta})\left\{(y_i - \mu_i)^2 - \sigma_i^2\right\}\right\} = \mathbf{0}, \tag{12.1}$$

where $\mathbf{a}(\mathbf{x}_i, \boldsymbol{\theta})$ and $\mathbf{b}(\mathbf{x}_i, \boldsymbol{\theta})$ are $q \times 1$ nonstochastic functions of $\boldsymbol{\theta}$, the $q \times 1$ unknown parameter vector to be estimated. Typically, $\boldsymbol{\theta} = (\boldsymbol{\beta}', \alpha)'$ where $\boldsymbol{\beta}$ are the parameters in the mean function, and the parameter α appears, in addition to $\boldsymbol{\beta}$, in the variance function. This class includes unweighted least squares where $\mathbf{a}(\mathbf{x}_i, \boldsymbol{\theta}) = \partial\mu_i/\partial\boldsymbol{\theta}$ and $\mathbf{b}(\mathbf{x}_i, \boldsymbol{\theta}) = \mathbf{0}$; and QL estimation, in which case $\mathbf{a}(\mathbf{x}_i, \boldsymbol{\theta}) = (1/\sigma_i^2)\,\partial\mu_i/\partial\boldsymbol{\theta}$ and $\mathbf{b}(\mathbf{x}_i, \boldsymbol{\theta}) = \mathbf{0}$.

Setting $\mathbf{b}(\mathbf{x}_i, \boldsymbol{\theta}) \neq \mathbf{0}$ in (12.1) yields estimating equations that are quadratic in $(y_i - \mu_i)$. These *quadratic estimating equations* (QEEs) are a potential refinement to the QL approach. QL estimation is an appropriate approach if the variance specification is doubtful, whereas the quadratic approach is better if the variance specification is more certain. Cubic and higher-order terms may be added if there is more information about higher moments, but the practical usefulness of such extensions is uncertain.

If $\mu_i = \mu(\mathbf{x}_i, \boldsymbol{\beta})$ and $\sigma_i^2 = \omega(\mathbf{x}_i, \boldsymbol{\beta}, \alpha)$ are correctly specified, and $\hat{\boldsymbol{\theta}}_{\mathsf{QEE}}$ is the solution to the QEE, then from the results of Crowder (1987) it is known that the estimator is consistent and asymptotically normal with variance $\mathsf{V}[\hat{\boldsymbol{\theta}}_{\mathsf{QEE}}] = \mathbf{A}_n^{-1}\mathbf{B}_n\mathbf{A}_n^{-1\prime}$, where

$$\mathbf{A}_n = -\sum_{i=1}^{n} \left\{ \mathbf{a}_i \frac{\partial\mu_i}{\partial\boldsymbol{\theta}'} + 2\sigma_i \mathbf{b}_i \frac{\partial\sigma_i}{\partial\boldsymbol{\theta}'} \right\}, \tag{12.2}$$

$$\mathbf{B}_n = \sum_{i=1}^{n} \sigma_i^2 \left\{ \mathbf{a}_i\mathbf{a}_i' + \sigma_i\gamma_{1i}\left(\mathbf{a}_i\mathbf{b}_i' + \mathbf{b}_i\mathbf{a}_i'\right) + \sigma_i^2\left(\gamma_{2i} + 2\right)\left(\mathbf{b}_i\mathbf{b}_i'\right)\right\}, \tag{12.3}$$

where $\mathbf{a}_i = \mathbf{a}(\mathbf{x}_i, \boldsymbol{\theta})$ and $\mathbf{b}_i = \mathbf{b}(\mathbf{x}_i, \boldsymbol{\theta})$ are $(k+1) \times 1$ vectors and γ_{1i} and γ_{2i} denote the skewness and kurtosis coefficients. The sandwich form of the variance matrix is used. Consistent estimation of $\boldsymbol{\theta}$ requires correct specification of the first two moments of y, while $\mathsf{V}[\hat{\boldsymbol{\theta}}_{\mathsf{QEE}}]$ depends on the first four moments. If $\mathbf{b}_i = \mathbf{0}$, the asymptotic covariance matrix does not depend on skewness or kurtosis parameters. This is consistent with earlier results for QL estimation.

As already noted, minimization of the first term only in the objective function corresponds to QL estimation. The second term is identically zero in some cases, such as the LEF density for which the variance function fully characterizes the distribution. In such a case specification of higher-order moments is redundant. In other cases, however, efficiency gains result from the inclusion of a correctly specified second term. An example of this follows.

Dean and Lawless (1989b) and Dean (1991), following Firth (1987), Crowder (1987), and Godambe and Thompson (1989), have discussed the estimation of a mixed Poisson model using extended QL approach. This employs the following specification of the first four moments of the NB2 model

$$\begin{aligned}
\mathsf{E}[y_i \mid \mathbf{x}_i] &= \mu_i = \mu_i(\mathbf{x}_i, \boldsymbol{\beta}) \\
\mathsf{E}[(y_i - \mu_i)^2 \mid \mathbf{x}_i] &= \sigma_i^2 = \mu_i(1 + \alpha\mu_i) \\
\mathsf{E}[(y_i - \mu_i)^3 \mid \mathbf{x}_i] &= \sigma_i^3 \gamma_{1i} = \sigma_i^2(1 + 2\alpha\mu_i) \\
\mathsf{E}[(y_i - \mu_i)^4 \mid \mathbf{x}_i] &= \sigma_i^4 \gamma_{2i} = \sigma_i^2 + 6\alpha\sigma_i^4 + 3\sigma_i^4,
\end{aligned} \tag{12.4}$$

where $\alpha \geq 0$, and γ_{1i} and γ_{2i} denote skewness and kurtosis coefficients.

Suppose one assumes that the first four moments are known, but does not wish to use the negative binomial distribution. The optimal quadratic estimating equations for estimation can be shown to be

$$\sum_{i=1}^{n} \frac{(y_i - \mu_i)}{\sigma_i^2} \frac{\partial \mu_i}{\partial \boldsymbol{\beta}} = \mathbf{0}, \tag{12.5}$$

$$\sum_{i=1}^{n} \left\{ \frac{(y_i - \mu_i)^2 - \sigma_i^2}{(1 + \alpha\mu_i)^2} - \frac{(y_i - \mu_i)(1 + 2\alpha\mu_i)}{(1 + \alpha\mu_i)^2} \right\} = 0. \tag{12.6}$$

Given correct specification of the first four moments, these equations yield the most efficient estimator for $(\boldsymbol{\beta}, \alpha)$. Given α, the solution of the first equation yields the QL estimate of $\boldsymbol{\beta}$. This is the special case of (12.1) with

$$\mathbf{a}(\mathbf{x}_i, \boldsymbol{\theta}) = \begin{bmatrix} (1/\sigma_i^2)(\partial \mu_i / \partial \boldsymbol{\beta}) \\ -(1 + 2\alpha\mu_i)/(1 + \alpha\mu_i)^2 \end{bmatrix},$$

$$\mathbf{b}(\mathbf{x}_i, \boldsymbol{\theta}) = \begin{bmatrix} \mathbf{0} \\ 1/(1 + \alpha\mu_i)^2 \end{bmatrix}.$$

The limit distribution can be obtained using (12.2) and (12.3).

Other estimators for α, given $\boldsymbol{\beta}$, have been suggested in the literature; for example, moment estimators that assume $\gamma_{1i} = \gamma_{2i} = 0$ and hence are less efficient than the previous one if the higher moment assumptions given earlier are correct. Dean and Lawless (1989b) have evaluated the resulting loss of efficiency in a simulation context. Dean (1991) shows that the asymptotic variance of $\boldsymbol{\beta}$ is unaffected by the choice of the estimating equation for α. An application to the mixed PIG regression is in Dean, Lawless and Willmot (1989). The practicality of improving efficiency of estimators based on higher order moment assumptions remains to be established.

12.2.2 *Generalized Method of Moments*

The literature generally does not motivate well the QEE estimator (12.1) and optimal cases such as (12.5) and (12.6). Results on optimal GMM provide a simple way to obtain the optimal formulation of the QEE.

From section 2.5.3, the optimal GMM estimator for general moment condition

$$\mathsf{E}[\boldsymbol{\rho}(y_i, \mathbf{x}_i, \boldsymbol{\theta}) \mid \mathbf{x}_i] = \mathbf{0}, \tag{12.7}$$

where $(y_i, \mathbf{x}_i)$ is iid, is the solution to the system of equations

$$\sum_{i=1}^{n} \mathbf{h}_i^*(y_i, \mathbf{x}_i, \boldsymbol{\theta}) = \mathbf{0}, \tag{12.8}$$

where

$$\mathbf{h}_i^*(y_i, \mathbf{x}_i, \boldsymbol{\theta}) = \mathsf{E}\left[\frac{\partial \boldsymbol{\rho}(y_i, \mathbf{x}_i, \boldsymbol{\theta})'}{\partial \boldsymbol{\theta}} \middle| \mathbf{x}_i\right] \times \{\mathsf{E}[\boldsymbol{\rho}(y_i, \mathbf{x}_i, \boldsymbol{\theta})\boldsymbol{\rho}(y_i, \mathbf{x}_i, \boldsymbol{\theta})' \mid \mathbf{x}_i]\}^{-1} \boldsymbol{\rho}(y_i, \mathbf{x}_i, \boldsymbol{\theta}). \tag{12.9}$$

We apply this result to estimation based on the first two moments, in which case

$$\boldsymbol{\rho}(y_i, \mathbf{x}_i, \boldsymbol{\theta}) = \begin{bmatrix} \rho_1(y_i, \mathbf{x}_i, \boldsymbol{\theta}) \\ \rho_2(y_i, \mathbf{x}_i, \boldsymbol{\theta}) \end{bmatrix} = \begin{bmatrix} y_i - \mu_i \\ (y_i - \mu_i)^2 - \sigma_i^2 \end{bmatrix}. \tag{12.10}$$

The first two moments are specified to be those of the NB2 model

$$\begin{aligned} \mu_i &= \mu_i(\mathbf{x}_i, \boldsymbol{\beta}) \\ \sigma_i^2 &= \mu_i(1 + \alpha\mu_i). \end{aligned} \tag{12.11}$$

Then $\boldsymbol{\theta} = (\boldsymbol{\beta}', \ \boldsymbol{\alpha})'$. Note that the conditional mean function is not restricted to be exponential. Note also that identification of $\boldsymbol{\theta}$ in this case requires that both $\rho_1(\cdot)$ and $\rho_2(\cdot)$ appear in $\mathbf{h}_i^*(\cdot)$ in (12.9).

For notational simplicity drop the subscript i and the conditioning on $\mathbf{x}_i$ in the expectation. The first two terms in the right-hand side of (12.9) are

$$\begin{aligned} \mathsf{E}\begin{bmatrix} \dfrac{\partial \rho_1}{\partial \boldsymbol{\beta}} & \dfrac{\partial \rho_2}{\partial \boldsymbol{\beta}} \\ \dfrac{\partial \rho_1}{\partial \alpha} & \dfrac{\partial \rho_2}{\partial \alpha} \end{bmatrix} &= \mathsf{E}\begin{bmatrix} -\dfrac{\partial \mu}{\partial \boldsymbol{\beta}} & \{-2(y - \mu) - 1 - 2\alpha\mu\}\dfrac{\partial \mu}{\partial \boldsymbol{\beta}} \\ 0 & -\mu^2 \end{bmatrix} \\ &= \begin{bmatrix} -\dfrac{\partial \mu}{\partial \boldsymbol{\beta}} & -(1 + 2\alpha\mu)\dfrac{\partial \mu}{\partial \boldsymbol{\beta}} \\ 0 & -\mu^2 \end{bmatrix}, \end{aligned} \tag{12.12}$$

and

$$\left\{\mathsf{E}\begin{bmatrix}\rho_1^2 & \rho_1\rho_2\\ \rho_1\rho_2 & \rho_2^2\end{bmatrix}\right\}^{-1}$$

$$= \left\{\mathsf{E}\begin{bmatrix}(y-\mu)^2 & (y-\mu)\{(y-\mu)^2-\sigma^2\}\\ (y-\mu)\{(y-\mu)^2-\sigma^2\} & \{(y-\mu)^2-\sigma^2\}^2\end{bmatrix}\right\}^{-1}$$

$$= \left\{\begin{bmatrix}\sigma^2 & \sigma^3\gamma_1\\ \sigma^3\gamma_1 & \sigma^4\gamma_2-\sigma^4\end{bmatrix}\right\}^{-1}$$

$$= \frac{1}{\sigma^6\left(\gamma_2-1-\gamma_1^2\right)}\begin{bmatrix}\sigma^4\gamma_2-\sigma^4 & -\sigma^3\gamma_1\\ -\sigma^3\gamma_1 & \sigma^2\end{bmatrix}, \tag{12.13}$$

using $\mathsf{E}[(y-\mu)^3\,|\,\mathbf{x}] = \sigma^3\gamma_1$ and $\mathsf{E}[(y-\mu)^4\,|\,\mathbf{x}] = \sigma^4\gamma_2$, where γ_1 and γ_2 denote skewness and kurtosis coefficients. Substituting (12.10) through (12.13) into (12.9) yields

$$\begin{bmatrix}\mathbf{h}_1^*(y_i,\mathbf{x}_i,\boldsymbol{\theta})\\ h_2^*(y_i,\mathbf{x}_i,\boldsymbol{\theta})\end{bmatrix} = \begin{bmatrix}\frac{\left(\sigma_i^4\gamma_{2i}-\sigma_i^4\right)-(1+2\alpha\mu_i)\sigma_i^3\gamma_{1i}}{\sigma_i^6\left(\gamma_{2i}-1-\gamma_{1i}^2\right)}\frac{\partial\mu_i}{\partial\boldsymbol{\beta}} & \frac{\sigma_i^3\gamma_{1i}-(1+2\alpha\mu_i)\sigma_i^2}{\sigma_i^6\left(\gamma_{2i}-1-\gamma_{1i}^2\right)}\frac{\partial\mu_i}{\partial\boldsymbol{\beta}}\\ \frac{\sigma_i^3\gamma_{1i}\mu_i^2}{\sigma_i^6\left(\gamma_{2i}-1-\gamma_{1i}^2\right)} & \frac{-\mu_i^2\sigma_i^2}{\sigma_i^6\left(\gamma_{2i}-1-\gamma_{1i}^2\right)}\end{bmatrix}$$

$$\times\begin{bmatrix}y-\mu_i\\ (y-\mu_i)^2-\sigma_i^2\end{bmatrix}. \tag{12.14}$$

The optimal GMM estimator solves (12.8) with $\mathbf{h}^*(y_i,\mathbf{x}_i,\boldsymbol{\theta})$ defined in (12.9). Its distribution can be obtained using (2.70) through (2.72) in Section 2.5.1. From (12.14), identification requires $\gamma_{2i}-1-\gamma_{1i}^2 \neq 0$ for all i.

Comparing (12.14) with (12.1), the optimal GMM estimator in this case is of the QEE form (12.1), with $\mathbf{a}(\mathbf{x}_i,\boldsymbol{\theta})$ and $\mathbf{b}(\mathbf{x}_i,\boldsymbol{\theta})$, respectively, equal to the first and second columns of the first matrix in the right-hand side of (12.14), which is a $(k+1)\times 2$ matrix.

Now specialize to the case in which the skewness and kurtosis parameters γ_{1i} and γ_{2i} are the functions given in (12.4). Then, in section 12.7 it is shown that

$$\begin{aligned}&\left(\sigma_i^4\gamma_{2i}-\sigma_i^4\right)-(1+2\alpha\mu_i)\sigma_i^3\gamma_{1i} = \sigma_i^4\left(\gamma_{2i}-1-\gamma_{1i}^2\right)\\ &\sigma_i^3\gamma_{1i}-(1+2\alpha\mu_i)\sigma_i^2 = 0\\ &\sigma_i^6\left(\gamma_{2i}-1-\gamma_{1i}^2\right) = 2(1+\alpha)\sigma_i^2.\end{aligned} \tag{12.15}$$

Using these results, (12.14) reduces to

$$\begin{bmatrix}\mathbf{h}_1^*(y_i,\mathbf{x}_i,\boldsymbol{\theta})\\ h_2^*(y_i,\mathbf{x}_i,\boldsymbol{\theta})\end{bmatrix} = \begin{bmatrix}\frac{1}{\sigma_i^2}\frac{\partial\mu_i}{\partial\boldsymbol{\beta}} & \mathbf{0}\\ \frac{(1+2\alpha\mu_i)\mu_i^2}{2(1+\alpha)\sigma_i^4} & \frac{\mu_i^2}{2(1+\alpha)\sigma_i^4}\end{bmatrix}\begin{bmatrix}y-\mu_i\\ (y-\mu_i)^2-\sigma_i^2\end{bmatrix}. \tag{12.16}$$

For σ_i^2 defined in (12.11), $\mu_i^2/\sigma_i^4 = 1/(1+\alpha\mu_i)^2$. Thus (12.16) yields the optimal QEE estimator defined in (12.5) and (12.6) on premultiplication of (12.6) by the constant $2(1+\alpha)$.

The optimal GMM estimator requires specification of $\mathsf{E}[\rho(y_i, \mathbf{x}_i, \boldsymbol{\theta})\rho(y_i, \mathbf{x}_i, \boldsymbol{\theta})' \mid \mathbf{x}_i]$, which in this example requires specification of the first four moments. Newey (1993) proposed a semiparametric method of estimation, which replaces these elements by nonparametric estimates. For example, an estimate of the (1, 1) element, $\mathsf{E}[(y_i - \mu_i)^2 \mid \mathbf{x}_i]$, may be formed from a kernel or series regression of $(y_i - \hat{\mu}_i)^2$ on an intercept, $\hat{\mu}_i$ and $\hat{\mu}_i^2$, where $\hat{\mu}_i$ is a consistent estimator. A similar treatment may be applied to the other two elements.

Unfortunately, even after determining that $\boldsymbol{\theta}$ is identified under GMM, this semiparametric method may run into practical difficulties. First, if the individually estimated elements are combined, there is no guarantee that the resulting estimate of $\mathsf{E}[\rho(y_i, \mathbf{x}_i, \boldsymbol{\theta})\rho(y_i, \mathbf{x}_i, \boldsymbol{\theta})' \mid \mathbf{x}_i]$ will be positive definite as required. Second, even if the procedure produces a positive definite estimate, the estimate may be highly variable. Finally, in small samples the resulting estimator may be biased, perhaps badly so, as indicated by several studies of the GMM method (Smith, 1997). The econometric literature includes several studies in which use of a constant rather the "optimal" matrix $\mathsf{E}[\rho_i\rho_i' \mid \mathbf{x}_i]$ produced better estimates.

12.3 Flexible Distributions Using Series Expansions

12.3.1 *Seminonparametric Maximum Likelihood*

Gallant and Nychka (1987) proposed approximating the distribution of an iid m-dimensional random variable $\mathbf{y}$ using a squared power series expansion around an initial choice of density or baseline density, say $f(\mathbf{y} \mid \boldsymbol{\lambda})$. Thus,

$$h_p(\mathbf{y} \mid \boldsymbol{\lambda}, \mathbf{a}) = \frac{(\mathcal{P}_p(\mathbf{y} \mid \mathbf{a}))^2 f(\mathbf{y} \mid \boldsymbol{\lambda})}{\int (\mathcal{P}_p(\mathbf{z} \mid \mathbf{a}))^2 f(\mathbf{z})\, d\mathbf{z}}, \tag{12.17}$$

where $\mathcal{P}_p(\mathbf{y} \mid \mathbf{a})$ is an m-variate p^{th} order polynomial, $\mathbf{a}$ is the vector of coefficients of the polynomial, and the term in the denominator is a normalizing constant. Squaring $\mathcal{P}_p(\mathbf{y} \mid \mathbf{a})$ has the advantage of assuring that the density is positive. This is closely related to the series expansions in Chapter 8, where $\mathcal{P}_p(\mathbf{y} \mid \mathbf{a})$ was not squared and emphasis was placed on choosing $\mathcal{P}_p(\mathbf{y} \mid \mathbf{a})$ to be the orthogonal or orthonormal polynomials for the baseline density $f(\mathbf{y} \mid \boldsymbol{\lambda})$.

The estimator of $\boldsymbol{\lambda}$ and $\mathbf{a}$ maximizes the log-likelihood $\sum_{i=1}^{n} \ln h_p(\mathbf{y}_i \mid \boldsymbol{\lambda}, \mathbf{a})$. Gallant and Nychka (1987) show that under fairly general conditions if the order p of the polynomial increases with sample size n then the estimator yields consistent estimates of the density. This result holds for a wide range of choices of baseline density. The estimator is called the *seminonparametric maximum likelihood estimator*. It is called seminonparametric to reflect that it is somewhere between parametric – in practice a specific baseline density needs to be chosen – and nonparametric.

This result provides a strong basis for using (12.17) to obtain a class of flexible distributions for any particular data. There are, however, several potential problems. First, the method may not be very parsimonious. Thus a poor initial choice of baseline density may require a fairly high-order polynomial, a potential problem even with relatively large data sets of, say, 1000 observations. Second, it may be difficult to obtain analytical expressions for the normalizing constant, especially in the multivariate case. Third, the normalizing constant usually leads to a highly nonlinear log-likelihood function with multiple local maxima. Finally, Gallant and Nychka (1987) establish only consistency. As with similar nonparametric approaches, it is difficult to establish the asymptotic distribution. One solution is to bootstrap, although the asymptotic properties of this particular bootstrap do not appear to have been established. Another solution is to select a high-enough-order polynomial to feel that the data is being well fit by the model, assume this is the density of the dgp, and apply standard maximum likelihood results. This is similar to starting with the Poisson, rejecting this in favor of NB2, and then using usual maximum likelihood standard errors of the NB2 model for inference.

Gallant and Tauchen (1989) and various coauthors in many studies have applied models based on (12.17) to continuous finance data. There the baseline density is the multivariate normal with mean μ and variance Σ, with a particular transformation used so that the normalizing constant is simply obtained as a weighted sum of the first $2p$ moments of the univariate standard normal. They advocate selecting the order of the polynomial on the basis of the BIC of Schwarz (1978), defined in section 5.7.1, which gives a relatively large penalty for lack of parsimony.

In the first application of these methods to count data, Gurmu, Rilstone, and Stern (1998) proposed using a series expansion to model the distribution of the heterogeneity term in the Poisson model with random heterogeneity. This method has also been applied by Gurmu and Trivedi (1996) and extended to hurdle models by Gurmu (1997). Cameron and Johansson (1997) instead use a series expansion to directly generalize and modify the Poisson density for the dependent variable. We present this study in sections 12.3.2 and 12.3.3 and defer presentation of the other studies to section 12.5.2, on flexible models for the heterogeneity term.

12.3.2 *General Results*

We begin with a quite general presentation for the univariate case, before specializing to count data with a Poisson density as a baseline in the next subsection. Derivations are given in Cameron and Johansson (1997).

Consider a scalar random variable y with baseline density $f(y \mid \lambda)$, where λ is possibly a vector. The density based on a squared polynomial series expansion is

$$h_p(y \mid \boldsymbol{\lambda}, \mathbf{a}) = f(y \mid \boldsymbol{\lambda}) \frac{P_p^2(y \mid \mathbf{a})}{\eta_p(\boldsymbol{\lambda}, \mathbf{a})}, \tag{12.18}$$

where $P_p(y \mid \mathbf{a})$ is a pth-order polynomial

$$P_p(y \mid \mathbf{a}) = \sum_{k=0}^{p} a_k y^k, \tag{12.19}$$

$\mathbf{a} = (a_0, a_1, \ldots, a_p)'$ with the normalization $a_0 = 1$, and $\eta_p(\boldsymbol{\lambda}, \mathbf{a})$ is a normalizing constant term that ensures that the density $h_p(y \mid \boldsymbol{\lambda}, \mathbf{a})$ sums to unity. Squaring the polynomial ensures that the density is nonnegative. This is just the univariate version of (12.17). It can be shown that

$$\eta_p(\boldsymbol{\lambda}, \mathbf{a}) = \sum_{k=0}^{p} \sum_{l=0}^{p} a_k a_l m_{k+l}, \tag{12.20}$$

where $m_r \equiv m_r(\boldsymbol{\lambda})$ denotes the rth moment (not centered around the mean) of the baseline density $f(y \mid \boldsymbol{\lambda})$.

The moments of the random variable y with density $h_p(y \mid \boldsymbol{\lambda}, \mathbf{a})$ can be readily obtained from those of the baseline density $f(y \mid \boldsymbol{\lambda})$ as

$$\mathsf{E}[y^r] = \frac{\sum_{k=0}^{p} \sum_{l=0}^{p} a_k a_l m_{k+l+r}}{\eta_p(\boldsymbol{\lambda}, \mathbf{a})}. \tag{12.21}$$

The rth moment of y generally differs from the rth moment of the baseline density. In particular, the mean for the series expansion density $h_p(y \mid \boldsymbol{\lambda}, \mathbf{a})$ usually differs from that for the baseline density $f(y \mid \boldsymbol{\lambda})$.

We consider estimation based on a sample $\{(y_i, \mathbf{x}_i),\ i = 1, \ldots, n\}$ of independent observations. Then $y_i \mid \mathbf{x}_i$ has density $h_p(y_i \mid \boldsymbol{\lambda}_i, \mathbf{a}_i)$, where regressors can be introduced by letting $\boldsymbol{\lambda}_i$ or $\mathbf{a}_i$ be a specified function of $\mathbf{x}_i$ and parameters to be estimated. As a simple example, suppose λ_i is a scalar determined by a known function of regressors $\mathbf{x}_i$ and an unknown parameter vector $\boldsymbol{\beta}$

$$\lambda_i = \lambda(\mathbf{x}_i, \boldsymbol{\beta}), \tag{12.22}$$

and the polynomial coefficients $\mathbf{a}$ are unknown parameters that do not vary with regressors. The log-likelihood function is then

$$\begin{aligned} \mathcal{L}(\boldsymbol{\beta}, \mathbf{a}) = \sum_{i=1}^{n} \{ & \ln f(y_i \mid \lambda(\mathbf{x}_i, \boldsymbol{\beta})) + 2 \ln P_p(y_i \mid \mathbf{a}) \\ & - \ln \eta_p(\lambda(\mathbf{x}_i, \boldsymbol{\beta}), \mathbf{a})\}, \end{aligned} \tag{12.23}$$

with first-order conditions that, given $\eta_p(\boldsymbol{\lambda}, \mathbf{a})$ in (12.20), can be reexpressed as

$$\frac{\partial \mathcal{L}}{\partial \boldsymbol{\beta}} = \sum_{i=1}^{n} \left\{ \frac{\partial \ln f(y_i \mid \lambda_i)}{\partial \lambda_i} - \frac{\sum_{k=0}^{p} \sum_{l=0}^{p} a_k a_l \partial m_{k+l,i} / \partial \lambda_i}{\sum_{k=0}^{p} \sum_{l=0}^{p} a_k a_l m_{k+l,i}} \right\} \frac{\partial \lambda_i}{\partial \boldsymbol{\beta}} = \mathbf{0}, \tag{12.24}$$

$$\frac{\partial \mathcal{L}}{\partial a_j} = \sum_{i=1}^{n} 2 \left\{ \frac{y^j}{\sum_{k=0}^{p} a_k y^k} - \frac{\sum_{k=0}^{p} a_k m_{k+j,i}}{\sum_{k=0}^{p} \sum_{l=0}^{p} a_k a_l m_{k+l,i}} \right\} = 0, \quad j = 1, \ldots, p. \tag{12.25}$$

Cameron and Johansson (1997) do not establish semiparametric consistency of this method. Instead, the density with chosen p is assumed to be correctly specified. Inference is based on the standard result that the MLE for $\boldsymbol{\beta}$ and $\mathbf{a}$ is asymptotically normally distributed with variance matrix equal to the inverse of the information matrix, under the assumption that the data are generated by (12.18) and (12.22).

In principle this method is very easy to apply, provided analytical moments of the baseline density are easily obtained. The maximum likelihood first-order conditions simply involve derivatives of these moments with respect to λ, and even then some optimization routines do not require specification of first derivatives.

In practice there are two potential problems. First, the objective function is very nonlinear in parameters and there are multiple optima. This is discussed in the next subsection. Second, these series expansion densities may not be very parsimonious or may not fit data very well. The usefulness can really only be established by applications.

12.3.3 *Poisson Polynomial Model*

The preceding framework can be applied to a wide range of baseline densities. Cameron and Johansson illustrated this method if baseline density is the Poisson, so $f(y \mid \mu) = e^{-\mu}\mu^y/y!$. They called this model the PPp model, for *Poisson polynomial of order p*. Then $\lambda = \mu$, and the normalizing constant $\eta_p(\mu, \mathbf{a})$ defined in (12.20) and the moments $\mathsf{E}[y^r]$ defined in (12.21) are evaluated using the moments $m_r(\mu)$ of the Poisson, which can be obtained from the moment generating function using $m_r(\mu) = \partial^r \exp(-\mu + \mu e^t)/\partial t^r \mid_{t=0}$.

As an example the PP2 model is

$$h_2(y \mid \mu, \mathbf{a}) = \frac{e^{-\mu}\mu^y}{y!} \frac{(1 + a_1 y + a_2 y^2)^2}{\eta_2(\mathbf{a}, \mu)}, \tag{12.26}$$

where

$$\eta_2(\mathbf{a}, \mu) = 1 + 2a_1 m_1 + \left(a_1^2 + 2a_2\right) m_2 + 2a_1 a_2 m_3 + a_2^2 m_4. \tag{12.27}$$

Note that μ here refers to the mean of the baseline density. In fact the first two moments of y for the PP2 density are

$$\begin{aligned}\mathsf{E}[y] &= \left(m_1 + 2a_1m_2 + \left(a_1^2 + 2a_2\right)m_3 + 2a_1a_2m_4 + a_2^2m_5\right)/\eta_2(\mathbf{a}, \mu)\\ \mathsf{E}[y^2] &= \left(m_2 + 2a_1m_3 + \left(a_1^2 + 2a_2\right)m_4 + 2a_1a_2m_5 + a_2^2m_6\right)/\eta_2(\mathbf{a}, \mu).\end{aligned} \tag{12.28}$$

Estimation requires evaluation of (12.27) and hence the first four moments of the Poisson density; evaluation of the mean and variance from (12.28) requires the first six moments of the Poisson density. These moments are

$$\begin{aligned}m_1 &= \mu\\ m_2 &= \mu + \mu^2\\ m_3 &= \mu + 3\mu^2 + \mu^3\\ m_4 &= \mu + 7\mu^2 + 6\mu^3 + \mu^4\\ m_5 &= \mu + 15\mu^2 + 25\mu^3 + 10\mu^4 + \mu^5\\ m_6 &= \mu + 31\mu^2 + 90\mu^3 + 65\mu^4 + 15\mu^5 + \mu^6.\end{aligned}$$

The PPp model permits a wide range of models for count data, including multimodal densities and densities with either underdispersion or overdispersion.

For the PPp model if the baseline density has exponential mean, so $\lambda_i = \exp(\mathbf{x}_i'\boldsymbol{\beta})$, the first-order condition (12.24) simplifies to

$$\frac{\partial \mathcal{L}_{\mathsf{PPp}}}{\partial \boldsymbol{\beta}} = \sum_{i=1}^{n} \left\{ y_i - \frac{\sum_{k=0}^{p}\sum_{l=0}^{p} a_k a_l m_{k+l+1,i}}{\sum_{k=0}^{p}\sum_{l=0}^{p} a_k a_l m_{k+l,i}} \right\} \mathbf{x}_i. \tag{12.29}$$

Using (12.21) with $r = 1$ and (12.20), (12.29) can be reexpressed as

$$\frac{\partial \mathcal{L}_{\mathsf{PPp}}}{\partial \boldsymbol{\beta}} = \sum_{i=1}^{n} (y_i - \mathsf{E}[y_i \mid \mathbf{x}_i])\mathbf{x}_i = \mathbf{0}. \tag{12.30}$$

Thus the residual is orthogonal to the regressors, and the residuals sum to zero if an intercept term is included in the model. The result (12.30) holds more generally if the baseline density is an LEF density with conditional mean function corresponding to the canonical link function.

As is common for many nonlinear models, the likelihood function can have multiple optima. To increase the likelihood that a global maximum is obtained Cameron and Johansson use fast simulated annealing (Szu and Hartley, 1987), a variation on simulated annealing (see Goffe, Ferrier, and Rogers, 1994), to obtain parameter estimates close to the global optima that are used as starting values for standard gradient methods. The advantage of simulated annealing techniques is that they permit movements that decrease the value of the objective function, so that one is not necessarily locked in to moving to the local maxima closest to the starting values. Cameron and Johansson find that using a range of starting values improves considerably the success of the Newton-Raphson method in finding the global maximum, but it is better still to use the fast simulated annealing method.

For the underdispersed takeover bids data introduced in section 5.2.5, Cameron and Johansson find that a PP1 model provides the best fit in terms of BIC and performs better than other models proposed for underdispersed data, namely Katz, hurdle, and double-Poisson.

12.3.4 *Modified Power Series Distributions*

The family of *modified power series distributions* (MPSDs) for nonnegative integer-valued random variables y is defined by the pdf

$$f(y \mid \lambda) = \frac{a(\lambda)^y b(y)}{c(\lambda)}, \tag{12.31}$$

where $c(\lambda)$ is a normalizing constant

$$c(\lambda) = \sum_{y \in I} a(\lambda)^y b(y), \tag{12.32}$$

$b(y) > 0$ depends only on y, and $a(\lambda)$ and $c(\lambda)$ are positive, finite, and differentiable functions of the parameter λ. If a distribution belongs to the MPSD class, then the truncated version of the same distribution is also an MPSD. The MPSD permits the range of y to be a subset, say T, of the set I of nonnegative integers, in which case the summation in (12.32) is for $y \in T$.

For the MPSD density, differentiating the identity $\sum_{y \in I} f(y \mid \lambda) = 1$ with respect to λ yields

$$\mathsf{E}[y] = \mu = \frac{a(\lambda)}{a'(\lambda)} \frac{c'(\lambda)}{c(\lambda)} = \left(\frac{\partial \ln a(\lambda)}{\partial \lambda} \right)^{-1} \frac{\partial \ln c(\lambda)}{\partial \lambda}, \tag{12.33}$$

where $a'(\lambda) = \partial a(\lambda)/\partial \lambda$ and $c'(\lambda) = \partial c(\lambda)/\partial \lambda$. The variance is

$$\mathsf{V}[y] \equiv \mu_2 = \frac{a(\lambda)}{a'(\lambda)} \frac{\partial \mu}{\partial \lambda} = \left(\frac{\partial \ln a(\lambda)}{\partial \lambda} \right)^{-1} \frac{\partial \mu}{\partial \lambda}.$$

Higher-order central moments, $\mu_r = \mathsf{E}[(y - \mu)^r]$, can be derived from the recurrence relation

$$\mu_r = \frac{a(\lambda)}{a'(\lambda)} \frac{d\lambda_{r-1}}{d\lambda} + r\mu_2\mu_{r-2}, \qquad r \geq 3, \tag{12.34}$$

where $\mu_{r-2} = 0$ for $r = 3$.

The MPSD family, proposed by Gupta (1974), is a generalization of the family of power series distributions (PSDs). The PSD is obtained by replacing $a(\lambda)$ in (12.31) by λ, in which case $c(\lambda) = \sum_{y \in I} b(y)\lambda^y$. This provides the motivation for the term *power series density*, as it is based on a power series expansion of the function $c(\lambda)$ with different choices of $c(\lambda)$ leading to different densities. An early reference for the PSD is Noack (1950). The generalized PSD family is obtained from the PSD if the support of y is restricted to a subset of the nonnegative integers. A generalization of the MPSD is the class of Lagrange probability distributions proposed by Consul and Shenton (1972). There is an extensive statistical literature on these families. Some discussion is given in Johnson, Kotz, and Kemp (1992), with more extensive discussion in various entries in Kotz and Johnston (1982–89). These densities have rarely been applied in a regression setting.

For nonnegative integer-valued random variables, the MPSD is a generalization of the LEF. To see this note that (12.31) can be reexpressed as $f(y|\lambda) = \exp\{-\ln c(\lambda) + \ln b(y) + \ln a(\lambda)y\}$. This is exactly the same functional form as the LEF defined in section 2.4.2, except it is parametrized in terms of λ rather than the mean μ. However, it is not a mean parameterization of the density. The difference is that the LEF places strong restrictions on $a(\lambda)$ and $c(\lambda)$. Here the restrictions are not as strong. The MPSD therefore includes the Poisson and the NB2 (with overdispersion parameter specified). For the Poisson, $a(\lambda) = \lambda$, $b(y) = 1/y!$ and $c(\lambda) = e^{\lambda}$. For the NB2, $a(\lambda) = [1 - \lambda/(\lambda + \alpha^{-1})]^{-1/\alpha}$, $b(y) = \Gamma(\alpha^{-1} + y)/[\Gamma(y+1)\Gamma(\alpha^{-1})$ and $c(\lambda) = \lambda/(\lambda + \alpha^{-1})$. The MPSD also includes the logarithmic series distributions.

The MPSD family is potentially very flexible. One modeling strategy is to begin with a particular choice of $a(\lambda)$ and $b(y)$, and then progressively generalize $b(y)$, which also changes the normalizing constant $c(\lambda)$. To be specific, the function $b(y)$ in (12.31) can be modified so that it also depends on additional parameters to be estimated, say $\mathbf{a}$, and consequently the term $c(\lambda)$ also depends on $\mathbf{a}$.

The PPp model presented in section 12.3.3 is an MPSD model. For example, the PP2 density (12.26) is (12.31) with $a(\mu) = \mu$, $b(y, \mathbf{a}) = (1 + a_1 y + a_2 y^2)^2/y!$, and $c(\mu, \mathbf{a}) = \eta_2(\mathbf{a}, \mu)/e^{-\mu}$. This results from choosing the baseline density, here the Poisson, to be an LEF density. With other choices of baseline density $f(y \mid \lambda)$ in (12.18), models found by series expansion as in section 12.3.2 need not be related to MPSD models.

12.4 Flexible Models of Conditional Mean

We now consider approaches in which a component of the conditional mean is nonparametric, meaning it has an unknown functional form. For example, the conditional mean function may be partially linear in the sense that it has one component linear in a subset of covariates, and another whose dependence on a second subset is of an unknown form (Robinson, 1988). Such an approach has been developed by Severini and Staniswalis (1994) in the general context of quasilikelihood estimation of GLM models.

Consider a model in which the conditional mean of y_i depends on two sets of covariates, $\mathbf{x}_i$ and $\mathbf{z}_i$, and is written in the form

$$\mathsf{E}[y_i \mid \mathbf{x}_i, \mathbf{z}_i] = \mu\big(\mathbf{x}_i'\boldsymbol{\beta} + \gamma(\mathbf{z}_i)\big), \tag{12.35}$$

where $\mu(\cdot)$ is a known function and $\gamma(\cdot)$ is an unknown smooth function. Such a model in which there is a parametric relation between y and $\mathbf{x}$, and a nonparametric one between y and $\mathbf{z}$, is referred to as a *partially parametric* model. In the context of the count regression typically $\mu(\cdot)$ is an exponential function.

The traditional parametric approach to obtaining a flexible specification with respect to a subset of covariates is to let $\gamma(\mathbf{z})$ be a polynomial function of $\mathbf{z}$. For example, in the analysis of recreational trip data in Chapter 6, we considered cost variables that entered the model quadratically rather than linearly. Even greater generality can be achieved by treating this component nonparametrically.

There is a considerable literature for more general treatment of $\gamma(\mathbf{z})$ in the linear regression model, in which case $\mathsf{E}[y \mid \mathbf{x}, \mathbf{z}] = \mathbf{x}'\boldsymbol{\beta} + \gamma(\mathbf{z})$ and the model is called the *partially linear* model. For example, Robinson (1988) proposes estimation of $\boldsymbol{\beta}$ by OLS regression of $y - \hat{\mathsf{E}}[y \mid \mathbf{z}]$ on $(\mathbf{x} - \hat{\mathsf{E}}[\mathbf{x} \mid \mathbf{z}])$, where $\hat{\mathsf{E}}[y \mid \mathbf{z}]$ and $\hat{\mathsf{E}}[\mathbf{x} \mid \mathbf{z}]$ are nonparametric kernel density estimates of $\mathsf{E}[y \mid \mathbf{z}]$ and $\mathsf{E}[\mathbf{x} \mid \mathbf{z}]$.

For count models there are several additional complications. The conditional mean function $\mu(\cdot)$ is nonlinear, the conditional variance is not constant, and usually this nonconstancy is controlled for by modeling the conditional variance as a function of the conditional mean. We present an estimator due to Severini and Staniswalis (1994), whose methods can be applied whenever quasilikelihood estimation is feasible.

The observations are assumed to be independent with conditional mean and variance

$$\begin{aligned} \mathsf{E}[y_i \mid \mathbf{x}_i, \mathbf{z}_i] &= \mu\left(\mathbf{x}_i'\boldsymbol{\beta} + \gamma(\mathbf{z}_i)\right) \\ \mathsf{V}[y_i \mid \mathbf{x}_i, \mathbf{z}_i] &= \phi\upsilon(\mathsf{E}[y_i \mid \mathbf{x}_i, \mathbf{z}_i]), \end{aligned} \tag{12.36}$$

where the functions $\mu(\cdot)$ and $\upsilon(\cdot)$ are specified. Let $\sum_{i=1}^{n} q(\mu(\mathbf{x}_i'\boldsymbol{\beta} \mid \eta_i))$ denote the quasilikelihood function, where $\eta_i = \gamma(\mathbf{z}_i)$. The flexibility of the approach results from the use of moment specification rather than the full distribution, and from the use of a potentially flexible functional form for the conditional mean.

Estimation is complicated because there is a parametric and a nonparametric component of the model. If $\boldsymbol{\beta}$ is treated as a fixed parameter then a quasilikelihood estimate of $\gamma(\mathbf{z}_i)$ can be obtained using a generalization of the weighted quasilikelihood method of Staniswalis (1989). Specifically, for given $\boldsymbol{\beta}$, given kernel function $K(\cdot)$, bandwidth parameter $b > 0$, and observables $\mathbf{z}$, the quasilikelihood estimator satisfies the equation

$$\sum_i K\left(\frac{\mathbf{z} - \mathbf{z}_i}{b}\right) \frac{\partial q\left(\mu\left(\mathbf{x}_i'\boldsymbol{\beta} + \eta(\boldsymbol{\beta})\right)\right)}{\partial \eta} = 0. \tag{12.37}$$

Denote this estimator as $\hat{\eta}(\boldsymbol{\beta})$. Treating η as a given infinite dimensional nuisance parameter, maximum quasilikelihood estimates of $\boldsymbol{\beta}$ satisfy the equation

$$\frac{\sum_i \partial q\left(\mu\left(\mathbf{x}_i'\boldsymbol{\beta} + \hat{\eta}(\boldsymbol{\beta})\right)\right)}{\partial \boldsymbol{\beta}} = \mathbf{0}, \tag{12.38}$$

which is a parametric estimation problem. In general these equations are solved iteratively. The interested reader should refer to the original article for details of the asymptotic properties of this estimator.

In practice the user of this method needs to determine which variables constitute the **z** subset and which ones the **x** subset. Although such choices are context-specific, given the constraint that γ should be smooth, continuous variables arc the natural candidates for **z**. If the sample size is large and the dimension of **z** not too large, then a computationally simpler alternative seems to approximate $\gamma(\mathbf{z})$ by a quadratic in **z**, as for instance in the recreational data analysis of Chapter 6, and then treat the estimation parametrically.

An alternative class of flexible models of the conditional mean, one embedded in the GLM framework, is the *generalized additive* model due to Hastie and Tibshirani (1990). Then the linear component $\mathbf{x}'\boldsymbol{\beta}$ in the GLM class model is replaced by an additive model of the form $\sum_{j=2}^{k} f_j(x_j)$, where $f_j(\cdot)$ are nonparametric univariate functions, one for each covariate. Thus

$$\mathsf{E}[y_i \,|\, \mathbf{x}_i] = \mu\left(\beta_1 + \sum_{j=2}^{k} f_j(x_{ij})\right),$$

where x_{ij} is the jth component of $\mathbf{x}_i$, and $\mu(\cdot)$ is specified. For Poisson regression $\mu(\cdot) = \exp(\cdot)$ and the conditional variance is a multiple of $\mu(\cdot)$.

12.5 Flexible Models of Conditional Variance

Let us reconsider the mixture density

$$h(y_i \,|\, \mathbf{x}_i) = \int f(y_i \,|\, \mathbf{x}_i, \nu_i) g(\nu_i)\, d\nu_i, \tag{12.39}$$

introduced in Chapter 4, where the density $f(y_i \,|\, \mathbf{x}_i, \nu_i)$ is the Poisson with conditional mean $\mu_i \nu_i = \exp(\mathbf{x}_i'\boldsymbol{\beta})\nu_i$. Unlike Chapter 4, the distribution of the unobserved heterogeneity component is treated as unknown. In this section we consider flexible models for the mixture density $g(\nu_i)$, leading to more flexible models for $h(y_i \,|\, \mathbf{x}_i)$. The first method considers mixtures of densities, while the second method uses a series expansion.

At the end of this section we present an adaptive estimation procedure that provides efficient estimates of the conditional mean parameters, controlling for heteroskedasticity by nonparametric estimation of the conditional variance.

12.5.1 *Mixture Models for Unobserved Heterogeneity*

As in section 4.8, consider a discrete representation of $g(\nu)$, so that the marginal distribution may be written as

$$h(y_i \,|\, \mathbf{x}_i, \boldsymbol{\beta}) = \sum_{j=1}^{C} f(y_i \,|\, \mathbf{x}_i, \boldsymbol{\beta}, \nu_j)\pi_j(\nu_j), \tag{12.40}$$

where ν_j, $j = 1, \ldots, C$, is an estimated support point for the distribution of unobserved heterogeneity and π_j is the associated probability with $\pi_j \geq 0$ and $\sum_j \pi_j = 1$.

For the Poisson with exponential mean, this representation of heterogeneity may be interpreted as a random-intercept model in which the intercept is $(\beta_0 + \nu_j)$ with probability π_j. This is detailed in section 4.8. The subpopulation with each intercept is treated as a "type," and the number of types, C, is estimated from the data along with $(\pi_j, \boldsymbol{\beta})$.

The method has both a nonparametric component, because it avoids distributional assumptions on ν, and a parametric component, the density $f(y \mid \mathbf{x}, \boldsymbol{\beta}, \nu)$. It is standard terminology in the statistic literature to call the estimator an SPMLE if C is taken as given and maximum likelihood estimation is done for the unknown parameters $(\boldsymbol{\beta}, \pi_j)$.

As an example, if $f(y_i \mid \mathbf{x}_i, \boldsymbol{\beta}, \nu_j)$ in (12.40) is the Poisson density with parameter $\mu_i \nu_j$, with $\mu_i = \mu(\mathbf{x}_i, \boldsymbol{\beta})$, the log-likelihood is

$$\mathcal{L}_{\mathsf{SP}}(\boldsymbol{\beta}, \boldsymbol{\pi}) = \sum_{i=1}^{n} \left[y_i \ln(\mu_i) - \ln(y_i!) + \ln\left(\sum_{j=1}^{C} \exp(-\mu_i \nu_j) \nu_j^{y_i} \pi_j \right) \right]. \tag{12.41}$$

Estimation of this model is discussed in section 4.8.

12.5.2 *Series Expansions for Unobserved Heterogeneity*

This section outlines estimation of the Poisson model with exponential mean and a random heterogeneity component ν whose density $g(\nu)$ is modeled by a series expansion. The method was proposed by Gurmu, Rilstone, and Stern (1998), who call it SPMLE. The goal is a flexible model specification that avoids strong parametric assumptions about the distribution of ν.

If y conditional on μ and ν is $\mathsf{P}[\mu\nu]$ distributed, the mixture density (12.39), suppressing the subscript i, is

$$\begin{aligned} h(y \mid \mu) &= \int \frac{e^{-\mu\nu}(\nu\mu)^y}{y!} g(\nu)\, d\nu \\ &= \frac{\mu^y}{y!} \int \nu^y e^{-\mu\nu} g(\nu)\, d\nu. \end{aligned} \tag{12.42}$$

Gurmu et al. propose approximating the unknown mixture density $g(\nu)$ by a squared p^{th}-order polynomial expansion of form (12.17), say $g_p^*(\nu)$, and analytically calculating the integral in (12.42) with respect to $g_p^*(\nu)$ rather than $g(\nu)$. The two-parameter gamma is used as the baseline density, because this restricts $\nu > 0$, and more importantly because the leading term in the expansion is then the gamma, which from Chapter 4 leads to $h(y \mid \mu)$ being the standard NB2 density. An orthonormal polynomial series expansion is used (see Chapter 8) in which the orthogonal polynomials for the gamma are the orthonormal generalized Laguerre polynomials.

Specifically, the approximating density is

$$g_p^*(\nu \mid \lambda, \gamma) = f(\nu \mid \lambda, \gamma) \frac{P_p^2(\nu \mid \lambda, \gamma, \mathbf{a})}{\eta_p(\lambda, \gamma, \mathbf{a})}, \tag{12.43}$$

where $f(\nu \mid \lambda, \gamma)$ is the two-parameter gamma density

$$f(\nu \mid \lambda, \gamma) = \frac{\nu^{\gamma-1}\lambda^{\gamma}}{\Gamma(\gamma)} e^{-\lambda\nu}, \tag{12.44}$$

$P_p^2(\nu \mid \alpha, \gamma, \mathbf{a})$ is the pth-order orthonormal generalized Laguerre polynomial

$$P_p^2(\nu \mid \lambda, \gamma, \mathbf{a}) = \sum_{k=0}^{p} a_k \eta_k^{-1/2} Q_k(\nu) \tag{12.45}$$

with the kth-order orthogonal generalized Laguerre polynomial defined by

$$Q_k(\nu) = \sum_{l=0}^{k} \binom{k}{l} \frac{\Gamma(k+\gamma)}{\Gamma(l+\gamma)\Gamma(k+1)} \lambda^l (-\nu)^l, \tag{12.46}$$

orthonormalization is achieved by premultiplying $Q_k(\nu)$ in (12.45) by $\eta_k^{-1/2}$ with

$$\eta_k = \frac{\Gamma(k+\gamma)}{\Gamma(\gamma)\Gamma(k+1)}, \tag{12.47}$$

and orthonormalization leads to the normalizing constant being simply

$$\eta_p(\lambda, \gamma, \mathbf{a}) = \sum_{k=0}^{p} a_k^2. \tag{12.48}$$

Clearly, evaluating $\int \nu^y e^{-\mu\nu} g(\nu)\, d\nu$ in (12.42) is not straightforward for $g(\nu) = g_p^*(\nu \mid \lambda, \gamma)$ defined by (12.43) through (12.48). Gurmu et al. observe that if ν has density $g(\nu)$, the moment generating function of ν is

$$\mathsf{M}_\nu(t) = \int e^{t\nu} g(\nu)\, d\nu,$$

with y^{th}-order derivative

$$\mathsf{M}_\nu^{(y)}(t) = \partial^y \mathsf{M}_\nu(t)/\partial t^y = \int \nu^y e^{t\nu} g(\nu)\, d\nu.$$

Thus (12.42) can be re-expressed as

$$h(y \mid \mu) = [\mu^y/y!]\mathsf{M}_\nu^{(y)}(-\mu). \tag{12.49}$$

Gurmu et al. obtain the analytical expression for $\mathsf{M}^*_{\nu,p}(t)$, the moment generating function for $g^*_p(\nu|\lambda,\gamma)$ defined by (12.43) through (12.48), and its yth-order derivative $\mathsf{M}^{*(y)}_{\nu,p}(t) = \partial^y \mathsf{M}^*_{\nu,p}(t)/\partial t^y$. Evaluation at $t = -\mu$ yields

$$\mathsf{M}^{*(y)}_{\nu,p}(-\mu) = \left(1+\frac{\mu}{\lambda}\right)^{-\gamma} \frac{\Gamma(\gamma)}{(\lambda+\mu)^y} \left(\sum_{k=0}^{p} a_k^2\right)^{-1} \sum_{k=0}^{p}\sum_{l=0}^{p} a_k a_l \left(\eta_k \eta_l\right)^{1/2}$$
$$\times \sum_{r=0}^{k}\sum_{s=0}^{l} \binom{k}{r}\binom{l}{s} \frac{\Gamma(\gamma+r+s+y)}{\Gamma(\gamma+r)\Gamma(\gamma+s)} \left(-1-\frac{\mu}{\lambda}\right)^{-(r+s)}. \tag{12.50}$$

Premultiplication by $[\mu^y/y!]$ yields at last the approximating density for the count variable.

The log-likelihood function for a sample of size n is

$$\ln \mathcal{L}(\boldsymbol{\beta},\gamma,\lambda,\mathbf{a}) = \sum_{i=1}^{n} \left\{ y_i \ln \mu_i - \ln(y_i!) + \ln\left(\mathsf{M}^{*(y_i)}_{\nu,p}(-\mu_i)\right)\right\}, \tag{12.51}$$

where in practice $\mu_i = \exp(\mathbf{x}_i'\boldsymbol{\beta})$. The MLE is obtained in the usual way. Identification requires that $\mathsf{E}[\nu_i] = \mathsf{M}^{*(1)}_{\nu,p}(0) = 1$ and $a_0 = 1$. A formal statement and proof of the semiparametric consistency of this procedure is given in Gurmu et al. (1998), but to date its asymptotic distribution as $p \rightarrow \infty$ has not been established.

This type of mixture representation generalizes the treatment of heterogeneity but does not alter the specification of the conditional mean in any way. One advantage of using Laguerre polynomial expansion is that the leading term is the gamma density, which has been used widely as a mixing distribution in count and duration literature. Thus, if higher terms in the expansion vanish and $\gamma = \lambda$, we obtain the popular NB2 model of the earlier chapters, with $\gamma = \lambda = \alpha^{-1}$. Further, if $\gamma^{-1} = \lambda^{-1} \rightarrow 0$ and $a_j = 0$ for $j \geq 1$, the Poisson model is obtained. Unlike semiparametric methods based on discrete mixtures, such as that in the preceding subsection, the series expansion method provides smooth estimation of the distribution of unobserved heterogeneity.

This form of heterogeneity representation is computationally demanding. The complexity of the last term in the log-likelihood hinders an analytical study of the likelihood. As with other series-based likelihoods there remains a possibility of multiple maxima and at present no test is available for a global maximum. Gurmu et al. compute the standard errors by computer-intensive bootstrap methods. Alternatively, if the estimated value of p is treated as correct, one can use the outer product of numerically evaluated gradients of (12.51). As in other studies, information criteria are used to select the number of terms p in the expansion.

Gurmu et al. show that this method can be extended to Poisson models with censoring, truncation, and excess zeros and ones. They apply the model to censored data on the number of shopping trips to a shopping mall in a month taken by 828 shoppers, where 7.9% of the observations are right-censored due to the highest category being recorded as 3 or more and the data are somewhat overdispersed with sample variance 2.1 times the sample mean. They prefer a model with $p = 2$, meaning two terms more than the NB2. Application by Gurmu and Trivedi (1996) to uncensored data is presented in section 12.6. In Gurmu (1997) the method is extended and applied to the hurdle model, leading to a model that nests the hurdle specifications considered in section 4.7. Although appealing in principle, a potential problem with the hurdle specification is overfitting due to estimation of two parts of the model.

12.5.3 *Nonparametric Estimation of Variance*

An alternative to flexible specification of the variance function is to impose no algebraic form on the variance function but to treat it nonparametrically. In ideal circumstances one can obtain estimates of the conditional mean parameters that are as efficient if the variance function is unspecified as they are if it is specified. Then the estimation method is called *adaptive*. Note that this is more ambitious than methods presented in Chapter 3 for unknown variance function. There, if the variance function was not specified or at least not assumed to be correctly specified, the goal was to obtain consistent parameter estimates and valid standard errors. Efficient estimation was not a goal.

Here we present the adaptive method of Delgado and Kniesner (1997) for heteroskedasticity of unknown functional form in the exponential model. This is a generalization of the adaptive method of Robinson (1987) for the linear regression model with heteroskedasticity.

For the linear model, Robinson introduced a semiparametric WLS estimator for the linear regression model in which the weights, the inverse of the square root of the error variance σ_i^2, are consistently estimated from residuals $\hat{u}_i = y_i - \mathbf{x}_i'\hat{\beta}$, generated by the first-stage regression of y on $\mathbf{x}$. The approach lets σ_i^2 be a continuous or discrete nonparametric function of the regressors $\mathbf{x}_i$. The estimated variances $\hat{\sigma}_i^2$ are obtained by nonparametric regression of $\hat{u}_i^2$ on $\mathbf{x}_i$. The nonparametric regression uses the method of k nearest neighbors (see, for example, Altman, 1992), rather than kernel methods. Here k can be viewed as a smoothing parameter, similar to the bandwidth in kernel methods, which determines the number of observations that are used in estimating each σ^2. A technical requirement is that the degree of smoothness should increase with the sample size, albeit at a slower rate. The properties of the estimator depend on the choice of the number of nearest neighbors. Values of $k = n^{1/2}$ and $k = n^{3/5}$ have been used in empirical work. The resulting WLS estimator is shown to be adaptive. Formally this means it attains the semiparametric efficiency bound among estimators, given the specification of the conditional mean.

Relatively few changes are required to extend the Robinson approach to nonlinear regression. Delgado and Kniesner (1997) apply Robinson's approach to a count regression in their study of the factors determining absenteeism of London bus drivers. Assuming an exponential conditional mean, and then following Robinson, they estimate the conditional variances σ_i^2 by

$$\hat{\sigma}_i^2 = \sum_{j=1}^{n} \left(y_j - \exp(\mathbf{x}_j'\tilde{\beta})\right)^2 w_{ij}, \tag{12.52}$$

where $\tilde{\beta}$ is an initial root-n consistent estimator for β, such as the NLS estimator or the Poisson MLE. The w_{ij} are k nearest neighbor weights that equal $1/k$ for the k observations $\mathbf{x}_j$ closest to $\mathbf{x}_i$ and equal 0 otherwise. The semiparametric WLS estimator $\hat{\beta}_{\mathsf{SP}}$ solves the first-order conditions

$$\sum_{i=1}^{n} \left(y_i - \exp(\mathbf{x}_i'\hat{\beta}_{\mathsf{SP}})\right) \exp(\mathbf{x}_i'\hat{\beta}_{\mathsf{SP}})\mathbf{x}_i\hat{\sigma}_i^{-2} = \mathbf{0}. \tag{12.53}$$

Under regularity conditions, $\hat{\beta}_{\mathsf{SP}}$ is root-n consistent and asymptotically normal with variance matrix estimate

$$\hat{\mathsf{V}}[\hat{\beta}_{\mathsf{SP}}] = \left(\sum \mathbf{x}_i\mathbf{x}_i'\hat{\mu}_i^2\hat{\sigma}_i^{-2}\right)^{-1}.$$

A robust sandwich variant of this estimate is

$$\begin{aligned}\hat{\mathsf{V}}_{\mathsf{RS}}[\hat{\beta}_{\mathsf{SP}}] = &\left(\sum \mathbf{x}_i\mathbf{x}_i'\hat{\mu}_i^2\hat{\sigma}_i^{-2}\right)^{-1} \sum \mathbf{x}_i\mathbf{x}_i'\hat{\mu}_i^2\hat{u}_i^2\hat{\sigma}_i^{-4} \\ &\times \left(\sum \mathbf{x}_i\mathbf{x}_i'\hat{\mu}_i^2\hat{\sigma}_i^{-2}\right)^{-1},\end{aligned}$$

where $\hat{u}_i = y_i - \exp(\mathbf{x}_i'\hat{\beta}_{\mathsf{SP}})$ is the raw residual.

The results reported by Delgado and Kniesner (1997) appear to be more sensitive to the specification of the conditional mean than the estimator for the conditional variance. Indeed, their results suggest that the changes resulting from the use of the nonparametric variance estimation compared with the NB assumption are not large, even though the latter makes a very strong assumption that variances depend on the mean. A possible reason for this is that in practice the NB variance specification is a good approximation to heteroskedasticity of unknown form. However, more experience with the comparative performance of alternative approaches is desirable.

Delgado (1992) extended Robinson's approach to the estimation of a multivariate (multiequation) nonlinear regression. This estimator is a WLS estimator based on k nearest neighbor estimates of the conditional variance matrices. The approach is an attractive alternative to likelihood-based methods in those cases in which the likelihood involves awkward integrals that cannot be simplified analytically. Multivariate count regressions with unrestricted patterns of dependence, and mixed multivariate models with continuous and discrete variables, fall into this category.

12.6 Example and Model Comparison

In this section we illustrate some of the above modeling approaches, using the recreational trips data analyzed in section 6.4. Recall that these data on number of boating trips in a year are very overdispersed, with sample variance 17.6 times the sample mean. They were very poorly fit by Poisson and Poisson hurdle models, reasonably well fit by the NB2 model, and best fit by NB2 hurdle model.

Here we investigate whether the more flexible distributions presented in this chapter perform as well or better than the NB2 hurdle model.

In Table 12.1 we present estimates from two flexible distribution models. We also reproduce the NB2 model estimates given in section 6.3. The first estimates in the table are NLS estimates from regression with exponential mean, along with heteroskedastic consistent standard errors, because this is viewed as a flexible method for modeling the first moment, although not the entire distribution.

In this literature it has become standard to refer to the estimator without referring to the model actually being estimated. Here for clarity we introduce acronyms for the models. First, the model of Gurmu et al. (1997) is called the PGP model for Poisson–gamma polynomial model, indicating that the basic model is Poisson with heterogeneity modeled by an orthogonal series expansion around a baseline gamma density. Second, the model of Cameron and Johansson (1997) is called the PP model, following their terminology. Third, a similar model based on polynomial series expansion around a baseline NB2 density is called the NB2P model. The suffix p denotes the order of the polynomial or number of mixture terms. To select p we use the minimum CAIC, $\text{CAIC} = -2 \ln \text{L} + (1 + \ln n)k$, where k is the number of free parameters.

The first flexible approach considered is the SPMLE of Gurmu et al. (1997) applied to the PGP model. This reproduces the estimates first reported in Gurmu and Trivedi (1996). The CAIC selects the specification with $p = 3$. The coefficient estimates are given in Table 12.1, along with absolute t ratios based on bootstrapped standard errors. Asymptotic standard errors for the SPMLE can instead be computed by viewing the log-likelihood with $p = 3$ as a valid specification. Compared with NB2 estimates, allowing for more terms in the Laguerre expansion increases the log-likelihood and substantially reduces the value of the CAIC. The coefficient estimates are plausible, all the three terms in the expansion are significant, and compared with the NB2 specification the *FC3* coefficient is now significant. The previously reported NBH model still has an edge, in terms of CAIC, over this model and estimator.

Next consider PP models. Cameron and Johansson (1997) found that for an application with mildly overdispersed data the PP model was not parsimonious, with a PP5 model needed to outperform NB2, which fit their data exceptionally well. This lack of parsimony is confirmed here. Results for the boating-trip data based on PP4 specification are given in Table 12.1. The CAIC steadily fell from 3318 for PP0, or Poisson, to 2907 for PP1, 2756 for PP2, and 2684 for PP3. But a fourth-degree polynomial has a CAIC value, 2484, still well below that of NB2. As expected, the parameter estimates for the PP4 model differ

Table 12.1. *Recreational trips: flexible distribution estimators and t ratios*

	NLS		NB2 MLE		PGP3 SPMLE		PP4 MLE		NB2P1 MLE	
Variable	Coefficient	t ratio	Coefficient	t ratio	Coefficient	t ratio	Coefficient	t ratio	Coefficient	t ratio
ONE	1.678	8.53	−1.120	5.04	−1.327	5.27	.956	13.68	−.661	−5.30
SO	.280	6.99	.722	16.45	.315	20.05	.189	13.49	.716	24.57
SKI	.487	3.90	.621	4.38	.339	3.20	.225	6.02	.362	4.50
I	−.140	2.91	−.026	.64	−.031	.65	−.036	3.00	−.010	.48
FC3	.942	8.56	.669	1.48	1.098	3.65	.387	5.20	1.078	4.43
C1	−.034	4.35	.048	4.62	.025	2.88	.777	3.44	.017	1.94
C3	−.037	8.74	−.092	15.30	−0.071	11.91	−2.408	13.60	−.060	12.54
C4	.045	6.13	.038	4.43	.042	4.91	1.219	6.51	.041	7.50
$\ln(\gamma)/\alpha$					−.033	.69			.936	11.02
a1					.748	8.26	−.798	33.32	−.519	14.37
a2					.507	4.36	.256	18.84		
a3					.271	2.52	−.032	14.69		
a4							.001	12.72		
− ln L			825		790		1198		796	
CAIC			1717		1668		2484		1647	

Note: NLS, NLS estimates of the exponential conditional mean model with robust sandwich t ratios; NB2 MLE, usual NB2 model estimated by MLE; PGP3 SPMLE, Poisson model with series expansion for heterogeneity around gamma baseline density with t ratios calculated from bootstrap standard errors; PP4, fourth-order series expansion around Poisson baseline density; NB2P1, first-order series expansion around NB2 baseline density. The PP4 and NB2P1 models, like the NB2 model, are estimated by MLE with t ratios based on Hessian estimate of variance matrix.

Table 12.2. *Recreational trips: cumulative predicted probabilities*

Counts	Empirical	Poisson	PP4	NB2P1	NB2H
0	0.633	0.420	0.544	0.653	0.623
1	0.736	0.640	0.740	0.747	0.730
2	0.794	0.744	0.787	0.797	0.739
3	0.845	0.805	0.813	0.835	0.836
4	0.871	0.850	0.847	0.862	0.866
5	0.891	0.885	0.880	0.883	0.889
6–8	0.923	0.945	0.901	0.921	0.930
9–11	0.947	0.971	0.944	0.942	0.952
12–14	0.955	0.983	0.949	0.956	0.965
15–17	0.977	0.988	0.972	0.965	0.974
18–62	0.999	0.998	1.000	0.994	0.997
63–100	1.000	1.000	1.000	0.996	1.000
$-\ln$ L		1529	1198	796	725
CAIC		2998	2484	1647	1321

Note: PP4, fourth-order series expansion around Poisson baseline density; NB2P1, first-order series expansion around NB2 baseline density; NB2H, hurdle model using NB2 density; Empirical, actual cumulative relative frequency. Remaining columns give cumulative predicted frequencies.

from that of other models, because the mean in this model is not equal to the mean $\exp(\mathbf{x}'\boldsymbol{\beta})$ in the baseline Poisson density. One should instead compare the derivative of the conditional mean function with respect to regressors.

It would appear to be much better to use as baseline density for the series-expansion method of Cameron and Johansson (1997) the NB2 density rather than the Poisson. And from section 12.3.2 there is no need to be restricted to the Poisson. NB2P models nest PP models and are therefore still capable of modeling underdispersed data, whereas a Poisson with heterogeneity term modeled by a series expansion is capable of modeling only overdispersion. Table 12.1 also provides estimates of the NB2P model with $P = 1$. This model has a higher log-likelihood (-796) than any other model in Table 12.1 except PGP3 and is clearly the most parsimonious, with CAIC of 1657. The advantage comes from modeling overdispersion in a more parsimonious fashion than the PP formulation.

Table 12.2 presents the empirical and fitted probabilities for the Poisson, PP4, NB2P1, and NB2 hurdle (NB2H) models. It confirms that the NB2P1 does much better than the PP4 model in explaining the data. Even for the PP4 specification the zero frequency and frequencies higher than two are underestimated, suggesting a failure to model overdispersion. Closer examination of the data suggests that the estimation method may have been particularly sensitive to a single large count of 88. If $P = 5$ was tried this appeared to lead to numerical instability, not surprising because 88^5 is a large number relative to most others in the sample.

From Table 12.2 the NB2P1 is outperformed by the NB2H, even using CAIC, which penalizes the NB2H model for its additional parameters. We also compared the SPMLE results with those obtained by applying the constrained and unconstrained versions of the FMNB2 model, introduced in section 6.4. These are not reported in detail to save space. The chi-square goodness-of-fit tests rejected both variants of this model and confirmed that NB2H was the preferred model overall. It appears that for this data a hurdle specification is needed.

12.7 Derivations

We derive the section 12.2 result on optimal GMM for NB2 first four moments. For notational simplicity we drop the subscript i in (12.14). From (12.4), $\gamma_1\sigma^3 = \sigma^2(1 + 2\alpha\mu)$ and $\gamma_2\sigma^4 = \sigma^2 + 6\alpha\sigma^4 + 3\sigma^4$. Then

$$\begin{aligned}(\sigma^4\gamma_2 - \sigma^4) - (1 + 2\alpha\mu)\gamma_1\sigma^3 &= \sigma^4\gamma_2 - \sigma^4 - (\sigma\gamma_1)\gamma_1\sigma^3\\ &= \sigma^4\gamma_2 - \sigma^4 - \sigma^4\gamma_1^2\\ &= \sigma^4\{\gamma_2 - 1 - \gamma_1^2\},\end{aligned}$$

$$\begin{aligned}\sigma^3\gamma_1 - (1 + 2\alpha\mu)\sigma^2 &= \sigma^2(1 + 2\alpha\mu) - (1 + 2\alpha\mu)\sigma^2\\ &= 0,\end{aligned}$$

and

$$\begin{aligned}\sigma^6(\gamma_2 - 1 - \gamma_1^2) &= \sigma^2(\sigma^2 + 6\alpha\sigma^4 + 3\sigma^4) - \sigma^6 - \sigma^4(1 + 2\alpha\mu)^2\\ &= \sigma^4\{1 + 6\alpha\sigma^2 + 2\sigma^2 - (1 + 2\alpha\mu)^2\}\\ &= \sigma^4\{1 + 6\alpha\mu(1 + \alpha\mu) + 2\mu(1 + \alpha\mu)\\ &\qquad - (1 + 4\alpha\mu + 4\alpha^2\mu^2)\}\\ &= \sigma^4\{2(1 + \alpha)\mu(1 + \alpha\mu)\}\\ &= 2(1 + \alpha)\sigma^6.\end{aligned}$$

This yields (12.15).

12.8 Count Models: Retrospect and Prospect

In this concluding section we provide a brief retrospective look at the contents and attempt to present a glimpse into possible future developments.

This book opens with reference to the vast statistical literature on iid univariate count distributions. A major thrust of the work of the recent decades has been to translate and extend analysis of counts to more general regression models. Hence, most of the book is devoted to regression models for counts in a variety of data situations, including cross-section, time series, and panels.

Parametric count models are especially useful if the response variable takes relatively few values and the counts are small. In most cases there is an advantage in working with the exponential mean specification. It is important that the inherent heteroskedasticity of count data be modeled, an effective parsimonious approach being to specify the variance as a function of the mean. We have emphasized parametric models based on discrete distributions, although models based on discretization of a latent continuous distribution, such as the ordered probit model, may also be used.

Count models are dual to waiting time models. The latter are often more attractive and may well be more suitable for structural (as opposed to reduced form) modeling. In general, however, they require more data and may also call for more complex estimation procedures. Although analyzing counts instead may lead to information loss, it can still be informative about the role of covariates.

Significant additional complications arise from the presence of unobserved heterogeneity, truncation, censoring, joint dependence, measurement errors, and nonrandom sampling. These complications, generally studied extensively in the linear setting but less so for nonlinear models, have also been considered in detail here. A variety of parametric and semiparametric estimators have been presented.

Use of flexible functional forms for the density and moments of count models has also been given considerable attention. These developments are practically significant in many areas in which large heterogenous samples are available.

In the future we expect considerable emphasis to be given to application of computationally intensive methods to counts. At the most basic level this includes more widespread use of bootstrap methods and nonparametric and semiparametric regression methods in simple cross-section settings.

At the frontier we expect this to lead to models that better accommodate empirical realities that are currently underdeveloped in certain areas. For example, the available estimation and inference procedures for multivariate counts, models for nonrandom samples, and measurement errors are largely restricted to special models. Sometimes to handle one specific complication, others are suppressed. The simultaneous presence of several complications often results in models that may be conveniently analyzed by numerical methods only. This lack of an analytical solution is increasingly becoming less of a barrier.

In dealing with models with a flexible representation of heterogeneity, in section 4.9, for example, it is shown why the Monte Carlo simulation approach is an attractive estimation strategy. Additional examples of this approach are cited in discussion of measurement error and selection bias models. The potential for application of such methods also is indicated in the context of maximum likelihood estimation of multivariate models. This arises because the kernel of the likelihood is often an integral that must be numerically evaluated. Bayesian analyses of these models typically share this feature also.

These examples appear to us as harbingers of an emerging new generation of reduced form and structural models, exploiting advances in simulation-based estimation that are already penetrating other areas of econometrics and statistics.

12.9 Bibliographic Notes

Optimal GMM in a variety of settings is covered in Newey (1993). Johnson, Kotz, and Kemp (1992, pp. 70–77) provide an informative account of the power series family of distributions. The articles by Cameron and Johansson (1997) and Gurmu et al. (1998) provide additional details on the computational aspects of their respective estimators. For the generalized additive models approach to flexible specification of the conditional mean, Hastie and Tibshirani (1990) is an authoritative reference, and a good guide to the relevant software is Hilbe (1993). Applied aspects of nonparametric regression are dealt with in Härdle (1990). A relatively nontechnical introduction to kernel and nearest-neighbor nonparametric regression is given by Altman (1992). A recent survey of regression methods is given by Härdle and Linton (1994).

APPENDIX A

Notation and Acronyms

AIC: Akaike information criterion
ARMA: autoregressive moving average
BHHH: Berndt-Hall-Hall-Hausman algorithm
BIC: Bayes information criterion
BP: binary Poisson
Boot: bootstrap
CAIC: consistent Akaike information criterion
CB: correlated binomial
cdf: cumulative distribution function
CFMNB: slope-constrained finite mixture of negative binomials
CFMP: slope-constrained finite mixture of Poissons
CM: conditional moment (function or test)
Cov: covariance
CP: correlated Poisson
CV: coefficient of variation
DARMA: discrete ARMA
dgp: data generating process
Diag: diagonal
E: mathematical expectation
$\mathcal{EL}$: expected value of log-likelihood function
$\mathrm{E}[y \mid \mathbf{x}]$: conditional mean of y given $\mathbf{x}$
Elast: elasticity
EM: expectation-maximization (algorithm)
$f(y \mid \mathbf{x})$: conditional density of y given $\mathbf{x}$
FE: fixed effects
FMNB-C: C-component finite mixture of negative binomial
FMP-C: C-component finite mixture of Poisson
GEC(k): generalized event count model
GLM: generalized linear model
GLS: generalized least squares
GMM: generalized method of moments
iid: independently identically distributed

IM: information matrix (criterion or test)
INAR: integer-valued autoregressive (model)
INARMA: integer ARMA
L[τ, **z**]: Laplace transform
L: likelihood function
$\mathcal{L}$: log-likelihood function
LEF: linear exponential family
LEFN: linear exponential family with nuisance parameter
LM: Lagrange multiplier
LR: likelihood ratio
mgf: moment generating function
m($s; \pi_1, \dots, \pi_n$): multinomial distribution
M(t): moment generating function
MLE: maximum likelihood estimator
MLH: maximum likelihood Hessian
MLOP: maximum likelihood outer product
MPSD: modified power series distribution
N[μ, σ^2]: normal distribution with mean μ and variance σ^2
N[0, 1]: standard normal distribution
NB: negative binomial
NB1: NB distribution with linear variance function
NB2: NB distribution with quadratic variance function
NB1FE: negative binomial 1 fixed effects model
NBH: negative binomial hurdle
NLIV: nonlinear instrumental variable (method)
NLIV2: sequential two-step NLIV
NLS: nonlinear least squares
NPML: nonparametric maximum likelihood
N($s, s+t$): number of events observed in interval ($s, s+t$)
OLS: ordinary (linear) least squares
OP: outer product
OPG: outer product of the gradient (score) vectors
P[μ]: Poisson distribution with mean μ
pdf: probability density function
PFE: Poisson fixed effects (model)
pgf: probability generating function
PGP: Poisson–gamma polynomial (model)
PIG: Poisson inverse Gaussian mixture
PML: pseudomaximum likelihood
PPp: polynomial Poisson (model) of order p
PRE: Poisson random effects (model)
PSD: power series distribution
QEE: quadratic estimating equation
QGPML: quasigeneralized PML
QGPMLE: QGPML estimator

QL: quasi likelihood
QVF: quadratic variance function
RE: random effects
RS: robust sandwich (variance estimator)
SC: Schwarz Bayesian information criterion
SPGLS: semiparametric generalized least squares
T_{CM}: conditional moment test (statistic)
$\mathsf{T}_{\mathsf{GoF}}$: chi-square goodness-of-fit test (statistic)
T_{H}: Hausman test (statistic)
T_{LR}: likelihood ratio test (statistic)
T_{LM}: Lagrange multiplier (score) test (statistic)
T_{W}: Wald test (statistic)
T_{Z}: standard normal test (statistic)
V: variance
$\mathsf{V}[y \mid \mathbf{x}]$: conditional variance of y given $\mathbf{x}$
WLS: weighted least squares
ZIP: zero-inflated Poisson

APPENDIX B

Functions, Distributions, and Moments

For convenience we list in this appendix expressions and moment properties of several univariate distributions that have been used in this book, most notably the Poisson and negative binomial. But first we define the gamma function, a component of these distributions.

B.1 Gamma Function

Definition. The gamma function, denoted by $\Gamma(a)$, is defined by

$$\Gamma(a) = \int_0^\infty e^{-t} t^{a-1}\, dt, \qquad a > 0.$$

Properties of the gamma function include

1. $\Gamma(a) = (a-1)\Gamma(a-1)$
2. $\Gamma(a) = (a-1)!$ if a is a positive integer
3. $\Gamma(0) = \infty, \quad \Gamma(\frac{1}{2}) = \sqrt{\pi}$
4. $\Gamma(na) = (2\pi)^{(1-n)/2}(n)^{na-1/2} \prod_{k=0}^{n-1} \Gamma(a + \frac{k}{n})$, where n is a positive integer.

Definition. The incomplete gamma function, denoted by $\gamma(a, x)$, is defined by

$$\gamma(a, x) = \int_0^x e^{-t} t^{a-1}\, dt; \qquad a > 0, \quad x > 0.$$

The ratio $\gamma(a, x)/\Gamma(a)$ is known as the *incomplete gamma function* ratio or the gamma cdf.

The derivative of the logarithm of the gamma function is the *digamma function*

$$\frac{d \ln \Gamma(a)}{da} = \psi(a).$$

The digamma function obeys the recurrence relation

$$\psi(a+1) = \psi(a) + 1/a,$$

and the jth derivative $\psi^{(j)}(a+1)$ with respect to a obeys the recurrence relation

$$\psi^{(j)}(a+1) = (-1)^j j! a^{-j-1} + \psi^{(j)}(a).$$

B.2 Some Distributions

B.2.1 *Poisson*

The Poisson density for the count random variable y is

$$f(y) = \frac{e^{-\mu}\mu^y}{y!}; \qquad y = 0, 1, \ldots; \quad \mu > 0.$$

Then $y \sim \mathsf{P}[\mu]$ with mean μ, variance μ, moment generating function (mgf) $\exp[\mu(e^t - 1)]$ and pgf $\exp[\mu(t-1)]$.

B.2.2 *Logarithmic Series*

The logarithmic series density for the positive valued count random variable y is

$$f(y) = \alpha\frac{\theta^y}{y}; \quad y = 1, 2, \ldots; \quad 0 < \theta < 1, \quad \alpha = -[\log(1-\theta)]^{-1}.$$

Then y has mean $\alpha\theta/(1-\theta)$, variance $\alpha\theta(1-\alpha\theta)/(1-\theta)^2$, mgf $\log(1-\theta e^t)/\log(1-\theta)$ and pgf $\log(1-\theta t)/\log(1-\theta)$.

B.2.3 *Negative Binomial*

The negative binomial density for the count random variable y with parameters α and P is

$$f(y) = \binom{\alpha+y-1}{\alpha-1}\left(\frac{P}{1+P}\right)^y\left(\frac{1}{1+P}\right)^\alpha; \quad y = 0, 1, \ldots; \quad P, \alpha > 0.$$

Then y has mean αP, variance $\alpha P(1+P)$ and pgf $(1+P-Pt)^{-\alpha}$.

Different authors use different parameterizations of the negative binomial (Johnson, Kotz, and Kemp, 1992). In this book we have used $\mu = \alpha P$, which leads to

$$f(y) = \binom{\alpha+y-1}{\alpha-1}\left(\frac{\mu}{\alpha+\mu}\right)^y\left(\frac{\alpha}{\alpha+\mu}\right)^\alpha,$$

which has mean μ and variance $\mu(1+\mu/\alpha)$ and pgf $(1+\mu/\alpha-\mu t/\alpha)^{-\alpha}$.

The special case of the *geometric distribution* is obtained by setting $\alpha = 1$. *Pascal distribution* is obtained by setting α equal to an integer.

B.2.4 *Gamma*

The gamma density for the positive continuous random variable y is

$$f(y) = \frac{e^{-y\phi} y^{\alpha-1} \phi^{\alpha}}{\Gamma(\alpha)}; \qquad y > 0; \quad \phi > 0, \quad \alpha > 0.$$

Then y has mean α/ϕ, variance α/ϕ^2 and mgf $\exp[\phi/(\phi-1)^{\alpha}]$.

B.2.5 *Lognormal*

The lognormal density for the positive continuous random variable y is

$$f(y) = \frac{1}{\sigma y \sqrt{2\pi}} \exp\left[-\frac{1}{2\sigma^2}(\ln y - \xi)^2\right];$$
$$y > 0; \quad -\infty < \xi < \infty, \quad \sigma > 0, \quad \alpha > 0.$$

Then y has mean $\exp[\xi + (1/2\sigma^2)]$ and variance $\exp(2\xi + \sigma^2)[\exp(\sigma^2) - 1]$.

B.2.6 *Inverse Gaussian*

The inverse Gaussian density for the positive continuous random variable y is

$$f(y) = \sqrt{\frac{\theta}{2\pi y^3}} \exp\left[-\frac{\theta(y-\mu)^2}{2\mu^2 y}\right]; \quad y > 0; \quad \theta > 0, \quad \mu > 0.$$

Then y has mean μ and variance μ^3/θ.

B.3 Moments of Truncated Poisson

The kth-order factorial moments of truncated Poisson can be derived conveniently in terms of the mean of the regular Poisson μ, the mean of the truncated Poisson θ, the adjustment factor δ, and the truncation point $r-1$. Both θ and δ are defined in section 4.5. Let $\mathsf{E}[y^{(k)}]$ represent the kth descending factorial moment of y, and $y^{(k)} = \prod_{z=0}^{k-1}(y-z)$, $k \geq 1$. For the left-truncated Poisson model the factorial moments can be derived using

$$\mathsf{E}[y^{(k)}] = \mu^{k-1} + \delta \sum_{j=0}^{k-2} \mu^j \pi_j,$$

where

$$\pi_j = \prod_{i=0}^{k-2-j} (r-1-i).$$

Hence the first four factorial moments of the left-truncated Poisson are

$$
\begin{aligned}
\mathsf{E}[y^{(1)}] &= \theta \\
\mathsf{E}[y^{(2)}] &= \mu\theta + \delta(r-1) \\
\mathsf{E}[y^{(3)}] &= \mu^2\theta + \delta[(r-1)(r-2) + (r-1)\mu] \\
\mathsf{E}[y^{(4)}] &= \mu^3\theta + \delta[(r-1)(r-2)(r-3) \\
&\qquad + (r-1)(r-2)\mu + (r-1)\mu^2].
\end{aligned}
$$

Given the factorial moments, the uncentered and central moments can be obtained easily using the standard relationships between the three. For details see Gurmu and Trivedi (1992).

APPENDIX C

Software

Many widely used regression packages, including LIMDEP, STATA, TSP, and GAUSS, support maximum likelihood estimation of standard Poisson and negative binomial regressions, the latter of these in a separate count module. LIMDEP also supports the QGPML versions of the standard models, maximum-likelihood estimation of truncated or censored Poisson, geometric and negative binomial models, and ZIP and sample selection models. STATA also supports the generalized negative binomial regression in which the overdispersion parameter is further parameterized as a function of additional covariates. In addition, any statistical package with a generalized linear models component will include maximum likelihood and QGPML estimation of the Poisson, although not necessarily negative binomial. Thus, regression packages cover the models in Chapter 3 and roughly half of those in Chapter 4. The packages vary somewhat in the provision of diagnostics such as overdispersion tests and goodness-of-fit measures.

At the time of writing (late 1997) there is virtually no specialized software for the models presented in Chapters 7 through 12. A notable exception is estimation of basic panel count data models, which is provided by both LIMDEP and TSP. For models for which off-the-shelf software is not available, one needs to provide at least the likelihood function, for maximum likelihood estimation, or the moment conditions and weighting matrix, for GMM estimation. In principle this can be done using many regression packages, or using matrix programming languages such as GAUSS, MATLAB, S-PLUS, or SAS/IML. In practice numerical problems can be encountered if models are quite nonlinear. For much of our work we have successfully used the MAXLIK optimization routine in GAUSS. Further information is available from accameron@ucdavis.edu or trivedi@indiana.edu or http://www.econ.ucdavis.edu/count.html.

Software for simulation-based estimation is even less readily available. Template programs and algorithms may provide a useful starting point. For Markov-chain Monte Carlo methods a good reference to such resources is Gilks, Richardson, and Spiegelhalter (1996). This work contains several articles on Bayesian estimation of mixtures using Gibbs sampling.

References

Aitchison, J., and C.H. Ho (1989), "The Multivariate Poisson-Log Normal Distribution," *Biometrika*, 76, 643.

Aitkin, M., and D.B. Rubin (1985), "Estimation and Hypothesis Testing in Finite Mixture Models," *Journal of Royal Statistical Society B*, 47, 67–75.

Akaike, H. (1973), "Information Theory and an Extension of the Maximum Likelihood Principle," in B.N. Petrov and F. Csaki, eds., *Second International Symposium on Information Theory*, 267–281, Budapest, Akademiai Kaido.

Alcañiz, M. (1996), *Modelos de Poisson Generalizados con una Variable de Exposicion al Riesgo*, Ph.D. dissertation, University of Barcelona, Spain.

Al-Osh, M.A., and A.A. Alzaid (1987), "First Order Integer Valued Autoregressive (INAR(1)) Process," *Journal of Time Series Analysis*, 8, 261–275.

Altman, N.S. (1992), "An Introduction to Kernel and Nearest-Neighbor Nonparametric Regression," *American Statistician*, 46, 175–185.

Alzaid, A.A., and M.A. Al-Osh (1988), "First-Order Integer-Valued Autoregressive (INAR(1)) Process: Distributional and Regression Properties," *Statistica Neerlandica*, 42, 53–61.

Alzaid, A.A., and M.A. Al-Osh (1990), "An Integer-Valued pth-Order Autoregressive Structure (INAR(p)) Process," *Journal of Applied Probability*, 27, 314–324.

Alzaid, A.A., and M.A. Al-Osh (1993), "Some Autoregressive Moving Average Processes with Generalized Poisson Distributions," *Annals of the Institute of Mathematical Statistics*, 45, 223–232.

Amemiya, T. (1974), "The Nonlinear Two-Stage Least Squares Estimator," *Journal of Econometrics*, 2, 105–110.

Amemiya, T. (1984), "Tobit Models: A Survey," *Journal of Econometrics*, 24, 3–61.

Amemiya, T. (1985), *Advanced Econometrics*, Cambridge, MA, Harvard University Press.

Andersen, E.B. (1970), "Asymptotic Properties of Conditional Maximum Likelihood Estimators," *Journal of the Royal Statistical Society B*, 32, 283–301.

Andersen, P.K., O. Borgan, R.D. Gill, and N. Keiding (1993), *Statistical Models based on Counting Processes*, New York, Springer-Verlag.

Andrews, D.W.K. (1988a), "Chi-Square Diagnostic Tests for Econometric Models: Theory," *Econometrica*, 56, 1419–1453.

Andrews, D.W.K. (1988b), "Chi-Square Diagnostic Tests for Econometric Models: Introduction and Applications," *Journal of Econometrics*, 37, 135–156.

Arellano, M., and S. Bond (1991), "Some Tests of Specification for Panel Data: Monte Carlo Evidence and an Application to Employment Equations," *Review of Economic Studies*, 58, 277–298.

Arnold, B.C., and D.J. Strauss (1988), "Bivariate Distributions with Exponential Conditionals," *Journal of the American Statistical Association*, 83, 522–527.

Arnold, B.C., and D.J. Strauss (1992), "Bivariate Distributions with Conditionals in Prescribed Exponential Families," *Journal of the Royal Statistical Society B*, 53, 365–375.

Australian Bureau of Statistics (1978), Australian Health Survey 1977–78 [machine-readable file], Australian Bureau of Statistics, Canberra.

Baltagi, B.H. (1995), *Econometric Analysis of Panel Data*, Chichester, UK, John Wiley.

Barlow, R.E., and F. Proschan (1965), *Mathematical Theory of Reliability*, New York, John Wiley.

Barmby, T.A., C. Orme, and J.G. Treble (1991), "Worker Absenteeism: An Analysis Using Micro Data," *Economic Journal*, 101, 214–229.

Berndt, E., B. Hall, R. Hall, and J. Hausman (1974), "Estimation and Inference in Nonlinear Structural Models," *Annals of Economic and Social Measurement*, 3/4, 653–665.

Bishop, Y.M.M., S.E. Feinberg, and P.W. Holland (1975), *Discrete Multivariate Analysis: Theory and Practice*, Cambridge, MA, MIT Press.

Blonigen, B. (1997), "Firm-Specific Assets and the Link between Exchange Rates and Foreign Direct Investment," *American Economic Review*, 87, 447–465.

Blundell, R., R. Griffith, and J. Van Reenan (1995a), "Dynamic Count Models of Technological Innovation," *Economic Journal*, 105, 333–344.

Blundell, R., R. Griffith, and J. Van Reenan (1995b), "Market Share, Market Value and Innovation in a Panel of British Manufacturing Firms," Discussion Paper 95-19, Department of Economics, University College London.

Blundell, R., R. Griffith, and F. Windmeijer (1995), "Individual Effects and Dynamics in Count Data," Discussion Paper 95-03, Department of Economics, University College London.

Böhning, D. (1995), "A Review of Reliable Maximum Likelihood Algorithms for Semiparametric Mixture Models," *Journal of Statistical Planning and Inference*, 47, 5–28.

Böhning, D., E. Dietz, R. Schaub, P. Schlattmann, and B.G. Lindsay (1994), "The Distribution of the Likelihood Ratio for Mixtures of Densities from the One-Parameter Exponential Family," *Annals of the Institute of Statistical Mathematics*, 46, 373–388.

Bortkiewicz, L. von (1898), *Das Gesetz de Kleinen Zahlen*, Leipzig, Teubner.

Boswell, M.T., and G.P. Patil (1970), "Chance Mechanisms Generating the Negative Binomial Distributions," in G.P. Patil, ed., *Random Counts in Models and Structures*, volume 1, 3–22, University Park, PA, and London, Pennsylvania State University Press.

Bourlange, D., and C. Doz (1988), "Pseudo-maximum de Vraisemblance: Experiences de Simulations dans le Cadre d'un Modele de Poisson" (Pseudo Maximum Likelihood Estimators: Monte-Carlo Experimentation in the Case of a Poisson Model [with English summary]), *Annales d'Economie et de Statisques*, 10, 139–176.

Brännäs, K. (1992), "Limited Dependent Poisson Regression," *The Statistician*, 41, 413–423.

Brännäs, K. (1994), "Estimation and Testing in Integer Valued AR(1) Models," Umea Economic Studies No. 355, University of Umeå.

Brännäs, K. (1995a), "Explanatory Variables in the AR(1) Model," Umea Economic Studies No. 381, University of Umeå.

Brännäs, K. (1995b), "Prediction and Control for a Time Series Count Data Model," *International Journal of Forecasting*, 11, 263–270.

Brännäs, K. (1996), "Count Data Modelling: Measurement Errors in Exposure Time," Umea Economic Studies No. 423, University of Umeå.

Brännäs, K., and P. Johansson (1992), "Estimation and Testing in a Model with Serially Correlated Count Data," in E. von Collani and R. Göb, eds., *Proceedings of the Second Würzburg-Uneå Conference in Statistics*, University of Würzburg.

Brännäs, K., and P. Johansson (1994), "Time Series Count Regression," *Communications in Statistics: Theory and Methods*, 23, 2907–2925.

Brännäs, K., and P. Johansson (1996), "Panel Data Regression for Counts," *Statistical Papers*, 37, 191–213.

Brännäs, K., and G. Rosenqvist (1994), "Semiparametric Estimation of Heterogeneous Count Data Models," *European Journal of Operations Research*, 76, 247–258.

Breslow, N. (1990), "Tests of Hypotheses in Overdispersed Poisson Regression and Other Quasi-likelihood Models," *Journal of American Statistical Association*, 85, 565–571.

Breusch, T.S., and A.R. Pagan (1979), "A Simple Test for Heteroscedasticity," *Econometrica*, 47, 1287–1294.

Browning, M. (1992), "Children and Household Economic Behavior," *Journal of Economic Literature*, 30, 1434–1475.

Burguette, J., A.R. Gallant, and G. Souza (1982), "On the Unification of the Asymptotic Theory of Nonlinear Econometric Methods," *Econometric Reviews*, 1, 151–190.

Cameron, A.C. (1991), "Regression Based Tests of Heteroskedasticity in Models Where the Variance Depends on the Mean," Economics Working Paper Series No. 379, University of California, Davis.

Cameron, A.C., and P. Johansson (1997), "Count Data Regressions Using Series Expansions with Applications," *Journal of Applied Econometrics*, 12, 3, 203–224.

Cameron, A.C., and L. Leon (1993), "Markov Regression Models for Time Series Data," presented at Western Economic Association Meetings, Lake Tahoe, NV.

Cameron, A.C., and P.K. Trivedi (1985), "Regression-based Tests for Overdispersion," Econometric Workshop Technical Report No. 9, Stanford University.

Cameron, A.C., and P.K. Trivedi (1986), "Econometric Models Based on Count Data: Comparisons and Applications of Some Estimators," *Journal of Applied Econometrics*, 1, 29–53.

Cameron, A.C., and P.K. Trivedi (1990a), "Regression-based Tests for Overdispersion in the Poisson Model," *Journal of Econometrics*, 46, 347–364.

Cameron, A.C., and P.K. Trivedi (1990b), "Conditional Moment Tests and Orthogonal Polynomials," Indiana University, Department of Economics, Working Paper 90-051.

Cameron, A.C., and P.K. Trivedi (1990c), "Conditional Moment Tests with Explicit Alternatives," Economics Working Paper Series No. 366, University of California, Davis.

Cameron, A.C., and P.K. Trivedi (1990d), "The Information Matrix Test and Its Implied Alternative Hypotheses," Economics Working Paper Series No. 372, University of California, Davis.

Cameron, A.C., and P.K. Trivedi (1993), "Tests of Independence in Parametric Models: With Applications and Illustrations," *Journal of Business and Economic Statistics*, 11, 29–43.

Cameron, A.C., and P.K. Trivedi (1996), "Count Data Models for Financial Data," in G.S. Maddala and C.R. Rao, eds., *Handbook of Statistics, Volume 14, Statistical Methods in Finance*, Amsterdam, North-Holland.

Cameron, A.C., P.K. Trivedi, F. Milne, and J. Piggott (1988), "A Microeconometric Model of the Demand for Health Care and Health Insurance in Australia," *Review of Economic Studies*, 55, 85–106.

Cameron, A.C., and F.A.G. Windmeijer (1996), "R-Squared Measures for Count Data Regression Models with Applications to Health Care Utilization," *Journal of Business and Economic Statistics*, 14, 209–220.

Cameron, A.C., and F.A.G. Windmeijer (1997), "An R-squared Measure of Goodness of Fit for Some Common Nonlinear Regression Models," *Journal of Econometrics*, 77, 329–342.

Campbell, M.J. (1994), "Time Series Regression for Counts: An Investigation into the Relationship between Sudden Infant Death Syndrome and Environmental Temperature," *Journal of the Royal Statistical Society A*, 157, 191–208.

Carroll, R.J., D. Ruppert, and L.A. Stefanski (1995), *Measurement Error in Nonlinear Models*, London, Chapman and Hall.

Chamberlain, G. (1987), "Asymptotic Efficiency in Estimation with Conditional Moment Restrictions," *Journal of Econometrics*, 34, 305–334.

Chamberlain, G. (1992a), "Efficiency Bounds for Semiparametric Regression," *Econometrica*, 60, 567–596.

Chamberlain, G. (1992b), "Comment: Sequential Moment Restrictions in Panel Data," *Journal of Business and Economic Statistics*, 10, 20–26.

Chen, T.T. (1979), "Log-linear Models for Categorical Data with Misclassification and Double Sampling," *Journal of the American Statistical Association*, 74, 481–488.

Chesher, A. (1984), "Testing for Neglected Heterogeneity," *Econometrica*, 52, 865–872.

Chesher, A. (1991), "The Effect of Measurement Error," *Biometrika*, 78, 451–462.

Chesher, A., and M. Irish (1987), "Residual Analysis in the Grouped and Censored Normal Linear Model," *Journal of Econometrics*, 34, 33–62.

Chib, S., E. Greenberg, and R. Winkelmann (1998), "Posterior Simulation and Bayes Factors in Panel Count Data Models," *Journal of Econometrics*, in press.

Christmann, A. (1994), "Least Median of Weighted Squares in Logistic Regression with Large Strata," *Biometrika*, 81, 413–417.

Christmann, A. (1996), "On Outliers and Robust Estimation in Regression Models with Discrete Response Variables," paper presented at Workshop on Statistical Modelling of Discrete Data and Structures, Sonderforschungbereich 386, University of Munich.

Cincera, M. (1997), "Patents, R&D and Technological Spillovers at the Firm Level: Some Evidence from Econometric Count Models for Panel Data," *Journal of Applied Econometrics*, 12, 265–280.

Cochran, W.G. (1940), "The Analysis of Variance When Experimental Errors Follow the Poisson or Binomial Law," *Annals of Mathematical Statistics*, 11, 335–347.

Cohen, A.C. (1960), "Estimation in a Truncated Poisson Distribution When Zeros and Ones Are Missing," *Journal of the American Statistical Association*, 55, 342–348.

Collings, B.J., and B.H. Margolin (1985), "Testing Goodness of Fit for the Poisson Assumption When Observations Are Not Identically Distributed," *Journal of the American Statistical Association*, 80, 411–418.

Conniffe, D.C. (1990), "Testing Hypotheses with Estimated Scores," *Biometrika*, 77, 97–106.

Consul, P.C. (1989), *Generalized Poisson Distributions: Properties and Applications*, New York, Marcel Dekker.

Consul, P.C., and F. Famoye (1992), "Generalized Poisson Regression Model," *Communications in Statistics: Theory and Method*, 21, 89–109.

Consul, P.C., and G.C. Jain (1973), "A Generalization of the Poisson Distribution," *Technometrics*, 15, 791–799.

Consul, P.C., and L.R. Shenton (1972), "Use of Lagrange Expansion for Generating Discrete Generalized Probability Distributions," *SIAM Journal of Applied Mathematics*, 23, 239–248.

Cox, D.R. (1955), "Some Statistical Models Related with Series of Events," *Journal of the Royal Statistical Society B*, 17, 129–164.

Cox, D.R. (1961), "Tests of Separate Families of Hypotheses," in *Proceedings of the Fourth Berkeley Symposium on Mathematical Statistics and Probability*, 105–123. Berkeley, University of California Press.

Cox, D.R. (1962a), "Further Results on Tests of Separate Families of Hypotheses," *Journal of the Royal Statistical Society B*, 24, 406–424.

Cox, D.R. (1962b), *Renewal Theory*, London, Methuen.

Cox, D.R. (1981), "Statistical Analysis of Time Series: Some Recent Developments," *Scandinavian Journal of Statistics*, 8, 93–115.

Cox, D.R. (1983), "Some Remarks on Overdispersion," *Biometrika*, 70, 269–274.

Cox, D.R., and P.A.W. Lewis (1966), *The Statistical Analysis of Series of Events*, London, Methuen and Co.

Cox, D.R., and E.J. Snell (1968), "A General Definition of Residuals [with discussion]," *Journal of the Royal Statistical Society B*, 30, 248–275.

Cragg, J.G. (1971), "Some Statistical Models for Limited Dependent Variables with Application to the Demand for Durable Goods," *Econometrica*, 39, 829–844.

Cramer, H. (1946), *Mathematical Methods of Statistics*, Princeton, NJ, Princeton University Press.

Creel, M.D., and J.B. Loomis (1990), "Theoretical and Empirical Advantages of Truncated Count Data Estimators for Analysis of Deer Hunting in California," *Journal of Agricultural Economics*, 72, 434–441.

Crepon, B., and E. Duguet (1997a), "Estimating the Innovation Function from Patent Numbers: GMM on Count Data," *Journal of Applied Econometrics*, 12, 243–264.

Crepon, B., and E. Duguet (1997b), "Research and Development, Competition and Innovation: Pseudo-maximum Likelihood and Simulated Maximum Likelihood Method Applied to Count Data Models with Heterogeneity," *Journal of Econometrics*, 79, 355–378.

Crowder, M.J. (1976), "Maximum Likelihood Estimation for Dependent Observations," *Journal of the Royal Statistical Society B*, 38, 45–53.

Crowder, M.J. (1987), "On Linear and Quadratic Estimating Functions," *Biometrika*, 74, 591–597.

Daley, D.J., and D. Vere-Jones (1988), *An Introduction to the Theory of Point Processes*, New York, Springer-Verlag.

Davidson, R., and J.G. MacKinnon (1981), "Several Tests for Model Specification in the Presence of Alternative Hypotheses," *Econometrica*, 49, 781–793.

Davidson, R., and J.G. MacKinnon (1993), *Estimation and Inference in Econometrics*, Oxford, Oxford University Press.

Davison, A.C., and A. Gigli (1989), "Deviance Residuals and Normal Scores Plots," *Biometrika*, 76, 211–221.

Davison, A.C., and E.J. Snell (1991), "Residuals and Diagnostics," in D.V. Hinkley, N. Reid, and E.J. Snell, eds., *Statistical Theory and Modelling: In Honor of Sir David Cox, FRS*, 83–106, London, Chapman and Hall.

Davutyan, N. (1989), "Bank Failures as Poisson Variates," *Economic Letters*, 29, 333–338.

Dean, C. (1991), "Estimating Equations for Mixed Poisson Models," in V.P. Godambe, ed., *Estimating Functions*, Oxford, Oxford University Press.

Dean, C. (1992), "Testing for Overdispersion in Poisson and Binomial Regression Models," *Journal of the American Statistical Association*, 87, 451–457.

Dean, C.B. (1993), "A Robust Property of Pseudo Likelihood Estimation for Count Data," *Journal of Statistical Planning and Inference*, 35, 309.

Dean, C.B. (1994), "Modified Pseudo-likelihood Estimator of the Overdispersion Parameter in Poisson Mixture Models," *Journal of Applied Statistics*, 1994, 21, 523.

Dean, C.B., and R. Balshaw (1997), "Efficiency Lost by Analyzing Counts Rather Than Event Times in Poisson and Overdispersed Poisson Regression Models," *Journal of the American Statistical Society*, 92, 1387–1398.

Dean, C.B., D.M. Eaves, and C.J. Martinez (1995), "A Comment on the Use of Empirical Covariance Matrices in the Analysis of Count Data," *Journal of Statistical Planning and Inference*, 48, 197–206.

Dean, C., and F. Lawless (1989a), "Tests for Detecting Overdispersion in Poisson Regression Models," *Journal of the American Statistical Association*, 84, 467–472.

Dean, C., and J.F. Lawless (1989b), "Comment on Godambe and Thompson," *Journal of Statistical Planning and Inference*, 22, 155–158.

Dean, C., J.F. Lawless, and G.E. Willmot (1989), "A Mixed Poisson-Inverse Gaussian Regression Model," *Canadian Journal of Statistics*, 17, 171–182.

Deb, P., and P.K. Trivedi (1997), "Demand for Medical Care by the Elderly: A Finite Mixture Approach," *Journal of Applied Econometrics*, 12, 313–326.

Delgado, M.A. (1992), "Semiparametric Generalized Least Squares in the Multivariate Nonlinear Regression Model," *Econometric Theory*, 8, 203–222.

Delgado, M.A., and T.J. Kniesner (1997), "Count Data Models with Variance of Unknown Form: An Application to a Hedonic Model of Worker Absenteeism," *Review of Economics and Statistics*, 79, 41–49.

Diggle, P.J., K-Y Liang, and S.L. Zeger (1994), *Analysis of Longitudinal Data*, Oxford, Clarendon Press.

Dionne, G., M. Artis, and M. Guillen (1996), "Count Data Models for a Credit Scoring System," *Journal of Empirical Finance*, 3, 303–325.

Dionne, G., D. Desjardins, C. Labergue-Nadeau, and U. Maag (1995), "Medical Conditions, Risk Exposure, and Truck Drivers' Accidents: An Analysis with Count Data Regression Models," *Accident Analysis and Prevention*, 27, 295–305.

Dionne, G., and C. Vanasse (1992), "Automobile Insurance Rate Making in the Presence of Asymmetrical Information," *Journal of Applied Econometrics*, 7, 149–165.

Duan, N. (1983), "Smearing Estimate: A Nonparametric Retransformation Method," *Journal of the American Statistical Association*, 78, 605–610.

Durbin, J. (1954), "Errors in Variables," *Review of the International Statistical Institute*, 22, 23–32.

Durbin, J., and S.J. Koopman (1997), "Monte Carlo Maximum Likelihood Estimation for non-Gaussian State Space Models," *Biometrika*, 84, 669–684.

Eagleson, G.K. (1964), "Polynomial Expansions of Bivariate Distributions," *Annals of Mathematical Statistics*, 35, 1208–1215.

Eagleson, G.K. (1969), "A Characterization Theorem for Positive Definite Sequences on the Krawtchouk Polynomials," *Australian Journal of Statistics*, 11, 29–38.

Efron, B. (1979), "Bootstrapping Methods: Another Look at the Jackknife," *Annals of Statistics*, 7, 1–26.

Efron, B. (1986), "Double Exponential Families and Their Use in Generalized Linear Regressions," *Journal of the American Statistical Association*, 81, 709–721.

Efron, B., and R.J. Tibshirani (1993), *An Introduction to the Bootstrap*, London, Chapman and Hall.

Eggenberger, F., and G. Polya (1923), "Über die Statistik Verketteter Vorgänge," *Zeitschrift für Angerwandte Mathematik and Mechanik* (*Journal of Applied Mathematics and Mechanics*), 1, 279–289.

Eicker, F. (1967), "Limit Theorems for Regressions with Unequal and Dependent Errors," in L. LeCam and J. Neyman, eds., *Proceedings of the Fifth Berkeley Symposium on Mathematical Statistics and Probability*, 59–82, Berkeley, University of California Press.

Englin, J., and J.S. Shonkwiler (1995), "Estimating Social Welfare Using Count Data Models: An Application to Long-Run Recreation Demand Under Conditions of Endogenous Stratification and Truncation," *Review of Economics and Statistics*, 77, 104–112.

Everitt, B.S., and D.J. Hand (1981), *Finite Mixture Distributions*, London, Chapman and Hall.

Fahrmeier, L., and H. Kaufman (1987), "Regression Models for Non-stationary Categorical Time Series," *Journal of Time Series Analysis*, 8, 147–160.

Fahrmeier, L., and G.T. Tutz (1994), *Multivariate Statistical Modelling Based on Generalized Linear Models*, New York, Springer-Verlag.

Fan, J. (1992), "Design-Adaptive Nonparametric Regression," *Journal of the American Statistical Association*, 87, 998–1004.

Feinstein, J.S. (1989), "The Safety Regulation of U.S. Nuclear Power Plants: Violations, Inspections, and Abnormal Occurrences," *Journal of Political Economy*, 97, 115–154.

Feinstein, J.S. (1990), "Detection Controlled Estimation," *Journal of Law and Economics*, 33, 233–276.

Feller, W. (1943), "On a General Class of 'Contagious' Distributions," *Annals of Mathematical Statistics*, 14, 389–400.

Feller, W. (1968), *An Introduction to Probability Theory and Its Applications*, volume 1, edition 3, New York, John Wiley.

Feller, W. (1971), *An Introduction to Probability Theory*, volume 2, New York, John Wiley.

Feng, Z.D., and C.E. McCulloch (1996), "Using Bootstrap Likelihood Ratios in Finite Mixture Models," *Journal of the Royal Statistical Society B*, 58, 609–617.

Fienberg, S.E. (1981), "Deciding What and Whom to Count," in R.G. Lehnan and W.G. Skogan, eds., *The NCS Working Papers*, volume 1, U.S. Department of Justice.

Firth, D. (1987), "On the Efficiency of Quasi-likelihood Estimation," *Biometrika*, 74, 223–245.

Firth, D. (1991), "Generalized Linear Models," in D.V. Hinkley, N. Reid, and E.J. Snell, eds., *Statistical Theory and Modelling: In Honor of Sir David Cox, FRS*, 55–82, London, Chapman and Hall.

Fleming, T.R., and D.P. Harrington (1991), *Counting Process and Survival Analysis*, New York, John Wiley.

Gallant, A.R., and D.W. Nychka (1987), "Seminonparametric Maximum Likelihood Estimation," *Econometrica*, 55, 363–390.

Gallant, A.R., and G. Tauchen (1989), "Seminonparametric Estimation of Conditionally Constrained Heterogeneous Processes: Asset Pricing Applications," *Econometrica*, 57, 1091–1120.

Gauthier, G., and A. Latour (1994), "Convergence Forte des Estimateurs des Paramètres d'un Processus GENAR(p)," *Les Annales des sciences mathematics du Quebec*, (with extended English abstract) forthcoming.

Geil, P., A. Melion, R. Rotte, and K.F. Zimmermann (1997), "Economic Incentives and Hospitalization," *Journal of Applied Econometrics*, 12, 295–311.

Gelfand, A.E., and S.R. Dalal (1990), "A Note on Overdispersed Exponential Families," *Biometrika*, 77, 55–64.

Gilks, W.R., S. Richardson, and D.J. Spiegelhalter (1996), *Markov Chain Monte Carlo in Practice*, London, Chapman and Hall.

Godambe, V.P., and M.E. Thompson (1989), "An Extension of Quasi-Likelihood Estimation," *Journal of Statistical Planning and Inference*, 22, 137–152.

Goffe, W.L., Ferrier, G.D., and J. Rogers (1994), "Global Optimization of Statistical Functions with Simulated Annealing," *Journal of Econometrics*, 60, 65–99.

Goldstein, H. (1995), *Multilevel Statistical Models*, edition 2, London, Edward Arnold.

Good, D., and M.A. Pirog-Good (1989), "Models for Bivariate Count Data with an Application to Teenage Delinquency and Paternity," *Sociological Methods and Research*, 17, 409–431.

Gourieroux, C., and A. Monfort (1991), "Simulation Based Inference in Models with Heterogeneity," *Annales D'Economie Et De Statistique*, 20/21, 70–107.

Gourieroux, C., and A. Monfort (1995), *Statistics and Econometrics Models*, volumes 1 and 2, translated by Q. Vuong, Cambridge, Cambridge University Press. (Originally published as *Statistique et modèles économetriques*, 1989).

Gourieroux, C., and A. Monfort (1997), *Simulation Based Econometric Methods*, Oxford, Oxford University Press.

Gourieroux, C., A. Monfort, and A. Trognon (1984a), "Pseudo Maximum Likelihood Methods: Theory," *Econometrica*, 52, 681–700.

Gourieroux, C., A. Monfort, and A. Trognon (1984b), "Pseudo Maximum Likelihood Methods: Applications to Poisson Models," *Econometrica*, 52, 701–720.

Gourieroux, C., A. Monfort, E. Renault, and A. Trognon (1987a), "Generalized Residuals," *Journal of Econometrics*, 34, 5–32.

Gourieroux, C., A. Monfort, E. Renault, and A. Trognon (1987b), "Simulated Residuals," *Journal of Econometrics*, 34, 201–252.

Gourieroux, C., and M. Visser (1997), "A Count Data Model with Unobserved Heterogeneity," *Journal of Econometrics*, 79, 247–268.

Greene, W.H. (1994), "Accounting for Excess of Zeros and Sample Selection in Poisson and Negative Binomial Regression Models," Discussion Paper EC-94-10, Department of Economics, New York University.

Greene, W.H. (1997a), *Econometric Analysis*, edition 3, New York, MacMillan.

Greene, W.H. (1997b), "FIML Estimation of Sample Selection Models for Count Data," Discussion Paper EC-97-02, Department of Economics, Stern School of Business, New York University.

Greenwood, M., and G.U. Yule (1920), "An Inquiry into the Nature of Frequency Distributions of Multiple Happenings, with Particular Reference to the Occurrence of Multiple Attacks of Disease or Repeated Accidents," *Journal of the Royal Statistical Society A*, 83, 255–279.

Grogger, J. (1990), "The Deterrent Effect of Capital Punishment: An Analysis of Daily Homicide Counts," *Journal of the American Statistical Association*, 85, 295–303.

Grogger, J.T., and R.T. Carson (1991), "Models for Truncated Counts," *Journal of Applied Econometrics*, 6, 225–238.

Gupta, C.R. (1974), "Modified Power Series Distribution and Some of its Applications," *Sankhya*, Series B, 36, 288–298.

Gurmu, S. (1991), "Tests for Detecting Overdispersion in the Positive Poisson Regression Model," *Journal of Business and Economic Statistics*, 9, 215–222.

Gurmu, S. (1993), "Testing for Overdispersion in Censored Poisson Regression Models," Discussion Paper 255, The Jefferson Center for Political Economy, University of Virginia.

Gurmu, S. (1997), "Semiparametric Estimation of Hurdle Regression Models with an Application to Medicaid Utilization," *Journal of Applied Econometrics*, 12, 225–242.

Gurmu, S., P. Rilstone, and S. Stern (1995), "Nonparametric Hazard Rate Estimation," Department of Economics, Discussion Paper, University of Virginia.

Gurmu, S., P. Rilstone, and S. Stern (1998), "Semiparametric Estimation of Count Regression Models," forthcoming *Journal of Econometrics*.

Gurmu, S., and P.K. Trivedi (1992), "Overdispersion Tests for Truncated Poisson Regression Models," *Journal of Econometrics*, 54, 347–370.

Gurmu, S., and P.K. Trivedi (1993), "Variable Augmentation Specification Tests in the Exponential Family," *Econometric Theory*, 9, 94–113.

Gurmu, S., and P.K. Trivedi (1994), "Recent Developments in Models of Event Counts: A Survey," Discussion Paper 261, The Jefferson Center for Political Economy, University of Virginia.

Gurmu, S., and P.K. Trivedi (1996), "Excess Zeros in Count Models for Recreational Trips," *Journal of Business and Economic Statistics*, 14, 469–477.

Haab, T.C., and K.E. McConnell (1996), "Count Data Models and the Problem of Zeros in Reaction Demand Analysis," *American Journal of Agricultural Economics*, 78, 89–98.

Haight, F. A. (1967), *Handbook of the Poisson Distribution*, New York, John Wiley.

Hall, A. (1987), "The Information Matrix Test in the Linear Model," *Review of Economic Studies*, 54, 257–265.

Hall, B.H., Griliches, Z., and J.A. Hausman (1986), "Patents and R and D: Is There a Lag?," *International Economic Review*, 27, 265–283.

Hamilton, J.D. (1989), "A New Approach to the Economic Analysis of Nonstationary Time Series and the Business Cycle," *Econometrica*, 57, 357–384.

Hamilton, J.D. (1994), *Time Series Analysis*, Princeton, NJ, Princeton University Press.

Hannan, M.T., and J. Freeman (1987), "The Ecology of Organizational Founding: American Labor Unions, 1836–1985," *American Journal of Sociology*, 92, 910–943.

Hansen, L.P. (1982), "Large Sample Properties of Generalized Method of Moments Estimators," *Econometrica*, 50, 1029–1054.

Härdle, W. (1990), *Applied Nonparametric Methods*, Cambridge, UK, Cambridge University Press.

Härdle, W., and O. Linton (1994), "Applied Nonparametric Methods," in R.F. Engle and D. McFadden, eds., *Handbook of Econometrics*, volume 4, Amsterdam, North–Holland.

Harvey, A.C. (1989), *Forecasting, Structural Time Series Models and the Kalman Filter*, Cambridge, UK, Cambridge University Press.

Harvey, A.C., and C. Fernandes (1989), "Time Series Models for Count or Qualitative Observations [with discussion]," *Journal of Business and Economic Statistics*, 7, 407–417.

Harvey, A.C., and N. Shephard (1993), "Stuctural Time Series Models," in G.S. Maddala, C.R. Rao, and H.D. Vinod, eds., *Handbook of Statistics, Volume 11, Econometrics*, Amsterdam, North–Holland.

Harville, D. (1977), "Maximum Likelihood Estimation of Variance Components and Related Problems," *Journal of the American Statistical Association*, 72, 320–340.

Hastie, T.J., and R.J. Tibshirani (1990), *Generalized Additive Models*, New York, Chapman and Hall.

Hausman, J.A. (1978), "Specification Tests in Econometrics," *Econometrica*, 46, 1251–1271.

Hausman, J.A., B.H. Hall, and Z. Griliches (1984), "Econometric Models for Count Data with an Application to the Patents–R and D Relationship," *Econometrica*, 52, 909–938.

Hausman, J.A., G.K. Leonard, and D. McFadden (1995), "A Utility-Consistent, Combined Discrete Choice and Count Data Model: Assessing Recreational Use Losses due to Natural Resource Damage," *Journal of Public Economics*, 56, 1–30.

Hausman, J.A., A.W. Lo, and A.C. MacKinlay (1992), "An Ordered Probit Analysis of Transaction Stock Prices," *Journal of Financial Economics*, 31, 319–379.

Heckman, J. J. (1976), "The Common Structure of Statistical Models of Truncation, Sample Selection, and Limited Dependent Variables and a Simple Estimator for Such Models," *Annals of Economics and Social Measurement*, 5, 475–492.

Heckman, J.J. (1984), "The χ^2 Goodness of Fit Test for Models with Parameters Estimated from Micro Data," *Econometrica*, 52, 1543–1547.

Heckman, J., and B. Singer (1984), "A Method of Minimizing the Impact of Distributional Assumptions in Econometric Models for Duration Data," *Econometrica*, 52, 271–320.

Hendry, D. F. (1995), *Dynamic Econometrics*, Oxford, Oxford University Press.

Hilbe, J. M. (1993), "Generalized Additive Models Software," *American Statistician*, 47, 59–64.

Hill, S., D. Rothchild, and A.C. Cameron (1998), "Tactical Information and the Diffusion of Peaceful Protests," in D.A. Lake and D. Rothchild, eds., *The International Spread of Ethnic Conflict: Fear, Diffusion, and Escalation*, Princeton, NJ, Princeton University Press.

Hinde, J. (1982), "Compound Poisson Regression Models," in R. Gilchrist, ed., *GLIM 82: Proceedings of the International Conference on Generalised Linear Models*, New York, Springer-Verlag.

Holly, A. (1982), "A Remark on Hausman's Specification Test," *Econometrica*, 50, 749–759.

Holly, A. (1987), "Specification Tests: An Overview," in T.F. Bewley, ed., *Advances in Economics and Econometrics: Theory and Applications*, volume 1, Fifth World Congress, 59–97, Cambridge, UK, Cambridge University Press.

Honda, Y. (1988), "A Size Correction to the Lagrange Multiplier Test for Heteroskedasticity," *Journal of Econometrics*, 38, 375–386.

Horowitz, J.L. (1997), "Bootstrap Methods in Econometrics: Theory and Numerical Performance," in D.M. Kreps and K.F. Wallis, eds., *Advances in Economics and Econometrics: Theory and Applications*, volume 3, Seventh World Congress, Cambridge, UK, Cambridge University Press.

Hsiao, C. (1986), *Analysis of Panel Data*, Cambridge, UK, Cambridge University Press.

Huber, P.J. (1967), "The Behavior of Maximum Likelihood Estimates under Nonstandard Conditions," in L. LeCam and J. Neyman, eds., *Proceedings of the Fifth Berkeley Symposium on Mathematical Statistics and Probability*, 221–234, Berkeley, University of California Press.

Imbens, G.W., and T. Lancaster (1994), "Combining Micro and Macro Data in Microeconometric Models," *Review of Economic Studies*, 61, 655–680.

Jacobs, P.A., and P.A.W. Lewis (1977), "A Mixed Autoregressive Moving Average Exponential Sequence and Point Process," *Advances in Applied Probability*, 9, 87–104.

Jacobs, P.A., and P.A.W. Lewis (1978a), "Discrete Time Series Generated by Mixtures I: Correlational and Runs Properties," *Journal of the Royal Statistical Society B*, 40, 94–105.

Jacobs, P.A., and P.A.W. Lewis (1978b), "Discrete Time Series Generated by Mixtures II: Asymptotic Properties," *Journal of the Royal Statistical Society B*, 40, 222–228.

Jacobs, P.A., and P.A.W. Lewis (1983), "Stationary Discrete Autoregressive Moving Average Time Series Generated by Mixtures," *Journal of Time Series Analysis*, 4, 19–36.

Jaggia, S. (1991), "Specification Tests Based on the Generalized Gamma Model of Duration – With an Application to Kennan Strike Data," *Journal of Applied Econometrics*, 6, 169–180.

Jaggia, S., and S. Thosar (1993), "Multiple Bids as a Consequence of Target Management Resistance: A Count Data Approach," *Review of Quantitative Finance and Accounting*, 3, 447–457.

Jewel, N. (1982), "Mixtures of Exponential Distribuhtions," *Annals of Statistics*, 10, 479–484.

Jin-Guan, D., and L. Yuan (1991), "The Integer-Valued Autoregressive (INAR(p)) Model," *Journal of Time Series Analysis*, 12, 129–142.

Johansson, P. (1995), "Tests for Serial Correlation and Overdispersion in a Count Data Regression Model," *Journal of Statistical Computation and Simulation*, 53, 153–164.

Johansson, P. (1996), "Speed Limitation and Motorway Casualties: A Time Series Count Data Regression Approach," *Accident Analysis and Prevention*, 28, 73–87.

Johansson, P., and M. Palme (1996), "Do Economics Incentives Affect Work Absence: Empirical Evidence Using Swedish Micro Data," *Journal of Public Economics*, 59, 195–218.

Johnson, N.L., and S. Kotz (1969), *Discrete Distributions*, Boston, Houghton Mifflin.

Johnson, N.L., S. Kotz, and N. Balakrishnan (1994), *Continuous Univariate Distributions*, edition 2, New York, John Wiley.

Johnson, N.L., S. Kotz, and N. Balakrishnan (1997), *Discrete Multivariate Distributions*, New York, John Wiley.

Johnson, N.L., S. Kotz, and A.W. Kemp (1992), *Univariate Distributions*, edition 2, New York, John Wiley.

Johnston, J., and J. DiNardo (1997), *Econometric Methods*, edition 4, New York, McGraw-Hill.

Jordan, P., D. Brubacher, S. Tsugane, Y. Tsubono, K.F. Gey, and U. Moser (1997), "Modeling Mortality Data from a Multi-Center Study in Japan by Means of Poisson Regression with Errors in Variables," *International Journal of Epidemiology*, 26, 501–507.

Jorgensen, B. (1987), "Exponential Dispersion Models [with discussion]", *Journal of the Royal Statistical Society B*, 49, 127–162.

Jorgensen, B. (1997), *The Theory of Dispersion Models*, London, Chapman and Hall.

Jorgenson, D.W. (1961), "Multiple Regression Analysis of a Poisson Process," *Journal of the American Statistical Association*, 56, 235–245.

Jung, C.J., and R. Winkelmann (1993), "Two Apects of Labor Mobility: A Bivariate Poisson Regression Approach," *Empirical Economics*, 18, 543–556.

Jupp, P.E., and K.V. Mardia (1980), "A General Correlation Coefficient for Directional Data and Related Regression Problems," *Biometrika*, 67, 163–173.

Kalbfleisch, J.D., and R.L. Prentice (1980), *The Statistical Analysis of Failure Time Data,* New York, Wiley.

Katz, L. (1963), "Unified Treatment of a Broad Class of Discrete Probability Distributions," in G.P. Patil, ed., *Classical and Contagious Discrete Distributions*, Calcutta, Statistical Publishing Society.

Keane, M.P., and D.E. Runkle (1992), "On the Estimation of Panel-Data Models with Serial Correlation When Instruments Are Not Strictly Exogenous," *Journal of Business and Economic Statistics*, 10, 1–9.

Kennan, J. (1985), "The Duration of Contract Strikes in U.S. Manufacturing," *Journal of Econometrics*, 28, 5–28.

Kianifard, F., and P.P. Gallo (1995), "Poisson Regression Analysis in Clinical Research," *Journal of Biopharmaceutical Statistics*, 5, 115–129.

King, G. (1987a), "Presidential Appointments to the Supreme Court: Adding Systematic Explanation to Probabilistic Description," *American Political Quarterly*, 15, 373–386.

King, G. (1987b), "Event Count Models for International Relations: Generalizations and Applications," *International Studies Quarterly*, 33, 123–147.

King, G. (1989a), "A Seemingly Unrelated Poisson Regression Model," *Sociological Methods and Research*, 17, 235–255.

King, G. (1989b), "Variance Specification in Event Count Models: From Restrictive Assumptions to a Generalized Estimator," *American Journal of Political Science*, 33, 762–784.

Kingman, J.F.C. (1993), *Poisson Processes*, Oxford, Oxford University Press.

Kocherlakota, S., and K. Kocherlakota (1993), *Bivariate Discrete Distributions*, New York, Marcel Dekker.

Koenker, R. (1982), "A Note on Studentizing a Test for Heteroskedasticity," *Journal of Econometrics*, 17, 107–112.

Kotz, S., and N.L. Johnson (1982–89), *Encyclopedia of Statistical Sciences*, vol. 1–9, New York, John Wiley.

Laird, N. (1978), "Nonparametric Maximum Likelihood Estimation of a Mixing Distribution," *Journal of the American Statistical Association*, 73, 805–811.

Lambert, D. (1992), "Zero-Inflated Poisson Regression with an Application to Defects in Manufacturing," *Technometrics*, 34, 1–14.

Lancaster, H.O. (1969), *The Chi-squared Distribution*, New York, John Wiley.

Lancaster, T. (1984), "The Covariance Matrix of the Information Matrix Test," *Econometrica*, 52, 1051–1054.

Lancaster, T. (1990), *The Econometric Analysis of Transitional Data*, New York, Cambridge University Press.

Landwehr, J.M., D. Pregibon, and A.C. Shoemaker (1984), "Graphical Methods for Assessing Logistic Regression Models [with discussion]," *Journal of the American Statistical Association*, 79, 61–83.

Lawless, J.F. (1987a), "Regression Methods for Poisson Process Data," *Journal of the American Statistical Association*, 82, 808–815.

Lawless, J.F. (1987b), "Negative Binomial and Mixed Poisson Regressions," *The Canadian Journal of Statistics*, 15, 209–225.

Lawless, J.F. (1995), "The Analysis of Recurrent Events for Multiple Subjects," *Applied Statistics: Journal of the Royal Statistical Society C*, 44, 487–498.

Lee, L.-F. (1983), "Generalized Econometric Models with Selectivity," *Econometrica*, 51, 507–512.

Lee, L.-F. (1986), "Specification Test for Poisson Regression Models," *International Economic Review*, 27, 689–706.

Lee, L.-F. (1997), "Specification and Estimation of Count Data Regression and Sample Selection Models: A Counting Process and Waiting Time Approach," presented at the North American Summer Meetings of the Econometric Society, Pasadena, CA.

Leon, L.F., and C.-L. Tsai (1998), "The Assessment of Model Adequacy for Markov Regression Time Series Models," forthcoming *Biometrics*.

Leroux, B.G. (1992), "Consistent Estimation of a Mixing Distribution," *Annals of Statistics*, 20, 1350–1360.

Lewis, P.A.W. (1985), "Some Simple Models for Continuous Variate Time Series," *Water Resources Bulletin*, 21, 635–644.

Li, W.K. (1991), "Testing Model Adequacy for Some Markov Regression Models for Time Series," *Biometrika*, 78, 83–89.

Liang, K.-Y., and S. Zeger (1986), "Longitudinal Data Analysis Using Generalized Linear Models," *Biometrika*, 73, 13–22.

Lindeboom, M., and G.J. van den Berg (1994), "Heterogeneity in Models for Bivariate Survival: The Importance of Mixing Distribution," *Journal of the Royal Statistical Society B*, 56, 49–60.

Lindsay, B.G. (1995), *Mixture Models: Theory, Geometry and Applications*, NSF-CBMS Regional Conference Series in Probability and Statistics, volume 5, IMS-ASA. Hayward, CA: Institute of Mathematical Statistics.

Lindsay, B.G., and K. Roeder (1992), "Residual Diagnostics in the Mixture Model," *Journal of the American Statistical Association*, 87, 785–795.

Liu, R.Y. (1988), "Bootstrap Procedures under Some Non-i.i.d. Models," *Annals of Statistics*, 16, 1696–1700.

Long, J.S. (1997), *Regression Models for Categorical and Limited Dependent Variables*, Thousand Oaks, CA, Sage Publications.

Lu, M.Z., and G.E. Mizon (1996), "The Encompassing Principle and Hypothesis Testing," *Econometric Theory*, 12, 845–858.

Luceño, A. (1995), "A Family of Partially Correlated Poisson Models for Overdispersion," *Computational Statistics and Data Analysis*, 20, 511–520.

MacDonald, I.L., and W. Zucchini (1997), *Hidden Markov and Other Models for Discrete-Valued Time Series*, London, Chapman and Hall.

Maddala, G.S. (1983), *Limited Dependent and Qualitative Variables in Econometrics*, Cambridge, Cambridge University Press.

Mammen, E. (1993), "Bootstrap and Wild Bootstrap for High Dimensional Linear Models," *Annals of Statistics*, 21, 255–285.

Manski, C.F. (1995), *Identification Problems in the Social Sciences*. Cambridge, MA, Harvard University Press.

Manski, C.F., and D. McFadden, eds. (1981), *Structural Analysis of Discrete Data with Econometric Applications*, Cambridge, MA, MIT Press.

Marshall, A.W., and I. Olkin (1990), "Multivariate Distributions Generated from Mixtures of Convolution and Product Families," in H.W. Block, A.R. Sampson, and T.H. Savits, eds., *Topics in Statistical Dependence*, IMS Lecture Notes Monograph Series, volume 16, 371–393. Hayward, CA, Institute of Mathematical Statistics.

Mátyás, L., and P. Sevestre (1995), *The Econometrics of Panel Data: A Handbook of the Theory with Applications*, edition 3, Nordrecht, The Netherlands, Kluwer Academic Publishers.

Mayer, W.J., and W.F. Chappell (1992), "Determinants of Entry and Exit: An Application of Bivariate Compounded Poisson Distribution to U.S. Industries, 1972–1977," *Southern Economic Journal*, 58, 770–778.

McCallum, J., C. Raymond, and C. McGilchrist (1995), "How Accurate Are Self Reports of Doctor Visits? A Comparison Using Australian Health Insurance Commission Records," National Center for Epidemiology and Population Health, The Australian National University.

McCullagh, P. (1983), "Quasi-likelihood Functions," *The Annals of Statistics*, 11, 59–67.

McCullagh, P. (1986), "The Conditional Distribution of Goodness-of-Fit Statistics for Discrete Data," *Journal of the American Statistical Association*, 81, 104–107.

McCullagh, P., and J.A. Nelder (1989, 1983), *Generalized Linear Models*, editions 1 and 2, London, Chapman and Hall.

McFadden, D., and P. Ruud (1994), "Estimation by Simulation," *Review of Economics and Statistics*, 76, 591–608.

McGilchrist, C.A. (1994), "Estimation in Generalized Mixed Models," *Journal of the Royal Statistical Society B*, 56, 61–69.

McKenzie, E. (1985), "Some Simple Models for Discrete Variate Time Series," *Water Resources Bulletin*, 21, 645–650.

McKenzie, E. (1986), "Autoregressive Moving-Average Processes with Negative Binomial and Geometric Marginal Distributions," *Advances in Applied Probability*, 18, 679–705.

McKenzie, E. (1988), "Some ARMA Models for Dependent Sequences of Poisson Counts," *Advances in Applied Probability*, 22, 822–835.

McLachlan, G.J., and K.E. Basford, (1988), *Mixture Models: Inference and Application to Clustering*, New York, Marcel Dekker.

Meghir, C., and J.-M. Robin (1992), "Frequency of Purchase and Estimation of Demand Equations," *Journal of Econometrics*, 53, 53–86.

Merkle, L., and K.F. Zimmermann (1992), "The Demographics of Labor Turnover: A Comparison of Ordinal Probit and Censored Count Data Models," *Reserches Economiques de Louvain*, 58, 283–307.

Mizon, G.E., and J.-F. Richard (1986), "The Encompassing Principle and Its Application to Testing Non-nested Hypotheses," *Econometrica*, 54, 657–678.

Montalvo, J.G. (1997), "GMM Estimation of Count-Panel-Data Models with Fixed Effects and Predetermined Instruments," *Journal of Business and Economic Statistics*, 15, 82–89.

Moore, D.F. (1986), "Asymptotic Properties of Moment Estimators for Overdispersed Counts and Proportions," *Biometrika*, 73, 583–588.

Moran, P.A.P. (1971), "Maximum Likelihood Estimation in Non-standard Conditions," *Proceedings of the Cambridge Philosophical Society*, 70, 441–450.

Morrison, D.G., and D.C. Schmittlein (1988), "Generalizing the NBD Model for Customer Purchases: What Are the Implications and Is It Worth the Effort?," *Journal of Economics and Business Statistics*, 6, 145–166.

Moschopoulos, P., and J.G. Staniswalis (1994), "Estimation Given Conditional from an Exponential Family," *The American Statistician*, 48, 271–275.

Mukhopadhyay, K., and P.K. Trivedi (1995), "Regression Models for Under-reported Counts," preprint. Paper presented at Econometric Society World Congress, Tokyo.

Mullahy, J. (1986), "Specification and Testing of Some Modified Count Data Models," *Journal of Econometrics*, 33, 341–365.

Mullahy, J. (1997a), "Instrumental Variable Estimation of Poisson Regression Models: Application to Models of Cigarette Smoking Behavior," *Review of Economics and Statistics*, 79, 586–593.

Mullahy, J. (1997b), "Heterogeneity, Excess Zeros and the Structure of Count Data Models," *Journal of Applied Econometrics*, 12, 337–350.

Mundlak, Y. (1978), "On the Pooling of Time Series and Cross Section Data," *Econometrica*, 46, 69–85.

Murphy, K., and R. Topel (1985), "Estimation and Inference in Two Step Econometric Models," *Journal of Business and Economic Statistics*, 3, 370–379.

Nagin, D.S., and K.C. Land (1993), "Age, Criminal Careers and Population Heterogeneity: Specification and Estimation of a Nonparametric, Mixed Regression Model," *Criminology*, 31, 327–362.

National Medical Expenditure Survey (1987), National Center for Health Services Research and Health Care Technology, Rockville, Maryland.

Nelder, J.A., and D. Pregibon (1987), "An Extended Quasi-likelihood Function," *Biometrika*, 74, 221–232.

Nelder, J.A., and R.W.M. Wedderburn (1972), "Generalized Linear Models," *Journal of the Royal Statistical Society A*, 135, 370–384.

Newell, D.J. (1965), "Unusual Frequency Distributions," *Biometrics*, 21, 159–168.

Newey, W.K. (1984), "A Methods of Moments Interpretation of Sequential Estimators," *Economics Letters*, 14, 201–206.

Newey, W.K. (1985), "Maximum Likelihood Specification Testing and Conditional Moment Tests," *Econometrica*, 53, 1047–1070.

Newey, W.K. (1990a), "Efficient Instrumental Variable Estimation of Nonlinear Models," *Econometrica*, 58, 809–838.

Newey, W. (1990b), "Semiparametric Efficiency Bounds," *Journal of Applied Econometrics*, 5, 99–136.

Newey, W.K. (1993), "Efficient Estimation of Models with Conditional Moment Restrictions," in G.S. Maddala, C.R. Rao, and H.D. Vinod, eds., *Handbook of Statistics, Volume 11, Econometrics*, 419–454, Amsterdam, North-Holland.

Newey, W.K., and D. McFadden (1994), "Large Sample Estimation and Hypothesis Testing," in R.F. Engle and D. McFadden, eds., *Handbook of Econometrics*, volume 4, Amsterdam, North-Holland.

Newey, W.K., and K.D. West (1987a), "A Simple, Positive Semi-definite, Heteroscedasticity and Autocorrelation Consistent Covariance Matrix," *Econometrica*, 55, 703–708.

Newey, W.K., and K.D. West (1987b), "Hypothesis Testing with Efficient Methods of Moments Estimators," *International Economic Review*, 28, 777–787.

Newhouse, J.P. (1993), *Free for All? Lessons from the Rand Health Insurance Experiment*. Cambridge, MA, Harvard University Press.

Neyman, J. (1939), "On a New Class of Contagious Distributions Applicable in Entomology and Bacteriology," *Annals of Mathematical Statistics*, 10, 35–57.

Neyman, J. (1965), "Certain Chance Mechanisms Involving Discrete Distributions," in G.N. Patil, ed., *Classical and Contagious Discrete Distributions*, 1–14, Calcutta, Statistical Publishing House.

Nickell, S. (1981), "Biases in Dynamic Models with Fixed Effects," *Econometrica*, 49, 1399–1416.

Noack, A. (1950), "A Class of Random Variables with Discrete Distributions," *Annals of Mathematical Statistics*, 21, 127–132.

Ogaki, M. (1993), "Generalized Method of Moments: Econometric Applications," in G.C. Maddala, C.R.Rao, and H.D. Vinod, eds., *Handbook of Statistics, Volume 11, Econometrics*, Amsterdam, North-Holland.

Okoruwa, A.A., J.V. Terza, and H.O. Nourse (1988), "Estimating Patronization Shares for Urban Retail Centers: An Extension of the Poisson Gravity Model,"*Journal of Urban Economics*, 24, 241–259.

Ozuna, T., and I. Gomaz (1995), "Specification and Testing of Count Data Recreation Demand Functions," *Empirical Economics*, 20, 543–550.

Pagan, A.R. (1986), " Two Stage and Related Estimators and Their Applications," *Review of Economic Studies*, 53, 517–538.

Pagan, A., and F. Vella (1989), "Diagnostic Tests for Models Based on Individual Data: A Survey," *Journal of Applied Econometrics*, 4, S29–S59.

Page, M. (1995), "Racial and Ethnic Discrimination in Urban Housing Markets: Evidence from a Recent Audit Survey," *Journal of Urban Economics*, 38, 183–206.

Palmgren, J. (1981), "The Fisher Information Matrix for Log-Linear Models Arguing Conditionally in the Observed Explanatory Variables," *Biometrika*, 68, 563–566.

Patil, G.P. (1970), ed., *Random Counts in Models and Structures*, volumes 1–3, University Park, PA, and London, Pennsylvania State University Press.

Patterson, H.D., and R. Thompson (1971), "Recovery of Inter-block Information When Block Sizes Are Unequal," *Biometrika*, 58, 545–554.

Pesaran, M.H. (1987), "Global and Partial Non-Nested Hypotheses and Asymptotic Local Power," *Econometric Theory*, 3, 677–694.

Phillips, P.C.B. (1987), "Time Series Regression with a Unit Root," *Econometrica*, 55, 277–301.

Pierce, D. (1982), "The Asymptotic Effect of Substituting Estimators for Parameters in Certain Types of Statistics," *Annals of Statistics*, 10, 475–478.

Pierce, D.A., and D.W. Schafer (1986), "Residuals in Generalized Linear Models," *Journal of the American Statistical Association*, 81, 977–986.

Pinquet, J. (1997), "Experience Rating through Heterogeneous Models," Working Paper No. 9725, THEMA, Université Paris X-Nanterre.

Pohlmeier,W., and V. Ulrich (1995), "An Econometric Model of the Two-Part Decision-making Process in the Demand for Health Care," *Journal of Human Resources*, 30, 339–361.

Poisson, S.-D. (1837), *Recherches sur la Probabilité des Jugements en Matière Criminelle et en Matière Civile*, Paris, Bachelier.

Pope, A., J. Schwartz, and M. Ransom (1992), "Daily Mortality and PM10 Pollution in Utah Valley," *Archives of Environmental Health*, 47, 211–217.

Pregibon, D. (1981), "Logistic Regression Diagnostics," *Annals of Statistics*, 9, 705–724.

Pudney, S. (1989), *Modelling Individual Choice: The Econometrics of Corners, Kinks and Holes*, New York, Basil Blackwell.

Qin, J., and J. Lawless (1994), "Empirical Likelihood and General Estimating Equations," *Annals of Statistics*, 22, 300–325.

Ramaswamy, V., E.N. Anderson, and W.S. DeSarbo (1994), "A Disaggregate Negative Binomial Regression Procedure for Count Data Analysis," *Management Science*, 40, 405–417.

Robert, C.P. (1996), "Mixtures of Distributions: Inference and Estimation," in W.R. Gilks, S. Richardson, and D.J. Spiegelhalter, eds., *Markov Chain Monte Carlo in Practice*, 441–464, London, Chapman and Hall.

Robinson, P.M. (1987), "Asymptotically Efficient Estimation in the Presence of Heteroskedasticity of Unknown Form," *Econometrica*, 55, 875–891.

Robinson, P.M. (1988), "Root-N Consistent Semiparametric Regression," *Econometrica*, 56, 931–954.

Ronning, G., and R.C. Jung (1992), "Estimation of a First Order Autoregressive Process with Poisson Marginals for Count Data," in L. Fahrmeir, et al., eds., *Advances in GLIM and Statistical Modelling*, New York, Springer-Verlag.

Rose, N. (1990), "Profitability and Product Quality: Economic Determinants of Airline Safety Performance," *Journal of Political Economy*, 98, 944–964.

Ross, S.M. (1996), *Stochastic Processes*, edition 2, New York, John Wiley.

Ruser, J.W. (1991), "Workers' Compensation and Occupational Injuries and Illnesses," *Journal of Labor Economics*, 9, 325–350.

Sargan, J.D. (1958), "The Estimation of Economic Relationships using Instrumental Variables," *Econometrica*, 26, 393–415.

Santos Silva, J.M.C. (1997), "Unobservables in Count Data Models for On-site Samples," *Economics Letters*, 54, 217–220.

Schall, R. (1991), "Estimation in Generalized Linear Models with Random Effects," *Biometrika*, 78, 719–727.

Schmidt, P., and A. Witte (1989), "Predicting Criminal Recidivism Using Split-population Survival Time Models," *Journal of Econometrics*, 40, 141–159.

Schneider, A.L. (1981), "Differences Between Survey and Police Information about Crime," in R.G. Lehnan and W.G. Skogan, eds., *The NCS Working Papers*, volume 1, U.S. Department of Justice.

Schwartz, E.S., and W.N. Torous (1993), "Mortgage Prepayments and Default Decisions: A Poisson Regression Approach," *AREUEA Journal: Journal of the American Real Estate Association*, 21, 431–449.

Schwarz, G. (1978), "Estimating the Dimension of a Model," *Annals of Statistics*, 6, 461–464.

Sellar, C., J.R. Stoll, and J.P. Chavas (1985), "Validation of Empirical Measures of Welfare Change: A Comparison of Nonmarket Techniques," *Land Economics*, 61, 156–175.

Severini, T.A., and J.G. Staniswalis (1994), "Quasi-likelihood Estimation in Semiparametric Models," *Journal of American Statistical Association*, 89, 501–511.

Shaban, S.A. (1988), "Poisson-Lognormal Distributions," in E.L. Crow and K. Shimizu, eds., *Lognormal Distributions*, 195–210, New York, Marcel Dekker.

Shaked, M. (1980), "On Mixtures from Exponential Families," *Journal of Royal Statistical Society B*, 42, 415–433.

Shaw, D. (1988), "On-Site Samples' Regression Problems of Non-negative Integers, Truncation and Endogenous Stratification," *Journal of Econometrics*, 37, 211–223.

Shephard, N. (1995), "Generalized Linear Autoregression," Nuffield College, Oxford University.

Shephard, N., and M.K. Pitt (1997), "Likelihood Analysis of Non-Gaussian Measurement Time Series," *Biometrika*, 84, 653–667.

Shiba, T., and H. Tsurumi (1988), "Bayesian and Non-Bayesian Tests of Independence in Seemingly Unrelated Regressions," *International Economic Review*, 29, 377–395.

Simar, L. (1976), "Maximum Likelihood Estimation of a Compound Poisson Process," *Annals of Statistics*, 4, 1200–1209.

Singh, A.C., and G.R. Roberts (1992), "State Space Modelling of Cross-Classified Time Series of Counts," *International Statistical Review*, 60, 321–335.

Smith, R.J. (1997), "Alternative Semi-parametric Likelihood Approaches to Generalised Method of Moment Estimation," *Economic Journal*, 107, 503–519.

Smyth, G.K. (1989), "Generalized Linear Models with Varying Dispersion," *Journal of the Royal Statistical Society B*, 51, 47–60.

Solow, A. R. (1993), "Estimating Record Inclusion Probability," *American Statistician*, 47, 206–209.

Staniswalis, J. (1989), "The Kernel Estimate of a Regression Function in Likelihood-Based Models," *Journal of the American Statistical Association*, 84, 426–431.

Steutel, F.W., and K. Van Harn (1979), "Discrete Analogues of Self-Decomposability and Stability, *Annals of Probability*, 7, 893–899.

Stroud, A.H., and D. Secrest (1966), *Gaussian Quadrature Formulas*, Englewood Cliffs, NJ, Prentice Hall.

Stukel, T. (1988), "Generalized Logistic Models," *Journal of the American Statistical Association*, 83, 426–431.

Szu, H., and R. Hartley (1987), "Fast Simulated Annealing," *Physics Letters A*, 122, 157–162.

Tauchen, G. (1985), "Diagnostic Testing and Evaluation of Maximum Likelihood Models," *Journal of Econometrics*, 30, 415–443.

Taylor, H.M., and S. Karlin (1994), *An Introduction to Stochastic Modelling*, revised edition, San Diego and New York, Academic Press.

Teicher, H. (1961), "The Identifiability of Mixtures," *Annals of Mathematical Statistics*, 32, 244–248.

Terza, J.V. (1985), "A Tobit-Type Estimator for the Censored Poisson Regression Model," *Economics Letters*, 18, 361–365.

Terza, J.V. (1998), "Estimating Count Data Models with Endogenous Switching: Sample Selection and Endogenous Switching Effects," *Journal of Econometrics*, 84, 129–139.

Terza, J.V., and P.W. Wilson (1990), "Analyzing Frequencies of Several Types of Events: A Mixed Multinomial-Poisson Approach," *Review of Economics and Statistics*, 72, 108–115.

Thall, P.F., and S.C. Vail (1990), "Some Covariance Models for Longitudinal Count Data with Overdispersion," *Biometrika*, 46, 657–671.

Titterington, D.M., A.F. Smith, and U.E. Makov (1985), *Statistical Analysis of Finite Mixture Distributions*, Chichester, UK, John Wiley.

U.S. National Center for Health Statistics (1965), *Health Interview Responses Compared with Medical Records*, Vital and Health Statistics Series 2 No. 7 Public Health Service, Washington, U.S. Government Printing Office.

U.S. National Center for Health Statistics (1967), *Interview Data on Chronic Conditions Compared with Information Derived from Medical Records*, Vital and Health Statistics Series 2 No. 23 Public Health Service, Washington, U.S. Government Printing Office.

Van Duijn, M.A.J., and U. Böckenholt (1995), "Mixture Models for the Analysis of Repeated Count Data," *Applied Statistics: Journal of the Royal Statistical Society C*, 44, 473–485.

van Praag, B.M.S., and E.M. Vermeulen (1993), "A Count-Amount Model with Endogenous Recording of Observations," *Journal of Applied Econometrics*, 8, 383–395.

Vuong, Q.H. (1989), "Likelihood Ratio Tests for Model Selection and Non-nested Hypothesis," *Econometrica*, 57, 307–333.

Wagner, G.G., R.V. Burkhauser, and F. Behringer (1993), "The English Language Public Use File of The German Socio-Economic Panel," *Journal of Human Resources*, 28, 429–433.

Wang, P., I.M. Cockburn, and M.L. Puterman (1998). "Analysis of Patent Data – A Mixed Poisson Regression Model Approach," *Journal of Business and Economic Statistics*, 16(1), 27–41.

Watermann, J., R. Jankowski, and I. Madan (1994), "Under-reporting of Needlestick Injuries by Medical Students," *Journal of Hospital Infection*, 26, 149–151.

Wedderburn, R.W.M. (1974), "Quasi-likelihood Functions, Generalized Linear Models, and the Gauss-Newton Method," *Biometrika*, 61, 439–447.

Wedel, W., W.S. DeSarbo, J.R. Bult, and V. Ramaswamy (1993), "A Latent Class Poisson Regression Model for Heterogeneous Count Data," *Journal of Applied Econometrics*, 8, 397–411.

Weiss, A.A. (1995), "Simultaneity and Sample Selection in Poisson Regression Models," unpublished discussion paper.

West, M., and P. J. Harrison (1997, 1990), *Bayesian Forecasting and Dynamic Models*, edition 2, New York, Springer.

West, M., P.J. Harrison, and H.S. Migon (1985), "Dynamic Generalized Linear Models and Bayesian Forecasting [with discussion]," *Journal of the American Statistical Association*, 80, 73–97.

White, H. (1980), "A Heteroskedasticity-Consistent Covariance Matrix Estimator and a Direct Test for Heteroskedasticity," *Econometrica*, 46, 817–838.

White, H. (1982), "Maximum Likelihood Estimation of Misspecified Models," *Econometrica*, 50, 1–25.

White, H. (1994), *Estimation, Inference, and Specification Analysis*, Cambridge, UK, Cambridge University Press.

White, H., and I. Domowitz (1984), "Nonlinear Regression with Dependent Observations," *Econometrica*, 52, 143–161.

Whittemore, A.S., and G. Gong (1991), "Poisson Regression with Misclassified Counts: Application to Cervical Cancer Mortality Rates," *Applied Statistics*, 40, 81–93.

Williams, D.A. (1987), "Generalized Linear Model Diagnostics Using the Deviance and Single Case Deletions," *Applied Statistics*, 36, 181–191.

Windmeijer, F.A.G., and J. M. C. Santos Silva (1997), "Endogeneity in Count Data Models: An Application to Demand for Health Care," *Journal of Applied Econometrics*, 12, 281–294.

Winkelmann, R. (1997, 1994), *Count Data Models: Econometric Theory and Application to Labor Mobility*, Berlin, Springer-Verlag.

Winkelmann, R. (1995), "Duration Dependence and Dispersion in Count-Data Models," *Journal of Business and Economic Statistics*, 13, 467–474.

Winkelmann, R., and K.F. Zimmermann (1991), "A New Approach for Modeling Economic Count Data," *Economics Letters*, 37, 139–143.

Winkelmann, R., and K.F. Zimmermann (1992), "Recursive Probability Estimators for Count Data," in G. Haag, U. Muller, and K.G. Troitzsch, eds., *Economic Evolution and Demographic Change*, 321–329, New York, Springer.

Winkelmann, R., and K.F. Zimmermann (1993), "Poisson Logistic Regression," SELAPO, University of Munich.

Winkelmann, R., and K.F. Zimmermann (1995), "Recent Developments in Count Data Modelling: Theory and Application," *Journal of Economic Surveys*, 9, 1–24.

Wong, W.H. (1986), "Theory of Partial Likelihood," *Annals of Statistics*, 14, 88–123.

Wooldridge, J.M. (1990a), "A Unified Approach to Robust, Regression-Based Specification Tests," *Econometric Theory*, 6, 17–43.

Wooldridge, J.M. (1990b), "An Encompassing Approach to Conditional Mean Tests with Applications to Testing Nonlinear Hypotheses," *Journal of Econometrics*, 45, 331–350.

Wooldridge, J.M. (1990c), "Distribution-Free Estimation of Some Nonlinear Panel Data Models," Working Paper No. 564, Department of Economics, Massachusetts Institute of Technology.

Wooldridge, J.M. (1991a), "On the Application of Robust, Regression-Based Diagnostics to Models of Conditional Means and Conditional Variances,"*Journal of Econometrics*, 47, 5–46.

Wooldridge, J.M. (1991b), "Specification Testing and Quasi-Maximum Likelihood Estimation," *Journal of Econometrics*, 48, 29–55.

Wooldridge, J.M. (1997), "Multiplicative Panel Data Models without the Strict Exogeneity Assumption," *Econometric Theory*, 13, 667–679.

Wu, D. (1973), "Alternative Tests of Independence between Stochastic Regressors and Disturbances," *Econometrica*, 41, 733–750.

Yannaros, N. (1993), "Analyzing Incomplete Count Data," *Statistician*, 42, 181–187.

Zeger, S.L. (1988), "A Regression Model for Time Series of Counts," *Biometrika*, 75, 621–629.

Zeger, S.L., and K.-Y. Liang (1986), "Longitudinal Data Analysis for Discrete and Continuous Outcomes," *Biometrics*, 42, 121–130.

Zeger, S.L., K.-Y. Liang, and P.S. Albert (1988), "Models for Longitudinal Data: A Generalized Estimating Equation Approach," *Biometrics*, 44, 1049–1060.

Zeger, S.L., and Qaqish B. (1988), "Markov Regression Models for Time Series: A Quasi-Likelihood Approach," *Biometrics*, 44, 1019–1031.

Author Index

Subject Index

D

E

Other titles in the series:

Christopher Sims, Editor *Advances in econometrics – Sixth World Congress (Volume II)*, 0 521 56609 6

Roger Guesnerie *A contribution to the pure theory of taxation*, 0 521 23689 4, 0 521 62956 X

David M. Kreps and Kenneth F. Wallis, Editors *Advances in economics and econometrics – Seventh World Congress (Volume I)*, 0 521 58011 0, 0 521 58983 5

David M. Kreps and Kenneth F. Wallis, Editors *Advances in economics and econometrics – Seventh World Congress (Volume II)*, 0 521 58012 9, 0 521 58982 7

David M. Kreps and Kenneth F. Wallis, Editors *Advances in economics and econometrics – Seventh World Congress (Volume III)*, 0 521 58013 7, 0 521 58981 9

Donald P. Jacobs, Ehud Kalai, and Morton I. Kamien, Editors *Frontiers of research in economic theory: The Nancy L. Schwartz Memorial Lectures*, 1983–1997 0 521 63222 6, 0 521 63538 1